# The Political Economy of Income Distribution in Egypt

The Political Economy of Income Distribution in Developing Countries
Henry Bienen, General Series Editor

I. Turkey
Ergun Özbudun and Aydin Ulusan, editors
II. Nigeria
Henry Bienen and V.P. Diejomaoh, editors
III. Egypt
Gouda Abdel-Khalek and Robert Tignor, editors
IV. Mexico
Pedro Aspe and Paul Sigmund, editors

The Political Economy of Income Distribution in Developing Countries series is prepared under the auspices of the
Research Program in Development Studies
Woodrow Wilson School of Public and International Affairs
Princeton University

# The Political Economy of Income Distribution in Egypt

Edited by

Gouda Abdel-Khalek and Robert Tignor

The Political Economy
of Income Distribution in Developing Countries
Henry Bienen, General Series Editor

Holmes & Meier Publishers, Inc.
New York • London

First published in the United States of America 1982 by
Holmes & Meier Publishers, Inc.
30 Irving Place
New York, N.Y. 10003

*Great Britain:*
Holmes & Meier Publishers, Ltd.
131 Trafalgar Road
Greenwich, London SE10 9TX





LIBRARY OF CONGRESS CATALOGING IN PUBLICATION DATA

Main entry under title:

The Political economy of income distribution in
Egypt.

**Library of Congress Cataloging in Publication Data**

Main entry under title:

The Political economy of income distribution in Egypt.

(The Political economy of income distribution in developing countries; v. 3)
Includes index.
1. Income distribution—Egypt—Addresses, essays, lectures. 2. Egypt—Economic policy—Addresses, essays, lectures. 3. Egypt—Economic conditions—1952– —Addresses, essays, lectures. I. Abdel-Khalek, Gouda. II. Tignor, Robert L. III. Series: Political economy of income distribution in developing countries; v. 3.
HC830.P64 1981 339 2′0962 80-26932
ISBN 0-8419-0633-5 AACR1

MANUFACTURED IN THE UNITED STATES OF AMERICA

# Contents

**Preface**

1. Overview 1
   *Gouda Abdel-Khalek and Robert Tignor*

2. Equity in Egypt's Recent Past: 1945–1952 20
   *Robert Tignor*

3. The Politics of Income Distribution in Egypt 55
   *Ali E. Hillal Dessouki*

4. Interconnections between Income Distribution and Economic Growth in the Context of Egypt's Economic Development 88
   *Ibrahim Hassan El-Issawy*

5. Impact of Taxation on Income Distribution: An Exploratory Attempt to Estimate Tax Incidence in Egypt 132
   *M. Reda A. El-Edel*

6. The Agricultural Output Pricing Policy and the Implicit Taxation of Agricultural Income 165
   *Karima Korayem*

7. Impact of Agricultural Policies on Income Distribution 198
   *Ahmed H. Ibrahim*

8. The Development of the Share of Agricultural Wage Labor in the National Income of Egypt 236
*Amr Mohie-Eldin*

9. Income Distribution in Egyptian Agriculture and Its Main Determinants 268
*Mohaya A. Zaytoun*

10. Patterns of Urban Growth and Income Distribution in Egypt 307
*John Waterbury*

11. Educational Expansion and Income Distribution in Egypt, 1952–1977 351
*Mahmoud Abdel-Fadil*

12. Social Mobility and Income Distribution in Egypt, 1952–1977 375
*Saad Eddin Ibrahim*

13. Foreign Economic Aid and Income Distribution in Egypt, 1952–1977 435
*Gouda Abdel-Khalek*

14. The Open-Door Economy: Its Roots and Welfare Consequences 469
*Fouad Ajami*

**List of Contributors** 517

**Index** 519

## A Note on Transliteration

The Arabic in this volume has been transliterated according to the method adopted in Holmes and Meier publications, except that common place names, such as Cairo and Alexandria, and personal names, such as Nasser and Sadat, appear in their customary English spelling.

# Preface

*The Political Economy of Income Distribution in Egypt* is the third volume of a series of case studies in income distribution undertaken in Turkey, Nigeria, Egypt, and Mexico. Just as Volumes I and II on Turkey and Nigeria brought together scholars from Princeton and other universities in the United States with scholars at Turkish and Nigerian universities, so this volume is a collaborative effort of American and Egyptian scholars. Egyptians from Cairo University, American University, and al-Azhar University and individuals from the Institute of National Planning in Cairo participated in this project.

The institutional home for the Egyptian study was the Center for Sociological and Criminological Research, directed by Dr. Ahmad Khalifa. We received great support from the United States Agency for International Development in Cairo and especially from Mission Director, Donald Brown, and from Peter Davis, John Chang, and James Norris. We acknowledge our appreciation to them. Jonathan Silverstone, Chief, Civic Participation Division of AID's Bureau for Program and Policy Coordination was once again a helpful colleague on this project.

Special thanks are owed to Professor Bent Hansen of the University of California, Berkeley, who was an important discussant of the first-draft papers. Professor Charles Issawi of Princeton University also played this role and was a continuously helpful critic and a friendly presence at all stages of our work. Professor John P. Lewis helped in setting up the study.

My special thanks go to Dr. Gouda Abdel-Khalek, who even though he moved to Kuwait as a World Bank representative during part of the project period, was able to continue to direct the Egyptian team. Professor Robert Tignor, Chairman of Princeton University's History Department, ably carried out his responsibilities despite his University administrative burdens. Professor Ergun Ozbudun and Professor Vremudia Diejomaoh attended meetings on the Egyptian study and contributed their insights from the Turkish and Nigerian projects. Professor Michael Danielson and Dean Donald Stokes of Princeton were also helpful participants and Dean Stokes made valuable inputs into survey work carried out by Dr. Hoda Magahid at the Center for Sociological and Criminological Research.

Jerri Kavanagh, Office Coordinator of the Research Program in Development Studies, took on many important responsibilities. She has been administrative cverseer, travel agent, keeper of budget and records. Thanks are due also to RPDS staff, Shirley Canty, Delores Wilson and Michael Padulo.

Henry Bienen
Director, Research Program in Development Studies
Princeton University
December, 1980

# CHAPTER 1

# *Overview*

Gouda Abdel-Khalek and Robert Tignor

## Scope, Purpose and Data

In few developing countries have questions of the distribution of income and social justice occupied such a prominent position as they have in Egypt. In the 1930s and 1940s, while other less developed countries were still marshalling their energies to bring an end to colonial rule, Egyptian intellectuals were grappling with the question of how wealth should be divided. In 1952 the Egyptian military came to power and began a process of realizing the twin goals of social justice and economic development. The purpose of this volume is to understand what Egyptians meant when they spoke of a more equitable society, to describe the present distribution of wealth and poverty and how it came about, and to consider the policy implications of what transpired.

Societies pursue many objectives, some of which may be in conflict with each other. National independence, power, economic growth, social mobility, and political liberty often rank high on the list. Equity has, at times, occupied a very high place in the hierarchy of values of widely different peoples. All these concepts are complex and do not lend themselves to simple definitions—much less measurement—and this is certainly true of equity, the topic to which this volume addresses itself. Equity has, at various times, meant either equality or proportion, the first of these notions suggesting that all people should be treated as identically as possible, while the second suggests treating them in proportion to some specified criterion—say need, merit, work, or ability—and therefore unequally. There is also the fundamental difference between equality of opportunity and equality of result; the first bids us give everyone an equal chance in the race, knowing that some will do better than others and emerge as winners, while the second urges us to take measures that will ensure that all will get equal shares, or as nearly equal as possible.

This volume is concerned with the question of income distribution and can obviously not address itself to all these broad, equity-related issues. But it is essential that they be kept in mind both in assessing Egypt's performance during the period under review and in comparing its experience with that of other countries.

We are not simply interested in providing a more complete picture of income distribution than has existed before; we want also to understand the reasons for the present arrangements. What impact have government policies had on the distribution of income? What has been the role of private initiatives? What has been the impact of Egypt's external links? What effect has the massive transfer of foreign resources had on this distribution? Answers to these and other questions have taken us into many areas of Egyptian society. We have tried to chart changes in the distribution of income over a number of decades. One of the chapters (Chapter 2 by Robert Tignor) provides a historical background by looking at Egypt's concern with equity in the 1930s and 1940s. The other papers focus on the period from 1952 until the present. The authors show that Egyptian conceptions of equity changed over time and that equity concerns assumed prominence during certain periods but were not as important at other times. An effort has been made to understand these changes in commitment to equity, so pronounced a feature of the last twenty-five years. Was it because of external events, changing attitudes toward social justice among political leaders, or a response to domestic pressures?

In a society so centralized and dominated by its government, it is not surprising that many of the essays focus on the government as an agent of income distribution. Some of the chapters, most notably those on education and land reform, evaluate the government's commitment to more equitable distribution. Others, especially those dealing with agricultural policies (Ahmed Hassan and Karima Korayem) spell out some of the intended and unintended consequences of government policy on the distribution of income in the agricultural sector and between agriculture and the rest of the economy.

In a volume dealing with the distribution of income, the first question that needs to be answered is what to include as income. We would of course like to take a broad view and take into account all sources of income: work, property, remittances, the value of basic goods and services provided for by the government, and receipts. But the reality is that the data on many of these elements are sparse, and we have been forced to limit our purview to salaries and wages and income from agricultural, commercial, and industrial activities.

Although compelled to take a narrow view of monetary income, we have also been aware that salaries, wages, profits, and rents do not give a full picture of a person's social and economic well-being. For centuries the Egyptian state has played a major role in the lives of its people. In recent times it has assumed heavy responsibilities for education, health, sanitation, housing, transportation, food supplies, and so forth. It is therefore imperative to pay attention to governmental provision of goods and services and to treat it as a form of income that is often unevenly distributed.

Since our main purpose is to give a precise and revealing profile of income distribution, we present this distribution from many perspectives. We make the obvious breakdowns between rural and urban and agricultural and nonagricultural, and find some disparities between these two sectors. We have also looked at the distribution of income by factor shares (labor vs. property) in both the rural and urban sectors and traced changes in distribution over time. As has been customary in income distribution studies, we have presented a household expenditure distribution profile. This profile has been presented on a national level, disaggregated into rural and urban sectors, and also analyzed on a per capita basis. The extent of equality or disparity has been estimated, using the most popular measure of disparity, viz the Gini coefficient. As indicated in the relevant papers, caution has to be emphasized. The data are frustratingly scarce. Those that we have are likely to make income distribution seem more equitable than it really is. Survey efforts have encountered difficulty in obtaining information on the very poor who do not have stable dwelling places; at the other end, the rich often do not report their income fully. Moreover, in a country in which the economy and society are so thoroughly penetrated by the state, the Gini coefficient cannot measure the impact of many public goods and services on household income. Finally, the coefficient itself is so highly aggregated as to be misleading in many ways. While values of the Gini coefficient based on Egyptian data do not reveal as bleak a picture as is generally found in third world countries, they do not give a good sense of the grinding poverty that has submerged such a large proportion of the Egyptian population.

As in other developing countries, the Egyptian income data are not abundant. Many basic sources are lacking. What is available has many shortcomings. Indeed, in the 1960s many important government annual surveys either were not undertaken or their results were not published. Although the government has once again begun to collect this vital information, most of the new surveys have not yet been published. There is no published survey of income distribution, although at present the National Center for Social and Criminological Research is carrying out an ambitious 4000 household survey dealing with this subject and many related topics.

The main distributional data source has been the household expenditure surveys carried out in 1958/59, 1964/65, and 1974/75. Many of the scholars writing in this volume have used these surveys as a primary source. Ibrahim El-Issawy uses them simply to give a picture of the distribution of expenditure groups. Reda El-Edel, however, seeks to transform expenditure data into income data. By estimating savings by expenditure groups, according to the formulas used by the World Bank in its study of Egypt, and then by allocating direct taxes to these expenditure groups, he produces estimates of personal income distribution which he uses to calculate Gini coefficients for the years 1958/59, 1964/65 and 1974/75.

Other data have been employed. The government conducted population censuses in 1960, 1966, and 1976, although the 1966 census was only a sample census and the full findings of the 1976 census were not available in time for the work reported here. Various ministries—Agriculture, Economy, and Industry—have conducted relevant surveys. Some of this material has been published, and some of it has had to be studied in unpublished form at the ministries themselves. Several of the chapters were based on the authors' own minisurveys. Saad Eddin Ibrahim's important study of social mobility rested heavily on a questionnaire he distributed to over six hundred households in Cairo. Mohaya Zaytoun's analysis of income distribution in agriculture is based on unpublished survey materials at the Ministry of Agriculture and preliminary findings from the income distribution survey of the National Center for Social and Criminological Research. Ahmed Hassan's analysis of the distributional impacts of government agriculture policies on different groups of landholders draws on his own field work conducted in four Egyptian governorates in 1970.

Although the data are not as full as one would like, there is enough material scattered about in published and unpublished studies and in private surveys to enable us to provide a fuller portrait of income distribution in contemporary Egypt than we have had before.

## Profile of Income Distribution—Rural Egypt

The most visible aspect of poorly distributed wealth prior to 1952 was in the rural sector where twelve thousand land owners possessed 35 percent of the arable land. Soon after coming to power, the military carried out a land reform measure (1952) and subsequently (in 1961 and 1969) lowered the ceiling on land ownership. The essays in this volume suggest that these reforms had a considerable initial income equalizing impact. Issawy, for instance, claims that the rural income distribution improved in the 1950s and the first half of the 1960s, but has deteriorated since the mid-1960s.

While there is consensus that land reform reduced the massive disparity of income in the rural sector up to the mid-1960s, there is also agreement that rural poverty has increased in the last decade. The impact of inflation, sluggish agricultural growth, and an expanding population has been little short of disastrous in the countryside. The major work on this subject is Samir Radwan's "The Impact of Agrarian Reform on Rural Egypt, 1952–1975," (World Employment Programme Research, *Working Papers*), which many of the authors in this work cite. Using the household expenditure surveys and estimating the income needed to sustain minimum food, housing, and clothing requirements, Radwan concludes that while the proportion of those families living below this minimum level—his poverty line—declined from 35 percent in 1958/59 to 26.8 percent in 1964/65, it rose dramatically to 43.3 percent in 1974/75. Although the countryside no longer contained the great extremes of wealth and poverty that characterized the rural sector in the pre-Nasser era, over 40 percent of the population was unable to support itself at a minimally acceptable level in the mid-1970s.

The most studied rural group has been the landholders. Numerous works have charted the rise of the landed grandees in the nineteenth and twentieth centuries and have shown their increasing political influence. Other works have sought to calculate the impact of land reform on this group, but these latter works have been stymied by one basic problem: Egypt's last agricultural census was carried out in 1961—nearly twenty years ago—and numerous changes have occurred in the countryside since then. Not only have two additional land reform schemes been enacted (in 1961 and 1969), but land has also changed hands as a result of land sales, population migration, land lease, and/or land inheritance. Using unpublished material available at the Ministry of Agriculture, Mohaya Zaytoun updates our information on landholding distribution to 1977/78. She finds that 82 percent of the landholders held 45 percent of the land in that year and that 2.4 percent of the landholders (those with 10 feddans or more) held 22.3 percent of the land. Her findings corroborate the conclusion that the middle peasants (those owning over ten feddans) have become the real power in the countryside and are successors to the dispossessed landed elite. Yet, by using these landholding figures to calculate the Gini coefficient for landholding, she obtains a figure of 0.411, which is substantially lower than the 1950 landholding value of the coefficient of 0.758. Egyptian land reform would appear to have made a difference in the lives of landowners. Analyzing the main determinants of income of landholders in agriculture, she also concludes that crop rotation patterns increase the income disparity while livestock and dairy production tends to be income equalizing.

In the countryside, the poorest element is the agricultural wage laborer. Both Amr Mohie-Eldin and Ibrahim El-Issawy find some relative improvement in their lot in the first part of the Nasser era. Issawy found that the relative share of rural wages in GDP rose from 17 percent in 1951/52 to 33 percent in 1965/66 and then began to decline. Amr Mohie-Eldin found that the share of rural wages in value added in agriculture showed a steady increase from 1959 until 1966, then a decline until 1974, and again an increase since 1975. He also discovered that the share of wage labor in agricultural income increased steadily from 8 percent in 1952 to 10 percent in 1976.

These different statistics give a mottled picture of the economic condition of the rural worker. Although they show that wages rose in proportion to other aggregates such as GDP or agricultural value added, they cannot refute the fact that the poorer segments of Egyptian society, including the rural wage laborers, find it more difficult to maintain minimum standards of living. Mohie-Eldin shows that the quality of life of agricultural wage earners is rather low, with some 20 percent calorie intake deficiency, and with one quarter of the children suffering severe malnutrition, according to surveys carried out in the late 1970s.

### Profile of Income Distribution—Urban Egypt

Egypt has become an increasingly urbanized country in the twentieth century. According to the 1976 population census, 44 percent of the population lives in cities with populations of 20,000 or more. Although many of these so-called cities are probably not much more than swollen agricultural communities and do not have many of the features associated with urban life, the population of Greater Cairo is 22 percent of Egypt's total and Alexandria accounts for another 6 percent. The major centers attracting rural migrants are, as they have been throughout most of the twentieth century, Cairo, Alexandria, and the Canal cities.

The income data for the urban sector tend to be scanty. Using the household expenditure surveys, Issawy calculated a Gini coefficient of consumption expenditures (not income distribution) in the urban areas falling from 0.40 in 1964/65 to 0.37 in 1974/75. He also found a rising trend in the share of industrial and nonagricultural wages as a part of GDP from the 1950s up to 1974. Still these are not clear and well-established trends.

Perhaps the most revealing picture of urban income distribution comes from Saad Eddin Ibrahim's Cairo survey. He identified six socioeconomic groups among the 634 households he surveyed, from the "rock-bottom" poor, constituting 11 percent, to the top 1 percent of these households. He estimates, on the basis of assumptions about the cost of living in urban areas related to rural areas, that the proportion of those living at or below a minimum standard of housing, food, and clothing fell from 30 percent in 1958/59 to 28 percent in 1964/65, but rose to 35 percent in 1974/75.

### National Income Distribution Profile

Although Egypt's intersectoral income differences are significant, they are not as large as those found in many LDCs. Both Issawy and Waterbury note that the per capita income differential between rural and urban sectors fluctuated between 1.6 and 2.2 between 1953 and 1975. Waterbury concluded that this gap was "a far cry from 3.0 ratios found in several LDCs." The wage rate differential between agriculture and nonagriculture was higher, varying between 3.7 and 5.5. Yet despite these obvious intersectoral disparities, the pattern of intrasectoral disparities is not really very different from one sector (rural) to another (urban). The economy-wide Gini coefficient of household expenditure distribution as calculated by Issawy, declined from 0.42 in 1958/59 to 0.40 in 1964/65 and 0.38 in 1974/75.

Although the chapters in this volume have different emphases, they suggest that Egypt under Nasser made strides in achieving a relatively high degree of income equality. The wide disparities of income within and between sectors which mark some LDCs are not nearly so pronounced in Egypt. Although the country is poor and a large proportion of its population lives at or even below a minimum standard of living, the Nasser years seem to have reduced the accumulation of huge assets in the hands of a few. Also, through its education, public health, public services, and food-subsidy programs the Egyptian government sought to secure an economic and social floor for all of its people.

## Socio-Political Dynamics and Periodization

The years between 1952 and 1980 have witnessed a mixed record with respect to equity achievements. In nearly all of the essays that survey these three decades, the authors see different periods during which attitudes and policies toward equity changed. Most of the authors would agree that the period from 1952 to 1956 saw the military consolidate power and carry out a limited number of programs with equity content. The most important was the land reform scheme which was introduced almost immediately after the military came to power. It limited a person's holdings to 200 feddans. Nineteen fifty-six to 1960 witnessed the nationalization or Egyptianization of large segments of the economy previously in the hands of foreigners. These measures themselves were sparked by foreign-policy issues, notably the British-French-Israeli invasion of Egypt in 1956 which brought in its wake the Egyptianization of almost all British and French assets in Egypt. Since foreigners held such a predominant position in the Egyptian economy, this action not only enabled the Egyptian state to achieve greater control of its economic affairs, but also saw the transfer of vast resources into private Egyptian hands. Between 1960 and 1966 Egypt entered its most socialist and egalitarian phase, marked by the National Charter of 1962, the nationalization of large-scale industrial and commercial concerns, and a second land reform scheme (1961). Land was again distributed to the smaller peasants, and the bureaucracy grew rapidly in the wake of the nationalization drives.

By the end of the 1960s, however, the Egyptian economy had entered a period of stagnation, and, though the commitment to equity remained, the capacity to improve living standards was limited. The war in Yemen and the costly war of 1967 were a huge drain on Egyptian resources as were the large, continuous military expenses involved in keeping Egypt's military establishment in a state of war readiness. This stagnation was broken only in the second half of the 1970s when under President Sadat new economic and political policies, called *Infitah* (the Opening), ushered in an era of economic liberalization, the encouragement of foreign investment, and the rebirth of a local bourgeoisie. The Infitāh seems to have had income-skewing tendencies, for the regime has been more concerned to promote economic growth than to secure equity.

The chapters dealing with politics pay particular attention to the role of the leader. Gamal Abd al-Nasser and Anwar al-Sadat have left their mark on the last three decades, and if one wants to understand national issues, one must start with the personality and the policies of the Egyptian president. Still, political analysts have tried to be sensitive to the sources of presidential support, for no political leader, no matter how powerful, can rule without regime support or a "constituency" and must also be wary of political opposition.

Nasser's and Sadat's equity policies were in fact not enacted in a political vacuum. The government's commitment to equity was always an ambiguous matter, even in the early 1960s when its socialist pronouncements were so evident. According to Ali Dessouki, many of the state's income redistributing programs stemmed from a desire to eliminate opponents and to build regime legitimacy rather than from a genuine commitment to the goals of equity or income redistribution. Dessouki contends that the land reform act of 1952 was intended to destroy the economic powers of the large landholders who opposed the military and to win support among the smaller holders, tenant farmers, and agricultural laborers. By the same token, although the expropriations and nationalizations of the late 1950s and early 1960s undoubtedly had enormous wealth-distributing consequences, they were, according to Dessouki, in part preventive steps to undercut opposition from those social elements in Egypt who were thought to be in league with foreign enemies.

Whatever the reality—and Dessouki does not deny that even in its early years, the regime's "implicit ideology" entailed vague socialist and populist leanings as well as a concern for social justice and the plight of the poor—these equity programs were carried out in a bureaucratic and technocratic fashion. Although the leaders endeavored to redistribute income, the reform programs themselves came from the top down. While securing regime support, the program did not sustain participatory political institutions. The effort to establish a mass single party was not successful. Thus a marked feature of the income distributional efforts was that they were conferred by a powerful autocratic state and had little popular input. This provides some explanation for the absence of resistance to the later reversal away from egalitarian measures under Sadat.

Fouad Ajami believes that the regime's "implicit ideology" was populist. Under Nasser the state implemented programs that benefitted and secured the support of large and influential segments of the Egyptian population. But the Nasser brand of populism was a diffuse one. In striving to appeal to many groups (medium-sized landholders, landless laborers, bureaucrats, industrial workers, students), it went in many directions at the same time. The state tried to be many things to many groups. It tried to achieve industrial dynamism while at the same time guaranteeing job security to the industrial workers. The result was plants with labor forces too large for their productive capacities. University graduates were guaranteed state positions, and the civil service swelled to alarming proportions. Economic planning was supposed to ensure the efficient allocation of resources, but because of competing interest groups, the planners could not perform their function. By the mid-1960s Egypt's economic problems were legion: a stagnant agriculture; an industrial sector with excess capacity; and a bureaucracy overgrown and unwieldy. But the real death blow to the left-populist experiment was administered in the Arab-Israeli war of 1967. The regime lost legitimacy. The ground was prepared for an overt turn to the right, which was crystallized in Sadat's Infitāh announcements in 1973 and 1974. As Ajami and Dessouki demonstrated, the roots of Infitah can be traced back into the latter Nasser years; the policy was not just the brainchild of Anwar al-Sadat.

One of the most important sources of regime support has been the government bureaucracy. Indeed, many of the income distributing policies, in particular the nationalizations of industries and commercial establishments, resulted in an extraordinary expansion in the size and powers of the state bureaucracy. Under Nasser the number of ministries rose from 15 in 1952 to 28 in 1970. Public agencies expanded from 1 in 1957 to 38 in 1962 and 46 in 1970. At the same time employment in the civil service and public sector rose from 350,000 in 1951/52 to 1,200,000 in 1969/70. In the 1960s the salaries of bureaucrats increased at a rate almost double that at which national income was expanding. Thus the new government may be seen to have used the bureaucracy as a foundation stone for its support.

What then have been the major equity policies enacted by the government? How have they contributed to the redistribution of income? Within the confines of this essay it would not be possible to describe all of the redistributive and equity programs implemented by the state. Many of them are discussed at great length in this volume. Some of them warrant attention here, however, since they shed light on the present "division of the pie" in Egypt and the processes by which this has come into being.

The first equity measure carried out by the state following military takeover was a land reform scheme, enacted just a few months after the military seizure of power. One must not exaggerate the impact of the three land reform programs. In fact less than 900,000 feddans of land were redistributed, a relatively small 13 percent of the total arable land, and only 9 percent of rural families benefitted. Moreover, as Samir Radwan points out in his study of the redistributive impact of the land reforms, while the Gini coefficient of landholding declined from 0.611 before 1952 to 0.383 in 1965, if the landless population were included in the calculations, the Gini coefficient remained very high and was altered little by land redistribution.[1] Moreover, the biggest gainers from the changes wrought in Egypt were the middle-sized owners, those possessing over 20 feddans. By 1965 they were estimated to own one-fourth of Egypt's arable land while constituting only 5 percent of the total landowning population.[2]

Another aspect of the land reform scheme was legislation designed to regulate agricultural wages and to fix the maximum rental that landowners could charge tenants on their land. Both of these measures were intended to alleviate rural poverty, but they were only fitfully enforced.

## Taxation

The land reform measures were the most dramatic equity programs enacted by the government. But there were other important programs. Taxation, education, and agricultural policies, among others, were all areas in which the government was able to affect the distribution of income.

The taxation structure in Egypt is a cumbersome set of rules that has evolved slowly into its present form and requires a thoroughgoing overhaul. The prevailing arrangements, as noted by El-Edel, seem to be largely motivated by revenue augmentation rather than allocational or distributional purposes. Little is known about the redistributive impact of taxation. Indeed, because of the fact that the bulk of Egyptian tax revenue stems from indirect taxes, many people have concluded that the tax system is regressive. Reda El-Edel disputes this point and argues that Egyptian taxes are slightly progressive. Although most of the taxes are commodity taxes (mainly customs duties), the higher rates tend to be on luxury items. According to El-Edel, taxation has been a powerful fiscal tool and a potentially important instrument of income redistribution. Over the last ten years (1967–1977) 21 percent of Egypt's GDP was redistributed through taxes, and over the last twenty-five years (1952–1977) the amount of tax revenue collected increased nearly ten times and, as a proportion of GDP, rose from 15 percent to 21 percent.

Using household budget survey data to derive income data, and allocating indirect taxes and subsidies to different income groups, El-Edel reaches a number of interesting conclusions. First, subsidies came to play a larger role, particularly after 1974/75, in moderating income inequality. This is borne out by a recent ILO study on food subsidy in Egypt,[3] which concludes that the cost of living of the urban poor would rise significantly if food subsidies were removed. Second, gross direct and indirect taxes have a progressive effect.

## Education

Another area in which the government made an impact on equity was education. While the population doubled between 1947 and 1976, the literate pool tripled. Government expenditure on education rose from less than 3 percent of GDP in 1952–1953 to about 4.1 percent in 1970–1971. The greatest expansion occurred at the secondary and university levels where pupil enrollments expanded approximately four times while enrollments at the primary level were not quite doubling.

Of course education does not automatically lead to all those goals of which its advocates speak, such as higher incomes and social mobility. Many studies show that heavy expenditures on education without reference to the manpower needs of the society produce unemployment, discontent, and even endemic political instability. It would appear, however, that for at least a decade and a half, Egyptian educational thrusts ameliorated the life of its recipients. Saad Ibrahim's minisurvey of Cairo is apposite in this regard. He found that no fewer than 48 percent of the fathers of his respondents were illiterate while only 23 percent of the respondents were. Moreover, 15 percent of the respondents had a university education while only 4 per cent of their fathers did. When these figures are coupled with Saad Ibrahim's findings on occupational mobility, one is led to conclude that education was an engine of income and social mobility. Saad Ibrahim's Cairo survey demonstrated, for example, a large-scale move into nonmanual professions from manual occupations, especially farming. No fewer than 29 percent of the persons surveyed had fathers who worked in agriculture; one of the most marked moves was into the professions. It would be hard to argue that education was not a factor in these social and occupational transformations.

Having said this, one must qualify one's remarks. There is a dark side to Egyptian education. The few surveys conducted on university students (and cited in the Abdel-Fadil chapter) indicate that positions in the most prestigious university faculties (engineering, economics, and medicine) tend to be monopolized by sons and daughters of the elite. Although Saad Ibrahim's Cairo survey stressed occupational mobility, he also noticed a slowing of mobility in the career patterns and educational opportunities of the sons of respondents. Equally worrisome has been the government's commitment to finding positions within the state bureaucracy for all university graduates. This policy has had the effect of honeycombing the public bureaucracy with vast numbers of redundant employees. Ibrahim el-Issawy believes that this policy contributes to equity but impedes economic growth.

Since Pharaonic times education has been linked with the bureaucracy. In recent times success in secondary school and in the university facilitated entry into the comfortable and secure existence of government employment. In the Nasser years this relationship was formalized by guaranteeing positions within the government bureaucracy to university graduates. A bloated bureaucracy was the unhappy result. There is now a move underway to untie education and public service. Additionally, Egypt's immediate manpower projections suggest a declining need for the graduates of the traditionally prestigious fields of learning. According to a recent study carried out by William B. Clatanoff, in the next few years, Egypt will have a great need for people with technical training, particularly graduates of industrial secondary schools, and teachers. On the other hand, universities are producing many more graduates than the country can efficiently absorb, and Clatanoff predicts an overproduction even of scientists and engineers at a time when industrial technicians are in short supply.[4]

These manpower predictions have been affirmed by many social scientists; they will have far-reaching implications for status and income in contemporary Egypt. Without powerful governmental regulating mechanisms, skilled and even unskilled men and women will fare much better financially than university graduates in law, the humanities, and even engineering and science. Already some evidence of these changes is at hand. Wages for skilled and unskilled labor have increased rapidly, not merely in the booming construction industry, but even in the rural sector. Meanwhile, university graduates often wait several years before securing a supposedly permanent job.

Finally, the educational system has always had difficulty keeping pace with Egypt's increasing population. In the last decade and a half problems of overcrowded classrooms and insufficient teachers have become palpable—not merely at the primary-school level but even within the universities. It has become increasingly difficult to receive a good quality public education, and families have turned in larger numbers to private schooling. And within the public schools, success does not seem possible without some form of private tutoring. These different forms of private schooling cost money and hence are more readily available to the rich than the poor. Abdel-Fadil believes that in the last decade education has become a force for maintaining existing privilege and no longer serves as the powerful instrument of social equity it had been in the 1950s and 1960s.

## Subsidies

In Egypt's highly regulated economy there are many kinds of subsidies. Textile mills receive cotton at a price below the world price. Indeed, textile manufacturers often receive cotton from the state at a price below that which the state itself paid the cultivators. Farmers themselves obtain seeds, fertilizers, and other inputs at a government-subsidized rate, and in return they deliver certain crops (cotton, rice, onions) at low, fixed prices. But the most important subsidies for the rank and file of the population are those on food and essential commodities. The main food subsidies are for wheat and flour, but there are other important ones on sugar, edible oil, and maize. These supports have assumed a large and controversial place in the state budget. Whereas they constituted only 2 percent of public expenditure in 1962/63, they rose to 30 percent of public expenditure in 1975/76 and accounted for no less than 11 percent of GDP.

These price supports have been a worry to government officials and especially to international economic organizations like the International Monetary Fund. Because of their mode of financing, they are highly inflationary and held to discourage rational economic behavior. Yet Ibrahim El-Issawy concludes that the food subsidies "play a significant role in maintaining the real income of the medium and lower (urban) income classes." Reda El-Edel introduced subsidies into his study of taxation, treating them as negative indirect taxes. He found that they were a powerful mechanism for equality. He estimates that in 1974/75, subsidies brought down the Gini coefficient (of national income distribution) from 0.399 to 0.366.

Perhaps in the long run the Egyptian economy could be made more dynamic and responsive if these large subsidies were dismantled. The critics claim that the subsidies give economic planners and individual consumers and producers the wrong economic signals and produce a misallocation of resources. But the middle and lower classes regard the subsidies as an important protection against the ravages of inflation and a guarantor of minimum standards. This fact was made apparent in January, 1977 when the government's program for slashing subsidies (and consequently raising the price of many commodities) resulted in widespread rioting and violence, only suppressed through the intervention of the military.

## Urban Biases

Not all government policies have contributed, or have been designed to contribute, to income equalization. Some of the income-skewing policies have come under scrutiny in this volume. John Waterbury explores the question of whether Egyptian policies, seen in their broad outlines, display an urban bias and bear responsibility for the influx of people into the cities. While concluding that the recurrent expenditures in the public budget were divided proportionately between the urban and rural populations, he points out that the investment budget, on the other hand, displays a very marked urban tilt. Cairo, Alexandria, and the Canal Zone cities, representing 22 percent of the nation's population, have obtained 56 percent of investment. The same urban prejudice is apparent in the Five Year Plan (1978–1982) where nearly 40 percent of all proposed investment will be concentrated in these same primary cities. This imbalance in expenditures has resulted in enormous differences in the provision of public services. Pure water and electricity, for example, are far more available in the cities than the countryside and no doubt are a factor in the move from rural to urban Egypt.

Urban migration is an extensively studied phenomenon in the Third World, and the same combination of push-and-pull factors that account for urban growth elsewhere appears to be at work in Egypt. Rural poverty and urban opportunity draw people to Egypt's cities. Egypt's cities are perceived as havens of new opportunities, as suggested by a 1964 study of migration in Cairo. Thirty-eight percent of the migrants were unemployed before coming to Cairo and 57 percent were unskilled. Yet the overwhelming majority felt that their economic and social situations had improved, and they related this improvement to better housing conditions and easier access to health and education.[5]

Another perspective on urban bias is the government's discrimination against agriculture—with its attendant income-skewing tendencies—a problem studied by Karima Korayem. Examining the four major export crops—cotton, rice, onions, and groundnuts—which were subjected to compulsory delivery at varying dates starting in the mid-1960s, she calculates the implicit tax the farmer pays on each crop. She finds the following implicit taxation rates over the period 1965 to 1978: cotton 22 percent to 84 percent; rice 34 percent to 64 percent; onions 47 percent to 86 percent; and groundnuts 8 percent to 57 percent. These rates are higher than the taxation rates obtaining for nonagricultural incomes; for example the maximum rate of tax on professional and noncommercial incomes is 43.5 percent. Additionally, no exemptions are permitted for the poorer farmers as is usually the case in nonagricultural taxation. Moreover, as the compulsorily-delivered crops are grown disproportionately by smaller and poorer holders, one would have to assume that this implicit tax is also highly regressive.

Since Korayem's paper does not measure the subsidy on the government's main inputs into agriculture (water, fertilizers, and pesticides), it does not purport to answer the question whether agriculture is more heavily taxed—on a net basis—than nonagriculture. But it does afford a perspective on the mentality of the government. It shows that the state is willing to impose heavy indirect taxes on the farmer even though these taxes may reduce cultivators' initiatives. The state does so because this implicit tax is easy to collect and has thus far been politically expedient. Although a tax on agricultural income would be fairer, it would require a large administration and would be difficult to collect.

## Agricultural Policies

Within the agricultural sector itself, a series of policies were examined by Ahmed Hassan. These policies—consolidation of land use and crop rotations, compulsory marketing of certain crops, and agricultural credit—were developed in connection with the land reform measures adopted after July 1952. On the one hand, the measures sought to protect the recipients of the redistributed land from unscrupulous moneylenders and to offer cultivators a safe and secure market. But on the other hand, they were also designed to regulate agricultural production, to ensure that certain crops were grown, and to extract resources from agriculture for use in other sectors. In practice, however, all three agricultural policies have disadvantaged smaller cultivators in favor of large holders. The small holders have found themselves growing more of the compulsorily delivered crops (whose government-regulated price precludes high profits), and they have benefitted less from the agricultural cooperatives and their credit provisions.

The agricultural papers in this volume provide general insights into the issue of equity in the agrarian sector. One can see that the state deprived the very large owners of their estates. It endeavored to protect the poor—the tenants and the landless—by issuing decrees on rents and agricultural wages, but these were not carefully observed or enforced. In fact, the group that benefitted most from the state's actions was the middle holders, who were able to devote a disproportionate share of their land to vegetables, fruits, and other high-value crops which could be sold freely, while the small holders shouldered the burden of growing cotton, rice, and other crops which had to be marketed through the state at fixed low prices.

## Labor Exportation

Although the state has of course been a major agent working for equity, nonetheless, there have been many nongovernmental forces affecting the distribution of income. At present probably the two most powerful are Egypt's booming construction industry and the migration of Egyptian workers to Arab oil-producing countries. Amr Mohie-Eldin holds these two factors directly responsible for the rise of rural wages, for they have drawn persons out of the agricultural economy and created labor shortages during peak rural work seasons. Construction has boomed in the last five years as a result of the vast reconstruction effort in the Canal Zone, Sadat's economic liberalization policies, and his hospitality to foreign capital. The construction industry has revolved around housing (a desperately needed commodity), public works (roads, bridges, etc.), and the expansion of tourist and business facilities.

Almost since accounts of modern Egypt were written, it has been an axiom that the inhabitants of Egypt would refuse to leave the Nile basin. It was not many years ago that the Egyptian state contemplated with many reservations a project for resettling small numbers of Egyptian peasants in sparsely-inhabited parts of Iraq. As late as 1965 only 100,000 Egyptians were living abroad. Now, however, these hoary principles are being shattered. At the time of the 1976 census no fewer than 1.4 million Egyptians were estimated to be living outside the country. The major areas of out-migration are the Arabian peninsula and Libya. At first, educated Egyptians were the ones to find employment abroad, but with the great investment and building booms taking place in underpopulated oil-rich countries like Saudi Arabia and Libya, skilled and unskilled workers have found employment abroad.

Egyptian workers leave the country for periods ranging from one to four years. Their remittances constitute an important element in the Egyptian economy (cash transfers were equal to 2.2 billion U.S. dollars in 1979). Just how long and how extensive this labor migration will be is hard to ascertain. According to a study by Birks and Sinclair, the underpopulated Arab oil countries will have a rising need for labor of all kinds for another decade. But these two authors believe that the Arab countries of the Persian Gulf will come increasingly to rely on South Asian rather than Arab labor. Pakistani, Indian, and Korean laborers are prepared to live in their own enclaves separate from the rest of the population, while the Arab workers live and intermingle with the local populations and accelerate the pace of social change more rapidly than the rulers of these states desire. Should this scenario take place, Egypt will lose a truly important new income source and an economic safety valve that has begun to have an impact on many lives, not merely of those who emigrate but of those who remain behind to enjoy remittances and who are able to find work because others are outside the country.[6]

## External Linkages

As a vitally important geopolitical area, Egypt, understandably, has been a large recipient of foreign aid. Grants and concessionary loans have had an impact on income distribution, according to Gouda Abdel-Khalek. Starting from a low level (about 1 percent of investment and imports between 1952 and 1959), aid rose dramatically. It constituted 32 percent of investment in 1960–1964, 26 percent in 1965–1969, and 37 percent in 1970–75. It assumed even more importance after 1975. The aid had certain clearly defined characteristics over the entire time period. Most of it was bilateral, and a high proportion came from a few sources and was used for a few purposes. One-third of the aid originated in the Arab states and Iran, and went largely for balance-of-payments support. Twenty-one percent came from the United States, mainly in the form of food aid, while 13 percent came from the Soviet Union and was used largely for the construction of the Aswan Dam and for general industrialization.

Abdel-Khalek recognizes how difficult it is to trace the distributional impacts of these aid inflows. Still, the aid was on an extraordinarily large scale. The total was LE 3088 million or LE 77 per person over a 24-year period. Without aid Egypt would have had to apply far more stringent measures to face the problems of stagnant exports and a falling savings rate. One-fifth to one-third of Egypt's investment and growth depended on aid transfers. Although the distributive impact is hard to assess, Abdel-Khalek concludes that Soviet industrialization projects probably benefitted more the middle classes, which were able to purchase the durables manufactured in the new Soviet-financed industries, while the High Dam and the American food aid benefitted all of Egypt's classes. The repayment of the loans fell heavily on the agricultural population through the system of compulsory delivery of specified crops. In Abdel-Khalek's view, aid from nonsocialist sources worsens the income distribution via a variety of subtle mechanisms: denationalization of the public sector, subsidization of the private sector, the reinstitution of market forces, and pressure to eliminate subsidies.

In October, 1974 President Anwar al-Sadat formally announced a new policy, called *Infitah*. The main emphasis of the policy was economic liberalization and provision of incentives to foreign investment. Having concluded that domestic savings were too small to fuel the growth of the economy, the leaders hoped to attract foreign investment and to make the market a more important force for allocation decisions. The Infitāh developed in the post-1973 era and was a response to changing political and economic realities in the Middle East. Egypt was eager to attract petrodollars from the Gulf and to make the country an industrial center for the Middle East. In a move designed to signal this change, Sadat expelled his Russian advisers and sought a close rapprochement with the United States. The Infitah anticipated an alliance of Western technical know-how, Arab oil money, and an abundant and cheap Egyptian skilled labor force producing for Arab markets. Moreover, the Egyptian leaders also hoped to profit from the strategic importance of Egypt and the desire of conservative Arab oil countries and the United States to support Egypt for geopolitical reasons.

Although these international factors were important in the elaboration of the Infitah policy, both Ali Dessouki and Fouad Ajami refer also to the domestic forces. They place the roots of Infitah in the latter Nasser years. Referring to the Nasser period as the populist interlude, Ajami argues that this populist course was destined to be short in view of two sets of factors: the converging pressures from outside (the cost of the Yemen war, the withdrawal of United States aid in 1965, and the regional accommodation of the conservative Arab states) and the course's own limits. Elements from the pre-1952 era who had been able to preserve their wealth and connections despite the Nasser expropriation and nationalization joined with high-level state bureaucrats and public-sector leaders, now anxious to increase their wealth in an expanding private sector.

What impact, if any, has the Infitāh had upon the distribution of income? Unfortunately, nearly all the data employed in this study were drawn from pre-1975 publications. No clear statistical pattern emerges.

The regime remains committed ideologically to social justice. Although Sadat has criticized many of Nasser's policies, he has never suggested that the quest for social justice was incorrect. The most enduring commitment to equity has been the subsidies. Yet the regime has reintroduced profit incentives and market forces. It has stressed that progressive taxation will be a major instrument of income redistribution. Most of the scholars in this volume believe that Infitah has produced a new skewing of income and the growth of a new middle class.

Ajami argues that prospects for redistribution and welfare under the turn to the right indicated by Infitāh are not bright. Abdel-Khalek argues elsewhere[7] that there are several reasons to expect Infitah to have detrimental effects on income distribution. First, Infitāh tends to cause public expenditure to run ahead of public revenue, leading to a mounting budgetary deficit that is largely covered by inflationary methods (borrowing from the Central Bank). Second, by encouraging more capital intensive projects, it tends to depress the share of wages in GDP. Third, the tax and customs duties exemption under the Infitah law (Law 43 for 1974 amended by Law 32 for 1977) lead to a greater concentration of wealth. Finally, Infitah will change the sociopolitical matrix in Egypt; landowners, traders and comprador elements will gain power and strength, while peasants, workers, bureaucrats and even the productive segment of national capitalists will be weakened.

## Conclusion

Egypt was the first African and Middle Eastern country to evince interest in equity. Since the end of World War II, intellectual and political leaders have championed equity goals. Nonetheless, the radical socialist directions taken by some Third World countries were not followed in Egypt. Before 1952 equity was not translated into political action. After 1952 the new rulers retained all political power in their own hands, snuffing out most of the liberal and parliamentary safeguards of the preceding period while advancing on the social and economic front. Land was redistributed. Foreign control of the economy was done away with, and many wealthy Egyptians were stripped of their assets. Education became an instrument of social mobility as graduates of Egypt's expanding universities moved into the bureaucracy and other segments of the public sector. While these reforms may be said to have had a tilt toward the middle segments of Egyptian society, the state also sought to create a floor of minimum standards of living for the poor. It provided price subsidies on basic foodstuffs, enacted a maximum land rental law, and controlled the rents of unfurnished apartments.

By the mid-1960s, however, the Egyptian economy had begun to stagnate. Following the 1967 war a move away from state economic controls started, with a concomitant de facto declining interest in equity. The invocation of the virtues of private enterprise and free market forces has not gone unnoticed. These calls have produced opposition, even violent outbursts like the January, 1977 riots. Although it is difficult to obtain information about opposition in Egypt, there appear to be potentially powerful groups which will oppose efforts to turn away from the social gains and commitments of the Nasser years. Urban workers have registered some displeasure from time to time. Students are always a reservoir of radical sentiments, and there is now a growing religious revival in Egypt. One of its emphases is social justice.

However one may feel about the policies of the Nasser years, they did bring important social and equity gains for many Egyptians. Available statistics do not permit facile generalizations, but they reveal a relatively equitable distribution of income, at least by Third World standards. Still, Egypt's resource base is so narrow, its cultivable land so limited, and its population expanding so rapidly that one cannot be sanguine about future economic prospects. Perhaps the equity gains will be maintained and the distribution of income will remain fairly equal. But unless the economy can be invigorated and high growth rates achieved, the numbers living at or below the poverty level will continue to grow.

## Notes

1. Samir Radwan, "The Impact of Agrarian Reform on Rural Egypt, 1952–75," World Employment Programme Research *Working Papers*, International Labour Office (Geneva, 1977), pp. 20–23.

2. Mahmoud Abdel-Fadil, *Development, Income Distribution, and Social Change in Rural Egypt, 1952–1970: A Study of the Political Economy of the Agrarian Transition* (Cambridge, 1975), p. 11.

3. Karima Korayem, "The Impact of the Elimination of Food Subsidies on the Cost of Living of Egypt's Urban Population," ILO, World Employment Programme, *WP* 91 (August, 1980).

4. William B. Clatanoff, "Manpower Projections for Planning Education and Training," (AID Mimeo, 1978), p. 32.

5. This is referred to in Joint Housing and Community Upgrading Team, "Housing and Community Upgrading for Low-Income Egyptians," (Cairo, 1977), p. 10.

6. Stace Birks and Clive Sinclair, "Aspects of International Labour Migration in the Arab Near East: Implications for USAID Policy," (Washington, 1979).

7. Gouda Abdel-Khalek, "The Open Door Economic Policy in Egypt: Its Contribution to Investment and Equity Implications," Ch. IX in Malcolm H. Kerr and El Sayed Yassin (eds.), *Rich and Poor States in the Middle East: Egypt and the New Arab Order* (Boulder, Colo.: Westview Press, forthcoming).

# CHAPTER 2

# *Equity in Egypt's Recent Past: 1945–1952*

Robert Tignor

Equity emerged as an important political and social concern in Egyptian politics at the conclusion of World War II. In the seven years before the military coup d'etat of July 1952, Egyptian politicians and intellectuals debated questions of wealth and poverty, the maldistribution of income, and ways to secure a decent standard of living for all citizens. But the government failed to effect meaningful redistributive programs, and this was one of the major reasons for the intervention of the military in politics.

Egypt was the first Middle Eastern and African country to manifest concern over social questions. Even most Latin American countries were not deeply troubled by these questions in the 1940s. Only in China and parts of Southeast Asia did the issues assume prominence early, and there these questions often resulted in the enactment of far-reaching programs of social reform. Most of the African and Middle Eastern states, on the other hand, tended to follow the dictum of Kwame Nkrumah to "seek ye first the political kingdom," postponing their quest for equity until after political independence had been won.

Why was it that Egypt experienced an early concern with equity? Why did the politicians of the 1940s describe themselves as socialists and propose programs designed to alleviate poverty and to redistribute wealth? And why, in the final analysis, did these various pre-Nasser governments accomplish so little? These are some of the questions posed in this chapter.

The answers to these questions are complex, but they are intimately bound up with a host of interrelated factors: Egyptian social structure; European predominance in the Egyptian economy and polity; the nationalist movement, which was engendered to combat this European influence; and a nationalist ideology stressing antiforeign, populist, and egalitarian themes.

By the twentieth century, the Egyptian economy and polity was dominated and penetrated by European capital. Few other African countries were so deeply involved in the international economic order—a penetration manifesting itself in numerous branches of European banking houses, land mortgages held by those firms, foreign control over commerce, and

the presence of British troops and administrators. While other colonial countries also had foreign banks, foreign troops, and foreign control of overseas commerce, in Egypt this foreign economic presence penetrated into the countryside and into the lives of ordinary peasants. It was a day-to-day reality of all urban dwellers. Because of intense nineteenth-century European contacts with Egypt, the construction of the Suez Canal, and the widespread cultivation of cotton, almost no part of the country was insulated from world economic forces. Moreover, a whole host of institutions, such as the Capitulations (legally sanctioned foreign privileges) and the Mixed Courts administered by foreign and Egyptian judges, set off the Europeans from the rest of the Egyptian population and rendered them a privileged and wealthy elite. They became the natural targets of nationalist hostility.

As a consequence, Egyptian nationalism always had a strong economic and, on occasions, an egalitarian component. The nationalists were not simply struggling with a distant colonial office or foreign office in London and Paris, but with a very palpable local and, in many cases, oppressive foreign economic presence. Consequently, nationalism projected populist and egalitarian messages, portraying the foreign capitalists in Egypt as exploiters and creators of gross inequalities. One can discern these themes even in the revolution of 1919, which was preeminently a political movement striving first and foremost for political independence. But there were also forceful economic undercurrents; nationalists called for an end to exploitation and the removal of gross disparities of wealth.

These same emphases receded from time to time in the ebb and flow of nationalism, but they were powerfully renewed after the Second World War. Ironically, the rise of a native Egyptian bourgeoisie was a factor in the resurgence of interest in the distribution of wealth. Many of these new men of industry and commerce aspired to the influence and wealth exercised by the foreign bourgeoisie in Egypt. In their efforts to unseat this solidly entrenched elite they were not averse to attributing the skewed distribution of wealth in the country to the foreign economic presence. They also argued that these disparities would quickly disappear under an autonomous Egyptian capitalism. Moreover, by this time the Egyptian ruling element had become factionalized. People who derived their wealth primarily from industry and commerce espoused different political and economic interests from those whose well-being stemmed from the land. These two factions often sought to depict their opponents as responsible for the poverty and suffering afflicting the country.

An additional factor was democratic politics. Parties competed for elections, and in the years after World War II students and workers began to become influential in elections. The different political parties sought to win their support by making appeals for social justice. But in the final analysis, power remained in the hands of the well-to-do; the nationalist ideology was controlled and manipulated. The efforts of workers and

students to organize for independent political action did not succeed and, as a consequence, no meaningful social and economic reform was carried out before 1952. The last Wafdist ministry had ties with left-wing elements and a commitment to enact redistributive programs. But the power centers in the party were in the hands of the large landowners and the large industrialists, and no significant program ever materialized.

## Nature and Sources of Egyptian Inequality

Although no studies were made of the distribution of income on a national scale prior to 1952, there is unanimity among commentators that Egypt's wealth was grossly maldistributed in this period. The portrait of the nature and sources of inequality must, however, be drawn from scattered pieces of evidence.

The basis of Egypt's wealth as a predominantly agricultural country and a cotton export economy was the land. Unfortunately, landholding statistics are somewhat flawed because the separate holdings of single people were not grouped together and often appeared in the statistics as separate entries. A more definitive view of the concentration of landed wealth was put forth at the time of the land reform scheme. According to Sayyid Marᶜī, 1,758 Egyptians owned estates larger than 200 *feddans* (207.6 acres). Their holdings totaled 656,640 feddans, or approximately one-tenth of Egypt's arable surface.[1] Of these 1,758 large landowners, 425 were members of the royal family, whose landholdings totaled 179,157 feddans.[2] The largest landowner in the country was King Farūq, whose estate totaled 28,109 feddans.[3] Three other families had holdings over 10,000 feddans—Badrawī-ᶜAshūr, Sirāj al-Dīn Shahīn, and ᶜAmr.[4]

According to Samir Radwan, the Gini coefficient for the distribution of land ownership increased from 0.696 in 1896 to 0.758 in 1952.[5] A feature of Egypt's rural scene, in addition to the concentration of large estates in the hands of a few families, was the large and ever increasing size of the rural landless population. The 1950 agricultural census reported 3,442,000 agricultural laborers.[6]

Because of the compactness and relative smallness of Egypt's arable area, this highly uneven distribution of land prevailed throughout the country. In certain provinces, however, inequality reached particularly high levels. In Lower Egypt the provinces of Buhayra and Gharbīya contained a large number of big estates. More than half of Buhayra province was in the hands of large landowners, while Gharbīya had a few extremely large estates, including the holdings of Badrawī-ᶜAshūr (18,000 feddans) and Sirāj al-Dīn (3,300 feddans).[7] In Upper Egypt, land in Minyā, Qinā, and Aswān provinces was heavily concentrated. In Qinā seventy people owned 44,352 feddans, and in Aswān, thirteen owned 74,350. A privately owned land company—the Kom Ombo Company—possessed more than one-half of the privately owned land of Aswān province.[8] The

area around Naj Hammādī in Qinā province, a lucrative sugar-growing region, contained numerous big estates belonging to the industrialist Ahmad ʿAbbūd (over 5,000 feddans), Prince Yūsuf Kāmal (over 16,000 feddans) and King Farūq (over 6,500 feddans). Minyā province was the home area of such large landowners as the Sultān, Shaʿrawī, and Lutfāllah families.[9]

Another aspect of inequality in land distribution was the disparity between Egyptian and foreign property holders. Even as late as 1949, foreigners owned 233,013 feddans, and their average holding was 61 feddans compared with less than 2 feddans for Egyptian landowners. According to the *Annuaire Statistique*, 233 foreigners possessed 173,896 feddans.[10] Much of this foreign-owned land was in the possession of European-run land development companies. A few of these firms farmed the land themselves, but most of them purchased land for the purpose of preparing it for cultivation and then selling it to private landholders. Still, there were a number of private foreign landowners.

The concentration of lands was paralleled by the concentration of industrial and commercial wealth. In this area definitive statistics are even more difficult to find, but one can obtain a representative portrait of inequality by focusing on the boards of directors of industrial and commercial joint stock companies. To be sure, there were many privately owned firms and partnerships, but increasingly in the twentieth century Egyptian and foreign businessmen saw the advantages of establishing limited joint stock companies. Moreover, a high proportion of the large-scale industrial and commercial businesses of Egypt were conducted as joint stock company undertakings.

An examination of the directors of the boards of these firms reveals the concentration of wealth. Of the 1,008 directors listed in the *Stock Exchange Yearbook* for 1946, only 227 appear to have been Egyptians.[11] A few individuals served on the boards of many companies, suggesting not only the presence of industrial and commercial cartels but also the existence of large personal fortunes. The following individuals served on the boards of 12 or more companies in 1946: Hafiz ʿAfīfī (33); Hussayn Sirrī (30); Muhammad Ahmad Farghalī (29); ʿAlī Amīn Yahya (23); ʿAbd al-Maqsūd Ahmad (22); Muhammad Mahmūd Khalīl (20); Hasan Mazlūm (17); Maurice N. Mosseri (15); Ahmad Sāddiq (15); Michel Salvago (14); Aslan Qattawi (14); Muhammad Shukrī (14); Tawfīq Dūss (13); Silvio Pinto (13); ʿAbd al-Rahmān Hamada (13); and Henry A. Barker (12).[12] Although some of these directors were foreigners, they warrant inclusion in a description of the bourgeoisie in Egypt. Not only did they derive their wealth in Egypt, but all of them resided there.

These macrostatistics reveal a society with a badly skewed distribution of wealth. Sometimes general indicators are not nearly as telling as specific illustrations, for which the Egyptian evidence is bountiful. For instance, the head of the land reform scheme, Sayyid Marʿī, estimated

that the Egyptian royal family derived a yearly income of £E12m. (12 million Egyptian pounds) from its agricultural estates in 1951; in addition its members had substantial investments in other economic activities.[13] The king had widespread estates in Upper Egypt. One of his *taftishes* (farms) there totaled 6,615 feddans and was valued at £E1,700,000. It had approximately 25,000 renters and agricultural laborers. A renter was said to make £E10 per year per feddan and the king £E40.[14]

Another glimpse into the extremes of wealth and poverty is provided by ᶜAsim al-Disūqī in his study of the large landowners in the twentieth century. He claims that in 1946–1947 the average yearly income of a family owning between 100 and 200 feddans was £E5105. Those families holding between 200 and 500 feddans were said to have an average annual income of £E10,941 and those over 500 feddans averaged close to £E50,000 per year. There were 2,125 Egyptian families who owned between 100 and 500 feddans. On the other hand, the average income of a person owning less than 1 feddan was £E28 and 5 feddans £E150.[15] According to an Egyptian government survey, the average rural wage for an adult male in 1945 was 9.3 piastres per day. Thus if one assumed that the rural laborer worked 260 days per year, his gross income for the year would be approximately £E24, a little less than the person owning less than 1 feddan and one-sixth the income of the owner of 5 feddans. Additionally, this figure of £E24 is based on an assumption of relatively steady employment during the year—an assumption not applicable to many agricultural laborers.[16]

Two other microstudies shed further light on income distribution before 1952. An Egyptian sociologist, Hamed Ammar, in his study of 238 households in a village in Sharqīya province published in 1944 found that 40 percent of the inhabitants lived on an annual income of £E5 or less while only 5.5 percent had incomes exceeding £E50.[17] A similar portrait of extraordinary and widespread poverty was revealed in the Rockefeller Foundation study of 1,071 families in Sindbis, Qalyūbīya province, in 1948. The investigators found that 5 percent of the population obtained less than £E12 per year, 61 percent had between £E12 and £E60, 27 percent between £E60 and £E120, and only 7 percent more than £E120.[18]

There were many reasons for the maldistribution of wealth, and this is not the place to offer a detailed exposition of those factors. It is clear that the state represented the interests of the wealthy and played a crucial role in increasing and sustaining these disparities of wealth. In the nineteenth century the gradual introduction of private property rights and the distribution of state lands to the wealthy and influential enabled a few families to accumulate large tracts of land. State support for private capital—even monopoly capital—enabled a few business firms to dominate many aspects of the economy. Other policies assisted the wealthy and had adverse effects on the poor. In particular, tariff and labor policies benefitted the rich at the expense of the poor.

Egypt did not acquire the freedom to regulate its own tariffs until 1930. Prior to that date the country was precluded from raising the tax on most items above 8 percent ad valorem. In 1930, however, tariff independence was obtained, and the government proceeded to erect modest tariff barriers for the purpose of protecting important import substituting industries, like textiles, cereals, and food processing. These industries began to advance under the aegis of tariff protection but, as they were unable to manufacture commodities at or below the world market price, the ordinary Egyptian had to finance this progress by spending a high proportion of his meager income on these locally made manufactures.

One can illustrate this contention and learn something about the sources of inequality by considering state policy toward textiles, cereals, sugar, and oil, all of which were vital products to the Egyptian population and were produced within the country.

The Egyptian cotton industry was prohibited from importing foreign raw cotton, ostensibly because these imports might introduce into the country cotton diseases that would infect the valuable locally grown crop. No doubt, however, powerful Egyptian cotton cultivators were also interested in securing for themselves a privileged local market. The result was that Egypt's burgeoning textile industry was forced to use expensive, albeit durable, long-staple Egyptian cotton to manufacture cloth for local consumption. The prices of locally made products were far from competitive with the extremely cheap and popular Japanese, Italian, and Indian textiles, which had begun to dominate world markets in the 1930s. The Egyptian government raised its tariff barriers to keep these products out of the local market. While this action enabled the domestic textile industry to thrive, the local consumer had to spend more to clothe himself and his family.

Similarly the state kept the sugar industry alive despite its inability to produce competitively by world standards. Two groups supported a high sugar tariff—large landowners based in Upper Egypt on whose estates sugar was cultivated, and the managers and owners of the Egyptian Sugar Company. In addition, the government found these arrangements beneficial, for, according to an accord negotiated between the government and the Sugar Company in 1931, the profits made by the company after it had paid a 5 percent dividend to its shareholders went mainly to the state.[19] These profits constituted a significant part of state revenues in the 1930s when the company was realizing handsome profits. That these profits were substantial—and no doubt paid for by the ordinary consumer—is indicated by the fact that between 1930/1931 and 1943/1944 the state received £E17,847,350 in the form of various payments from the company while the company was itself realizing a profit of only £E334,763.[20]

The government's cereals policies also imposed a heavy burden on the consumer. In the 1930s the state cut off the import of grain by raising the tariffs. The result of these tariff policies was to raise the price of wheat and maize to more than double that of imported grains. According to Charles Issawi, the bulk of Egypt's wheat was consumed by Egypt's urban population, whose expenditure on bread represented over 50 percent of their household expenditures. Town workers, Issawi felt, paid a subsidy of some £E5 million per year to Egypt's wheat-growing landlords and tenants and its millers.[21]

A final example of a high-priced necessity was kerosene, used by a large number of Egyptians for cooking and heating. Kerosene was supplied by two Western-run oil exploration and refining companies based in Egypt. These were the Anglo-Egyptian Company, a subsidiary of Shell Oil, and the American Socony-Vacuum Company. According to the agreement negotiated between these companies and the Egyptian government, the companies were supposed to supply the domestic market at a price below that prevailing for oil in the world. In fact, through various subterfuges the companies conspired to fix prices and to sell oil and kerosene on the domestic market at inflated prices. In the view of British and American embassy officials, the companies were able to make exorbitant profits in Egypt in the interwar years, largely again because they held monopoly powers over the marketing of an indispensable product.[22]

A final area of policy in which a fundamentally inegalitarian and, in this case, predominantly capitalist view prevailed was labor policy. When Egypt gained its nominal independence in 1922, labor conditions were regulated by only one law. This decree, enacted in 1909, provided restrictions against the employment of children in cotton ginneries, tobacco factories, and spinning, weaving, and cotton pressing plants.[23] After the First World War the state recognized the need to enact more comprehensive labor regulations, and a governmental committee, chaired by ᶜAbd al-Rahman Ridā, put forward far-reaching proposals based largely on legislation prevailing in Europe at the time. The Ridā Commission, for instance, made the employer responsible for providing housing, food, schooling, and health care, limited the working day to nine hours, and prohibited the employment of children under twelve. It also recognized the right of workers to organize unions and federations of unions.[24] Even before the report was published, Egypt's leading industrialist group, the Egyptian Federation of Industries, began to marshall opposition. Spokesmen for the federation argued that industrial conditions in Egypt were different from those in Europe, that Egypt was at an early stage of industrial growth and was seeking to attract foreign and domestic capital through the cheapness and docility of its labor force, and that the Egyptian worker was different from his European counterpart, having more limited needs and a more restricted social horizon.[25] The federation's campaign proved successful. It was buttressed by a report written by a labor expert from the International Labor Office, M. H. Butler, sent to advise the Egyptians. Butler agreed with the industrialists that Egypt should not have "a rigid and comprehensive code regulating the conditions of employment on Western European lines." Rather he counseled Egyptians to look to the industrial regulations in existence at that time in Japan, India, Palestine, and French North Africa.[26]

As a consequence of these pressures, Egypt's new labor laws, as enacted in the 1930s, made no provision for old age, sickness, and unemployment insurance. Although the legislation regulated the employment of women and children, it also permitted the employment of nine- and twelve-year-old children and in general was well below the international standard.[27]

One may wonder whether tougher legislation would have made much difference in labor relations, for even these far from stringent regulations were only sporadically enforced. What, in fact, the debate over labor legislation provided was insight into the mentality of the ruling elite, especially the rising industrial element, which was anxious to pare labor costs to the bone.

## Equity as a Political Issue

Despite the obvious disparities in wealth in Egypt, equity questions did not become politically salient until after World War II. The war had a decisive and radicalizing impact on Egypt. It generated vast social changes and dislocations in Egyptian society. Many Egyptians left the countryside and found employment in Egyptian industries. The large contingent of British armed forces stationed in Egypt employed 140,000 workers. In addition the British force had numerous contracts with Egyptian manufacturing firms.[28] Although the war years generally saw a slowdown in Egyptian economic activities because of the disruption of international trade, 1941 was the single most expansive year for Egyptian industries.[29] Many domestic firms found themselves in an advantageous position because they no longer had to compete with cheap European manufactures.[30] On the other hand, rampaging inflation injured the poor urban dwellers and the peasants, who were compelled to pay high prices for necessities. The cost of living nearly tripled between 1939 and 1945.[31] Finally at the close of the war the demobilization of British troops and the gradual resumption of international trade produced industrial dislocations and led to crises of unemployment. The years 1946 and 1947 were marked by widespread strikes while the period from 1950 to 1952 saw the postwar inflationary crisis come to a head.

These social and economic changes resulted in increased attention being given to the gross disparities of wealth within Egyptian society. Concern for social problems came to occupy a major place in the thinking of literate Egyptians, second only to the goal of achieving political independence from the British. The evidence for this assertion comes from a wide variety of sources—literature, journalism, leftist thought, the rise of new political parties, and the transformation of the political and economic programs of established parties.

An important barometer for Egyptian thinking—at least the thought of literate urban dwellers—is literature. Although the novel has had but a short history in Egypt, its practitioners have developed a talent for articulating the country's burning issues. Beginning in 1945 a series of novels had as their theme the misery and poverty among the masses and the need for radical redistributive changes.

Three novelists were the most powerful exponents of social concerns in the 1940s. In 1946 and 1947 Lūwīs ᶜAwad wrote *al-ᶜAnqa' (The Phoenix),* "one of the most violent expressions of revolt to come out of Egypt," but he was unable to publish his manuscript until after the overthrow of the monarchy in 1952.[32] ᶜAwad was a member of a Marxist study group and believed that Egypt needed radical social reform. ᶜAdīl Kāmil's one novel, *Milim al-Akbār* (1944), contained an arresting description of social injustice. Undoubtedly the most influential literary critic of this period was Najīb Mahfūz. Having written three historical novels during the Second World War, Mahfūz abruptly changed his orientation in 1945; between 1945 and 1952 he wrote nine novels, all of them realistic portraits of the impoverished classes in Egypt. His *Midhaq Alley,* for example, depicted life in the slums of Cairo. According to a literary critic of Mahfūz, "the social theme is dominant in most of these stories. Mahfūz's interest in the impoverished classes of Cairo is of a less detached and a more militant nature. . . . The suffering of these people is portrayed with much passion and bitterness."[33]

The novels of this period reveal an interest in communism and socialism and, indeed, there was an increased attraction toward leftist thought, as manifested by the proliferation of leftist study groups and even secret cells after 1945. Although these communist and socialist societies had a small membership, the impact of their ideas was not slight. These groups in particular influenced the thinking of the left wing of the Wafd party.

Toward the end of the Second World War and in 1946, a host of new communist, socialist, and leftist groups came into existence. They spoke out against poverty, maldistribution of land, foreign economic domination, and called for a variety of political, social, and economic reforms. Their programs included, in most cases, limitation on the size of landed estates, a more progressive system of taxation, and state control of public utilities. In July 1946 Egypt's autocratic prime minister, Ismāᶜīl Sidqī, sought to repress the left, arresting their leaders and suspending the publication of their newspapers.[34] Among the persons arrested were Salāma Mūsa, Egypt's Coptic socialist, Muhammad Mandūr, a left-wing Wafdist and editor of the highly influential newspaper *al-Wafd al-Misrī,* known for its exposition of socialist ideas, and Henri Curiel, a long-standing participant in communist and socialist activities in Egypt. Among the leftist publications that were suspended at the time were *al-Wafd al-Misrī, al-Fajr al-Jadīd, al-Talīᶜa, Um Durmān,* and *al-Damīr.*

The ideas espoused by these leftist organizations and their publications were not as radical as their critics contended, but they forcibly interjected into the political arena such themes as Egyptian control over the economy, the gross disparities of wealth, the need to secure decent standards of living for the poor, the desirability of enacting redistributive programs, and the need for public and democratic control of Egyptian resources.

Accompanying the proliferation of leftist organizations was the emergence of organized labor as a force in Egyptian society and politics. The industrial labor force was on the rise in the 1940s; the numbers organized into trade unions were increasing. According to estimates made by the British in 1944, the trade union movement encompassed approximately 100,000 members, of whom 36,000 were in textiles.[35] The economic officer in the American embassy estimated trade union strength the next year at 489 unions with 140,000 members; 39,500 were in textiles; 20,000 in transportation, and 17,000 in food processing.[36] Like unions in most developing countries, these organizations were badly fragmented. Although they represented less than half of the urban work force, they had considerable support in Egypt's large modernized industries. Most labor leaders were not interested in theoretical socialist ideas and radical programs of social reform, however. Their concerns were focused on shorter working hours, improved working conditions, and higher pay.

Nevertheless, certain unions and workers were under the influence of socialist leaders. The textile factory at Shubra al-Khaymā employed 7,000 workers and suffered a paralyzing and bitter strike in 1946.[37] One of the strike leaders was Yūsuf Darwīsh, who was on the board of the leftist newspaper *al-Fajr al-Jadīd.* He disseminated this newspaper among the workers.[38] An even more influential strike organizer was Saᶜd ᶜUthmān, who was president of a textile workers union in Shubra and had been president of the General Union for Textile Workers in Cairo from 1938 to 1943. Saᶜd ᶜUthmān was also on the board of the leftist newspaper *al-Damīr,* which was the organ of one of the most influential leftist organizations, the Committee of Workers for National Liberation *(Lajna ᶜUmmāl al-Tahrīr al-Qawmī).* ᶜUthmān's ambition was to unite socialist thought and the labor movement. Like many programs of self-pronounced socialists, his program was not extremely radical. It consisted mainly of nationalist and democratic appeals. But Saᶜd ᶜUthmān also favored programs with such potentially redistributive implications as state control over public utilities, education for all, land limitation, distibution of surplus lands to small peasants, recognition of labor unions, the right to strike, and a limitation on working hours.[39]

Equity concerns also infused Egypt's political parties, although the issues tended to be articulated more energetically by the extremist parties that were on the fringe of the established political order. The extremist party with the largest following in Egypt was the Muslim Brotherhood, founded in 1928 by Hasan al-Bannā. Its call for a return to pristine Islam was attractive to many students and workers. Many of these elements were angered because of their limited career prospects and were intrigued by the seductive appeals of an almost millennial vision of the world. Criticizing the Muslim Brothers for their simplistic social and economic program, critics argued that a return to purified Islam, as practiced in the earliest Islamic period, offered no meaningful solution to Egypt's problems of poverty, population explosion, and lack of political development. Indeed, many spokesmen for the Muslim Brotherhood were perplexingly vague about these pressing social issues. Yet at the same time there were Brethren intellectuals whose message contained powerful social criticisms.

The writings of Sayyid Qutb, Khalid Muhammad Khalīd, and Muhammad al-Ghazzālī were of this genre. Sayyid Qutb's *al-ᶜAdala al-Ijtimā-ᶜīya fī-l-Islām,* published around 1945 and subsequently translated into English, argued that primitive Islam provided safeguards against exploitative capitalism and ensured a decent standard of living to all. The establishment of a truly Islamic society, he contended, would enable Egypt and other Middle Eastern states to chart a middle course between the rampant individualism and social unconcern of capitalism and the oppressive state controls of communism. Sayyid Qutb also wrote a searing indictment of Egyptian conditions of oppression and inequality called *Maᶜraka al-Islām w-al-Ra'smālīya,* published in 1952.[40]

A less influential political group was Young Egypt; yet its swing toward equity matters and radical social and economic programs provides further proof of the saliency of this issue after World War II. Young Egypt was founded as a quasi-fascistic organization in 1933. It was mainly the creation of two young Egyptians—Ahmad Husayn and Fathī Radwān. During the 1930s its appeal was strongest among the young, especially students and workers. Before World War II its ideological orientation was primarily nationalist and religious. It extolled the use of Arabic and counseled Egyptians to purchase and use only Egyptian-made goods. During these years the social content of Young Egypt was muted, limited to a very large extent to railing against the corruption and inefficiency of the established parties and the parliamentary system.

Thus Young Egypt's political transformation after the war was revealing. It renamed itself the Socialist party, and in the 1950 election it succeeded in having Ibrāhīm Shukrī elected. Shukrī spoke in Parliament in favor of redistributive reform programs, calling for a fifty-feddan limitation on land, free education, free health care, social insurance, and the abolition of titles.[41] Ahmad Husayn also became an exponent of those programs. He now characterized the capitalist elite as exploiters and monpolists.[42]

The established parties, as might be expected, were less equity-conscious than the Muslim Brotherhood and Young Egypt. Yet even these political leaders could not resist the new currents of thought sweeping through Egypt. *Socialism (Ishtirākīya)* had become a fashionable word, albeit always carefully distinguished from *communism*. Politicians sought to persuade their electorates that they were indeed socialist, as evidenced by an interview given by ᶜAbd al-ᶜAzīz al-Sufānī, a former minister of state and secretary of the Watanī party. In it he claimed that the Watanī party was socialist since it was concerned about the welfare of the people. But the only radical reform he championed, at least in this interview, was the nationalization of public utilities.[43]

While the Saᶜdists, the Liberal Constitutionalists, the Watanists, and the Kutla bloc of Makram ᶜUbayd sporadically made socialist claims, their commitment to altering the distribution of wealth was weak. Quite the contrary was the case of the Wafd, Egypt's most popular party since its founding during the 1919 revolution. Its ties with the masses—in the cities and the countryside—were always closer than those of the other parties and always more important to its own self-image. Its leadership had undergone many changes and numerous defections since the first appearance of the party. Following the Anglo-Egyptian treaty of 1936, new elements entered the party. Many of the new leaders represented the landed class, such as ᶜAbd al-Fattāh al-Tawīl, Muhammad Sulaymān al-Wakīl, Muhammad al-Hifnī al-Tarrāzī, Ahmad Mustafa ᶜAmr, Fahmī Wīssa, Sayyid Bahnis, and Fu'ad Sirāj al-Dīn Shāhīn.[44] While some of these individuals, like Sirāj al-Dīn, had ties with student and labor organizations and even helped to foment riots and strikes, there can be no question that they gave the Wafd a powerful and exceedingly conservative orientation.[45]

At the same time the Wafd also spawned an activist and imposing left-wing movement. In the years immediately after the war this leftist orientation began to make its influence felt. Its most articulate spokesman was Dr. Muhammad Mandūr, an exponent of nationalism, democracy, and socialism. As editor of the influential leftist newspaper *al-Wafd al-Misrī*, he wrote articles favoring tighter state regulation of the economy and attacking the maldistribution of wealth. A series of articles written in June 1946 under the title "Pashāwāt wa Ra'smālīyīn" (Pashas and Capitalists) argued that a few families in Egypt monopolized most of the wealth and that these families were growing wealthier by the year, leaving the rest of the people to experience poverty, ignorance, and sickness.[46]

The Wafd came to power for the first time after World War II in 1950. Its electoral triumph was an impressive one, demonstrating once again that it was still Egypt's most popular party. In this open election, it won 228 of the 319 Chamber of Deputies seats.[47] Great expectations surrounded the Wafd's coming to power. Programs involving a substantial redistribution of wealth were expected. The failure of the Wafd to carry out even a minimally acceptable program condemned this party to be overthrown in the July 1952 coup.

The Wafd's failure was not one of ideas, for it had a radical left wing whose intellectual energies and socialist proclivities could have been exploited to good effect. Nor was its failure the result of faulty planning. Shortly after the party came to power, it created a new Ministry of National Economy, the goal of which was to tackle questions involving the poor. A great deal of fanfare surrounded the establishment of this ministry. It was given the task of securing reasonable standards of living, providing work for the unemployed, food for the poor, knowledge for the ignorant, and medicines for the sick.[48] Its minister, Muhammad al-Wakīl, speaking on the occasion of its creation, said that the ministry must secure a decent level of living for all the people and must devise programs that would spread income to the middle and lower classes.[49] Another important new government organization was the Department of Social Support, under the Ministry of Social Affairs. Its task was to compel landowners to provide health and social services to those who lived and worked on their estates, to facilitate the distribution of state lands to small peasants, and to enact a program of free secondary education. Despite these meritorious programs, the Wafd succeeded in implementing little significant social legislation.

In part this failure stemmed from the fact that political issues always assumed precedence over social concerns in colonial Egypt. In the two years before the Nasser coup, the Wafd was engaged in a bitter and often violent struggle with the British to gain complete independence. But the basic reason for failure was the fact that the Wafdist party and its ministry represented the conservative wing of the party. A number of the most important ministerial offices were held by ultraconservatives and large landowners. ᶜUthmān Muharram was minister of public works. ᶜAbd al-Fattāh al-Tawīl was justice minister. Sirāj al-Dīn was at the Interior and Muhammad Muhammad al-Wakīl headed up the sensitive and potentially important Ministry of National Economy. The only person in the Wafdist ministry with credentials as a social reformer was Dr. Ahmad Husayn at the Ministry of Social Affairs.

Thus the new waves of thought concerning equity and social justice came to be focused on the Wafdist ministry. They were rudely dashed by its incapacity to implement at least a fraction of the social program that had entered the thinking of literate, and no doubt illiterate, Egyptians after the Second World War.

## The Causes of the Concern with Equity in Egypt

It is easy to marshall evidence demonstrating the gross disparities of income in Egypt prior to 1952. Equally straightforward is the argument and evidence for the saliency of equity and distributive questions after the ending of the Second World War. Much more difficult questions to answer are why equity came to the fore as a political concern when it did and why equity questions were expressed in the manner in which they were. On the surface these questions might seem to have easy and obvious answers. Equity became important because the maldistribution of income was so extreme in Egypt and tending to become even worse. This is, indeed, part of the answer, but only a part. In fact, it is clear from examining other societies that poorly distributed income does not automatically lead people to turn their thoughts to equity or to call for the redistribution of wealth.

Why did equity become a salient political issue when it did? What were the factors causing Egyptian politicians to turn their attention to this question? The answers to these quesions will also shed light on how equity questions were framed in pre-Nasser Egypt and why in the final analysis little was accomplished.

One must first consider some basic social and economic facts about Egypt. The evolving Egyptian social structure helps to account for much of the attention paid to equity, but equally important were ideological themes articulated within the corpus of Egyptian nationalism. In particular, nationalist leaders and a rising Egyptian bourgeoisie developed a populist and in some ways egalitarian ideology as a weapon with which to challenge the foreigners and their control over the Egyptian polity and economy. Once implanted in people's consciousness, these ideas could not be and were not confined to the foreigners, but inevitably were used to call attention to disparities of wealth among Egyptians themselves.

One obvious and important point needs to be made at the outset. Egypt, unlike many Asian and African countries, is a compact country geographically and ethnically. There are few significant regional and geographical variations. Thus the problems that affect one part of Egypt affect the entire country, and hence issues and problems are rarely articulated in regional terms but quickly become national matters. In many Asian and other African states the issues that trouble one region are of lesser relevance to other areas. Poverty and income distribution might be a concern of a heavily populated African district, experiencing problems of a growing landless class, but of little interest to other less populated districts. Regional demands for income distribution are not supported at the national level.

Since the Egyptian concern with equity was intimately linked to Egyptian social structure, one must consider the classes and class segments that constituted Egyptian society. Peasants, workers, and students played a role in the concern with equity. In the final analysis, however, their influence was contained by the wealthy, who manipulated equity issues for their own ends and failed to implement major legislation. Still, peasants, workers, and students must be taken into account. Equity appeals were directed at them. One would also like to understand why these groups, singly or in alliance, were not able to bring about social changes favorable to their condition.

A crucial feature of twentieth-century Egyptian life was that the country's great agricultural advances had occurred in the previous century. According to Patrick O'Brien, Egyptian agricultural output expanded twelve times between 1821 and 1872–1878, and the per capita productivity rose nearly six times.[50] But from this point onward, agricultural growth became less vigorous. Again according to O'Brien, agricultural output grew at a rate of 1.2 percent between 1895 and 1960, a commendable achievement in light of the earlier triumphs. Yet the agricultural growth rate was not able to keep pace with Egypt's expanding population and began to fall behind population growth rate during the Second World War.[51] Nor were industry and commerce able to take up much of the slack during the pre-Nasser period. Prior to 1930 Egypt was precluded from erecting protective tariff barriers, and the country made only slight progress in industrializing. In the 1930s and 1940s a considerable amount of industrial innovation took place. Entrepreneurs established import-substitution industries, especially in food processing and textiles. Yet the overall industrial growth rate was not outstanding; according to Mabro and Radwan, Egyptian industries did not create many new employment opportunities.[52]

The slowing down of the Egyptian economy and the continued expansion of the population posed serious problems to all segments of Egyptian society. Around these groups equity questions revolved, and the groups themselves were often combattants in the struggle to alter the distribution of income.

In comparison with the rest of Africa and the Middle East, Egypt has an extraordinarily large rural nonlandowning population. The precise figures and percentages are difficult to obtain, but large numbers of the rural population did not own so much as a single feddan in 1950. Not all of these landless persons were simply agricultural wage laborers, however. Indeed, the most prevalent agricultural arrangements were sharecropping, cash renting, and leaseholding.[53] Here the contrast with tropical Africa is striking for, despite the poverty of the African countryside, most heads of rural households did, in fact, own some land and could provide at least part of their own subsistence. Egyptian rural conditions were much closer to those prevailing in China, India, and parts of Southeast Asia.

Not surprisingly, then, the lot of the *fellahin* (peasants) became a concern of Egyptian politicians and intellectuals. Already by the 1930s the tendency of literate Egyptians to romanticize the countryside and to glorify the stable and hardy Egyptian peasants, the reputed successors of pharaonic civilization, had given way to portraits of rural poverty and to the enunciation of the three great evils of Egyptian rural life—poverty, ignorance, and sickness. From the 1930s onward, all Egyptian regimes were committed, in theory if not in practice, to eradicating these ills. And yet within Egypt there never did originate an authentic peasant-supported political movement like that of the Communist party in China and Ho Chi

Minh in Vietnam. To be sure, during the 1919 revolution peasants rose in revolt against the British and their Egyptian collaborators, destroying communication links with the cities and in some cases even proclaiming short-lived breakaway republics. But these movements were not well organized or coherent. Some of them were spontaneous acts of violence while others were orchestrated and guided by local rural magnates. They subsided under coercion and did not spawn rurally based action groups. In 1938 the Fellah party was created, but this was the work of educated urban people and had no support in the countryside.[54] Similarly, the few halting efforts made by certain Egyptian socialists after World War II to put themselves in touch with the peasantry were unsuccessful. Again, after the Second World War peasants carried out acts of violence against their landlords. But this movement, if it could be called that, was cut short by the coup d'etat of 1952.[55]

Just why Egypt did not produce a powerful peasant movement and why concern for the fellah was confined to the educated, urban elements are difficult questions to answer. The answers must be speculative since few studies have penetrated the Egyptian countryside. Again the compactness of Egypt is a factor. There were no regions in Egypt where a peasant-based movement could emerge and gain strength free from the power of the central government. Additionally, the peasantry were bound closely through debt obligation and rent payments to the rural magnates. Those who appeared likely to cause trouble might find themselves unemployed. Finally, the goal of those obtaining an education, even those of peasant stock, was to gain admittance to the government bureaucracy and to leave the countryside for a better urban life. Individuals who might have been organizers of peasant discontent tended to cut their ties with the peasantry. Perhaps also the landless peasantry were too poor and vulnerable to contemplate organizing resistance.

The second group consisted of the urban industrial and commercial wage laborers and the urban unemployed and semiemployed. Egypt experienced a remarkable growth in its urban population, much of it stemming from a sluggish agriculture and declining land/man ratios. People flocked into the cities in search of new employment opportunities. Indeed, the urban population of Egypt, according to definitions used by the Egyptian government, increased from 1.3 million in 1882 to 12.2 million in 1966, and the urban proportion of the population rose from 19 percent in 1882 to 40 percent in 1966.[56] By 1947 the population of Cairo had risen to over 2 million and that of Alexandria to over 900,000. Cairo experienced a per annum growth rate of 5.9 percent between 1937 and 1947, second only to Suez, which grew at a rate of 11.6 percent during this decade. The provinces from which the highest proportions of Cairo immigrants came were Minūfīya, Qalyūbīya, and Aswān.[57]

At the same time that the cities were growing, the agricultural labor force was declining from 69 percent of the total work force in 1907 to 58.4

percent in 1947.[58] Not much of this decline was taken up by industrial activity, however; manufacturing, construction, and electricity only rose from 9 percent of the total labor force in 1907 to 9.9 percent in 1947. But the tertiary sector of commerce, transportation, and services greatly expanded from 18.9 percent of the total in 1907 to 26.3 percent in 1947. Many of those who worked in the tertiary sector were engaged in petty trading and domestic services and were little more than hangers-on in their urban communities.

Nonetheless, Egyptian industries did offer employment to substantial numbers. Mahmoud Anis estimated the industrial work force in 1945 at 577,500, assuming 361,336, as reported by the industrial census of 1945, and adding 51,200 proprietors of small establishments and 165,000 engaged by the allied forces.[59] As we have observed, a relatively large proportion of this work force (approximately 140,000) was unionized. Of this work force 30 percent were engaged in weaving and spinning, 20 percent in food processing, and 25 percent more in mechanical industries, flax and jute, cotton ginning, carpentry and wood working, tobacco, and chemicals. Thus eight main industrial branches supported three-quarters of Egypt's working population in manufacturing.

This urban work force constituted a potentially formidable element in Egyptian politics, exposed as it was to various leftist ideas and organizers. Moreover, in the period between 1945 and 1952 it faced severe problems of unemployment and inflation. The severity of the unemployment problem fluctuated during these years. It was most marked in 1946 as a result of war demobilization and the discharging of large numbers of people employed by British troops and by war-related industries. The unemployment figures are not reliable, but some evidence of the seriousness of the problem may be seen by considering the fact that the government held numerous meetings with leading industrialists in which remedies to the problem of unemployment were sought. Eventually the government raised £E38,000 in contributions for the unemployed from such leading firms as the Filature Nationale, the textile firms at Kafr al-Dawār, the Egyptian Copper Company, the Salt and Soda Company, and Rabbath Shop. Government officials estimated that the most sorely affected city was Alexandria, where the unemployed work force was said to be 50,000.[60]

Inflation was another severe problem. It was felt most acutely during the war years, and again between 1949 and 1951. Wholesale prices increased by 17 percent in 1949, and the cost of living rose 9 percent.[61] Inflation and unemployment, coupled with traditional irritants like dangerous and unhealthy working conditions, poor pay, and long hours, produced a series of major strikes, particularly in 1946 and 1947.

Yet the laboring population, while far more activist and volatile than the peasants, did not generate a powerful labor movement or meaningful labor-oriented political activity. Again the reasons are not easy to discern.

From the earliest days of labor activity, the movement was always fragmented and lacked dynamic leadership. The pre-World War I unions tended to be organized and led by European workers, who brought to Egypt their knowledge of European trade unionism. After the First World War various establishment groups vied with each other to bring the slowly evolving union membership under their own control. In 1924 the Wafd, impressed and frightened by a number of strikes, delegated one of its front-line leaders, ᶜAbd al-Rahman Fahmī, to bring as many unions as possible under the umbrella leadership of their party. Similarly a renegade member of the royal family, former *nabil* ᶜAbbās Halīm, sought to federate trade unions during the interwar years. These efforts at federation were only partially successful, in some measure because the state itself was opposed to any nationwide federated union structure. Not only was union leadership at the federation level uncertain and fragmented, but it was also politically and economically conservative. ᶜAbbās Halīm and the Wafdist labor organizers were not champions of radical social or political programs. They saw the unions at best as bargaining organs working for better wages, working conditions, and social services.

Another reason for organized labor's relative weakness was the fact that there was so much labor turnover. This appears to have been less of a problem in Cairo and Alexandria, where a permanent wage-earning proletariat had come into being. But outside these two cities the evidence for considerable labor turnover was marked. Although there was little large-scale industrial activity in Upper Egypt, Lower Egypt did have a number of factories. In 1945 Lower Egypt had more than 40,000 unionized workers.[62] The city of al-Mahalla al-Kubra was one of the major textile centers in Egypt. In al-Mahalla al-Kubra and other Lower Egyptian industrial cities, workers tended to come into the city from the countryside and to work for a period of time and then return to their homes. Moreover, the Misr Spinning and Weaving Company at al-Mahalla al-Kubra encouraged this kind of labor force. Its managers preferred the more malleable and cheaper fellah worker to the permanent worker, who was viewed as more likely to be a political activist.[63] In this kind of a setting union organizers found it difficult to create independent labor organizations. Indeed, contrary arrangements prevailed. The managers of large factories organized company unions that never put forward radical demands.

Although equity and socialist ideas circulated among the urban workers and the unemployed and although serious strikes occurred in Cairo, al-Mahalla al-Kubra, Kafr al-Dawār, and Alexandria, labor never became a powerful political force. A genuine labor party was never organized.

The third and last group consisted of the students. In the same fashion as the cities were growing, so was the student population, with concomitantly dangerous results for political stability. During the British occupation of Egypt (1882–1914) British officials had worked to see that educational funds, minimal though they might be, were spent on mass elementary education. Their educational program was motivated in part by political goals. They were fearful of creating in Egypt, as they thought they had in India, a class of educated but alienated intellectuals who would take out their wrath on the British as colonial rulers. The British officials in Egypt had been only partially successful in implementing this policy, so powerfully was it resented and resisted by the well-to-do in Egypt. The British made a last forceful push in this direction during World War I, when the government debated proposals for expanding elementary education.[64] But this program was never implemented. Once Egyptian politicians took over the reins of power, as they did beginning in 1924, they expended the lion's share of educational revenues on primary, secondary, and university education despite paying lip service to the ideals of schooling for the masses. According to F. O. Mann, a British educational advisor sent to Egypt to make a report on education in 1928, four-fifths of Egyptian educational revenue went for "Europeanized" schooling (primary, secondary, and higher) and only one-fifth for elementary mass education.[65]

The results of this educational program are clearly to be seen. In 1948/1949 there were 527,138 students in schools other than Muslim schools, that gave only a rudimentary education.[66] The census of 1947 indicated that 369,760 Egyptians held primary, secondary, or university certificates.[67]

| | |
|---|---|
| Holders of lower educational certificates | 198,897 |
| Holders of secondary or intermediate education certificates | 113,430 |
| Holders of higher educational certificates | 55,512 |
| Holders of higher educational certificates from abroad | 1,921 |

While these numbers may not seem impressive for a population in which the literacy rate was around 30 percent among men and 12 percent for women in 1947, the comparisons with 1921–1922, for instance, are striking. In that academic year there were only 168,851 students in schools other than Muslim schools.[68] The literacy rate of Egyptian males in the 1917 census was approximately 12 percent and for females a meager 2 percent.[69] Also, the top-heavy nature of these statistics is clear since university graduates accounted for nearly one-sixth of the total educated population and were almost one-third of the graduates of primary schools.

The expansion of Westernized schooling, especially secondary and university training, created a problem known in Egypt as "black-coated unemployment"—the inability of secondary and university graduates to find employment. This problem was first noted in the 1930s. It greatly troubled Egypt's minister of finance, ᶜAbd al-Wahāb, who indicated that for a twenty-year period (1915–1935) government service had absorbed the whole output of government schools. Between 1915 and 1925, he noted, the permanently established civil service was increased from 15,000 to 33,000. But no further expansion had taken place, and the service now contained a very large number of young men. Finance Minister Wahāb estimated that only about 10 percent of successful candidates leaving schools could hope to find government employment in 1935.[70]

ᶜAbd al-Wahāb was concerned that a top-heavy educational system would lead to student discontent and political radicalism. His fears were justified. Egyptian students had been a potent political force during the 1919 revolution as they had been in nationalist demonstrations before World War I. They were to become active again in the 1930s and 1940s. Young Egypt and the Muslim Brotherhood both derived a great deal of support from students. Moreover, the activist student policy pursued by Young Egypt persuaded the Wafd to intensify its own efforts among students. Young Egypt organized the Green Shirts in imitation of European fascist youth organizations and as a paramilitary group. In response the Wafd created the Blue Shirts organization, drawing its support from students and workers.

As a force in Egyptian politics, students had considerable potential to disrupt normal life. They used this capability on many occasions. Their support was cultivated by all the political parties, although the Wafd, the Muslim Brotherhood, and Young Egypt probably had the largest student followings. The desire of the established parties to curry student favor undoubtedly pushed politics in radical directions, even toward equity issues. While most students aspired to secure lucrative government positions, it was clear to many by the 1930s that their occupational opportunities were severely limited. Thus their leaders evinced concern about income disparities within the government bureaucracy, the high rate of profits accuring to industrial and commercial capitalists, and the concentration of landed wealth in the hands of a few pashas. Inevitably some of the young were drawn to socialist and revolutionary programs.

Yet the impact of students, like peasants and workers, was a limited one. Students did not create autonomous political parties. A few individuals sought to create ties with the impoverished peasantry. In 1946 just before Sidqī introduced his repressive policies, students and socialist-labor leaders tried to forge an alliance between the students and the working class. Their call for a general strike, however, was not popularly supported, and their new umbrella organization of students and workers proved short-lived.

Workers, peasants, and students were important factors in Egypt's political arena, interjecting themselves with force from time to time. But their action was not continuous, and they were not well organized. They did not make equity a prominent political issue after the Second World War. That, in fact, was done by Egypt's ruling elite. They did so partly because they were mindful of the threats to the established order posed by these three groups, and hence they were attentive to issues touching upon poverty, justice, and equity. But they also used questions of equity as a way of trying to win political support for their faction and to embarrass their rivals.

Egypt's ruling elite was composed of many different groups—large landowners, members of the upper reaches of the state bureaucracy, professionals (lawyers, teachers, doctors, journalists, and engineers), and people possessing urban, industrial, and commercial wealth. The elite also included many non-Egyptians who, nonetheless, resided in Egypt. As these people intended to live out their lives in Egypt and anticipated their children inheriting their wealth and businesses, they rightfully belong in any discussion of Egypt's ruling groups.

Many scholars have described the Egyptian elite as a single, almost monolithic, group. They have pointed out the dominant position of large landowning families in Parliament, in parties, on the boards of industrial and commercial firms, in the professions, and in the civil service; and they have drawn the conclusion that in pre-Nasser Egypt the power of the large landowners was preeminent and largely unchallenged. In fact, the Egyptian ruling elite was much more fragmented than many have believed. The very fragmentation of the elite, coupled with a fear of the poorer elements in Egyptian society and a desire to win their support and channel their frustrations, caused the issue of equity to be framed as it was in pre-Nasser Egypt. In the period immediately after the Second World War, equity was largely an ideological issue, at times a rhetorical tool, employed by the elite primarily to further their own interests.

Equity was first interjected into Egyptian politics by Egypt's aspiring rulers—its nationalists—mainly as an instrument with which to challenge foreign domination over the Egyptian economy and polity. There were probably few countries in 1920, for example, where foreign capital was so deeply and solidly entrenched and where so many aspects of economic life were under the control of foreigners. China, for example, did not have such massive foreign economic involvement, for foreign businesses were largely confined to the coast. In tropical Africa, many parts of the Middle East, and parts of Southeast Asia, the colonial authorities were hard-pressed to attract foreign investment. Latin America had substantial amounts of overseas investment, but many Latin American states also had an indigenous entrepreneurial class. Only India and South Africa seem to parallel Egypt as to the extent and predominance of foreign investment. But India was a huge, sprawling country, and it contained many relatively untouched regions. South Africa also had a large European settler population, which was making strides in indigenizing its wealth.

Egypt's involvement with foreign capital stemmed in large measure from Khedive Ismāᶜīl's rule (1863–1879). The Egyptian cotton boom, associated with the American Civil War, attracted European financiers and merchants to the country. By 1920 virtually all of Egypt's international trade was in foreign hands. Europe's leading banks had established branches in Egypt, and through loans to cultivators they were instrumental in financing the export of cotton. In addition, there were a number of European-run land development companies that prepared new land for cultivation and then sold the land to Egyptian farmers. The most heavily capitalized companies in Egypt were land mortgage companies like the Crédit Foncier Egyptien, a predominantly French firm that lent money to landowners, using their land as surety. The Egyptian state debt was close to £E100m. in 1914, and most of it was held by investors living outside the country. In short, the Egyptian economy was deeply penetrated by foreign capital. Even the land, the vast majority of which was owned by Egyptians themselves, was mortgaged to foreign banks and mortgage companies.

Foreign economic dominance was paralleled by foreign political rule. Egypt had been occupied by a British army since 1882. At first the British sought to minimize their political influence. They did not incorporate Egypt into their empire or declare a protectorate over the country. But by the outbreak of World War I, British officials held dominant positions in virtually every Egyptian ministry. Moreover, the country was proclaimed a British protectorate in 1914. Even within Egyptian society itself a so-called Turkish element had always enjoyed a preeminent social and political position. Most of these Turkish families had come to Egypt from other parts of the Ottoman Empire in the nineteenth century and had become staunch supporters of Egypt's ruling family. The Turkish ruling elite continued to have family ties outside of Egypt; in many cases they possessed wealth and landed estates in other parts of the Ottoman Empire. They took pride in their Turkish heritage and, though there was a steady Egyptianization of this elite, it had not been completely absorbed as late as 1920.

Thus aspiring native-born Egyptians had two powerful forces to vie with—foreign capital and a Turco-British political alliance. In trying to gain some maneuvering room for themselves, they found it advantageous to espouse a nationalist ideology with strong populist and even equity emphases. This explosive combination first revealed itself during the nationalist outbursts of 1919–1924. The exiling of Zaghlul in March 1919 provoked demonstrations and violence all over the country. Although the intensity of the reaction surprised the Wafdist leadership, they sought to take advantage of it. They championed a nationalist ideology, picturing the Wafd and its leadership as springing from the people. Implicit was the notion that, once in power, the Wafd party would create a regime representing the will of the people. Indeed, Wafdist leaders resisted efforts to describe their organization as a political party, preferring to see the Wafd as an overarching national congress and an embodiment of the popular will.

Just how elitist, in fact, the Wafdist leadership was can be seen from the fact that of its forty-two original prominent leaders, thirty-six were large landowners themselves or from large landowning families. Twenty-two were professionals of whom sixteen were lawyers or judges. Nine of these men had Turkish wives, and four were Turks themselves, despite the fact that in their pronouncements the Wafdist leadership often stressed their purely Egyptian roots, thus differentiating themselves from the foreign groups within Egyptian society.[71] Saᶜd Zaghlūl proved to be exceedingly skilled at these populist appeals. Like other popularly supported contemporary Egyptian leaders, he knew the language of the Egyptian masses. He was a master of colloquial Egyptian Arabic. He portrayed himself as a leader of purely Egyptian stock—a peasant and the son of peasants *(al-fallāh, ibn al-fallāhīn)*.[72] His Egyptian Muslim roots were stressed, including his birth in the countryside, his Muslim schooling, his education at al-Azhar, his common dress, and his liking for common foods like *fūl* (Egyptian beans). Wafdist orators took pleasure in describing Zaghlūl as a peasant employee *(fallāh muwazzif)* and a genuine Egyptian *(misrīyūn sammīm)*.[73]

Just as the characterization of the Wafd as a purely Egyptian political party contained gross exaggerations, so the description of Zaghlūl as a man of the people and a person from lowly peasant stock was a far cry from the truth. Zaghlūl was not from a poor peasant family, although his roots were in the countryside. His father had been ᶜUmdah of Abyāna and owned more than 100 feddans of land, and Zaghlūl had married into a leading Turco-Egyptian family.[74]

Zaghlūl's nationalism was of a "seek ye first the political kingdom" kind, however, His goal was *al-istiqlāl al-tāmm* (complete independence). He apparently thought little about the economic and social dimensions of independence. At least he spoke little about these matters, averring at one juncture that, despite Egypt's numerous economic difficulties, the country's primary responsibility must be to realize its independence and to forge a strong spirit of national unity.[75] When in power he devoted little attention to economic issues.

Yet Zaghlūl's populist nationalism did have an equity tinge to it and helped to implant such concerns within Egyptian nationalist ideology. His attack was launched against foreign and non-Egyptian groups—the British occupiers, the aristocratic Turkish collaborators, and foreign capitalists. These groups were seen to be exploiting Egypt, monopolizing its wealth, and impoverishing the rank and file. The implication was that, once these foreign influences had been removed, all segments of Egyptian society would enjoy the wealth that previously had gone into the pockets of a few rich foreigners.

The same kind of populist thrust, with equity implications, can also be seen in the emergence of a native-born Egyptian bourgeoisie after World War I. The leading exponent of the group was Talᶜat Harb. Not only was Talᶜat Harb an unusually successful entrepreneur, he was also an extraordinarily capable propagandist for this nascent bourgeoisie. He founded

Bank Misr in February 1920 and shortly thereafter a number of industrial and commercial companies. He owed a great deal of his success to his publicizing capabilities. Talᶜat Harb was an unabashed Egyptian nationalist.

Unlike Zaghlūl, Talᶜat Harb believed that political and economic independence must go hand in hand. In an essay published in 1911 he argued in favor of the creation of a genuinely national bank that would endow the country with the financial resources capable of diversifying the economy. He believed that Egypt's weakness and poverty stemmed from foreign economic domination. In several essays he attacked the Belgian company that administered Cairo's tramways and the French-run Sugar Company, arguing that these foreign firms impoverished Egyptians for the purpose of making large profits for their foreign shareholders. The creation of Egyptian industries, he contended, would result in the economic betterment of the Egyptian people. Egyptian-run firms would produce necessities and sell them at a fair price. They would also offer employment to Egyptians at fair wages. Talᶜat Harb sought to win shareholders and depositors for his bank on the grounds that this financial institution, with an entirely Egyptian board of directors and stockholders, would have the welfare of all Egyptians at heart and would contribute to general Egyptian well-being. Talᶜat Harb's appeal was broadcast widely, for his bank had a large number of small Egyptian stockholders and was not simply financed by a few superwealthy landlords and merchants.[76]

Talᶜat Harb stood for a capitalist strategy of economic development and a trickle-down effect for the poor. He did not favor redistributive economic programs. He argued for light taxation and protective tariffs for nascent Egyptian industries. He never championed land limitation or land redistribution, and he was an ardent advocate of the right of private property. Yet such an unregenerate capitalist can be seen to have made a contribution to the concern about equity and the distribution of wealth. He assaulted the foreign community in Egypt because of its inordinate wealth and the concentration of so much political and economic power in its hands.

The populism of Egypt's aspiring nationalists, politicians, and entrepreneurs helped to focus attention on Egypt's problems of unequal income distribution, exploitation, and poverty. Egypt's bourgeoisie sought to use nationalism and populism to unseat the foreigners. But the bourgeoisie had, of course, introduced explosive new ideas into the political arena—ideas that could be and were used against themselves.

Although these equity concerns became muted once the passions of the revolution subsided, they were from time to time revived. Their most energetic and articulate spokesman was Makram ᶜUbayd of the Wafd party. Having originally made his mark as Zaghlūl's most spellbinding orator, ᶜUbayd kept alive the ideological flame of populism in the 1930s and during the Second World War. While serving as the Wafd's minister of finance in 1936 and 1942, he elaborated budgets with social reform content. His 1936 budget—which he called a democratic budget—argued that the nation's revenue had been put at the service of the government and its bureaucrats and needed to be redirected toward the people. In particular he called attention to the misery of the fellahin and warned that, if present trends continued, the poor would be enslaved to the rich and the rich to the foreigner.[77] Again in 1942, with the Wafd returning to power, ᶜUbayd promulgated an "equilibrium" budget—a budget that he claimed would achieve not merely fiscal but also social equilibrium and that would remove some of the gross inequalities in Egyptian life.[78]

ᶜUbayd's budgetary proposals proved to be more facade than reality. Their redistributive content was severely limited. The main emphasis was on the distribution of state lands to small holders, the reduction of the taxes paid by poor peasants, and the provision of social services to poor rural communities. Like the other Egyptian politicians of this age, he trusted economic expansion and the trickling down of wealth to the poor rather than elaborate redistributive programs. Yet his oratorical skills and his ability to coin the apt phrase kept issues of inequality, poverty, and exploitation in the popular consciousness.

Interest in equity, poverty, exploitation, and the maldistribution of income became so central a focus of the Egyptian political vocabulary by 1945 that different factions within the political elite began to try to enhance their own image and embarrass their opponents with reference to these issues. Also, no intelligent and far-seeing Egyptian politician could ignore the growth of peasant discontent, the rise of an alienated student population, the spread of socialist ideas, and the growing urban working and unemployed population. It would appear that equity issues were introduced into Egyptian politics by Egyptian political and economic leaders aspiring to positions of power held by foreigners. Once implanted, these ideas were taken up by different segments or factions of this ruling elite in their competition for power.

The view presented here runs counter to certain recent studies of Egyptian politics, for it assumes that the Egyptian ruling elite was fragmented and that the motive force behind the interjection of equity issues into Egyptian politics was a competition for power among different segments of that elite. Several recent studies of Egyptian political history, however, seem to have concluded that Egypt's ruling class was a unified and coherent one. One of the best of these works is ᶜAsim al-Disūqī's study of the large landowners between 1920 and 1952. He contends that the large landowners were the dominant element in Egyptian politics and that they were strongly represented in all of the major political parties. He has also demonstrated that large landowners served on the boards of important industrial and commercial firms. Yet one is not yet entitled to conclude from these findings that the Egyptian ruling elite was unified and that the dominant element was the landed group.

In the first place, although certain individuals did, in fact, have large landholdings, it is not clear that they saw their interests in the same light as the majority of large landowners. Talᶜat Harb was a large landowner, according to Disūqī, but it is probable that his family estates were not enormous. As head of Bank Misr and the far-flung Misr commercial and industrial empire, he was inclined to view political and economic affairs from the standpoint of those commercial and industrial interests rather than from the vantage point of a large landholder. ᶜAlī Amīn Yahya had substantial estates, but he too was the head of a far-flung commercial and industrial cartel. When issues arose in which these interests clashed, as they did over taxation and tariff policy, his position could not be as clear as a large landowner without commercial and industrial holdings.

Further evidence of individuals who had large landed estates but did not have the same political interests can be seen in the markedly different careers of two of Egypt's wealthiest persons—Ahmad ᶜAbbūd and Muhammad Badrāwī-ᶜAshūr. In terms of economic interests they seem to be men cut from the same cloth. Both had enormous estates. Muhammad Badrāwī-ᶜAshūr's holdings were more than 18,000 feddans while ᶜAbbūd owned close to 5,000 feddans. They were both on the boards of commercial and industrial firms. Muhammad Badrāwī-ᶜAshūr was one of the early investors in Bank Misr and held a large portion of the stock of the Misr Spinning and Weaving Company. ᶜAbbūd was the founder or managing director of a number of Egypt's largest business concerns, including the Khedivial Mail Line, the Sugar Company, and the Fertilizer Company.

Yet these men had come to their positions of economic preeminence in radically different ways. The Badrāwī-ᶜAshūr estate dated back to the nineteenth century, and the family owed its wealth to landowning and agriculture. Although he had large industrial and commercial investments, Muhammad Badrāwī-ᶜAshūr thought of himself as a fellah, or at least as having sprung from peasant roots. He gave money to various industrial and commercial companies and allowed his name to be used as a board member, largely as a favor to friends and for patriotic reasons. He was one of Egypt's many "sleeping board members" because he took little interest in company activities. In short, he looked upon his shareholding in these companies as a kind of tribute paid to nationalist sensitivities. He believed that Egypt's wealth was in the land and would always be so, and his primary economic goal was to accumulate larger and larger estates for himself and his family.[79]

Ahmad ᶜAbbūd's pathway to success was very different. He came from a family of modest means, studied engineering at Glasgow University, and became a construction engineer in the Ottoman Empire before settling in Egypt after World War I. There he made a fortune in business. One of his important enterprises was the Egyptian Sugar Company, of which he became managing director. As part of this undertaking he acquired nearly 5,000 feddans of lucrative sugar estates at Armant in Upper

Egypt. ᶜAbbūd was a far cry from the typical Egyptian landlord. Based in Cairo and Alexandria and traveling regularly to Europe and North America on business trips, he looked upon himself as an industrialist and an entrepreneur. His world and his attitudes could hardly be described in the same terms as those of Muhammad Badrāwī-ᶜAshūr.

One could add more career histories. But perhaps more compelling evidence can be obtained by determining how many of Egypt's large landowners served on boards of Egyptian joint stock companies. The companies, especially those operating primarily in Egypt, were anxious to attract the interest and financial support of landed magnates and were eager to appoint them to their boards.

I have compiled an almost complete list of the 1,758 individuals who lost land in 1952 because their estates exceeded 200 feddans. *The Egyptian Stock Exchange Yearbook* also issued annual lists of directors of joint stock companies, and I have elected to use the list for 1946, the year before new legislation compelled business firms in Egypt to increase substantially the number of Egyptian joint stock company directors and caused them to appoint many people with little or no interest in these firms. The 1946 list of board members contains 1,008 names, of which 227 appear to be Egyptians.

The first point to be made is that there still existed a chasm between foreign and Egyptian communities. Foreigners dominated industry and commerce while Egyptians were preeminent on the land. Of the 227 Egyptians who sat on the boards, it appears that 46 were large landholders subject to the land reform law of 1952. This proportion of 20 percent seems relatively small in light of the fact that land was the major source of wealth for Egyptians. One would expect more wealthy magnates to have become involved in industrial and commercial joint stock companies by the end of World War II. To be sure, a number of wealthy families, like the Abāzas, ᶜAmrs, Badrāwīs, Dūsses, Sharīfs, and others were represented on these firms by family members whose landholdings were less than 200 feddans. But by the same token the figure of 46 Egyptian board members also contains powerful industrialists, like Hafiz ᶜAfīfī and ᶜAbd al-Rahmān Hamāda, leading businessmen in the Misr empire, who used some of their assets to purchase large (400 feddans) but not massive estates and who were not landed aristocrats.

The proof for the fragmentation and tension within Egypt's ruling elite does not rest on career histories or statistical studies of joint stock company directors. It stems in very large part from the political arena where these different segments—especially the landed magnates and the industrial and commercial leaders—began to vie for political preeminence. Their competition involved efforts to win parliamentary elections and to gain popular support; here they began to exploit equity and justice appeals.

Competition among Egypt's ruling segments was muted in the 1930s.

Most of the industrialists and large merchants were foreigners and felt constrained from speaking out openly on issues that might threaten landed interests. There was some concealed enmity over the new tariff structure of 1930. Several landed groups complained that the Egyptian Federation of Industries had exercised inordinate influence in the drafting of this legislation, claiming that the tariffs benefitted industry much more than agriculture. But the real diversity of interests and potential for conflict only became clear after the abolition of the Capitulations in 1937. For the first time Egypt had substantial fiscal autonomy, and its politicians set about reforming the system of taxation. The landed element and the industrial and commerical groups attacked each other as these new taxes were brought into existence, arguing that the tax burdens were unfairly distributed. The industrialists complained that landholders paid only a small tax (the land tax) and had many price supports while their own companies were forced to bear heavy charges. Heated debates arose over the surplus profits tax on joint stock companies enacted in the early years of World War II. Two of Egypt's leading industrialists, Ismāᶜīl Sidqī and Hafiz ᶜAfīfī, led the assault on this tax, claiming that the only pathway to economic growth in Egypt was through industrialization. Therefore, they concluded, industries should be relatively unencumbered with taxes.[80]

Debates over the distribution of tax burdens increased in intensity after the Second World War as ministries put forward expensive programs for alleviating poverty and redressing social injustices. The industrialists and the agriculturalists, if one might be permitted to use those terms, made the argument that their own approaches would deal with these problems more effectively.

Perhaps the best way to illustrate the contention that equity was brought into Egyptian politics through the competition of opposing factions is to consider the way in which the question of the fellah became a central concern in Egyptian politics. The fellah first became a major political issue in the 1930s, largely as a result of the depression. Declining world prices for cotton and the inability of large landowners to meet their debt payments caused many to consider ways in which they could improve their agricultural productivity. The fellah entered their consciousness as an instrument of production. If the Egyptian peasant could be made a more efficient farmer, Egypt's agricultural economy might withstand the shocks of the international capitalist system. Illustrative of this concern was the publication in 1930 by the Ministry of Agriculture of a journal called *Zamīl al-Fallāh*. Written in simple language and capable, it was hoped, of being read to peasant farmers, the journal contained all manner of agricultural advice on how to increase yields on the land.

ᶜAlī Islām was a landlord who thought clearly and intelligently about the fellah as an instrument of production. He was a large landowner from Banī Suwayf. A speech he delivered in 1937 sums up many of the themes of this period.[81] The Egyptian peasant, he argued, was the source of

Egyptian wealth and, therefore, his miserable existence was a major reason for Egypt's poverty. The best way to better his lot was through a generalized program of agricultural development, with emphasis on irrigation projects and drainage, increased crop yields, and industrial development. To ᶜAlī Islām, "the sickness of Egypt was not the result of the distribution of wealth but the lack of wealth," and so he favored increasing the country's material wealth. Programs of social services, like education and health care for the peasantry, could follow after the country had been put on the pathway of economic development.

Thus the concern for the fellah entered the Egyptian political arena in the 1930s, primarily because of the landlords' desire to increase national wealth. The poverty and misery of the peasantry were admitted, but the leading figures in this debate did not call for the redistribution of wealth. Even in the moving and socially sensitive writings of Bint al-Shatī *(Qadīya al-Fallāh* and *al-Rīf al-Misrī)* there was no demand for income distribution.

By the 1940s, however, a concern with the maldistribution of wealth in the countryside had entered the debate. Also, the fellah question was being used as a stick with which to beat one's political opponents. The focal point of this debate proved to be a severe epidemic of malaria and famine in Qinā and Asyūt provinces during World War II. Many peasant farmers lost their lives, and the matter was vigorously debated in Parliament. Critics of the Wafd, the party in power at that time, charged the government with administrative mismanagement and held it responsible for the loss of lives. Mustafa al-Nahhās, the Wafdist prime minister, sought to counter these accusations by pointing out that Qinā and Asyūt were areas of extreme poverty and that the poor were the ones to die from malnutrition and malaria. Nahhās added that the two hardest hit areas were between ᶜIdfū in the south and Naj Hammādī in the north and that this territory was characterized by great extremes of poverty and wealth.[82] Indeed this was an area noted for its large estates, many of which were under the control of the royal family. In this way the malaria problem was used by factions within the ruling elite to attempt to embarrass their foes. The king and opposition political parties sought to embarrass the Wafd by claiming that the problem stemmed from the Wafd's giving essential supplies to British troops and thereby depriving Egyptians.[83] In short, both sides called attention to the poverty and misery of the countryside and sought to blame their political opponents. Although the Wafd did not go on record as favoring land redistribution, they argued that poverty in Upper Egypt stemmed from inordinate wealth and maldistribution of landed property.

Once the question of poverty had been introduced into Egyptian politics as an issue for embarrassing one's opponents, it continued to be employed in that fashion. As we have observed, after World War II fissures appeared within the Egyptian ruling elite. The landed class quarreled with the industrial and commercial bourgeoisie over a wide range of issues, including taxation and strategies of economic development. Inevitably, the question of peasant poverty was interjected into this duscussion. A large landowner, Muhammad al-Manzalāwī, became a champion of the downtrodden peasantry in many of these parliamentary debates. Although his concern may have been genuine, it is also clear that he used this issue to criticize policies drawn up to favor industrial and commerical interests. In particular he was a strong advocate of the surplus profits tax enacted during the Second World War, arguing that this tax would help the state carry out needed reforms for the peasantry.[84] Yet, one cannot help but feel that he was anxious to see the increasing financial burdens of the state—military as well as social—borne by those possessing industrial and commerical wealth.

## Conclusion

Egypt's first equity crisis came to a head after the Second World War. At that time the major political organs were concerned about poverty and disparities of wealth, and they were committed to alleviating misery. Only the extreme groups and the left wing of the Wafd, however, favored redistributing wealth from the rich to the poor. The other parties believed that poverty could be reduced by traditional programs of economic growth channeled through a dynamic middle class.

This concern with equity stemmed only partly from the gross disparities of wealth in Egypt. That there was enormous inequality was clear despite a lack of definitive statistics. Disparities were clear in the distribution of land, the vast numbers of rural landless, and the rising tide of migration to the cities. Inequality was also clear in the consolidation of industrial and commercial power in the hands of a few. Yet disparities and even grinding poverty do not lead automatically and inevitably to widespread concern with economic and social justice. Many societies have tolerated huge inequalities for long periods of time. Ironically, in Egypt the moving forces behind the demands for equity were the rising Egyptian middle and lower middle classes. They aspired to the wealth and power of the solidly entrenched European political and economic elites. Eager to accelerate their quest for power, they mobilized powerful ideological appeals. One of their most effective arguments was that foreigners exploited Egypt, impoverished its people, and created inequality. They also contended that attainment of political and economic independence would bring an end to these injustices. Their appeal was directed to the masses, especially workers and students, whom they portrayed as victims of foreign exploitation. But the ideology remained in their hands.

Although few reforms were carried out prior to 1952, the framing of redistributive issues was an important legacy for the new military government. It would, of course, be a mistake to believe that the military simply carried out the programs that the civilian politicians had been unable to realize before 1952. The military regime had its own dynamic. In addition, the military leaders had been raised in a different social and ideological milieu. They were most strongly influenced by the ideas of the communists, the Muslim Brothers, and Young Egypt. But many of the social programs they considered and eventually implemented had been vigorously debated prior to 1952. Land reform was only the most obvious of these programs. The pre-1952 Parliaments and parties had also debated the nationalization of the Suez Canal and public utilities, and they had taken large strides in Egyptianizing the joint stock companies operating in the country.

Alistair Hennesy has observed that egalitarian urban populism was a common feature of twentieth-century Latin America.[85] Much of his analysis is readily applicable to pre-Nasser Egypt. Egyptian populist nationalism, like Latin American populism, grew out of similar social circumstances. Both ideologies were conditioned in large part by the influx of marginal groups into the cities, the weakness of the middle class, the failure of the working class to develop autonomous labor organizations, and the inability of the peasantry to create a sense of class identity. Thus large numbers of poorly organized but highly volatile and marginalized groups were available to be manipulated by segments of the middle and lower middle class in competition with each other for power. Their appeal usually took the form of populist and egalitarian programs and was consciously transclass in its emphasis. In Egypt the communality and solidarity of the people were stressed. As in most populist movements evil, privileged forces were held accountable for the backwardness and divisions plaguing Egypt. These were often seen as imperialist elements—the British as a neocolonial power, and foreign capital through its domination of the Egyptian economy. The solution to these problems was thought to take place through the restoration of political autonomy to the Egyptian people and its natural leaders. No other far-reaching changes were contemplated, except perhaps for enhancing the powers of the state so as to enable it to protect a hard-won independence and to secure an elusive economic development.

## Notes

1. *Al-Ahrām,* August 4, 1954.

2. *Al-Ahrām,* May 28, 1954. In a recent study ᶜAsim al-Disūqī estimated that 2,541 landowners in addition to the royal family owned estates of 100 feddans or more. See Disūqī, *Kibār Mullāk al-'Arādī al-Ziraᶜīya* (Cairo, 1975), p. 21.

3. *Al-Ahrām,* May 28, 1954.

4. Disūqī, p. 31.

5. Samir Radwan, "The Impact of Agrarian Reform on Rural Egypt, 1952–75," World Employment Programme Research, *Working Papers* (Geneva, 1977), p. 5. Alan R. Richards developed the following table of Gini coefficients for landownership, 1900–1952, in his work "Accumulation, Distribution, and Technical Change in Egyptian Agriculture, 1800–1940" (Ph.D. diss., University of Wisconsin, 1975), p. 239:

| | | | |
|---|---|---|---|
| 1900 | .6608 | 1933 | .7608 |
| 1913 | .7726 | 1945 | .7594 |
| 1920 | .7744 | 1952 | .7508 |

6. See chapter 8 by Amr Mohie-Eldin in this volume. Samir Radwan estimated the number of rural landless families in 1950 as 1.6 million or over 60 percent of the rural population. See Radwan, p. 5. Hassan Riad in *L'Égypte Nasserienne* (Paris, 1964), pp. 16–17, on the other hand, claimed that, even after the first land reform, 80 percent of the rural population were without any land.

7. *Al-Ahrām,* September 10, 1954.

8. Gabriel Baer, *A History of Landownership in Modern Egypt, 1800–1952* (New York, 1962) p. 137.

9. *Al-Ahrām,* April 3, 1955.

10. Égypte, Ministère des Finances, Departement de la Statistique. *Annuaire Statistique, 1947–49,* pp. 310–311.

11. *Egyptian Stock Exchange Yearbook, 1946.* By law every firm operating principally in Egypt had to have at least two Egyptian directors. Thus a certain number of the Egyptian directors were selected in response to the law and were not really influential board members.

12. The list of seventeen people reflects three kinds of people serving on the boards of business firms. First were the Egyptian political personalities, like Muhammad Mahmūd Khalīl and Husayn Sirrī, selected in part because of their political influence and as a way of satisfying government requirements. Second, there were powerful Egyptian financiers like Muhammad Ahmad Farghālī and ᶜAlī Amīn Yahya. Finally, there were influential foreign businessmen like Michel Salvago and Henry A. Barker.

13. *Al-Ahrām,* May 28, 1954.

14. *Al-Ahrām,* February 27, 1953.

15. Disūqī, p. 77.

16. Bent Hansen, "Marginal Productivity, Wage Theory, and Subsistence Wage Theory in Egyptian Agriculture," United Arab Republic, Institute of National Planning, *Memo no. 547,* March 1965.

17. Abbas M. Ammar, *The People of Sharqiyya: Their Racial History, Sociology, Physical Characteristics, Demography, and Conditions of Life* (Cairo, 1944), 1: 306.

18. As quoted in Charles Issawi, *Egypt at Mid-Century: An Economic Survey* (New York, 1954), p. 88.

19. *Revue d'Égypte Économique et Financière* 17, no. 592, (December 18, 1943): 5–6.

20. Ibid., vol. 19, no. 673 (July 7, 1945): pp. 4–5.

21. Charles Issawi, *Egypt: An Economic and Social Analysis* (New York, 1947), p. 69.

22. No. 970, High Commissioner to Foreign Office, September 12, 1919, Public Record Office (PRO) Foreign Office (FO) 141/426.

23. *Sahīfa al-Tijāra wa-l-Sināᶜa* 13, no. 3 (March 1936): 301–317.

24. This report has been published in *al-Talīᶜa* 1, no. 5: 153–162.

25. *L'Égypte Industrielle* 1, no. 3 (1928): 47–51.

26. M. H. Butler, *Report on Working Conditions in Egypt* (Cairo, 193?).

27. See the general review article by Mahmud Jamāl al-Dīn Zakī, "Qanūn al-ᶜAmal," in al-Jamāᶜīya al-Misrīya lil-Iqtisād al-Siyāsī wa-l-Ahsā' wa-l-Tashrīᶜ, *Buhūth al-ᶜĪd Khamsīnī* (Cairo, 1960), pp. 595–618.

28. Report by M. T. E. Evans, Second Secretary of His Majesty's Embassy in Cairo on Conditions of Labor and Trade Unions in Egypt, Received in the Foreign Office, July 28, 1944, PRO FO 471/41380.

29. Robert Mabro and Samir Radwan, *The Industrialization of Egypt, 1939–1973: Policy and Performance* (Oxford, 1976), p. 82.

30. Samir Radwan argues that, while capital formation suffered during World War II, company profits soared by 126 percent and industry expanded. See Samir Radwan, *Capital Formation in Egyptian Industry and Agriculture, 1882–1967* (London, 1974).

31. Great Britain, Department of Trade, *Egypt, 1951*, p. 89.

32. Hilary Kilpatrick, *The Modern Egyptian Novel: A Study in Social Criticism* (London, 1974), p. 51.

33. Sasson Somekh, *The Changing Rhythm: A Study of Najib Mahfuz's Novels* (Leyden, 1973), p. 47.

34. *Al-Ahrām,* July 12 and 14, 1946.

35. Killearn to Eden, June 30, 1944, PRO FO 371/41380.

36. No. 1684, Carol B. Lyon to Secretary of State, July 8, 1946, U.S. National Archives 883.504/7–846.

37. *Économiste Égyptien,* February 10, 1946.

38. No. 979, Campbell to Bevin, September 1, 1946, PRO FO 371/53327.

39. Saᶜd ᶜUthmān, "Mudhakkirāt," *al-Kātib* 11, no. 124: 170–171.

40. The major work on this subject is Richard P. Mitchell, *The Society of the Muslim Brothers* (London, 1969).

41. *Al-Ahrām,* March 2, 1950.

42. See the pamphlet of Ahmad Husayn, *al-Ishtirākīya Allatī Nadᶜa Illayha* (Cairo, 1950).

43. *Al-Ahrām,* February 20, 1950.

44. Rashīd al-Barrāwī, *Haqīqa al-Inqilāb al-Akhīr fī Misr* (Cairo, 1952), p. 148.

45. J. Patterson to Secretary of State, June 28, 1948, U.S. National Archives, 883.00/6–2848.

46. *Al-Wafd al-Misrī,* July 1946, and ᶜAbd al-ᶜAzīm Ramadān, "Hizb al-Wafd bayn al-Yamīn wa-l-Yisār," *al-Kātib* 13, no. 147 (June 1973): 56–65.

47. *Al-Ahrām,* January 12, 1950.

48. Ibid., January 14, 1950.

49. Ibid., May 5, 1950.

50. Patrick O'Brien, "The Long-Term Growth of Agricultural Production in Egypt, 1821–1962," in P. M. Holt, ed., *Political and Social Change in Modern Egypt* (London, 1968).

51. Bent Hansen and Michael Wattlesworth, "Agricultural Output and Consumption of Basic Foods, 1886/87–1967/68," *International Journal of Middle Eastern Studies* 9, no. 4 (November 1978): 449–469.

52. Mabro and Radwan, p. 83.

53. Alan Richards, "Land and Labor on Egyptian Cotton Farms, 1882–1940," manuscript kindly lent by the author.

54. "Wathā'iq Barāmaj Ahzāb al-ᶜUmmāl wa-l-Fallāhīn fī-l-Thalāthināt," *al-Talīᶜa* 6, no. 10 (October 1970): 153–161.

55. Baer, p. 221, and no. 508, Killearn to Eden, Apr. 5, 1945, enclosing memorandum

by W. Stuart, March 30, 1945, PRO FO 371/45920.

56. Abdel-Fattah Nassef, *The Egyptian Labor Force: Its Dimensions and Changing Structure, 1907–1960* (Philadelphia, 1970), pp. 26ff. The government definition of *urban* includes Cairo, Alexandria, Port Said, Ismailia, Suez, the capitals of the other governorates, and the capitals of districts within nonurban governorates.

57. Egypt, Ministry of Finance and Economy, *Population Census of Egypt, 1947*, pp. 48–49, 68–69.

58. Nassef, *The Egyptian Labor Force*, p. 103.

59. Mahmoud Amin Anis, *A Study of the National Income of Egypt* (Cairo, 1950), p. 786.

60. *Al-Ahrām*, June 3 and June 9, 1946.

61. Great Britain, Department of Trade, *Egypt, 1951*, p. 89.

62. No. 1684, Carol B. Lyon to Secretary of State, July 8, 1946, U.S. National Archives, 883.504/7–846.

63. Abdel Kader Ibrahim, "The Labor Problem in Industrialization in Egypt" (Ph.D. diss., Princeton University, 1957), pp. 90ff.

64. No. 142, Wingate to Balfour, July 3, 1917, PRO FO 371/2927 f. 141957.

65. Mann to British Residency, n.d., PRO FO 371/13879.

66. Égypte, Ministère des Finances, Departement de la Statistique, *Annuaire Statistique*, 1947–1948 and 1948–1949, p. 229.

67. Egypt, Ministry of Finance and Economy, *Population Census of Egypt, 1947*, p. 4.

68. Égypte, Ministère des Finances, Departement de la Statistique, *Annuaire Statistique*, 1921–1922, p. 61.

69. Egypt, Ministry of Finance, Statistical Department, *The Census of Egypt in 1917* (Cairo, 1921), vol. 2, p. 5.

70. This information is contained in No. 310, Lampson to Simon, March 23, 1935, PRO FO 371/19044.

71. Louis Joseph Cantori, "The Organizational Basis of an Elite Political Party: The Egyptian Wafd" (Ph.D. diss., University of Chicago, 1966), p. 38, and Disūqī, *Kibār Mullāk al-'Arādī al-Zira$^{c}$īya*, p. 224.

72. Muhammad Bahī al-Dīn Barakāt, *Safahāt min al-Tā'rīkh* (Cairo, 1961), p. 137.

73. Ahmad Qāsim Jūda, ed., *al-Makramīyāt* (Cairo, n.d.), p. 24.

74. Muhammad Ibrāhīm al-Jazīrī, *Athār al-Za$^{c}$īm Sa$^{c}$d Zaghlūl* (Cairo, 1927), vol. 1, pp. 255–257.

75. Ibid., vol. 1, p. 237.

76. Robert L. Tignor, "Bank Misr and Foreign Capitalism," *International Journal of Middle Eastern Studies* 8, no. 2 (1977): 161–181.

77. *Annales de la Chambre des Députés*, 6th Legislature, 1st Sess., July 8, 1936, pp. 43ff. Also *Économiste Égyptien*, July 12, 1936; and *Mijalla Ghurfa al-Qāhira* 1, no. 7 (July 1936): 3–7.

78. *Annales de la Chambre des Députés*, 9th Legislature, 1st Sess., May 14, 1945, pp. 3ff.

79. Much of this interpretation comes from an interview with Husām al-Dīn Badrāwī and $^{c}$Alī al-Dīn Badrāwī in London, June 28, 1977.

80. *Économiste Égyptien*, February 2, 1941 and *Révue d'Égypte Économique et Financière* 15, no. 457 (May 17, 1941), p. 5.

81. Alī Islām, *Wasā'il Tahsīn Halla al-Fallāh al-Iqtisādīya* (Cairo, 1937).

82. *Annales de la Chambre des Députés*, 8th Legislature, 3rd Sess., February 28, 1944, pp. 149–168.

83. Tel., No. 351, Killearn to Foreign Office, February 25, 1944, PRO FO 371/41326.

84. *Économiste Égyptien,* March 2, 1941.

85. Alistair Hennessy, "Latin America" in *Populism: Its Meaning and National Characteristics,* ed. Ghita Ionescu and Ernest Gellner (London, 1969), pp. 28–61.

ical mix that led, among other factors, to a series of intraelite conflicts and purges.

To say that, however, is not to argue that Nasser and his colleagues were void of any ideological commitments. It would be more accurate to describe Nasser as having an implicit ideology. In fact, a great deal of Nasser's ideas in the 1960s can be found in embryonic form in his speeches of the early 1950s. One notices a line of thinking, of accumulative nature, developing over time and unfolding itself in relation to Nasser's performance as a national leader.[4]

The ideological development of the new regime is better understood in the wider context of creating a new political order. It was linked to the development of a political structure that was characterized by the absence of political competitiveness and the existence of a single political organization: the Liberation Rally (1953–1956), the National Union (1956–1962) and the Arab Socialist Union (1963–1977).[5] In addition to the absence of political competiveness, the regime had a number of authoritarian features, such as limited political participation, centralization of power, supremacy of the executive over the legislature, and suppression of political dissent. There was a clear imbalance between politics and administration. Output institutions (bureaucracy, police, and army) far outgrew input institutions (interest groups and political parties). The government penetrated almost all intermediary associations and groups, bringing them under its legal and financial control.

The ideological development was also linked to Egypt's external relations and foreign policy concerns. One may argue that Egyptian politics, at least since the midnineteenth century, cannot be studied divorced from its regional and international context. In Nasser's case, the nationalization of the Suez Canal Company, though debated among the ruling elite since 1952, was timed as a reaction to the West's withdrawal of its offer to finance the High Dam project. The Egyptianization of British and French firms was related to those countries' military attack on Egypt in 1956, and of Belgian firms as a show of protest over its policy in the Congo. Nasser's intensive socialization program in 1962–1964 was undoubtedly influenced by the Syrian secession of September 1961.

The development of a new ideology proceeded in a gradual and piecemeal fashion. It developed in four major phases. The first phase was from July 1952 to around January 1956, which was a period of maintaining law and order and stabilizing the new regime in the face of diverse opposition. Economically, it was characterized by the encouragement of free enterprise. The second phase was from 1956 to the promulgation of the "socialist" decrees in July 1961. During this period, Nasser defined his ideology as "cooperative, democratic socialism," which was essentially a reformist set of ideas. It was an attempt to remedy the social problems resulting from a free-market situation and was described economically as guided capitalism. The third phase started in 1961 and gathered momentum in May 1962 with the promulgation of the National Charter. During this phase, the problems of social justice and ID came to be leading national issues and central questions of policymaking. In the 1970s under Sadat, there developed a fourth phase, that is characterized by the adoption of an open-door economic policy.

The first phase is described as "statist" because the primary objective of the regime was law and order. The immediate goal was to consolidate power and to mobilize mass support. The new regime sought discipline. The officers forcefully punished violent manifestations of both left and right. In order to consolidate their power, the army, police, and civil service were purged. The press was censored. Political parties were requested to purge themselves of corrupt elements and, on January 16, 1953, they were banned.

Social justice was one of the six famous principles of the revolution. The others were liquidation of colonialism, liquidation of feudalism, putting an end to the domination of power by capital, establishment of a strong national army, and establishment of sound democratic life. In his "philosophy of the revolution," Nasser wrote of the necessity of going through two revolutions: a political revolution that achieves independence and national freedom, and a social revolution whose objective is social justice. On June 16, 1953, the Liberation Rally, the sole legitimate political organization, released an eleven-point program that included two points of social significance: the establishment of "a social system in which all citizens shall be entitled to protection against the ravages of unemployment, illness and old age, *i.e.*, a welfare state," and the establishment of "an economic system designed to encourage a fair distribution of wealth, full exploitation of natural and human resources and the maximum investment of new capital."[6]

As early as 1954, Nasser developed the link between democracy and social justice. "I can't understand how there can be freedom if I am not free to find my bread and make a living, and free to find employment," he wondered.[7] Nasser also emphasized the need for national unity and cooperation among classes. At this stage, he did not identify his regime with any particular social group: "the revolution's government is the government of all the classes of the nation, the government of peasants and workers, of officials and students, financiers and businessmen, of the weak and poor and the strong and rich and of mere beginners and those who have achieved success. It is a government that looks at Egypt as one big family . . ." Nasser told the people on July 23, 1954. Interestingly, Sadat was to repeat almost the same words twenty-five years later.

The main feature of the concept of social justice in this phase was its vagueness. Moreover, it was not reflected in policies, with the exception of the Land Reform Law, which was issued on September 9, 1952, six weeks after the army took over, and which was motivated by a combination of political and social considerations.

On January 16, 1956, Nasser announced the end of the three-year transitional period and presented the people with a new constitution. The ideology of the regime, which was called "cooperative, democratic socialism," showed greater concern with the issues of social justice.[8] This phase of ideological development was predicated on two main concepts: social democracy and national unity. As to the first, Nasser believed that political democracy required certain social and economic requisites. Before political freedom could be established, there must be social and economic democracy involving the removal of class barriers and the insurance of more social mobility in society.[9]

Nasser referred to the term *socialism* for the first time in February 1955; and after his return from the Bandung conference (April 1955), where he met with Nehru and Chou En Lai, he used it more frequently. On December 5, 1957, Nasser announced the idea of "socialist, democratic and cooperative society." He defined his ideal society in a variety of ways, such as a society without exploitation, a society of owners,[10] a controlled economy, and a controlled capitalist economy.[11]

The second pillar of Nasser's thought was the concept of national unity. He envisaged the stage Egypt was going through as one of national construction and economic development. For him the fulfillment of that vision required the highest degree of national unity and the minimizing of social and class conflicts.[12] The goal was the achievement of a national consensus transcending class differences. All Egyptians "have one goal and one aim: to work for the welfare of the nation with no individual, no group or party working for its own benefit, but all of us working together for the benefit of this nation," Nasser asserted.[13]

The idea of reconciling class differences was embodied in the 1956 constitution, whose preamble reiterated the six principles of the revolution. Part II, entitled "The Basic Constituents of the Egyptian Society," made social solidarity the cornerstone of society (Article 4). The authors of the constitution conceived an active role for the government in the socioeconomic sphere to ameliorate inequality in the distribution of wealth and income.

Three areas of the constitution had direct bearing on distributional issues. The first was that economic life was to be regulated according to the principles of social justice. The constitution emphasized that the economy was to be planned along those principles (Part II, Article 7). Taxation policies were also to be based on social justice (Part II, Article 22). Private business was free provided that it did not prejudice public welfare (Part II, Articles 8 and 9). The law was to ensure harmony between private capital and public policies (Part II, Article 10). The second area was land reform, which had been introduced four years earlier, but now was given a constitutional sanction. Law was to limit landownership so as to prevent "the return of feudalism" (Part II, Article 12). Thus, the constitution opened the door for further land reforms. The third area was that of social rights. The constitution established a number of social obligations on the part of the government. Every citizen had the right to social security, medical care, housing, and education (Part II, Article 21). The state was responsible for the ensuring of a decent standard of living for all citizens and the provision of social, cultural, and health services. Egyptians had the right to education (Part III, Article 49). Primary education (up to the sixth grade) was compulsory, and free in governmental schools (Part III, Article 51). Similarly, it was a government responsibility to establish hospitals and ensure medical care (Part II, Article 56).

The inclusion of these equity-related issues in the constitution was not without significance. First, it established norms and values in the body politic and affected people's expectations from the government. Second, it provided the legal basis for distributive policies. Third, the constitutional recognition of a social right was more likely to transform it into a political issue, create a constituency of its beneficiaries, and establish a source of support for these policies.

The third stage of the regime's ideological evolution was described variously as state capitalism, state socialism, the hegemony of the state bourgeosie, nationalitarian development, or simply the takeover of economy by bureaucracy.[14] It was characterized by an increasing attention given to distributive issues and the frequent use of nationalization and sequestration as means of achieving them. Its ideas were articulated in the National Charter, which was announced and adopted in 1962. The charter, a document of ten chapters, reflected Nasser's thinking after ten years of governing. For the first time, Nasser and his associates explicitly recognized the existence of class struggle.[15] The charter laid a special emphasis on the concept of socialism.[16] As in most developing countries, socialism was seen as an instrument to establish a society based on justice rather than on market forces, and on industrialization as opposed to the production of raw materials. Also, socialism was perceived as a means for mobilizing the resources of society and stimulating the masses to increase production. The basic principle of Nasser's socialism was "sufficiency and justice," that is, increase in production and justice in its distribution. The government, therefore, must interfere to ensure equitable distribution of wealth and income. The objective of the government's intervention was to resolve class conflict through the reduction of economic disparities and the extension of social services and educational opportunities.

These ideological developments were embodied in the constitution. Thus, whereas the constitutions of 1956 and 1958 included a general reference to social justice, welfare, and the use of taxation policy, in the 1964 constitution Egypt was described as "a democratic socialist state"

(Article 1) whose economic system was based on socialism (Article 9). The economy was to be directed by a development plan, and people controlled all the means of production (Articles 10 and 12). The forms of ownership were mentioned in the following order: state (the public sector), cooperative, and private.

The drive for socialization continued, with ups and downs, until 1967. In 1966, Nasser referred to the need to nationalize wholesale trade and the construction sector. In the countryside a committee presided over by Field Marshal ᶜAbd al-Hakīm ᶜAmir, the first vice-president, launched a controversial campaign against big landowners. The defeat of 1967 was a turning point that put in motion a new train of events.

From the foregoing analysis, it seems that Nasser and his colleagues did not begin with a coherent concept of social justice. The concept developed over time from their experience in government. As will be shown from our analysis of land reform and nationalization laws, distributional policies were used as a means to maintain political stability and as an instrument of control. Behind this, there existed a basic concept of national power and the unity of the nation.

The regime's approach to economic development showed its preoccupation with the notion of unity. For the Egyptian elite, socialism was not so much a matter of ideological belief as it was a pragmatic means of solving the problems of economic development. The aim of socialism was conceived of as minimizing conflict through means of rational planning.[17] Like economics, politics can, and must be, planned and administered. In both spheres, it is denied that pluralism could produce a better state of affairs. Indeed, socialism and the absence of competitive politics were perceived as two sides of the same coin. If socialism is the ideology of economic development and the single party is the ideology of political development, both constitute the strategy for achieving national power. National power and the strength of the state were basic ideas to Nasser. His approach to social problems was colored by this nationalistic vision. Social and class cleavages were essentially unwanted because they undermined national unity. Social injustices were equally unwanted because they might lead to political instability and the weakening of the nation.[18]

Nothing shows the weakness of Nasser's system of institutions more than what has happened in Egypt since his death in 1970. When Sadat assumed power, little was known about him. Soon he was to develop his own style of governance. In the confrontation with his opponents, led by ᶜAlī Sabrī, in May 1971, he acted fast, outmaneuvered them, and had them sent to jail. Between May 15, 1971, and October 6, 1973, Sadat gradually consolidated his position. The war of 1973 and the aura of victory gave him the necessary power and legitimacy to be more critical of Nasser's views and policies.

In a piecemeal fashion, Sadat started to introduce a new set of ideas and policies that represented a new phase of ideological development and led to a radical alteration of Nasser's Egypt. Changes have affected almost all aspects of the country's socio-economic and political structure, as well as its foreign policy and international alliances. A close reading of Sadat's views and ideas reveals a system of thinking very similar to the guided capitalism phase and highly critical of the socialist one.

On the whole, Sadat is much less interested in ideological legitimation than Nasser was. The key concept in his thinking is *infitāh* (opening or open-door policy). The basis of Egypt's new economic policy was laid out in November 1974 in the October Paper, which called for a vigorous investment program that would mobilize Egyptian domestic capital, Arab and foreign resources. In a major speech on the occasion of his reelection for presidency, Sadat articulated the main features of his policy. Private initiative was to be encouraged. and individuals could earn freely as long as they paid due taxes.[19] The socialist ideas and policies of Nasser were strongly criticized as sacrificing individuals for the state.[20] They led to inhuman and illegal practices such as torture, confiscation, and sequestration of property for political reasons. Sadat was particularly critical of the mid-1960s campaign to liquidate "the remnants of feudalism," and he blamed Marxists and "Centers of Powers" for this deviation.[21] Hence, Nasserite socialism failed completely.[22] Instead, Sadat calls his brand of ideology "democratic Socialism" and identifies it with European social democratic experiences.

Democratic socialism is a vague system of ideas that is not taken seriously by the regime itself. In a basic document, attributed to Dr. Sūfī Abū Tālib, the former president of Cairo University and in 1980 the speaker of Parliament, the key concept is balance: between society and individual, material and spiritual considerations, public and private sectors, and planning and individual initiative.[23]

Democratic socialism does not recognize nationalization or sequestration as legitimate policy options.[24] It emphasizes the importance of individual initiative, free enterprise, and foreign investment.[25] Its main instrument of social justice is progressive taxation. In a statement on February 4, 1975, Sadat emphasized the importance of taxes as an instrument to achieve three objectives: (1) sharing public responsibility; (2) imposing a ceiling on large incomes; and (3) reducing luxury consumptions. The real problem of this line of thinking is the inefficiency of Egypt's taxation system. It is hard on salaried people, while lax on private activities. Hence it is doubtful that existing taxation policy can be used effectively as the main strument of ID.

The infitah is not merely an economic policy. It is rather an orientation, a guiding principle. It has implications in all spheres of society, such as government, administration, political organization, migration, employment, and foreign policy. In Egypt, economic liberalization has been accompanied by a corresponding process of limited political liberalization. How much congruence and/or divergence between economic and political liberalization will exist in the future is yet to be seen. There is enough evidence, however, to show that economic liberalization has already outpaced the political one.

The infitāh was justified in terms of (1) the failure of the socialist experience; (2) the opportunity presented by Arab capital of the oil-producing countries; and (3) the international context of détente. To these one must add the growth of a strong professional and entrepreneurial elite for whom the public sector exhausted its functions as a channel for professional and social promotion—or at least it was no longer the only available one.[26]

Economically, the two essential elements of the open-door policy were, first, to attract export-oriented foreign enterprises by the establishment of duty-free zones, and, second, to attract foreign capital through a liberal investment policy. The goal of the policy was to set the stage for the development of the Egyptian economy through joint ventures and projects bringing together Egyptian labor, management, and other resources; Arab and foreign capital; and Western technology and management expertise.

The policy raises a number of interesting reseach issues whose answers have important policy implications. One issue is related to the genesis of the policy and to what extent it can be traced back to the economic policies of Nasser after 1967.[27] Another issue is what kind of society it may lead to, capitalist or mixed economy, and to what extent it provides a solution to the problems of Egypt's economic development. A third issue is which classes and groups stand to gain or lose from the policy. The last issue has a direct bearing on ID. The infitāh policy has been criticized for its adverse effect on ID. Its critics argue that, in a country like Egypt, it will increase the gap between the "haves" and the "have-nots." It encourages luxury and unproductive consumption. It enhances bureaucratic corruption, the growth of parasitic capitalism, and tax evasions.[28] On top of this, foreign capital will not commit itself to the projects that Egypt needs most. Sadat once admitted some of these points and asked for rectification,[29] but no major action has since taken place.

## III. Land Reform

After the formation of ID as an issue in Egyptian politics in the 1940s, an increasing number of politicians and writers emphasized the importance of land reform. People from different walks of life—reformist bourgeoisie, socialists, and industrialists—advocated its necessity.

Land reform was the first distributive issue to be raised by the new regime. The issue caused the first major confrontation between the officers and the representatives of the ancient regime and led to the resignation of Prime Minister ᶜAlī Māhır. After 1952 three land reform laws were enacted. Law 178 of 1952 put a ceiling of 200 *feddans* on personal ownership, plus 100 feddans for a dependent wife and children. Excess land was to be appropriated by the government and redistributed, in parcels of 2 to 5 feddans, to peasants. Owners were to be compensated by government bonds. The law also fixed the rent of the land at seven times the land tax and established a minimum wage for agricultural labor. Law 127 of 1961 decreased the ceiling to 100 feddans per person, and Law 50 of 1969 lowered it further to 50 feddans per person and 100 feddans for the family.

The agrarian reform policy was not confined to limiting ownership size but involved a number of policies that may be grouped as follows:

1. Policies aimed at changing the pattern of land ownership,
2. Policies aimed at regulating landowner-tenant relations,
3. Policies aimed at creating agricultural cooperatives and organizing crop rotation,
4. Policies aimed at improving the conditions of agricultural labor.[30]

The first law, enacted on September 9, 1952, only six weeks after the army takeover, initiated a broad debate in the country. Introducing the law on August 11, 1952, General Muhammad Naguib argued that the land reform policy "was designated to narrow the gap between classes, raise the standard of living of the peasant and divert capital to investment in industry."[31] In his book *Revolt on the Nile,* Sadat stated that land reform was the main objective of the revolution. It was a means of striking at feudalism, the core of political corruption in the country.[32] Major Jamāl Sālim, who was the driving force behind the first land reform, was quoted as saying, "Land reform represents a main turning point in the life of the large base of the Egyptian people. Therefore, the revolution must place all its weight behind it."[33] In his speeches on the occasions of land distribution, Nasser emphasized the political significance of the law. It aimed at achieving political liberty for peasants. For him it was not merely a matter of ownership, but the achievement of their freedom and dignity.[34]

All the members of the Revolutionary Command Council agreed on the law. Naguib was hesitant for a while, and Khālid Muhī' al-Dīn, a leftist, advocated a more radical land reform.[35] The authors of the law had several social and economic objectives in mind, not to mention the political one. In fact, the immediate objective was political, to weaken the political and economic power of landowners, who constituted the greater part of the old ruling elite. Another objective was to incorporate the peasantry into the body politic as a source of support and legitimacy.[36] The new leaders made sure of appearing among the peasants distributing land ownership certificates. In September 1952, Naguib made a tour in the delta, traditionally a Wafdist stronghold. The trip ended in great triumph. The campaign was extended during February, March, and April 1953 to all parts of the country. Sayyid Marᶜī, whose career was associated with land reform from 1952 until he became speaker of the National Assembly in 1971, recounts in his memoirs how he organized a number of public appearances in the countryside for Nasser and other officers during the fateful days of 1954 and the Nasser-Naguib power struggle.[37] The law was also designed to correct the maldistribution of the landownership system and to divert capital to industry. One may add another social-psychological factor that has to do with the social background of Nasser and his associates. Given their social origins from middle and lower middle classes, they had no sympathy toward large landowners, which was not the case for the pre-1952 ruling elite. The officers could issue a land reform law with no personal or familial interests being threatened. On the other hand, because of the same social origins, many of them kept their connections with their villages and were in a position to know the abuses of large landowners.

The conflict over land reform was not between peasants and large landowners but between two elites, the new officer ruling elite and that of the old regime. The new elite perceived the land reform as a major legitimacy device and a means to create a new constituency of support. The old ruling elite, the *pashas* and *beys* of pre-1952, were opposed to the concept of land reform. Similarly, most political parties took a hesitant and critical view of the idea. The majority party, *al-Wafd,* was more in favor of progressive taxation, minimum wage income for agricultural labor, regulating tenant-owner relations, and selling government land to small farmers.

In a meeting arranged between the officers and the leaders of the majority party, Fu'ād Sirāj al-Dīn, the general secretary of al-Wafd, refused to approve the idea of putting a ceiling on land ownership and suggested, as a substitute, increasing land tax. Nasser commented that taxes would increase the government revenue but would not achieve the objective of the revolution, which was the liberation of the peasants. Other political parties such as the Sa<sup>c</sup>dists and the Liberal Constitutionalists maintained similar positions.

There were other political groups that had more egalitarian visions of society. Only one week after the army takeover in July, the Muslim Brothers released a communique on the expected reforms from the new regime. They advocated social reform and attacked maldistribution in land, suggesting a ceiling on land ownership and the distribution of excess land to peasants.[38] The Brothers did not approve of the Land Reform Law of 1952, however. In a meeting with Nasser, their leader asked that the ceiling be raised from 200 to 500 feddans. Nasser rejected the proposal.[39]

Other than the Muslim Brothers, no political group of sizable support endorsed land reform. There were some small political parties that advocated the reform such as the new Nationalist party. The Socialist party of Ahmad Husayn and Ibrāhīm Shukrī called for the reduction of the ceiling to 50 feddans. Also, Ahmad Qutb, the leader of the Peasant party, proposed a ceiling of 50 feddans and a reduction of 40 percent in land rents.[40]

The various social classes took different stands on the land reform issue. The peasants, who were the direct beneficiaries of the policy, were in a state of surprise. The majority of them did not believe that the government would take the lands from rich and powerful pashas and distribute it to them. Large landowners opposed the law and used almost every possible means to stop it. They perceived it as a blow to their political power and prestige in the countryside. They tried to pressure the ruling officers through petitions, messengers, and even force. In Upper Egypt, a large landowner, ᶜAdlī Lamlūm, attempted to prevent land reform officials from implementing the law. The army moved swiftly, and he was arrested. Another incident was caused by al-Badrāwī ᶜAshūr Pasha, but he was persuaded by Marᶜī not to resist.[41] Some of them appealed to the courts to declare the law unconstitutional. Another group stopped the water pumps needed to irrigate the land. As late as September 4, five days before the issuing of the law, a group of large landowners met the prime minister and presented a memorandum refuting the arguments on which the law was based. According to them, the law would prove detrimental to the country. It was unfair to landowners and contrary to religious beliefs and to the constitution.

The officers were faced with a broad alliance of political parties, including the majority party, against the land reform. Even the prime minister and two members of the tutelage council (a council to perform the functions of the king till the infant crown prince reached eighteen years of age) opposed the reform. The officers did not surrender and identified the land reform issue with the revolution. They considered the reform an issue of vital importance, especially Jamāl Sālim, who gave it all his effort and concern.[42]

A second land reform law was issued nine years later. The explanatory memorandum of the land reform law of July 26, 1961, stated that this law was due to "the crystalization of the socialist ideology through the past nine years . . . and due to the revolutionary will of the people to liquidate gaps between the classes and to give every individual a chance to forge his place in society according to his capabilities and achievement." Its objective was to "broaden the base of landowners and to convert the largest number from tenants to owners."[43] The second land reform was closely associated with the "transition to socialism" and the nationalization laws. Since the constituency of these laws was basically the workers, it seems that the government wanted to create a stake for the peasants in the process. The 1969 reform was already set in the National Charter of 1962.[44]

The redistributive effects of the agrarian reform have been limited. The distribution of about 13 percent of the cultivated area to some 9 percent of the rural population has for all practical purposes eliminated the large landowners, slightly improved the lot of small peasants, and consolidated the position of the medium stratum, which represents the dominant economic and political power in rural Egypt now. There was an initial improvement for small peasants due to the introduction of a package of reforms, but they were offset through the effect of inflation and an increase in cultivation and cooperative expenses. In practice, the reform has not affected the position of the landless peasants. Further, the basic structure of inequality in land ownership continued to exist. In 1970 5.2 percent of the landowners, owning between 5 and 50 feddans, possessed 32 percent of all cultivatable land.[45]

The effectiveness of the cooperative system that was established by the land reform law was impeded by its centralization and bureaucratic control. Cooperatives were no doubt successful as an instrument of government control over Egyptian agriculture. They controlled the sale of agricultural inputs, such as seeds and fertilizers, and were responsible for implementing the agricultural cycle (crop rotation). It is this bureaucratic feature of the reform that was primarily responsible for the nonemergence of active peasant organizations and for the lack of strong peasant constituency for reform policies.

Politically, the land reform succeeded in eradicating the power base of large landowners. Whether it liberated the peasant is more doubtful. It "benefited those who already had a stake, however small, in village society."[46] The class of rich peasants (20–50 feddans) maintained its dominant position through an alliance with local officials that ensured them a great deal of influence in the agricultural cooperatives.

The implementation of the first land reform had a technocratic rather than political emphasis. Land reform officials at the local level were not responsible to the peasants, and in most cases they collaborated with rich landowners. Some officials were involved in illegal practices such as "land smuggling." In 1965 it was revealed that a number of families owned more than the limit of 100 feddans. Some had 1364 feddans and in one case 25,000 feddans. In al-Buhayra province alone 1,400 cases were discovered. Forged documents were used to retain the land within the family or to increase land ownership. Large landowners, it was revealed, had their relatives or friends in all official structures in the village: political, administrative, cooperative, and even the police. In some cases, landowners reverted to open acts of terror, the best-known of them happening in Kamshīsh village in Minūfīya province.[47]

The Arab Socialist Union's analysis of these incidents attributed them to "the opportunist and reactionary pockets in the administrative apparatus" who allied themselves with the remnants of feudalism. Public officials had thus indulged in acts of corruption that upset the aims of the land reform. This situation was made possible by two factors. First, there was a high degree of centralization and an absence of peasant participation. Second, the lack of an ideological focus of the reform, the absence of viable political institutions, and the dependence on bureaucracy inclined bureaucrats to see the project as "a technical endeavor necessitated by purely economic considerations."[48]

In February and March of 1965, the weekly *Rūz al-Yūsuf* published a series of articles on the smuggling of land. The assassination in Kamshīsh, of political activist Salāh Husayn, instigated by the large landowning al-Fiqqī family in the village, exposed the situation in rural Egypt. The Arab Socialist Union viewed the incident as an attempt by the large landowners to sabotage the socialist goals of the revolution. The Arab Socialist Union advocated radical measures to curb feudal influences in the countryside. Nasser accepted this view and established a high-ranking committee headed by Field Marshal ᶜAbd al-Hakīm ᶜĀmir, the first vice-president, to "liquidate the remnants of feudalism." Members of the committee came primarily from the army, intelligence, and the Arab Socialist Union and relied in their work on reports from these organizations rather than from normal bureaucratic channels. Up to February 1967, the committee had ordered the sequestration of 200,000 feddans and the dismissal of 939 local officials. It also evicted 220 large landowners from their villages. Since their presence was perceived as an impediment to reform policies, they were required to live in the cities.

In fact, the local bureaucrats were far from being technical and neutral. Many of them had closer connections with the privileged classes than with the peasants. Officials in the land reform authority included employees who worked on the former king's farms and the Ministry of *Awkaf* (religious endowments) and were brought up in the tradition of respect and loyalty to big families and contempt for the peasants. Nasser himself complained more than once of the attitudes of government officials toward the peasants. The land reform experience illustrated how bureaucracy can be resistant to social change when policies tend to challenge its employees' views or interests.[49]

The reform was not without positive political consequences. For a while, it cultivated a new consciousness in the villages and mobilized peasants behind the revolutionary regime. One manifestation of peasant participation has been their representation in Parliament. The number of peasant members of Parliament (maximum ownership of 10 feddans) was 64, 77, and 61 at the parliamentary elections of 1969, 1971, and 1976, representing 17.8 percent, 19.15 percent and 16.9 percent of the total membership. There is also the impression that land reform initiated a certain degree of social mobility whose magnitude has not been examined empirically yet.[50]

### IV. Nationalization and the Socialist Transformation

The majority of Egyptians were not involved in the "socialist revolution" that took place in their country in the early 1960s. On July 22, 1961, the government issued a number of nationalization laws. These were followed by other laws in 1962, 1963, and 1964, bringing distribution issues to the heart of Egyptian politics. The political environment of the laws was different from that of the land reform of 1952. There was no public debate of the laws prior to their promulgation, and no political parties existed to discuss them. Faithful to his way of doing things, Nasser acted first and then ideologically legitimized his action in the National Charter of 1962.

During the "socialist" era a number of policies were introduced that had direct impact on distribution issues.

- A strong public sector was created through Egyptianization and nationalization. All banks, insurance companies, most of the export and import trade, and important industrial and commercial firms were nationalized. The stock exchange was closed. The public sector was charged with the responsibility of increasing production and redistributing income.
- A profit-sharing scheme requested firms to distribute 25 percent of their net profits to the benefit of their workers and employees. Also, membership of companies' boards was reorganized. The number was limited to seven, including two elected representatives of the personnel, one weekly paid worker, and one salaried employee. Hours of work were reduced to forty-two hours a week.
- At least 50 percent of members of all political and local elected councils, including Parliament, were to be peasants and workers.
- The use of progressive tax and putting a ceiling on large incomes. The income of senior officials of the public sector was not to exceed £E5,000 a year. Private income was subject to a tax that reached 90 percent for incomes exceeding £E10,000 a year.
- Limiting the ownership of shares in companies to a maximum of £E10,000. Excess holdings were to be transferred to the government in return for fifteen-year, 4 percent-interest government bonds.
- All levels of education, including university, became free.
- And, finally, as mentioned earlier, the promulgation of a second land reform, which set a ceiling of 100 feddans per family.

The laws of 1961–1964 crippled the economic power of the industrial, financial, and commercial classes of Egypt, further weakened the position of large landowners, and enhanced the role of the technocratic-bureaucratic elite, which occupied top positions in the public sector. The influence of the private sector was further curtailed by the sequestration measures of October 1961 and January 1962, which expropriated the properties of 850 of the wealthiest Egyptian families. On the other side, the government extended its control over the economy, thus having not only military and political hegemony but economic as well.

Nasser explained the change in his thinking by the failure of capitalists to shoulder their share of the first Five Year Plan despite the encouragement and guarantees given to them. According to him, they continued to invest in quick-profit projects such as housing. The only way to finance industry, therefore, was nationalization. For Nasser, the 1952 revolution remained a political one, and reactionary and conservative elements were still maintaining their privileges. After the laws, the political revolution acquired a socioeconomic dimension. It was a necessary step to protect the revolution, to keep its zeal, and to create a more egalitarian social structure.

In fact, as late as 1958 Nasser was still not clear about the implications of "socialism" and the role of the private sector. P. J. Vatikiotis reports a change in Nasser's attitudes toward private enterprise in 1958–1959.[51] The year 1960 was associated with two fundamental economic changes. First, three leading banking institutions, the National Bank, Bank Misr, and Banque Belge, were completely nationalized. Second, the general organization for the implementation of the Five Year Plan was established, an indication of the adoption of a central planning approach.

The "socialist" laws have been subject to a number of interpretations. Some consider them a manifestation of economic nationalism and a further step for enhancing the Egyptianization of the economy. Others take them as the manifestation of an authoritarian polity in the sphere of economics. Authoritarian systems tend to penetrate all aspects of society and weaken autonomous sources of power and potential political opposition. Thus, such sources of power as *al-Azhar,* trade unions, professional associations, universities, and student unions were being brought under state control so the economy was to be dominated. The net result of these laws, in Anwar Abdel Malek's words, was the "assertion of hegemony over decision-making in the economic, social and ideological fields, accompanied by a tighter grip on the whole of the public life."[52]

The core issue in the socialist laws was state power, not only in the political administrative area, but also over society and the economy. Nationalization was a means to exercise direct control over the allocation of economic resources in the country in order to finance the first Five Year Plan and to use economic power in the service of Egypt's active foreign policy and leadership role in the Arab world. The expansion of government controls appeared desirable in the hope that external pressures, particularly those emanating from the two superpowers, would be best faced by a planned economy.

The feeling of insecurity on the part of the ruling elite and the perception of capitalists as a hostile force became evident in Nasser's thinking after the Syrian secession of September 1961 and the role played in it by big businessmen and landowners. Nasser continued to refer to reactionism and conservatism as the main enemies of the revolution. The Syrian secession seems to have influenced him.[53] It was the first major setback of Nasser's political career, and the secession challenged his role as a leader of Arab nationalism. According to Nasser, government control over

Egypt's economic resources was necessary to "forestall an attack on the revolution by the wealthy middle classes."[54] In fact, it was more of a preventive measure to liquidate possible adversaries, rather than a response to an immediate danger.[55] The situation was aggravated by an emerging alliance between a number of conservative Arab governments, led by Saudi Arabia, against Nasser's social and economic policies. Nasser perceived the regime's position to be domestically insecure and regionally isolated. His reaction was a more intensive nationalization and sequestration campaign. In a number of cases political opponents were sequestrated. The climax of this process was the establishment in 1965 of a committee (intended to liquidate feudal influences) whose practices are still debated in Egypt. In 1978 a court verdict condemned the use of torture by the military police while investigating big landowners at the time.

There is not much available data on how the first nationalization laws of July 1961 were passed, or who participated in the consultative process. It seems that Nasser was the prime mover of these laws, assisted by two economist technocrats, ᶜAbd al-Munᶜim al-Qaysūnī and Hasan ᶜAbbās Zākī. Strangely enough, neither had great sympathy for socialism, and both are known for their support of a liberal economic policy. Al-Qaysūnī attempted to limit the scope of nationalization by confining it to basic industries such as textiles, cement, and mines. Nasser was not to be persuaded. Muhammad H. Haykal, editor of the daily *al-Ahrām* and a confidante of Nasser, and Dr. Muhammad Labīb Shukayr, a professor of economics at Cairo University, minister of planning, and later a speaker of Parliament, drafted the explanatory memorandum that accompanied the law.[56]

Nasser's views apparently were not shared by a number of his closest associates. In two meetings held on October 12 and 13, 1961, attended by Nasser, ᶜĀmir, Sadat, Baghdādī, Kamāl al-Dīn Husayn, and Zakāriyā Muhī' al-Dīn, there was a discussion on what course of action Egypt must take after the Syrian secession. Baghdādī and Husayn expressed their doubts about Nasser's social revolution. Muhī' al-Dīn emphasized the importance of stability, stating that people must be told of the limits of socialism.[57] In his autobiography, Sadat also took a critical view of the socialist laws.[58]

In 1964, this conflict between members of the ruling elite came to the fore when Baghdādī and Husayn were removed from their posts. Both had been leading members of the regime since 1952. Baghdādī had served as minister of war (June 1953), minister of social affairs (April 1954), speaker of Parliament (July 1957), and vice-president of the Repubic (March 1958). Husayn also had occupied important posts such as minister of education, secretary general of the National Union, and vice-president of the Republic. Both claim that they differed with Nasser on the issue of democracy.[59] According to them, they grew uneasy with Nasser's individualistic style of governing, lack of consultation, and absence of political liberties. Distributive issues were not, however, entirely absent. Baghdādī opposed the nationalization laws of 1963.[60] Husayn was also concerned about the drift of Egypt to the left. In the discussion of the National Charter in 1962, he was not enthusiastic about some of Nasser's radical views. In particular, he objected to the reference to scientific socialism, and he emphasized Islam as a source of social values.[61] He thought that Egypt was moving toward communism and did not condone the excessive resort to nationalization of private property. At one point, he rejected the idea of celebrating the First of May as Labor Day since he viewed that as a communist practice.

The position of various political groups at the time is difficult to determine. As mentioned earlier, under Nasser, political parties were banned, and a single political organization existed. Two political trends, however, warrant attention—the Islamic and the communist. As early as the mid 1950s Islamic organizations and publications were brought under the close supervision of the government. A survey of Islamic journals published in Egypt during 1961 shows their role as apologists for the regime's policy. They provided an Islamic legitimation for Nasser's socialism. For instance, in 1961–1962, *al-Azhar* magazine published a number of essays on Islam and socialism.[62] One issue reports a meeting headed by Shaykh al-Azhar to discuss the charter. The meeting issued a statement that concluded that "the National Charter is in conformity with the principles of Islam"[63] and thanked the president for issuing it. Other publications such as *Islamic Forum, Islamic Youth,* and *Islamic Affairs* took the same line.

Communist groups took different stands on Nasser's social policies. One group viewed the regime's social and economic policy as a step toward socialism. This view motivated the two largest communist groups, in a rare move in the history of communist organizations, to dissolve themselves in April 1965 and join, as individuals, the Arab Socialist Union. This group cooperated with the regime and constituted a radicalizing force within it. It emphasized the concepts of class consciousness, public ownership, and the universality of socialist principles. Socialism, it argued, is one and the same; what differs from one country to another is the specific form it takes, depending on local circumstances and problems.[64] In the post-1967 era, this group took a more critical line and advocated further socialization. Marxist writers proposed new taxes on capitalist agriculture,[65] socialization of agriculture.[66] and bridging the gap between wages. They criticized the growing privileges of the middle class and warned against its consequences.

There were other Marxists, however, who did not consider Nasser's regime as socialist. They described Egypt as a democratic national revolution,[67] noncapitalist development,[68] petit bourgeois revolution, and state capitalism.[69]

The main shortcoming of Nasser's socialist experience was its technicist-bureaucratic nature. The public sector and national planning were introduced by decrees and without the support of an active political party. They were imposed from above and implemented largely by administrative means. Since the regime did not have a disciplined party or mass organization, it relied on the existing powerful bureaucracy. Many public enterprises were run by individuals who had no faith in socialism. One Egyptian economist concludes that public sector was in fact the private property of the state; "the Egyptian economy remained a capitalist society run by the state and hence controlled by state machinery."[70]

As in the land reform experience, the government did not encourage the development of an active trade-union movement. On the contrary, the thrust of the policy was control and manipulation. The genesis of this policy goes back to the days of the Nasser-Naguib power struggle in March 1954 when the workers, instigated by the liberation-rally officials, proved to be the crucial factor in support of Nasser. Later, trade unions were brought under the influence of the Ministry of Labor, which interfered in their budgets and elections. The ministry made sure that leadership positions were filled by progovernment elements. In a fiery essay in June 1966, the counselor of the General Federation of Trade Unions demanded the abolition of the ministry and the transfer of its functions to the labor movement.[71]

The workers' rights of 1961 did not lead to the mobilization and politicization of the working class. The official line was that Egyptian workers did enjoy many rights, many more than the labor movement had asked for at the time. The government provided social and economic security and symbolic representation (a worker is always appointed as a minister, and 50 percent at least of the seats of Parliament and all elected councils are for workers and peasants) in exchange for its control over the labor movement. The outcome of the provision of social rights and political controls of trade unions was to preempt the labor movement as an active political actor, thus preventing the development of a labor constituency for "socialism."

Also, similar to the land reform experience, the reliance on bureaucracy resulted in a prevailing technical administrative approach to problems. The bureaucracy grew rapidly. The number of ministries increased from 15 in 1952 to 28 in 1970. Likewise, the number of public agencies expanded from 1 in 1957 to 38 in 1962 and 46 in 1970. Employment in the civil service and public sector increased from 350,000 in 1951/1952 to 770,000 in 1962/1963 to 1,200,000 in 1969/1970. Thus, the bureaucracy enjoyed an increase of about 70 percent at a time when the increase in national employment or population did not exceed 20 percent. Between 1962/1963 and 1969/1970 the salaries increased by 123 percent in contrast to an increase of national income of 68 percent. Bureaucratic growth outpaced the rate of growth in population, employment, and production.

To this steady expansion, one must add the complex structure of public bureaucracy, civil service, and public sector, both vertically and horizontally. At the central level the civil service consisted in 1969 of 1,600 administrative units including ministries, departments, public authorities, public organizations, public companies, and independent public bodies. The structure was characterized by a high degree of centralization, compartmentalism, and interagency jealousies, organizational instability and duality of the old bureaucracy (ministries), and the new bureaucracy (public organizations and central agencies).[72] Within the bureaucratic elite a tension existed between career civil servants and the military, who were appointed in almost every ministry and public agency. The tension became public when Muhammad H. Haykal wrote a series of articles in 1961 on the crisis of intellectuals in Egypt, referring in particular to the relation between "men of expertise" and "men of confidence."

Another aspect of the bureaucracy was the social origin of administrative-managerial leaders in Egypt. According to M. Berger's study, conducted in the early 1950s, administrators came from middle and upper classes. They were mostly sons of landowners and civil servants. A noticeable degree of inbreeding existed; 40 percent of the top bureaucrats were sons of civil servants. The picture did not change much in the 1960s. In a study of the new managerial elite in Egypt, Sami Kassem concluded that 90 percent of the managers' fathers belonged to upper (21 percent) and middle (69 percent) classes.[73]

The role of bureaucracy and the absence of a strong political party or active labor movement led to a discussion of the emergence of a new class in Egypt. The issue was raised for the first time in *al-Ahrām* on April 28, 1964. The new class was identified as consisting of the administrative bureaucratic elite in the civil service and the public sector. Nasser did not approve of this definition. According to him, the administrative elite contributed to the society and was rewarded accordingly. The concept of the new class must be used, in his view, in reference to parasitic capitalists such as wholesale traders. He was ready, however, to attack some elements of the bureaucracy who belonged to the old regime and did not believe in the socialist transformation.

The new class whose interests were enhanced under "socialism" consisted of a number of strata. On the one side there were those bureaucratic elements that performed the crucial economic functions of capitalists and that enjoyed many privileges. They represented a privileged group compared to the society at large and to the rest of the civil service. Among them there were a number of army officers who moved to civilian life. On the other side there was the private sector in the wholesale trade and construction. Finally, there was a group of people who were full-time *apparatchik* of the Arab Socialist Union, who made use of their positions to improve their lot.[74] The emergence of a "new class" is important in understanding the evolution of the open-door economic policy. While the interests of this new class were linked for a while with the public sector and the "socialist experience," in the 1970s many of its members recognized the existence of other options. The structure of relations that produced this stratum became a decade later an impediment to the furthering of its interests.

## V. The Open-Door Economic Policy

The term *economic opening* appeared for the first time on April 21, 1973, in a government statement. Initially, it referred to the role of Arab and foreign capital in the housing and construction sectors. In 1974, it acquired a high political sanction when the October Paper, issued by the president and approved in a referendum, adopted it. Parliament organized three public hearing sessions in March of 1975 on the open-door policy.[75] During 1974–1975 a number of laws and decisions were taken to introduce the open-door policy, the most important of which was the law of foreign and Arab investment.

When Dr. ᶜAbd al ᶜAzīz Hijāzī's cabinet did not proceed with economic liberalization as quickly as expected by the president, in 1975 Sadat installed a new cabinet headed by a former police officer, Mamdūh Sālim, with the mandate of giving a push to the infitāh policy and of overcoming all obstacles facing it. Mr. Sālim defined these obstacles as twofold: the attachment to socialist slogans and the bureaucratic inefficiency.[76]

The open-door policy emerged gradually and in a piecemeal fashion. In 1973 and 1974 it was portrayed as compatible with socialism. In his October Paper, Sadat took pains to explain that the shift in economic policy was in no way a break with Egypt's socialist tradition. Rather, says the document, new circumstances called for new solutions and greater flexibility. Five years later, in August 1979, Sadat informed representatives of chambers of industry and commerce that capitalism was no longer a crime in Egypt.[77]

In practice, the policy meant a free market and capitalist economic relations. Throughout its development, the policy invited broad discussion on the part of various groups in society. A particular group whose position was crucial in this process was the bureaucratic-technocratic elite of the public sector. In the early 1970s, this elite was clearly indecisive. The majority still favored the public sector, which provided them with rewarding positions. A minority preferred a full return to a capitalist society. A third group perceived their place in the public sector as a stepping stone to private business. They thought of using the capital gained from salaries or corruption and the contacts they developed while in office to set up their own business. As foreign capital and investment opportunities increased, more of this group lost enthusiasm for public enterprises and tied their future to that of the private sector.[78] This process of shifting loyalties had taken place once before in Egyptian history.

What happened in the early 1970s resembles to a great extent the situation of post-Muhammad ᶜAlī and the collapse of Egypt's industrial effort in midnineteenth century. The open-door policy was also undoubtedly encouraged by foreign policy considerations—namely, the rapprochement with the United States and the close cooperation, until 1977, with Saudi Arabia and the Gulf oil producing states.[79]

In the process of adopting the new economic policy, Egypt's political regime changed its symbols and constituency. While Nasser symbolized revolution, anticolonialism, social equity, and socialism, Sadat emphasized the symbols of love, peace, and faith. The regime's constituency also underwent a noticeable change. Nasser's constituency consisted primarily of the middle and lower middle classes, urban and rural. Sadat's policies, on the other side, appealled to the upper middle class and those elements of the old bourgeosie that surfaced again. The privileged class that benefitted from infitāh consisted of diverse groups that had different social backgrounds and economic activities. It consisted of rentiers, importers, wholesale merchants, urban contractors, real estate manipulators, and rural landlords involved in capitalist agriculture. Thus the open-door policy had its supporters in the upwardly mobile segment of the population, particularly among those involved in entrepreneurial activities.

To review the various views on the open-door policy, we will take as a case study the discussion in Parliament of the law of Arab and foreign investment. The discussion took place over six meetings and eleven days between May 21 and June 1, 1974. It involved members of the legislative, economic, and budget committees of Parliament.

Dr. Sharīf Lutfī, then the head of the Arab and International Cooperation Agency, defended the bill on two grounds: the need for Arab investment and for Western technology.[80] The leader of the Liberal Socialist party, Mustafa Kāmil Murād, added that socialism was firmly established in Egypt and, therefore, there should be no fear of foreign capital. He argued further that the law was insufficient. The whole economy must be restructured to achieve economic liberalization and the laws regulating the activities of banking, insurance, employment, foreign exchange, and foreign trade must be changed accordingly.[81]

There were a number of objections to the law raised by independent members Ahmad Tāhā and Dr. Mahmūd al-Qādī. In their view the law contradicted the National Charter and the constitution. Second, it would lead to the subordination of the Egyptian economy to foreign interests. Third, it did not ensure labor rights such as minimum wage and labor participation in management that were included in the constitution (Articles 26 and 27). On this particular point, Tāhā and al-Qādī were supported by Dr. Jamāl al-ᶜUtīfī, the chairman of the Legislative Committee.[82] Another member objected to the idea that buildings financed by foreign capital would be exempted from the rent control laws.[83]

Another issue that provoked discussion was which sectors should be open to foreign capital. One group defended a restrictive approach and wanted foreign capital accepted only in areas where Egypt lacked capital or expertise. The government, however, pushed for a more liberal policy, and virtually no serious restrictions were imposed.[84]

In practice, the infitah policy opened wide the doors of the Egyptian economy to foreign investment. The policy invited severe criticism. Many people, while accepting the rationale of the open-door policy, have been critical of its implementation since 1974. First of all, the policy has tended to be consumer-oriented rather than productive-oriented. Egyptian markets were filled with all kinds of goods that enhanced a consumerist spirit in society. Second, the policy created an envrionment conducive to bureaucratic corruption and parasitic capitalism. Some flagrant examples of corruption came to the public eye such as those related to the Pyramids' plateau project and the ᶜAmirīya project.[85] Another example was a proposal to sell the cinema industry to a firm in which Saudi interests and the information minister's son had shares. Accusations were directed at individuals close to the president such as ᶜUthmān Ahmad ᶜUthmān, a multimillionaire contractor, and Sayyid Marᶜī, an agricultural capitalist. Both are the president's relatives by marriage. Opposition papers referred to the practice of accepting commissions and bribes on the part of senior civil servants. There was also the story of an agreement with Austria to use Egypt as a dumping ground for nuclear waste from Europe. The fact that the official who negotiated the agreement—Ahmad Sultān, former vice-prime minister and minister of electricity—faced charges of accepting bribes from American companies further hurt the government's image.[86] Third, the open-door policy could have been very useful had Egypt defined its priorities and needs. Not only did a set of priorities not exist, but government agencies made little effort to develop one. For instance, in the debates on the ᶜAmirīya textile project, ministers of planning and industry used different stastistics to defend different positions, a clear instance of elite fragmentation. Another example was the contradictory views held by the ministers of economy and trade in 1975 on the controversial policy of own-import.[87] Finally, a number of critics discussed the impact of the open-door policy on ID and the widening gap between the many poor and the few rich.

In two major policy statements in February 1975 and May 1978, Sadat referred to taxes as an instrument for achieving social justice. Critics doubt the effectiveness of taxes to achieve this objective. Tax revenues are around 14 percent of the gross national income.[88] Tax law was modified in 1978 in favor of large income groups. According to the previous law of 1973, taxes on incomes exceeding £E10,000 were 95 percent. The tax was changed to 70 percent on incomes exceeding £E70,000 and 80 percent on incomes exceeding £E100,000.[89] In a country in which per capita income does not exceed $280 or £E200, Egyptian tax law must be seen as generous. About 70 percent of the tax revenue comes from indirect taxes. Foreign and mixed investment projects are exempted from taxes for an average of five years and are allowed, under certain conditions, to import their production needs without paying tariffs. Also exempted from paying taxes are the construction companies and consulting offices engaged in the construction of new towns. On the other side, however, the law exempts peasants owning less than 3 feddans from land tax, taxes capitalist agriculture (gardens), and increases the level of nontaxable income.

The most organized political opposition to the policy has come from the left. The left in Egypt consists of diverse groups and organizations. First, the National Progressive Unionist Organization (NPUO) is a legitimate political party representing an alliance of Nasserites, Arab nationalists, and Marxists. In addition, there exist a number of clandestine illegal groups such as the Egyptian Communist party, the Egyptian Workers Communist party, and the Revolutionary Trend.

The leftist party (NPUO) is headed by Khālid Muhī' al-Dīn, a former Free Officer who was removed from power in 1954. According to its program, socialism is a historical necessity in Egypt. However, the party does not aim at the immediate establishment of socialism. At this stage, its main task is the defense of workers' rights and political freedoms. It demands the protection of the Egyptian economy from foreign domination and asserts the importance of planning and the role of the public sector. It is highly critical of the infitah policy and its consequences on the poor. According to the party the policy leads to inflation, the concentration of wealth in a few hands, foreign influence, and the development of parasitic capitalism.

ID cannot be achieved through taxation policy, the party suggests. In Egypt the bulk of tax revenues is derived from indirect tax, while no direct taxes are imposed on many capitalist activities. Further, ID cannot be achieved through segmental or partial policies; it must be the thrust of all economic policies, such as planning, consumption, saving, wages, and investment.[90]

The *Da'wa* magazine, the spokesman of the Muslim Brothers, does not dwell on ID issues in detail. To the extent that it deals with the problem, it has been critical of the maldistribution of income and wealth. The solution lies in a return to the economic principles of Islam, in particular *Zakāt* (Islamic tax).

Other political parties do not offer an alternative to the economic policy of the government. For instance, the neo-Wafd party, which existed for one hundred days before it dissolved itself in 1978, advocated a more active role for the private sector. The role of the public sector was to be confined to heavy industry and basic services. ID was to be achieved through taxation; taxes must be imposed on all incomes, and wages must increase in correspondence to prices. The program of the Liberal Socialist party approved a limited public sector confined to heavy and basic industries. The private sector was to be encouraged by all means. Shares of some public sector firms might be sold to individuals, and mixed projects between the two sectors were to be planned.[91] According to the Liberal Socialists, the main instrument of ID was taxation policy. The Labor party, headed by Ibrāhīm Shukrī, while accepting the policy of open door in theory, criticized the way it has been implemented.

Writers of different persuasions also warned about the widening gap between the rich and the poor. For instance, Dr. Muhammad Hilmī Murād, a respected public figure who was the president of ᶜAyn Shams University, minister of education, vice-president of the neo-Wafd party and a member of Parliament, wrote regularly in Egypt and abroad on the shortcomings of the open-door policy in the area of social justice. He criticized the flagrant consumerism of the rich and the government's expenditures on youth parades and ceremonial activites.[92] Another writer, Dr. Lutfī ᶜAbd al-ᶜAzīm, a German-educated liberal economist and the editor of *al-Iqtisādī* (the Economist), who was a major advocate of the open-door policy, kept referring to the social problems resulting from the policy, such as consumerism and maldistribution of income. In November 1976 he wrote that luxury consumption by the rich represented "social provocation" and could lead to class antagonism and instability.[93]

The president of the General Federation of Chambers of Commerce wrote an unpublished report in 1978 criticizing the way in which the open-door policy was implemented. The report referred to many shortcomings, among them the failure of Egypt to decide its economic priorities and the tendency on the part of foreign capital to invest in quick-profit projects. The report emphasized that the open-door policy must not be a means for the enrichment of the few.[94]

The most important political event related to the open-door policy was the January 18 and 19, 1977, riots. Major Egyptian cities witnessed massive and violent demonstrations after a government decision, in response to a demand by the IMF (International Monetary Fund) and some Arab oil producing countries, to discontinue subsidies for a number of basic commodities. The increases, announced on January 17 in a presentation of the budget for 1977 in the People's Assembly, would have increased the price of rice 16 percent, sugar 3.3 percent, gas 31 percent, cigarettes 12 percent, and household cooking gas 46 percent. Import duties on a wide range of luxury products would have doubled.[95] Demonstrations erupted in a violent reaction to the decisions. The riots—the most widespread, and violent since Black Saturday, January 26 a quarter of a century ago—left an official death toll of about seventy. An estimated 800 were injured, and 1,270 were arrested. Economic decisions were shelved, a curfew was imposed, and the army was called in to maintain law and order. The government accused extreme leftist elements and the NPUO of inciting the riots. Political observers have been skeptical of this interpretation, seeing the events as an expression of popular social discontent and an outburst of the long-suffering masses to unexpected price increases.

What has the open-door policy produced up to now? The results of the infitah so far are limited. Throughout the year 1979 the investment authority approved 200 projects as compared with 163 in 1978 (22 percent increase). The capital of 1979 projects totaled £E521.3 million as compared to £E313.6 million in 1978 (66 percent increase). The total number of projects approved, according to a report by the authority covering its activities until the end of December 1979, was 766 projects involving a capital of £E2,277 million; out of these only slightly over one-third (37 percent) started actual production and another one-third (36 percent) were under some stage of implementation. These projects employed 19,553 workers, all Egyptians but for 283. Wages reached £E22.2 million a year, out of which £E2.5 million went to foreign employees. Egyptians and Egyptian firms were surprisingly the main contributor to these projects (58 percent), followed by Arab countries (16 percent), the United States (7 percent), EEC (European Economic Community) countries (7 percent), and other states (12 percent).[96]

The hoped-for flood of Western capital, petrodollars, and big business into the country has not yet taken place. One reason perhaps is that, no matter how many enticements foreign businesses are offered, it will be hard to attract them to an area considered among the most politically unstable in the world. The infitah itself has indirectly increased regional instability. In order to work, the policy demands Egypt's shift from a wartime to a peacetime economy. But the price of peace has been high; Egypt's peace agreement with Israel has cost her the goodwill of other Arab countries. Until the political problem is solved or until foreign businessmen feel investment there is worth the risk, the influx of foreign businesses into Egypt will remain small.

The foreign businesses that do come are confronted by an array of problems. For one, the nation's communications and transportation systems are greatly overburdened, especially in the capital. Egypt's bureaucracy is another on the list of aggravations that foreign investors must put up with. A whole new category of middlemen has sprung up to assist the bewildered foreigner make his way through government rules and regulations. The regime is inefficient in handling the growing corruption and has done little to stem it. Although a few investigations have taken place, more often the guilty are ignored.[97] Other obstacles include rampant inflation and the steady migration of Egypt's best skilled labor to the Gulf states.

So, despite everything, the fanfare surrounding the policy, the government's backing, and the incentives offered foreign businesses, the opening is off to a slow start. This is not to say that the potential is not there. It is. But the question is whether the Egyptian regime will be able to make that potential a reality.

The foreign investors who come to Egypt are cautious. They are aware of the obstacles they face and accordingly choose investment projects with the lowest risk factor and the greatest possibilities for profit. Unfortunately, most of these projects are not developmental. A good deal of foreign capital has gone for tourism, hotel facilities, and the construction of middle- and high-income apartments. Foreign banks are also not moving in the directions desired by the government, but have gravitated toward import finance, hoping to obtain a slice of the profits to be had from Egypt's hefty import business.[98]

In 1977 the Central Bank of Egypt released two important reports. The first indicated that the then twenty foreign banks whose total capital did not exceed £E26 million transferred to their head offices abroad £E160 million. Thus, instead of bringing foreign currency into the country, foreign banks were exporting Egyptian deposits for investment abroad. The other report mentioned that in March 1977 there were forty-one persons whose bank deposits totaled £E119.3 million, an average deposit of £E2.9 million per person.[99]

All these examples underline an important point—the government in advocating the open-door policy, has lost control over the direction of investment. Capital is not being directed into the areas where it is most needed.

When Sadat signed the peace treaty with Israel, he made his people a promise: peace would have a significant and tangible impact on their lives. "Peace is not an abstract. It means a better life for people. We have shaken off prejudice. Now we must destroy poverty, ignorance, hunger."[100] Fed by the promises of the government, the expectations of Egyptians were high. So far, though, the regime has failed to deliver the much-heralded infitah.

Despite the disappointing results of the infitah, the government is determined to pursue the policy. Sadat seems convinced that the infitah needs a little more time. "Wait until 1980," he reassured workers when they told him the burdens of everyday life were becoming unbearable.[101] That was 1977. The year 1980 came, and still no relief was in sight.

The outcome of Egypt's recent policies is an economy neither wholly socialist nor capitalist. The policies have brought some of the ills of Western economies but few of the benefits. Western cars, refrigeration, and clothes are now everywhere and contribute to the balance of payment deficit. Even the real object of the open-door policy, foreign investment, has yet to appear in a significant quantity.

Where all of this will lead Egypt is an open question. From the perspective of the ID issue, it seems clear that the provocative consumerist behavior of a class of *nouveau riche* represents an invitation to social unrest. Egypt is in a real sense at the crossroads. The future of its economic policies is closely linked to foreign policy considerations, problems of war and peace in the region and, most importantly, its domestic situation—namely, political stability and social priorities.

## VI. Conclusion

Distribution problems lie at the heart of political investigation. Politics is the process of resolving conflicts over the distribution of scarce resources and values. In the broadest sense, all political decisions are directly or indirectly of a distributive nature. The political process is defined as the authoritative allocation of values in terms of who gets what, when, and how.[102] Different political systems involve different arrangements and mechanisms of handling conflicts over resource allocation.

Works in comparative politics refer to the distributive capacity and performance as major indicators of evaluating political systems. According to this line of thinking, distributive performance refers to "the allocation of money, goods, services, honors, statuses and opportunities of various kinds to individuals and groups in the society.[103] It deals with three basic questions:

- How large is the distributive activity of the political system?
- How does the political system allocate its resources among different social activities and sectors—and through what kind of instruments?
- Who are the main beneficiaries of these resources?

As it appears from the previous analysis, Egypt stands as an example of an "unfinished revolution." The nature of the post-1952 political system, the absence of institutionalized restraints, and the pragmatic nature of the elite have given the leadership a free hand in shaping the social policy of the country. The transition of power from Nasser to Sadat ushered in a new train of events—politically from one-party structure to controlled multipartism, and economically from national planning to open-door policy. In brief, a new socioeconomic priority set and commitments that directly affect ID have emerged. From the analysis presented in this chapter, it seems that Egypt has experienced two processes of ID: the first was toward a more egalitarian structure that was the outcome of a conscious policy on the part of the government, and the second was a reverse redistributive process in favor of the more privileged groups in society.

A striking feature of the Egyptian experience is that distributive policies did not create their political constituency. The nonemergence of a "political constituency" may be attributed to the nature of the distributional policies themselves. They were characterized by a high degree of centralization, limited popular participation, and heavy reliance on bureaucracy. Issues of ID were not articulated by their direct beneficiaries, but by representatives of the ruling elite. Further, in the absence of competitive politics or some degree of political freedom, direct beneficiaries could not develop a political constituency. This explains in part the ease by which Egypt moved from one set of distributive policies to another.

In developing countries that are characterized by a low degree of political institutionalization, power is usually personified in one man. The type of leader, his perception of equity issues, and his commitment to them are crucial factors in the formation of the ID issue. Notwithstanding objective socioeconomic factors, personal and subjective considerations cannot be disregarded. No analysis of the situation in Egypt can overlook the differences between Nasser and Sadat. Further, the absence of political competitiveness or at least active popular participation is a major factor limiting the social impact of distributional policies. It creates a tension between norms of distribution and the structure of representation. It leads to bureaucratic corruption and the nonemergence of a constituency of beneficiaries. The major shortcoming of Nasser's regime was its failure to build up institutions and develop constituencies capable of providing continuity to its ID policies. Another perspective is, perhaps, the failure of the regime to go beyond its middle-class base. That is to say, that the "revolution" was not "revolutionary" enough.

One problem with the present-day regime under Sadat is that it looks too much outside Egypt for a solution. The Egyptian ruling elite is better advised to look more to the inside and to provide solutions to the problems of social and economic organization. There are problems that no amount of Western capital or foreign expertise can resolve—namely, bureaucratic inefficiency, corruption in high places, widespread apathy, elite cynicism, consumerism and lavish expenditures, and the need for more democratization and participation in policymaking.

Below the quiet surface of Egypt's polity and society, strong currents are under way. Life is getting harder for an increasing number of Egyptians, while symbols of luxury consumption are becoming more visible in the streets of urban centers. Peace with Israel has been justified in terms of its positive economic effects. Unless the government proceeds swiftly to curb luxury consumption and to ameliorate the maldistribution of income, a recurrence of January 1977 events should be a surprise to nobody.

## Notes

1. P. J. Vatikiotis. *Nasser and His Generation* (London, 1978), pp. 21–98. For Nasser's connections, see ᶜAbd al-ᶜAzīm Ramadān, *Nasser and 1954 Crisis* (in Arabic) (Cairo, 1977); and for Sadat, see his autobiography, *The Search for Identity* (New York, 1978).

2. David E. Apter. *Choice and the Politics of Allocation* (New Haven, 1971), p. 28.

3. Malcolm H. Kerr, "The Emergence of a Socialist Ideology in Egypt," *Middle East Journal,* 16, no. 2 (November 1962), p. 127. See also Anwar Sadat, *Revolt on the Nile* (London, 1957), p. 53.

4. For this idea I am indebted to Professor Saad Ibrahim of the American University in Cairo.

5. On this development, see Ali E. Hillal Dessouki, "The Transformation of the Party System in Egypt, 1952–1977," in Dessouki, ed., *Democracy in Egypt: Problems and Prospects* (Cairo, 1978), pp. 7–24.

6. Muhammad Naguib, *Egypt's Destiny* (New York, 1959), pp. 184–185.

7. Nasser's speech of April 30, 1954.

8. On the concept of socialist, democratic and cooperative society, see Francois Bertier, "L'Idéologie Sociale de la Revolution Égyptienne," *Orient,* no. 6 (1958), pp. 49–71; "Principles of Socialist Cooperative Democracy," *Egyptian Economic and Political Review* 7, no. 9 (1961), pp. 18–29.

9. Nasser's speech of November 23, 1959. He expressed the same idea, though in less sophisticated manner, in an early speech on the second anniversary of the revolution in 1954. See Hassan Khedr and Amin Hassouna, *Egypt's Republic in Its First Year,* published in English by the Department of Public Relations of the Egyptian Armed Forces (Cairo, 1957), p. 79.

10. Jean and Simonne Lacouture, *Egypt in Transition,* (New York, 1958), p. 22.

11. Nasser's press interview with a group of American editors, January 27, 1958.

12. Nasser's interview with the daily *al-Ahrām,* July 2, 1959. See also his interview with the *New York Times,* November 3, 1959.

13. Nasser's speech of November 14, 1958.

14. On these conceptualizations, see Vatikiotis, *Nasser and His Generation,* p. 220; Anwar Abdel Malek, *Egypt: Military Society* (New York, 1968), p. 369; Mahmoud Hussein, *Class Conflict in Egypt, 1945–1970* (New York, 1973), p. 160; and Lūwīs ᶜAwad, *The Seven Veils of Nasserism* (in Arabic) (Beirut, 1975), p. 53.

15. *The Charter,* (Cairo: Information Department, n.d.), p. 42.

16. Fayez Sayegh, "The Theoretical Structure of Nasser's Socialism," in Sami Hanna and George Gardner, eds., *Arab Socialism* (Leiden, 1969), pp. 98–141.

17. Isaiah Berlin once remarked, "It is populist ideas which lie at the base of the socialist economic policy pursued by the emergent countries today." Cited in Peter Worsely, *The Third World* (London, 1964), p. 172.

18. Maxime Rodinson, "The Political System," in P. J. Vatikiotis, ed., *Egypt Since the Revolution* (London, 1968), pp. 87–89.

19. Sadat's speech of September 16, 1976.

20. Sadat's speech of May 1, 1977.

21. Sadat uses this term, *centers of power,* in reference to a number of senior associates of Nasser's with whom he had a power struggle in May 1971.

22. Sadat's speech of June 26, 1977.

23. Sūfī Abū Tālib, *Democratic Socialism* (in Arabic) (Cairo, 1978).

24. Sadat's speech of January 19, 1977.

25. Sadat's speech of March 1, 1978.

26. Nazih N. Ayubi, "Bureaucracy and Political Development in Egypt, 1952–1970," (Ph.D. diss., University of Oxford, 1975).

27. See an essay on the genesis of the policy under Nasser: Mark Cooper, "Egyptian State Capitalism in Crisis: Economic Policies and Political Interest, 1970–1971," *International Journal of Middle East Studies* 10, no. 4 (November 1979), pp. 481–516.

28. See criticism of the policy in Fu'ād Mursī, *This Economic Infitah* (in Arabic) (Cairo, 1976), and the monthly leftist *al-Talīᶜa* (The Vanguard), the issues of April 1974, pp. 5–20; April 1975, pp. 10–23; and October 1976, pp. 43–55.

29. Sadat's speech of March 2, 1978.

30. On these policies, see Samir Radwan, "The Impact of Agrarian Reform on Rural Egypt, 1952–1975," World Employment Program Research, working paper (Geneva, International Labor Office, 1977), p. 8 ff.

31. *Al-Misrī,* August 11, 1952.

32. A. al-Sadat, *Revolt on the Nile,* p. 156.

33. Sayyid Marᶜī, *Political Papers* (in Arabic) (Cairo, 1978), p. 266.

34. Nasser's speeches of April 19, 1954, and May 20, 1954.

35. Ahmad Hamrūsh, *The Story of the July 23rd Revolution* (in Arabic) (Beirut, 1977), vol. 4, pp. 430, 481; and ᶜAbd al-Latīf al-Baghdādī, *Memoirs,* (in Arabic) (Cairo, 1977), vol. 1, p. 102.

36. Springborg refers to the officers' desire to gain American sympathy and support. I found no evidence for such an interpretation. See Robert D. Springborg, "The Ties that Bind: Political Associations and Policy Making in Egypt," Ph.D. diss. Stanford University, (1974), p. 243.

37. Marᶜī, *Political Papers,* pp. 299–305.

38. A. Ramadān, *Nasser and 1954 Crisis,* pp. 109–110 and 273–286 and, by the same author, *Social and Political Struggle in Egypt,* (in Arabic) (Cairo, 1975), p. 55. See also the Brothers journal *al-Daᶜwa* 26, no. 17 (October 1977), pp. 32–34.

39. Ramadān, *Nasser and the Crisis of March 1954,* pp. 111–112.

40. Ramadān, *Social and Political Struggle in Egypt,* p. 55.

41. Sayyid Marᶜī, *Political Papers,* pp. 253–255.

42. Ibid., p. 266.

43. *Al-Ahrām,* July 26, 1961.

44. In the late 1960s a broad debate took place on reclaimed lands and whether they should be distributed to peasants or be cultivated by governmental companies. On this debate, see Robert Springborg, "Patriomonialism and Policy Making in Egypt: Nasser and Sadat and the Tenure Policy for Reclaimed Land," *Middle Eastern Studies* 15, no. 1 (January 1979), pp. 49–69.

45. Samir Radwan, *Impact of Agrarian Reform,* pp. 14–23; F. ᶜAbd al-Fattāh, *Contemporary Village Between Reform and Revolution,* (in Arabic) (Cairo, 1975), p. 207; John Waterbury, "Egypt: The wages of Dependency," in A. Udovitch, ed., *The Middle East: Oil, Conflict and Hope* (Lexington, 1976), p. 307.

46. Raymond W. Baker, *Egypt's Uncertain Revolution under Nasser and Sadat* (Cambridge, Mass., 1978), p. 205.

47. Nazih N. Ayubi, *op. cit.,* pp. 250–252. See an account of these cases in Baker, *op. cit.,* pp. 205–209.

48. Ayubi, "Bureaucracy and Political Development," p. 354.

49. Ibid., pp. 354–355.

50. In this regard, see the study of Illiya Harik, *The Political Mobilization of Peasants* (Bloomington, 1974). It remains to be seen whether or not Harik's conclusions can be generalized to other villages in Egypt.

51. P. J. Vatikiotis, *The Egyptian Army in Politics* (Bloomington, 1961), p. 137.

52. Anwar Abdel Malek, "The Crisis in Nasser's Egypt," in I. L. Genziher, ed., *A Middle East Reader* (New York, 1969), p. 135. See a similar view in Robert Mabro, *The Egyptian Economy* (Oxford, 1974), p. 128.

53. Robert Stephens, *Nasser* (New York, 1971), pp. 344–346.

54. R. Baker, *Egypt's Uncertain Revolution,* pp. 61–62.

55. Waterbury, "Egypt," p. 306.

56. Interview with Mr. Muhammad H. Haykal in June 1979.

57. Baghdādī, *Memoirs* vol. 2, pp. 141–153.

58. Sadat, *The Search for Identity,* pp. 142–147.

59. Hamrūsh, *July 23rd Revolution,* pp. 149–151.

60. Baghdādī, *Memoirs,* vol. 2, p. 231.

61. Samī Juhār, *The Silenced Talk* (in Arabic) (Cairo, 1975), p. 56.

62. See, for instance, *al-Azhar* 33, no. 7 (December 1961), pp. 791–804; no. 8 (January 1962), pp. 910–921 and pp. 940–944; no. 9 (February 1962), pp. 1035–1037, 1098–1107; vol. 34, no. 1 (June 1962), p. 4; no. 2 (July 1962), pp. 132–136 and no. 4 (November 1962), pp. 487–493.

63. *Al-Azhar* 34, no. 2 (July 1962), pp. 132–136.

64. Hamrūsh, *July 23rd Revolution,* vol. 2, pp. 244–245 and *al-Talīᶜa* 1, no 7 (July 1965), p. 48.

65. *Al-Talīᶜa,* 3, no. 9 (September 1967), pp. 35–36.

66. *Al-Talīᶜa,* 4, no. I (January 1968), pp. 75–77.

67. Salāh ᶜIssā, "The Future of Democracy in Egypt," *al-Kātib,* (September 1974), pp. 12–13.

68. *Al-Talīᶜa,* 7, no. 12 (December 1971), p. 67.

69. Fu'ād Mursī, "Abdel Nasser and the Revolutionary Theory," *al-Talīᶜa* 7, no. 9 (September 1971), pp. 11–12.

70. Gouda Abdel Khalek, "The Open Door Policy in Egypt: A Search for Meaning, Interpretation and Implication," in Herbert M. Thompson, ed., *Studies in Egyptian Political Economy* (Cairo, 1979), p. 83.

71. *Al-Talīᶜa* 2, no. 6 (June 1966), pp. 47–57.

72. Ayubi, "Bureaucracy and Political Development, pp. 212–213.

73. See a study by Sami Kassem, "Managerial Elite in Egypt" (Ph.D. diss., University of Michigan, Ann Arbor, 1967), pp. 118–120.

74. ᶜĀdil Ghunaym, "On the Issue of New Class in Egypt," *al-Talīᶜa,* 4, no. 2 (February 1968), pp. 82–93; and Ahmad Mukhtār Qutb, "Socialism and the New Class", *al-Iqtisādī,* no. 225 (January 1, 1965), p. 40.

75. *Al-Ahrām,* March 8 and 15, 1975.

76. See the text of a memorandum, presented by the prime minister and approved by the Council of Ministers, in *al-Akhbār,* June 10, 1975.

77. *Al-Ahrām,* August 19, 1979.

78. Ayubi, "Bureaucracy and Political Development," pp. 375, 423.

79. Waterbury, "Egypt," p. 324.

80. Preparatory discussions of the law on Arab and foreign investment and free zones, (in Arabic) (Cairo, n.d.), pp. 79–81.

81. Ibid., p. 85.

82. Ibid., pp. 94, 253.

83. Ibid., p. 188.

84. Ibid., pp. 91–92, 166, 269–370.

85. *Ruz al-Yūsuf* of December 18, 1978, and January 22, 1979.

86. Faris Glubb, "Sadat's Fading Hopes," *Middle East International,* no. 85 (July 1978), pp. 12–13.

87. This system permits Egyptians to import consumer and capital goods by means of foreign exchange from their earnings abroad, without requiring license for a total value of up to £E5,000 each year.

88. *Al-Ahālī,* March 1, 1978.

89. *Al-Ahrām,* March 3, 1978, and *Ruz al-Yūsuf,* no. 2572 of September 21, 1977.

90. See the program of the party and its weekly newspaper *al-Ahālī* of February 5 and March 1, 1978.

91. The Liberal Socialist party platform. See also *al-Jumhūrīya,* March 16, 1976, and *al-Ahrām,* April 9, 1976.

92. See his articles in *al-Sha*ᶜ*b* weekly, September and October 1979.

93. *Al-Iqtisādī* (Economist), no. 484 (October 15, 1975), pp. 6–7; no. 510 (November 15, 1976), pp. 4–7; and no. 531 (October 1, 1977), pp. 4–7.

94. ᶜIzzat Ghidān, "*Ṭawabit* of the Open Door Policy" (in Arabic), mimeographed, July 11, 1978, pp. 3–6.

95. *Middle East Economic Journal* 21, no. 3 (January 21, 1977), pp. 18–19.

96. These statistics are from a report by the Investment Authority for Arab and Foreign Capital covering its activities until December 31, 1979, mimeographed.

97. Alan Mackie, "Lid Comes Off the Cairo Corruption Cauldron," *Middle East Economic Digest,* October 1, 1976, p. 7.

98. Assem Abdul Mohsen, "Egypt: Foreign Investors Want Bankable Projects," *Middle East,* September 1979, pp. 5–43.

99. *Ruz al-Yūsuf,* no. 2575, September 17, 1977.

100. "The Promise of Peace," *Time,* December 24, 1979, p. 19.

101. Baker, *Egypt's Uncertain Revolution,* p. 168.

102. The conceptualization of the political system as a mechanism of distribution and allocation goes back to Max Weber. See David Easton, *The Political System* (New York, 1953) and Harold Lasswell, *Politics: Who Gets What, When, How* (New York, 1936). An elaborate analysis of the distribution crisis is in Joseph Lapalombara, "Distribution: A Crisis of Resource Management," in *Crises and Sequences of Political Development,* Leonard Binder, Lucian Pye, et al, eds, (Princeton, 1971), pp. 233–282.

103. A. Almond and G. Powell, *Comparative Politics* (Boston, 1978), p. 299.

# CHAPTER 4

# *Interconnections between Income Distribution and Economic Growth in the Context of Egypt's Economic Development*

Ibrahim Hassan El-Issawy

## I. Introduction

The purpose of this chapter is to describe and analyze the interconnections between growth and distribution in Egypt during the past twenty to twenty-five years. Taking account of the changing institutional framework as well as the growth and distribution policies that have been pursued in Egypt during this period, an attempt is made to deal with some questions of profound policy implications. How did changes in income distribution affect growth performance? What was the impact of economic growth on inequality? Were the two goals of growth and equity compatible or contradictory? How does one explain the relationship between growth and distribution?

In order to understand the *interaction* between growth and distribution in a *specific country setting,* and to work out the *net effect* of each phenomenon on the other, a quantitative model of some sort is needed.[1] Given the absence of a fully developed comprehensive theory of income distribution that is relevant to the conditions of underdeveloped countries and the paucity and unreliability of distribution data, the construction of a meaningful model is probably an overambitious (some may even say impossible) task. In these circumstances, a more modest aim had to be pursued. We shall attempt to ascertain from available data the general trends in growth and distribution over time, and to find out how they were *associated* in recent Egyptian experience (parts II–IV). We then proceed to examine the *main* links, causes, and mechanisms that may have led to the observed associations (part V). The growth-effects of a selected number of distributive measures are first discussed. This is followed by an analysis of the distribution effects of growth policies. In both cases, the analysis is admittedly *partial* and the treatment *nonexhaustive*. The main results of this study (summarized in part VI) are consequently tentative and may be regarded as a set of conjectures calling for further investigation.

## II. Changes in Incomc Distribution

Identification of the changes that occurred in the distribution of income in Egypt during the past twenty to twenty-five years is no easy task. The data are scarce, fragmentary, and speculative. Many of the statistics presented on aspects of the distribution of income are inferential, indirect, and based on assumptions that do not lend themselves to empirical verification. No matter how sophisticated the procedures by which some of the distributions were derived, it must be recognized that elaborate structures were built on shaky foundations. What is known about the distribution of income is mainly derived from information pieced together from sources that were not explicitly designed for the purpose. Coverage of all income or expenditure groups has not been achieved. This shortcoming is particularly serious in the case of informal activities and informal income transfers whose impact on the distribution of income may be considerable. The figures are difficult to interpret, owing to the diversity of definitions and methods used in their derivation, on the one hand, and the fact that the nature of the assumptions upon which they are based is not always disclosed, on the other.

### *A. Distribution of Income in the Rural Sector*

Three elements will be used in this section to construct a broad and tentative picture of the changes in the rural distribution of income over the past twenty-five years. They are: (a) the relative shares of wages and property income in agricultural GDP (gross domestic product); (b) the distribution of agricultural income by socioeconomic groups; and (c) the distribution of household expenditure in rural areas.

Before proceeding, mention should be made of two recent estimates of the *personal* distribution of rural or agricultural income. The first estimate was carried out by the World Bank on the basis of the 1974/75 family budget survey.[2] This estimate is unreliable for two reasons: (a) highly arbitrary assumptions were used concerning the saving behavior of the population in the various income groups, and (b) incorrect percentages were used for dividing the total population into rural and urban, and the estimate of average family size in rural areas is open to question, so that the total number of rural households is incorrectly specified. The other estimate is that of A. Mohie-Eldin.[3] It relates to the agricultural sector only in 1976. According to this estimate the share of the poorest 60 percent in agricultural income was 41 percent, and that of the middle 30 percent and richest 10 percent was 30.4 percent and 28.6 percent respec-

*TABLE 4.1.*
*Relative Shares of Wages and Property Income in Agricultural GDP, 1951/1952–1976*

| *Period* | *Wages as Percent of GDP* | *Property Income as Percent of GDP* |
|---|---|---|
| 1951/52 | 17.0 | 83.0 |
| 1959/60 | 24.2 | 75.8 |
| 1960/61–64/65 | 27.8 | 72.2 |
| 1965/66–66/67 | 32.9 | 67.1 |
| 1967/68–69/70 | 30.0 | 70.0 |
| 1970/71–1974 | 25.3 | 74.7 |
| 1975–1976 | 25.3 | 74.7 |

NOTES AND SOURCES:
The percentages shown for 1959/60 and the following periods are annual averages computed from the agricultural GDP and wage series of the Ministry of Planning, compiled from the ministry's (a) *Follow-up Reports,* several numbers, (b) *Indicators of Economic Growth for the ARE, 1959/60–1971/72,* July 1972, and (c) *Proposals for the Five Year Plan, 1976–1980,* Memo. 28, June 1976. They are based on the values of the relevant variables in fixed prices. The GDP and wages series were deflated by the national cost of living index (1959/60 = 100) up to 1966/67 and by the rural cost of living index (1966/67 = 100) for subsequent years. The 1951/52 percentages were taken from M. Abdel-Fadil, *Development, Income Distribution, and Social Change in Rural Egypt, 1952–1970* (Cambridge U.P., 1974), p. 64. They were calculated from GDP and wages in current prices. The share of property income is calculated as a residual. Unfortunately, available data do not permit further disaggregation of property income.

tively. No further reference will be made to this estimate, owing to the lack of comparable estimates for earlier years.

Table 4.1 summarizes the available information of the relative shares of wages and property income in agricultural GDP during the period 1952–1976. Wages in this table refer to paid and imputed wages. The wage series is subject to three types of errors, namely (a) errors in estimating annual average wage rates by farm operation; (b) errors in calculating imputed wages; and (c) errors in estimating agricultural employment which arise from inaccurate estimation of both labor requirements by crop and actual number of working days per year.[4] Property income is calculated as a residual. Its accuracy hinges, therefore, on the degree of precision in the estimation of the wage component and agriculture's GDP itself.

Some authors have argued that official statistics tend to overestimate wages and underestimate property income; but it is not difficult to find counterarguments.[5] Since we are concerned with trends over time rather than with precise magnitudes at specific points in time, this bias is not important.

TABLE 4.2.
*Percentage Distribution of Agricultural Income by Socioeconomic Groups, 1950–1965*

| *Socioeconomic Groups* | *1950* Mead | *1950* Fadil | *1950* Mabro | *1960* Mead | *1961* Fadil | *1965* Mabro |
|---|---|---|---|---|---|---|
| *Landless Peasants* | 5.4 | 5.3 | 9.0 | 5.0 | 9.7 | 8.0 |
| *Holders of:* | | | | | | |
| Below 2 feddans | 6.5 | ... | ... | 7.0 | ... | ... |
| Below 5 feddans | ... | 15.0 | 17.5 | ... | 28.0 | 34.0 |
| 2–50 feddans | 43.7 | ... | ... | 52.0 | ... | ... |
| 5–50 feddans | ... | 25.0 | ... | ... | 32.3 | ... |
| 5–100 feddans | ... | ... | 48.5 | ... | ... | 54.0 |
| 50 feddans & over | 31.2 | 39.0 | ... | 29.0 | 17.0 | ... |
| 100 feddans & over | ... | ... | 25.0 | ... | ... | 4.0 |
| *Rental Payments* | 13.1 | 15.7 | ... | 7.0 | 13.0 | ... |

NOTES AND SOURCES:
This table was compiled from D. Mead, *Growth and Structural Change in the Egyptian Economy,* R. D. Irwin (Homewood, Ill., 1967), p. 78; M. Abdel-Fadil, *op. cit.,* p. 58; R. Mabro, *op. cit.,* p. 221. Another estimate of the income distribution is available for 1958. This is Samir Amin's attempt (see *L'Égypte Nasserienne* (Paris, 1964), chap. 1, published under the pseudonym of Hassan Riad). His estimate is not included in table 4.2 because it suffers from a number of serious errors as pointed out in S. Radwan, *op. cit.,* pp. 32–33.

It is clear from table 4.1 that the relative shares of wages in agricultural GDP moved upward during the period 1951/52–1966/67. It rose from 17 percent in 1951/52 to around 33 percent in the middle 1960s. After 1966, a movement in the opposite direction is observed, with the share of wages falling to 25 percent by the end of the 1960s, and fluctuating around this level in the first half of the present decade. The share of wages in 1976 (25.7 percent) was only 1.5 percentage points above its 1959–60 level.

Clearly, most of the improvement in the distribution of agricultural income by factor shares achieved between 1952 and the middle 1960s has been eroded in the post-1967 period. The improvement up to 1966/67 was largely the result of the agrarian reforms of 1952 and 1961, the expansion of employment, and a rise in real wage rates in agriculture, particularly in the first half of the 1960s. After 1966, total agricultural wages stagnated, owing to a much slower rate of employment growth and a downward movement in real wage rates.[6] The distribution of income in agriculture by socioeconomic groups is shown for the years 1950, 1960, 1961, and 1965 in table 4.2. The diversity of methods of estimation and schemes of classification raise difficulties concerning the accuracy and comparability of the different estimates. A serious problem concerns the estimation of the number of landless peasants. It is highly likely that their numbers are underestimated. This is bound to affect the relative shares of the other socioeconomic groups in the agricultural population. Other problems arise from the difficulties of estimating: (1) net returns per *feddan* by farm size; (2) actual, as distinct from statutory, rent per feddan; and (3) income from livestock production and off-farm sources. Of the estimates shown in table 4.2, Fadil's estimate for 1950 and Mead's estimate for 1960 ought to be interpreted cautiously because a problem of double-counting (with respect to the treatment of rental payments) probably exists in the former and highly arbitrary assumptions were used (regarding the share of the landless and the structure of holdings) to arrive at the latter.[7]

In spite of these problems, it is not difficult to ascertain the *general movement* in the relative shares of landholding groups over time. The share of the very big landowners (50 feddans and over or 100 feddans and over) declined between 1950 and 1965; that of the small peasants (less than 2 feddans) improved only slightly between 1950 and 1965. The medium and rich farmers (5–50 feddans) managed to consolidate their position and raise their share during the 1950–1961 period. The position of the landless group is problematical in view of the difficulties in ascertaining their true number. The evidence suggests that the share of this group improved substantially (according to Fadil) between 1950 and 1961, or declined slightly between 1950 and 1960 (according to Mead) and between 1950 and 1965 (according to Mabro). Another attempt, by A. Mohie-Eldin, suggests steady improvement in the share of the landless between 1960 and 1976.[8] What is clear from most of these estimates, however, is that the share of the landless either remained virtually unchanged or improved slightly between 1950 and 1965, and probably improved since the mid-1960s as a result of increasing labor shortages in Egyptian agriculture. Moreover, the pace of improvement, if any, was fairly slow, and the share itself remains very modest.

Another admittedly indirect and imperfect indicator of the changes in the rural income distribution is available from the three family budget surveys of 1958/59, 1964/65, and 1974/75. The percentage shares of the population in different expenditure classes, together with estimates of the Gini coefficients of concentration are shown in table 4.3. Given the shortcomings of household consumption surveys in underdeveloped countries, particularly in rural areas, it is believed that the patterns of household consumption that emerge from such surveys are poor indicators not only of income distribution but also of the distribution of consumption itself. They tend to reflect the pattern of consumption of the middle-income classes rather than of the rural population at large. This is because *neither the very rich nor the very poor households are adequately represented in such surveys.*[9] Furthermore, if the pattern of saving is properly taken into account, much higher Gini coefficients would emerge for the distribution of income than is suggested by the distribution of household consump-

*TABLE 4.3.*
*Relative Shares in Household Expenditure and Gini Coefficients of Its Distribution in Rural Areas*

| | *Family Budget Survey* | | |
|---|---|---|---|
| *Items* | *1958/59* | *1964/65* | *1974/75* |
| *Relative Share of:* | | | |
| Lowest 40 percent | 17.65 | 19.00 | 18.84 |
| Lowest 60 percent | 34.24 | 35.26 | 35.46 |
| Middle 30 percent | 37.74 | 37.28 | 37.80 |
| Top 10 percent | 28.02 | 27.46 | 26.74 |
| *Gini Coefficient* | 0.37 | 0.35 | 0.35 |

NOTES AND SOURCES:
Computed from the results of the 1958/59 and 1964/65 family budget surveys cited in O. El-Kholie, *op. cit.*, p. 42, 47, and 48, and the 1974/75 survey given in CAPMS, *Family Budget Survey by Sample in the ARE; The Combined Results of the Four Rounds, 1974–1975* (Cairo, September 1978).

tion. Therefore, the findings from the family budget surveys need to be treated with extreme prudence.

Table 4.3 makes clear that the rural distribution of household consumption has not undergone any substantial change between the late 1950s and the middle 1970s. A small improvement occurred between 1958/59 and 1964/65, but practically no change was observed in the decade ending 1974/75.[10] The relative share of the poorest 40 percent increased and that of the top 10 percent decreased between 1958/59 and 1964/65. The relative share of the top 10 percent continued to decline up to 1974/75, but so did the share of the poorest 40 percent. The middle 30 percent of rural households experienced some slight decline in their share between 1958/59 and 1964/65, but managed to reverse this trend by 1974/75. The constancy of the Gini coefficient at 0.35 between 1964/65 and 1974/75 conceals an important trend in rural poverty that was revealed in a recent study of rural poverty. According to this study, the proportion of rural households unable to secure a minimum level of consumption fell from 35 percent in 1958/59 to 26.8 percent in 1964/65, and rose sharply to 43.3 percent in 1975/75.[11]

The trends in rural poverty suggest that the share of wages in agricultural income increased up to the mid-1960s and declined afterward; the real wage rates rose in the first half of the 1960s and then declined after 1966, and the agrarian reforms had little influence on the position of the landless groups. Rural income distribution has worsened since the mid-1960s[12] largely as a result of two factors: (1) the limited effects of the agrarian reforms, and (2) inflationary pressures that, in the absence of

*TABLE 4.4.*
*Relative Share of Wages and Property Income in Industrial and Nonagricultural Income*

| | *Industrial Sector* | | *Nonagricultural Sector* | |
|---|---|---|---|---|
| *Period* | *Wages* | *Property Income* | *Wages* | *Property Income* |
| 1952 | 41.8 | 58.2 | n.a. | n.a. |
| 1959/60 | 48.1 | 51.9 | 53.7 | 46.3 |
| 1960/61–64/65 | 45.7 | 54.3 | 53.2 | 46.8 |
| 1965/66–66/67 | 45.7 | 54.3 | 54.6 | 45.4 |
| 1967/68–69/70 | 47.0 | 53.0 | 57.6 | 42.4 |
| 1970/71–1974 | 48.3 | 51.7 | 60.3 | 39.7 |
| 1975–1976 | 43.3 | 56.7 | 52.2 | 47.8 |

NOTES AND SOURCES:
The percentages shown were calculated from Ministry of Planning, *op. cit.*, except for 1952, whose percentage was privately estimated from employment, wages, and income in manufacturing using data cited in R. Mabro, *op. cit.*, p. 222. The wages and income series were converted into constant price series using as deflator the national cost of living index (1959/60 = 100) up to 1966/67, and the urban cost of living (1966/67 = 100) afterwards. The 1952 percentage was calculated from current price series. The share of property income was derived as a residual.

increases in money wages and incomes, inevitably led to a substantial rise in the cost of living.

On the basis of the foregoing it seems safe to conclude that the rural income distribution improved in the 1950s and the first half of the 1960s, and deteriorated from the mid-1960s onward.

### *B. Distribution of Income in the Urban Sector*

Distribution data are much weaker for the urban sector. With the exception of two recent attempts to estimate the urban income distribution,[13] almost nothing is known about the income shares of different socioeconomic groups.

The movements over time of the share of wages in industrial and nonagricultural (NA) income are shown in table 4.4. An upward trend is observed for the share of wages in the two sectors up to 1974, except for the period 1960–1967, where the share remained virtually constant in industry. After 1974, a significant decline is observed, with wages accounting in 1975–1976 for a smaller percentage in both sectors than in 1959/60 (43.3 percent against 48.1 percent in industry and 52.2 percent against 53.7 percent in NA). The share of property income has been moving in the opposite direction. Note, however, that a significant part of property income in industry and certain subsectors of the services sector accrues to the state, particularly since the 1961 nationalizations.

The sluggish behavior of the share of wages in NA between 1960/61 and 1966/67 may be explained as follows: Between 1960/61 and 1963/64, total NA real wages increased (due to a rise in both real wage rates and employment), but so did value added in all NA sectors except housing. Between 1963/64 and 1966/67 a decline in total NA real wages occurred (owing to a decline in real wage rates coupled with employment expansion at much slower rates), whereas NA value added continued to increase. After 1966, total NA real wages were moving along an upward trend due to a continuous rise in NA real wage rates and expansion of NA employment, coupled with a much slower growth of NA value added. Finally, between 1975 and 1976 real wage rates declined whereas employment continued to increase, but the resulting increase in total NA wages was less rapid than the increase in NA value added so that the share of wages declined.[14]

Household expenditure surveys suggest that inequality in the distribution of urban household consumption remained virtually unchanged between 1958/59 and 1964/65 (see table 4.5). This finding appears consistent with the stagnation in the share of wages in NA income between 1960 and 1966. This does not necessarily imply that income inequality remained constant during this period. Income inequality may have declined. Large scale nationalization and confiscation of property in the early 1960s deprived the upper-income classes of a significant source of income. Their share in total income must have fallen, and there would have been a rise in the share of the poorer sections of the urban population (mainly industrial workers). That the rich continued to maintain their share in urban consumption is not surprising. Consumption habits do not respond instantaneously to changes in income. Indeed, the downward adjustment took

*TABLE 4.5.*

*Relative Shares in Household Consumption and Gini Coefficients of Its Distribution in Urban Areas*

| | *Family Budget Survey* | | |
|---|---|---|---|
| *Item* | *1958/59* | *1964/65* | *1974/75* |
| *Relative Share of:* | | | |
| Lowest 40 percent | 16.41 | 16.49 | 18.31 |
| Lowest 60 percent | 30.89 | 31.25 | 34.39 |
| Middle 30 percent | 38.73 | 37.99 | 38.01 |
| Top 10 percent | 30.38 | 30.76 | 27.60 |
| *Gini Coefficient* | 0.40 | 0.40 | 0.37 |

NOTES AND SOURCES: As for table 4.3.

place later, when the share of the top 10 percent fell from 30.7 percent in 1964/65 to 27.6 percent in 1974/75. Expropriated groups and the rich tend to increase consumption expecting to be hit by future expropriations.

The urban distribution of consumption apparently became more egalitarian in 1974/75 as compared with 1964/65. The Gini coefficient has fallen from 0.40 to 0.37. The share of the urban poor (lowest 40 percent or 60 percent) has increased and that of the rich (top 10 percent) has declined, while the middle stratum (middle 30 percent) continued to enjoy the same share. These developments seem consistent with the rising share of real wages in industrial and NA real income between 1966 and 1974.

Available evidence suggests that income inequality in the urban sector has been reduced in the 1950s and continued to decline up to 1974. This trend appears to have been reversed after 1974. Note, however, that the data base from which these conclusions were derived is very weak. My results regarding the periods up to 1958/59 and after 1974 are based entirely on developments in the share of wages in industrial and NA income. Nevertheless, these findings are not implausible as will be seen when distribution and growth policies are analyzed.

### C. *Intersectoral Inequality*

A number of indicators of disparities in the distribution of income between urban (U) and rural (R) areas, or between agricultural (A) and nonagricultural (NA) activities are shown in table 4.6. These indicators include U/R of NA/A disparities in labor productivity, wage rates, household consumption, and per capita income. All ratios were calculated from the relevant variables, after correcting current values for price changes in the different sectors.

The NA/A productivity ratio is found to be of the order of 2.8–3.3 for the 1952–76 period.[15] Examination of the changes in this ratio over time reveals a clear upward trend, particularly since the early 1960s. Productivity differences remained practically constant between 1952 and 1964/65, but tended to increase steadily afterward. Changes in the intersectoral productivity ratio obviously reflect the differential rates of growth of labor productivity in A and NA; productivity tended to increase faster in NA than in A for most of the years under consideration.[16] Note, however, that productivity differentials reflect, not only the effects of distributive policies, but also differences in the nature and scope of technical change as well as differences in the price structure and policies in the two sectors.

Wage rate differences between A and NA are more pronounced than productivity differences. The NA/A wage ratio ranged from 3.7 to 5.5 during the period 1959/60–1976. The larger spread of wage differences is due to the tendency of wages to increase faster than productivity, particularly in NA, which is dominated by service sectors. Wage differences

*TABLE 4.6.*
*Changes in Intersectoral Inequality*

| *Period* | *(1) NA/A Productivity Ratio* | *(2) NA/A Wage Rate Ratio* | *(3) U/R Consumption Ratio* | *(4) U/R Per Capita Income Ratio* |
|---|---|---|---|---|
| 1952 | 2.77 | ... | ... | ... |
| 1953 | ... | ... | ... | 1.64 |
| 1958/59 | ... | ... | 1.83 | ... |
| 1959/60 | ... | 5.50 | ... | ... |
| 1960 | ... | ... | ... | 1.84 |
| 1964/65 | ... | ... | 1.62 | 2.21 |
| 1959/60–64/65 | 2.84 | 5.21 | ... | ... |
| 1965/66–66/67 | 2.92 | 4.18 | ... | ... |
| 1967/68–69/70 | | 4.32 | ... | ... |
| 1970 | ... | ... | ... | 1.96 |
| 1972 | ... | ... | ... | 1.90 |
| 1970/71–1974 | 3.10 | 4.99 | ... | ... |
| 1974/75 | ... | ... | 1.73 | ... |
| 1975 | 3.28 | 3.50 | ... | 1.93 |

NOTES AND SOURCES:
*Column 1:* The 1952 ratio was arrived at by adjusting the IBRD estimate of 3.5 (IBRD, *op. cit., Statistical Appendix,* vol. 6, p. 19) downward, since the latter was based on a wider definition of agricultural employment than that used in the Ministry of Planning series, which is used from 1959/60 onward. The other ratios were calculated from sectoral value added (1959/60 prices) and employment figures obtained from the Ministry of Planning *(op. cit.)* and IBRD, *Statistical Appendix, op. cit. Column 2:* computed from employment and annual wages. Total wages were deflated by the national cost of living index (1959/60 = 100) up to 1966/67 for both A and NA and by the sectoral (U and R) cost of living indices (1966/67 = 100), after 1966/67. *Column 3:* Calculated from the results of the three family budget surveys (sources given earlier), after adjustment for changes in the cost of living. *Column 4:* K. Korayem estimates in "Distribution of Income between Urban and Rural Areas in Egypt," in the Egyptian Society of Political Economy, Legislation and Statistics (ESPE). *The Egyptian Economy in a Quarter of a Century 1952–1977* (Cairo, 1978), p. 73. (in Arabic). The R/U ratios given in the sources were converted into U/R to conform with other ratios in table 4.6.

tended to diminish between 1959/60 and 1966/67, owing to a systematic rise in real wage rates in A and much slower and uneven rise in NA wage rates.[17] The wage gap tended to widen after 1966/67, owing to a decline in real wage rates in A and a moderate but stready rise in NA real wage rates. In 1973, the NA/A wage ratio was 5.2, which is equal to the early 1960s ratio. After 1973, real wage rates increased faster in A than in NA so that the wage gap appears to have narrowed somewhat in recent years.[18] The NA/A wage ratio fell from 5.2 in 1973 to 4.9 in 1974 and 3.5 in

1975. Available figures suggest that the ratio has risen to 3.8 in 1976 owing to a sharp drop in A wage rates and a slight rise in NA wage rates.

Distribution of consumption by households appears to be more egalitarian in R than in U as tables 4.3 and 4.5 clearly demonstrate. The rural Gini coefficients are consistently lower than the urban coefficients. The share of the poorest 40 percent or 60 percent of the population is higher and that of the richest 10 percent lower in R than in U in the three family budget surveys of 1958/59, 1964/65, and 1974/75. This suggests that the rural income distribution is more equal than the urban—a result that is similar to that found in other underdeveloped countries.[19] The differences are not considerable and may reflect statistical imperfections in the family budget surveys.

Taking account of changes in the cost of living in U and R, the gap in household consumption as measured by the U/R ratio appears to have decreased slightly between 1958/59 and 1964/65, and increased (also slightly) between 1964/65 and 1974/75, as shown in column 3 of table 4.6. Average expenditure per household in terms of 1966/67 prices rose between 1958/59 and 1964/65 from £E191.3 to £E264.7 in R and from £E350.8 to £E429.1 in U, but declined to £E225.8 in R and £E391 in U in 1974/75. Much of the deterioration in average consumption per household in both U and R and the widening of the U/R consumption gap is attributable to different rates of inflation in the rural and urban sectors, particularly since 1973.[20]

Estimates of the U/R per capita real income gap are shown in column 4 of table 4.6. According to these estimates, which were derived by K. Korayem, the real income gap steadily increased between 1953 and 1964, tended to decline in the second half of the 1960s, and remained virtually constant in the first half of the 1970s. These findings are hard to reconcile with the findings based on the first three columns of table 4.6. They conflict with the observation that the U/R gap narrowed from the late 1950s up to the mid-1960's in terms of the wage and consumption ratios or remained constant in terms of the productivity ratio. The reduction of income differences in the second half of the 1960s is not supported by the analysis of the productivity and wage ratios. This finding is also in conflict with the findings of a Ministry of Planning study of regional growth in which the ratio of per capita income in the urban governorates to per capita income in the provinces remained constant (at 2:1) throughout the 1964/65–1969/70 period.[21] The constancy of the income ratio in the first half of the 1970s is at variance with the findings from the productivity, wage, and consumption ratios analysis, which indicated a widening of the gap. It is believed that the income series from which the income ratios were derived misrepresents developments over time in U and R incomes and probably underestimates the magnitude of the income gap at any point in time owing to an upward bias in the estimate of rural per capita income.[22]

Available evidence does not permit firm conclusions concerning trends in intersectoral income disparities. The broad picture may be stated as follows: The U/R income gap probably narrowed somewhat in the late 1950s and first half of the 1960s, either remained constant or continued to narrow in the second half of the 1960s, and tended to widen in the first half of the 1970s. It should be noted, however, that the changes in most of the indicators used in the analyses were *very marginal*. This suggests that the underlying structural forces making for intersectoral inequality remained virtually unchanged during the period under consideration.

### *D. Distribution of Income Nationally*

In assessing the distribution of income on a national level, three types of distributional data are considered: (1) relative shares of wages and property income in GDP, (2) distribution of household consumption, and (3) distribution of income by persons.

The relative shares in GDP of wages and property income are shown in table 4.7 for the period from 1959/60 to 1976.

The first half of the 1960s witnessed a steady increase in the share of wages. Employment and real wages increased by impressive rates during this period.[23] This period was one of major structural change, with the industrial sector growing much faster than the agricultural sector. In view of the large component of self-employed peasants in agriculture, it is not surprising that the share of wages should rise at the national level. In the period 1965/66–1974, the share of wages was fairly stable around the 49 percent mark. This was largely due to the slowing down of the rates of

*TABLE 4.7.*
*Relative Shares of Wages and Property Income in GDP*

| *Period* | *Wages as Percent of GDP* | *Property Income as Percent of GDP* |
|---|---|---|
| 1959/60 | 44.8 | 55.2 |
| 1960/61–64/65 | 46.1 | 53.9 |
| 1965/66–69/70 | 49.2 | 50.8 |
| 1970/71–1974 | 49.6 | 50.4 |
| 1975–1976 | 44.1 | 55.9 |

NOTES AND SOURCES:
Percentages computed from Ministry of Planning Wage and GDP series (Ministry of Planning documents noted for table 4.1), in constant prices. From 1959/60 to 1969/70, GDP is in 1959/60 prices, and wages are deflated by the implicit GDP deflator (1959/60 = 100). From 1970/71 to 1976, GDP is in constant 1970 prices, and wages are deflated by the implicit GDP deflator (1970 = 100). The figures shown are average percentages for the relevant periods, except for 1959/60. Note that since 1966/67, the cost of living index is given for rural and urban areas only.

*TABLE 4.8.*
*Relative Shares in Total Household Consumption and Gini Coefficients of Its Distribution*

| *Items* | *1958/59* | *1964/65* | *1974/75* |
|---|---|---|---|
| *Relative Share of:* | | | |
| Lowest 40 percent | 16.25 | 17.05 | 17.62 |
| Lowest 60 percent | 30.56 | 31.63 | 33.62 |
| Middle 30 percent | 37.31 | 32.24 | 37.86 |
| Top 10 percent | 32.13 | 31.13 | 28.52 |
| *Gini Coefficients* | 0.42 | 0.40 | 0.38 |

NOTES AND SOURCES:
The nationwide distribution was calculated from the rural and urban distributions of household expenditure (sources noted earlier for tables 4.3 and 4.5) as follows: (1) the population of households in each sector is estimated using estimates of the rural and urban populations and average family size in each sector, (2) the fractions of households in each sector in the survey are then transformed into fractions in the nation's population by multiplying the former by the ratio of the total number of households in the sector to the total number of households in the total population, (3) the fractions of household consumption for each expenditure group in the survey are transformed into a fraction in total consumption by multiplying the former by the ratio of the sector's total consumption to the nation's total consumption. The sector's total consumption is estimated from its estimated number of households and average consumption per household in the survey. The nation's total consumption is the sum of total consumption of the two sectors.

increase of employment and wage rates and the sluggish growth of GDP itself during this period. The year 1970 marks an important turning point, for the share of wages began to decline falling from 50 percent in 1970/71 and 1971/72 to 49.6 percent in 1973, and 49.1 percent in 1974 and 45.6 percent in 1975. By 1976, the share of wages (42.6 percent) was 2.2 percentage points below its 1959/60 level. An interesting feature of these developments is the downward trend of employment rates and the upward trend of real wage rates during most of the 1959/60–1976 period. The trend in real wages should be cautiously interpreted in view of the inadequacy of the official GDP deflator and its tendency to understate increases in the price level.

An attempt was made to combine the rural and urban distributions of consumption obtained from each of the three family budget surveys of 1958/59, 1964/65, and 1974/75, so as to secure a nationwide distribution of household consumption. The results are presented in table 4.8.

A clear pattern emerges from table 4.8. The degree of inequality in the distribution of household consumption has been declining between 1958/59 and 1974/75. This improvement is reflected in the steady fall of the Gini coefficient, the diminishing share of the richest 10 percent and the

*TABLE 4.9.*
*The Personal Distribution of Income*

| *Relative Shares of Income Groups* | *Early 1950s* | *1972* | *1975* | *1976* |
|---|---|---|---|---|
| Lowest 60 percent | 18.0 | 29.8 | 34.9 | 33.7 |
| Middle 30 percent | 38.5 | 37.0 | 30.2 | 31.7 |
| Top 10 percent | 43.5 | 33.2 | 34.9 | 34.6 |

NOTES AND SOURCES:
Relative income shares in the early 1950s were interpolated from data given in C. Issawi's description of the income distribution estimated by a *UK Trade Mission to Egypt, The Sudan and Ethiopia,* (London, 1955), p. 51. See C. Issawi *Egypt in Revolution* (Oxford U.P., 1963), p. 118. It is not clear from Issawi's account to which year these estimates relate. The 1972 relative shares were computed from Price Planning Agency, *Distribution of Personal Incomes,* Memo. 18, (Cairo, January 1973) (in Arabic). The 1975 shares are based on the estimates of a World Bank Mission to the Ministry of Planning, unpublished memo, April 1976. Income shares in 1976 were computed by combining the agricultural and nonagricultural distributions estimated by A. Mohie-Eldin in R. Ekaus et al., *op cit.,* section 5.

rising share of the poorest 40 percent and 60 percent of the population. Changes in relative shares of the rich and poor have been very small, and the share of the middle 30 percent remained virtually constant in the three survey years.

Much has been said about the shortcomings of the family budget surveys and their limited capacity to provide reliable indications of the distribution of income. The pooling of the rural and urban distributions of household consumption creates further technical problems. The distribution of income is likely to be much more unequal than suggested by the Gini coefficients and relative shares of table 4.8. The data tend to reflect changes in the *middle class,* in the broadest sense, rather than in the Egyptian population at large.

Table 4.9 sheds some light on the changes in the distribution of income by persons. Little information is available for this type of income distribution in the 1950s, and none exists for the 1960s, when most of the important distributional measures were taken. The estimate relating to the early 1950s is highly suspect. The share of the poorest 60 percent of the population is obviously understated, for it diverges considerably from their share in household consumption in 1958/59 given in table 4.8. Some doubt surrounds the estimate of the share of the middle 30 percent, particularly in the 1975 distribution. The fall in the share of this group between 1972 and 1975 is hard to interpret except in terms of methodological differences between the two estimates. It is probable that the share of the middle 30 percent was underestimated and that of the poorest 60 percent overestimated in 1975. The share of the richest 10 percent appears to be reasonably estimated in all the distributions shown in table 4.9, except perhaps for the early 1950s distribution, where an upward bias may be present.

In spite of their shortcomings, the estimates presented in Table 4.9 provide some indication of the trends in income inequality between the early 1950s and middle 1970s. Income inequality declined up to 1972, as clearly demonstrated by the significant increase in the share of the poorest 60 percent and the appreciable reduction in the share of the richest 10 percent of the population. This trend has been reversed in recent years. The share of the richest 10 percent rose after 1972, and the share of the poorest 60 percent declined after 1975. The reversal of the earlier trend toward equality is also clearly demonstrated by the fact that 30 percent of the total income was appropriated by the top 4 percent of households in the early 1950s, whereas the same proportion of income was appropriated by 8 percent of the richest households in 1972. In contrast, the richest 5 percent of households obtained once again around 30 percent of the nation's income in 1975.[24]

These findings are supported by the analysis of the share of wages in total income and the changing distribution of household consumption discussed in section D. The share of wages has been rising throughout most of the period and only began to decline after 1974. Inequality in the distribution of household consumption diminished steadily between 1958/59 and 1974/75. The analysis of sectoral and intersectoral inequality also revealed a reduction of inequality in both the rural and urban distributions as well as in intersectoral inequality during the decade ending 1964. In the next decade (ending 1974), the rural distribution deteriorated, the urban distribution may have continued to improve, and intersectoral inequality either diminished or remained constant. Overall income inequality probably remained constant during that decade. After 1974, both sectoral and intersectoral inequality increased, which, together with the decline in the share of wages and the share of the poorest 60 percent in total income, constitute sufficient evidence of increasing overall inequality.

These trends in overall inequality appear consistent with the evolution of the social and economic policies pursued in the past twenty to twenty-five years. The reduction of inequality up to 1964 is largely attributable to the distributional policies carried out during this period, particularly those in 1961, which redistributed income from the rich to the poor (as in the case of the land reforms) or took income and wealth away from the rich and placed them at the government's disposal (as in the case of nationalization). After 1964, distributional efforts became weaker, and some of the benefits of the earlier distributional policies were dissipated, owing to some negative effects of those policies and the natural process of differentiation in a society in which the basic sources of inequality were far from being eradicated.

Low-end poverty was not a primary concern of distribution and other policies. It is not surprising, therefore, that overall inequality remained constant between 1964 and 1974. After 1974, inflation played a significant role in redistributing income from the poor to the rich. The sharp rise in prices was not matched by commensurate increases in money incomes, particularly wage income, and the rural poor were hit harder than the urban poor because prices tended to increase faster in the rural areas.[25] The *infitāh* policy, with its greater tolerance of income inequalities, has led to considerable gains by income groups. Dramatic rises in the value of assets and real estate have brought enormous windfall gains to their owners and the intermediaries. Certain sections of the upper strata of the farming population managed also to increase their incomes considerably (mainly fruit, vegetable, and barseem growers), whereas farmers subject to the government-imposed cropping system and price controls have not done so well.[26] In these circumstances, overall income inequality tends to increase.

## III. Changes in Growth Performance

Estimates in real GDP growth rates for several periods between 1952 and 1977 are shown in table 4.10. The estimates are known to suffer from a number of weaknesses, which may obscure actual growth performance.[27] A time series covering the past twenty-five years is bound to be inconsistent because modifications in definitions, coverage, and methods of valuation are normally introduced without proper adjustment of previous years estimates. The GDP contribution of agriculture is believed to be understated owing to insufficient coverage, undervaluation of nonmarketed output, and the use of administered prices that are well below export prices. The use of administered prices causes similar problems of undervaluation in other sectors, mainly housing. Incomplete coverage of such sectors as construction, small industries, and personal services leads to serious underestimation of their contribution to output growth. On the other hand, the contribution of government services is grossly overstated.[28] Given these shortcomings, it is hard to determine whether on balance official GDP at current prices is over- or underestimated. In contrast, it is almost certain that the official GDP series at constant prices overstates the real rate of economic growth owing to a lack of realism in the official GDP deflators.[29] The available figures relate to gross output, whereas a proper assessment of growth performance should be based on changes in net output, that is, after allowing for depreciation. Since we are concerned with major directions of change in output growth, rather than with point estimates, these defects do not seriously affect our appraisal of growth performance. Nevertheless, analysis of growth-distribution connections is bound to be affected by the inadequate coverage and insufficient breakdown of the construction and personal and informal service sectors.

TABLE 4.10.

*Average Annual Rates of Real GDP Growth*

| *Period* | *Agriculture* | *Industry* | *Electricity*[a] | *Construction* | *Trans. & Comm.*[c] | *Housing* | *Trade & Finance* | *Other Services* | *GDP Economy* |
|---|---|---|---|---|---|---|---|---|---|
| 1) 1952/53–54/55 | −1.1 | 4.5 | ... | 2.0 | 3.0 | 2.5 | −1.8 | 4.1 | 1.3 |
| 2) 1954/55–59/60 | 4.2 | 7.0 | ... | 10.1 | 8.6 | 3.3 | 5.8 | 2.0 | 4.8 |
| 3) 1959/60–64/65 | 3.3 | 8.5 | 18.0[b] | 10.4 | 11.1 | 1.9 | 3.3 | 4.1 | 6.0 |
| 4) 1964/65–69/70 | 1.5 | 2.8 | 9.4 | 4.2 | −6.2 | 2.0 | 4.5 | 6.2 | 3.0 |
| 5) 1969/70–1973 | 1.6 | 3.3 | 3.6 | −0.2 | 6.5 | 1.4 | 4.5 | 7.7 | 4.2 |
| 6) 1973–1976 | 2.2 | 11.6 | 10.4 | 6.2 | 13.5 | 8.6 | 7.7 | 5.7 | 7.1 |
| 7) 1977 | −0.1 | 16.4 | 10.3 | 12.3 | 15.3 | 5.9 | 5.9 | 9.3 | 8.3 |

NOTES AND SOURCES:

[a]Electricity included in industry for the first two subperiods.

[b]Includes public utilities which are part of "other services" in other years.

[c]Includes Suez Canal. Average annual compound rates of growth.

Rows 1 and 2 are calculated from the GNP Series at 1954 market prices given in B. Hansen and G. Marzouk, *Development and Economic Policy in the UAR* (Egypt) (North Holland, 1965), p. 320.

Row 3 is based on the GDP Series in 1959/60 prices cited in B. Hansen, *Economic Development in Egypt* (Rand Corporation, 1969), p. 16.

Rows 4 and 5 are calculated from Ministry of Planning, *op. cit.*, on the basis of GDP in 1959/60 and 1970 prices, respectively.

Row 6 is computed from GDP at 1970 prices given in IBRD, *op. cit.*, *Statistical Appendix*, vol. 6, p. 24.

Row 7 is derived from GDP in 1976 prices given in NBE, *Economic Bulletin* 31, no. 3 (1978), p. 246.

## A. Overall Growth

Examination of Egypt's growth performance reveals a number of significant turning points. The economy was fairly stagnant in the period 1952–55, as a result of the slack following the Korean boom and the uncertainties accompanying a major change of political regime. Performance was extremely poor up to 1954, with the rate of GDP growth well below the rate of population growth. After 1954 the economy grew, and GDP tended to expand at respectable rates for the decade 1955–1965. During this decade the government launched its first Industrialization Program (1957–59) and its first Five Year Plan (1960/61–64/65). The average annual rate of GDP growth rose steadily from 2.9 percent in the middle 1950s to 5 percent in the second half of the 1950s, and 6 percent in the first half of the 1960s.

The year 1963/64 marks a significant turning point. Growth performance reached a peak. The rate of growth declined steadily from 8.6 percent in 1963/64 to 5.3 percent in 1964/65, 0.5 in 1966/67, and became negative in 1967/68. A short-lived recovery occurred in 1968/69 and 1969/70 (6 percent–7 percent rate of growth). On the average, the annual rate of growth in the second half of the 1960s was one-half of the rate achieved in the first half. The economy's performance was as sluggish as it had been in the period 1953/54–1956/57 (3 percent rate of growth in both periods). The downturn in growth performance was the outcome of failure to increase the rate of savings, growing inefficiency of production and administration, population pressure, and the impact of the Yemen and 1967 wars.

GDP increases continued to be small in the first four years of the 1970s, though the average annual rate of growth (4.2 percent) was higher than in the second half of the 1960s (3 percent). Recovery was unbalanced; little progress was achieved in the principal producing sectors. The growth was largely contributed by the rapid expansion of the service sectors (8 percent), and increased expenditure on public administration and defense. Developments after 1974 contrast sharply with the sluggish performance of the preceding ten years. Official figures imply an average rate of real growth of the order of 8 percent between 1974 and 1977. Though industrial production increased at impressive rates, agriculture continued to lag. A large part of recent growth is, therefore, attributable to the rapid expansion of the tertiary sector, which grew vigorously under the *infitah* policy, the reopening of the Suez Canal, and the recovery of tourism.[30]

## B. Sectoral Growth

Growth of the sectoral components of real GDP are also shown in table 4.10. The broad picture is clear. Throughout the twenty-five years surveyed, agriculture grew comparatively slowly. Except for the decade 1955–65, agriculture growth lagged behind population growth. A marked decline in agricultural GDP growth is observed between 1965 and 1973 (1.5 percent rate of growth, which is well below the 2.5 percent rate of the early 1950s). In contrast, the rate of growth of industry has been high, except in the period 1964/65–1973, in which the economy as a whole passed through a contractive phase. The trickle-down effect of industrial growth, particularly to agriculture, was very modest. Industry "does not seem to have imported a growth momentum to sectors other than the services. There are strong backward linkages with agriculture because a large proportion of industry is represented by textiles and food processing. Industry, however, may not have stimulated new demands from agriculture. It simply diverted output away from direct export (e.g., cotton) or direct consumption (e.g., foodstuffs) into a different use, namely the domestic manufacturing of textiles and processed food. Industry supplies agriculture with fertilizers and little else. . . . Egyptian industry has not attempted so far to contribute more directly to productivity growth in agriculture by developing input and implements adapted to local conditions."[31]

The growth of the tertiary sector reveals another peculiar feature of Egypt's economic growth in the past twenty-five years. With the exception of housing, whose growth declined sharply between the mid-1950s and early 1970s, the tertiary sector grew at fast rates, and these cannot be *totally explained in terms of the growth of the primary and secondary sectors*. Much of the growth was attributable to the sluggish performance of agriculture and its inability to absorb additional workers (hence the massive migration from the rural sector), the indiscriminate expansion of education, the expansion of the civil service and public administration that accompanied increased government intervention in the economy, the expansion of the armed forces, particularly after the 1967 war, and the social welfare objectives that dominated policymaking since 1961. The expansion of the service sector may have contributed more to employment than to real output growth.

## IV. Patterns of Association between Growth and Distribution

The directions of change in growth performance and income inequality are charted in table 4.11 on the basis of the analysis of parts II and III.

It is immediately clear from table 4.11 that the pattern of association between growth and inequality is by no means uniform. Rapid growth, whether sectoral or nationwide, appears to be associated with less inequality in certain periods and greater or constant inequality in other periods. In the decade covering the second half of the 1950s and first half of the 1960s, growth in the urban and rural sectors and the economy as a whole was rapid, and inequality tended to diminish at the sectoral, intersectoral, and overall levels. The slower growth, sectorally as well as nationwide, in the next decade appears to have been associated with increased inequality in the rural sector, less inequality in the urban sector,

*TABLE 4.11.*
*Growth-Distribution Association Patterns*

| | *Rural* | | *Urban* | | | *Nation-Wide* | |
|---|---|---|---|---|---|---|---|
| *Period* | *G* | *I* | *G* | *I* | *Intersectoral Inequality* | *G* | *I* |
| 1955–59 | + | – | + | – | – | + | – |
| 1960–64 | + | – | + | – | – | + | – |
| 1965–70 | – | + | – | – | – /0 | – | 0 |
| 1971–74 | – | + | – | – | + | – | 0 |
| 1975–77 | – | + | + | + | + | + | + |

SYMBOLS AND NOTES
G = Growth; I = Inequality.
The signs should be interpreted as follows:
G: + = high, – = low; I: + = increase, – = decrease, 0 = no change.
In the context of growth, *rural* may be interpreted as agricultural, and *urban* as nonagricultural.

and less or constant intersectoral inequality in the second half of the 1960s and greater intersectoral inequality in the first half of the 1970s. The overall distribution of income probably remained constant during the decade ending 1974. In recent years (1975–77), inequality appears to have increased (sectorally, intersectorally, and overall), whereas growth has been very rapid in the urban sector and the economy as a whole, and very sluggish in the rural sector.[32]

The nonuniformity of the association between growth and inequality should not be interpreted as implying a random relationship between those variables. My view is that growth and inequality are indeed linked, though the relationship between them is by no means formal or mechanical and should not be expected to be of the same nature in all circumstances and time periods. The mode or character of growth, the social and political framework, the initial distribution of productive assets and foreign relations are all powerful determinants of whether or not the fruits of growth are broadly distributed and of the extent to which distributional measures may stimulate or retard growth. Empirical evidence on these matters is far from being conclusive, and its relevance is highly questionable. The conventional practice of testing growth-distribution hypotheses (such as the Kuznets hypothesis) by using *cross-country* data suffers from serious problems of data comparability, bypasses country-specific characteristics, entails fairly arbitrary assumptions concerning the growth path of the individual countries, and provides no guarantee that the patterns of growth-distribution association found in the *cross-country* sample will be of the same nature as those that characterize *intracountry* data.[33] Recent studies, focusing on country-specific experiences, support the *diversity hypothesis* that emerged from my examination of the Egyptian case.[34]

Before 1952, Egypt had a basically private enterprise economy, except for some "feudal" elements in agriculture. Distribution of income and wealth was extremely skewed, and absentee landownership was widespread. Fiscal and monetary policies were mainly designed to promote the interests of big landowners, merchants, and industrialists. Some measures were, however, adopted to foster economic growth (improvements in irrigation, protective tariffs to assist import substitution, and so forth), but they were incapable of coping with the country's problems, especially in view of the rapid growth of population and the deterioration in the external terms of trade. The 1952 Revolution attempted in its early years to promote economic growth with no major change in the country's institutional framework, with the exception of the long-overdue land reform. Much faith was placed in the efficacy of private enterprise and its capacity to set the economy on a path of rapid growth. Neither domestic nor foreign private enterprise responded to the incentives offered by the new regime. Though possessing no coherent ideology or clear ideas about the manner in which growth and equity objectives could be realized, the revolution was soon forced to a more positive role in directing the economic affairs of the country. The private enterprise phase of the revolution (1952–56) gave way to a phase of "guided capitalism" (1956–60), and later to a phase labeled "Socialist transformation."[35]

Since 1956, the government has followed an increasingly energetic interventionist policy. Industrialization was the backbone. The foundations of a growing public sector were laid through the nationalization of the Bank Misr Group in 1957 and the NBE (National Bank of Egypt) in 1960. Commencing with the "Socialist Decrees" of 1961, the large-scale nationalization and sequestration drive created a sizeable public sector and placed under government control a great part of the productive apparatus. This tight control of the economy began to weaken in the late 1960s. By the mid-1960s, the private sector, having absorbed the shock of the "Socialist Decrees," began to accommodate itself to the new situation and sought new avenues of profit from within the system. Hence "the emergence of a 'new' private sector consisting mostly of small firms, repair workshops and commercial intermediaries, often established in discreet partnership with public sector employees."[36] A tendency toward liberalization began, particularly after the 1967 war, and continued with greater force in the late 1960s and early 1970s. Examples of this tendency include relaxation of controls over export trade and foreign exchange dealings in the late 1960s and the lifting of sequestrations and promulgation of the first foreign investment law in the early 1970s. By 1973/74, the forces working for opening the economy had already gathered momentum. The official declaration of the new policy of infitāh came as a natural development of previous moves.[37]

A new era began in 1973/74.The scope for private domestic and foreign enterprise was officially broadened and legitimatized. The leading roles of the public sector and planning were gradually curtailed, and the mangement of the economy increasingly relied on indirect controls and market forces. Equity concerns waned, and a *grow first, redistribute later* policy was firmly adhered to. Social justice was to be achieved by "narrowing" rather than "liquidating" class differences, and greater faith was placed in a tax system whose efficiency and redistributive capacity were highly questionable. "Democratic Socialism" was now officially upheld as a substitute for the old "Marxist-oriented Socialism" of the 1960s.[38] Almost any kind of private economic activity was welcome, so long as the treasury exacted its share in the form of taxes.

These institutional phases coincide with changes in growth and distribution. They were also accompanied by changes in social and economic policies, Egypt's trade partners, sources of external finance, and variations in the character of growth and the concept of equity. Nevertheless, the movement from one phase to the other did not constitute a complete change in the sociopolitical and economic environment. Certain elements of *continuity* can be discerned throughout the total period. The following are probably the most important: (1) heavy reliance on foreign loans for financing investment; (2) a development policy with import-substitution orientation; (3) a sizeable and growing public sector; and (4) an enormous and steadily growing defense burden.

To what extent did these elements of continuity and discontinuity in the development environment influence the nature of the relationship between growth and equity?

## V. Growth-Effects of Distributional Changes

Numerous distributive measures have been taken by the Egyptian government since 1952. Since some of these measures are the subject of separate studies in this project, my treatment will be focused on what may be regarded as the *principal* distribution policies.

Though motivated by a variety of political and social justice considerations, the first (1952) land reform was also designed to release investible funds from agriculture in favor of industrial development.[39] Much of the capital released from agriculture on account of the land reform was not, however, invested in industry. It was invested partly in agriculture (mainly in the orchards subsector), and partly in urban housing, commercial and speculative activities outside agriculture. Despite the generous tax exemptions allowed to industry, "total industrial net investment hardly increased at all from 1953 . . . until the effects of the Five Year Industrial Plan of 1957 made themselves felt in 1958/59, and since government industrial investment increased (from 1954 onwards), there must actually have been a fall in private industrial investment."[40] Indeed, the effect on the propensity to save and invest on the part of the expropriated landlords was on the whole negative, especially following the land reforms of 1961 and 1969, which involved a large measure of confiscation.

Moreover, the acts of violence and abuse to which some landlords were subjected at the hands of the Committee for the Liquidation of Feudalism in the mid-1960s caused them to refrain from productive investment activities. They spent lavishly and wastefully on consumer goods or nonproductive investments or hoarded their money to protect themselves against an uncertain future or in anticipation of a more favorable investment climate.

These negative effects were to some extent overcome by another factor, namely, the tendency of land redistribution to lag behind land sequestration. This lag, which amounted to four or five years in the first land reform, meant that the land reform involved a transfer of the income of the sequestrated land to the state.[41] Significant resources became available to the state and must have contributed to the financing of growth during the transitional period.

The land redistribution program, together with such complementary measures as rent control, security of tenure, better terms of finance, the supervised cooperative, and the unified crop rotation, were expected to foster agricultural growth by promoting incentives to improve productivity and intensify production. Though the impact of the land reform per se on agricultural productivity and output growth is difficult to assess, there appears to be general agreement that there was some increase in yields. "Its extent does not seem to have been very considerable and its incidence has been by no means universal."[42] My view, however, is that although the initial impact of the land reform was positive, its beneficial effects on growth were gradually dissipated. Three factors were at work. First, in spite of the government's attempt to secure economies of scale through the unified crop rotation, the supervised cooperatives, and antifragmentation clauses in the land reform act itself, the land reform reinforced an already existing trend toward subdivision and fragmentation of holdings.[43] Second, a large part of the benefits of the cooperatives did not flow to those most in need of cooperative services. Productivity of the mass of small holders may not have increased significantly.[44] Third, the land reform did not affect the lot of farm workers, and their productivity continued to be very low.

The growth-effects of the land reforms have been mixed. However large the initial positive effects were, they were gradually eroded. The return was a limited one, and in time holdings became more fragmented. High rates of agricultural growth in the second half of the 1950s and first half of the 1960s (following the 1952 and 1961 land reforms) were followed by sluggish growth after the impact of the first two reforms weakened. No further spur was given by the reform of 1969.[45]

Land reclamation proceeded at a very slow pace in the 1950s. The area reclaimed amounted to 78,800 feddan, at an average rate of 10,000 feddan per annum.[46] The 1960s witnessed an energetic land reclamation program, particularly during the period of the first Five Year Plan. The area reclaimed between 1960/61 and 1964/65 was 536,400 feddan, or an average of over 100,000 feddan per annum. In the second half of the 1960s, the land reclamation program was severly curtailed; only 275,800 feddan were reclaimed, or an average of 55,000 feddan per annum. Land reclamation programs were modest after 1967 and were practically stopped in the early 1970s. No more than 21,000 feddan were reclaimed during this period. By 1973, the total area reclaimed was 912,000 feddan, of which 183,500 were still under preparation and 179,600 were not available for farming purposes (wells, military zones, public, utilities, and so forth). The new cultivated area amounted to 548,900 feddan (around 10 percent of the old land area) of which 150,000 feddan were distributed to new owners, 160,000 were rented to tenant cultivators, and the rest (240,000, of which one-third was classified as submarginal) was farmed by the state.

In 1975, the value added generated in the new land sector was £E30 million, which represented no more than 2 percent of total agricultural value added. The new land sector employed 199,000 workers, with a total wage bill of £E21.4 million in that year, or 4.7 percent of both the total number of workers and total wages in agriculture.

Clearly, the impact of land reclamation on the growth of output has been very limited. Productivity of the new owners and tenants is modest compared with the old land sector. The land itself is not as rich, and the new cultivators lack infrastructural services.

From the mid-1950s to the mid-1960s Egypt witnessed a continuous expansion of the public sector. This sector emerged first through the initiation of new projects (mostly in the form of mixed companies), and later through the Egyptianization of foreign firms and nationalization of foreign and domestic enterprises.[47] Egyptianization involved a shift of ownership and control from foreigners to Egyptians (in effect to the Egyptian government). Nationalization eliminated the very high income brackets and deprived certain groups from the right of controlling the use of a large part of the nation's economic surplus. Both measures led to a change in the relative distribution of income without much transfer of income from the rich to the poor. Nevertheless, the new public-sector-based institutional framework facilitated the introduction and enforcement of a variety of measures that benefited wage and salary earners.[48]

The emergence and expansion of the public sector had an impact on labor productivity and domestic savings.

The numerous benefits accruing to the workers in nationalized industries were expected to promote incentives and increase productivity. It is not clear whether these objectives have been accomplished. My view is that the stimulus to productivity was small and short-lived. The positive effects on productivity were gradually negated because of the indiscriminate application of the profit-sharing system and the tendency on the part of the workers to abuse the sick leave and the protection against arbitrary dismissal. Further detrimental effects on productivity resulted from the application of a rigid pay scale and promotion system to the public sector and the welfare-oriented employment policy of the government. The bureaucracy expanded in a political setting that allowed little public debate and criticism. In the absence of a truly comprehensive plan even in the first half of the 1960s or a well-coordinated investment program since 1964, problems of inefficiency were bound to increase.[49] The political system, in the 1960s and 1970s, provided no built-in checks to inefficiency and never allowed any administrative reform sufficient time to prove itself useful or useless.

Despite its weak or even negative effects on productivity and efficiency, nationalization enabled the government to establish its control over a significant part of the nation's capital and economic surplus, without which the rapid growth attained particularly in the first half of the 1960s would have been impossible. The savings ratio rose from around 12 percent in the late 1950s to around 15 percent in 1966/67. A rise in public consumption since 1967 has reduced the savings ratio in the late 1960s to 8–9 percent. The rate has continued to decline sharply reaching a low point of 4.5 percent in 1974 (which is one-half of the 1952/53 ratio). Signs of recovery are evident since 1975. The savings ratio rose to 7 percent in 1975 and *apparently* doubled between 1975 and 1976.

The share of public savings in total savings rose from 44.3 percent in 1959/60 to 93.4 percent in 1964/65. It dropped to around 70–75 percent in the second half of the 1960s largely due to stagnation in the public business sector's net surpluses. By 1976, only 60 percent of total savings came from public sources.[50] The developments in the first half of the 1970s are attributable to the dramatic increases in the current budget deficit and to the remarkable increases in private savings. The first factor is directly related to a rapid increase of public consumption and the subsidization program. The second is closely related to the infitah policy.

The nationalization movement, coupled with increasing government involvement in development, has led to a situation where the public sector became responsible for the greatest part of capital formation. By 1964/65, the public sector contributed 94.3 percent of the total gross domestic investment, leaving only 5.7 percent for the private sector. The relative shares of the public and private sector have not changed much since that time, with the public sector's share fluctuating around 90 percent from 1964/65 up to 1976. The stability of the relative shares in investment is rather surprising, given the upward trend in private savings noted earlier. Three reasons can be offered to explain the disparity between the private sector's shares in savings and investment. First, a large proportion of private savings was hoarded, particularly in the 1960s and early 1970s. Second, a large part of private savings tends to be invested in fields that require a large amount of circulating rather than fixed capital, notably trade and service activities. Third, a part of private savings is not invested by the private sector itself and is used to finance public sector investments, as is the case with post office savings, deposit accounts, and investment certificates.

On balance, Egyptianization, nationalization, and the growth of the public sector were instrumental in reinforcing Egypt's growth capabilities since the late 1950s. They afforded great opportunities for mobilizing domestic savings and facilitated the redirection of investments into productive channels. The beneficial effects could have been greater and more durable had appropriate measures been taken to overcome the problems of low productivity and inefficiency in the public sector. Growing inefficiency contributed to the sluggishness of growth after 1964, but was not, of course, the only reason for the slowdown in growth performance.[51]

The government committed itself in the early 1960s to employ all graduates of technical schools, universities, and other higher education institutions in the civil service and public sector. This policy gave school-leavers and college graduates access to employment and income, and its equity implications are, therefore, beyond doubt. But efficiency and growth have been jeopardized. It proved impossible to reorganize production so as to absorb the additional workers. Many of the jobs assigned to graduates were fictitious. They contributed nothing to output growth. Labor costs rose without a commensurate rise in productivity. This policy "transfers income from the economy to the educated at the cost of future economic growth."[52]

The government's employment policy was by no means restricted to the employment of the educated. Employment expansion became a general objective and was probably considered an indicator of success. Excessive employment was one of the major causes of loss in public sector industries. A striking example was found in the Abū-Zaᶜabal pharmaceutical complex, in which all construction workers had to be maintained on the payroll of the firm. Whereas the number of workers required was originally estimated at 898, costing £E196,000, in the first year of operation the plant employed 2,245 workers, at a cost of more than £E500,000.[53]

Egypt's tax system has been ineffective in redistributing income and promoting growth. From the point of view of distributive justice, the tax burden tends to be unequally distributed. This is due to two factors: (1) the tax system relies heavily on indirect taxes whose burden falls disproportionately on the poor, and (2) direct taxes, though progressive on paper, tend to be regressive in practice, owing to widespread tax evasion and avoidance on the part of personal businesses and noncommercial professions and the disproportionate direct tax burden borne by government and public sector employees.[54] From the point of view of incentives and output growth, the tax system is of limited value. On the one hand, the tax base is narrow and cannot be easily broadened for technical as well as political considerations. Taxation of agriculture tends to be mild. Most high-income groups manage to escape the tax net. On the other hand, the incentive effect of the tax system proved to be weak and in some instances negative. The tax exemptions introduced in the early 1950s to promote industrial investment were unsuccessful.[55] Furthermore, examination of the marginal rates of taxation has shown that the tax system tends to favor incomes from rents of land and buildings and discriminates against incomes from labor, particularly for the high-income strata.[56] The inability to enforce existing tax laws means that the tax system in reality bears very little relation to economic activity and economic development.

Subsidies on basic consumer goods have become one of the major mechanisms of redistributing income and attacking poverty in recent years. The subsidies constituted an insignificant proportion of public expenditure prior to 1973. They amounted to £E15 m. in 1962/63 and £E51 m. in 1970/71, accounting for 2 percent and 4 percent, respectively, of public expenditure.[57] Since 1973, however, there have been dramatic increases in the subsidies. They rose from £E89 m. in 1973 to £E491 m. in 1975. Over one-half of the latter figure was devoted to the bread subsidy. In 1976, the subsidies amounted to nearly 30 percent of total government expenditure and 11 percent of GDP. Despite the leakage of a part of these subsidies to nontarget groups, they played a significant role in maintaining the real income of the medium and lower income classes.[58] The political disturbances of January 1977, following a government proposal to cut the subsidies, is indicative of the significant contribution they make to the standards of living of the ordinary people in Egypt.

Finally, the farm input subsidies played a positive role in agricultural growth. Subsidization made such inputs as fertilizers, pesticides, fodder, and credit more accessible to the small farmer and hence increased productivity. It is probable that the disincentive effect of the government's policy of pricing agricultural products would have been more strongly felt in the absence of the farm input subsidies.[59]

The last thirty years witnessed a marked expansion in social insurance, social security, education, health, and housing schemes.

In education, the expansion in terms of number of students and classes has been tremendous. The total number of students more than tripled between 1952 and 1976, rising from 2.2 m. to 6.8 m. The number of graduates from secondary schools and universities more than doubled in the seven years from 1967/68 to 1974/75. Moreover, the recent population census of 1976 has shown a drop in the percentage of illiterates from 70.5 percent in 1960 to 56.5 percent in 1976, and a dramatic rise in the percentage of those with higher qualifications from 0.8 percent to 2.2 percent of the population during the same period. Growth in numbers or in educational expenditure does not necessarily imply a parallel growth in the educational level of the population and their productivity. Educational expansion has not been accompanied by an improvement in quality of the education. Signs of deterioration are evident in the rise in the number of pupils per class and the student/teacher ratio.[60] The deterioration in the quality of public education has led in recent years to a considerable expansion of costly private tuition and greater demand for private schooling.

The impact of education on productivity has been small and has declined over time. Moreover, the expansion in education did not respond to major development needs. General and formal education still predominate. The ratio of general to technical secondary school graduates was 2.0 in 1965/66, 2.7 in 1967/68, and 1.4 in the period 1970/71–1974/75. The ratio of graduates from the arts to the sciences faculties was 1.2 in 1967/68, 0.8 in 1971/72 and 1.5 in 1974/75. Enrollment in the arts faculties as a percentage of total university enrollment rose from 21.6 percent in 1968 to 42 percent in 1972. Technical education and on-the-job training tend to expand very slowly and bear little relation to real-world problems. The links between technical schools and colleges and industry are practically nonexistent. Learning in such institutions leans heavily on matters of theory. Schools and colleges are generally poorly equipped and inadequately staffed. Quality dropped considerably, particularly in the science faculties. Expansion of education may have reduced income differentials based on unequal opportunity of education, but it is doubtful that the economic performance of the population and growth of the economy benefited much from such expansion.

With respect to health services, the growth in number of medical units and number of beds has been impressive, though growth has been slower than in the field of education.[61] The total number of beds in hospitals increased from 35,744 in 1952 to 64,213 in 1965 and 78,928 in 1975. Rural medical units increased from 1,112 in 1964 to 1,916 in 1972, with an increase in the number of beds from 7,649 to 8,383. Expansion has been slow since 1965. Number of beds in rural units increased by around 200 beds from 1968 to 1973, and the number of units increased by around 300 during this period. Services in the field of endemic diseases increased by less than 400 in terms of number of units and by 274 in terms of number of beds during the 1968–1973 period. Improvements in health are reflected in the drop of death rates from 17.8 in 1952 to 12.2 in 1971 and in child mortality rates from 37.5 in 1960 to 23.6 in 1972.

The fall in death rates may have had some positive impact on productivity. However, the productivity-effects of the expansion in health services should not be exaggerated. The health sector expanded along traditional lines, promoting curative rather than preventive services. Hospitals and health centers are poorly staffed and equipped, particularly in the rural areas. Of course, the health of the population is not only a function of the provision of medical services. It also depends on levels of nutrition and the availability of other amenities, like housing and drinking water. Whereas housing accounted for 28.2 percent of total investment over the period 1952–60, its share dropped to 8.2 percent in 1960–72 and rose to 11 percent in 1976.[62] The neglect of this sector has led to serious problems. Between 1970 and 1977, the proportion of families in need of proper housing rose from 21.7 percent to 31.9 percent.[63] As regards drinking water, the 1976 census has shown that 25.2 percent of Egyptian families had no access to a source of clean water. The proportion of rural families lacking access to clean water was 36.3 percent, which contrasts sharply with the corresponding proportion in urban areas (12.3 percent). These indicators suggest that the improvement in people's health may not have

*TABLE 4.12.*
*Sectoral Allocation of Investments*
*(Percentages)*

| *Period* | *Agricul-ture* | *Indus-try* | *Elec-tricity* | *Transpor-tation* | *Hous-ing* | *Ser-vices* | *Other sectors* |
|---|---|---|---|---|---|---|---|
| 1952/53–56/57 | 11.4 | 23.8 | 6.0 | 14.7 | 32.5 | 9.8 | 1.8 |
| 1957/58–59/60 | 14.9 | 25.7 | 4.0 | 18.8 | 23.1 | 12.1 | 1.4 |
| 1960/61–64/65 | 23.4 | 26.6 | 7.4 | 19.3 | 10.7 | 10.0 | 2.6 |
| 1966–1970 | 20.4 | 29.1 | 13.9 | 15.9 | 12.8 | 6.2 | 1.7 |
| 1971–1975 | 9.8 | 33.7 | 5.2 | 27.7 | 10.5 | 6.0 | 7.1 |
| 1976 | 7.9 | 30.4 | 4.7 | 29.7 | 10.0 | 5.3 | 12.0 |

NOTES AND SOURCES:
*Agriculture* includes land reclamation, irrigation and the High Dam. *Industry* includes mining and petroleum. *Transportation* includes communications. *Others sectors* include trade, finance, and public utilities. Sources: up to 1965 from R. Mabro, *op. cit.*, p. 187. Other years from Ministry of Planning documents noted under table 4.1.

been sufficiently great to bring about an appreciable rise in productivity.

In Egypt during the past twenty to twenty-five years some redistributive measures enhanced growth; others did not. The 1952 and 1961 land reforms and the Egyptianization and nationalization measures were a spur to economic development. Land reclamation and distribution, expansion of social services, and taxation reform did not effect growth. The official employment policy was a powerful deterrent to growth.

Policies intended to spur growth also have had distributional effects, some facilitating equality and others impeding it. The impact of economic growth on the distribution of income will be assessed by analyzing the distributive implications of the following components of growth policies: (1) the sectoral allocation of investment; (2) the regional allocation of investment and industries; (3) industrial development strategy; (4) choice of technology and employment creation; (5) financing of growth.

Changes in the sectoral allocation of investment are shown in table 4.12. The share of agriculture rose steadily from the early 1950s to the middle 1960s, after which it sharply declined. The share of industry increased systematically throughout the whole period, and has been much larger than the share of agriculture except during the first Five Year Plan. The ratio of the relative share of industry to that of agriculture exhibits rapid fluctuations, falling from 2.09 in the period 1952/53–1956/57, to 1.72 in the period 1957/58–1959/60, and 1.14 between 1960/61 and 1964/65, and then rising to 1.39 in 1966/70, 3.44 in 1971–75 and 3.85 in 1976. The statistics reveal a clear bias in favor of industry, particularly in the 1950s, and a reasonable balance in the 1960s, particularly in the first half of that decade.

The neglect of agriculture starting in the late 1960s and continuing to the present is consistent with the deterioration in the rural income distribu-

TABLE 4.13.

*Allocation of Investments Within the Agricultural Sector*

| *Period* | *Private Sector* | | *Public Sector* | | *Horizontal Public Invest.* | | *Vertical Public Invest.* | | *Total Agr. Invest. (£E m.)* |
|---|---|---|---|---|---|---|---|---|---|
| | *£E m.* | *% total* | *£E m.* | *% total* | *£E m.* | *% of public* | *£E m.* | *% of public* | |
| 1960–65 | 17.0 | 8.3 | 188.3 | 91.7 | 154.5 | 82.0 | 33.8 | 18.0 | 205.3 |
| 1966–70 | 9.5 | 4.4 | 208.6 | 95.6 | 176.2 | 84.5 | 32.4 | 15.5 | 218.1 |
| 1970–75 | 13.0 | 6.5 | 186.1 | 93.5 | 127.4 | 68.5 | 58.7 | 31.5 | 199.1 |
| 1960–75 | 39.5 | 6.4 | 583.0 | 93.6 | 458.1 | 78.6 | 124.9 | 21.4 | 622.5 |

NOTES AND SOURCES:
Ministry of Planning figures cited in INP, *An Economic and Technical Study of the Prospects of the Fertilizer Industry and Agricultural Development in the ARE up to 1985* (INP, April 1978), p. 15 (in Arabic). Note that the share of the private sector in agricultural investment is underestimated, owing to inadequate statistical coverage. Total agricultural investment does not include irrigation and drainage projects and the High Dam.

TABLE 4.14.
Regional Distribution of Industrial Establishments

| Region | 1952 % of establishments | 1952 % of labor force | 1966/67 % of establishments | 1966/67 % of labor force | 1972 % of establishments | 1972 % of labor force |
|---|---|---|---|---|---|---|
| Greater Cairo | 49.3 | 37.4 | 51.6 | 44.1 | ... | ... |
| Alexandria | 19.2 | 25.4 | 14.6 | 20.8 | ... | ... |
| Canal Zone | 3.4 | 3.1 | 2.8 | 3.6 | ... | ... |
| Main Cities | 71.9 | 65.9 | 69.0 | 68.5 | 51 | 55 |
| Lower Egypt | 19.8 | 25.4 | 20.6 | 26.5 | 30 | 29 |
| Upper Egypt | 8.1 | 6.6 | 10.0 | 6.4 | 19 | 16 |
| Frontier Gov. | 0.2 | 2.1 | 0.4 | 1.6 | ... | ... |

NOTES AND SOURCES:
1952 and 1966/67, from R. Mabro and S. Radwan, *op. cit.*, p. 94; the data cover establishments employing ten workers and more. The 1972 distributions are taken from A. al-Jirītlī, *op. cit.*, p. 43; the data refer to establishments with twenty-five workers and more.

tion during this period. The emphasis on industrial growth partly explains the improvement in the urban income distribution up to 1973/74. After 1973/74, the beneficial distributive effects of industrial growth weakened, owing to the greater, though by no means dominant, role private investments played in industrial growth.[64]

The extent to which the rural population benefited from agricultural investments should not be exaggerated, since a large part of this investment did not take place in the traditional (old-land) sector, even during the first Five Year Plan period. As table 4.13 shows, over 80 percent of the public sector's investments in agriculture went into horizontal development in the 1960s. The share of horizontal development in public sector agricultural investments declined to a little over two-thirds in the first half of the 1970s. Since the return on this type of investment has been very low, this probably explains the poor growth performance of agriculture, relative to industry, over the past twenty-five years. Thus, whereas there has not been any visible discrimination against agriculture in terms of the sectoral allocation of investments in the 1960s, the particular pattern of investment allocation within the agricultural sector itself implied a discrimination against the majority of the rural population who live in the old-land sector. The continuation of this allocation pattern in the first half of the 1970s, together with the sharp decline in the share of agriculture in total investment, exacerbated the problems of low incomes and productivity in the Egyptian countryside and partly explains the widening of the rural-urban income gap during this period.

Regarding other sectors, changes in the investment share of the housing sector are worthy of comment. A sharp decline in the share of this sector occurred in the late 1950s, followed by a much sharper decline in the first

TABLE 4.15.
*Distributional Consequences of the Regional Allocation of Investments (1964/65–69/70, Average Annual Percentages)*

| *Region* | *% Share in Population* | *% Share in Income* | *% Share in Wages* | *% Share in Household Consumption* |
|---|---|---|---|---|
| *Urban Governorates* | 22.5 | 36.5 | 44.0 | 33.7 |
| *Provinces:* | 77.5 | 63.5 | 56.0 | 66.3 |
| Lower Egypt | 42.3 | 35.0 | 33.0 | 36.6 |
| Upper Egypt | 34.0 | 28.0 | 22.4 | 29.1 |
| Frontier Gov. | 1.2 | 0.5 | 0.6 | 0.6 |

NOTES AND SOURCES:
Urban governorates include Cairo, Alexandria, Port Said, and Suez. *Source:* Ministry of Planning, "Basic Features of Regional Growth. . . ," *op. cit.* Note that these are crude estimates which involve a large measure of guesswork owing to the lack of adequate regional data.

half of the 1960s. Housing accounted for nearly one-third of total investment between 1952/53 and 1956/57, a little less than one-fourth between 1957/58 and 1959/60, and around 10–12 percent afterwards. This bias against investment in housing clearly explains the serious housing problems that Egypt has been facing since the mid-1960s. In spite of the income-equalizing effect of rent control,[65] the shortage of housing has led to sharp increase in land values and actual rents (if key-money is taken into account).

The main characteristic of the regional allocation of investment and industries is concentration in the main cities and urban governorates. In the first Industrialization Program of 1958–60, nearly 80 percent of the investments were devoted to Cairo, Alexandria, and Aswān. In the first Five Year Plan, the share of Greater Cairo was 25 percent of total investments, 31 percent of industrial investments, 46 percent of investments in transportation and communications, 43 percent of investments in housing, and 50 percent of investments in public utilities. The same trend continued in the Transitional Plan of 1974/75, with Greater Cairo and Alexandria accounting for 60 percent of industrial investments and the urban governorates 65 percent. Despite much talk about regional planning in recent years, the 1978–82 Five Year Plan still reflects a lopsided regional distribution of investments, with Greater Cairo accounting for nearly one-fourth of total investments and about 50 percent going to three urban governorates, namely, Greater Cairo, Alexandria, and Buhayra.[66]

The urban bias of growth policies is also evident from table 4.14, which shows the regional distribution of the relatively large industrial establishments and the associated distribution of employment. No major change appears to have occurred from 1952 till 1966/67, and the figures for 1972 (though not comparable with those for earlier years) still demonstrate a marked concentration of industries in urban areas.

Some indications of the implications of this urban bias in allocation of investments and industries is given in table 4.15.

The disturbing thing about these regional imbalances is that government policies do not appear to have seriously attempted to contain the natural tendencies making for concentration of economic activities in the urban centers. On the contrary, government policies reinforced those tendencies. A recent study of the regional distribution of employment in the public sector has shown that of the total public sector employment in 1972, Cairo accounted for 36 percent and Alexandria 21 percent. Furthermore, employment in certain activities that by their very nature do not require to be concentrated in the capital city or in the major urban centers (e.g. public sector activities relating to agriculture, land reclamation, irrigation, and drainage) tended also to be concentrated in Cairo and Alexandria.[67]

Industrial development consistently followed a strategy of import-substitution in the pre- as well as in the post-Revolution periods.[68] Initially, the emphasis was on establishing industries that use local materials (such as textiles and food processing). There has been a shift of emphasis since the mid-1950s toward the establishment of industries producing consumer goods (including consumer durables), and also, though to a smaller extent, intermediate and capital goods. This policy had serious implications for agricultural growth and income distribution in the rural areas. The emphasis on consumer goods (to the extent that by 1970/71, 63 percent of the value added in the industrial sector was contributed by consumer-goods industries) was partly at the expense of the needs of the agricultural sector for intermediate and capital goods.[69] This was reflected in the modest agricultural rates of growth, the deterioration in the food situation, and the rapid increase in food imports. Agriculture became increasingly incapable of meeting the demands of the rising population and the growing industrial sector.

The bias in favor of consumer goods would be beneficial from the distributional point of view if the composition of the *product mix* corresponded to the needs of mass consumption. The initiation and rapid expansion of consumer durables (television sets, refrigerators, washing machines, butane stoves, automobiles, and so forth) seem to be out of line with a policy focusing on the basic needs of the rural and urban poor. The rapid increase in the prices of such simple commodities as kerosene stoves, lamps, pots and pans, shoes, low-quality textiles, bicycles, and so forth, which are required by the rural and urban poor alike, indicates the low priority assigned to their production. It is not easy to determine whether emphasis on producing consumer durables catering to the middle and upper income groups has been excessive. It has been reported that public investment in the "capital-goods, consumer-durables" sector accounted for 10 percent of total public industrial investment in the period 1957/58–1964/65.[70] Most of the 16.4 percent of total investments in the first Five Year Plan, which were officially reported as

TABLE 4.16.
*Average Annual Growth Rates of Employment*

| *Period* | *Agriculture* | *Industry* | *Services* | *Economy* |
|---|---|---|---|---|
| 1960–64/65 | 2.2 | 8.6 | 3.3 | 3.5 |
| 1964/65–69/70 | 1.4 | 2.4 | 3.4 | 2.2 |
| 1969/70–1973 | 0.8 | 1.8 | 3.1 | 1.8 |
| 1973–1976 | 0.1 | 4.7 | 3.4 | 2.1 |

NOTES AND SOURCES:
Computed from Ministry of Planning data after smoothing the series, sources as for table 4.1.

investments in "machine and transportation equipments," were used for the production of these consumer durables.[71] Egypt's automobile industry has been consistently interested in the production of private cars rather than buses, tractors, and lorries.[72] In Egypt's biggest industry—the textile industry—cheap, low-quality textiles such as "damūr" and "kastūr" did not keep pace with rising demand while high quality and expensive textiles did.[73] Emphasis has been given to the production of expensive commodities at a time when the country still imported pins, nails, paper clips, and so forth, and when the production of simple goods in domestic demand could have been easily expanded.[74]

The growth policies followed up to 1960 have not led to significant increases in the labor-absorptive capacity of the economy. Total employment increased at an average rate of less than 1 percent per annum between 1947 and 1960—much lower than the average rate of population growth (2.5 percent).[75] Because of the large share of agricultural employment and the already very high labor intensity of agricultural techniques, agricultural growth did not entail much employment creation. Despite the rapid growth of industrial output after World War II, manufacturing employment expanded very slowly (1.9 percent per annum) during the same period. This was no doubt the outcome of the adoption of capital intensive technology in the new industries (petroleum, chemicals, paper, metals, pharmaceuticals, and so forth) and the gradual shift of previously established industries to such techniques. In these circumstances, the bulk of the increase in the labor force had to seek jobs in the tertiary sector. This sector's share of total employment rose from 24 percent in 1937 to 31 percent in 1960. The overexpansion of the tertiary sector may have led to some improvement in the distribution of income. The implications for growth are, however, serious since little real economic surplus is created in this way.

Although the rates of total and industrial employment growth were considerably higher after 1960 than in the previous two decades, agriculture's labor-absorptive capacity remained very limited, and the expansion of employment in the tertiary sector continued unabated, as table 4.16 clearly demonstrates. Government employment policies reinforced employment growth in the tertiary sector.

Since the late 1950s, the bulk of development financing came from public sector surpluses, involuntary savings, and foreign loans. This pattern still persists even in the infitah era. The public sector's share in gross domestic savings has risen from 49 percent in 1958/59 to 93 percent in 1964/65. It dropped to 75 percent in 1969/70 and 60 percent in 1976.[76] Foreign financing played a major role throughout the post-1960 period. Foreign financing as a ratio of gross fixed investment amounted to 30–35 percent between 1961 and 1964, 27.4 percent in the 1965/66–1969/70 period. The ratio has been rising steadily from 38.5 percent in 1969/70 to around 50 percent between 1970 and 1973, and to 73 percent in 1974 and 1975.[77] Preliminary analysis of foreign aid in the 1960s suggests that it did not favorably affect the distribution of income. Further analysis of the terms of aid, particularly in recent years, has revealed that aid is detrimental to the attainment of greater equity and tends to reinforce the trends toward increasing inequality.[78]

One question of particular importance in discussing the distributive impact of development financing is whether the agricultural sector has been squeezed, through price administration and other policies, for the purposes of financing industrial growth. A relevant issue in this connection is whether there has been a tendency to let the terms of trade of agriculture *vis-à-vis* industry to deteriorate as a means of financing industrialization. This is a controversial question. Bent Hansen believes that there has been a clear tendency of the terms of trade to deteriorate, and that this tendency has been detrimental to agricultural growth.[79] The calculations of Abdel-Fadil show that the terms of trade have not turned greatly against agriculture during the period 1960–1970. It emerges from his analysis that there has been a slight deterioration in the mid-1960s, after which the terms of trade (whether between agricultural output and manufactured consumer goods or between the former and manufactured agricultural inputs and consumer goods bought by farmers) remained fairly stable.[80] Further support of the proposition that methods of financing industrial growth did not entail a worsening of the rural income distribution is also available from a recent study of the resource inflows to and outflows from agriculture. By comparing the resource inflows (mainly in the form of investment) and the resource outflows (mainly through the land, defense, and national security taxes, and price differentials of cotton and rice), it was found that the outflows and inflows almost cancel out during the period 1960–71. Furthermore, when the resource inflows are augmented by the price subsidy on imported fertilizers, the agricultural sector turns out to be a net receiver of resources during this period.[81] Thus, it is appears safe to conclude that the financing of development did not entail a redistribution of income from the rural to the urban sector.

Some elements of the growth policies pursued in the past twenty to twenty-five years appear to explain part of the observed changes in income distribution. The improvement in the rural distribution in the late

1950s and first half of the 1960s and its deterioration after 1964/65 are partly attributable to fluctuations in the allocation of investments among sectors as well as within agriculture and the declining labor-absorptive capacity of agriculture. The steady improvement in the urban distribution up to 1973/74 was partly the outcome of emphasis on industrial investments and the overexpansion of employment in the services sector. The worsening of the sectoral and nationwide distributions after 1973/74 can be partly explained in terms of the lack of employment growth in agriculture and its slow pace in industry, the increased bias against agricultural growth in the allocation of investment, the changing nature of the services sector, and the adverse terms of foreign aid. That the changes in income distribution throughout the period have been moderate can be partly explained by certain elements of *continuity* in growth policies. They include the urban bias in the allocation of investment and location of industries, the high capital intensity of production techniques in industry and the resulting low capacity for employment creation, and the excessive dependence on foreign resources in financing growth.

## VI. Conclusions

A comprehensive analysis of the links between growth and distribution is a very difficult task. Though the analysis presented in this chapter is partial and based on circumstantial evidence, some important insights have been gained.

The twenty-five year period was characterized by a marked *diversity* in the patterns of association between growth and equity. Three phases can be clearly distinguished.

The first phase covers the period from the late 1950s to the mid-1960s. Growth was rapid, and inequality declined sectorally as well as intersectorally. Growth and distribution policies were vigorous during this phase. The land reforms of 1952 and 1961, Egyptianization and nationalization, and the expansion of the social insurance and security systems are examples of distributive measures that were instrumental in fostering growth. The growth-effects of other redistributive measures were limited (land reclamation and taxation) or negative (the official employment policy). Some of the improvement in the distribution of income can be attributed to certain elements of the growth policy, mainly the relatively balanced allocation of investment between agriculture and industry and the absence of a squeeze on agriculture as a means of financing growth. Nevertheless, the distributive impact was not great, particularly in the case of agriculture. This period was relatively peaceful. Military expenditure was modest and foreign aid abundant.

The second phase covers the period from 1964/65 to 1973/74. Growth was relatively sluggish (for reasons primarily related to the Yemen and the 1967 war), and inequality increased in the rural sector, decreased in the urban sector, and remained constant or slightly diminished intersectorally. Overall, inequality remained fairly constant. The growth-effects of distributional changes during this phase were limited, and the beneficial growth effects of earlier distributive measures were gradually eroded. The greater emphasis on industrial growth and the overexpansion of the services sector provide partial explanations of the deterioration in the rural distribution and the improvement in the urban distribution during this phase.

The third phase covers the period from 1973/74 to the present. Growth has been rapid, except in agriculture, and inequality increased sectorally and intersectorally. The infitah era witnessed a slackening of inequality-reducing measures and encouraged private enterprise to contribute to growth regardless of distributional consequences. The subsidization program played a significant role in protecting the standards of living of the poor (though inflation negated a large part of the benefits), as well as in supporting growth. Much of the growth during this phase was related to the increase in foreign exchange earnings (from tourism, the Suez Canal, and remittances of Egyptians working abroad), as well as foreign borrowing. Growth policies contributed to the increase in inequality through the neglect of agriculture, the lack of employment growth in agriculture and its slow growth in industry, the changed character of the services sector, and the acceptance of inequality-promoting terms of foreign aid.

In general, the links between growth and distribution appear to have been particularly strong in the first and third phases, with the growth effects of distributional changes dominating the former and the distribution-effects of growth policies dominating the latter. Both phases witnessed major changes in the institutional framework of development and drastic shifts in socioeconomic thinking. Nevertheless, it is clear that marked fluctuations occurred in growth performance without being associated with commensurate changes in the distribution of income during the whole period. This is probably due to the relative independence of the primary determinants of growth and distribution. The marked fluctuations in growth were primarily the outcome of fluctuations in foreign aid inflows and foreign exchange earnings generated by extraneous factors, mainly the ups and downs of foreign political relations and the wars of 1967 and 1973. The marginal nature of distributional changes is attributable to the limited scope of the distributive policies pursued, the little attention paid to problems of low-end poverty, and the persistence of certain inequality-promoting elements in growth policies. The latter include the urban bias in the allocation of investments and location of industries, the middle-class orientation of the product mix of manufacturing, the high capital intensity of production techniques, the excessive dependence on foreign aid, and the failure to activate the latent economic surplus.

## Notes

1. Given the multiplicity of factors that affect distribution and growth, it is very difficult—indeed, impossible—to decide, without a model, which part of GNP growth could be attributed to growth policies and which part could be attributed to distributional policies. Similarly, it becomes very difficult to apportion the observed changes in the distribution of income to growth and distribution measures.

2. See IBRD, *Arab Republic of Egypt, Economic Management in a Period of Transition,* (6 volumes), vol. 1, *Final Report No. 1815 EGT, May 1978,* Annex 1.1.

3. See: R. Ekaus et al., *Multi-sector General Equilibrium Policy Models for Egypt,* Report of the Cairo University/MIT Technological Planning Program, 1978(?), section 5.

4. According to Ministry of Planning sources, agricultural employment is calculated on the basis of standard norms of labor *requirements* (in man-days) per crop, which may not reflect actual labor use in agriculture. In transforming requirements in terms of man-days into number of laborers, the Ministry of Planning assumes 185 work days per year, which is greater by 5 work days than the norm used by the Ministry of Agriculture. This partly explains why the Ministry of Planning employment figures fall short of the population and agricultural census figures. Mabro's guess that the Ministry of Planning employment series is restricted to male adults was rejected by the ministry's sources. See R. Mabro, *The Egyptian Economy, 1952–1972* (Oxford, 1974), p. 207.

5. See M. Abdel Fadil, *op. cit.*, p. 63; and S. Radwan, "The Impact of Agrarian Reform on Rural Egypt, 1952–1972," *ILO Working Paper, WEP 10–61 WP–13,* Geneva, January 1977, p. 31. Their arguments are based on assumptions concerning the official calculation of wages and property income that are not supported by Ministry of Planning sources, as explained in note 4. The crucial factor is the precision with which average wage per farm operation and labor requirements are calculated. The underestimation of agricultural employment in the Ministry of Planning series may suggest that wages are understated. Since it is not known whether wage rates are over- or underestimated, the credibility of the wage component of agricultural GDP remains an open question.

6. Agricultural employment increased at an average annual rate of 1.8 percent between 1960/61–1966/67 and 0.7 percent between 1966/67 and 1976. Total agricultural real wages were practically constant at around £E192 million between 1970 and 1974, and began to rise in 1975 (£E217.8 million) and 1976 (£E231.8 million), all in 1966/67 prices. The question of wages is further discussed in section C of part II.

7. These estimates are discussed in detail in M. A. Zaytoun's project paper.

8. According to this source, the share of the landless increased from 7.1 percent in 1959/60 to 8.7 percent in 1966/67 and 11.5 percent in 1976. See A. Mohie-Eldin's project paper.

9. Moreover, respondents are prone to underreport their consumption for a variety of psychological reasons. Another serious problem relates to the estimation of autoconsumption of the rural people.

10. O. El-Kholie's analysis of the 1958/59 and 1964/65 surveys suggests that no change occurred in the rural distribution between the survey years. This finding is based on a comparison of the coefficient of variation of the two distributions, which is not a proper measure of the degree of inequality, i.e., the concentration of the distribution. See O. El-Kholie, "Disparities of Egyptian Personal Income Distribution as Reflected by Family Budget Data," *L'Égypte Contemporaine* 64, no. 354, pp. 33–55. My results are, however, similar to those of S. Radwan (*op. cit.*, p. 43) and IBRD (*op. cit.*, Annex 1.1), for the period 1958/59–1964/65, but diverge from their findings for the decade ending 1974/75, which were based on the first round of 1974/75 survey only; my results are based on the complete four-round survey.

11. These findings were reported by S. Radwan (*op. cit.*, pp. 37–42). The 1974/75

proportion was recalculated by me from the combined results of the four-round 1974/75 survey, which turned out to be very close to Radwan's estimate (44 percent). Note that the proportion of rural households below Radwan's poverty line in 1974/75 is much higher than the corresponding estimate made by the World Bank (IBRD, *op. cit.*, pp. 44), namely 35 percent (which rises to 36 percent on the basis of the four-round survey). The difference is attributable to the fact that Radwan's poverty line (£E270) is higher than the bank's (£E240).

12. S. Radwan, *op. cit.*, p. 42.

13. One of these studies was done by the World Bank (IBRD, *op. cit.*, Annex 1.1) on the basis of the 1974/75 family budget survey. The estimated personal income distribution is unreliable for reasons similar to those stated with respect to the rural distribution in section A, part II, The other study was done by A. Mohie-Eldin (in R. Ekaus et al., *op. cit.*,). It showed that nonagricultural incomes were distributed as follows in 1976: 30 percent to the lowest 60 percent of the *nonagricultural* population, 32.4 percent to the middle 30 percent, and 37.6 percent to the top 10 percent.

14. The index number of real NA wage rates (1959/60 = 100) dropped to 96.9 in 1960/61 and rose to 112.8 in 1962/63 and 117.1 in 1963/64, after which a downturn began so that the index was 101.0 in 1966/67. The downward movement continued up to 1968/69, after which NA wage rates index (1966/67 = 100) increased steadily up to 1973 (index = 110.9). This trend was reversed after 1973 with the index falling to 106.3 in 1974 and to 102–103 in 1975 and 1976. NA employment and value added growth rates are shown in tables 4.16 and 4.10, respectively.

15. These ratios appear in line with the ratios computed for other underdeveloped countries. Compare, for instance, with the ratio cited in K. Dervis & S. Robinson, "The Structure of Income Inequality in Turkey: 1950–1973," in *The Political Economy of Income Distribution in Turkey,* ed. by E. Ozbudun and A. Ulusan (New York, 1980), p. 98, which ranged from 2.2 to 3.5 in 1960.

16. Development in productivity in A and NA can be seen from the following productivity indices, which were calculated from the data used in constructing column 1 of table 4.6:

| | 1959/60 = 100 | | | 1969/70 = 100 | | |
|---|---|---|---|---|---|---|
| Sector | 1964/65 | 1966/67 | 1969/70 | 1974 | 1975 | 1976 |
| A | 101.8 | 96.0 | 101.8 | 103.2 | 108.7 | 112.3 |
| NA | 112.9 | 116.3 | 118.0 | 113.5 | 124.2 | 126.2 |

17. The differential growth of real wages in A and NA is quite evident from the following index numbers of real wages, which were calculated from the data sources noted for column 2 of table 4.6:

| | 1959/60 = 100 | | 1966/67 = 100 | | | | |
|---|---|---|---|---|---|---|---|
| Sector | 1964/65 | 1966/67 | 1969/70 | 1973 | 1974 | 1975 | 1976 |
| A | 133.8 | 137.1 | 89.6 | 87.0 | 88.3 | 119.6 | 110.8 |
| NA | 112.9 | 101.0 | 102.1 | 110.9 | 106.3 | 102.3 | 103.5 |

18. NA real wage rates fell in 1974 and 1975. Between 1973 and 1975, money wage rates appear to have risen by 57.8 percent in A and 14.8 percent in NA, whereas real wage rates registered a rise of 22.1 percent in A and a drop of 6.3 percent in NA.

19. Compare with the findings of M. S. Ahluwalia, in H. Chenery et al. *Redistribution with Growth* (Oxford, 1976), p. 21.

20. The cost of living index tended to move at similar rates in both U and R between 1966/67 and 1971/72 (around 3 or 4 percent per year). Since 1973 cost of living increased faster in R than in U as the following figures clearly indicate.

Annual Rates of Increase in Consumer Prices (%)

| Sector | 1973 | 1974 | 1975 | 1976 |
|---|---|---|---|---|
| R | 11.5 | 14.0 | 12.2 | 11.8 |
| U | 5.2 | 10.8 | 9.7 | 10.2 |

These rates were calculated from the official index of consumer prices (1966/67 = 100) cited in NBE (National Bank of Egypt), *Economic Bulletin,* several issues. The faster rise in rural prices calls for some explanation. My belief is that this finding reflects the lop-sided distribution of the state-managed shops which handle most of the goods in short supply and a significant part of the subsidized items of consumption. These shops tend to be concentrated in the urban areas. Moreover, it is believed that the urban index does not fully reflect the rise in urban cost of living since many items are valued at official rather than actual market prices. The index, for example, would portray a totally untrue picture of the cost of urban housing, where key-money figures have been rocketing. It is also my impression that the *weights* used in constructing the urban index bear very little relation to the actual pattern of consumption, which have been greatly influenced by the availability of imported consumer goods in the infitah era.

21. See Ministry of Planning, *Basic Features of Growth in Governorates during the Period 1964/65–1969/70* (Cairo, April 1972). Urban governorates include Cairo, Alexandria, Port Said, and Suez. The provinces include Lower and Upper Egypt and the frontier governorates.

22. Rural per capita income is overestimated as is recognized by the author (K. Korayem, *op. cit.*, p. 67) because of the assumption that rural NA per capita income equals per capita income in NA activities as a whole, and the inclusion in agricultural income of the rent that accrues to absentee landowners who normally reside in urban areas. Other difficulties with Korayem's estimates arise from the arbitrary classification of the rural population between A and NA activities, the deflation procedure and the use of annual figures rather than two- or three-year averages, particularly for rural income.

23. Annual increases in employment between 1959/60 and 1976 are shown in table 4.16, using Ministry of Planning figures. The following index number was constructed for real wage rates at the national level.

| Base: 1959/60 | | | | Base: 1970 | |
|---|---|---|---|---|---|
| Year | Index | Year | Index | Year | Index |
| 1960/61 | 92.9 | 1965/66 | 124.0 | 1971/72 | 101.9 |
| 1961/62 | 98.8 | 1966/67 | 122.9 | 1973 | 103.9 |
| 1962/63 | 109.8 | 1967/68 | 120.5 | 1974 | 105.5 |
| 1963/64 | 117.0 | 1968/69 | 125.8 | 1975 | 103.7 |
| 1964/65 | 119.8 | 1969/70 | 131.9 | 1976 | 103.8 |

24. Information derived from the sources noted for table 4.9.

25. The official cost of living indices (1966/67 = 100) as reported in NBE, *op. cit.*, developed as follows:

| | 1967/68 | 68/69 | 69/70 | 70/71 | 71/72 |
|---|---|---|---|---|---|
| U | 102.0 | 106.1 | 109.2 | 113.6 | 116.3 |
| R | 101.8 | 105.6 | 113.6 | 117.9 | 117.6 |
| | 73 | 74 | 75 | 76 | 77 |
| U | 122.4 | 135.7 | 148.9 | 164.2 | 185.1 |
| R | 131.2 | 149.6 | 167.9 | 187.8 | 206.7 |

26. See IBRD, *op. cit.*, pp. 43–45.

27. A detailed appraisal of GDP estimates can be found in B. Hansen and D. Mead, *The National Income of the UAR (Egypt),* INP memo. 355 (Cairo, July 1963), and B. Hansen,

"Planning and Economic Growth in the UAR (Egypt), 1960–1965," in P. J. Vatikiotis, ed., *Egypt Since The Revolution* (London, 1968). See also R. Mabro and S. Radwan, *The Industrialization of Egypt, 1939–1973* (Oxford, 1976), pp. 41–43, for a brief account.

28. R. Mabro (*op. cit.*, p. 171) suggests that conventional national accounts concepts of government output imply an upward bias of the order of 15 to 20 percent in Egypt's GDP.

29. It has been suggested that real GDP growth rates for the period 1959/60–1971/72 contain an upward bias of the order of 15 to 20 percent on account of the use of unrealistic deflators. See R. Mabro and S. Radwan, *op. cit.*, p. 43.

30. Note, however, that the Suez Canal and tourism are very important earners of foreign exchange, and, together with remittances of Egyptians working abroad, they must have played a significant role in financing growth in recent years.

31. IBRD, *op. cit.*, vol. 1, p. 27.

32. It may be objected that comparison of developments in both growth and distribution in 1952–64/65 period with developments after 1964/65 is somewhat inappropriate, if not unfair. For, it may be argued, the earlier period was largely characterized by *once-for-all* changes (e.g., land reform and nationalization), which released enormous funds to finance both growth and redistribution, and that by the mid-1960s the impetus thus given to growth and equality was dying out. While I recognize this fact, and indeed it is included in the analysis that follows, I fail to see that it renders the comparison inappropriate. Moreover, I do not consider that the scope for structural change was totally exhausted by the measures that were taken in the 1950s and 1960s. But this is obviously a matter of opinion.

33. Consider, for example, the crucial assumption made by I. Adelman, C. T. Morris, and S. Robinson that "In its growth path, a typical underdeveloped country will embody the average characteristic of the groups of countries which are associated with successive levels of development" (see "Policies for Equitable Growth" in *World Development* 4, no. 7 (1976), p. 562). What this assumption amounts to is that there is a *universal, uniform* growth path which countries of different social, political, and economic structures must follow. For a critical review of available theoretical propositions and empirical evidence, see I. El-Issawy, "Distribution, Growth, and Development" (a paper presented to the Fourth Annual Conference of Egyptian Economists, Cairo, May 1979) (in Arabic).

34. See *World Development* 6, no. 3 (March 1978), which contains a set of papers presented in a recent conference. The lessons from this conference are summarized in Paul Streeten's Introduction (pp. 241–243) as follows: "There is no correlation between either point inequality (inequality at any given time) or changes in inequality (over time) and rates of growth." There is a vast *variety* of experiences: fast growers with equality (e.g., Taiwan 1964–68, and Korea) and fast growers with inequality (e.g., Puerto Rico, Colombia, and Phillippines); fast growers that have become more equal (e.g., Taiwan 1959–64 and since 1968) and fast growers that have become less equal (e.g., Mexico, Brazil, Peru, Argentina, and Malaysia); slow growers that have been unequal and slow growers that remained unequal (e.g., India); slow growers that have become more equal (e.g., Sri Lanka) and slow growers that have become less equal (e.g., some states in India). The major determinants of the link between growth and inequality reduction are antipoverty policies, the social and political structure, cultural factors, the amount of human capital formation, the initial distribution of assets, and foreign trade.

35. Institutional changes up to the late 1960s are well documented in the standard texts of C. Issawi, *op. cit.*, P. O. Brien, *The Revolution in Egypt's Economic System* (Oxford, 1966); Hansen and G. Marzouk, *op. cit.*; on more recent developments, see; F. Mursī, *This Economic Infitah* (Cairo, 1976) (in Arabic); A. al-Jirītlī, *Twenty Five Years* (Cairo, 1977) (in Arabic); G. Amin, "Some Issues of the Economic Infitah in Egypt" and G. Abdel-Khalek, "The Significance of the Economic Infitah Policy for the Structural Transformations of the Egyptian Economy," both published in ESPE, *op. cit.*, pp. 403–426 and 363–402, respectively. See also IBRD, *op. cit.*, vol. I. Compare my findings with those of S. E. Ibrahim's project paper (section II).

36. R. Mabro, *op. cit.*, p. 131.

37. Further analysis of the origins of infitah will be found in F. Ajami's project paper.

38. Official interpretations of the "socialist transformation" phase of the 1960s are highly contradictory—ranging from "state capitalism" to "Marxism."

39. Detailed descriptions of Egypt's land reforms can be found in C. Issawi, *op. cit.*, B. Hansen and G. Marzouk, *op. cit.*, G. Saab, *The Egyptian Agrarian Reform 1952–1962* (Oxford, 1967); S. Radwan, *op. cit.*, and M. Abdel-Fadil, *op. cit.*, See also: M. Zaytoun's project paper.

40. B. Hansen and G. Marzouk, *op. cit.*, p. 268. In view of the fact that a large proportion of the capital diverted from agriculture went into apartment building, a law was passed in 1956 with the object of limiting investment in building. See C. Issawi, *op. cit.*, p. 53 and p. 163.

41. See R. Mabro, *op. cit.*, pp. 218–219. Up to 1958, the area sequestrated was 560,756 feddans, whereas the area distributed was only 268,943 feddans. See S. Radwan, *op. cit.*, p. 16.

42. C. Issawi, *op. cit.*, p. 163. Further evidence in support of this conclusion can be found in al-Nashratī, *Agrarian Reform in the U. A. R.*, (Cairo: Agrarian Reform Organization, 1966) (in Arabic), and G. Saab, *op. cit.*, pp. 109–113; B. Hansen and G. Marzouk, *op. cit.*, pp. 91–92, and E. Eshag and A. Kamal, "Agrarian Reform in the UAR," *Bulletin of the Oxford University Institute of Economics and Statistics* 30, no. 2 (May 1968), pp. 95–98.

43. The antifragmentation clauses were never observed, and actual land distribution gave an impetus to further subdivision of holdings. See Fathī ᶜAbd al-Fattāh, *The Contemporary Village* (Cairo, 1975), (in Arabic), pp. 160–163.

44. This was one of the reasons behind forming the Committee for Liquidating Traces of Feudalism in 1966. See Arab Socialist Union, *Victories of the Peasants* (Cairo, 1966), pp. 95–123, where numerous examples of land reform evasion and domination of cooperatives by influential landlords are given.

45. The 1969 land reform (which reduced the ownership ceiling to 50 feddans per person and 100 per family) was of a very limited effect on the pattern of land distribution. Probably no more than 35,000 feddans were requisitioned. See S. Radwan, *op. cit.*, p. 19, and F. Abdel-Hamid, *The Agrarian Question in Developing Countries and the Agrarian Reform in Egypt* (Cairo, 1973), p. 115.

46. The figures mentioned in this and the following paragraph were obtained from the Ministry of Planning, unpublished memos, and *The Five Year Plan 1978–82*, vol. 4 (in Arabic).

47. For an account of the origins and growth of the public sector, see the references given in note 35. See also I. S. ᶜAbd Allah, *Organization of the Public Sector* (Cairo, 1969), pp. 247–270, and M. Murād, *By Whom was Egypt Governed?* (Cairo, 1975) (both in Arabic).

48. Examples of these benefits include minimum wage legislation, upper ceiling on incomes and salaries, reduction of work hours, profit sharing, generous sick leave, protection against unfair dismissal, and equality of wages for women and men.

49. For an assessment of the problem of efficiency in the public sector and planning, see: B. Hansen, "Economic Development of Egypt," in C. A. Cooper and S. S. Alexander, eds., *Economic Development and Population Growth in the Middle East* (New York, 1972), Ch. V, and R. Mabro *op. cit.*, chap. 6.

50. The figures noted in this and the next paragraph are based on a savings series compiled from B. Hansen and G. Marzouk, *op. cit.*, p. 325; Ministry of Planning, *op. cit.*, S. A. Sakr, "Savings and Strategy of Development in Egypt", in ESPE, *Strategy of Development in Egypt* (Cairo 1978) (in Arabic), and M. Abdel-Fattah Ibrahim, "Strategy of Financing Industrial Development," (a paper presented to the INP/ECA Preparatory Seminar for the African Conference on Policies and Strategies of Industrial Development, INP, Cairo, September 1978). Note that, despite the fall in the share of public savings in total

savings in the 1970s, public business sector surpluses continued to increase from £E102 m. in 1971/72, to £E222 m. 1973, £E360 m. in 1974, £E623 m. in 1975, and £E960 m. in 1976. The increase in the "savings counterpart of private investment" between 1973 and 1975 is dramatic: £E38 m. in 1973, £E176 m. in 1975. Voluntary savings also increased from £E58 m. in 1973 to £E120 m. in 1976.

51. Other factors include the dislocation caused by the war of 1967, the rising defense burden, the failure to check increases in consumption (particularly public consumption), inflationary pressures and the slow-down in foreign aid flows. On the impact of the war on growth, see I. ᶜIssawī and M. A. Nassar, "An Attempt to Estimate Egypt's Economic Losses which Resulted from the Arab-Israeli War since 1967," in ESPE, *The Egyptian Economy . . .*, pp. 127–156 (in Arabic). On the fluctuations in aid flows, see G. Abdel-Khalek's project paper.

52. R. Mabro, *op. cit.*, p. 227.

53. See H. Handūsā, "The Public Sector in Egyptian Industry, 1952–1977," in ESPE, *op. cit.*, pp. 496–518.

54. See M. ᶜAbd al-Fadīl, "Development of the Tax Structure in Egypt," in ESPE, *The Egyptian Economy . . .*, pp. 49–64. More on the tax system and its distributive implications in R. El-Edel's project paper, where a different verdict is reached.

55. See B. Hansen and G. Marzouk, *op. cit.*, p. 268.

56. See B. Hansen and G. Marzouk, *op. cit.*, p. 267, and M. Abdel-Fadil, *op. cit.*, p. 51 et seq.

57. Figures in this paragraph are taken from IBRD, *op. cit.*, vol. 1, p. 40, and *The Financial and Economic Statement on the General State Budget, Fiscal Year 1976*, (Cairo: Government Press, 1975), pp. 67–68.

58. See R. El-Edel's project paper on the effect of the subsidies.

59. Farm input subsidies and price policies are discussed in A. H. Ibrahim's project paper.

60. The figures and trends noted in this and the next paragraph are based on data from: CAPMAS, *Statistical Handbook, Statistical Yearbook,* and *Statistical Indicators for the ARE,* several issues; A. El-Grietly, *op. cit.*, p. 111; and al-Ahrām al Iqtisādī, "Egypt's Population," Supplement, May 1, 1977, p. 32. Further analysis of educational trends will be found in M. Abdel-Fadil's project paper.

61. The ratio of investment in the health sector to investment in the education sector ranged from 0.25 to 0.50 over the period 1964/65–1976, according to Ministry of Planning Figures (unpublished). Other figures in this paragraph were taken from the sources noted in note 60.

62. See Ministry of Planning, The 1978–82 Five Year Plan, vol. 5, August 1977.

63. As estimated in IDCAS, "Principal Features of Housing in Egypt," unpublished memo, Cairo, October 1978.

64. Industry's share in private investment rose from 3.2 percent in 1964/65 to 6.9 percent in 1968/69, and continued to rise until it reached 14.4 percent in 1971/72 and 17.7 percent in the first half of the 1970s. Sources as given for table 4.1.

65. Rentals of residential buildings were enormously reduced in 1955, 1958, and 1961.

66. All figures given in this paragraph refer to *planned* rather than actual shares. They were taken from M. H. Fag El-Nour, "Regional Development and Investment Allocation in the UAR" (a paper presented to the Long-Range and Regional Planning Seminar, Warsaw, Central School of Planning and Statistics, 1971) and H. Subhī, "A General View of Some Problems of Regional Planning in Egypt", *INP Seminar Paper,* June 1978 (in Arabic). Further discussion of regional disparities and biases will be found in J. Waterbury's project paper.

67. See M. H. Fāj al-Nūr, *The Regional Structure of Employment in the Public Sector in the ARE* (INP, Cairo, December 1977), p. 10 (in Arabic). Cairo's share in public sector employment by activity was 16 percent in agriculture, 31 percent in land reclamation, and 71 percent in irrigation and drainage in 1972.

68. A detailed account of the evolution of this strategy can be found in A. Muhī al-Dīn, "Evaluation of Industrialization Strategy and the Alternatives for the Future in Egypt," in ESPE, *Development Strategy in Egypt,* (Cairo, 1978), pp. 177–207; M. al-Saᶜīd, "Industrial Development in the ARE and the Strategy of Satisfying the Basic Needs of the Population," in ESPE, *ibid.,* pp. 209–232.

69. The number of tractors produced by Al-Nasr Automobile Company accounted for 20 percent of its production between 1958 and 1977. See Adel Gazarine, "The Automobile Industry in Egypt", (a paper presented to the INP/ECA Seminar), *op. cit.*

70. See R. Mabro and S. Radwan, *op. cit.,* p. 114.

71. See Mabro, *op. cit.,* p. 183.

72. While the number of private cars produced has increased by 3,555 percent, the number of buses and lorries produced increased by 217 percent and 208 percent respectively, between 1959/60 and 1964/65. See ᶜAli Sabrī, *The Years of Socialist Transformation and Evaluation of the First Five Year Plan,* (Cairo, 1965(?)), p. 57. Furthermore, of the total production of Al-Nasr Automobile Company during the period 1958–77, private cars accounted for 55 percent, buses 4.5 percent, and lorries 7 percent. See ᶜAdil Jazarīn, *op. cit.*

73. It is not necessarily implied that expensive long-staple cotton should have been used to produce popular textiles.

74. Bent Hansen discussed the economics of producing consumer durables in Egypt and showed that neither the domestic market for such commodities was big enough, nor were the skills required for their production available. He argued also for a future industrial policy focusing on the basic needs of the poor on the grounds that the "people in the lowest income brackets do not demand sophisticated high-quality products. Demonstration effect and the need of living up to the Western Joneses are typically middle and upper class phenomena. The poor classes have simpler needs to think upon." See: B. Hansen, "Economic Development . .," *op. cit.,* p. 38 and p. 61.

75. The figures quoted in this paragraph were cited in R. Mabro, *op. cit.,* pp. 204–205.

76. Sources: as in note 50.

77. Source: Ministry of Planning, *op. cit.;* M. ᶜAbd al-Fattāh Ibrāhīm, *op. cit.,* and G. ᶜAbd al-Khāliq, "Development, Self-Reliance and Equity", (a paper presented to the Fourth Annual Conference of Egyptian Economists, Cairo, May 1979), p. 5. Note that the aim of a large proportion of foreign loans in recent years was to repay old debts rather than to finance development. The ratio of debt servicing to exports has risen from 19.4 percent in 1967 to 32 percent in 1974. See: M. ᶜAbd al-Fattāh Ibrāhīm, *op. cit.,* p. 14.

78. See: G. Abdel-Khalek's project paper, where the structure of foreign loans and their distributive implications are discussed. See also: G. 'Abd al-Khāliq, "Development, Self-Reliance. . . ," *op. cit.*

79. B. Hansen, "Economic Development. . . ," *op. cit.,* p. 88.

80. The terms of trade between agricultural output and manufactured agricultural inputs alone, showed a tendency to improve throughout the period under discussion. See: M. Abdel-Fadil, *op. cit.,* pp. 98–102.

81. See E. Montasser, "Agricultural Prices, Growth and Sectoral Terms of Trade in Egypt," in *Proceedings of the FAO/SIDA Seminar on Agricultural Sector Analysis in the Near East and North Africa* (INP, Cairo, October, 1975), p. 19.

# CHAPTER 5

# *Impact of Taxation on Income Distribution: An Exploratory Attempt to Estimate Tax Incidence in Egypt**

M. Reda A. El-Edel

## I. Introduction

In Egypt, as in many other countries, taxes have been conceived, not only as a means for providing budget revenues, but also as a major instrument for effecting a socially desirable income distribution. Over the last ten years, and on the average, about 21 percent of the country's GDP (Gross Domestic Product) was redistributed through taxes.

This chapter is an exploratory attempt to investigate the effect of taxes on income distribution and to display the general tendencies of this effect over the period 1958/1959–1974/1975. It is exploratory because up to the present time there has not been a thorough study on taxation and income distribution in Egypt. It seems that applied economists dealing with the Egyptian economy have been apprehensive of this field, perhaps due to the lack and contradictory nature of data not only on income distribution but also on taxes themselves.

## II. The Formal System in Evolution

The present Egyptian tax system was born at the end of the 1930s by Law 14 of 1939. Since then the law has had several amendments. In this

*I am indebted to Professor Dr. ᶜAli Lutfī, Minister of Finance, Egypt, for his encouragement; to Mr. Sayyid ᶜAlī Tāhā, a postgraduate student at the Faculty of Commerce of ᶜAin-Shams University, for much of the underlying data; and to Mr. ᶜAbd al-Rahmān Nuwayrī, research assistant at the Arab Planning Institute, for helping to calculate Gini coefficients and draw the figures.

Special thanks go to the participants of the Luxor Conference (January 1979) and the Lisbon Conference (November 1979) for their constructive criticism and advice. The editors have thought it prudent to publish only the most important tables referred to in the text of the chapter. The rest of the tables are available on request from the Research Program in Development Studies at Princeton University.

*TABLE 1.1.*

*Tax on Wages and Salaries (The Original Tax)*

| *Date* | *Exemption and Rates* | *The Individual Basis* |
|---|---|---|
| From September 1952 | Income up to £E 150 is exempted.<br>The rates are:<br>2% for the first £E 120<br>3% for the next £E 180<br>4% for the next £E 200<br>5% for the next £E 300<br>7% for the next £E 400<br>9% for the more than that | Law 147 for 1952 |
| From August 1960 | Income up to £E 250 is exempted.<br>The rates are:<br>2% for the first £E 100<br>3% for the next £E 150<br>4% for the next £E 150<br>5% for the next £E 150<br>7% for the next £E 200<br>9% for the next £E 300<br>11% for the next £E 300<br>13% for the next £E 500<br>15% for the next £E 1,000<br>18% for the next £E 2,000<br>22% for more than that | Law 199 for 1960 |
| From May 1974 | Income exempted £E 260<br>No change in the rates structure | Law 53 for 1974 |

section, interest is focused on the major developments from the end of the 1950s to 1974/1975. The exposition will be made in two subsections devoted to taxes on incomes and wealth and on goods and services.

### *Taxes on Incomes and Wealth*

#### *Tax on Wages and Salaries*

This tax is levied with progressive rates on income derived from employment, comprising wages, salaries, and other emoluments, including payment in kind. The evolution of this tax since 1952 may be seen in table 1. To this tax must be added, of course, the defense tax since 1956 and the national security tax since 1967, which are progressive.

#### *Taxes on Professionals and Noncommercial Professions*

This tax is levied on the net profits of self-employment in free and other noncommercial professions equal to accrued business revenue less business expenses. Over the period 1952–1959, it had a flat rate of 11 percent

(Law 147 for 1952). Since 1960 its rates have become progressive: 11 percent for the first £E1,500; 13 percent for the second £E500; 15 percent for the next £E1,000; 18 percent for the next £E2,000 and 22 percent for more than that (Law 199 of 1960). Exempted from this tax are wages and salaries.

### *Tax on General Income*

The general income tax is levied on the total net income of individuals (but not companies) residing in Egypt and on nonresidents' income accruing in Egypt. Tax is due on the basis of income from real estate, movable property, professional earnings, and other income earned in the preceding calendar year, including capital gains. To this tax must be added also a defense tax of progressive character.

Since 1952 this tax has had a relatively heavy progressive scale, starting at a rate of 8 percent for income over £E1,000 and reaching a rate of 80 percent for incomes over £E30,000 until 1960. Since then the progressivity of this tax has increased. Its maximum rate reaches 95 percent for incomes over £E10,000.

### *Tax on Income from Movable Property*

This tax is levied on income from movable property comprising interest, dividends, and royalties earned in Egypt by individuals and companies, or earned abroad by Egyptian residents. Interest on capital invested in Egypt by nonresidents is also taxable. The basic tax rate since 1952 has been fixed at 17 percent of taxable income (Law 147 for 1952). To this tax must be added proportional rates of duties of city councils of provinces, the defense tax since 1956, and national security tax since 1967—which increase the total tax rate to 40.55 percent.

### *Tax on Profits*

A tax is levied annually on accrued net profits earned in Egypt by both foreign and domestic companies engaged in manufacturing, commerce, and mining; profits of stock and real estate brokers; and profits of commercial leasing activities. Taxable profits include capital gains but exclude distributed profits on which movable property tax has been paid. The tax base is actual profits (gross income less operating expenses and allowances) in cases where adequate records are maintained; otherwise the Tax Department assesses the tax on the basis of estimated profits. For partnerships, personal exemptions are £E500 provided income from this source does not exceed twice the applicable exemption. Since 1952, the tax rate has been fixed at 17 percent of taxable profits. To this must be added taxes of proportional rates for local councils, defense, and national security.

### *Agricultural Land Tax*

This tax is levied on all arable land on the basis of the annual rental value of the land as assessed every ten years by the Central Administration. The tax is paid by the landowner annually. Between 1953 (Law 370 for 1953) and 1973, taxable landowners whose tax liability did not exceed £E4 were exempted. Later, according to Law 51 for 1973, properties of less than three feddans became exempt. The basic rate is 14 percent of the annual rental value. To this tax must be also added defense and national security taxes.

### *Tax on Buildings*

Buildings located in major urban districts are subject to this tax, including buildings used for residential purposes, hotels, shops, warehouses, and manufacturing plants. The tax is levied on the basis of the annual rental value, as assessed by the Central Administration, or on actual rental income when the building is rented. Tax is paid by the owner. According to Law 56 of 1954, the basic tax rate on nonresidential buildings is 10 percent of the annual rental value, and tax rates for residential buildings are:

| *Rent per Room per Month* (£E) | *(Percent)* |
|---|---|
| Less than 3 | 10 |
| 3–5 | 15 |
| 5–8 | 20 |
| 8–10 | 30 |
| Over 10 | 40 |

Additional taxes (defense, national security, and other taxes) result in a total tax rate of 20.5 to 68.2 percent for residential buildings and 23.2 percent for nonresidential buildings.

### *Estate and Inheritance Taxes*

*Estate Tax.* According to Law 159 of 1952 amended by Law 202 of 1960, an estate tax is levied on the total value of the estates of deceased persons, including the real (fixed assets) and personal property of Egyptian nationals and resident foreigners, and rural property in Egypt owned by deceased nonresident foreign nationals. This tax is in addition to the succession duty. The value of the estate is calculated net of debts and obligations, and the first £E5,000 of the net value of the estate is not subject to tax. Tax is levied at the rate of:

| *Net Value of Estate* (£E) | *Marginal Tax Rate* (Percent) |
|---|---|
| Up to 5,000 | 0 |
| 5,001–10,000 | 5 |
| 10,001–25,000 | 10 |
| 25,001–50,000 | 20 |
| 50,001–100,000 | 30 |
| More than 100,000 | 40 |

*Succession Duty.* The juridical basis is Law 142 of 1944, amended by Law 217 of 1951, by Law 159 of 1952, and by Law 202 of 1960. Succession duty is payable by all persons to whom a succession accrues. Bequests subject to duty include the real and personal property of Egyptian nationals and foreign residents, and real property in Egypt owned by deceased nonresident foreign nationals. The duty payable is determined on the basis of the value of the bequest and the relationship of the recipient to the deceased. In certain cases, gifts made by the deceased during the five years preceding death are taxable. This tax is in addition to the estate tax. The value of the estate is calculated net of debts. Items exempt from duty include the family house, up to £E2,000 of personal life insurance policies, all employer-provided life insurance, and collections of books, art, and so forth. Each heir who is a descendant, spouse, or parent may deduct £E500 from the net value of the bequest. Since 1960 the basic tax rates have been:

| *Taxable Value of Inheritance* (£E) | *Marginal Tax Rate* (Percent) |
|---|---|
| Up to 5,000 | 5 |
| 5,001–10,000 | 6 |
| 10,001–15,000 | 7 |
| 15,001–20,000 | 8 |
| 20,001–25,000 | 9 |
| 25,001–30,000 | 10 |
| 30,001–35,000 | 11 |
| 35,001–45,000 | 12 |
| 45,001–55,000 | 15 |
| 55,001–65,000 | 18 |
| More than 65,000 | 22 |

Applicable tax rates double the above schedule for brothers and sisters, and for relatives other than parents. Tax rates are three times the above schedule for nephews, nieces, and other collateral heirs, and four times the above schedule for all other heirs.

### *Taxes on Goods and Services*

This sub-section has been extracted from a summary of the Egyptian tax system made by I.M.F.

### *Selective Excises*

*Selective Excises on Goods*. According to Ministerial Decree 76 of 1960 and Customs Law 66 of 1963 as amended, these taxes are payable by the importer or manufacturer of alcoholic beverages, sugar, coffee, motor fuels, cement, and a range of consumer durables. Gasoline taxes are earmarked for road construction. Excise duties paid on locally manufactured products are refunded if these products are exported. Under the program of investment incentives for approved undertakings, this tax may be excused (or reduced) for specific periods. Rates of excise duty are mostly specific—for example, cement, £E1.400 per 100 kilograms; beer in bottles £E4.360 per 100 kilograms; gasoline, £E0.018 to £E0.025 per liter (depending upon the grade); tape recorders and refrigerators, 20 percent of value.

*Selective Excises on Energy*. According to stamp duty law (Law 224 of 1951, as amended, and Law 25 of 1967), these duties are levied on the consumption of gas and of electricity supplied for lighting and domestic purposes. The duty is payable by the consumer. Homes for the poor, hospitals, and dispensaries not run for profit are exempt. The duty on energy consumption is £E0.004 per cubic meter of gas, and £E0.010 per kilogram of butagas (bottled gas).

*Additional Selective Excise (Price Differentials)*. These taxes are levied on a range of consumption items through the price control program. This is achieved by setting both the ex-factory price and the wholesale price of each item, with the difference accruing to the government. Items taxed include cigarettes and tobacco, refrigerators, automobiles, household fuels, soaps, and building materials. Exported goods are exempt. Typical rates include: cigarettes, £E0.025 to £E0.050 per pack; refrigerators, £E5 to £E45 per unit; automobiles, £E100 per car; kerosene £E0.01 per liter; tires, £E2.3 to £E9.66 each; soaps, £E21.78 per ton; cement, £E1.1 per ton.

### *Selective Tax on Services*

*Hotel Tax*. This tax is levied at 2 percent of the total hotel bill.

*Airport Tax*. It is levied on all passengers departing on international flights at £E1 per ticket.

### *Taxes on International Trade, Imports and Exports*

*Customs Duties*. (Customs Law 66 of 1963, as amended). The customs tariff consists of a single column based on the Brussels Tariff Nomenclature. Most duties are ad valorem and are applied to a fair market CIF (cost, insurance, and freight) import price. Specific duties are levied on only a few important items (for example, tobacco); the valuation of imports for the purpose of assessing customs duties is based upon the exchange rate applicable to the transaction, with "own-exchange" imports being valued at the parallel. Goods in transit and goods that enter specified free zones are exempt. Customs (as well as excise) duties may be refunded on imports that are embodied in exports if the reexportation takes place within one year after the duties are paid. Ad valorem customs duties are in a range of 10 percent to 40 percent for many industrial supplies, while capital goods enter duty free. Customs duties on consumer goods are generally higher and are in the range of 100 percent to 300 percent for many consumer durables (color television sets, refrigerators, passenger cars, tape recorders, and so forth). The specific duty of £E6.1 per kilogram of unmanufactured tobacco yielded an ad valorem equivalent rate of approximately 1,000 per cent in 1973 and 1974.

*Customs Statistical Duty* (Law 174 of 1956, as amended). This is an additional customs duty levied on all imports. Valuation and other conditions for collecting these duties are the same as for customs duty. Imports of wheat are exempt from the statistical duty. The duty is 1 per cent of the CIF value of imports.

*Economic Development Tax* (Presidential Decree 6 of 1969). This tax on imports is levied in addition to the customs duty and the statistical tax. Exempt imports include books, newspapers, and cattle imported by public enterprises for meat. The basic rate is 10 percent of the value of imports. Certain essential consumer goods imports, as determined by the Ministry of Supply, are subject to a preferential rate of 5 percent; these include milk, flour, edible fats and oils, and sugar.

*Surtax on Import and Export Duties* (Presidential Decree 165 of 1963). This tax is levied as a proportion of the principal import or export customs duty applicable. The rate of tax is 3 percent of the principal customs duty payable on imports or exports.

*Maritime Tax on Imports and Exports* (Ministerial Decree 6 of 1959). An additional tax based on the value of imports and exports is collected and earmarked for port development and the nationally owned shipping companies. Imports exempt from the customs duties are exempted from this tax. Also, imports of personal effects valued no greater than £E20 are exempt. The tax is 3 percent of the dutiable imports arriving by sea.

*National Defense Tax* (Ministerial Decree 119 of 1973). This tax is levied on many imports subject to excises that are also produced domestically. Rates are mostly specific. Examples of specific rates are £E4 per hectoliter of beer and £E0.065 milliemes per liter of wine.

*Export Customs Duty* (Customs Law 66 of 1963 as amended, and Ministerial Order 95 of 1977). Specific or ad valorem customs duties are levied on the export of a small number of commodities, such as raw hides and skins, metal waste and scrap, and antiques. A variable levy is imposed on exports of 1977 winter potatoes equal to all or part of the difference between the FOB export price and the estimated export cost. The tax proceeds are earmarked for the Export and Import Price Stabilization Fund. Illustrative export duty rates are £E11 per metric ton of metal

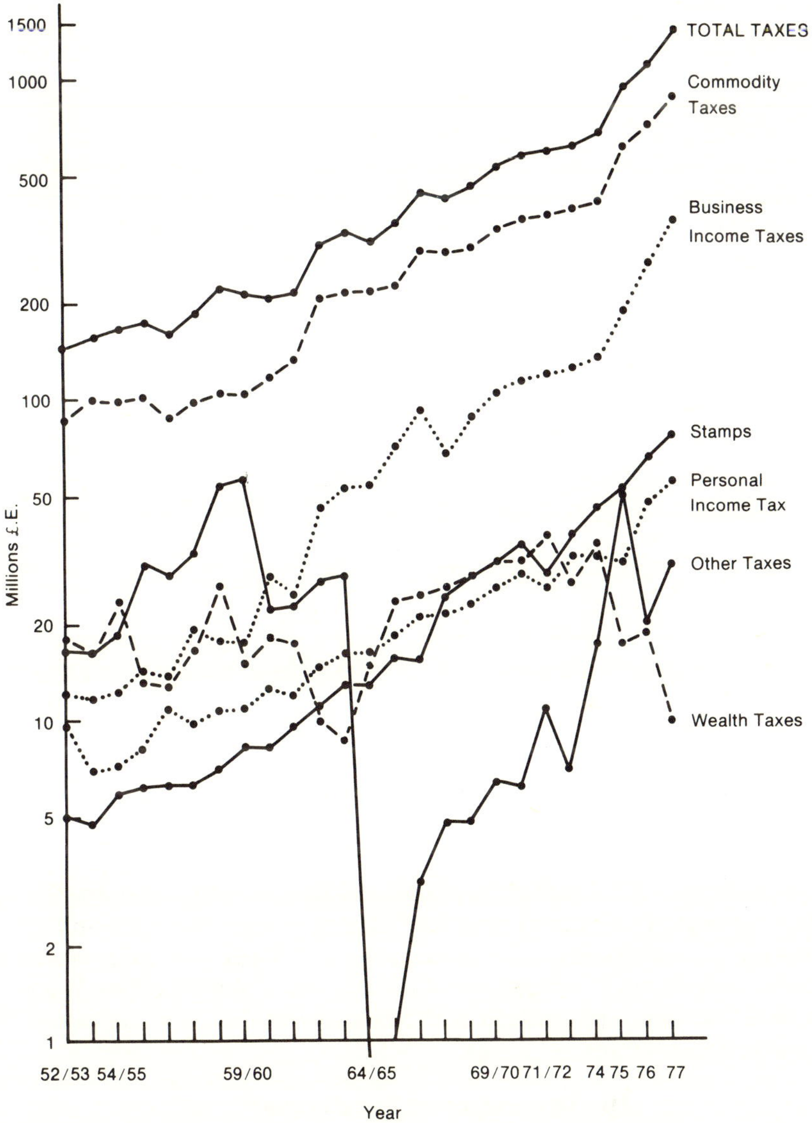


*FIGURE 1.*
*Evolution of Tax Structure in Egypt (1952/53–1977)*

*TABLE 1.2.*
*Development of Tax Structure in Egypt 1952/53–1977*

| *Description* | *52/53* | *53/54* | *54/55* | *55/56* | *56/57* | *57/58* | *58/59* | *59/60* | *60/61* | *61/62* | *62/63* |
|---|---|---|---|---|---|---|---|---|---|---|---|
| 1. **BUSINESS INCOME TAX** | **8.1** | **7.5** | **7.3** | **8.2** | **8.5** | **10.5** | **8.0** | **8.2** | **13.3** | **11.2** | **14.8** |
| a. Profit Tax | 3.3 | 2.8 | 2.5 | 3.5 | 4.0 | 5.8 | 4.6 | 4.7 | 7.3 | 6.8 | 6.9 |
| b. Movable Capital Tax | 4.8 | 4.7 | 4.8 | 4.7 | 4.5 | 4.7 | 3.4 | 3.5 | 3.2 | 2.2 | 3.5 |
| c. Others | | | | | | | | | 2.8 | 2.2 | 4.4 |
| 2. **PERSONAL INCOME TAX** | **6.3** | **4.5** | **4.3** | **4.6** | **6.8** | **5.4** | **4.9** | **5.1** | **6.1** | **5.6** | **4.8** |
| a. Wages & Salaries | 2.3 | 2.2 | 2.2 | 2.4 | 2.9 | 2.4 | 2.4 | 2.5 | 3.2 | 3.5 | 3.8 |
| b. Free Professionals | 0.2 | 0.2 | 0.2 | 0.2 | 0.2 | 0.2 | 0.1 | 0.2 | 0.2 | 0.2 | 0.1 |
| c. General Income Tax | 3.8 | 2.1 | 1.9 | 2.0 | 3.7 | 2.8 | 2.4 | 2.4 | 2.7 | 1.9 | 0.9 |
| 3. **WEALTH TAX** | **11.9** | **10.4** | **14.2** | **7.5** | **8.0** | **9.0** | **11.9** | **7.1** | **8.8** | **8.0** | **3.2** |
| a. Inheritance Taxes | 2.1 | 0.7 | 1.0 | 1.2 | 1.3 | 1.6 | 1.2 | 0.2 | 1.5 | 1.2 | 1.2 |
| b. Land Tax | 9.2 | 9.2 | 7.2 | 5.8 | 6.2 | 6.9 | 6.0 | 6.4 | 6.2 | 5.8 | 1.8 |
| c. House Bldgs. | 0.6 | 0.5 | 6.0 | 0.5 | 0.5 | 0.5 | 4.7 | 0.5 | 1.1 | 1.0 | 0.2 |
| 4. **STAMPS** | **3.4** | **3.1** | **3.5** | **3.6** | **3.9** | **3.5** | **3.2** | **3.8** | **3.9** | **4.3** | **3.6** |
| 5. **COMMODITY TAXES** | **59.0** | **63.9** | **59.4** | **58.3** | **54.8** | **53.8** | **47.8** | **48.7** | **57.1** | **60.4** | **64.7** |
| a. Customs | 51.0 | 52.9 | 48.1 | 46.2 | 41.7 | 43.8 | 36.7 | 37.8 | 47.7 | 47.4 | 48.7 |
| b. Prodctn. Taxes | | | | | | | | | 8.7 | 8.4 | 10.3 |
| c. Consumption & Other Excises | 8.0 | 11.0 | 11.3 | 12.1 | 13.1 | 10.0 | 11.1 | 10.9 | 0.7 | 4.6 | 5.7 |
| d. Price Differen. | | | | | | | | | | | |
| 6. **OTHER TAXES** | **11.3** | **10.6** | **11.3** | **17.8** | **18.0** | **17.8** | **24.2** | **27.1** | **10.8** | **10.5** | **8.9** |
| TOTAL | 100 | 100 | 100 | 100 | 100 | 100 | 100 | 100 | 100 | 100 | 100 |

waste and scrap; £E1.2 per metric ton of raw hides and skins; mature 1977 winter potatoes: FOB export price and £110 per ton up to £E310 and 90 percent of the excess in export price above £E310 per ton; 1977 winter potatoes in peat moss: 100 percent of the difference in FOB export price and £E122 per ton, up to £E350; and 90 percent of the excess in export price above £E350 per ton.

## III. Development of Tax Revenues

Over twenty-five years (1952–1977), the level of tax revenues has increased nearly tenfold. It rose from £E148.652 million to £E1,451.361 million. Taken as percentage of the GDP, it rose from 14.8 percent in 1952 to 21 percent in 1975.*

*In 1952, GDP at 1954 prices amounted to £E1,004 million (see reference 17, p., 319). In 1975 it reached £E4,778.8 million at current prices (see reference 5).

| *Shares* | | | | | | | | | | | | | |
|---|---|---|---|---|---|---|---|---|---|---|---|---|---|
| *63/64* | *64/65* | *65/66* | *66/67* | *67/68* | *68/69* | *69/70* | *70/71* | *71/72* | *1973* | *1974* | *1975* | *1976* | *1977* |
| **15.8** | **16.8** | **20.2** | **20.7** | **15.8** | **18.8** | **19.2** | **19.7** | **19.9** | **20.4** | **20.3** | **19.6** | **23.0** | **25.3** |
| 8.0 | 8.6 | 10.4 | 12.3 | 10.3 | 9.7 | 9.4 | 9.5 | 9.5 | 8.8 | 9.7 | 11.6 | 12.8 | 13.9 |
| 3.4 | 3.6 | 3.8 | 3.6 | 5.1 | 7.0 | 6.9 | 7.4 | 8.7 | 9.3 | 9.2 | 6.3 | 8.0 | 9.1 |
| 4.4 | 4.6 | 6.0 | 4.8 | 0.4 | 2.1 | 2.9 | 2.8 | 1.7 | 2.3 | 1.4 | 1.7 | 2.2 | 2.3 |
| **4.8** | **5.1** | **5.2** | **4.7** | **5.0** | **4.9** | **4.8** | **4.8** | **4.3** | **5.1** | **4.9** | **3.2** | **4.1** | **3.8** |
| 3.7 | 4.0 | 4.1 | 3.9 | 4.2 | 4.1 | 4.1 | 4.1 | 3.8 | 4.5 | 4.3 | 2.8 | 3.6 | 3.2 |
| 0.2 | 0.2 | 0.2 | 0.2 | 0.2 | 0.2 | 0.1 | 0.2 | 0.2 | 0.3 | 0.3 | 0.2 | 0.3 | 0.3 |
| 0.9 | 0.9 | 0.9 | 0.6 | 0.6 | 0.6 | 0.6 | 0.5 | 0.3 | 0.3 | 0.3 | 0.2 | 0.2 | 0.3 |
| **2.6** | **4.6** | **6.6** | **5.4** | **6.0** | **6.0** | **5.7** | **5.4** | **6.3** | **4.3** | **3.3** | **1.7** | **1.6** | **0.7** |
| 0.6 | 0.6 | 0.6 | 0.4 | 0.5 | 0.5 | 0.5 | 0.4 | 0.4 | 0.4 | 0.4 | 0.2 | 0.3 | 0.3 |
| 1.7 | 1.7 | 2.4 | 2.0 | 1.9 | 2.4 | 2.3 | 2.2 | 2.8 | 1.5 | 0.2 | 1.0 | 0.8 | 0.0 |
| 0.3 | 2.3 | 3.6 | 3.0 | 3.6 | 3.1 | 2.9 | 2.8 | 3.1 | 2.4 | 2.7 | 0.5 | 0.5 | 0.4 |
| **3.9** | **4.1** | **4.3** | **3.4** | **5.6** | **6.0** | **5.8** | **6.2** | **4.9** | **6.0** | **6.8** | **5.4** | **5.7** | **5.4** |
| **64.3** | **69.0** | **63.4** | **64.9** | **66.5** | **63.3** | **63.2** | **62.8** | **62.9** | **63.1** | **62.3** | **64.5** | **63.8** | **62.8** |
| 50.2 | 52.1 | 48.2 | 34.4 | 33.3 | 28.6 | 32.0 | 33.6 | 32.0 | 32.5 | 34.4 | 41.4 | 39.9 | 40.5 |
| 10.1 | 14.3 | 12.9 | 10.0 | 11.9 | 10.5 | 9.7 | 10.7 | 11.3 | 10.6 | 10.2 | 6.9 | 6.2 | 6.0 |
| 4.0 | 2.6 | 2.3 | 2.7 | 3.7 | 3.7 | 1.5 | 0.8 | 0.9 | 0.6 | 0.3 | 1.0 | 1.6 | 2.8 |
| | | | 17.8 | 17.6 | 20.5 | 20.0 | 17.7 | 18.7 | 19.4 | 17.4 | 15.2 | 16.1 | 13.5 |
| **8.6** | **0.5** | **0.3** | **0.9** | **1.1** | **1.0** | **1.3** | **1.1** | **1.7** | **1.1** | **2.4** | **2.6** | **1.8** | **2.0** |
| 100 | 100 | 100 | 100 | 100 | 100 | 100 | 100 | 100 | 100 | 100 | 100 | 100 | 100 |

Table 1.1 and figure 1 illustrate the development of tax revenues. Table 1.2 indicates the evolution of the tax revenues structure through this period. Taxes were grouped into six groups of thirteen subgroups. The first group includes business income tax and consists of three subgroups: profit tax, movable capital tax, and others. The second group embraces personal income tax and is composed of three categories of taxes: wages and salaries, free professionals, and general income. The third group is represented by a wealth tax and includes three subgroups: inheritance taxes (estate tax and succession duty), land tax, and tax on buildings. The fourth group consists of stamp taxes. The fifth is designed for commodity and services taxes and comprises four subgroups: custom duties, production duties, consumption and other commodity and services excises and price differentials. The sixth group includes other taxes.

Egyptian taxation has the following tendencies:

1. A dominance of commodity taxes. Their average annual share amounted to 60 percent. When stamp duties are added, all explicit indirect taxes attain, on average, 65 percent.
2. The next group is the tax on business income. Its revenues amounted to 25.3 percent of all tax revenues in 1977. However, it is noticeable from table 1 that this was not so during the 1950s, when wealth taxes had a share larger than that of business income tax. The relative change toward an increase of share of business income tax has occurred since 1962/1963. This seems to be a natural consequence of putting a large number of businesses under state ownership by the Nationalization Acts of 1961 and 1962.
3. A dependence on foreign trade—mainly imports. From table 1, it is evident that revenues from custom duties had the largest share in tax revenues in every single year. Their average annual share exceeds 41.4 percent of all tax revenues. In some years it approaches and even exceeds 50 percent.
4. A minor share of personal income tax did not exceed the 6.8 percent of 1956/1957. One has to notice also the structural disproportion inside this group, the majority of which comes from *taxes on wages and salaries*. The other subgroups (namely, taxes on free professionals and general income tax) have the smallest shares. Taxes on free professionals rose by 0.1 percentage point from 1952/1953 to 1977. And the share of general income tax declined from 3.8 per cent in 1952/1953 to 0.3 percent in 1977.
5. A quick look at table 1 suggests the idea that changes in taxes have been motivated to an extent, by purposes of revenue augmentation, rather than allocational or distributional purposes. The increase of tax revenues comes from sources of easy-to-collect types. The increases of shares of these types in 1977 with relation to 1952/1953 applies to: commodity taxes—from 59 percent to 62.8 percent; stamps—from 3.4 percent to 5.4 percent; and tax on business income—from 8.1 percent to 25.3 percent.

However, this does not mean that taxes in Egypt have no allocational or distributional effects. They do have. The next sections examine the distributional effects of Egyptian taxes.

## IV. The Procedures

The main goal of the procedural operation is twofold:

- To determine the distribution of household income according to size expenditure groups;
- To allocate different types of taxes and their total to these groups.

### *Estimation of Income Distribution*

The method for estimating income distribution consists of the following steps:

### *Allocation of Household Population to Various Size Expenditure Groups*

Here it was necessary to determine the total number of households for rural and urban sectors. Then shares of each expenditure group were determined from the corresponding Family Budget Survey (FBS).

For 1958/1959, the number of households was calculated from the *Annual General Statistics of 1960* published by Department of Statistics and Census in 1962 (table 11, p. 26). The total of urban families was calculated from the *General Census of Population for 1960*. By subtracting this total from the national total, the total number of rural families was obtained. Then allocation of rural and urban families was made according to shares derived from the FBS.

For 1964/1965, family expenditure shares were calculated for both rural and urban sectors from the FBS of 1964/1965. Here the basis was the average of both the first and third rounds of the budget survey. The totals of rural and urban families were assumed to be represented by totals of dwelling units for both sectors. The assumption is considered to be a reasonable one since the difference between columns of families and dwelling units in the FBS is rather a minor one. It follows the calculation of household allocation according to the derived shares.

For 1974/1975, total families and their allocation between rural and urban sectors were extracted from the *Results of the General Census of Population in November 1976* (see reference 14). Shares of family allocation according to expenditure intervals were derived from the corresponding average shares in FBS (1974/1975) for its four rounds. However, we have to notice the difference between division of population between rural and urban sectors as indicated by the census and the estimate by the World Bank (see reference 8). The World Bank Report estimates rural population at 0.4279 and urban sector at 0.5721 while the census estimates were 0.5351 for rural sector and 0.4649 for urban sector. It has been thought more expedient to make the calculations on the basis of census data.

Estimation of the number of families and their allocation among the various expenditure intervals is tabulated in column 1 of tables 2.7a, 2.7b, 3.7a, 3.7b, 4.7a, 4.7b for the years 1958/1959, 1964/1965 and 1974/1975, respectively.

### *Determination of Income Distribution*

*Determination of Distribution of Household Consumption.* This was made in two stages: First, preparing a table of the average per-household consumption expenditure in each expenditure interval for each expenditure item. The total gives a column of survey expenditure per household (column 2 in tables 2.7a, 2.7b, 3.7a, 3.7b, for the corresponding years).

## TABLE 2.7a.

*Inferred Income Distribution for Rural/Agricultural Households 1958/59*

(£E.)

| Expenditure Intervals | No. of Households Mln. | Survey Expenditure/ Household | Total Expenditure Mln. £E. 1 × 2 | Saving/ Household | Total Saving Mln. £E. 1 × 4 | Disposable Income/ Household 2 + 4 | Total Disposable Income Mln. £E. 3 + 5 | Direct Tax/ Household 9 ÷ 1 | Total Direct Tax Mln. £E. | Total Income/ Household 6 + 8 | Total Income 7 + 9 |
|---|---|---|---|---|---|---|---|---|---|---|---|
| | 1 | 2 | 3 | 4 | 5 | 6 | 7 | 8 | 9 | 10 | 11 |
| – 25 | 0.046 | 20.609 | 0.948 | 0.319 | 0.015 | 20.928 | 0.963 | — | — | 20.928 | 0.963 |
| 25 – | 0.300 | 39.147 | 11.744 | 0.834 | 0.250 | 39.981 | 11.994 | — | — | 39.981 | 11.994 |
| 50 – | 0.493 | 62.609 | 30.886 | 1.687 | 0.832 | 64.296 | 31.698 | — | — | 64.296 | 31.698 |
| 75 – | 0.477 | 87.333 | 41.658 | 2.779 | 1.326 | 90.112 | 42.984 | — | — | 90.112 | 42.984 |
| 100 – | 0.803 | 121.081 | 97.228 | 4.537 | 3.643 | 125.618 | 100.871 | — | — | 125.618 | 100.871 |
| 150 – | 0.477 | 168.623 | 80.433 | 7.456 | 3.557 | 176.079 | 83.990 | 7.887 | 3.762 | 183.966 | 87.752 |
| 200 – | 0.264 | 213.678 | 56.411 | 10.635 | 2.808 | 224.313 | 59.219 | 10.083 | 2.662 | 234.396 | 61.881 |
| 250 – | 0.144 | 260.667 | 37.536 | 14.330 | 2.064 | 274.997 | 39.600 | 12.354 | 1.779 | 287.351 | 41.379 |
| 300 – | 0.137 | 324.153 | 44.409 | 19.872 | 2.722 | 344.025 | 47.131 | 15.467 | 2.119 | 359.492 | 49.250 |
| 400 – | 0.095 | 434.305 | 41.259 | 30.818 | 2.928 | 465.123 | 44.187 | 20.874 | 1.983 | 485.997 | 46.170 |
| 600 – | 0.020 | 655.700 | 13.114 | 57.171 | 1.143 | 712.871 | 14.257 | 100.300 | 2.006 | 813.171 | 16.263 |
| 800 – | 0.003 | 845.667 | 2.537 | 83.737 | 0.251 | 929.404 | 2.788 | 141.667 | 0.425 | 1071.071 | 3.213 |
| 1000 – | 0.007 | 1444.000 | 10.108 | 186.839 | 1.308 | 1630.839 | 11.416 | 339.000 | 2.373 | 1969.839 | 13.789 |
| TOTAL | 3.266 | 143.378 | 468.271 | 5.846 | 22.847 | 149.224 | 491.098 | 5.239 | 17.109 | 154.463 | 508.207 |

NOTES:
Column 1—from Table 2.1a.
Column 2—Calculated from the Family Budget Survey 1958, table 5.
The formula that saving/household = 0.003405 $(\text{Expenditure/household})^{1.5}$ given and used in (14, table 1.4) have been adopted here to estimate Column 4.
Column 9—from Table 2.6a.
Note that the division of Column 11 or Column 7 by Column 1 does not exactly give 10 or 6 due to approximations

TABLE 2.7b.

*Inferred Income Distribution for Urban/Non-Agricultural Households 1958/59*

(£E.)

| Expenditure Intervals | No. of Households Mln. | Survey Expenditure/ Household | Total Expenditure Mln. £E. 1 × 2 | Saving/ Household | Total Saving Mln. £E. 1 × 4 | Disposable Income/ Household 2 + 4 | Total Disposable Income Mln. £E. 3 + 5 | Direct Tax/ Household 9 ÷ 1 | Total Direct Tax Mln. £E. 1 × 8 | Total Income/ Household 6 + 8 | Total Income 7 + 9 |
|---|---|---|---|---|---|---|---|---|---|---|---|
| | 1 | 2 | 3 | 4 | 5 | 6 | 7 | 8 | 9 | 10 | 11 |
| – 25 | 0.004 | 18.500 | 0.074 | 0.708 | 0.003 | 19.208 | 0.077 | — | — | 19.208 | 0.077 |
| 25 – | 0.039 | 40.436 | 1.577 | 2.287 | 0.089 | 42.723 | 1.666 | — | — | 42.723 | 1.666 |
| 50 – | 0.098 | 62.561 | 6.131 | 4.401 | 0.431 | 66.962 | 6.562 | — | — | 66.962 | 6.562 |
| 75 – | 0.151 | 87.894 | 13.272 | 7.329 | 1.107 | 95.225 | 14.379 | — | — | 95.225 | 14.379 |
| 100 – | 0.359 | 124.638 | 44.745 | 12.376 | 4.443 | 137.014 | 49.188 | 2.340 | 0.840 | 139.354 | 50.028 |
| 150 – | 0.307 | 169.212 | 51.948 | 19.678 | 6.041 | 188.890 | 57.989 | 3.235 | 0.993 | 192.125 | 58.982 |
| 200 – | 0.213 | 219.061 | 46.660 | 28.837 | 6.142 | 247.898 | 52.802 | 6.690 | 1.425 | 254.588 | 54.227 |
| 250 – | 0.160 | 264.398 | 42.568 | 38.435 | 6.150 | 302.833 | 48.718 | 8.450 | 1.352 | 311.283 | 50.070 |
| 300 – | 0.226 | 333.133 | 75.288 | 54.359 | 12.285 | 387.492 | 87.573 | 10.597 | 2.395 | 398.089 | 89.968 |
| 400 – | 0.184 | 467.603 | 86.039 | 90.397 | 16.633 | 558.000 | 102.672 | 20.766 | 3.821 | 578 766 | 106.493 |
| 600 – | 0.079 | 652.038 | 51.511 | 148.849 | 11.759 | 800.887 | 63.270 | 33.177 | 2.621 | 834 064 | 65.891 |
| 800 – | 0.026 | 820.308 | 21.328 | 210.040 | 5.461 | 1030.348 | 26.789 | 52.808 | 1.373 | 1083.156 | 28.162 |
| 1000 – | 0.036 | 1413.028 | 50.869 | 474.858 | 17.095 | 1887.886 | 67.964 | 258.722 | 9.314 | 2146.608 | 77.278 |
| TOTAL | 1.882 | 261.429 | 492.010 | 37.789 | 87.639 | 299.218 | 579.649 | 12.824 | 24.134 | 312.042 | 603.783 |

NOTES:

Column 1—from Table 2.1b.

Column 2—Calculated from the Family Budget Survey 1958, table 1.

Colume 4—The formula that Saving/household = 0.00894 (Expenditure/Households)$^{1.5}$ given and used in (14, table 1.5) has been adopted here to estimate Column 4.

Column 9—from Table 2.6b.

Note that division of 11 by 1 does not exactly give 10 due to approximations.

## TABLE 3.7a.

*Inferred Income Distribution for Rural/Agricultural Households 1964/65*

(£E.)

| Expenditure Intervals | No. of Households Mln. | Survey Consumption Expenditure/ Household | Total Expenditure Mln. £E. 1 × 2 | Saving/ Household | Total Saving Mln. £E. 1 × 4 | Disposable Income/ Household 2 + 4 | Total Disposable Income Mln. £E. 8 + 5 | Direct Tax/ Household 9 ÷ 1 | Total Tax Mln. £E. | Total Income/ Household 6 + 8 | Total Income 7 + 9 |
|---|---|---|---|---|---|---|---|---|---|---|---|
| | 1 | 2 | 3 | 4 | 5 | 6 | 7 | 8 | 9 | 10 | 11 |
| – 25 | 0.011 | 19.917 | 0.219 | 0.303 | 0.003 | 20.220 | 0.222 | — | — | 20.220 | 0.222 |
| 25 – | 0.106 | 38.263 | 4.056 | 0.806 | 0.086 | 39.069 | 4.142 | — | — | 39.069 | 4.142 |
| 50 – | 0.173 | 64.324 | 11.128 | 1.757 | 0.304 | 66.081 | 11.432 | — | — | 66.081 | 11.432 |
| 75 – | 0.262 | 88.480 | 23.182 | 2.834 | 0.743 | 91.314 | 23.925 | — | — | 91.314 | 23.925 |
| 100 – | 0.768 | 124.551 | 95.655 | 4.733 | 3.635 | 129.284 | 99.290 | — | — | 129.284 | 99.290 |
| 150 – | 0.616 | 174.176 | 107.292 | 7.827 | 4.822 | 182.003 | 112.114 | 1.338 | 0.824 | 183.341 | 112.938 |
| 200 – | 0.478 | 221.956 | 106.095 | 11.259 | 5.382 | 233.215 | 111.477 | 1.713 | 0.819 | 234.928 | 112.296 |
| 250 – | 0.308 | 276.183 | 85.064 | 15.628 | 4.814 | 291.811 | 89.878 | 2.143 | 0.660 | 293.954 | 90.538 |
| 300 – | 0.407 | 335.336 | 136.482 | 20.909 | 8.510 | 356.245 | 144.992 | 2.592 | 1.055 | 358.837 | 146.047 |
| 400 – | 0.283 | 468.923 | 132.705 | 34.576 | 9.785 | 503.499 | 142.490 | 3.696 | 1.046 | 507.195 | 143.536 |
| 600 – | 0.066 | 661.484 | 43.658 | 57.929 | 3.823 | 719.413 | 47.481 | 11.030 | 0.728 | 730.443 | 48.209 |
| 800 – | 0.028 | 767.507 | 21.490 | 72.400 | 2.027 | 839.907 | 23.517 | 9.214 | 0.258 | 849.121 | 23.775 |
| 1000 – | 0.032 | 1345.871 | 43.068 | 168.121 | 5.380 | 1513.992 | 48.448 | 27.125 | 0.868 | 1540.125 | 49.316 |
| TOTAL | 3.538 | 228.970 | 810.094 | 13.939 | 49.314 | 242.909 | 859.408 | 1.769 | 6.258 | 244.678 | 865.666 |

NOTES:
Column 1—from Table 3.1a.
Column 2—Calculated from the Family Budget Survey for 1964/65 as an average of table 18b for first and third rounds of survey.
Column 4—Calculated by the same method and assumption as Table 2.7b.
Column 8—from Table 3.6a.

## TABLE 3.7b.

*Inferred Income Distribution for Urban/non-Agricultural Households 1964/65*

(£E.)

| Expenditure Intervals | No. of Households Mln. | Survey Consumption Expenditure | Total Expenditure Mln. £E. 1 × 2 | Saving/ Household | Total Saving Mln. £E. 1 ×4 | Disposable Income/ Household 2 + 4 | Total Disposable Income Mln. £E. 8 + 5 | Direct Tax/ Household 9 ÷ 1 | Total Tax Mln. £E. | Total Income/ Household 6 + 8 | Total Income 7 + 9 |
|---|---|---|---|---|---|---|---|---|---|---|---|
| | 1 | 2 | 3 | 4 | 5 | 6 | 7 | 8 | 9 | 10 | 11 |
| – 25 | 0.003 | 19.583 | 0.059 | 0.771 | 0.002 | 20.354 | 0.061 | — | — | 20.354 | 0.061 |
| 25 – | 0.027 | 40.556 | 1.095 | 2.297 | 0.062 | 42.853 | 1.157 | — | — | 42.853 | 1.157 |
| 50 – | 0.048 | 62.892 | 3.019 | 4.436 | 0.213 | 67.328 | 3.232 | — | — | 67.328 | 3.232 |
| 75 – | 0.087 | 86. 66 | 7.557 | 7.200 | 0.626 | 94.066 | 8.183 | — | — | 94.066 | 8.183 |
| 100 – | 0.259 | 123.992 | 32.114 | 12.280 | 3.180 | 136.272 | 35.294 | 4.919 | 1.274 | 141.191 | 36.568 |
| 150 – | 0.343 | 173.634 | 59.556 | 20.349 | 6.980 | 193.983 | 66.536 | 6.910 | 2.370 | 200.893 | 68.906 |
| 200 – | 0.273 | 220.985 | 60.329 | 29.217 | 7.976 | 250.202 | 68.305 | 8.941 | 2.441 | 259.143 | 70.746 |
| 250 – | 0.229 | 272.669 | 62.441 | 40.045 | 9.170 | 312.714 | 71.611 | 11.122 | 2.547 | 323.836 | 74.158 |
| 300 – | 0.344 | 338.264 | 116.363 | 55.333 | 19.034 | 393.597 | 135.397 | 17.948 | 6.174 | 411.545 | 141.571 |
| 400 – | 0.328 | 476.589 | 156.321 | 92.536 | 30.352 | 569.125 | 186.673 | 29.768 | 9.764 | 598.393 | 196.437 |
| 600 – | 0.142 | 669.164 | 95.021 | 153.956 | 21.862 | 823.120 | 116.883 | 45.592 | 6.474 | 868.712 | 123.357 |
| 800 – | 0.073 | 850.811 | 62.109 | 220.722 | 16.113 | 1071.533 | 78.222 | 59.370 | 4.334 | 1130.903 | 82.556 |
| 1000 – | 0.116 | 1501.835 | 179.213 | 517.643 | 60.047 | 2019.478 | 234.260 | 143.534 | 16.650 | 2163.012 | 250.910 |
| TOTAL | 2.272 | 365.404 | 830.197 | 77.296 | 175.617 | 442.700 | 1005.814 | 22.900 | 52.028 | 465.600 | 1057.842 |

NOTES:
Column 1 from Table 3.1b.
Column 2—Calculated from the Family Budget Survey for 1964/65 as an average of table 18A for first and third rounds of the Survey.
Column 4—Calculated by the same method and assumption as table 2.7b.
Column 8—from Table 3.6b.

*TABLE 4.7a.*

*Inferred Income Distribution for Rural/Agricultural Households 1974/75*

0.003405

(£E.)

| Expenditure Intervals | No. of Households Mln. | Survey Consumption Expenditure/ Household | Total Expenditure Mln. £E. 1 × 2 | Saving/ Household | Total Saving Mln. £E. 1 ×4 | Disposable Income/ Household 2 + 4 | Total Disposable Income Mln. £E. 3 + 4 | Direct Tax/ Household 9 ÷ 1 | Total Tax Mln. £E. | Total Income/ Household 6 + 8 | Total Income 7 + 9 |
|---|---|---|---|---|---|---|---|---|---|---|---|
| | 1 | 2 | 3 | 4 | 5 | 6 | 7 | 8 | 9 | 10 | 11 |
| 0– 50 | 0.067 | 32.037 | 2.146 | 0.617 | 0.041 | 32.654 | 2.187 | — | — | 32.654 | 2.187 |
| 50– 75 | 0.076 | 31.736 | 4.692 | 1.652 | 0.126 | 63.388 | 4.818 | — | — | 63.388 | 4.818 |
| 75– 100 | 0.099 | 87.676 | 8.680 | 2.795 | 0.277 | 90.471 | 8.957 | — | — | 90.471 | 8.957 |
| 100– 150 | 0.269 | 127.005 | 34.165 | 4.874 | 1.311 | 131.879 | 35.476 | — | — | 131.879 | 35.476 |
| 150– 200 | 0.395 | 173.539 | 68.548 | 7.784 | 3.075 | 181.323 | 71.673 | — | — | 181.323 | 71.623 |
| 200– 250 | 0.470 | 225.519 | 105.994 | 11.532 | 5.420 | 237.051 | 111.414 | 2.249 | 1.057 | 239.300 | 112.471 |
| 250– 300 | 0.450 | 274.570 | 123.556 | 15.492 | 6.971 | 290.062 | 130.527 | 2.751 | 1.238 | 292.813 | 131.765 |
| 300– 350 | 0.384 | 322.805 | 123.957 | 19.748 | 7.583 | 342.553 | 131.540 | 3.245 | 1.246 | 345.798 | 132.780 |
| 350– 400 | 0.317 | 367.186 | 116.398 | 23.958 | 7.595 | 591.144 | 123.993 | 3.710 | 1.176 | 394.854 | 125.109 |
| 400– 500 | 0.417 | 438.811 | 182.984 | 31.300 | 13.052 | 470.111 | 198.036 | 4.458 | 1.859 | 474.569 | 197.895 |
| 500– 600 | 0.229 | 534.934 | 122.500 | 42.128 | 9.647 | 577.062 | 132.147 | 5.467 | 1.252 | 582.529 | 133.399 |
| 600– 800 | 0.219 | 679.801 | 148.876 | 60.352 | 13.217 | 740.153 | 162.093 | 9.256 | 2.027 | 749.406 | 164.120 |
| 800–1000 | 0.099 | 848.981 | 84.049 | 84.230 | 8.339 | 933.211 | 92.388 | 11.676 | 1.156 | 944.889 | 93.544 |
| 1000–1400 | 0.061 | 1146.227 | 69.920 | 132.137 | 8.060 | 1278.364 | 77.980 | 16.000 | 0.976 | 1294.361 | 78.956 |
| 1400–2000 | 0.020 | 1527.178 | 30.544 | 203.213 | 4.064 | 1730.391 | 34.608 | 21.650 | 0.433 | 1752.020 | 35.041 |
| 2000– | 0.020 | 2816.719 | 56.334 | 509.017 | 10.180 | 3325.736 | 66.514 | 41.600 | 0.832 | 3367.300 | 67.346 |
| TOTALS | 3.592 | 357.278 | 1283.343 | 27.550 | 98.958 | 384.828 | 1382.301 | 3.690 | 13.252 | 388.518 | 1395.553 |

NOTES:

Column 1 from Table 4.1 (1).

Column 2—Calculated from the Family Budget Survey for 1974/75 as an average computed from the first and third rounds of the survey.

Column 4—Calculated according to the same method used for calculating the corresponding column for the preceding years.

Column 9—from Table 4.6a.

*Inferred Income Distribution for Urban/Non-Agricultural Households 1974/75*

0.008894 (£E.)

| Expenditure Intervals | No. of Households Mln. | Survey Consumption Expenditure/ Household | Total Expenditure Mln. £E. 1 × 2 | Saving/ Household | Total Saving Mln. £E. 1 × 4 | Disposable Income/ Household 2 + 4 | Total Disposable Income Mln. £E. 3 + 5 | Direct Tax/ Household 9 ÷ 1 | Total Tax Mln. £E. | Total Income/ Household 6 + 8 | Total Income 7 + 9 |
|---|---|---|---|---|---|---|---|---|---|---|---|
| | 1 | 2 | 3 | 4 | 5 | 6 | 7 | 8 | 9 | 10 | 11 |
| 0– 50 | 0.013 | 26.828 | 0.349 | 1.236 | 0.016 | 28.064 | 0.365 | — | — | 28 064 | 0.365 |
| 50– 75 | 0.022 | 63.310 | 1.393 | 4.481 | 0.099 | 67.799 | 1.492 | — | — | 67 799 | 1.492 |
| 75– 100 | 0.030 | 88.571 | 2.657 | 7.414 | 0.222 | 95.985 | 2.879 | — | — | 95.985 | 2.879 |
| 100– 150 | 0.108 | 126.895 | 13.705 | 12.713 | 1.373 | 139.608 | 15.078 | 7.694 | 0.831 | 147.302 | 15.909 |
| 150– 200 | 0.155 | 176.039 | 27.286 | 20.774 | 3.220 | 196.813 | 30.506 | 10.794 | 1.673 | 207.607 | 32.179 |
| 200– 250 | 0.223 | 224.470 | 50.057 | 29.911 | 6.670 | 254.381 | 56.727 | 13.982 | 3.118 | 268.363 | 59.845 |
| 250– 300 | 0.268 | 273.515 | 73.302 | 40.232 | 10.782 | 313.747 | 84.084 | 17.239 | 4.620 | 330.986 | 88.704 |
| 300– 350 | 0.267 | 322.530 | 86.115 | 51.517 | 13.755 | 374.047 | 99.870 | 20.584 | 5.496 | 394.631 | 105.366 |
| 350– 400 | 0.262 | 372.358 | 97.558 | 64.236 | 16.830 | 436.594 | 114.388 | 24.015 | 6.292 | 460.609 | 120.680 |
| 400– 500 | 0.462 | 444.405 | 205.315 | 83.323 | 38.495 | 527.728 | 243.810 | 33.850 | 15.639 | 561.578 | 259.449 |
| 500– 600 | 0.347 | 544.704 | 189.012 | 113.652 | 39.437 | 658.356 | 228.449 | 44.841 | 15.560 | 703.197 | 244.009 |
| 600– 800 | 0.419 | 676.424 | 283.422 | 156.468 | 65.560 | 832.892 | 348.982 | 59.759 | 25.039 | 892.651 | 374.021 |
| 800–1000 | 0.206 | 875.053 | 180.261 | 230.223 | 47.426 | 1105.276 | 227.687 | 83.612 | 17.224 | 1188.888 | 244.911 |
| 1000–1400 | 0.204 | 1108.810 | 226.197 | 328.385 | 66.990 | 1437.195 | 293.187 | 110.397 | 22.521 | 1547.592 | 315.708 |
| 1400–2000 | 0.088 | 1572.299 | 138.362 | 554.498 | 48.796 | 2126.797 | 187.158 | 174.068 | 15.318 | 2300.865 | 202.476 |
| 2000– | 0.046 | 2149.336 | 98.870 | 886.246 | 40.767 | 3035.582 | 139.637 | 152.522 | 11.616 | 3288.104 | 151.253 |
| TOTALS | 3.120 | 536.494 | 1673.861 | 128.346 | 400.438 | 664.840 | 2074.299 | 46.457 | 144.947 | 711.297 | 2219.246 |

NOTES:
Column 1 from Table 4.1 (4).
Column 2—Calculated as in Table 4.7a.
Column 4—Calculated according to the same method used for calculating the corresponding column for the preceding years.
Column 9—from Table 4.6b.
Note that the division of column 11 or 7 by column 1 does not exactly give 10 or 6 due to approximations.

The data sources here for 1958/1959 and 1964/1965 are the corresponding Family Budget Surveys. For 1974/1975 the source is the World Bank Report (see reference 8). Second, multiplying the average expenditure by the number of households in each expenditure interval gives the total consumption expenditure allocated to various expenditure groups (column 3 in tables 2.7a, 2.7b, 3.7a, 3.7b for corresponding years).

*Determination of Household Saving.* Here the formulas used in reference 8, annex 1.1 to determine saving per household of rural and urban sector were adopted for the 1958/1959 and 1964/1965 calculations.

For the rural sector, the formula is:

$$\frac{\text{Saving}}{\text{Household in rural sector}} = 0.003405 \left(\frac{\text{Expenditure}}{\text{Household}}\right)^{1.5}$$

For the urban sector the formula has the following form:

$$\frac{\text{Saving}}{\text{Household}} = 0.008894 \left(\frac{\text{Expenditure}}{\text{Household}}\right)^{1.5}$$

Results of calculations are tabulated in column 4 (of tables 2.7a, 2.7b, 3.7a, 3.7b for 1958/1959 and 1964/1965, respectively), which assigns saving/houshold for each expenditure group. Then multiplication of this column by the households column gives the total saving in million Egyptian pounds, represented by column 5 of these tables.

*Total Disposable Income.* This is determined by adding elements of column 5 to those of column 3 of the total consumption results in total disposable income, which is illustrated in column 7 of these tables.

Allocation of direct nonshifted taxes was then made (see page 0). It is represented by column 9 in the tables cited.

*Expenditure Intervals of Total Income Distributed.* Adding column 9 of total direct nonshifted taxes to column 7 of total disposable income gives total income distributed with respect to expenditure intervals and represented by column 11 in tables 2.7a, 2.7b; 3.7a, 3.7b; 4.7a, 4.7b, for 1958/1959, 1964/1965, and 1974/1975, respectively.

## *Tax Allocation*

Having obtained the pattern of income distribution, we next allocate the various types of taxes. Statistical data are discouragingly scarce. However as Musgrave and others put it in their pioneering investigation of the distribution of tax payment by income groups for 1948 in the United States (see reference 23), the economist cannot plead complete absence of information. There is some empirical evidence to work with, and some conclusions may be reached deductively. In the case of Egypt, such empirical evidence is very scarce. Therefore, the area of assumptions has to be a wide one. Mobilizing the maximum possible energies, relatively good reliable data regarding taxes on goods and services of the years under investigation were obtained. On the other hand, data regarding direct taxes, in general, were much more scarce. Therefore, procedures for allocating taxes will be different according to the type of tax. The primary task for allocation of taxes on goods and services and shifted direct taxes is to allocate them for different types of expenditure items. With respect to direct nonshifted taxes, the job is to allocate them among the various expenditure groups of the spending units.

### *Allocation of Indirect and Shifted Direct Taxes*

The starting point is to select the taxes to be allocated. Here a distinction between taxes, duties, and fees is irrelevant. Therefore, this group of taxes comprises a wide range of taxes that could be classified as follows:

- Custom taxes
- Taxes on goods and services:
  - Production excises
  - Consumption excises
  - Price differentials
  - Other selective excises
- Stamps that in general represent taxes on services
- Social insurance contributions
- Subsidies treated as negative taxes

*Commodity and Services Taxes.* The main assumption is that these taxes are shifted 100 percent to consumers. This assumption is asserted by a number of observations on the mechanism of performance of the Egyptian market (for example, the imperfections that cause a high degree of shiftability of customs, consumption, and production taxes): some taxes are shifted by their very nature (price differentials); demand elasticity in a number of cases (taxes on free professionals in case of doctors, artists, etc.); fixation of a tax for a long period in a situation of imperfections helps to increase the degree of shiftability as in the case of taxes on profits and business contributions for social insurance. Here taxes and contributions have become costs to be shifted forward by enterprises. Backward shifting seems to be rare in the Egyptian conditions due to the relative rigidity of the money wage.

Therefore, it might be legitimate to assume that all these types of taxes are fully shifted to consumers. Having established this assumption, the next step was allocating these taxes.

Tables 2.3, 3.3, and 4.3 (available on request) give the outcome of allocating taxes to expenditure items for 1959/1960, 1964/1965, and 1974/1975, respectively. Methods of allocation could be summarized as follows:

*Custom Taxes*

A distinction was made between three main groups of imports: Consumption, intermediate, and investment goods. Data on taxes on imported goods for 1959 and 1964/1965 were easy to find (see reference 1, tables 84, 85, and 86). For 1974/1975, taxes were calculated in three stages: First, by grouping imports into consumption, intermediate, and investment goods. Second, by applying general prevailing and available custom rates to the items in the groups, the possible tax receipts were determined. Third, from the latter, shares of different items in tax receipts were calculated and applied to the actual receipts of customs taxes drawn—as an average of 1974/1975—from the Ministry of Finance Budget Report Accounts of these years. The results of the third stage were three columns allocating taxes to different items of consumption, intermediate, and investment goods. Note that the similar columns corresponding to 1959/1960 and 1964/1965 were readily available (see reference 1).

Then comes the allocation of the obtained allocated taxes to the expenditure items as classified in the FBS and in this chapter. For consumption goods the problem was rather minor. Here allocation was to an extent either a direct one or an aggregation of a number of items that are considered parts of the items in the FBS classification. With respect to intermediate goods, a dependence on flows of intermediate imported goods (published and included in reference 1, table 74, p. 205) was made. This means that taxes on imported intermediate goods were fully shifted forward to consumption goods of domestic production. For imported investment goods only 10 percent of their taxes was considered for allocation. This percent was assumed on the basis of an assumed prevailing rate of capital depreciation. Their allocation was undertaken, in principle, on the basis of shares of different sectors in investments by foreign currencies. A relatively more detailed indication on allocation methods and sources is included in the footnotes of tables 2.3, 3.3, and 4.3.

In short, the calculations were made to ensure the full shifting of taxes on imported goods. Nevertheless, in a comment made on a draft of this chapter, Professor B. Hansen argued that if there is a tariff on a commodity both produced in the country and imported, then the burden on the consumer exceeds the revenue because the price tends to increase also for the domestically produced part of the total supply. Hence the estimation of the tax burden on the assumption of only full shifting tends to involve a downward bias. But it is not clear how this would affect the impact on distribution. Hansen's argument is represented in figure 2.

The assumption of full shifting made in this chapter implies that the indirect tax rate will be equal to C D E F/O B D H. According to Hansen's argument, the burden should be defined as A B D F/O B D H. This means that taxes on imported goods induce further price increases in the

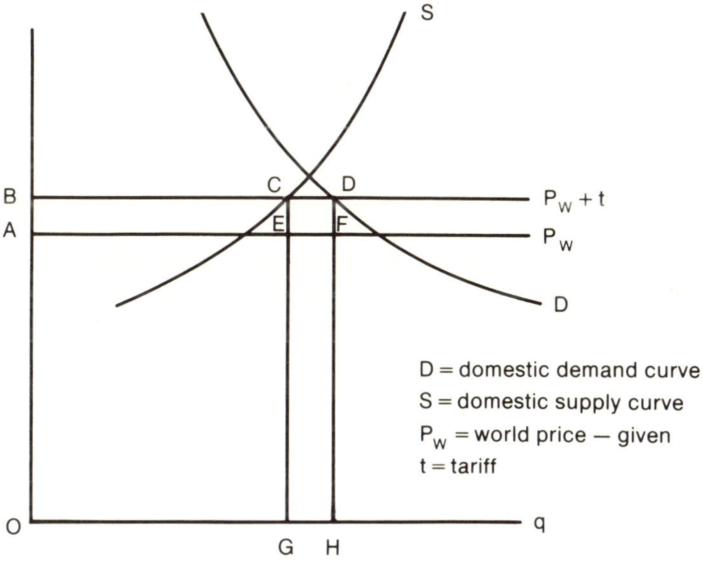


*FIGURE 2.*

domestically produced ones. Though day-to-day observations assure this argument, it was not possible in the framework of this chapter to calculate the impact of further price increases induced by tariff on income distribution.

*Taxes on Commodities and Services*

This group includes production and consumption excises, price differentials, some selective excises, and stamps. Major parts of these taxes were found easy to allocate by their titles. They are addressed to particular commodities and services. Other parts (for example, taxes on petroleum products) were allocated according to flows of intermediate goods to the different sectors using petroleum products as an intermediate and final consumption good. More detailed indication is referred to in the footnotes of tables 2.3, 3.3, and 4.3.

*Shifted Direct Taxes*

The fully shifted direct taxes are assumed to consist of:

1. Business income taxes, namely taxes on profits and movable property. Some business income taxes, for example, Atāwāt, are incorporated in the previous section of taxes on commodities and services. The allocation of taxes on profits and movable property was made according to shares of different sectors in business profits.

2. Social insurance contributions of private and public business enterprises. Contributions of agencies of government sector are not treated here. They are considered as a part of public expenditures. The idea behind the assumption of shiftability of these taxes on business income and social insurance contribution is that their rates are fixed for a relatively long time, and it might be legitimate to assume that enterprises treat them as costs to be covered through forward shifting. Allocation of business contributions to social insurance was run according to shares of different subsectors in business sector wages.
3. Taxes on building were allocated to expenditure item of dwelling.
4. Tax on free professionals. This tax was allocated between different types of services depending on the share of the corresponding professions in the tax receipts. The idea behind the shifting assumption is that the price of the services presented by these professionals is determined through a market that is dominated by the sellers due to the observed low elasticities of demand on these services.

*Subsidies.* Subsidies are treated in this chapter because of their importance in Egypt's economic and political life at the present time. (It is outside the framework of this chapter to offer solutions for this problem.) However, the purpose of this treatment is to estimate the effect of subsidies on income distribution. In this chapter, subsidies are considered to be negative indirect taxes and are manifested in the net taxes estimated as gross taxes, excluding subsidies. Allocation of subsidies follows generally the same methods as allocating taxes on goods and services. The task of allocating the subsidies was facilitated by the fact that the major part of subsidies are for food and beverages.

After allocating gross and net indirect and shifted taxes to different items of consumer expenditures (as illustrated in tables 2.3, 3.3, and 4.3), tax content ratios for gross taxes excluding subsidies and for net taxes including subsidies have then to be calculated. Their estimations are illustrated in tables 2.5, 3.5, and 4.5 (available on request) for 1958/1959, 1964/1965, and 1974/1965, and 1974/1975, respectively. In these tables, columns of total consumption expenditure were taken as a sum of total consumption expenditure of rural and urban sectors derived from tables 2.2a, 2.2b, 3.2a, 3.2b, and 4.2a, 4.2b (available on request); and columns of gross and net taxes are taken from tables 2.3, 3.3, and 4.3 for the respective years.

The next step was to allocate indirect and shifted taxes (gross and net) to spending household groups. This was done through multiplying gross and net tax content ratios obtained from the previous step by tables of consumption expenditure. The results of multiplication were four tables for each year of calculation:

1. For gross tax contents of expenditure items for the rural sector, 2.4.1a, 3.4.1a, 4.4.1a (available on request)

2. For net tax contents of expenditure items for the rural sector, 2.4.2a, 3.4.2a, 4.4.2a (available on request)
3. For gross tax contents of expenditure items in the urban sector, 2.4.1b, 3.4.1b, 4.4.1b (available on request)
4. For tax contents of expenditure items in the urban sector, tables 2.4.2b, 3.4.2b, 4.4.2b (available on request)

### *Allocation of Direct Nonshifted Taxes*

For rural agricultural households, this group of taxes consists of two types (land tax and inheritance taxes). For urban nonagricultural households, it embraces four types of taxes:

- Taxes on wages and salaries
- Employees' contribution to social insurance
- Inheritance taxes
- General income tax

As stated earlier, data required for allocation of these taxes are extremely scarce. Therefore, the only solution to this problem is to make certain assumptions. A number of alternatives based on different criteria were calculated. Some led to unusual results, whereas others produced contradictory conclusions. The alternatives reflected in tables 2.6a, 2.6b, 3.6a, 3.6b, 4.6a, and 4.6b represent some reasonable possible conclusions. The allocation was undertaken as follows:

*Allocation of Land Tax among Rural Spending Families.* This was made according to their shares in disposable income.

*Inheritance Taxes for Rural Households.* Their allocation was run in two stages: (1) Determination of shares of the taxable categories of spending units. These shares were calculated by applying the tax rates to a calculated possible value of the subject of inheritance (land) for each category. (2) Multiplying these obtained shares by the total tax revenues of rural sector. The latter was not available and therefore, it was assumed that it constituted 50 percent of the total revenues of inheritance taxes.

*Wages and Salaries.* Its allocation was made in the following steps:

1. Determining the taxed income for each taxable spending unit.
2. Applying tax rates to get the possible tax per family.
3. Multiplying the possible tax per family by the number of families in each taxable spending category to get the total possible tax for each class.
4. Getting shares of each class in this total possible tax.
5. Multiplying these shares into the actual tax revenues to obtain the allocation of the actual taxes.

*Allocation of Employee Contributions to Social Insurance.* This was carried out according to the shares of spending units in their total disposable income.

*Inheritance Taxes of Urban Household.* These were allocated along the same lines of inheritance taxes in rural sector but with application on buildings, which are assumed to be the main form of wealth in the urban sector.

*General Income Tax.* By its nature, this tax applies to the last expenditure interval for 1958/1959 and 1964/1965. For 1974/1975 it applies to the last three categories. Its allocation among them was carried out according to their shares in their total disposable income. Tables 3.6 and 4.6 (available on request) outline the allocation of different types of taxes to the spending groups in rural and urban sectors for 1959/1960, 1964/1965, and 1974/1975, respectively. The column total in each table represents the total direct nonshifted taxes assigned to each spending group. However, one has to notice that the pattern of allocation according to shares in the disposable income does not produce any changes in income distribution. This result is not astonishing as taxes allocated by this method are determined by proportional rate, namely, land tax and employee contributions to social insurance.

## Main Findings

The main findings are illustrated in figures 2.a, 2.b, 3.a, 3.b, 4.a, and 4.b and tables 2.8a, 2.8b, 2.8c, 3.8a, 3.8b, 3.8c and 4.8a, 4.8b, 4.8c (available on request) in rural, urban total society and for 1958/1959, 1964/1965, and 1974/1975, respectively. One should underline the following conclusions:

### *The Impact of Taxes on Income Distribution in 1958/1959*

The impact of total net taxes on income distribution in the urban sector seems to be larger than that in the rural sector. The same conclusion holds with respect to the impact of gross total taxes on income distribution.

The main direction of the tax impact is to increase the shares of the lower spending groups and to decrease those of the upper groups, though to a rather slight degree.

Note that the conclusions in the case of the rural sector are particularly due to the effect of direct taxes because indirect taxes, either gross or net, have an extremely minor impact. Further, if land taxes were to be excluded, due to their proportional allocation, then the likely reasonable conclusion is that the taxes in the rural sector in 1958/1959 have an impact mainly through inheritance taxes.

With respect to the urban sector, the effect of indirect taxes, either gross or net, is also a very minor one. The main role here is played by direct taxes. Employee contributions were not considered for 1958/1959, and they have no role to play due to the method of its allocation.

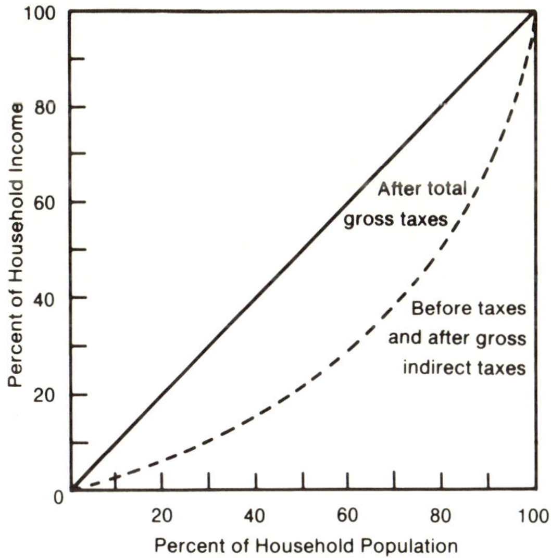


*FIGURE 2.a.*
*Taxes and Income Distribution in Egypt (1958/1959)*
*Excluding Subsidies*

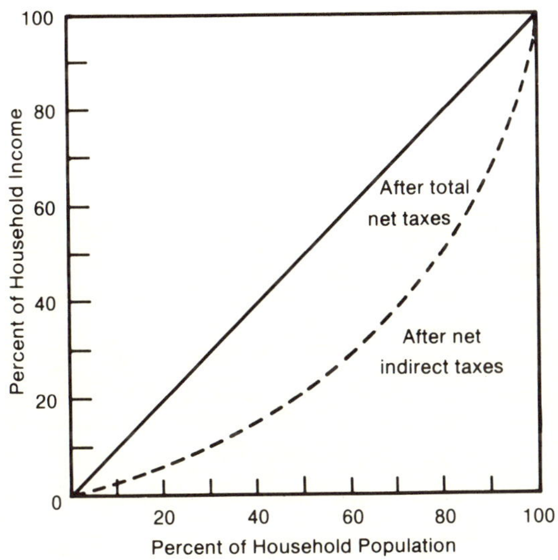


*FIGURE 2.b.*
*Including Subsidies*

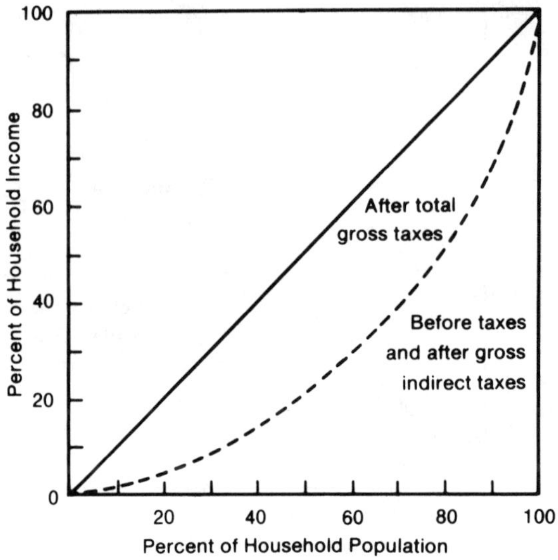


*FIGURE 3.a.*

*Taxes and Income Distribution in Egypt (1964/1965)*
*Excluding Subsidies*

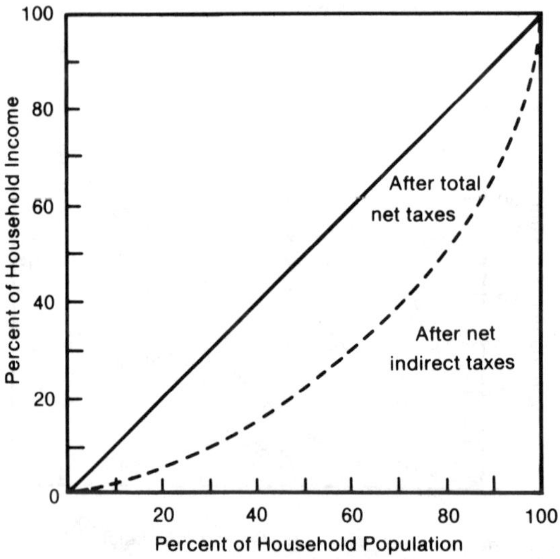


*FIGURE 3.b.*

*Including Subsidies*

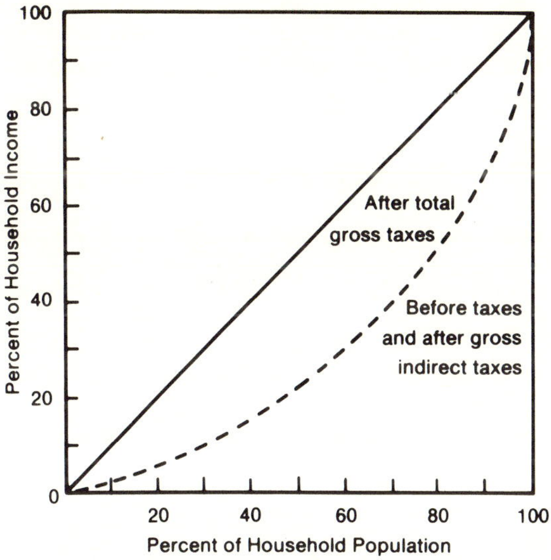


*FIGURE 4.a.*
*Taxes and Income Distribution in Egypt (1974/1975) Excluding Subsidies*

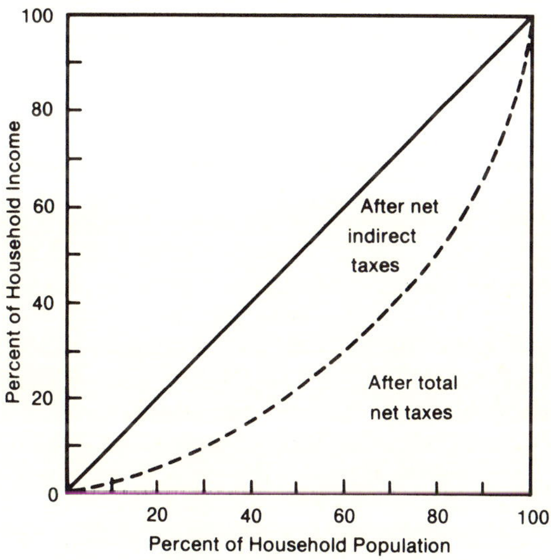


*FIGURE 4.b.*
*Including Subsidies*

Therefore, one can conclude that the impact of taxes in this sector is due to other direct taxes, namely, taxes on general income, inheritance, and wages and salaries. It is difficult to trace the role played by each type.

As for society at large as illustrated by table 2.8c, the same conclusions also hold.

### *The Impact of Taxes on Income Distribution in 1964/1965*

Total net taxes have a noticeable impact in both rural and urban sectors. The same conclusion holds with respect to gross indirect taxes. For the society at large, total net taxes have an impact that seems to be larger than that of 1958/1959. The direction of impact is still the same—a progressive one manifesting itself in increasing the shares of lower spending groups while decreasing those of upper group.

With respect to the impact of gross indirect taxes in the rural sector, the situation in 1964/1965 differs from that of 1958/1959. These taxes have a more noticeable impact as can easily be seen from a comparison of columns 7 and 4 of table 3.8a. Adding up subsidies improves the distribution toward equality in both rural and urban sectors.

Assessment of the role played by direct taxes reveals a rather different role in comparison to that of 1958/1959. Here direct taxes have a slight effect on the rural sector. This can be seen by comparing columns 13 and 4 of table 3.8a. The situation is not the same in the urban sector. Comparison of column 13 and 4 in table 3.8a reveals greater impact from direct taxes.

Subsidies play a larger role than in 1958/1959 in both rural and urban sectors. Such a proposition is seen by comparing columns 10 and 3 of tables 3.8a and 3.8b.

As a whole, the impact of net total taxes on income distribution seems to be more progressive in 1964/1965 than that of 1958/1959, as suggested through comparing columns 3 and 19 of tables 2.8c and 3.8c.

### *The Impact of Taxes on Income Distribution in 1974/1975*

Total net taxes have a larger impact on income distribution in the urban sector than in the rural sector. However, the impact in both sectors seems to be greater than that in 1958/1959 and 1964/1965.

In the rural sector, both gross and net indirect taxes have a relatively significant role in improving shares of lower groups, whereas direct taxes have a very minor role.

In the urban sector, gross indirect taxes have a slight effect, whereas subsidies exert a significant role as seen from comparison of columns 10 and 4 of table 4.8b. Direct taxes in 1974 / 1975 have larger impact than in previous years but less than that of the indirect taxes.

*TABLE 2.9.*
*Effective Tax Rates in 1958/59*

| *Expenditure Categories* | *Income before Taxes Mln* | *Gross Total Tax Mln LE* | *Gross Tax Rate Percent* | *Net Total Tax Mln LE* | *Net Tax Rate (Percent)* |
|---|---|---|---|---|---|
| – 25 | 1.040 | 0.103 | 0.0990 | 0.090 | 0.0865 |
| 25 – | 13.660 | 1.696 | 0.1242 | 1.530 | 0.1120 |
| 50 – | 38.260 | 5.186 | 0.1355 | 4.737 | 0.1238 |
| 75 – | 57.363 | 8.063 | 0.1406 | 7.411 | 0.1292 |
| 100 – | 150.059 | 21.445 | 0.1429 | 19.815 | 0.1320 |
| 150 – | 143.609 | 25.015 | 0.1742 | 23.575 | 0.1642 |
| 200 – | 112.898 | 19.687 | 0.1744 | 18.604 | 0.1648 |
| 250 – | 89.917 | 15.753 | 0.1752 | 14.958 | 0.1664 |
| 300 – | 137.230 | 23.527 | 0.1714 | 22.096 | 0.1610 |
| 400 – | 150.011 | 26.060 | 0.1737 | 24.959 | 0.1664 |
| 600 – | 81.379 | 16.023 | 0.1969 | 15.536 | 0.1909 |
| 800 – | 31.646 | 6.288 | 0.1987 | 6.124 | 0.1935 |
| 1000 – | 94.410 | 24.455 | 0.2590 | 23.960 | 0.2538 |
| TOTAL | 1101.482 | 193.301 | 0.1755 | 183.395 | 0.1665 |

SOURCE: Table 2.8 c

Subsidies in 1974/1975 are more significant than in both 1958/1959 and 1963/1964 in both rural and urban sectors.

### *Overall Impact of Taxes on Income Distribution*

The overall assessment of the impact of taxes on income distribution is represented by tables 2.9, 3.9, and 4.9 for 1958/1959, 1964/1965, and 1974/1975, respectively. From these tables the following conclusions can be drawn:

1. In all the years under consideration the Egyptian tax system exhibits a degree of progressivity. It is higher in 1964/1965 and 1974/1975 than in 1958/1959.
2. Subsidies play a larger role in 1974/1975 than in 1964/1965; and the latter is, in its turn, larger than that of 1958/1959.
3. The main findings of calculations are represented by estimation of Gini coefficients in the years under consideration.

*Gini Coefficients of Income Distribution before and after Taxes*

| | *1958/1959* | *1964/1965* | *1974/1975* |
|---|---|---|---|
| Income before taxes | 0.4446 | 0.4313 | 0.4043 |
| Income after gross indirect taxes | 0.4402 | 0.4276 | 0.3985 |
| Income after total gross taxes | 0.4300 | 0.4184 | 0.3885 |
| Income after net indirect taxes | 0.4400 | 0.4257 | 0.3659 |
| Income after total net taxes | 0.4300 | 0.4170 | 0.3792 |

From this table, these conclusions follow:

1. Gross indirect taxes have a progressive effect. They help to decrease the Gini coefficients in the three years—from 0.4446 to 0.4402 in 1958/1959; from 0.4313 to 0.4276 in 1964/1965; and from 0.4043 to 0.3985 in 1974/1975. Notice that this effect of gross taxes seems to be increasing over the period 1958/1959–1974/1975.
2. Direct taxes have a similar direction of impact. Implicit in total gross taxes they help to decrease the coefficients from 0.4402 to 0.4300 in 1958/1959; from 0.4276 to 0.4184 in 1964/1965; and from 0.3985 to 0.3885 in 1974/1975.

*TABLE 3.9.*

*Effective Tax Rates in 1964/1965*

| *Expenditure Categories* | *Income before Taxes Mln* | *Gross Total Tax Mln LE* | *Gross Tax Rate (percent)* | *Net Total Tax Mln LE* | *Net Tax Rate (percent)* |
|---|---|---|---|---|---|
| – 25 | 0.283 | 0.030 | 0.1060 | 0.024 | 0.0848 |
| 25 – | 5.299 | 0.641 | 0.1210 | 0.547 | 0.1032 |
| 50 – | 14.664 | 1.908 | 0.1301 | 1.658 | 0.1131 |
| 75 – | 32.108 | 4.491 | 0.1309 | 3.959 | 0.1233 |
| 100 – | 135.858 | 22.109 | 0.1627 | 19.966 | 0.1470 |
| 150 – | 181.844 | 32.127 | 0.1767 | 29.086 | 0.1600 |
| 200 – | 183.042 | 32.292 | 0.1764 | 29.734 | 0.1624 |
| 250 – | 164.696 | 29.351 | 0.1782 | 27.153 | 0.1649 |
| 300 – | 287.618 | 53.387 | 0.1856 | 49.787 | 0.1731 |
| 400 – | 339.973 | 66.003 | 0.1941 | 62.186 | 0.1829 |
| 600 – | 171.566 | 35.264 | 0.2055 | 33.557 | 0.1956 |
| 800 – | 106.331 | 22.180 | 0.2086 | 21.271 | 0.2000 |
| 1000 – | 300.226 | 69.433 | 0.2313 | 67.318 | 0.2242 |
| TOTAL | 1923.508 | 369.216 | 0.1919 | 346.246 | 0.1800 |

SOURCE: Table 3.8 c

*TABLE 4.9.*
*Effective Tax Rates in 1974/75*

| *Expenditure Intervals* | *Income Before Taxes Mln. £E* | *Gross Total Tax Mln. £E* | *Gross Tax Rate (percent)* | *Net Total Tax Mln. £E* | *Net Tax Rate (percent)* |
|---|---|---|---|---|---|
| 0– 50 | 2.552 | 0.411 | 0.1611 | –0.001 | –0.0002 |
| 50– 75 | 6.310 | 1.157 | 0.1834 | 0.164 | 0.0260 |
| 75– 100 | 11.836 | 2.393 | 0.2022 | 0.598 | 0.0505 |
| 100– 150 | 51.385 | 11.425 | 0.2223 | 3.969 | 0.0772 |
| 150– 200 | 103.802 | 23.478 | 0.2262 | 8.741 | 0.0842 |
| 200– 250 | 172.316 | 42.309 | 0.2455 | 18.886 | 0.1096 |
| 250– 300 | 220.469 | 54.993 | 0.2494 | 26.148 | 0.1186 |
| 300– 350 | 238.152 | 59.964 | 0.2518 | 29.015 | 0.1218 |
| 350– 400 | 245.849 | 62.300 | 0.2534 | 31.713 | 0.1290 |
| 400– 500 | 457.344 | 121.158 | 0.2649 | 66.877 | 0.1462 |
| 500– 600 | 377.408 | 103.186 | 0.2734 | 60.855 | 0.1612 |
| 600– 800 | 538.141 | 150.118 | 0.2790 | 92.831 | 0.1725 |
| 800–1000 | 338.455 | 95.312 | 0.2816 | 61.377 | 0.1813 |
| 1000–1400 | 394.664 | 113.423 | 0.2874 | 77.748 | 0.1970 |
| 1400–2000 | 237.517 | 71.301 | 0.3002 | 52.671 | 0.2218 |
| 2000– | 218.599 | 74.724 | 0.3418 | 60.114 | 0.2750 |
| TOTALS | 3614.799 | 987.552 | 0.2732 | 591.706 | 0.1637 |

SOURCE: Table 4.8c.

3. Subsidies have contributed to decreasing the coefficients in the three years. They decrease the coefficient corresponding to gross indirect taxes from 0.4402 to 0.4400 in 1958/1959, from 0.4276 to 0.4257 in 1964/1965, and from 0.3985 to 0.3659 in 1974/1975. Notice here also that impact of subsidies has increased over the period 1958/1959–1974/1975.
4. There exists a trend toward more equity over the period 1958/1959–1974/1975.

## Sources and References

1. Ministry of Planning, *The Detailed Plan of the Fifth Year* (Cairo, 1966) (in Arabic).

2. Ministry of Planning, "Sectoral Interrelationships in 1964/1965," in *The Detailed Plan of the Fifth Year.*

3. Ministry of Planning, *The Detailed Plan of the Second Year* (Cairo, 1963) (in Arabic).

4. J. R. Lotz, "Taxation in the United Arab Republic (Egypt)," in *IMF Staff Papers,* 13, no. 1, March 1966.

5. Ministry of Planning, *The Transitional Plan, July 1974–December 1975* (Cairo, 1975) (in Arabic).

6. R. S. Eckaus, Nazli Choucri, and Amr Mohie Eldin, *Multisector General Equilibrium Policy Models* (Cairo University/MIT Technological Planning Program, 1978).

7. Ministry of Planning, *Preliminary Report of Follow-up 1976 Plan* (Cairo, 1977) (in Arabic).

8. World Bank, *Arab Republic of Egypt, Economic Management in a Period of Transition,* vol. 4, May 8, 1978.

9. World Bank, *Arab Republic of Egypt, Economic Report,* vol. 6, March 22, 1977.

10. Central Agency for Public Mobilization and Statistics, *Monthly Bulletin of Foreign Trade for 1974 and 1975* (Cairo, 1974 and 1975).

11. World Bank, *Arab Republic of Egypt, Survey of Small Scale Industry,* December 2, 1977.

12. Department of Statistics and Census, *General Annual Statistics, 1960* (Cairo, 1962).

13. Central Agency for Public Mobilization and Statistics, *Survey of Family Budget* (in Arabic).

14. Al-Ahrām al-Iqtisādī, *Egyptian Population: The Results of the General Census of Population in November 1976,* 1 May 1977, Tables 24, 26.

15. Central Agency for Auditing, *A Statistical and Analytical Study of Sovereign Revenues, 1964–1974* (in Arabic).

16. International Monetary Fund, *A Report on the Egyptian Tax System,* 1978.

17. B. Hansen and G. Marzouk, *Development and Economic Policy in the U.A.R. (Egypt)* (North Holland, 1965).

18. Department of Taxes, *Tax Guide* (Cairo, 1968) (in Arabic).

19. Department of Taxes, *Laws and Executive Rules regarding Income Taxes according to the Last Amendments in 1 January 1970* (in Arabic).

20. Al-Najjār, ᶜAbd al-Hādī, *Income Taxes in Egyptian Legislation, 1976/1977* (Cairo, 1976) (in Arabic).

21. Ministry of Planning, *Preliminary Report of Following-up 1976 Plan* (Cairo, July 1977) (in Arabic)

22. C. R. Webb, *Tax Policy and the Incidence of Taxation in Peru,* Research Program in Economic Development, Woodrow Wilson School, Princeton University, Discussion Paper No. 27, September 1972.

23. R. A. Musgrave, J. J. Carroll, L. D. Cook, and L. Frane, "Distribution of Tax Payments by Income Groups: A Case Study for 1948," in *National Tax Journal,* vol. 4, no. 1, March 1951.

# CHAPTER 6

# *The Agricultural Output Pricing Policy and the Implicit Taxation of Agricultural Income**

Karima Korayem

## I. Introduction

The examination of the prevailing tax system in Egypt reveals that agriculture is privileged as compared to other economic activities. With the exception of the land tax, which is relatively low, agricultural income is exempted from the different types of taxes that are imposed on the incomes generated in the other sectors of the economy.[1] This picture is misleading. Agricultural income is actually taxed implicitly through the price differential policy applied on the main agricultural crops, including the major export crops. The main objective of this chapter is to show how high this implicit tax rate is as compared to the explicit rates of the specific income taxes imposed on the nonagricultural incomes in Egypt.

The relevance of this implicit tax imposed on agriculture to the income distribution issue is twofold. First, if the tax is considered, not only as a tool to collect revenue to the government, but also as a means to improve income distribution among sectors and to establish justice among the different groups of population, which should be the case, then taxing agricultural income will be questionable if the share of agriculture in the national-income cake is small in relation to its population size. Second, taxing agricultural income implicitly this way may turn out to be regressive, thus worsening the relative position of the small farmers as compared to the rich farmers. In this case an explicit progressive tax on agricultural income will make the income distribution within the agricultural sector more equitable than what is prevailing under this disguised tax policy.

The chapter is divided into four sections besides the introduction,

*The author acknowledges the helpful comments and suggestions made by her colleagues in this project. Special debt is owed Professor Robin Barlow, Director, Center for Research on Economic Development, University of Michigan, for valuable comments.

which forms section I. In section II, a summary of the structure of the tax system in Egypt is presented to show the prevailing tax rates to which we shall compare the implicit tax rates involved in the price differential policy of the relevant crops.

However, not all the agricultural crops are subject to this implicit tax policy, since there is more than one type of agricultural pricing policy applied in Egypt. These different types of policy and their impact on farmers' incomes is discussed in section III. The estimation of the disguised tax of the major export crops, which are those subject to the highest implicit tax rates, is made in section IV. Finally, the implied impact of this disguised tax on the income distribution issue is discussd in section V.

## II. The Structure of the Direct Tax System in Egypt:[2]

The direct tax system in Egypt consists of specific taxes that are levied on different types of incomes and properties, and a general income tax that is imposed on the incomes subject to the specific income or property taxes. The incomes that are not subject to any of the specific taxes are not subject to the general income tax. In other words, according to the tax system in Egypt, income is either taxed twice or not at all.

One may differentiate between three groups of direct taxes in Egypt:

1. Specific Income Taxes: They consist of the tax on wages, salaries, pensions, and annuities; the tax on commercial and industrial profits; the tax on professional and noncommercial incomes; and the tax on agricultural profits from fruit orchards, poultry farms, and some other sources.
2. The Property Taxes: They consist of the tax on the agricultural lands; the tax on buildings; and the tax on interest, dividends, and other income from "movable" capital.
3. The General Income Tax: Only those incomes that are subject to specific taxes (income or property taxes) are subject also to the general income tax.

## III. The Pricing Policy of Agricultural Crops in Egypt

Most crops are marketed cooperatively.[3] They include cotton, rice, onions, sesame, beans, wheat, groundnuts, lentils, soya beans, sugarcane, barley, and potatoes.[4] However, not all of them are subject to the same pricing policy.

One may differentiate between three types of pricing policy applied to the agricultural crops in Egypt.[5]

The first type is the pricing policy of the crops that are compulsorily delivered, totally or partly, to the cooperatives at a relatively lower price. According to this policy, the government buys the compulsory delivery quota at a price lower than that prevailing on local and/or world markets. The remainder of the crop is left to the farmer. The compulsory delivery

TABLE 6.1.
*A Summary of the Tax Structure in Egypt*

| *Types of Tax* | *Exemption* | *The Tax Rate (percent)* |
|---|---|---|
| *Specific Income Taxes* | | |
| Tax on wages, salaries, pensions, and annuities | £E600 per person without dependents plus £E60 per dependent | Progressive tax rate: 4.5%–32.5% |
| Tax on commercial and industrial profits | £E600 per person | Flat tax rate: 37.2% below £E500 a year after the deduction of personal exemption; 39.7% above £E500 a year |
| Tax on professional and noncommercial income | £E600 per person | Progressive tax rate: 32%–43.5% |
| Tax on the returns from fruit orchards, specified plants, nurseries, poultry farms, and livestock-raising projects | Fruit orchards (3 feddans or less); the specified plants (1 feddan); desert land and land under reclamation (for 10 years) | Flat tax rate: 23.9% for 10 feddans & less; 47.6% above 10 feddans |
| *Property Taxes* | | |
| Tax on rent of agricultural land | Owners and holders of three feddans and less | Flat tax rate: 30.1% plus Gihad tax |
| Tax on rent of buildings (after subtracting 20% for expenses) | Buildings with an annual rental value of £E18 or less | Progressive tax rate: 19–51% |
| Tax on interest dividends and other income from "movable" capital | No exemptions | Flat rate: 40.55% |
| *General Income Tax* | | |
| A tax on all incomes that are subject to the specific income taxes and the property taxes | £E1,200 per person without dependents plus £E75 for each dependent, with a maximum of £E300 | Progressive rate: 8%–90% |

SOURCE:
B. Hansen and C. Marzouk, *Development and Economic Policy in the UAR* (Egypt), (Amsterdam: North Holland Publishing Company, 1965), pp. 156–262; J. K. Lotz, "Taxation in the United Arab Republic (Egypt," *IMF Staff Papers* 13, March 1966, pp. 121–153; "The Tax Guide," presented by Dr. ᶜAlī Lūtfī, minister of finance; an annex distributed with *al-Ahrām al-Iqtisādī,* March 15, 1979 (Arabic); *Official Gazette,* no. 29, July 20, 1978 (Arabic).

quota system includes cotton, rice, onions, groundnuts, wheat,[6] beans, lentils, and sesame. The quota that should be delivered to the coopeeratives ranges from a minimum of 27.6 percent for wheat to a maximum of 100 percent for cotton.

The second type of pricing policy applied is that the cooperatives buy the crop from the farmer at a price relatively close to the market price.

The third type of pricing policy is that the cooperatives buy the crop at the price agreed upon between the farmers and the producers that process it. This price is determined by means of a contract signed by the farmers and the manufacturers early in the agricultural season. The contract also determines the quantity and quality of the crop that will be delivered to the cooperatives. This pricing policy is applied mainly to sugarcane.

Cooperatives have been used as the main channel for marketing crops since the Nationalization Acts of 1961, which nationalized foreign trade and a large portion of wholesale trade in Egypt. Thus, the government had to take over the role of the private sector in the wholesale trade marketing of many of the inputs and outputs of the different sectors in the economy, including the agricultural sector. The cooperatives were, then, the best tool to use for marketing agricultural inputs and outputs. To use this tool effectively, membership in cooperatives, which was voluntary except for the Land Reform beneficiaries, became compulsory, since the cooperatives became the only channel open to farmers for agricultural inputs, outputs, and credits.

Having unified the agricultural marketing channel for most of agricultural inputs and outputs, the government then easily enforced the prices it wanted for these goods. Government interference in fixing the prices of agricultural outputs did not start, however, with the cooperative marketing of the crops. Its roots go as far back as World War I, when cotton regulations were applied.[7] But the increasing intervention of the government in the prices and quantities of agricultural products started during World War II.[8] During that war, the government fixed the price of wheat and the minimum area planted to it, to ensure enough supply to feed the Egyptian population and the Allied armies. It also manipulated cotton prices, to protect farmers, when those prices fell sharply during the war. The government, through the Egyptian Cotton Commission, bought cotton from farmers at prices higher than world prices and sold it when world prices recovered after the war. Cotton continued to be subject to government regulation in the postwar period because of its relative importance as the main cash crop and the main source of foreign exchange to the country.[9]

Looking at the three types of the pricing policy applied to the agricultural crops in Egypt, we can see that the first type—the pricing of crops subject to compulsory delivery quotas—squeezes the farmers' income in favor of the Treasury. The government makes profits by buying the crop from the farmers at low prices and reselling it in domestic and / or foreign markets at higher prices. These price differentials, which are especially high in the case of the export crops, should go to the farmers. Thus, one cannot say, as some do[10] that the two main goals of this policy are to ensure the increasing urban population with a sufficient quantity of agricultural products at stable prices, and to increase exports of the main agricultural export crops.

The increase in government revenue is another important goal. I believe that this third goal is the most important one motivating the pricing policy of the crops subject to the compulsory delivery quotas because neither the first nor the second goal explains satisfactorily the large price differentials kept by the government, especially with respect to the export crops. For example, regarding the first goal, since 1976 wheat has not been subject to the compulsory delivery system, although it is a basic food commodity. Regarding the second goal, sufficient quantities of the export crops could have been secured through other policies, as, for example, by giving price incentives to farmers to produce the required crops. Moreover, the crop-rotation system would ensure sufficient supply of the different crops.

The profits that the government realizes by means of the compulsory delivery quota system represent, in fact, a disguised tax that the farmers pay on their incomes.[11] The heaviness of the burden of this disguised tax on the farmers' income is what we intend to find out in the next section.

Concentrating on the impact of the pricing policy of the crops subject to the compulsory delivery quota system does not necessarily imply that the two other types of pricing are "fair" to the farmers. I believe that the latter may not be favorable to the farmers, but in a lesser degree as compared to the compulsory delivery quota system. This is because the monopolistic position of the government enables it to impose the price it wants, and this may not be the "fair" price to the farmers. Even for sugarcane, where the price is agreed upon by the farmers and the manufacturers by means of a contract, the existence of the crop-rotation system and the nonavailability of marketing channels other than the cooperatives leave the farmers with little choice except to cultivate sugarcane in the specified areas and to sell it to the manufacturers at some price. Thus, the price that they accept is probably not the best they could get if production and marketing conditions were different.

What about the subsidized prices of agricultural inputs? Do they compensate for the disguised taxation of agricultural outputs?[12] Direct subsidies are paid by the authorities on fertilizers, pesticides, gypsum, improved seeds, fodder, fuels, and many minor items.[13] The two main subsidized agricultural inputs are fertilizers and pesticides.[14] Fertilizers are used in the cultivation of almost all crops. The outcome of the fertilizer pricing policy was the following: in the 1960s,[15] no net subsidy was actually paid to the farmers; while in the 1970s the subsidy payment rose as shown in table 6.2. This is because in the 1960s, the deficit paid by the

*TABLE 6.2.*
*The Fertilizers Subsidy*
*(1971/1972–1975)*
*(£E millions)*

| | *1971/1972* | *Second half of 1972* | *1973* | *1974* | *1975* | *1976* | *1977* | *1978* |
|---|---|---|---|---|---|---|---|---|
| Subsidy | 0.579 | 0.5 | 1.5 | 50.0 | 78.6 | 39.8 | 24.0 | 33.4 |

SOURCE: Technical Secretariat of Chemical Industries' Sector and Ministry of Agriculture

Fertilizers Stabilization Fund for some types of fertilizers was offset by the surplus realized in dealing with other types.[16] The situation changed in the 1970s with the rise in the cost of production in general and in oil prices in particular after 1973. At the same time the government kept fertilizer retail prices almost constant. The outcome of these factors was a net deficit, which started in the early 1970s and increased significantly after 1973. This net deficit, paid by the Fertilizers Stabilization Fund, represents the subsidy paid by the government to the farmers.

Comparing this subsidy with the profits that the government has made in cotton, rice, and onions, for example,[17] we see that the subsidized pricing policy of the agricultural inputs[18] was much lower than the implicit taxation of the agricultural outputs. And if the main purpose of the implicit taxes[19] is to subsidize the agricultural inputs sold to them, one wonders why the government does not leave the prices of agricultural inputs and outputs to be determined by the market and save itself the trouble and the cost of designing and implementing these policies.

Finally, how are the prices of the agricultural crops determined in Egypt? They are determined by a ministerial committee under the Ministerial Council on the basis of the prices suggested by the Ministries of Agriculture and Supply. The Ministry of Agriculture sets the price of the crop on the basis of the costs of production and the crop mixture per feddan in one year, given the crop-rotation system prevailing in Egypt. Thus, the price of the crop is not set on the basis of its cost of production only, but is based on the prices of the alternative crops as well. However, regarding the food crops (like wheat, rice, lentils, beans *(fūl),* sesame), the Ministry of Supply established a quota for each of them and has the upper hand in determining the prices suggested to the committee. The Ministry of Supply determines the price of the crop on the basis of its cost of production only. Therefore, there is usually a difference between the prices suggested by the two ministries for the same crop. A compromise between the two prices must be reached, but more weight is given to the price suggestion of the Ministry of Supply with regard to the food agricultural crops.

## IV. The Disguised Tax Paid on the Incomes of the Major Export Crops*

Since we cannot estimate the disguised tax paid on all the crops subject to the compulsory delivery quota system because of the data problems involved, a choice should be made regarding which of these crops are worthy of consideration. The objective of the chapter is to show that some of the agricultural incomes are heavily taxed implicitly as compared to the nonagricultural incomes that are explicitly taxed. Since the burden of the tax is measured by the rate and not by the amount of the tax paid, the criterion that will be used to guide us in our choice is the relatively high rate of the disguised tax paid. In order words, we shall choose the crops that are subject to the highest disguised tax rate.

The disguised tax per unit of output is the price differential between the government buying price and the selling price in the domestic and/or foreign markets.[20] The rate of this tax will then be equal to the ratio between the amount of the disguised tax paid and the total return from the crop before paying the tax. This ratio depends on two things: the extent of the price differential and the size of the compulsory delivery quota. The larger the difference between the government buying price from the farmers and the selling price of the crop in domestic and/or foreign markets and the greater the compulsory delivery quota, the greater will be the amount of the disguised tax paid relative to the total return from the crop and, hence, the higher will be the rate of the disguised tax paid.

Since prices in world markets are much higher than the corresponding prices in the domestic markets in Egypt, it is to be expected that the largest price differentials exist in crops that are exported. One finds also that export crops are the ones with the largest compulsory delivery quota, with the exception of sesame.[21] The crops that are subject to the compulsory delivery quota and are exported are cotton, rice, onions, and groundnuts.[22] Thus, those crops, which are also the major export crops of Egypt, are the ones that are subject to relatively high rates of disguised tax and, consequently, are the ones that we shall be interested in.

How high are the rates of the disguised tax paid on these crops as compared to the rates of the specific income taxes levied explicitly on nonagricultural incomes? Before answering this question, it is important to show the similarity between what we are trying to do and previous work in the area of taxing agricultural output. Although the implicit taxation of agricultural output under the price differential policy in Egypt has been recognized by several authors, no serious attempt has been made to estimate the "rate" of this implicit tax. What has been done in this regard is to estimate the price differential between the government buying price of the crop and its selling price in the domestic or foreign markets.[23]

*I am indebted to Professor Robin Barlow for clarification regarding the method of calculating the disguised tax.

TABLE 6.3.

*The Rate of the Disguised Tax Paid on Cotton Income*
*(£E millions)*

| Year | Return on cotton sold to domestic mills 1 | Return on cotton exported 2 | Farmers' net income from cotton[1] 3 | The disguised tax paid by farmers on cotton 4 (= 1 + 2 − 3) | Rate of the disguised tax (%) 5 (= 4 ÷ (1 + 2)) | Government profit from the price differential to domestic mills[2] 6 | Government profit from the price differential in cotton export[2] 7 |
|---|---|---|---|---|---|---|---|
| 1964/1965 | 9.1 | 40.0 | 30.0 | 19.1 | 38.9 | 3.0 | 16.1 |
| 1965/1966 | 0.3 | 12.5 | −3.5 | 16.3 | 127.3 | 4.2 | 11.7 |
| 1966/1967 | 3.4 | 19.5 | 12.1 | 10.8 | 47.2 | 3.4 | 9.5 |
| 1967/1968 | 8.2 | 30.4 | 23.7 | 14.9 | 38.6 | 1.1 | 13.7 |
| 1968/1969 | 8.3 | 41.9 | 34.0 | 16.2 | 32.3 | −1.3 | 17.5 |
| 1969/1970 | 7.0 | 41.3 | 37.5 | 10.8 | 22.4 | −2.6 | 13.4 |
| 1970/1971 | 14.0 | 89.3 | 68.6 | 34.7 | 33.6 | −6.5 | 29.5 |
| 1971/1972 | 18.4 | 95.4 | 78.3 | 35.5 | 31.2 | −7.0 | 43.3 |
| 1972/1973 | 12.8 | 116.7 | 72.6 | 56.9 | 43.9 | −14.0 | 71.0 |
| 1973/1974 | 3.1 | 238.2 | 42.1 | 199.2 | 82.6 | −13.1 | 212.2 |
| 1974/1975 | 12.8 | 151.0 | 23.2 | 115.0 | 80.2 | −21.6 | 136.7 |
| 1975/1976 | 2.6 | 71.2 | 11.8 | 62.0 | 84.0 | −0.6 | 62.5 |
| 1976/1977 | 10.5 | 99.2 | 23.7 | 86.0 | 78.4 | 0.0 | 86.0 |
| 1977/1978 | 52.2 | 67.7 | 84.2 | 35.7 | 29.8 | 0.0 | 35.8 |

SOURCE: Calculated from table 6.A.1 in the chapter appendix.

NOTES:

1. This column includes the sum of the farmers' return from producing extra long, long, and medium staples cotton. Farmers' return for each staple is calculated from table 1 in the chapter appendix by subtracting the cost of production per metric kantar of cotton from the government buying price and multiplying the outcome by the total quantity of cotton produced (= quantity consumed domestically + quantity exported). N.B.: The negative sign indicates losses.

2. The price differential with respect to selling to domestic mills (or cotton export) means the difference between government buying price from the farmers and government selling price to domestic mills (or export prices). This is estimated for extra long, long, and medium staples cotton, and the price differential for each type is multiplied by the quantity consumed domestically (or quantity exported). N.B.: The negative sign indicates losses.

Calculating the price differential of the agricultural crops is different from what we are trying to do in this chapter. Although the price differential is an indicator of the implicit taxation of the crop, it does not show the real tax burden imposed on the farmer's income generated from the cultivation of the relevant crop. This tax burden, which is measured by the rate of the disguised tax paid, is a function not only of the price differential but also of the quota that is compulsorily delivered to the government (for crops subject to a compulsory delivery quota), the amount exported, and the cost of production, as shown from the calculations in tables 6.3–6.6.

## *Cotton*

Cotton crop was delivered exclusively to the cooperatives from 1964.[24] Table 6.3 shows the rate of the disguised tax paid on cotton income between 1964/1965 and 1977/1978.

It is clear from the table that until 1967/1968, a very small portion of the government profits, which it realized under the cotton price differentials policy, was attributed to reselling the cotton in the domestic market (to domestic mills). Between 1968/1969 and 1975/1976, the government incurred losses in this market. These losses, which were made in spite of the monopolistic position of the government in the cotton trade, might be explained by two factors: First, the government was concerned to determine the buying price of cotton at a reasonable level to guarantee a certain level of income to the farmers, and also to avoid the farmers' refusal to cultivate cotton.[25] Second, the government fixed the sale price of cotton to the domestic mills relatively low, sometimes lower than its buying price from the farmer, to guarantee that cotton textile reached the Egyptian consumer at a relatively low price. However, starting in 1975/1976 (with the exception of the long staple cotton in 1975/1976), the government set the cotton sale price to the domestic mills equal to its buying price from the farmers (see table I in the chapter appendix).

The government makes up for whatever losses it may have in the domestic market by the high profit it realizes in cotton export. The large difference between the government buying price and the export price of cotton has been always the major source of government profit before 1968/1969 and its only source afterward. There was a big jump in this profit in the 1970s, especially in 1972/1973–1976/1977, as compared to what it was in the second half of the 1960s. During 1964/1965–1969/1970, government profit from export ranged between a minimum of £E9.5 million in 1966/1967 to a maximum of £E17.5 million in 1968/1969. During the 1970s, however, the minimum government profit from cotton export was £E29.5 million in1970/1971 and was as high as £E212.2 million in 1973/1974. This was due to the big increase in the prices of cotton on the world market in the 1970s, especially after 1973.[26] This government profit was thus a tax collected in disguise from the cotton growers' income.

*TABLE 6.4.*

*The Disguised Tax Paid on Rice (£E millions)*

| *Year* | *Return on exported rice* 1 | *Hypothetical return on rice sold domestically at free market price*[1] 2 | *Farmers' net income from the compulsory quota* 3 | *Farmers' net income from the free retention share*[2] 4 | *Total farmers' net income* 5 (= 3 + 4) | *The disguised tax paid by the farmers on rice* 6 (= 1 + 2 − 5) | *The rate of the disguised tax* 7 (= 6 ÷ (1 + 2)) | *Government profit from rice export* 8 |
|---|---|---|---|---|---|---|---|---|
| 1968 | 29.9 | 63.1 | 17.4 | 26.6 | 44.0 | 49.0 | 52.7 | 17.1 |
| 1969 | 36.5 | 54.5 | 16.0 | 25.6 | 41.6 | 49.4 | 54.3 | 18.8 |
| 1970 | 20.0 | 56.0 | 13.9 | 24.9 | 38.8 | 37.2 | 48.9 | 5.6 |
| 1971 | 13.1 | 52.9 | 9.2 | 22.0 | 31.2 | 34.8 | 52.7 | 3.4 |
| 1972 | 11.9 | 54.8 | 10.1 | 22.2 | 32.3 | 34.4 | 51.6 | 3.2 |
| 1973 | 18.2 | 55.0 | 11.0 | 21.1 | 32.1 | 41.1 | 56.1 | 12.3 |
| 1974 | 36.1 | 63.8 | 15.2 | 23.1 | 38.3 | 61.6 | 61.7 | 32.6 |
| 1975 | 21.0 | 75.0 | 19.7 | 26.6 | 46.3 | 49.7 | 64.8 | 18.3 |
| 1976 | 21.7 | 62.6 | 14.7 | 23.2 | 37.9 | 46.4 | 55.0 | 16.8 |
| 1977 | 12.7 | 71.6 | 21.6 | 26.6 | 48.2 | 36.1 | 42.8 | 7.0 |
| 1978 | 12.6 | 92.0 | 33.4 | 33.2 | 66.6 | 38.0 | 36.3 | 7.7 |

SOURCES: Calculated from table 6.A.2 in the chapter appendix.

NOTES:

1. This is not the actual net value (price less cost) of rice sold on the domestic market. It is, rather, calculated as if all such rice that is not exported had been sold at free market price.

2. The "free retention share" of rice means the remainder of the crop after the delivery of the compulsory quota (i.e., total production of rice minus the quantity delivered compulsory to the government).

Looking at the rate of this disguised tax as shown in table 6.3, one finds that, during the second half of the 1960s, and with the exception of 1965/1966,[27] the tax fluctuated between a minimum rate of 22.4 percent of the cotton income in 1969/1970 and a maximum of 47.2 percent in 1966/1967. During the 1970s the tax rate increased significantly. Over the period of 1973/1974–1976/1977, specifically, the disguised tax rate did not fall below 78.4 percent, and was reaching a maximum level of 84.0 percent. This was mainly due to the relatively high level of cotton export prices in those years. In 1977/1978, however, the rate dropped sharply—to 29.8 percent—because of the significant increase in the farmers' return share in cotton income. This relatively big increase in the farmers' net income from cotton is attributed to the increase in government buying price accompanied by a fall in the average cost of production of cotton (see table 6.A.1 in the chapter appendix).

### *Rice*

Rice was delivered on a fixed quota basis to the cooperatives in the second half of the 1960s. About 66 percent of the total crop is delivered compulsorily to the cooperatives at a price fixed by the government.[28] Those who fail to provide the predetermined compulsory quota have to pay a large fine.[29] The disguised tax paid on rice under the price differential policy is shown in table 6.4

It is clear from table 6.4 that, until 1977, the return to farmers from the 34 percent of rice production—their free retention share—was significantly greater than their return on the 66 percent of production delivered compulsorily to the government. During 1970–1973 in particular, the farmers' return on the free retention share was almost double, or more than the farmers' return on the compulsory quota.[30] In 1977, however, the situation improved relatively; the farmers' return on the free retention share was close to their return from the compulsorily delivered quota, and in 1978 the latter exceeded the former.

Comparing government profit from rice trade with farmers' return from rice cultivation, one finds that, during the whole period 1968–1978, government profit per ton of rice exported was greater than the farmers' return per ton of the compulsory delivery quota. However, the difference between the two returns was small until 1973, when the world prices started to jump. In 1973 and after, the export price of rice increased greatly, while this was not accompanied by a matching increase in the government buying price. The outcome was that the government profit per ton of exported rice jumped from £E7.8 in 1972 to £E47.1 in 1973, and to £E58.1 in 1978, while the farmers' return per ton of the compulsorily delivered rice increased from £E6.1 in 1972 to only £E7.3 in 1973 and reached £21.6 only in 1978.

TABLE 6.5.

*The Disguised Tax Paid on Onions (£E millions)*

| Year | *Return on exported onions* 1 | *Hypothetical return on onions sold domestically at market price*[1] 2 | *Farmers' net income from the compulsory quota* 3 | *Farmers' net income from the free retention share*[2] 4 | *Total farmers' net income* 5 (= 3 + 4) | *The disguised tax paid by the farmers on onions* 6 (= 1 + 2 − 5) | *The rate of the disguised tax* 7 (= 6 ÷ (1 + 2)) | *Government profit from the price differential in onion export*[3] 8 |
|---|---|---|---|---|---|---|---|---|
| 1968 | 3.4 | 2.3 | 0.2 | 1.2 | 1.4 | 4.3 | 75.4 | 3.3 |
| 1969 | 5.0 | 2.1 | −0.2 | 1.2 | 1.0 | 6.1 | 86.0 | 5.1 |
| 1970 | 4.5 | 2.5 | 0.4 | 1.4 | 1.8 | 5.2 | 74.3 | 4.3 |
| 1971 | 3.5 | 3.7 | 1.4 | 1.9 | 3.3 | 3.9 | 54.2 | 3.1 |
| 1972 | 3.5 | 6.7 | 0.9 | 3.6 | 4.5 | 5.7 | 55.9 | 3.1 |
| 1973 | 8.3 | 8.9 | 2.6 | 4.6 | 7.2 | 10.0 | 58.1 | 7.5 |
| 1974 | 6.4 | 10.8 | 3.5 | 5.4 | 8.9 | 8.3 | 48.3 | 5.6 |
| 1975 | 5.8 | 13.4 | 2.6 | 6.5 | 9.1 | 10.1 | 52.6 | 5.2 |
| 1976 | 6.5 | 13.7 | 2.5 | 6.6 | 9.1 | 11.1 | 55.0 | 6.1 |
| 1977 | 5.1 | 8.1 | 2.2 | 3.9 | 6.1 | 7.1 | 53.8 | 4.7 |
| 1978 | 3.6 | 11.0 | 2.5 | 5.3 | 7.8 | 6.8 | 46.6 | 3.2 |

SOURCE: Calculated from table 6.A.3 in the chapter appendix.

NOTES:

1. This is not the actual net value (price less cost) of onions sold on the domestic market. It is, rather, a calculation as if all the onions that are not exported were sold at the free market price.

2. The "free retention share" of onions means the remainder of the crop after the delivery of the compulsory delivery quota (i.e., total production of onions minus the quantity delivered compulsorily to the government).

3. Government net profit from onion export is lower than the government profit from the price differential between government buying price from the farmers and the onion export price, by an amount equal to the cost of transportation and the preparation of onions for export.

The price differentials between the government buying price of rice and the free market price and between the former and the export price represent the disguised tax paid by the farmer on each ton of rice sold on the domestic and foreign markets, respectively. The total amount of this tax ranged from a minimum of £E34.4 million in 1972 to a maximum of £E61.6 million in 1974, as shown in table 6.4.

Looking at the rate of this disguised tax, one finds that it did not go below 48.9 percent until 1977. This minimum rate is higher than the maximum rates of the specific taxes imposed on nonagricultural incomes (see table 6.1). In 1977 and 1978, although there was a relative decrease in the rate of the disguised tax on rice paid by the farmers, the rate was still high (42.8 percent and 36.3 percent in 1977 and 1978) as compared to the rates of the specific income taxes.

### *Onions*

The compulsory delivery quota for onions is about 57 percent of the crop.[31] Those who fail to deliver this quota are fined heavily.[32] Table 6.5 shows the disguised tax paid on onions under the price differential policy.

The price differential between the government buying price and export price is much higher than the price differential between the buying price and the domestic market price. This very high price differential in onion export[33] makes government profit in this respect in some years higher than the total farmers' return from onion cultivation (that is, their return on the compulsory delivery quota and the free retention share) as is clear from table 6.5. This made the rate of the disguised tax paid on onions income significantly high in some of the years 1968–78.

Comparing government profit realized from the onion price differential policy with the profits realized in the case of rice and cotton, one should differentiate between the absolute size of the profit and its ratio to the total return from the crop. Regarding the size of the profit, the government realized a smaller profit on onions than on rice and cotton. This means that the disguised tax paid by farmers on onions is relatively small as compared to the two other crops. It ranged from a minimum of £E3.9 million to a maximum of £E11.1 million during the period 1968–1978 as compared to a range of £E34.4 million to £E61.6 million for rice and £E10.8 million to £E199.2 million for cotton. But the tax rate on the return from onions is relatively high as compared to the tax rate on rice in most of the comparative years during 1968–1978, and also higher than the tax rate on cotton in the period before 1973/1974. The minimum level of the disguised tax rate on onions was 46.6 percent, and it soared to as high as 86 percent in 1969.

### *Groundnuts*

Groundnuts were introduced to the compulsory delivery system in 1970. The compulsory delivery quota is about 87 percent of the crop.[34]

*TABLE 6.6.*

*The Disguised Tax Paid on Groundnuts (£E millions)*

| *Year* | *Return on exported groundnuts* | *Hypothetical return on groundnuts sold domestically at free market price*[1] | *Farmers' net income from the compulsory-delivery quota* | *Farmers' net income from the free retention share*[2] | *Total farmers' net income* | *The disguised tax paid by the farmers on groundnuts* | *The rate of the disguised tax* | *Government profit from the price differential in groundnuts export*[3] |
|---|---|---|---|---|---|---|---|---|
| | *1* | 2 | 3 | 4 | 5 (= 3 + 4) | 6 (= 1 + 2 − 5) | 7 (= 6 ÷ (1 + 2)) | 8 |
| 1970 | 1.46 | 1.20 | 1.24 | 0.28 | 1.52 | 1.14 | 42.9 | 0.83 |
| 1971 | 1.61 | 0.92 | 1.13 | 0.26 | 1.39 | 1.14 | 45.1 | 0.91 |
| 1972 | 1.09 | 1.10 | 0.94 | 0.22 | 1.16 | 1.03 | 47.0 | 0.70 |
| 1973 | 1.04 | 0.98 | 0.79 | 0.20 | 0.99 | 1.03 | 51.0 | 0.73 |
| 1974 | 1.96 | 0.99 | 1.07 | 0.20 | 1.27 | 1.68 | 56.9 | 1.49 |
| 1975 | 2.01 | 1.73 | 1.82 | 0.35 | 2.17 | 1.57 | 42.0 | 1.26 |
| 1976 | 1.20 | 1.37 | 2.06 | 0.26 | 2.32 | 0.25 | 9.7 | 0.45 |
| 1977 | 2.15 | 1.28 | 2.85 | 0.32 | 3.17 | 0.26 | 7.6 | 0.59 |
| 1978 | 2.17 | 1.58 | 2.60 | 0.43 | 3.03 | 0.72 | 19.2 | 0.59 |

NOTES:

1. This is not the actual net value (price less cost) of groundnuts sold in the domestic market. It is, rather, calculated as if all the groundnuts that are not exported were sold at the free market price.

2. The "free retention share" of groundnuts means the remainder of the crop after the delivery of the compulsory quota (total production of groundnuts minus the quantity delivered compulsorily to the government).

3. Government net profit from groundnuts export is lower than the government profit from the price differential between government buying price from the farmers and the export price, by an amount equal to the cost of transportation and the preparation of groundnuts for export.

The price differentials between government buying price and export price, and between the former and the price in the domestic market, are relatively smaller for groundnuts than for rice and onions in most years. This has been reflected in the relatively low rate of disguised tax paid on groundnuts income, as shown in table 6.6, as compared to the other two crops. Comparing it with cotton, one finds that its rate was higher than the cotton rate until 1973/1974, when the disguised tax rate on cotton soared really high. Since 1976, the disguised tax rate on groundnuts has undergone a sharp drop. During 1976–1978, it was very low compared to previous years, and also compared to the rate of cotton, rice, and onions in comparable years. The increase in the farmers' return share in the groundnuts income in 1976 and after, in spite of the increase in the cost of production of groundnuts, was due mainly to the significant increase in the government buying price, which has compensated for and exceeded the cost increase (see table 6.A.4 in the chapter appendix).

However, it is worth noting that, among the four export crops that are subject to the compulsory delivery quota system, groundnuts is the least important, judging by its total production and the quantity exported relative to the other crops: cotton, rice, and onions. The relevant tables[35] reveal that, while the production of cotton and rice are in the million-tons range, and that of onions fluctuates around a half-million tons and reached seven hundred thousand tons in some years, the production of groundnuts is below forty thousand tons. The quantity of groundnuts exported is also relatively small as compared to the other three crops.

Comparing the rates of the disguised tax paid on the returns of cotton, rice, onions, and groundnuts with the rates of the explicit specific tax paid on nonagricultural incomes,[36] one finds that the minimum level of the disguised tax rates on rice before 1977 (48.9 percent) and on onions during the whole period (46.6 percent) was higher than the maximum rate of the specific taxes on nonagricultural incomes (43.5 percent). The minimum level that the tax rate on rice reached was 36.3 percent in 1978. In the case of groundnuts, the minimum rate of the disguised tax paid until 1976 was pretty close (42.0 percent) to the maximum rate of the specific tax on nonagricultural incomes. Starting in 1976, the situation improved. The disguised tax rate was 9.7 percent, 7.6 percent, and 19.2 percent in 1976, 1977, and 1978. In the case of cotton, in six of the fourteen years shown in table 6.3, the disguised tax rate was below the maximum level of the specific tax rate on nonagricultural income; the lowest level of the cotton tax rate during these six years was 22.4 percent. In the rest of the period of 1964/1965–1977/1978, it was above 43.5 percent. However, paying the 22.4 percent rate on cotton income as it was in 1969/1970 should be considered relatively high as compared to the explicit rates of the specific income taxes. This is because the specific income taxes are subject to personal exemption of £E600 (and £E660 with dependents), which does not apply to the disguised tax implied in the price differential policy of the agricultural crops.

The nonprivileged position of agricultural income becomes more obvious if we compare the maximum level that the disguised tax rate has reached for cotton, rice, onions, and groundnuts with the maximum level of the explicit rates on the specific incomes. The maximum rate is 43.5 percent in the case of the professional and noncommercial incomes as compared to a rate that has reached 86 percent for onions, 84 percent in the case of cotton, 64.2 percent for rice, and 56.9 percent for groundnuts. If we add to that the fact that most of the specific income taxes on nonagricultural incomes are progressive, and all of them are subject to personal exemptions of £E600 a year (without dependents), one can see clearly how heavy the relative burden of this disguised tax is as compared to the specific income taxes.

The burden of this disguised tax on farmers' incomes in general can be seen more clearly if we look at the area planted in the two export crops: cotton and rice.[37] These two summer crops cover about 50 percent of the total summer crops area.[38] Given the high price differentials and the large compulsory delivery quotas of cotton (100 percent) and rice (67 percent), a relatively high tax rate is paid implicitly on a major part of the farmers' income generated from summer crops.[39]

## V. Income Distribution and the Implied Tax of the Pricing Policy of the Agricultural Crops

A tax is a tool that is supposed to be used not only to collect governmental revenue but also to establish social justice by improving income distribution among sectors and among the population within each sector. In this section I try to sketch out broadly the impact of the disguised tax implied in the pricing policy of the crops subject to the compulsory delivery quota on the distribution of income among the sectors as well as within the agricultural sector in Egypt.

Looking at the income distributional issue at the sectoral level, one can see that taxing agriculture, explicitly or implicitly, will improve the income distribution among sectors if personal incomes in this sector are, generally, higher than the incomes in the other sectors in the economy. But with the nonavailability of income distribution data in Egypt, this comparison between the personal incomes level in the different sectors is not feasible. An alternative way to do it is to compare the average income in the agricultural sector (income per capita of farmers) with the average income in the rest of the economy (income per capita in the nonagricultural sectors) to find out whether agriculture is relatively better off than the other sectors and, hence, its taxation is justifiable, or worse off than the others, in which case its taxation will be questionable.

Comparing income per capita of farmers in the rural sector with income

*TABLE 6.7.*
*The Income per Capita of Farmers and the Urban Dwellers in Egypt*

| *Year* | *Income per capita in urban sector (£E)* *1* | *Income per capita of farmers (£E)* *2* | *The ratio of the income per capita of farmers to income per capita in the urban sector (%)* *3* *(= 2 ÷ 1)* |
|---|---|---|---|
| 1953 | 59.1 | 22.6 | 38.2 |
| 1960 | 77.8 | 32.1 | 41.3 |
| 1965 | 99.4 | 43.1 | 43.4 |
| 1970 | 109.4 | 51.4 | 47.0 |
| 1975 | 166.4 | 89.7 | 53.8 |
| 1978 | 258.2 | 104.6 | 40.5 |

SOURCE: K. Korayem, "The Rural-Urban Income Gap in Egypt and the Biasedness of Agricultural Pricing Policy against Farmers' Income," unpublished paper.

per capita in the urban sector, which includes all nonagricultural sectors. one finds from table 6.7 that the existing sectoral gap is quite large. Farmers' income per capita is less than half the average income of the urban dwellers in most years. Consequently, the pricing policy of the agricultural crops, with its implied tax involved, cannot be justified on the basis of improving the sectoral income distribution within the country.

We now look at the impact of the disguised tax of the pricing policy on income distribution within the agricultural sector. The tax affects the income distribution within the agricultural sector positively if it improves the relative position of the poor as compared to the rich, as in the case of a progressive tax; and affects it negatively if it worsens the relative position of the poor as compared to the rich, as is the case with a regressive tax. Thus, to examine the impact of the implied tax of the pricing policy on the income distribution within the agricultural sector, we shall try to answer the two following questions: First, who are the payers of this disguised tax? Second, how progressive or regressive is this disguised tax?

To answer the first question, let us look at table 6.8, which shows the percentage distribution of the area and the number of cultivators of crops subject to the compulsory delivery quota system, as classified by size of holdings. Although the most recent data available on the percentage distribution of the area and the cultivators of the crops by size of holdings are for 1961, I believe that the change that may have occurred is in favor of the large farmers. In other words, it is believed that fewer of the traditional crops, including the compulsorily delivered ones, will be cultivated

*TABLE 6.8.*

*The Percentage Distribution of the Areas Cultivated by the Compulsory Delivery Crops and the Number of Cultivators by Size of Holding*

| | *5 < feddans* | | *5–10 feddans* | | *10–50 feddans* | | *50 > feddans* | | *Total* | |
|---|---|---|---|---|---|---|---|---|---|---|
| *Crop* | *Cultivators* | *Area* | *Cultivators* | *Area* | *Cultivators* | *Area* | *Cultivators* | *Area* | *Cultivators* | *Area* |
| Wheat | 82.1 | 46.4 | 11.7 | 18.5 | 5.5 | 20.5 | 0.7 | 14.6 | 100 | 100 |
| Beans (fūl) | 62.3 | 28.7 | 22.3 | 20.2 | 13.7 | 29.8 | 1.7 | 20.3 | 100 | 100 |
| Winter onions | 68.4 | 33.8 | 17.4 | 19.2 | 12.1 | 30.4 | 2.1 | 16.6 | 100 | 100 |
| Lentils | 62.7 | 26.4 | 19.8 | 19.6 | 15.7 | 38.7 | 1.8 | 15.3 | 100 | 100 |
| Cotton | 80.2 | 38.0 | 12.9 | 18.7 | 6.1 | 24.4 | 0.8 | 18.9 | 100 | 100 |
| Rice | 62.7 | 25.7 | 24.1 | 22.3 | 11.4 | 27.5 | 1.8 | 24.5 | 100 | 100 |
| Sesame | 62.9 | 29.0 | 20.2 | 20.3 | 14.8 | 31.4 | 2.1 | 19.3 | 100 | 100 |
| Groundnuts | 67.5 | 29.6 | 17.8 | 17.2 | 12.3 | 27.3 | 2.4 | 25.9 | 100 | 100 |

SOURCE: Calculated from the Agricultural Census, 1961, table 26, as included by Ahmed Ibrahim in chapter 7.

by the large farmers. Given the crop-rotation system applied, the large farmers have more room to choose the crop composition in their holdings, which enables them to choose the crop mix with relatively high returns (fruits and vegetables).[40]

It is clear from table 6.8 that a good portion of the area cultivated by the compulsorily delivered crops falls within the small size holdings (less than five feddans). This ranged between a minimum of 25.7 percent of the crop area for rice, and a maximum of 46.4 percent of the crop for wheat. This means that the small farmers with their limited income pay the same "flat rate" disguised tax as the big farmers. This certainly does not narrow the income gap between the small and the big farmers. On the contrary, it worsens the relative position of the former since it takes from them the same tax rate as from the big farmers although their incomes are much lower, judging, not only by the size of the agricultural land they hold, but also by the composition of the crops they cultivate.[41]

Looking at the percentage distribution of the cultivators of the compulsorily delivered crops by size of holdings, we see from table 6.8 that those who cultivate the relevant crops are holders of less than five feddans, that is, small farmers. They represent 62–68 percent of the cultivators of beans, onions, lentils, rice, sesame, and groundnuts; and about 80 percent of the cultivators of wheat and cotton.

Looking more specifically at the cultivators of the crops that are heavily taxed (the export crops—cotton, rice, onions, and groundnuts), one finds that the holders of less than five feddans represent 80 percent of the cotton cultivators, 63 percent of the rice cultivators, 68 percent of the onion cultivators, and 67 percent of the groundnuts cultivators. This means that most of the cultivators of the crops that are subject to high disguised tax rates are small farmers.

Regarding the second question raised about the progressivity or regressivity of the disguised tax implied in the pricing policy, it is clear that it is a regressive tax. One may differentiate between two main reasons in this regard:

1. The flat rate of the tax. Large and small incomes are subject to the same disguised tax rate.
2. No personal exemption is allowed as in the case of the explicit specific taxes on nonagricultural incomes.

To summarize, the impact of the disguised tax involved in the pricing policy of the agricultural crops on income distribution with respect to the agricultural sector *vis-à-vis* the other sectors, and within the agricultural sector itself, is not a positive one. On the sectoral level, taxing agriculture widens the income gap among sectors, since the average income in agriculture is already much lower than the average income in other sectors. Also, within the agricultural sector, its distributional impact is negative.

The question that would be interesting to raise, then, is why does the government not eliminate the price differential policy of the agricultural crops and impose instead an explicit progressive tax on farmers' income? This would have a positive impact on income distribution within the agricultural sector since the income of the small farmers is probably below the personal exemption level (£E600 per person without dependents) and different rates would be applied to different sizes of income, which would improve the relative position of the small farmers as compared to the big farmers. However, this substitution between the disguised and explicit tax would not probably be welcomed by the government.

First, the government, through the price differential policy of the agricultural crops, takes a good portion of the farmers' income without running political risk. The same amount of revenue cannot be collected by the government from the farmers through an explicit progressive income tax, since this implies—given the personal exemption allowances, the progressive rate schedule, and the possibility of tax evasion—levying tax rates higher than the disguised tax rates already prevailing, which is not politically feasible. Moreover, it is doubtful that even the existing disguised tax rates can be levied explicitly by the government without encountering political difficulties. In most cases, these tax rates are too high to be announced openly.

Second, the administrative cost of collecting government revenue under the price differential policy is lower than for the explicit income tax. It is more difficult to know the size of the incomes subject to the tax than to know the crops cultivated by the farmers, given the compulsory application of the crops rotation system in Egypt. This makes the possibility of tax evasion in the disguised tax case a minimum as compared to the case of an explicit income tax.

Third, the prices of the agricultural crops are determined by a ministerial decree, which gives the government greater latitude in changing these prices and, hence, in changing the revenue collected from farmers. This cannot happen in the case of the explicit tax, which is issued by a law and, hence, cannot be changed without changing the law, which is more difficult to do politically.

In short, it is easier and more beneficial, politically and economically, to the government to tax farmers' income disguisedly by the price differential policy of the agricultural crops than to tax this income explicitly by a specific progressive income tax.

In concluding, a word of warning should be given to eliminate any misunderstanding of the situation of the Egyptian economy. The negative impact of the pricing policy of agricultural outputs on the farmers does not mean, though, that the relative position of the farmers in the economy has been deteriorating. This is just one policy among others that have been applied and that have their different impacts—positive as well as negative—on farmers' income and their standard of living in general. For example, some government policies have positive impacts on farmers' income, especially small farmers, such as the Land Reform Acts and the minimum wage policy for agricultural labor. The increase in government services to the rural population during the last twenty-five years is also one of the important policies that have had a positive impact on the standard of living of the rural population. This can be seen clearly, for example, in the increase in the number of health units in the rural areas, in the increase in the number of schools in these areas, and in the electrification of the villages. In other words, one can judge neither the role of the government *vis-à-vis* the farmers, nor the change in the relative position of the farmers in the economy on the basis of this agricultural pricing policy of outputs alone. The impact of this policy is just one piece of the picture; all the pieces should be put together. But this is beyond the scope of this chapter.

## Appendix

*TABLE 6.A.1.*

*Average Cost of Production, Prices, and Quantities of Cotton Produced (Extra Long Staple Cotton)*

| *Year* | *Average cost of production per metric kantar (£E)* 1 | *Average buying price per metric kantar (£E)* 2 | *Average selling price to domestic mills per metric kantar (£E)* 3 | *Average export prices per metric kantar (£E)* 4 | *Quantity consumed domestically (000 metric kantar)* 5 | *Quantity exported (000 metric kantar)* 6 |
|---|---|---|---|---|---|---|
| 1964/1965 | 12.8 | 17.3 | 19.9 | 20.7 | 406 | 4,070 |
| 1965/1966 | 16.2 | 17.3 | 19.9 | 19.7 | 843 | 4,006 |
| 1966/1967 | 14.8 | 17.3 | 19.9 | 19.7 | 454 | 3,375 |
| 1967/1968 | 13.4 | 17.9 | 19.9 | 21.9 | 455 | 2,833 |
| 1968/1969 | 12.7 | 19.7 | 19.9 | 24.8 | 469 | 2,728 |
| 1969/1970 | 13.8 | 21.0 | 19.9 | 24.3 | 516 | 3,281 |
| 1970/1971 | 13.5 | 24.1 | 20.9 | 29.9 | 592 | 3,669 |
| 1971/1972 | 12.5 | 24.1 | 20.9 | 31.8 | 557 | 3,473 |
| 1972/1973 | 14.1 | 25.2 | 20.9 | 39.4 | 692 | 3,003 |
| 1973/1974 | 16.5 | 24.5 | 20.6 | 65.4 | 708 | 2,805 |
| 1974/1975 | 20.2 | 26.3 | 20.3 | 60.6 | 725 | 2,409 |
| 1975/1976 | 22.2 | 27.2 | 27.2 | 51.1 | 683 | 1,995 |
| 1976/1977 | 27.3 | 33.7 | 33.7 | 67.1 | 691 | 1,791 |
| 1977/1978 | 23.7 | 37.5 | 37.5 | 51.5 | 842 | 1,797 |

*TABLE 6.A.1. continued*

*Average Cost of Production, Prices and Quantities of Cotton Produced (Long Staple Cotton)*

| *Year* | *Average buying price per metric kantar (£E)* 7 | *Average selling price to domestic mills per metric kantar (£E)* 8 | *Average export price per metric kantar (£E)* 9 | *Quantity consumed domestically (000 metric kantar)* 10 | *Quantity exported (000 metric kantar)* 11 |
|---|---|---|---|---|---|
| 1964/1965 | 14.9 | 16.0 | 15.7 | 126 | 2,309 |
| 1965/1966 | 14.9 | 16.0 | 14.8 | 127 | 2,442 |
| 1966/1967 | 14.9 | 16.0 | 14.6 | 154 | 1,831 |
| 1967/1968 | 15.1 | 14.7 | 15.5 | 239 | 1,924 |
| 1968/1969 | 15.1 | 14.7 | 16.4 | 369 | 1,783 |
| 1969/1970 | 15.1 | 14.7 | 15.8 | 601 | 2,968 |
| 1970/1971 | 17.2 | 17.4 | 21.1 | 932 | 2,119 |
| 1971/1972 | 17.2 | 17.4 | 24.7 | 1,004 | 2,078 |
| 1972/1973 | 17.9 | 17.4 | 28.2 | 890 | 2,754 |
| 1973/1974 | 17.9 | 17.4 | 58.6 | 1,250 | 2,352 |
| 1974/1975 | 19.9 | 17.4 | 51.3 | 1,251 | 1,689 |
| 1975/1976 | 20.6 | 20.3 | 37.1 | 1,752 | 854 |
| 1976/1977 | 28.7 | 28.7 | 54.8 | 2,038 | 782 |
| 1977/1978 | 31.7 | 31.7 | 43.8 | 3,031 | 714 |

TABLE 6.A.1. *continued*

*Average Cost of Production, Prices and Quantities of Cotton Produced (Medium Staple Cotton)*

| *Year* | *Average buying price per metric kantar (£E)* 12 | *Average selling price to domestic mills per metric kantar (£E)* 13 | *Average export price per metric kantar (£E)* 14 | *Quantity consumed domestically (000 metric kantar)* 15 | *Quantity exported (000 metric kantar)* 16 |
|---|---|---|---|---|---|
| 1964/1965 | 14.4 | 15.1 | 15.3 | 2,528 | 465 |
| 1965/1966 | 14.4 | 15.1 | 20.2 | 2,653 | 400 |
| 1966/1967 | 14.4 | 15.1 | 18.8 | 2,908 | 837 |
| 1967/1968 | 15.0 | 15.1 | 19.2 | 2,901 | 387 |
| 1968/1969 | 15.8 | 15.1 | 19.9 | 1,748 | 319 |
| 1969/1970 | 15.8 | 15.1 | 18.5 | 2,569 | 189 |
| 1970/1971 | 18.2 | 16.1 | 17.9 | 2,299 | 285 |
| 1971/1972 | 18.2 | 16.1 | 20.9 | 2,432 | 356 |
| 1972/1973 | 20.2 | 16.1 | 20.2 | 2,589 | 313 |
| 1973/1974 | 20.2 | 16.1 | 51.1 | 2,359 | 57 |
| 1974/1975 | 22.3 | 16.1 | 36.0 | 2,284 | 75 |
| 1975/1976 | 23.4 | 23.4 | 32.1 | 2,093 | 87 |
| 1976/1977 | 29.2 | 29.2 | 45.9 | 1,719 | 344 |
| 1977/1978 | 33.2 | 33.2 | 45.8 | 1,717 | 155 |

SOURCES:

Column 1 is taken from the Department of Agricultural Economy, Ministry of Agriculture. The average cost of production includes the rent of land.

Columns 2, 3, 4, 7, 8, 9, 12, 13, and 14 are taken from M. Abdel-Fadil, *Development, Income Distribution* pp. 94–95; the Technical Secretariat for Cotton Sector, and CAPMS, *Monthly Bulletin for Foreign Trade,* various issues. It is worth noting that in Abdel-Fadil's book, the price was in tallari. It has been converted into pounds as one tallari equals 0.2 pound. Also notice that one metric ton of cotton equals 20 metric kantar.

Columns 5, 6, 10, 11, 15, and 16 are taken from Central Agency for Public Mobilization and Statistics (CAPMS), *Statistical Indicators for the Arab Republic of Egypt, 1952–1972* (Arabic) 1973, pp. 94, 95; and National Bank of Egypt, *Economic Bulletin,* no. 1, 1978; and no. 1, 1979. It is worth noting that both issues are used simultaneously since some types of the extra long and the medium staple cotton are included in one, and not the other, issue. It is worth noting also that "other types of cotton" are included in the medium staple cotton. The classifications of cotton are as follows: extra long staple cotton includes Gīza 45, Gīza 59, Karnak, Minūfī, Gīza 68, and Gīza 70. Long

TABLE 6.A.2.

*Prices and Quantities of Rice Exported and Compulsorily Delivered to the Government*

| *Year* | Total production of rice in husk (000 ton) 1 | Quantity of exported bleached rice (000 ton) 2 | Average cost of rice production per ton in husk (£E)* 3 | Quantity of rice delivered compulsorily to the govern-ment (000 ton) 4 | Government buying price per ton of rice in husk (£E) 5 | Farmers' return per ton of the compulsorily delivered rice (£E) 6 ( = 5 − 3) | Farmers' return per ton of the free retention share (£E) 7 | Price per ton of bleached rice exported (£E) 8 | Government profit per ton of exported bleached rice (£E) 9 |
|---|---|---|---|---|---|---|---|---|---|
| 1968 | 2,586 | 497.9 | 21.4 | 1,706.8 | 31.6 | 10.2 | 30.2 | 81.4 | 34.3 |
| 1969 | 2,556 | 707.0 | 21.5 | 1,687.0 | 31.0 | 9.5 | 29.5 | 73.1 | 26.6 |
| 1970 | 2,604 | 612.5 | 20.3 | 1,718.6 | 28.4 | 8.1 | 28.1 | 53.0 | 9.1 |
| 1971 | 2,534 | 459.2 | 20.5 | 1,672.4 | 26.0 | 5.5 | 25.5 | 49.0 | 7.5 |
| 1972 | 2,507 | 405.5 | 20.7 | 1,654.6 | 26.8 | 6.1 | 26.1 | 50.1 | 7.8 |
| 1973 | 2,274 | 260.6 | 20.8 | 1,500.8 | 28.1 | 7.3 | 27.3 | 90.7 | 47.1 |
| 1974 | 2,242 | 136.1 | 25.7 | 1,479.7 | 36.0 | 10.3 | 30.3 | 291.3 | 239.8 |
| 1975 | 2,423 | 99.9 | 27.9 | 1,599.2 | 40.2 | 12.3 | 32.3 | 238.6 | 182.9 |
| 1976 | 2,300 | 190.7 | 40.3 | 1,518.0 | 50.5 | 9.7 | 29.7 | 153.9 | 87.9 |
| 1977 | 2,272 | 191.3 | 41.8 | 1,500.0 | 56.2 | 14.4 | 34.4 | 108.2 | 36.5 |
| 1978 | 2,345 | 132.6 | 44.5 | 1,547.7 | 66.1 | 21.6 | 41.6 | 139.7 | 58.1 |

SOURCES: Column 1: National Bank of Egypt, *Economic Bulletin*, various issues. Columns 2 & 8: CAPMS, *Monthly Bulletin of Foreign Trade*, various issues. Column 3: Ministry of Agriculture. (Note that one ton of rice equals 1.058 dariba). Column 4: The compulsory delivery quota is about 66% of the total production of rice (1.5 daribas for each of the first five feddans and 1.75 daribas for each feddan over and above the first five). See Abdel-Fadil, *Development, Income Distribution* p. 89, and *al-Ahrām*, October 3, 1978. Column 5: Ministry of Agriculture Column 7: It is calculated by subtracting the average cost of production per ton of rice (column 3) from the price of the ton of rice sold freely in the domestic market. The price of the free retention share is about £E20 per ton higher than the government buying price (data obtained through personal contacts; also see Abdel-Fadil, p. 89). Column 9: is calculated as follows: price per ton of bleached rice exported (column 8) minus government buying price per ton of rice in husk (column 5) plus the bleaching cost and marketing cost of the exported rice. The bleaching cost of rice was about £E4.178 per ton in 1970/1971; and the cost of marketing the exported rice was £E11.320 per ton in 1968/1969, 1969/1970 and 1970/1971 (for both costs, see CAPMS, Price Planning Agency, *Commodity Reports; Rice, August 1972*, pp. 97, 105–107). These two costs add up to £E15.5 per ton.

NOTES: *Includes land rent.

*TABLE 6.A.3.*

*Prices and Quantities of Onions Exported and Compulsorily Delivered to the Government*

| *Year* | *Total production of onions (000 ton)* | *Quantity exported of fresh onions (000 ton)* | *Price per ton of onions exported (£E)* | *Average cost of production per ton of onions* | *Government price differential per ton of exported onions (£E)* | *Quantity delivered compulsory to the government (000 ton)* | *Government buying price per ton of onions (£E)* | *Farmers' return per ton of the compulsory delivered onions (£E)* | *Farmers' return per ton of onions sold freely in the domestic market (£E)* |
|---|---|---|---|---|---|---|---|---|---|
| | *1* | *2* | *3* | *4** | *5 (= 3 − 7)* | *6* | *7* | *8 (= 7 − 4)* | *9* |
| 1968 | 444 | 82.1 | 53.3 | 11.8 | 40.6 | 253.1 | 12.7 | 0.9 | 6.40 |
| 1969 | 567 | 137.3 | 48.1 | 11.8 | 36.8 | 323.2 | 11.3 | −0.5 | 5.00 |
| 1970 | 437 | 90.8 | 61.4 | 12.2 | 47.4 | 249.1 | 14.0 | 1.8 | 7.30 |
| 1971 | 571 | 87.6 | 51.6 | 11.6 | 35.8 | 325.5 | 15.8 | 4.2 | 7.66 |
| 1972 | 487 | 105.1 | 43.4 | 10.2 | 29.8 | 277.6 | 13.6 | 3.4 | 17.43 |
| 1973 | 529 | 89.4 | 103.8 | 10.9 | 84.3 | 301.5 | 19.5 | 8.6 | 20.15 |
| 1974 | 730 | 103.4 | 73.0 | 10.7 | 54.0 | 416.1 | 19.0 | 8.3 | 17.20 |
| 1975 | 572 | 70.0 | 99.4 | 16.7 | 74.8 | 326.0 | 24.6 | 7.9 | 26.60 |
| 1976 | 652 | 66.1 | 121.3 | 22.5 | 92.1 | 371.6 | 29.2 | 6.7 | 23.40 |
| 1977 | 723 | 80.9 | 89.7 | 26.1 | 58.3 | 412.1 | 31.4 | 5.9 | 12.60 |
| 1978 | 599 | 57.4 | 88.5 | 25.5 | 55.6 | 341.4 | 32.9 | 7.4 | 20.40 |

NOTES:

*Includes rent of agricultural land.

SOURCES:

Column 1: National Bank of Egypt, *Economic Bulletin*, various issues.

Column 2: CAPMS, *Monthly Bulletin of Foreign Trade*, several issues.

Column 3: Calculated from CAPMS, *Monthly Bulletin of Foreign Trade*, various issues.

Columns 4 and 7: Department of Agricultural Economic, Ministry of Agriculture. Note that one ton equals 22.26 kantar.

Column 6: The compulsory delivery quota is about 57 percent of the total production of onions. Abdel-Fadil, *Development, Income Distribution*, p. 89 and *al-Ahrām*, March 18, 1978.

Column 9: Calculated by subtracting the average cost of production of the ton of onions (column 4) from the price of the ton of onions sold freely in the domestic market. This price was in 1968 £E5.5 per ton higher, on the average, than the government buying price from the farmer (Abdel-Fadil, p. 89; compare columns 1 and 2 in table 5.5). For 1971–1978, the price per ton of onions sold freely in the domestic market is taken as equal to the wholesale trade price after deducting 10 percent to cover the cost of marketing and transportation and the profit margin for the wholesale trader. The average wholesale trade price per ton of onions was as follows (£E):

| Year | 1971 | 1972 | 1973 | 1974 | 1975 | 1976 | 1977 | 1978 |
|---|---|---|---|---|---|---|---|---|
| Price | 21.4[1] | 30.7[1] | 34.5[1] | 31.0[2] | 48.13[3] | 51.0[4] | 43.0[4] | 51.0[5] |

1. Average price of ten months
2. Average price of four months
3. Average price of eight months
4. Average price of twelve months
5. Average price of six months

SOURCE: CAPMS, *Quarterly Issue of the Prices of Food Commodities*, several issues.

TABLE 6.A.4.

*Prices and Quantities of Groundnuts Exported and Compulsorily Delivered to the Government*

| Year | Total production of groundnuts (000 ton) 1 | Quantity exported of groundnuts (000 ton) 2 | Price per ton of groundnuts exported (£E) 3 | Average cost of production per ton of groundnuts[a] 4 | Government buying price per ton of groundnuts[b] (£E) 5 | Government price differential per ton of exported groundnuts 6 (= 3 − 5) | Quantity delivered compulsory to the government (000 ton) 7 | Farmers' return per ton of the compulsorily delivered groundnuts (£E) 8 (= 5 − 4) | Farmers' return per ton of groundnuts sold freely in the domestic market (£E) 9 |
|---|---|---|---|---|---|---|---|---|---|
| 1970 | 33 | 16.85 | 136.3 | 49.5 | 87.1 | 49.2 | 33.1 | 37.6 | 57.8 |
| 1971 | 33 | 17.56 | 139.2 | 47.7 | 87.1 | 52.1 | 28.7 | 39.4 | 59.6 |
| 1972 | 30 | 10.89 | 151.7 | 51.2 | 87.1 | 64.6 | 26.1 | 35.9 | 57.3 |
| 1973 | 26 | 9.05 | 167.3 | 52.0 | 87.1 | 80.2 | 22.6 | 35.1 | 57.7 |
| 1974 | 25 | 9.45 | 269.0 | 61.9 | 111.2 | 157.8 | 21.8 | 49.3 | 63.5 |
| 1975 | 28 | 10.0 | 273.4 | 72.9 | 147.4 | 126.0 | 24.4 | 74.5 | 95.9 |
| 1976 | 28 | 8.9 | 232.6 | 97.3 | 181.6 | 51.0 | 24.4 | 84.3 | 71.5 |
| 1977 | 30 | 14.3 | 266.9 | 116.5 | 225.7 | 41.2 | 26.1 | 109.2 | 81.3 |
| 1978 | 25 | 13.2 | 295.4 | 131.2 | 250.6 | 44.8 | 21.8 | 119.4 | 134.1 |

SOURCES:

Column 1: CAPMS, *Statistical Yearbook,* several issues, and unpublished data from the Ministry of Agriculture.

Column 2: CAPMS, *Monthly Bulletin of Foreign Trade,* several issues.

Column 3: Calculated from CAPMS, *Monthly Bulletin of Foreign Trade,* several issues.

Column 4 Calculated by dividing the average cost of production per feddan of groundnuts (taken from the Ministry of Agriculture) by the average productivity per feddan taken from CAPMS, *Statistical Yearbook,* several issues.

Column 5: Unpublished data from the Development and Agricultural Crerdit Bank, Department of Grain Marketing. The data was in ardab. I have converted it into tons as follows: one ton equals 13.4 ardab.

Column 7: The compulsory delivery quota is about 87 percent of the total production of groundnuts. See Ahmed Ibrahim in chapter 7.

Column 9: Calculated by subtracting the average cost of production per ton of groundnuts (column 4) from the price per ton of groundnuts sold freely in the domestic market. This price is taken as equal to the wholesale trade price after deducting 10 percent to cover the cost of marketing and transportation and the profit margin for the wholesale trader. The yearly average wholesale trade price per ardab of groundnuts was as follows (£E):

| Year | 1970 | 1971 | 1972 | 1973 | 1974 | 1975 | 1976 | 1977 | 1978 |
|---|---|---|---|---|---|---|---|---|---|
| Price | 8.9[1] | 8.9[1] | 9.0[1] | 9.1[2] | 10.4[3] | 14.0[4] | 14.0[5] | 16.4[5] | 22.0[6] |

SOURCE: CAPMS, *Quarterly Issue of the Prices of Food Commodities,* several issues.

1. Average of nine months
2. Average of ten months
3. Average of four months
4. Average of eight months
5. Average of twelve months
6. Average of six months

NOTES:

[a]Includes the rent of the agricultural land

[b]This is the average price of the prices of the two types of groundnuts bought by the government.

## Notes

1. Only very recently, in 1978, a tax was imposed on the return on some specified agricultural projects.

2. For a detailed description of the tax structure in Egypt, see Reda El-Edel in chapter 5.

3. The "cooperative" marketing in Egypt means, nevertheless, "governmental" marketing.

4. CAPMS, *The Annual Issue of the Cooperative Activity in the Agricultural Sector in UAR* (in Arabic), several issues.

5. For the three types of pricing policy, see S. Nassar, "Planning of Agricultural Prices," *L'Égypte Contemporaine,* April 1972 (in Arabic), p. 89.

6. Wheat was subject to the compulsory delivery quota until 1976. See Ahmed Hassan in chapter 7.

7. B. Hansen and C. Marzouk, *Development and Economic Policy In the UAR (Egypt),* (Amsterdam: North Holland Publishing Company), 1965, pp. 95–96.

8. Ibid., p. iii.

9. For the grain and the cotton policies applied by the government during the war and postwar periods, see Hansen and Marzouk, pp. 95–112.

10. S. Nassar, "Structural Changes and Socialist Transformation in Agriculture of the U.A.R. (Egypt)," *L'Égypte Contemporaine,* July 1969, p. 125.

11. This does not necessarily mean that the farmers were better off before government intervention in marketing, which followed the Nationalization Acts of 1961. Before that date the export and the wholesale trade were undertaken by the private sector, and farmers' income was also squeezed by the private traders. For example, looking at the relative situation of the main cash crop, cotton, we see that the farmers' selling price of cotton was about half its price at the cotton exchange (el-Gritly, *The Structure of Modern Industry in Egypt* [Cairo, 1948], as cited in Hansen and Marzouk, *Development and Economic Policy,* footnote 22, p. 105).

However, two points should be made clear. First, although there was a relatively large difference between the farmers' selling price and the traders' selling price of the main cash crop (cotton), its cultivation was relatively profitable so that the farmers tried in most of the years in the 1950s to exceed the maximum limit that the government imposed on cotton cultivation (Hansen and Marzouk, p. 98). This situation changed in the middle 1960s, when the farmers were complaining about cotton cultivation and were trying to avoid it (*al-Ahrām al-Iqtisādī,* no. 317, November 1, 1968, pp. 14–15). This implies that, although farmers' income was squeezed all the time, the price offered to the farmers by the traders was relatively profitable, given the cost of production of cotton and the price of the other competitive crops. Second, the fact that part of the farmers' income was appropriated by the private traders is not an excuse for the price differential policy applied by the government, since the role of the government should not be just a substitute to the role of the private traders in squeezing farmers' income.

12. The indices of the terms of trade between agricultural output and manufacture agricultural inputs, and between agricultural output and inputs from the agricultural sector are calculated by Abdel-Fadil for the period 1960–1970 (M. Abdel Fadil, *op. cit.* 98–103). The former index has been constructed also by Samir Radwan for the period 1960–1975 for each of the three groups: poor farmers, rich farmers, and all the farmers (S. Radwan, *op. cit.*, 73–77). The terms of trade between agricultural outputs and manufactured inputs (fertilizers, pesticides, and fuel) constructed by the two authors show an improvement in the prices of agricultural outputs as compared to the prices of manufactured inputs. This does not mean though that the farmers became better off during the period. This is because the

three manufactured inputs represent just part of the cost of production of the farmers. What matters is the change in the value added received by the farmers, which is determined by the price of the output and the prices of all the inputs of production. In other words, the change in the value added received by the farmers cannot be inferred by the change in the terms of trade between the agricultural outputs and the manufactured inputs. Only if the index of the terms of trade is constructed so as to include the agricultural outputs and all agricultural inputs, can the change in this index be taken as an indicator of the direction of the change in the value added, and hence the income, of the farmers. But even such an index, if constructed, cannot be used to answer the question that we are raising regarding whether the subsidy given to agricultural inputs compensates for the disguised taxation of the agricultural outputs.

13. It should be mentioned that, besides these direct subsidies, water is supplied free of charge to the farmers.

14. The subsidies on the imported fertilizers and the pesticides for cotton represented 95.5 percent of the inputs subsidy in 1975. See World Bank Report, *Arab Republic of Egypt: Economic Management in a Period of Transition,* vol. 3, 1978, table 10.4, p. 34.

15. The government established the Fertilizers Stabilization Fund in 1960.

16. The main idea of the fund is that the government fixes the retail prices of fertilizers, taking into consideration the production cost of the locally produced types. If the producer's price of the fertilizer locally produced or imported (after adding the determined margins) is above the fixed retail price, the price differential will be paid to the suppliers from the fund. On the other hand, if the producer's price is lower than the retail price, the difference in prices will be going to the fund to subsidize fertilizers whenever the producer's price is relatively higher than the fixed price level (F. Hammam and M. G. Abu-el-Dahab, *Fertilizer Distribution in the Arab Republic of Egypt,* ed. Eric O. Degnia [Paris: OECD Development Center, 1974], referred to in Abdel-Fadil, *Development, Income Distribution and Social Change in Rural Egypt, 1952–1970* [Cambridge: Cambridge Univ. Press, 1975], p. 144).

17. See tables 6.3, 6.4, and 6.5.

18. The subsidy on imported fertilizers represented 68.7 percent of the total subsidy on agricultural inputs in 1975. See the data from the General Authority for Agricultural Crops Stabilization Fund referred to in the World Bank Report, *Arab Republic of Egypt,* table 10.4, p. 34.

19. "Implicit" and "disguised" tax are used interchangeably.

20. The disguised tax equals the difference between the selling price in the domestic or foreign market and the government buying price.

21. The compulsory delivery quota for sesame is 99 percent. See Ahmed Hassan in chapter 7.

22. The other crops that are subject to the compulsory delivery quota system are sold on the domestic markets. These are beans, lentils, sesame, and wheat (until 1976).

23. Abdel-Fadil estimated the price differential of each of the compulsorily delivered crops (wheat, rice, and onions) as the ratio between the average price for free retention and the average price for compulsory purchases (Abdel-Fadil, *Development, Income Distribution,* p. 89). Hansen and Nashashibi estimated the price differential between domestic prices and international prices for nine major field crops. This has been called the "nominal de facto rate of protection" and is defined as "the difference between domestic and international price divided by the international price" (B. Hansen and Nashashibi, *Foreign Trade Regimes and Economic Development: Egypt* [New York: Columbia Univ. Press, 1975], pp. 162–165; the quotation is from p. 163).

24. After the nationalization of the cotton trade in 1961, all sales of raw cotton for export or local consumption were effected through the Egyptian Cotton Commission (ECC), which bought cotton at fixed prices and set selling prices for export and for local consump-

tion. But until 1964, the ECC buying price was set for the deliveries from the ginning mills. The price received by the farmers was lower than this fixed price by the margins of the mills and the intermediaries handling the cotton. To make these margins as small as possible, the cooperative societies and the Cooperative and Agricultural Credit Bank were ordered to compete with the private merchants at this stage of the cotton trade. From 1964, all trade went through the cooperative societies (see B. Hansen and G. Marzouk, p. 105).

25. It is worth noting, though, that the farmers at present are complaining about the nonprofitability of cotton and try to avoid its cultivation.

26. See table 6.A.1. in the chapter appendix.

27. In 1965/1966, the farmers incurred losses because of the cotton crop failure (see Price Planning Agency, *The Cotton; A study in a Series of Commodity Reports* [Cairo, May 1972] [in arabic], pp. 51–52). This resulted in a jump of the disguised tax rate to 127.3 percent as shown in table 6.3 in the text.

28. In the 1960s the government price was 1.5 daribas for each of the first five feddans and 1.75 daribas for each feddan over and above the first five (see M. Abdel-Fadil, *Development, Income Distribution,* p. 89). The Agricultural Committee recommends the decrease of the compulsory quota of rice from 1.5 ton to 1.25 ton (see *al-Ahrām,* [daily newspaper], October 3, 1978).

29. In the case of rice, the fine is £E50 for every nondelivered ton in the compulsory quota (see the Rice Committee's announcement to the rice producers in the daily Egyptian newspaper *al-Akhbār,* February 16, 1978).

30. During this period 1970–1973, the government buying price was relatively lower than in the previous and succeeding years. It is true that the average cost of production of rice was falling during this period, but this fall in cost was relatively smaller than the fall in government buying price (see table 6.A.2 in the chapter appendix). This has led to a decrease in the farmers' return on the compulsory delivery quota to £E9.2 million in 1971 as compared to £E13.9 million in 1970 and £E17.4 million in 1968, for example.

31. The minimum compulsory deliveries of onions are set at 4 tons per feddan in the three Middle Egypt governorates (Banî Suwayf, al-Minyā, and al-Fayyūm) and at 6 tons per feddan in the Upper Egypt governorates (Asyūt, Sawhāj, and Qinā), (see M. Abdel-Fadil, *Development, Income Distribution,* p. 89). The compulsory delivery quota of onions was set for 1977/1978 at 4 tons in al-Minyā, 6 tons in al-Fayyūm and Ismāᶜīlīya, 7 tons in Asyūt and Qinā, and 8 tons in Sawhāj (see *al-Ahrām,* March 18, 1978).

32. The fine for onions is £E20 for every nondelivered ton with a maximum of £E500 (see *al-Ahrām,* March 18, 1978).

33. See table 6.A.3 in the chapter appendix.

34. See Ahmed Ibrahim in chapter 7.

35. See tables 6.A.1, 6.A.2, 6.A.3, and 6.A.4 in the chapter appendix.

36. Tax on wages, salaries, pensions, and annuities; the tax on commercial and industrial profits; and the tax on professional and nonprofessional income, in table 6.1 in the text.

37. The area cultivated with the two other export crops, onions and groundnuts, is relatively very small. It is less than 1 percent of the summer crops area in the case of groundnuts and of the winter crops area in the case of onions (calculated from CAPMS, *The Statistical Yearbook, 1978*).

38. Cotton cultivation covers about 30 percent and rice about 20 percent of the total summer crops area. These figures are calculated from CAPMS, *Statistical Yearbook, 1978.*

39. Although wheat, which was subject to the compulsory delivery quota system until 1976, has been covering about 27 percent of the winter crops areas, it was much less important than cotton and rice regarding its burden on farmers' income. This is because of the relatively small compulsory delivery quota of wheat—27.6 percent of the crop only—and its relatively low price differential (e.g., the differential was £E1.1 per ardab in 1967/1968;

Abdel-Fadil, *Development, Income Distribution,* p. 89). Although I do not have data about the price differential of wheat in the 1970s, I do not expect a significant change in it. This is because wheat is sold totally in the domestic market and the government cares to keep its price, as a basic food commodity, at a low level. It may be worth noting also that the implicit tax on wheat cannot be considered as a good source of income to the government as it may appear to be if one considers the area variable alone and disregards the two other equally important variables: the price differential and the size of the compulsory delivery quota.

40. The large landholders have the right to organize the crop rotation in their lands apart from the crop rotation applied in the villages where their holdings are. See Ahmed Hassan in chapter 7.

41. A large portion of vegetables and most of the fruits are cultivated by the big farmers (see Ahmed Ibrahim in chapter 7, table 7.6). The yield per feddan of vegetables or fruit is much higher than the yield per feddan of traditional crops. For example, during 1967–76 the average yield per feddan of traditional crops ranged between a minimum of £E42.7 at current prices in the case of using a crop rotation of wheat and rice, and a maximum of £E103.5 in the case of cultivating clover rather than rice; while the average yield per feddan of vegetables ranged between £E284 and £E488 at current prices; and the average yield per feddan of fruit ranged between a minimum of £E143 and a maximum of £E938 at current prices (Ahmed Hassan in chapter 7, table 7.1). Thus, one can easily see that the average income of the big farmer per feddan of his agricultural land holding is relatively higher than the average income of the small farmer per feddan of his holdings.

# CHAPTER 7

# *Impact of Agricultural Policies on Income Distribution*

Ahmed H. Ibrahim

## I. Introduction

In Egypt, the distribution of agricultural income has been affected by a number of policies implemented in the last quarter of a century. Some policies aim directly and principally at improving income distribution in agriculture. For example, the Agrarian Reform Acts aimed at redistributing agricultural land ownership, and at affecting the distribution of income between the landowner and the tenant through regulating the rental relationship and fixing the rental value.

Other policies were intended not to affect the distribution of the agricultural income but to increase agricultural production and to speed up the growth of agricultural income. Nonetheless, they had a significant effect on agricultural income distribution. Among these policies were the consolidation of land use and the organization of the crop rotation (CLUOCR), cooperative marketing and compulsory delivery of agricultural crops (CMCDAC), and agricultural cooperative credit and supply of agricultural inputs (ACC). Because these three policies are interconnected, their effect on the distribution of income has been magnified. Each depends for its success on the implementation of the others.

This chapter will investigate these three policies and their effect on the distribution of agricultural income. Because of the scarcity of the data on income distribution in Egypt, we depend on the results of an unpublished field study carried out in 1970 in ten villages in four governorates. This study measured the effects of CLUOCR on income distribution among the landholders. Despite the smallness of the size of the sample, we draw on its results because of the absence of other samples or official statistical data. The field study serves at least as a pointer to the effect of crop rotation policy on distribution of the agricultural income.

## II. The Effects of the Consolidation of Land Use and Crop Rotations on Income Distribution

*Land consolidation* means the pooling of areas under a certain crop within a village, without violating or affecting the individual property or holding rights. *Crop rotation* means determining the sequence of the various crops planted on a plot of land.

The consolidation of land use and state-regulated crop rotation took place at first on those estates seized under the Agrarian Reform Act (ARA). The redistributed land was divided into three nearly equal pieces, each of which lay within a larger area.[1] This system was gradually expanded until by 1965 it covered all agricultural land in Egypt.[2]

The primary goal of the consolidation of land use and crop rotation was the growth of agricultural productivity. The state hoped to:

- increase the export value of the commercial agricultural crops, such as cotton, rice, and onions,
- supply the country with the staple agricultural products,
- meet the needs of local industry for agricultural raw materials,
- and produce supplies of vegetables and fruits sufficient to cover the need of the urban areas.

To meet these goals, decrees were issued by the Ministry of Agriculture to specify the zones and areas allotted to cultivating various crops and also to define the zones in which the cultivation of certain crops was forbidden.[3] Measures were also taken to encourage cultivators to expand production of fruit.[4]

Although the primary concern in devising this system was efficiency, the changes had equity or distributional effects many of which did not receive attention.

The consolidation of land use and controlled crop rotation have distributional effects because they enable some cultivators to increase income and wealth at the expense of others. The distributional effects are demonstrated by evidence derived from an unpublished field study conducted in 1970.[5] This study covered ten villages in four governorates. The governorates of al-Daqahlīya, al-Sharqīya, al-Gharbīya, and al-Minūfīya comprise 34.6 percent of the total number of holdings and about 33.7 percent of the total area of holdings in Egypt.[6] The results demonstrate that consolidated land use and crop rotations do not benefit small landholders (5 *feddans* and less), whose holdings are made up of one piece and who represent about 31 percent of the total number of landholders in the fourth Agricultural Census of 1961. These programs also fail to benefit another group of small landholders—those whose two holdings are in the block of a single crop.

The field study contained a number of findings important to an analysis of income distribution. First, a large proportion of the landholders, varying between 55 percent in Kafr al-Zayyāt and Shibīn al-Kūm and 100 percent in Dikirnis, Kafr Saqr, and Diyarb Nijm, held areas of land that lay wholly in one single crop block.[7] Those landholders could not diversify their crops and their sources of income, and they were obligated to purchase many commodities in the open market to cover the needs of their families. Those families whose entire holdings or larger part thereof were in cotton blocks suffered. They experienced a shortage of cereals. The suffering was particularly great because these holders were unable to accumulate sufficient stocks in the years they grew cereals to meet family needs during the years in which they grew cotton. Moreover, the low return they received from cotton cultivation left them with little money for buying cereals. The proportion of holders faced with a shortage of cereals in my 1970 field study amounted to 60 percent in Shibīn al-Kūm, 95 percent in Kafr Saqr, and 100 percent in Kafr al-Zayyāt, Dikirnis, and Diyarb Nijm. Related to the problems of the shortage of cereals in cases where the holding lies either wholly or in part in a cotton block is the shortage of winter and summer fodder needed for livestock. Approximately 50 percent in Shibīn al-Kūm, 90 percent in Kafr al-Zayyāt and Kafr Saqr, 95 percent in Dikirnis and 100 percent in Diyarb Nijm suffered from the shortage of fodder.

The rise of the prices of cereals and fodder and the rise of the rental value of agricultural land had distributional effects. For example, the annual rental value of one feddan in Shibīn al-Kūm in 1970 was £E70, more than double its annual rental value (which is about £E28 on the average) according to the Agrarian Reform Act. Naturally, those who benefit from the rise of the prices of cereals and fodder and the rise of the actual rental value of the agricultural land are middle and large landholders who can realize a surplus that they sell to the small landholders and the agricultural workers. In addition, they rent some areas of their holdings to small landholders. The large landholders benefit more than the middle ones from these positions. The large landholders organize the crop rotation (CR) in their own lands in the manner that they see fit, irrespective of the village to which they belong.[8] Also, they usually cultivate their land according to a three-year rotation in which cotton occupies only one-third of their holdings. On the other two-thirds they grow clover, wheat, and other cereals, and thus they are able to take advantage of the shortage in clover areas within the village border and the neighboring villages by raising land rental during the clover-growing season. This rental value amounted to about £E50 for the period of growing clover in Kafr al-Zayyāt in 1970.

Because of the shortage of fodder, small farmers were forced to sell the calves prematurely at considerable loss. Of the landholders included in this study, 35 percent in Kafr al-Zayyāt, 40 percent in Dikirnis, 50 percent in Diyarb Nijm, 10 percent in Kafr Saqr, and 20 percent in Shibīn al-Kūm suffered such losses. Some of them reported selling all their livestock, or part of it, during the year when their holdings lay in a cotton block, and then purchasing other livestock in the year when crops other than cotton were cultivated. To some of them selling livestock meant buying manure from others and hiring livestock or machinery. In my sample the proportion of those who sold their livestock in the cotton year amounted to 45 percent in Kafr al-Zayyāt, 40 percent in Dikirnis, 10 percent in Diyarb Nijm, 30 percent in Kafr Saqr, and 15 percent in Shibīn al-Kūm.

To compensate for the reduction of income caused by CLUOCR, some of the small farmers had to work for a wage, either in or outside agriculture. The proportion of those to the total number of landholders was 20 percent in Kafr al-Zayyāt, 10 percent in Dikirnis, 20 percent in Diyarb Nijm, 40 percent in Kafr Saqr, and 50 percent in Shibīn al-Kūm.

Some small landholders borrowed in order to cover the gap between their income from cotton and their necessary consumption needs. In my field study the proportion amounted to about 50 percent in Kafr al-Zayyāt, 25 percent in Diyarb Nijm, 20 percent in Kafr Saqr, and 5 percent in Shibīn al-Kūm. Some were forced to sell their wives' jewelry or copper utensils or to mortgage part of their land. Others contemplated breaking the crop rotation or not repaying debts to the agricultural cooperatives, or even leaving work in agriculture altogether. They all strove to increase their monetary income through selling egg, poultry, milk, and dairy products.

The system of CLUOCR also may have led to increasing disparities between different agronomic zones in Egypt—specifically between zones fit for growing vegetables and fruits on the one hand, and zones designated for growing traditional crops. Even within the same agronomic zone, CLUOCR has led to widening differences between growers of traditional crops and growers of nontraditional ones.[9] There are many reasons for this, the most important of which is that the system tends to force small farmers to grow traditional crops while at the same time allowing middle and large farmers to escape.

Large differentials occur in net income per feddan under different rotations (see table 7.1). The maximum annual net income of one feddan under long clover (five cuts) and maize in the period 1967–1977 amounted to about £E75 in 1966/1967 prices. The annual average net income of one feddan of cotton preceded by short clover (two cuts) was about £E44. Under vegetable rotation, the maximum average net income amounted to £E377 per feddan at 1966/1967 prices (cultivated with potatoes followed by cucumbers, then beans) equivalent to about five times the maximum average of the net income of one feddan under traditional crops. The minimum average net income per feddan under vegetables was about £E193, or more than one and one-half times the minimum average net

TABLE 7.1.

*Average net income per feddan[a] associated with different rotations of some principal traditional, vegetable and fruit crops. (Annual average for the period 1967–1977 in current prices and 1966/1967 prices)[b]*

| Rotation of Traditional Crops | Current prices | Constant prices | Rotations of Vegetable Crops | Current prices | Constant Prices | Fruit Crops Average of 1970 & 1977 | Current prices | Constant prices |
|---|---|---|---|---|---|---|---|---|
| Short clover followed by cotton | 60.5 | 43.7 | Summer potatoes, veg. marrow, cabbages | 402.7 | 289.3 | Citrus | 142.5 | 92.6 |
| Wheat then maize | 49.9 | 36.4 | Summer potatoes, eggplant, phaseolus | 487.9 | 348.8 | Grapes | 268.6 | 171.0 |
| Wheat then rice (1967–1976) | 42.7 | 24.0 | Summer potatoes, cucumber, phaseolus | 539.2 | 376.7 | Mangoes | 262.7 | 159.0 |
| Long clover (green) then maize | 103.5 | 75.5 | Summer potatoes, veg. marrow, phaseolus | 527.7 | 273.1 | Pears | 237.4 | 127.5 |
| Long clover (green) then rice (1967–1976) | 93.4 | 73.1 | Summer potatoes, eggplant, cabbages | 362.9 | 265.0 | Peach | 394.5 | 211.0 |
| Long clover then maize | 86.7 | 68.4 | Summer potatoes, cucumber, cabbages | 414.2 | 292.9 | Plum | 426.5 | 226.5 |
| Long clover then rice (1967–1976) | 73.7 | 66.0 | Winter tomatoes, eggplant | 369.6 | 264.3 | Bananas | 937.5 | 608.5 |
| Broad beans then maize | 58.2 | 41.6 | Winter tomatoes, cucumber | 420.8 | 292.3 | Gawafa | 367.5 | 207.6 |
| Winter onions then maize (1967–1975) | 54.2 | 45.0 | Winter tomatoes, veg. marrow | 409.3 | 288.6 | | | |
| Broad beans then rice (1967–1976) | 49.4 | 39.0 | Long clover (green), veg. marrow, phaseolus | 470.5 | 335.5 | | | |
| | | | Long clover (green), cucumber, cabbages | 357.0 | 255.3 | | | |
| | | | Long clover (green), veg. marrow, cabbages | 345.5 | 251.6 | | | |
| | | | Long clover (green), cucumber, phaseolus | 482.0 | 339.1 | | | |
| | | | Long clover (green), eggplant, phaseolus | 431.0 | 257.9 | | | |
| | | | Long clover (green), eggplant, cabbages | 306.0 | 227.4 | | | |
| | | | Long clover (seeds), veg. marrow, phaseolus | 461.4 | 328.3 | | | |
| | | | Long clover (seeds), cucumber, cabbages | 348.0 | 248.2 | | | |
| | | | Long clover (seeds), veg. marrow, cabbages | 336.4 | 244.5 | | | |
| | | | Long clover (seeds), cucumber, phaseolus | 473.0 | 332.0 | | | |
| | | | Long clover (seeds), eggplant, phaseolus | 425.0 | 306.3 | | | |
| | | | Long clover (seeds), eggplant, cabbages | 296.6 | 220.3 | | | |
| | | | Broad beans, veg. marrow, phaseolus | 423.6 | 301.5 | | | |
| | | | Broad beans, cucumber, cabbages | 310.2 | 221.4 | | | |
| | | | Broad beans, veg. marrow, cabbages | 298.6 | 221.0 | | | |
| | | | Broad beans, cucumber, phaseolus | 464.0 | 305.2 | | | |
| | | | Broad beans, cabbages, phaseolus | 415.0 | 277.3 | | | |
| | | | Broad beans, eggplant, cabbages | 284.0 | 193.5 | | | |

SOURCE: Computed from Ministry of Agriculture, unpublished data.

NOTES:

[a]This average was computed by deducting the total costs, including wages and rent, from the total value of production at farm prices. These prices equal the compulsory delivery prices as regards the traditional crops. The disparity of the rental value according to crops was taken into consideration. The rental value of a fruit feddan was computed as fourteenfold of land tax, estimated at £E4, this because the fertility of land planted by fruit trees is usually

income under traditional crops. In the case of bananas, maximum average net income per feddan was £E608. These disparities increase greatly if calculated according to current prices, because of the tremendous rise in the prices of vegetables and fruit.

## III. Cooperative Marketing and Compulsory Delivery of Some Agricultural Crops

The system of compulsory delivery complements land consolidation and crop rotation. According to this system, known as cooperative marketing,[10] cultivators are obliged to deliver at fixed prices specific quotas of those agricultural crops important for export earnings, domestic supplies, and local industry.[11] The compulsory delivery (CD) of crops enables the government to allocate supplies for export and local consumption and to distribute the parts allocated to local consumption in a fair manner, geographically.

Wheat was the first crop in Egypt to be put under compulsory delivery. In the 1940s the system was introduced to guarantee supplies to the British Occupation Forces and the urban population. In 1953, the system of cooperative marketing was applied to cotton grown by the beneficiaries of the Agrarian Reform Act,[12] as a means of protecting them against exploitation of merchants.

As part of the government's effort to mobilize the agricultural surplus, cooperative marketing was applied on an experimental level to cotton produced in the 1962/1963 season for nonbeneficiaries of the Agrarian Reform Act in al-Minūfiȳa governorate. Its application was extended gradually to include all the Egyptian governorates from the 1965/1966 season on.[13] The cooperative marketing of cotton was converted from a method for protecting small farmers against the exploitation of merchants to a technique for using the agricultural product to finance projects in the first Five Year Plan.

Outside cotton, the compulsory delivery extended gradually to include other crops. Beginning with important export crops, onions and rice were put under compulsory delivery in the 1963/1964 and 1966 seasons, respectively. Other crops were included as shown in table 7.2.

The application of compulsory delivery to cotton, onions and rice is related to the development priorities involved in the first Five Year Plan of 1960/1961–1964/1965. Emphasizing industrialization, the state realized that success depended on its ability to acquire the foreign currency needed for importing investment goods and raw materials.

To overcome the shortage of foreign financing, the state increased agricultural exports, which represented the major part of the Egyptian exports at that time. This was no easy task, owing to the dominance of the private sector over more than 95 percent of the agricultural production.[14] CD (compulsory delivery) of the export crops was deemed the answer.

*TABLE 7.2.*
*Development of the system of compulsory delivery and minimum of the quotas delivered for each crop*

| | *Date when crop first put under CD* | *Date when CD of crop was generalized* | *Minimum quota per feddan* | *Average yield per feddan in the period 1972–1977*[a] | *CD quota as % from the average yield* |
|---|---|---|---|---|---|
| Cotton | 1962/1963 | 1965/1966 | The whole yield | 5.32 kentar | 100.0 |
| Onions[b] | 1963/1964 | 1966/1967 | 4–6 tons[c] | 4.51–10.83 tons | 55.4–88.7 |
| Rice | 1966 | 1966 | 1.5 tons[d] | 2.18 tons | 69.0 |
| Wheat[e] | 1940s | 1940s | 2–4 ardab | 9.35 ardab | 21.5–43.0 |
| Broad beans | 1967 | 1967 | 1–2.5 ardab | 6.34 ardab | 15.8–39.4 |
| Lentils | 1967 | 1967 | 2 ardab | 4.35 ardab | 46.0 |
| Peanuts | 1966/1967 | 1966/1967 | (the whole yield except 1 ardab per feddan) | 11.54 ardab | 87.0 |
| Sesame[f] | 1966/1967 | 1966/1967 | (the whole yield except 4 kg. per feddan) | 4.27 ardab | 99.0 |

NOTES:
[a]Average yield per feddan at the national level except in the case of onions, in which the average yield per feddan is at the governorate level.
[b]The CD of onions is applied only on winter onions. It started in Asyūt and extended gradually to include in 1978 Asyūt, al-Ninyā, Sawhāj, al-Fayyūm, Qinā, and al-Ismāᶜilīya. It was decided it would include Banī Suwayf starting 1979. Qinā was to be excluded, to be allocated to producing seeds.
[c]These quotas were increased starting in the 1978 season to 6 tons for al-Ismāᶜilīya and al-Fayyūm, 7 tons for Asyūt and Qinā, and 8 tons for Sawhāj. In January 1979 another increase was stipulated, once more making the quota 5 tons per feddan in Minyā, 8 tons in Asyūt, and 7 tons in Banī Suwayf. As to the other governorates, the quotas remained as they were in 1978.
[d]This quota was reduced to 1.25 tons per feddan in Fayyūm and Kafr Saᶜd in Dumyāt, and 1 ton per feddan in Burullus in Kafr al-Shaykh and Abū al-Matāmīr in al-Buhayra.
[e]It was climinated from the CD in 1976, when the CD price became higher then the wholesale price for wheat.
[f]It was eliminated from CD in the 1977/1978 season; later it was reintroduced from the 1979/80 season, according to decree no. 42, 1979, of the minister of agriculture.
SOURCES: Collected and computed from The Principal Bank of Development and Agricultural Credit, unpublished data; Ministry of Agriculture, unpublished data; Central Agency of Public Mobilization and Statistics (CAPMS), *Annual Statistical Book of ARE, 1952–1977,* Provisional edition, Cairo, 1978.

After first applying compulsory delivery to export crops, the state extended the policy to include crops of importance for local supplies and industry. In 1967, two crops were added to the list: broad beans and lentils. Both represent the principal protein food for the masses. Two years later, two other crops were subjected to CD—peanuts and sesame, both important for domestic supplies and for industry.

## *The Distributional Effect of the CDAC*

Compulsory deliveries were created in order to facilitate economic development. Little thought was given to the effect of these policies on the distribution of agricultural income. Yet the distribution impacts were considerable. They varied according to the proportion of the crop delivered and the difference between the CD price and the free market price.

Cotton, sesame, and peanuts are sold almost entirely to the state. The other crops are not.

From the data of table 7.2, it is clear that the cultivators of winter onions have to deliver to the state a minimum quantity that varies in the light of the average yield in their respective governorates. It ranges from about 55.4 percent of the 1972–1977 average yield per feddan in Sawhāj to about 88.7 percent of the 1972–1977 average yield per feddan in al-Minyā. Small cultivators are sometimes obliged to deliver their products at CD prices, even if they have to buy additional quantities to cover their consumption.[15]

Despite the continuous increase in the per ton CD price for onions during the period 1971–1977, the same period witnessed oscillation in the quantities compulsorily delivered as shown in table 7.3. At the same time, prices remained far less than the free market prices (measured by wholesale prices). Table 7.4 contains data for the average per ton CD price for onions and the annual average wholesale price over the period 1971–1977. It is clear that the former was always less than the latter by some 24.5 percent to 56.3 percent of the wholesale price. The major part of this price differential represents part of the income of the onion cultivators channeled to the government as a result of the CD system.

The distributional effect of the CD in the case of rice is clearer than it is in the case of onions. The CD quota of rice is 1.5 tons per feddan, except for some regions where average yield per feddan is lower than the country average.[16] The regular CD quota of rice (1.5 tons per feddan) is equivalent to about 69 percent of the country's average yield for rice.[17] This average leaves the cultivator with a surplus of only 0.68 ton per feddan of unbleached rice, an amount hardly sufficient for the consumption of the typical peasant family. Small cultivators, those who grow rice in areas of less than one feddan, are forced to buy additional quantities of rice for their own consumption at prices higher than CD prices. This applies to nearly all those landholders of less than three feddans who grow rice. This group represents about 34 percent of the total rice cultivators, according to the data of the Fourth Agricultural Census of 1961.[18] This surplus of rice does not exceed about 0.6 ton of unbleached rice (in the subcategory of three feddans). This is equivalent to about 0.4 ton of bleached rice. This quantity is not sufficient for the consumption of a typical small farmer family composed of seven persons, assuming that the per capita rice consumption in rice zones amounts to 60 kg.—a little bit less than twice

*TABLE 7.3.*

*Quantities of onions cooperatively marketed compared with the total production of single winter onions[a] and average CD prices of onions for the period 1971–1977*

| | Total production of single winter onions in the country | | Total production of single winter onions in the governorates of CM | | | The quantities cooperatively marketed | | | |
|---|---|---|---|---|---|---|---|---|---|
| | Thousand tons[1] | % of total production of winter onions | Thousand tons[1] | % of total production of onions in these governorates | % of total production in the country | Thousand tons[2] | % of total production of single winter onions in the country | % of total production in the CM governorates | Average price of CD (£E/ton) |
| 1971 | 273.1 | 96.4 | 238.6 | 97.0 | 87.4 | 167.0 | 61.1 | 70.0 | 15.83 |
| 1972 | 257.4 | 96.4 | 223.5 | 96.7 | 86.8 | 168.8 | 65.6 | 75.5 | 13.41 |
| 1973 | 225.3 | 97.9 | 193.3 | 97.0 | 85.8 | 131.7 | 58.4 | 68.1 | 19.40 |
| 1974 | 331.7 | 92.3 | 290.7 | 92.9 | 87.6 | 212.8 | 64.2 | 73.2 | 19.05 |
| 1975 | 203.5 | 88.1 | 172.2 | 92.5 | 84.6 | 115.9 | 60.0 | 67.3 | 24.17 |
| 1976 | 214.1 | 89.3 | 167.8 | 91.7 | 78.3 | 103.7 | 48.4 | 61.8 | 28.89 |
| 1977 | 215.4 | 82.0 | 146.1 | 82.3 | 67.8 | 115.3 | 53.5 | 78.9 | 31.95 |

SOURCES: Collected and computed from:

1. Ministry of Agriculture, unpublished data.
2. Principal Bank of Development and Agricultural Credit (PBDAC), unpublished data.

NOTE:

[a]Only single winter onions are subjected to the CD. Their production represents the major part of production of winter onions, even though the proportion of the total winter onion production has declined in later years because of the increase of the production of onions jointly produced with other crops.

*TABLE 7.4.*

*Development of the average per ton CD price of onions compared with their wholesale price over the period 1971–1977*

| | *Average price of CD per ton (£E)* (1) | *Annual average of wholesale price per ton (£E)* (2) | *The difference between (2) and (1)* (3) | *Ratio of (2) to (1) (%)* | *Ratio of (3) to (2) (%)* |
|---|---|---|---|---|---|
| 1971 | 15.8 | 21.4[a] | 5.6 | 135.2 | 26.0 |
| 1972 | 13.4 | 30.7 | 17.3 | 228.9 | 56.3 |
| 1973 | 19.4 | 34.5[a] | 15.1 | 177.8 | 43.8 |
| 1974 | 19.0 | 31.0[b] | 11.9 | 192.7 | 38.5 |
| 1975 | 24.2 | 48.1[c] | 24.0 | 199.1 | 49.8 |
| 1976 | 28.9 | 50.8 | 21.9 | 175.9 | 43.2 |
| 1977 | 31.9 | 42.3 | 10.4 | 132.5 | 24.5 |

SOURCE: Collected and computed from: PBDAC, unpublished data; CAPMS, *Quarterly Bulletin of the Foodstuff Prices,* different issues

NOTES:
[a]Average for ten months
[b]Average for four months
[c]Average for eight months

the per capita rice consumption estimated by the Ministry of Planning for 1977. This is because of the very low consumption of rice outside its production zones, especially in Upper Egypt. Cultivators who grow enough rice to have a surplus are benefited. They can sell part of this surplus to small cultivators at prices much higher than those of CD. Thus the system leads to the redistribution of income from the small cultivators to the large ones.

The prices of the rice compulsorily delivered are determined annually by decisions of the Ministry of Supply. The period 1967–1978 witnessed continuous change in the prices of CD of rice. The price per ton increased from £E20 in 1967 to £E50 and £E65 in 1977 and 1978, respectively.[19] Despite the rise in the CD prices of rice, they were always less than the prices at which the cultivators sold their free shares. The average price of a dariba (945 kg.) of rice on the free market in 1967 was double the CD price.[20] This supports my contention that the CD of rice redistributes the income from the small to large and middle rice cultivators.

Compared to rice, the distributional effect of CD of wheat appears to be marginal. This results from two principal causes:

1. The CD quota of wheat is less than that of rice, varying from about 21.5 percent to 43 percent of the average wheat yield. Rice amounted to about 69 percent of the average yield.
2. The difference between CD price of wheat and its free market price is small.

*TABLE 7.5.*
*Production and CD quota of rice for different holding categories*

| Holding category | Average rice area[a] (feddan) | Average yield per feddan[b] (tons) | Total holding production (tons) | CD quota[c] (tons) | Total quantities delivered by holding (tons) | Retained quantity (tons) |
|---|---|---|---|---|---|---|
| < 1 feddan | 0.40 | 2.18 | 0.87 | 1.5 | 0.60 | 0.27 |
| 1–2 feddans | 0.64 0.76 | 2.18 | 1.39 | 1.5 | 0.96 | 0.43 } 0.54 |
| 2–3 feddans | 0.89 | 2.18 | 1.94 | 1.5 | 1.33 | 0.60 |
| 3–4 feddans | 1.22 | 2.18 | 2.66 | 1.5 | 1.83 | 0.83 |
| 4–5 feddans | 1.04 | 2.18 | 3.42 | 1.5 | 2.35 | 1.07 |
| Total of < 5 feddans | 1.04 | 2.18 | 2.27 | 1.5 | 1.56 | 0.71 |
| 5–10 feddans | 2.36 | 2.18 | 5.14 | 1.5 | 3.54 | 1.60 |
| 10–20 feddans | 4.62 | 2.18 | 10.07 | 1.5 | 6.93 | 3.14 |
| 20–50 feddans | 10.03 | 2.18 | 21.86 | 1.5 | 15.04 | 6.82 |
| 50 > feddans | 35.89 | 2.18 | 78.24 | 1.5 | 55.83 | 24.40 |
| Total of 10 > feddans | 10.09 | 2.18 | 22.00 | 1.5 | 15.13 | 6.86 |

SOURCES: Computed from Ministry of Agriculture, *The Fourth Agricultural Census, 1961,* section I, part II, p. 145; CAPMAS, *The Annual Statistical Book of ARE, 1952–1977,* Provisional Edition, Cairo, 1978, p. 42; PBDAC, unpublished data.

NOTES:
[a]According to the Fourth Agricultural Census, 1961
[b]Annual average for the period 1972–1977. It is a constant average for all categories and subcategories.
[c]CD quota since 1969

> For wheat the free market prices were higher than those of the CD by some 4.5 percent in 1972 and 18.1 percent in 1973.[21] This difference in the case of rice was not less than 40 percent up to 1977.

In 1975 the CD price for wheat exceeded the free market price, and after 1976 the government abandoned the system of CD for wheat.

The CD quota of lentils was equivalent to 46 percent of the average yield per feddan for the period 1972–1977. The difference between the CD prices of lentils and their free market price ranged from 8.4 percent to 38 percent.[22] The CD price of lentils surpassed the average wholesale price in 1977 by about 9 percent.[23]

The distributional effect of CD of broad beans is similar to that for lentils. In both cases, the effect is less than on rice and more than on wheat. The CD quota of broad beans ranged from 15.8 percent to 39.4 percent of the average yield per feddan for the period 1972–1977. The wholesale prices of broad beans were 26.3 percent to 85.7 percent higher than the CD prices.[24]

The agricultural crops that are subjected to CD are traditional crops,[25] cultivated mainly by small holders, as shown in table 7.A.2. of the chapter appendix. For according to the data of the Fourth Agricultural Census, 1961, the small landholders (less than 5 feddans) represented more than 80 percent of those who grew cotton, more than 82 percent of those who grew wheat, more than 68 percent of winter onion cultivators, about 67.5 percent of peanut cultivators, and 63 percent of rice cultivators. The crops having high return, notably vegetables and fruits, were not grown by the small holders who constituted about 84.1 percent of the total holders in 1961. They cultivated about 17.7 percent, 37.1 percent, 32.8 percent, and 29.5 percent of the total areas of fruits and of winter, summer, and autumn vegetables, respectively. The owners of ten feddans and more (about 5.5 percent of the total number of the holders in 1961) cultivated about 73.5 percent, 44.3 percent, 48.4 percent, and 52.6 percent of the total areas of fruits, and of winter, summer, and autumn vegetables, respectively.

On the other hand, table 7.A.3. of the chapter appendix shows that (according to the data of the Fourth Agricultural Census of 1961) the areas cultivated with fruits and vegetables within each category of holdings amounted to about 6.5 percent, 7.8 percent, and 10.5 percent of the total areas in the category of holdings less than 5 feddans, 5–10 feddans, and 10 feddans and more, respectively. This proportion amounted to about 11.6 percent in the subcategory of holdings from 50 feddans and more. This shows that the large landholders enjoy the biggest share of the areas of the crops that have high economic return, and that the share of these crops of the total area of their holdings is high in comparison with their share of the total area of the holdings of the small and middle landholders. Since the Fourth Agricultural Census was taken in 1961, there have been many changes in the areas of crops cultivated by large and small holders. Because of the ability of large holders to change the crop mix of their lands, I believe that their share in cultivating crops of high economic return has risen and that the share of these crops in the total area of their holdings has also increased at the expense of crops subject to CD. Nevertheless, the absence of the data about crop patterns and landholding size after 1961 obliged me to use the data of the Fourth Agricultural Census as an indicator of these tendencies. The CD of the crops mentioned is carried out at prices fixed by the government, and lower than free market prices.

The government fines farmers who fail to deliver their set quota, and these fines vary for every crop. In some cases they are equivalent to the CD price per unit; in the case of lentils they are double that price.[26] In addition to the fine, the crops are also confiscated, and the convicted farmer is denied access to credit and cannot obtain agricultural inputs at subsidized prices.

The ratio of the CD quotas to the average yield per feddan (as an annual average for the period 1972–1977) is highest for the principal export crops:[27] 100 percent for cotton; 55.4 percent to 88.7 percent for onions; and 87 percent and 69 percent for peanuts and rice, respectively. This ratio is lowest for staple crops: 21.5 percent to 43 percent for wheat, 16–39 percent for broad beans and about 46 percent for lentils.

The government tried to use the CD as a means of improving income distribution within the agricultural sector by relating the size of the CD quota to the size of landholding. In the first three years of its introduction to CD, the quota for rice varied according to the size of the area where rice was grown. The quota in 1966 and 1967 was 1.5 dariba per feddan up to five feddans and 1.75 dariba per feddan on estates in excess of five feddans. In 1968 this rate was 1.25 tons per feddan up to two feddans and 1.5 tons per feddan on larger holdings. This progressivity was, however, adopted in the case of rice only and abandoned after 1968.

The CD policy has created increasing income differentials between the cultivators of traditional crops and the cultivators of vegetables and fruits. It has also increased income differentials between the cultivators of traditional export crops and the cultivators of traditional nonexport crops subject to CD. The quota to be delivered is higher in the former case.

Income differentials have increased between the small cultivators and the large ones who produce crops subject to CD, especially those crops that the cultivator needs for his direct consumption, such as rice and onions. The system of CD forces the cultivator to deliver a fixed quota of his produce at a price that is less than that of the free market. The small cultivator is left without a surplus sufficient for his family's consumption and has to buy on the free market, usually from the large cultivators, who can naturally afford a surplus over their own consumption.[28]

## IV. The Provision of Agricultural Credit and Supply of Agricultural Inputs

A feature of agriculture in Egypt before July 1952 was that small cultivators, and particularly tenants, lacked an organized source of credit on reasonable terms. For this reason, in the design of the Agrarian Reform Act of 1952, financing was created for the beneficiaries of lands. Article 18 of the act created Agricultural Cooperative Societies for beneficiaries of confiscated land and for those who already owned land less than five feddans in these villages. It was mandated that these societies serve the members' interest, especially by providing them with the agricultural production inputs, such as seeds, fertilizers, livestock, and agricultural machinery.[29]

The Agrarian Reform Act protected the beneficiaries of redistributed land with financing on easy conditions. Yet it did not provide financing for small tenants (less than five feddans), who represented about 16 percent of the total number of landholders, (according to the data of the Third General Agricultural Census of 1950). Lacking property guarantees, which the Agriculture-Cooperative Credit Bank asked for,[30] the tenants were unable to obtain materials and cash needed for cultivation unless the actual landowners guaranteed to the bank that they would repay the loans. This happened only if tenants accepted stringent conditions imposed on them by landowners. In addition to injuring tenants, this system was detrimental to agriculture and the economy as a whole.

The government made efforts, starting in the agricultural year 1953–1954,[31] to devise a system for agricultural financing that would provide all cultivators with an opportunity of obtaining inputs to cultivate their lands on reasonable terms. In order to realize this objective a system of agricultural credit was started in 1957. Called "Agricultural Cooperative Credit" (ACC), the results were so encouraging that the experiment was made universal at the country level in 1961.[32] The Agricultural and Cooperative Credit Bank (ACCB) stopped dealing directly with the cultivators as individuals. It dealt only with the members of the Agricultural Cooperative Societies. These societies offered planting loans to members on the basis of actual holdings, not on the sufficiency of the guarantee. They replaced the property guarantee by a yield guarantee. Thus the ACC system furnished the tenant in particular with a regular source of credit on easy conditions. As a result, the Agricultural Cooperative Societies became the single channel through which inputs, such as fertilizers, flowed to cultivators.

The ACCB monopolized the supply of the agricultural inputs and restricted distribution to the cultivators through the Agricultural Cooperative Societies. As a consequence, the cultivators were obliged to become members of these societies, and this led to a great increase in the size of their memberships. The number of the societies increased from 1,727 societies in 1952 with about 0.5 million members[33] to 4,083 societies with about 1.5 million members in 1962,[34] one year after generalizing the ACC system. The number of the Agricultural Cooperative Societies reached 5,075 in 1973, and their membership totaled more than 3.2 million.[35]

Nonetheless, this vast expansion was not preceded by dissemination of information to the cultivators about the benefits of the cooperative societies. Thus these societies represented for the majority nothing more than a governmental agency providing them with agricultural inputs. Their administration was unwieldy. There were delays in supplying inputs and paying for crops delivered compulsorily to the state. Crops were weighed inaccurately, and final accounts were not carefully rendered. For these reasons the cultivators were not dissatisfied when the Agricultural Cooperative Societies were replaced by the village banks in 1976.[36]

On August 10, 1961, in the first year after generalizing the ACC system, Presidential Decree No. 1250 for 1961 was issued, abolishing the interest that the ACCB received on cultivators' loans. In Article 1, the decree

TABLE 7.6.
*Agricultural credits offered by the Agricultural and Cooperative Credit Bank according to holding categories, 1960*

| Holding Category | Borrowers Number (000) | % | Credits Offered £E (million) | % | Area Served Feddan (000) | % | Holder's average share (£E) | Feddan's average share (£E) |
|---|---|---|---|---|---|---|---|---|
| < 5 feddans | 366.5 | 68.9 | 6.368 | 23.2 | 790.0 | 28.1 | 17.29 | 8.02 |
| 5–10 feddans | 85.9 | 16.6 | 4.16 | 15.2 | 435.7 | 15.7 | 48.47 | 9.56 |
| 10 and more feddans | 79.0 | 14.5 | 16.866 | 61.6 | 1,566.4 | 56.2 | 213.5 | 10.77 |
| Total | 531.4 | 100 | 27.368 | 100 | 2,792.1 | 100 | 51.5 | 9.8 |

SOURCE: Collected and computed from Agricultural and Cooperative Credit Bank, *Board's Report* and *Auditors' Report* and *The General Assembly Meeting Resolution 1960,* (in Arabic) p. 24.

stated that "the Agricultural and Cooperative Credit Bank is to stop receiving interests on the loans it offers to cultivators, and to the cooperative societies, from the beginning of the agricultural year 1961/62, as regards planting loans; and from November 1, 1961, as regards other loans."[37] This decree exempted all cultivators, regardless of the size of their holdings, from paying any interest on the loans they obtained from the ACCB. It did not distinguish between small holders and the large holders (who can, because of their high incomes, depend on their own financing capabilities). It would have been possible to use this exemption to realize an improvement, even though a slight one, in the position of small holders. Yet, what such measures led to was the preservation of income disparities.

Large cultivators were able to take greater advantage of the exemption from interest on the loans offered by the ACCB. They held the greatest part of the cultivated land served by these loans, for which the bank demanded property guarantees that other cultivators were unable to provide. That the large and, to some extent, middle landowners took advantage of the exemption from interest on loans offered by ACCB can be shown by considering the distribution of agricultural loans among the various categories of holding in 1960. This is shown in table 7.6. It is clear that most of the benefits from the ACC, and the abolition of interest on agricultural loans, went to the middle and large cultivators.

The data in table 7.6 give clear evidence of agricultural capitalism in Egypt. The abolition of the interest payment on the loans of the Agricultural and Cooperative Credit Bank encouraged large holders to expand the sphere of their business and to increase their wealth through investing private capital in business and agricultural projects that give high return. This helps the growth of their wealth, and consequently the rise of their incomes and the increase of disparity between them and those of small holders.

The decision to abolish interest payments on all kinds of loans did not last long. On July 13, 1965, the Executive Committee of the Arab Socialist Union decided that, to cover administrative costs, cultivators whose holdings exceed ten feddans must pay 4 percent of the value of loans offered them. This was to begin in the agricultural year 1965/1966.[38] Whatever the real reasons of issuing this decision, it was the first effort by the state to use the policy of agricultural credit as a means of improving income distribution in agriculture. Nevertheless, this step was short-lived. Two years later the minister of agriculture and agrarian reform issued Decree No. 2069 for 1967, extending the requirement to pay interest to all cultivators, and also to the loans of the cooperative societies for various purposes, in rates as follows:

4.5 percent annually for short-term loans
5.0 percent annually for middle- and-long term loans

By issuing, and implementing, this last decree, the first initiative of using the policy of agricultural credit to narrow the income gap between small cultivators and large ones was abandoned.

## *Kinds of Agricultural Loans under the ACC System*

The most important agricultural loans in Egypt are of the following types:

1. Planting loans, which are offered for the purposes of plant production; they include the field crops loans, orchards loans, and vegetables loans.
2. Livestock loans
3. Agricultural machinery loans

### *Planting Loans*

Planting loans provide for the purposes of plant production. They include the field crops loans, which represent the major part of the total loans offered to the cultivators by the ACCB. They accounted for more than 80 percent of total planting loans given in the period 1970/1971–1978 (see table 7.A.5. in chapter appendix), followed by loans for orchards and vegetables. The planting loans are considered an important means for increasing agricultural production. For this reason, offering loans in kind (seeds, fertilizers, and pesticides) gained special attention and care.

Recognizing the importance of the loans in kind for agricultural production, the government decided in 1962/1963 to offer these loans to all holders.[39] The decision remained in effect until the agricultural year 1967/1968, when it was decided that loans in kind (except for seeds and pesticides) would be offered only to cultivators who had repaid their debt arrears to the end of the previous season. From 1975 on, loans in kind were denied to those who failed to deliver the compulsory delivery quotas of the relevant crops.

From February 1968 on, loans in cash were confined to the principal crops, namely cotton, sugarcane, rice, onions, and flax,[40] which are pivotal for export and industry. They also included fruit orchards. Besides confining these loans to certain crops, the government reduced their rates. For example, in the 1971/1972 season the loan for picking cotton was reduced from 5 pounds per feddan for holders, owners, and tenants alike to 2.5 pounds per feddan for tenants. Again, cultivators who fail to repay their loans were to be punished by depriving them of the right of getting loans in cash.

### *Loans for Livestock*

These loans come next in size to plant loans, especially since the year 1971/1972. Since that season the proportion of livestock loans to the total amount of loans offered to the cultivators by ACCB has increased almost regularly. The proportion was about 2 percent in 1961/1962, and crept to about 3 percent in 1971/1972. It then jumped to 8.7 percent in 1976 and 16.1 percent in 1978, as shown in Tables IV and V in chapter appendix.

The livestock loans are conditional on submitting property guarantees. Hence, they are offered only to the landowners. The most important schemes enabling the cultivators to obtain loans for the development of livestock are as follows:

1. *The Scheme of Fattening Calves.* Its execution began in 1964, with the object of developing livestock and increasing meat supply. The loan was conditional on providing as collateral one-half feddan for each head of calves.[41] With the rise of the price of agricultural land, however, the amount of the collateral was reduced to one-quarter of a feddan in all governorates starting in 1976/1977. The value of the loan per head rose too as a result of the rise of the prices of livestock from £E30 in 1964/1965 to £E50 in 1976/1977. The amount of the credits sanctioned for this scheme also rose from about £E315,000 in 1964/1965 to about £E841,000 in 1978.[42]
2. *The Scheme of Fattening Calves on Clover.* Its execution began together with the scheme of fattening calves. Loans were conditional on the ownership of agricultural land, since a loan for one calf was given on condition that the borrower owned, through registered deeds, not less than half a feddan.[43] The maximum loan was for fifty calves. The qualification that the borrower own land could be abandoned if he secured the guarantee of another person who owned the required area. The total amount of the loans provided within this scheme amounted to £E929,000 in 1978.
3. *The Scheme of Fattening Calves Year-Round.* This scheme began in 1970. Borrowing is conditional on the ownership of land by the borrower himself or by another person who guarantees him. In all cases, a loan for one calf required collateral of half a feddan at least. In reality, borrowing under this scheme was confined to those who owned at least two feddans. The minimum of calves for which loans were provided was four and the maxi-

*TABLE 7.7.*

*Number of calves for which loans were provided according to the size of the property of the borrower*

| *Size of land property* | *Number of calves* | *Size of land property* | *Number of calves* |
|---|---|---|---|
| < 5 feddans | 4 calves | 25 feddans | 12 calves |
| 6–10 feddans | 6 calves | 30 feddans | 15 calves |
| 11–15 feddans | 8 calves | 40 feddans | 17 calves |
| 16–20 feddans | 10 calves | 50 feddans | 20 calves |

SOURCE: The Principal Bank of Development and Agricultural Credit, unpublished data.

mum twenty. Table 7.7 shows the number of calves for which loans were provided according to the size of borrower's property.

In 1976, the state abolished the requirements linking property size and number of calves for which loans were provided. It also decided to abandon the maximum number of calves for which loans were provided and to provide the loans according to the real size of property of the borrower. The value of the loan for one calf was raised gradually from £E35 in 1970 to £E100 in 1976. The total amount of loans under this scheme also rose from £E3,660 in 1970 to about £E11.7 million in 1978. The amendments that were made to this scheme support the growth of agricultural capitalism and help to concentrate wealth in the hands of wealthy cultivators.

Livestock loans increased from about £E0.769 million in 1961/1962 to about £E21.47 million in 1978 (see table 7.A.4., chapter appendix), or 2,691 percent. The loans oscillated until 1975, when they amounted to £E2.37 million. The year 1976 witnessed a huge jump to about £E8.58 million, an increase of about 263 percent. The years 1977 and 1978 continued the trend. The major part of these livestock-raising loans found their way to individuals starting in 1977. The proportion of loans obtained by individuals to the total amount of livestock-raising loans amounted to 57.7 percent in 1977 and increased to 70.3 percent in 1978. Thus the ACC system provided further opportunities for the growth of agricultural capitalism. Besides providing property guarantees, repaying agricultural loans due and delivering compulsory quotas, the applicant for a year-round loan under the fattening of calves scheme[44] must have the equipment necessary for livestock raising, the most essential feature of which is adequate stables, usually available only to the large cultivators who cultivate their own land. In addition, the practice of permitting the borrower, from 1970 onward, to borrow under any of the schemes of livestock development mentioned above,[45] so long as his land property is sufficient to cover the guarantee, provided a further impetus to the growth of agricultural capitalism in the field of animal production.

The tendencies to support the growth of agricultural capitalism in the field of animal production carry over to the provision of the intermediate inputs necessary for animal production, namely fodder. This policy sides with the large breeders. It requires, as a condition to get fodders at subsidized prices, that the breeder must have five grouped heads or more in the case of meat livestock and ten grouped heads in the case of milk livestock.[46] Further still, the fodder quota per head increases with the increase of the number of heads held by the breeder. For livestock fattening, the breeder who holds five heads and more is given monthly 120 kilograms of fodder for each head. This quantity increases to 150 kilograms a head when the number of heads is more than fifty. As to milk livestock, holdings of grouped five heads and more are given 60 kilograms a head monthly all year, while holdings of grouped ten heads and more are given 120 kilograms a head monthly during summer (from June 1 to the end of November) and 90 kilograms a head monthly in winter (from December 1 to the end of May). What may raise a question in this matter is that the "Decision of the Minister of Agriculture No. 1719 for 1978 Concerning the System of Providing Fodders for the 1978 Season" relaxes the condition of tying the giving of fodder to the delivering of the produce.[47] It is surprising that this decision is the same that fixes a minimum of heads for which the breeder can get fodder.[48]

The 1978 decision of the minister of agriculture gives another evidence that the policy of providing fodder was put in a way that serves the growth of agricultural capitalism. It allocated 0.35 million tons of fodder to meat livestock held in groups of five heads and more. This quantity amounted to about 35 percent of all the quantity of fodder available for distribution among all livestock holders in 1978. This quantity is equal to the quantity assigned to what is known as "livestock of general census."[49] This is the number of livestock held by all cultivators, a number amounting in 1970 to about 2.115 million head of cows and about 2.01 million buffalos.[50]

### *Credit for Agricultural Machinery*

In the order of magnitude, credits for agricultural machinery rank third, after planting credits and livestock credits. The amount of machinery credits oscillated, reaching its maximum of £E4.89 million in 1978, twenty-one times its 1961/1962 level (which was about £E0.232 million). The share of machinery credits going to individuals amounted to about 62.3 percent and 87 percent of the total of these credits in 1977 and 1978, respectively.[51] The increase of the share of machinery credits going to individuals means the reduction of the share of credits to cooperative societies and local bodies, thus increasing the opportunities of the owners of agricultural machinery to exploit small cultivators and to add to their own wealth. This resulted from the bias embodied in the conditions for securing the repayment of these credits, which confine them to the large landowners. These conditions have evolved in a manner that restricts access to these credits within a certain category of cultivators. In 1961 it was stipulated that, to obtain a credit for purchasing agricultural machinery, the borrower must provide one feddan collateral for every £E30 borrowed. The borrower is entitled to a credit of £E20 per feddan owned. Thus getting a credit of £E1,000 to purchase agricultural machinery required owning 50 feddans or more. In addition, the applicant must provide, as a guarantee for this credit, deeds of more than 33 feddans.

In 1970 it was decided to provide loans for purchasing tractors on condition that the borrower should pay half the price of the tractor in advance. The other half is to be paid within two years through extending a credit not exceeding fifty pounds per feddan. Later in the same year it was decided to reduce the down payment to 25 percent of the price of the tractors to those who want to buy them on credit, the rest is to be paid in installments within three years.

In 1976 the value of one feddan of collateral was raised to £E75, and the credit was to be repaid in installments: 40 percent the first year, 35 percent the second year, and 25 percent the third. It was also decided to give credit for purchasing agricultural machinery to those who could provide the required property guarantee, irrespective of the area they hold and cultivate. This 1976 decision is considered as an acknowledgment on the part of the PBACC that anyone who can provide the required property guarantee has the right to get a credit for purchasing agricultural machinery so as to sell its services to other cultivators, who are often small cultivators. The opportunities for the owners of agricultural machines to exploit the small cultivators increased in the light of the diminishing of availability of these machines in the cooperatives and local organizations.

In 1977 it was decided that the property guarantee for tractor-purchasing loans was to be ten feddans at least. The actual area provided as guarantee is determined according to the value of each feddan, which the bank estimates before sanctioning the loan. To determine this area, it takes into account that the proportion of each feddan in the installments of various kinds of loans must not exceed 40 percent of its value estimated by the bank. In the same year, it was decided that the tractor loans could be paid over five installments.[52]

We see, therefore, that the conditions of providing loans for purchasing agricultural machinery in the different stages of their evolution have confined the benefit from them to those who own ten feddans at least or to those who can provide the guarantee of an owner of this area.

We may be in a position to deduce here, in general terms, the essential features of the agricultural credit policy in Egypt, since the generalizing of the implementation of the system of agricultural cooperative credit was completed in 1961. The most important of these features are as follows:

1. The system of the agricultural cooperative credit was a step on the way of agrarian reform in its broadest sense. It enabled tenants to enjoy the full advantages of regulating the tenancy relationship of the agricultural land. It has provided for tenants a regular source of credit on easy conditions. It has

enabled them to cultivate and serve suitably the land they hold without need to borrow from the usurers and dealers of agricultural inputs or from landowners who used to impose unfair conditions.

2. The state committed itself to supplying all cultivators with the agricultural inputs, especially seeds, fertilizers, and pesticides, regardless of cultivators' payment of arrears on previous loans. It probably perceived the importance of these inputs for increasing agricultural production. Then there was a change in the state's attitude beginning in the agricultural year 1967/1968, when the repayment of past loans became a precondition for obtaining new loans whether in cash or in the form of agricultural inputs. From the beginning of 1975 on, the commitment of the cultivator to deliver compulsory quotas of agricultural crops became a precondition for getting new loans or agricultural inputs at subsidized prices.
3. The agricultural credit policy failed to be a means of improving income distribution in agriculture, since it instituted the same terms for both small and large cultivators. It treated them equally also in not charging interest on all agricultural loans.
4. The loan terms for setting up orchards and livestock and purchasing agricultural machinery increase the disparity of incomes between the different sizes of landholders. Access to these loans is limited to those who can provide the property guarantee, and the guarantee itself is so large in some cases that only large landowners can provide it.

These loans mainly benefit the large owner-cultivators and, to some extent, the middle ones. Small landowners received smaller loans per feddan than large owners.[53] For example, the average loan per feddan made to holders of less than 5 feddans was 18.36 percent less than the average loan per feddan made to holders of 5 to 10 feddans and 36.13 percent less than the average loan made to holders of 10 feddans or more. (See table 7.8.)

From table 7.8 it is also clear that the average loan per feddan made to small cultivators (less than five feddans) of the total amount of agricultural loans provided to individuals in 1978 is equal only to about 81.6 percent and 63.9 percent of the average share of these loans per feddan in the categories of middle (5–10 feddans) and large (10 and more feddans) cultivators, respectively. These shares compared with those of 1960 (shown in table 7.6) denote a deterioration of the position of the average share per feddan of small cultivators. The same thing is true of the average loan per holder (borrower) made to small cultivators as a proportion of the total loans. The position of small holders deteriorated between 1960 and 1978. In 1960, the average loan per holder made to small holders was equal to 35.7 percent and 8.1 percent of the average loan per holder made to middle and large holders, respectively. These proportions decreased in 1978 to about 17.3 percent and 5.2 percent.

Evidently agricultural credit policy between 1960 and 1978 developed in a manner that gave large and middle holders greater advantages than the small ones, despite an increase of the share of small holders loans from

*TABLE 7.8.*

*Agricultural credits provided by Banks of Development and Agricultural Credit to individuals according to holding categories, in 1978*

| *Holding Category* | *Borrowers* (000) | % | *Credits provided* £E million | % | *Area served* feddan (000) | % | *Average share per borrower* (£E) | *Average share per feddan* (£E) |
|---|---|---|---|---|---|---|---|---|
| < 5 feddans | 2,651.4 | 93.2 | 71.07 | 56.25 | 3,459.0 | 64.7 | 26.80 | 20.54 |
| 5–10 feddans | 125.6 | 4.4 | 19.44 | 15.38 | 772.5 | 14.5 | 154.73 | 25.16 |
| 10 and more feddans | 69.3 | 2.4 | 35.84 | 28.37 | 1,114.6 | 20.8 | 517.54 | 32.16 |
| Total | 2,846.3 | 100.0 | 126.35 | 100.00 | 5,346.1 | 100.0 | 44.39 | 23.63 |

SOURCE: Collected and computed from the Principal Bank of Development and Agricultural Credit, unpublished data.

NOTES: The share of each holding category in the total amount of agricultural loans provided to individuals, and hence the average loan per feddan and per borrower (holder) in each category, was worked out on the following bases:

1. The average share per feddan of the loans of field crops is equal in each of the three categories, since the conditions of providing them apply to all cultivators in the same degree.
2. the total amount of orchard and vegetable loans was allocated to the various categories in the same proportion as the allocation of areas of orchards and vegetables to them. The basis for this allocation was the Fourth Agricultural Census of 1961. I have assumed that it represents their distribution in 1978, though I believe that change in these proportions occurred in favor of large and middle categories of cultivators.
3. The total amount of loans for livestock provided to individuals was divided equally among the areas across the three categories of holding after dropping the holders of less than three feddans, though I believe that the category of large holders in particular would secure a bigger share than that estimated on this basis.
4. Loans to purchase agricultural machinery were allocated to large owners only, since only they are able to provide the property guarantee required (ten feddans at least) for these loans.

23.2 percent of the total amount of agricultural credits in 1960 (as shown from table 7.6) to 56.25 percent of their total in 1978. The increase of the share of small holders loans in total agricultural credits in 1978 is due essentially to the increase of their proportion in the total number of landholders. It is also due to the increase of the proportion of their holdings to the total area served by these loans (see table 7.6).

## V. Conclusions of the Study

Despite the paucity of data facing the student of income distribution in Egypt, some tentative and general conclusions regarding the effect of the agricultural policies on income distribution within agriculture have been reached.

There is a strong interconnection among the different policies studied. The agricultural cooperative credit policy is connected with the policy of consolidation of land use and the organization of the crop rotation. The former policy ties the provision of agricultural credit to the holders' commitment to carry out the directions of the local agricultural departments regarding assignment of certain areas of their holdings to certain crops. This is realized by providing loans in cash and agricultural production inputs to each holder according to the area in his holding assigned to each crop by the local agricultural departments. Consolidation of land use and organization of the crop rotation is tied also to the policy of cooperative marketing and compulsory delivery of some agricultural crops. The commitment to carry out the former policy makes it possible to carry out the latter. The quotas of the compulsorily delivered crops imposed on the holder are imposed according to the area cultivated with this crop and the holders who grow it.

The agricultural cooperative credit policy and the policy of cooperative marketing and compulsory delivery of some agricultural crops are connected with each other. The former is used to induce the cultivators to carry out the latter. The commitment of the cultivators to deliver the compulsory quotas imposed on them is a precondition to obtaining the agricultural credit and production inputs.

The agricultural policies included in this study were formed and implemented at a time when talking about social justice and the inevitability of achieving an equitable distribution of income was frequent. Yet, these policies may have increased income inequality. They have given those with high incomes opportunities to increase their incomes at the expense of those with low incomes and in some cases at the expense of society in general. Large cultivators exploit the weak positions of the small ones to obtain additional incomes (as a result of implementing the CLUOCR or of CMCDAC, particularly of items of staple food consumption). For example, CLUOCR could have been implemented in a way that allowed small cultivators to diversify the sources of their income and to satisfy their various needs without resorting to large cultivators. Again, the state could have provided small cultivators with cereals at the same prices it paid for the compulsory delivery of these crops, and it could have supplied cultivators with fodder for their livestock at suitable prices. A progressive system could have been devised for the compulsory delivery of crops, by which the quotas of compulsory delivery would rise in proportion to the size of the area of the holding as a whole to the area cultivated in the crop itself.

That large cultivators, generally, and the landowners, in particular, enjoy easily available opportunities to increase their incomes at the expense of the society as a whole is realized by the agricultural cooperative credit policy implemented at present. This policy works to the advantage of landowners in general, and the large ones in particular. Loans for purchasing agricultural machinery, the setting up of orchards, and the development of livestock also help large holders. These loans also equate small and large cultivators, subjecting both to the same terms and conditions despite their unusual economic and financing condition. Even where overdue debts are annulled, large cultivators share in this annulment the same as do the small cultivators. Thus, the agricultural credit policy provides large cultivators with cheap credit compared to commercial banks. It restricts the access to some kinds of loans to large landowners, such as the loans for purchasing agricultural machinery, and those for setting up orchards. Such a policy offers this category of cultivators opportunities to increase their wealth and move ahead on the road of capitalist growth. It also grants them an additional means of exploiting small cultivators, through their ownership of agricultural machinery which they hire to others at exaggerated prices.

## Appendix

TABLE 7.A.1.

*Average net income per feddan[a] associated with different rotations of some principal traditional, vegetable and fruit crops at current prices in 1977*

| Rotations of traditional crops | Net income (LE) | Rotations of Vegetable Crops | Net income (LE) | Fruit Crops | Net income (LE) |
|---|---|---|---|---|---|
| Short clover followed by cotton | 93 | Summer potatoes, veg. marrow, cabbages | 586 | Citrus | 166 |
| Wheat then maize | 105 | Summer potatoes, eggplant, phaseolus | 768 | Grapes | 327 |
| Wheat then rice (1976) | 53 | Summer potatoes, cucumber, phaseolus | 1,034 | Mangoes | 367 |
| Long clover (green) then maize | 218 | Summer potatoes, veg. marrow, phaseolus | 903 | Pears | 411 |
| Long clover (green) then rice (1976) | 151 | Summer potatoes, eggplant, cabbages | 451 | Peach | 687 |
| Long clover then maize | 208 | Summer potatoes, cucumber, cabbages | 717 | Plum | 751 |
| Long Clover then rice (1976) | 120 | Winter tomatoes, eggplant | 538 | Bananas | 1,094 |
| Broad beans then maize | 106 | Winter tomatoes, cucumber | 804 | Gawafa | 587 |
| Winter onions then maize (1975) | 97 | Winter tomatoes, veg. marrow | 673 | | |
| Broad beans then rice (1976) | 81 | Long clover (green), veg. marrow, phaseolus | 874 | | |
| | | Long clover (green, cucumber, cabbages | 689 | | |
| | | Long clover (green), veg. marrow, cabbages | 558 | | |
| | | Long clover (green), cucumber, phaseolus | 1,006 | | |
| | | Long clover (green), eggplant, phaseolus | 740 | | |
| | | Long clover (green), eggplant, cabbages | 423 | | |
| | | Long clover (seeds), veg. marrow, phaseolus | 865 | | |
| | | Long clover (seeds), cucumber, cabbages | 679 | | |
| | | Long clover (seeds), veg. marrow, cabbages | 548 | | |
| | | Long clover (seeds), cucumber, phaseolus | 996 | | |
| | | Long clover (seeds), eggplant, phaseolus | 730 | | |
| | | Long clover (seeds), eggplant, cabbages | 413 | | |
| | | Broad beans, veg. marrow, phaseolus | 766 | | |
| | | Broad beans, cucumber, cabbages | 580 | | |
| | | Broad beans, veg. marrow, cabbages | 449 | | |
| | | Broad beans, cucumber, phaseolus | 897 | | |
| | | Broad beans, cabbages, phaseolus | 591 | | |
| | | Broad beans, eggplant, cabbages | 314 | | |

SOURCE: computed from Ministry of Agriculture, unpublished data.

NOTE:

[a]This average was computed by deducting the total costs, including wages and rent, from the total value of production at farm prices. These prices equal the compulsory delivery prices as regards the traditional crops. The disparity of the rental value according to crops was taken into consideration. The rental value of a fruit feddan was computed as 14-fold of land tax estimated at LE because the fertility of land planted with fruit trees in usually higher than that of the others.

TABLE 7.A.2.

*The relative distribution of the areas cultivated with traditional crops, fruits, and vegetables and the number of holders who cultivate them in the various holdings categories in 1961*

| | < 5 feddans | | 5–10 feddans | | 10–50 feddans | | 50 and more feddans | | Total | |
|---|---|---|---|---|---|---|---|---|---|---|
| | Number (%) | Area (%) | Number (%) | Area (%) | Number (%) | Area (%) | Number (%) | Area (%) | Number (%) | Area (%) |
| *Winter Crops* | | | | | | | | | | |
| Wheat | 82.1 | 46.4 | 11.7 | 18.5 | 5.5 | 20.5 | 0.7 | 14.6 | 100 | 100 |
| Long Clover | 80.6 | 46.4 | 12.7 | 18.6 | 5.9 | 19.8 | 0.8 | 15.2 | 100 | 100 |
| Short Clover | 79.7 | 41.2 | 13.2 | 19.7 | 6.3 | 22.4 | 0.8 | 16.7 | 100 | 100 |
| Broad beans | 62.3 | 28.7 | 22.3 | 20.2 | 13.7 | 29.8 | 1.7 | 20.3 | 100 | 100 |
| Barley | 63.1 | 29.6 | 19.8 | 17.5 | 14.5 | 27.6 | 2.6 | 27.3 | 100 | 100 |
| Fenugreek | 60.3 | 26.8 | 20.2 | 18.6 | 16.8 | 34.8 | 2.7 | 17.8 | 100 | 100 |
| Onions | 68.4 | 33.8 | 17.4 | 19.2 | 12.1 | 30.4 | 2.1 | 16.6 | 100 | 100 |
| Lentils | 62.7 | 26.4 | 19.8 | 19.6 | 15.7 | 38.7 | 1.8 | 15.3 | 100 | 100 |
| Flax | 57.9 | 19.8 | 22.5 | 12.3 | 14.8 | 21.6 | 4.8 | 46.3 | 100 | 100 |
| Total of Winter Crops | | 42.4 | | 18.9 | | 22.3 | | 16.4 | | 100 |
| *Summer Crops* | | | | | | | | | | |
| Cotton | 80.2 | 38.0 | 12.9 | 18.7 | 6.1 | 24.4 | 0.8 | 18.9 | 100 | 100 |
| Sugarcane (plant crop) | 70.6 | 36.2 | 16.4 | 17.5 | 11.5 | 28.0 | 1.5 | 18.3 | 100 | 100 |
| Sugarcane (ratoon) | 72.1 | 31.6 | 15.2 | 15.7 | 11.2 | 27.2 | 1.5 | 25.5 | 100 | 100 |
| Maize | 73.0 | 38.9 | 16.8 | 19.4 | 8.9 | 22.6 | 1.3 | 18.4 | 100 | 100 |
| Sorghum | 84.4 | 50.5 | 9.5 | 16.8 | 5.5 | 21.7 | 0.6 | 11.0 | 100 | 100 |

TABLE 7.A.2.—*Continued*

| | *< 5 feddans* | | *5–10 feddans* | | *10–50 feddans* | | *50 and more feddans* | | *Total* | |
|---|---|---|---|---|---|---|---|---|---|---|
| | *Number (%)* | *Area (%)* | *Number (%)* | *Area (%)* | *Number (%)* | *Area (%)* | *Number (%)* | *Area (%)* | *Number (%)* | *Area (%)* |
| Rice | 63.0 | 25.8 | 24.0 | 22.4 | 11.3 | 27.4 | 1.7 | 24.4 | 100 | 100 |
| Sesame | 62.9 | 29.0 | 20.2 | 20.3 | 14.8 | 31.4 | 2.1 | 19.3 | 100 | 100 |
| Peanuts | 67.5 | 29.6 | 17.8 | 17.2 | 12.3 | 27.3 | 2.4 | 25.9 | 100 | 100 |
| Onions | 69.9 | 32.5 | 16.1 | 16.1 | 11.9 | 30.5 | 2.1 | 20.9 | 100 | 100 |
| Total of Summer Crops | | 37.5 | | 19.0 | | 24.7 | | 18.8 | 100 | 100 |
| *Autumn Crops* | | | | | | | | | | |
| Maize | 81.7 | 48.5 | 12.0 | 17.9 | 5.5 | 19.0 | 0.8 | 14.6 | 100 | 100 |
| Sorghum | 74.8 | 39.1 | 14.9 | 17.5 | 8.8 | 24.0 | 1.5 | 19.5 | 100 | 100 |
| Rice | 51.2 | 18.3 | 26.9 | 17.8 | 18.2 | 29.0 | 3.7 | 34.7 | 100 | 100 |
| Total of Autumn Crops | | 47.8 | | 17.9 | | 19.3 | | 15.0 | 100 | 100 |
| Winter Vegetables | | 37.1 | | 18.6 | | 26.1 | | 18.2 | | 100 |
| Summer Vegetables | | 32.8 | | 18.8 | | 26.4 | | 22.0 | | 100 |
| Autumn Vegetables | | 29.5 | | 17.9 | | 25.9 | | 26.7 | | 100 |
| Total of Vegetables | | 33.1 | | 18.5 | | 26.3 | | 22.1 | | 100 |
| Fruit | | 17.7 | | 8.8 | | 23.9 | | 49.6 | | 100 |

SOURCE: Computed from Ministry of Agriculture, *The Fourth Agricultural Census, 1961, part I, section II* (in Arabic), pp. 119, 145, 171, 197, 233, 249.

TABLE 7.A.3.

*Distribution of cultivated land in the various holdings categories among traditional vegetables and fruit crops in 1961*

| | < 5 feddans | | 5–10 feddans | | 10–50 feddans | | 50 and more feddans | | Total of 10 & more feddans | |
|---|---|---|---|---|---|---|---|---|---|---|
| | Number (%) | Area (%) | Number (%) | Area (%) | Number (%) | Area (%) | Number (%) | Area (%) | Number (%) | Area (%) |
| *Winter Crops* | | | | | | | | | | |
| Wheat | 81.2 | 33.8 | 94.3 | 28.9 | 92.8 | 24.6 | 90.2 | 18.8 | 92.5 | 21.8 |
| Long clover | 64.7 | 22.8 | 82.7 | 19.6 | 80.5 | 16.0 | 84.9 | 13.0 | 81.0 | 14.6 |
| Short clover | 54.2 | 21.5 | 79.0 | 22.0 | 73.2 | 19.2 | 74.2 | 15.4 | 73.3 | 17.4 |
| Broad beans | 14.6 | 4.5 | 42.5 | 6.8 | 55.3 | 7.7 | 51.9 | 5.9 | 54.9 | 6.8 |
| Barley | 7.1 | 1.7 | 18.0 | 2.2 | 27.9 | 2.6 | 38.7 | 2.6 | 29.0 | 2.6 |
| Fenugreek | 2.3 | 0.6 | 6.3 | 0.8 | 11.1 | 1.2 | 14.0 | 0.7 | 11.4 | 1.0 |
| Onions | 3.4 | 0.7 | 7.0 | 0.9 | 10.3 | 1.1 | 13.4 | 0.6 | 10.6 | 0.9 |
| Lentils | 1.6 | 0.7 | 4.2 | 1.1 | 7.0 | 1.7 | 6.4 | 0.7 | 6.9 | 1.2 |
| Flax | 0.5 | 0.2 | 1.6 | 0.3 | 2.2 | 0.4 | 5.5 | 0.9 | 2.5 | 0.6 |
| Winter vegetables | | 1.5 | | 1.7 | | 1.7 | | 1.3 | | 1.5 |
| Total of Winter Crops | | 88.0 | | 84.3 | | 76.2 | | 59.9 | | 68.4 |
| *Summer Crops* | | | | | | | | | | |
| Cotton | 69.1 | 31.7 | 90.0 | 33.3 | 90.0 | 33.4 | 88.2 | 27.7 | 89.8 | 30.6 |
| Sugarcane (plant crop) | 2.3 | 1.0 | 4.4 | 1.1 | 6.5 | 1.3 | 6.5 | 0.9 | 6.5 | 1.1 |
| Sugarcane (ratoon) | 2.2 | 1.2 | 3.8 | 1.3 | 6.0 | 1.9 | 6.3 | 1.7 | 6.0 | 1.7 |
| Maize | 17.3 | 7.3 | 32.2 | 7.8 | 35.9 | 7.2 | 41.4 | 6.1 | 36.5 | 6.7 |
| Sorghum | 25.2 | 9.9 | 23.2 | 7.0 | 28.0 | 7.0 | 24.0 | 3.8 | 27.5 | 5.4 |

TABLE 7.A.3.—*Continued*

| | *< 5 feddans* | | *5–10 feddans* | | *10–50 feddans* | | *50 and more feddans* | | *Total of 10 & more feddans* | |
|---|---|---|---|---|---|---|---|---|---|---|
| | *Number (%)* | *Area (%)* | *Number (%)* | *Area (%)* | *Number (%)* | *Area (%)* | *Number (%)* | *Area (%)* | *Number (%)* | *Area (%)* |
| Rice | 9.4 | 5.7 | 28.9 | 10.6 | 28.7 | 9.9 | 33.9 | 9.5 | 29.3 | 9.7 |
| Sesame | 1.9 | 1.6 | 5.1 | 0.9 | 7.9 | 1.1 | 8.8 | 0.7 | 8.0 | 0.9 |
| Peanuts | 1.4 | 0.6 | 3.1 | 0.7 | 4.4 | 0.8 | 6.7 | 0.9 | 4.7 | 0.9 |
| Onions | 1.0 | 0.2 | 2.0 | 0.2 | 3.0 | 0.3 | 4.3 | 0.2 | 3.2 | 0.3 |
| Summer vegetables | | 2.9 | | 3.6 | | 3.9 | | 3.4 | | 3.7 |
| Total of Summer Crops | | 61.1 | | 66.5 | | 66.8 | | 54.9 | | 61.0 |
| *Autumn Crops* | | | | | | | | | | |
| Maize | 56.0 | 31.7 | 67.2 | 25.0 | 64.9 | 20.4 | 70.6 | 16.9 | 65.5 | 18.7 |
| Sorghum | 2.9 | 1.1 | 4.7 | 1.1 | 5.9 | 1.1 | 7.7 | 1.0 | 6.1 | 1.1 |
| Rice | 0.2 | 0.1 | 0.8 | 0.1 | 1.2 | 0.2 | 2.0 | 0.2 | 1.3 | 0.2 |
| Autumn vegetables | | 1.0 | | 1.4 | | 1.5 | | 1.7 | | 1.6 |
| Total of Nili Crops | | 33.9 | | 27.6 | | 23.2 | | 19.8 | | 21.6 |
| Fruits | 2.9 | 1.1 | 3.7 | 1.1 | 7.5 | 2.4 | 20.2 | 5.2 | 8.9 | 3.7 |

SOURCE: Computed from Ministry of Agriculture, *The Fourth Agricultural Census, 1961, part I, section II* (in Arabic), pp. 119, 145, 171, 197, 223, 249.

*TABLE 7.A.4.*

*Credits provided to cultivators by the ACCB distributed according to their objectives in the period 1961/1962–1978 (Million £E)*

| | *Planting Credits* | | | | *Machinery purchasing credits* | *Livestock credits* | *Total*[a] |
|---|---|---|---|---|---|---|---|
| | *Field crops* | *Vege- tables* | *Fruit orchards* | *Total* | | | |
| 1961/1962 | 34.60 | 0.46 | 1.71 | 36.77 | 0.23 | 0.77 | 37.77 |
| 1962/1963 | 43.85 | 0.55 | 1.94 | 46.34 | 0.58 | 1.51 | 48.43 |
| 1963/1964 | 50.68 | 0.001 | 0.002 | 50.69 | 0.73 | 1.11 | 52.53 |
| 1964/1965 | 55.63 | 1.52 | 1.50 | 58.65 | 0.91 | 1.30 | 60.86 |
| 1965/1966 | 86.31 | 1.52 | 1.49 | 71.33 | 2.17 | 1.93 | 75.42 |
| 1966/1967 | 76.27 | 1.50 | 1.35 | 79.12 | 2.77 | 2.32 | 84.21 |
| 1967/1968 | 69.39 | 2.39 | 1.54 | 73.32 | 2.53 | 0.98 | 76.83 |
| 1968/1969 | 61.62 | 2.57 | 1.18 | 65.37 | 1.89 | 0.98 | 68.24 |
| 1969/1970 | 72.62 | 1.79 | 1.19 | 75.60 | 2.11 | 2.34 | 80.05 |
| 1970/1971 | 70.04 | 1.70 | 1.68 | 73.42 | 1.12 | 0.44 | 74.98 |
| 1971/1972 | 70.86 | 1.43 | 1.90 | 74.19 | 1.25 | 2.33 | 77.77 |
| 1972 | 67.62 | 1.81 | 1.89 | 71.32 | 0.89 | 2.52 | 74.73 |
| 1973 | 73.81 | 2.71 | 2.29 | 78.81 | 0.96 | 3.22 | 82.99 |
| 1974 | 72.72 | 2.69 | 2.51 | 77.92 | 0.32 | 1.77 | 80.01 |
| 1975 | 72.97 | 2.92 | 2.60 | 78.49 | 0.39 | 2.37 | 81.25 |
| 1976 | 81.26 | 3.06 | 3.82 | 88.14 | 2.13 | 8.58 | 98.85 |
| 1977 | 92.85 | 4.53 | 3.65 | 101.03 | 1.73 | 15.86 | 118.62 |
| 1978 | 98.18 | 4.65 | 4.17 | 107.00 | 4.89 | 21.47 | 133.36 |

SOURCE: The Principal Bank of Development and Agricultural Credit, unpublished data.

NOTE: [a]The total doesn't include small loans provided for some purposes such as cleaning of drainage canals, setting up of honeybees' houses, manufacturing of carpets, and other nonagricultural purposes. The amount of these loans reached its maximum of £E1.25 million in 1978. It was about £E0.58 million in 1977.

TABLE 7.A.5.

*The relative distribution of credits provided to cultivators by ACCB according to their objectives in the period 1961/1962–1978*
*(percent)*

| | Planting Credits | | | | Machinery-purchasing credits | Livestock credits | Total |
|---|---|---|---|---|---|---|---|
| | Field crops | Vege-tables | Fruit orchards | Total | | | |
| 1961/1962 | 91.7 | 1.2 | 4.5 | 97.4 | 0.6 | 2.0 | 100 |
| 1962/1963 | 90.5 | 1.1 | 4.0 | 95.7 | 1.2 | 3.1 | 100 |
| 1963/1964 | 96.5 | ... | ... | 96.5 | 1.4 | 2.1 | 100 |
| 1964/1965 | 91.4 | 2.5 | 2.5 | 96.4 | 1.5 | 2.1 | 100 |
| 1965/1966 | 90.6 | 2.0 | 2.0 | 94.6 | 2.9 | 2.5 | 100 |
| 1966/1967 | 90.6 | 1.8 | 1.6 | 93.9 | 3.3 | 2.8 | 100 |
| 1967/1968 | 90.3 | 3.1 | 2.0 | 95.4 | 3.3 | 1.3 | 100 |
| 1968/1969 | 90.3 | 3.8 | 1.7 | 95.8 | 2.8 | 1.4 | 100 |
| 1969/1970 | 90.7 | 2.2 | 1.5 | 94.5 | 2.6 | 2.9 | 100 |
| 1970/1971 | 93.4 | 2.3 | 2.2 | 97.9 | 1.5 | 0.6 | 100 |
| 1971/1972 | 91.1 | 1.8 | 2.4 | 95.4 | 1.6 | 3.0 | 100 |
| 1972 | 90.5 | 2.4 | 2.5 | 95.4 | 1.2 | 3.4 | 100 |
| 1973 | 88.9 | 3.3 | 2.8 | 95.0 | 1.1 | 3.9 | 100 |
| 1974 | 90.9 | 3.4 | 3.1 | 97.4 | 0.4 | 2.2 | 100 |
| 1975 | 89.8 | 3.6 | 3.2 | 96.6 | 0.5 | 2.9 | 100 |
| 1976 | 82.2 | 3.1 | 3.9 | 89.2 | 2.1 | 8.7 | 100 |
| 1977 | 78.3 | 3.8 | 3.1 | 85.2 | 1.4 | 13.4 | 100 |
| 1978 | 73.6 | 3.5 | 3.1 | 80.2 | 3.7 | 16.1 | 100 |

SOURCE: Computed from table 7.A.4, this appendix.

*TABLE 7.A.6.*

*Indices of credits provided to cultivators by ACCB according to their objectives in the period 1961/1962–1978 (1961/1962 = 100)*

| | Planting Credits | | | | Machinery-purchasing credits | Livestock credits | Total |
|---|---|---|---|---|---|---|---|
| | Field crops | Vegetables | Fruit orchards | Total | | | |
| 1961/1962 | 100 | 100 | 100 | 100 | 100 | 100 | 100 |
| 1962/1963 | 127 | 118 | 113 | 126 | 249 | 197 | 128 |
| 1963/1964 | 146 | ... | ... | 138 | 315 | 144 | 139 |
| 1964/1965 | 161 | 330 | 87 | 159 | 392 | 169 | 161 |
| 1965/1966 | 197 | 330 | 87 | 194 | 934 | 250 | 200 |
| 1966/1967 | 220 | 324 | 79 | 215 | 1195 | 302 | 223 |
| 1967/1968 | 200 | 518 | 90 | 199 | 1089 | 128 | 203 |
| 1968/1969 | 178 | 558 | 69 | 178 | 814 | 127 | 181 |
| 1969/1970 | 210 | 388 | 70 | 206 | 907 | 305 | 212 |
| 1970/1971 | 202 | 368 | 99 | 200 | 484 | 57 | 198 |
| 1971/1972 | 205 | 311 | 111 | 202 | 538 | 303 | 206 |
| 1972 | 195 | 392 | 111 | 194 | 382 | 327 | 198 |
| 1973 | 213 | 587 | 134 | 214 | 412 | 419 | 220 |
| 1974 | 210 | 583 | 147 | 212 | 137 | 230 | 212 |
| 1975 | 211 | 633 | 152 | 213 | 169 | 308 | 215 |
| 1976 | 235 | 662 | 224 | 240 | 917 | 1116 | 262 |
| 1977 | 268 | 981 | 214 | 275 | 746 | 2061 | 314 |
| 1978 | 284 | 1008 | 244 | 291 | 2106 | 2791 | 353 |

SOURCE: Computed from table 7.A.4, this appendix.

*TABLE 7.A.7.*

*The relative distribution of planting credits provided to cultivators by the ACCB according to their objectives in the period 1961/1962–1978*

*(percent)*

| | *Field Crops* | *Vegetables* | *Fruit Orchards* | *Total* |
|---|---|---|---|---|
| 1961/1962 | 94.1 | 1.3 | 4.6 | 100 |
| 1962/1963 | 94.6 | 1.2 | 4.2 | 100 |
| 1963/1964 | 100.0 | ... | ... | 100 |
| 1964/1965 | 94.9 | 2.6 | 2.5 | 100 |
| 1965/1966 | 95.8 | 2.1 | 2.1 | 100 |
| 1966/1967 | 96.4 | 1.9 | 1.7 | 100 |
| 1967/1968 | 94.6 | 3.3 | 2.1 | 100 |
| 1968/1969 | 94.3 | 3.9 | 1.8 | 100 |
| 1969/1970 | 96.1 | 2.4 | 1.6 | 100 |
| 1970/1971 | 95.4 | 2.3 | 2.3 | 100 |
| 1971/1972 | 95.5 | 1.9 | 2.6 | 100 |
| 1972 | 94.8 | 2.5 | 2.6 | 100 |
| 1973 | 93.7 | 3.4 | 2.9 | 100 |
| 1974 | 93.3 | 3.4 | 3.2 | 100 |
| 1975 | 93.0 | 3.7 | 3.2 | 100 |
| 1976 | 92.2 | 3.5 | 4.3 | 100 |
| 1977 | 91.9 | 4.5 | 3.6 | 100 |
| 1978 | 91.8 | 3.3 | 3.9 | 100 |

SOURCE: Computed from table 7.A.4., this appendix.

TABLE 7.A.8.

*The planting credits provided to cultivators by ACCB according to their kinds in the period 1961/1962–1978*

| | Credits in kind | | | Credits in cash | | |
|---|---|---|---|---|---|---|
| | Total (million £E) | % of planting credits | Index (1961/1962 = 100) | Total (million £E) | % of planting credits | Index (1961/1962 = 100) |
| 1961/1962 | 21.62 | 58.8 | 100 | 15.15 | 41.2 | 100 |
| 1962/1963 | 30.13 | 65.0 | 139 | 16.20 | 35.0 | 107 |
| 1963/1964 | 32.55 | 64.2 | 151 | 18.13 | 35.8 | 120 |
| 1964/1965 | 34.57 | 59.0 | 160 | 24.07 | 41.0 | 159 |
| 1965/1966 | 47.23 | 66.2 | 218 | 24.09 | 33.8 | 159 |
| 1966/1967 | 53.61 | 67.8 | 248 | 25.51 | 32.2 | 168 |
| 1967/1968 | 52.20 | 71.2 | 241 | 21.12 | 28.8 | 139 |
| 1968/1969 | 46.04 | 70.4 | 213 | 19.33 | 29.6 | 128 |
| 1969/1970 | 51.80 | 68.5 | 240 | 23.79 | 31.5 | 157 |
| 1970/1971 | 49.74 | 67.7 | 230 | 23.68 | 32.3 | 156 |
| 1971/1972 | 50.24 | 67.6 | 232 | 23.95 | 32.4 | 158 |
| 1972 | 47.42 | 66.5 | 219 | 23.90 | 33.5 | 158 |
| 1973 | 51.24 | 65.0 | 237 | 27.57 | 35.0 | 182 |
| 1974 | 51.79 | 66.5 | 240 | 26.13 | 33.5 | 172 |
| 1975 | 49.24 | 62.7 | 228 | 29.25 | 37.3 | 193 |
| 1976 | 51.95 | 58.9 | 240 | 36.19 | 41.1 | 239 |
| 1977 | 59.70 | 58.9 | 276 | 41.53 | 41.1 | 274 |
| 1978 | 66.00 | 61.7 | 305 | 40.99 | 38.3 | 271 |

SOURCE: Collected and computed from the Principal Bank of Development and Agricultural Credit, unpublished data.

## Notes

1. Sa'd Hajrās, *Land Reform, History, Philosophy, & System* (in Arabic), ʿAyn Shams Bookshop, Cairo, 1970), pp. 319, 320.

2. See Office of the Project of Organizing the Crop Rotation, Ministry of Agriculture, *The Project of Organizing the Crop Rotation* (in Arabic), (Division of Agricultural Extension, Ministry of Agriculture, Cairo, 1962), p. 10; and Sa'd Hajrās, pp. 344–345.

3. For further details concerning decisions organizing consolidation of land use and organizing of the crop rotation, see Muhammad al-Saʿīd Muhammad, *Organizations of Agricultural Crops Production Starting Agricultural Year 1968/69*, (in Arabic), (General Department of Agricultural Extension, Ministry of Agriculture, Cairo, 1968), pp. 3–12; al-Sayyid Ahmad al-Khulī, *Crop Rotation Between Organization and Legislation*, "Ikhtarnā li-l-Fallāh" Series No. 100, (in Arabic), (Ministry of Agriculture, Cairo, 1979), pp. 49–54; and

Ministry of Justice, *Legislative Bulletin* (in Arabic), no. 11, November 1963, Cairo, 1964, p. 3843, and no. 1, January 1964, Cairo, 1964, pp. 51–52.

4. H. A. El Tobgy, *Contemporary Egyptian Agriculture,* 2nd ed., (Ford Foundation, Cairo, 1976), p. 164.

5. The results of this field study are reported in Ahmed Hassan, "The Role of Legislation in Fulfilling the Targets of the Agricultural Development Plan in the UAR, With Special Reference to Legislations of Consolidation of Land Use and Organizing of Crop Rotation," Institute of National Planning (INP) Diploma Research Paper, 1970.

The sample taken included only 100 landholders distributed among 10 villages in 5 districts in al-Gharbīya, al-Daqhālīya, al-Sharqīya and al-Minūfīya. Although the size of the sample was too small, it was sufficient for the purpose of the study at the time when it was made. I use the results of this study because of the absence of other studies and official data concerning the economic and social results of the CLUOCR. They help here merely as pointers to the distributional effect of the mentioned policy.

6. Computed from Ministry of Agriculture, *The Fourth Agricultural Census 1961,* part I, section II, (in Arabic), pp. 52–71.

7. According to my field study, the proportion of holdings constituted from one lot in the sample amounted to about 15 percent in Kafr al-Zayyāt, 45 percent in Dikirnis and Diyarb Nijm, 80 percent in Kafr Saqr and 35 percent in Shibīn al-Kūm. The proportion of holdings constituted from two lots in the sample amounted to about 30 percent in Kafr al-Zayyāt, 35 percent in Dikirnis and Diyarb Nijm, 15 percent in Kafr Saqr and 25 percent in Shibīn al-Kūm. This assures my belief that the two lots constituting one holding may lie in one single crop block. Furthermore, the study has shown, especially in Dikirnis and Diyarb Nijm, that three or even four lots which constitute a small holding and sometime middle one may lie in one single crop block.

8. In an interview with Muhammad-al-Sa'īd Muhammad, former director of agricultural legislations in the Ministry of Agriculture, who devoted most of his time to write about the legislation organizing the consolidation of land use and its implementation, he corroborated this fact that I deduced through my field study.

9. According to the Fourth Agricultural Census, 1961, the total number of fruit orchard holdings is 54,961; the total area is 141,178 feddans, distributed according to holding categories as follows:

| *Holding category (feddans)* | *Holding numbers* | *Percent of holders* | *Total area* | *Percent Average holding area (feddan)* | |
|---|---|---|---|---|---|
| | | | | *Percent of area* | *Average holding per feddan* |
| < 5 | 40,594 | 73.9 | 25,023 | 17.7 | 00.6 |
| 5–10 | 6,234 | 11.3 | 12,412 | 8.8 | 2.0 |
| 10–50 | 6,032 | 11.0 | 33,796 | 24.0 | 5.6 |
| 50 and more | 2,101 | 3.8 | 69,947 | 49.5 | 33.3 |
| Total | 54,961 | 100 | 141,178 | 100 | 2.6 |

Collected and computed from *The Fourth Agricultural Census,* part I, section III, (in Arabic), p. 26.

10. The term *Cooperative Marketing* is used in this study although I believe that what takes place is not cooperative marketing by any means. The Agricultural Cooperative Societies are no more than places where the accounts of farmers are settled, the values of their compulsorily delivered crops are paid after deducting the land taxes and their debts to the ACCB. There is no clearer evidence than the fact that there is no single characteristic of cooperative marketing known in the cooperative literature. The marketing operation known

in Egypt as cooperative marketing does not exceed the fact that the farmer delivers to the governmental centers the quantities he is obligated to deliver according to the law, where officials receive, weigh and inspect these quantities with a view to settling their prices according to qualities. It may be worth mentioning that I consider as cooperative marketing only the cooperative marketing of cotton produced by the beneficiaries of land redistributed as a result of agrarian reform, before the generalizing of what is known now as cooperative marketing.

11. Although sugarcane is an important industrial crop, it is, however, not included within the framework of cooperative marketing due to the fact that the sugar company is the only buyer, and was even before cooperative marketing was known in Egyptian agriculture. Furthermore, there is the costly and difficult transport of the sugarcane crop from Upper Egypt to the consumption centers in Cairo, Alexandria, and other towns in the delta. Although sugarcane marketing is done according to contracts concluded between the company on one hand and the farmer on the other, the bulletin of cooperative activity issued by the CAPMS includes these transactions as if they were cooperative marketing.

12. M. Abdel-Fadil, *Development, Income Distribution and Social Change in Rural Egypt (1952–1970)*, Cambridge University Press, London, 1975, p. 85.

13. The registers of the Principal Bank for Development and Agricultural Credit.

14. See Fu'ād Mursī, *This Economic Open Door* (Hadhā al-Infitāh al-Iqtisādī) (Dar al-Thaqāfa al-Jadīda, Cairo, 1976), p. 29.

15. There is a fine of £E20 for every ton a cultivator fails to deliver of the quantities assessed him.

16. The CD quota of rice amounts to 1.25 tons in Fayyūm and Kafr Sa'd in Dumyāt governorate, and 1 ton in Burullus in Kafr al-Shaykh governorate, and Abū al-Matāmīr in al-Buhayra governorate; from registers of PBDAC, unpublished data.

17. Computed as an annual average in the period 1972–1977 amounting to 2.18 tons: computed from CAPMS, *The Annual Statistical Book of ARE, 1952–1977*, p. 42.

18. The holders of less than three feddans number about 2.36 million. They represent about 83 percent of all land holders who borrowed from the Banks of Development and Agricultural Credit in 1978. Registers of the PBDAC, unpublished data.

19. The registers of the Principal Bank for Development and Agricultural Credit.

20. Massar, Saad, "Structural Changes and Socialist Transformation in Agriculture of the UAR" (Egypt), *L'Égypt Contemporaine*, no. 337, July 1969, p. 286.

21. Computed from CAPMS, *The Statistical Year Book, UAR, 1952–1977, Preliminary Version* (Cairo, 1978), p. 42, and the PBDAC, unpublished data.

22. Computed from CAPMS, *Quarterly Bulletin, Foodstuffs Prices*, various issues, and the registers of the PBDAC.

23. Computed from the registers of the Principal Bank for Development and Agricultural Credit, and CAPMS, *Quarterly Bulletin, Foodstuffs Prices*, various issues.

24. Computed from *Ibid.*

25. With the exception of potatoes in 1967 due to the arrêté (no. 47, 1967) issued by Ministry of Supply and Internal Trade imposing obligatory delivery from 1966/1967 crops. This procedure has not been repeated.

26. The lentil CD price has been fixed since the winter season of 1979 at £E35 per ardab, whereas the amount of the fine for not delivering one ardab increased to £E70.

27. With the exception of sesame, which is domestically industrialized and consumed.

28. By small, middle, and large cultivators I mean those who hold up to 5 feddans, 5–10 feddans, and 10 feddans and more, respectively.

29. According to the Article 19 of the Agrarian Reform Act number 178 for 1952; See Sayyid Mar'ī, *Land Reform in Egypt* (Cairo, 1957), pp. 113, 327.

30. It was and is still the only organized source of agricultural financing.

31. Kamal El Din Mohamed Nabih, "Agricultural Cooperative Credit Planning in UAR" (complementary paper to the Seventh Long-Term Training Course, Institute of National Planning, Cairo, 1968), pp. 34–35.

32. See Nabik, p. 36; also Sāmī Abū al-ᶜIzz and Ahmad Muhammad Abū al-Ghār, *Cooperative Financing* (al-Shabāb Library, Cairo, 1972), pp. 396–398, 400; also Mahāsin Murād Qutb "An Analytical Study on Debts Collection: Its Basis, Means, Stages Evolution and Suggestions for Its Supporting and Promotion," Research Department, PBDAC, 1976, unpublished study, p. 26.

33. Ministry of Agriculture, *Agricultural Economic Bulletin, 1978,* part I, (in Arabic), Cairo, 1980, p. 19.

34. Ministry of Agriculture, *Agricultural Economic Bulletin, 1963* (in Arabic), Cairo, 1963, p. 12.

35. Ministry of Agriculture, *Agricultural Economic Bulletin, 1978,* (in Arabic), part I, p. 19.

36. See Article 4 of Law 117 of 1976 concerning the Principal Bank for Development and Agricultural Credit, The PBDAC.

37. The agrarian year begins in October.

38. General Egyptian Organization for Agricultural and Cooperative Credit, *Circular No. 400 of 1965 to all of its branches in the governorates and the managers of the agricultural cooperative societies.*

39. Owners and tenants, those who had repaid their loans and those whose loans were overdue, all alike.

40. The registers of the PBDAC.

41. With the exception of al-Minūfīya governorate, where this collateral was only a quarter of a feddan. This was due to the small-size holdings prevailing in it.

42. The registers of the PBDAC.

43. With the exception of al-Minūfīya governorate, where it suffices that the borrower should own a quarter of a feddan as a condition to getting a loan for one calf.

44. The share of this scheme in the total of livestock loans for the individuals amounts to more than 77 percent.

45. Before 1970 it was forbidden to get loans for livestock within more than one of the mentioned schemes.

46. With the exception of milk livestock around the principal cities, where this number decreases to five heads.

47. The reason provided is that fodder is one of most important inputs of animal production, hence no restrictions should be put on it and fodder should not be permitted to be used in subsidizing the meat price.

48. The registers of the PBDAC.

49. "Decision of the Minister of Agriculture No. 1719 for 1978."

50. See Ahmed Hasan Ibrāhīm, "The Economic Relationships Between Agriculture and Industry in Egypt," (Ph.D. diss. (in German), High School of Economics, Berlin, GDR, 1977), p. 67.

51. The registers of the PBDAC. Data about the distribution of agricultural machinery credits between individuals on the one hand and cooperatives and local bodies on the other are not available for years before 1977.

52. The registers of the PBDAC.

53. Taking into consideration the ratio of population (more than 40 million) to the cultivated land area (about 6 million feddans only) in Egypt and the cropping intensity (about

two crops a year on the average in the same area), I consider the cultivators of less than 5 feddans as small cultivators and the cultivators of 10 and more feddans as the large ones. The cultivators between both categories, those with 5–10 feddans, are considered as middle cultivators. This classification may naturally differ from the classification of cultivators in other countries where the ratio of population to the cultivated land area notably differs from that in the case of Egypt.

# CHAPTER 8

# *The Development of the Share of Agricultural Wage Labor in the National Income of Egypt*

Amr Mohie-Eldin

## I. The Formation of the Agricultural Wage Labor Force

In dealing with the historical formation of the agricultural wage labor force, we start with a basic theoretical assumption and test it against historical evidence. This assumption is that the origins of the agricultural proletariat are tied with the creation of a free market for agricultural labor. The market is tied with the mode of production prevailing, the pattern of economic organization in agriculture, and hence, ultimately, the system of ownership of the means of production. Thus the development of a free market for labor in agriculture is closely connected with the development of private ownership in agriculture. Only when full private ownership was completed were the seeds of a free market for labor sown. With the formation of private ownership, a distinction was created between those who owned means of production and those who owned their labor force.

Before we examine this thesis in detail, a point of clarification should be made. The existence of a free market for wage labor, in which there is a free interaction of supply and demand for wage labor, is completely different as a social formation from the existence of some form of paid labor. In a slave system or semislave system, there can exist some form of paid labor, but a free market for wage labor is definitely absent. The corvée system that existed in Egypt for such a long time was in a sense paid labor, but that does not mean the existence of a free market for wage labor where labor is a free commodity. Corvée labor was forced labor. A free market for wage labor exists when labor becomes an independent factor of production able to supply its labor power freely to the highest bidder.

The system of land distribution and land utilization that existed during the Mamlūk period (1250–1517) was actually established during the Ayubid era (1171–1250). In this system, known in history as the "Military

Land Grant System," land was distributed among the sultan and his army men.[1] The share of the sultan and his family was decided first *(al-khāss al-sultānī)*.[2] Land was then distributed to the Mamlūk princes, who were the leaders of the sultan's army. Each prince was given an estate that sometimes included a large district (several villages).[3] Then land was granted to army officers according to rank.[4] The land grant system gave the holder only the right of utilization *(usufruct right)*, not full ownership.[5] Only the usufruct title was granted.[6] However, such a right was not permanent. The land was periodically redistributed under several occasions,[7] such as when a new sultan was appointed, when the sultan reshuffled his army officers, and when economic or political circumstances required redistribution.

The granting of land by the sultan created certain obligations on the part of the Mamlūk princes and top army men. The obligations entailed preparing an army to fight under the command of the sultan,[8] paying the *Kharāj* (land tax),[9] providing means of transport among different parts of the country, and participating in public works through the use of some form of corvée labor.[10]

The agricultural land of the villages in the areas granted by the sultan was allocated among the peasants of those villages. The power of distribution was exercised by the army officers, who were the day-to-day managers of those estates.[11] They also determined the rent the peasant had to pay and the share of the crop that he was allowed to take, which differed from region to region and from time to time.[12] The share of the crop was so low and the rent was so high that peasants often deserted their land.[13] When they did so, they were forced back to work on it.[14]

Peasants were part of the land they cultivated. They were transferred from one Mamlūk prince to another when land was distributed or when transfer of land took place through the selling of usufruct rights. Actually, the *Fallāh* was a serf who never owned the land.[15] It is clear that, under this pattern of agricultural organization, it was impossible for a free independent body of wage labor to exist, and hence there was no market for wage labor.

Historical evidence also shows that during the *Iltizām* (tax farming) system prevailing at the end of the Ottoman Empire—and even during that of Muhammad ᶜAlī, when the system was abolished—the Egyptian village as a unit had three major functions:

1. Village land was held in common and periodically redistributed among the peasants. The power of redistribution was held by the village shaykh, who held that power through the *Multazim* (tax farmer) or through the central authority since the time of Muhammad ᶜAlī. Those who were allotted land were asked to provide part of their labor freely on the Multazim's land and on large estates formed since Muhammad ᶜAlī.
2. The village was a fiscal unit, its inhabitants held responsible collectively for the payment of taxes.

3. The village as a whole, not the individual peasants, was responsible for the furnishing of labor for any required public works, that is, corvée labor.[16]

Under this system, it was impossible to generate a body of independent labor able to sell its labor power in a free market. The three functions held the village together as an autonomous unit. So long as private ownership in land was not granted, the three functions remained closely interconnected. (We shall follow the development of these functions to see when each ceased to exist. However, it is my belief that the collapse of the first function was bound to pave the way for the collapse of the other two.)

When Muhammad ᶜAlī abolished the Iltizam system[17] and land became fully owned by the state, he introduced new policies of land distribution out of which two new patterns of landholding emerged. First, there was the *Kharājī (Atharīya)* land, which represented land registered in the name of the village, cultivated by the peasants of the village, and on which the village paid taxes to the state. The second pattern represented the land granted by Muhammad ᶜAlī, which represented the seed of large land ownership.[18] These lands were tax-free, and their owners were allowed the use of corvée labor.[19]

The Kharājī (Atharīya) land was distributed among the peasant families of the village in the amount of 3–5 *feddans* per peasant family.[20] The village land was registered in the name of the village, not in the name of the holders. The village as a whole, not the individual peasant, was responsible for the payment of taxes.[21] Peasants had only the usufruct right, while title of ownership rested with the state. All historical records refer to private land redistribution, the power of which rested with the village shaykh.

Law 1846 *(Lā'iha al-Atyān)* legalized the existing pattern of land distribution, permitted the transfer of usufruct right, and gave the holders the right to mortgage their land.[22] The 1858 Saᶜīd law provided for inheritance of usufruct right according to Muslim law. As a result of Egypt's growing indebtedness during the time of Ismāᶜīl, the *Muqābala* law in 1871 was promulgated. This law freed anyone who paid six years' taxes in advance from his tax liability. Kharājiȳa owners paying Muqābala could enjoy full private-ownership rights in addition to tax concessions. In 1874, the Muqābala payment was made compulsory.[23] In this way, the greater part of land came under full private ownership. In 1891, those who did not pay the Muqābala were granted full private ownership. Thus, through the process of privatization of land ownership, a process of differentiation between those who owned land and those who did not started to take place.

This process of proletarianization of a large section of the peasant community took place as a result of several factors. First, when the Muqābala became compulsory, many small peasant landholders were not able to pay. Some of them transferred part of their land to large owners so that the latter would pay the Muqābala on the rest of the land, while others lost all their land to large landowners.[24] A second factor was the increasing burden of taxation on Kharājī land, which led large numbers of peasant cultivators to desert their land and flee to urban areas or to work on the estates of big landowners. Since land tax was the major source of revenue to the state, when these revenues fell short of expenditures, taxes on land were increased. The common responsibility of the village for the tax was an important element in the increasing burden of taxation. When a village was unable to fulfill its tax burden, the burden was transferred to nearby villages. The flight of peasants from their land due to tax burdens reached large dimensions; whole villages were deserted.[25] In 1856 a decree permitted peasants who wanted to leave their land due to the inability to pay the tax to do so. The area of deserted land in Sharqīya and in Daqhalīya provinces reached 67,000 feddans.[26] Moreover, when the ᶜuhda system was introduced, those who were not able to pay their tax arrears were expelled from their land,[27] and their estates were transferred to other peasants or taken over by the ᶜuhda holder. Another factor contributing to the process of proletarianization of an important section of the peasant community was the increased debt burden on the peasant population and the consequent mortgaging and dispossession of land. In 1858 a land law allowed the creditor who had held land under mortgage for over fifteen years to obtain usufruct right on it.[28] Another reason for the increase in loans and foreclosures was the legal sanction given to the acquisition of land by foreigners and the establishment in 1875 of a European court system in Egypt, known as the Mixed Courts, which brought about the introduction of mortgaging as known in the West.[29] (The dispossession of the fallāh's land as a result of mortgage is beyond the scope of this paper.[30]) Another factor that led fallāhīn to desert their land was corvée labor for public works or for military service. They fled either to towns or to large estates since labor working on those estates was exempted from corvée.

The second and third functions of the village dissolved as soon as private ownership developed. Thus, after the law of 1858, tax payment became the responsibility of the individual peasant landholder. While the supply of corvée labor remained the responsibility of the village during the reign of Saᶜīd and Ismāᶜīl, it became the duty of the individual peasant by the 1881 law.[31] Two subsequent laws (in 1887 and 1895) organized forced labor on individual bases. Gradually forced labor was abolished; what remained was the obligation to turn out to fight locusts and strengthen the dams in case of high floods.

## II. The Development of Agricultural Wage Labor

The definition of agricultural wage labor adopted in this chapter includes only those who do not either own or rent land, that is, landless laborers, whose only source of income is selling their labor power in the market at the prevailing wage rate. Thus, those who work on their own farms and also provide labor on other farms are excluded.

An estimation of the size of agricultural wage labor is of primary importance to this chapter in order to arrive at an estimate of their share in agricultural income. Difficulties in making such an estimate arise from the combination of the data on the size of the agricultural labor force, the absence of data on agricultural wage labor, and the vague definition used for wage labor in many sources.

In the face of these difficulties I have employed three methods for estimating agricultural wage labor, based on three different sources of data. The first method utilizes data for the agricultural labor force drawn from the Population Censuses and the Labor Force Sample Surveys. These sources show only the total agricultural labor force.

Table 8.1 gives support to the notion of a stable agricultural labor force between 1960 and 1976.[32] Over the entire period 1947–1976 the increase seems to have been only 8 percent.[33]

In the absence of concrete evidence to the contrary, we shall assume that the ratio of wage labor to the total agricultural labor force also remains constant. The data for agricultural wage labor in 1960 and 1966 were obtained from the 1960 and 1966 censuses.[34] The ratios of wage labor in agriculture to the total agricultural labor force were 34.5 percent and 33.3 percent, respectively. The Labor Force Sample Surveys were used to estimate the agricultural wage labor for 1973 and 1975. They give a ratio of wage labor to total agricultural labor force equal to 35 percent for the two years.[35] One may then assume the constancy of the ratio of agricultural wage labor in 1978, and hence estimate the agricultural wage labor for that year.

*TABLE 8.1.*

*Agricultural Labor Force and Agricultural Wage Labor 1947–1976*

| *Year* | *Agricultural Labor Force (In Thousands)* | *Agricultural Wage Labor (In Thousands)* | *Ratio of Wage Labor (%)* |
|---|---|---|---|
| 1947 | 4,086 | ... | ... |
| 1960 | 4,406 | 1,519 | 34.5 |
| 1966 | 3,973 | 1,323 | 33.3 |
| 1970 | 4,298 | ... | ... |
| 1973 | 4,422 | ... | 35.0 |
| 1975 | 4,425 | ... | 35.0 |
| 1976 | 4,422 | 1,548 | 35.0 |

SOURCES: For 1947, 1960, and 1976, the sources are the *Population Censuses*. The 1966 data are from the *Population Sample Census of 1966*. For the years 1970, 1973, and 1975, data are from *Labor Force Sample Surveys*, (Cairo: Central Agency for Public Mobilization and Statistics (hereafter CAPMS), May 1971, 1974, 1976).

*TABLE 8.2.*
*Agricultural Labor Force and Agricultural Wage Labor*

| *Year* | *Agricultural labor* | *Wage Labor (Permanent)* | *Nonwage Labor* |
|---|---|---|---|
| 1939 | 3,978 | 1,628 | 2,350 |
| 1950 | 3,442 | 1,058 | 2,384 |
| 1961 | 3,840 | 452 | 3,388 |

SOURCE: *Agricultural Censuses,* 1939, 1950, and 1961. The data for 1961 were adjusted to include only workers older than twelve years, to make them consistent with 1939 and 1950 data.

The ratio of females in agricultural wage labor and their age structure presented certain difficulties. In the 1960 census, the ratio of females to total agricultural labor force was 6.2 percent, while in the 1973 Labor Force Sample Survey, it was 2.3 percent. Again the ratio of females in wage labor in 1960 was 5.6 percent, and in 1975 it was 4.3 percent. Since the figures for 1975 do not seem to represent an economic phenomenon, but most probably a statistical aberration, I adopted the ratio of 1960.[36] For 1976, the same procedure was applied concerning the ratio of those in the age groups 6–12 to the total agricultural wage labor. The agricultural wage labor force in 1976, in which children included only male children of ages six to twelve, will be divided as follows:

(Thousands)

| Men | Women and Children |
|---|---|
| 1,254 | 205 |

This dual division is important for our analysis since women and children carry out separate activities at different times of the year and have different levels of money wages.

It should be noted, however, that both the ratio of females to total agricultural labor force and to wage labor force is exceptionally low. On family farms, which represent around 86 percent of the total number of farms, women participate in certain farm activities at specified times of the year. However, it seems that females who participate intermittently in farm activities were excluded from the definition of the labor force. Moreover, in wage labor where the sole source of income is the selling of labor power in the market, one would expect the female participation rate to be very high. That is why I consider that such ratios, whether provided by the census or the sample surveys, are very low.

The second method of estimating agricultural wage labor utilizes data from the Agricultural Censuses of 1939, 1950, and 1961.

Table 8.2 shows that if we compare 1939 figures with those of 1961, we would conclude that the agricultural labor force remained more or less constant.[37] However, between 1950 and 1961 the rate of growth was 1

*TABLE 8.3.*
*Agricultural Labor Force by Size of the Farm, 1961*
*(In Thousands)*

| | *Permanent Agricultural Labor Force* | | | | |
|---|---|---|---|---|---|
| | *Holders* | *Family Labor* | *Permanent Wage Labor* | *Temporary Agricultural Labor Force* | *Total Permanent Labor* |
| Below 5 feddans | 1,357 | 1,894 | 178 | 833 | 2,072 |
| Five feddans to less than 20 | 221 | 563 | 211 | 549 | 774 |
| More than 20 feddans | 33 | 88 | 209 | 469 | 297 |
| Total | 1,611 | 2,545 | 598 | 1,951 | 3,143 |

SOURCE: *1961 Agricultural Census,* vol. 1, part 4, table 58.

NOTE:

The data represent those who are six years old and over, in contrast to table 8.2., which represents only twelve years and over.

percent per annum. The ratio of wage labor showed a sharp drop between 1939 and 1961. This drop could not be accounted for by any changes that took place in agriculture during that period. The only factor that I could think of was the 1952 land reform, but this factor alone could not explain such a large decline in the size and ratio of agricultural wage labor. The reform affected a small pecentage (9 percent) of the cultivated area, and the number of families benefitting from this land distribution would not explain these changes.

Since results of the 1961 Agricultural Census are important, and widely used, they should be examined in some detail. Table 8.3 shows the agricultural labor force by the size of farm.

In the 1961 Agricultural Census, as table 8.3 indicates, the permanent labor force is 4,757,000. This result tallies with the results of the 1960 Population Census. Permanent wage labor represents 12.5 percent of the total permanent labor force. This is very low when compared with the Population Censuses or Labor Force Sample Surveys. However, permanent wage labor as a proportion of total labor increases with the size of the farm. It represents 8.5 percent of total permanent agricultural labor in small farms below 5 feddans, and 27.3 percent on farms between 5 and 20 feddans, while it jumps to 70.4 percent on farms above 20 feddans—a logical development since farms below 5 feddans are family farms depending largely on family labor (95 percent).

The Agricultural Census of 1961 presents for the first time data on the temporary labor force. The labor force jumps to 6,708,000 and is more than 2 million in excess of the 1960 Population Census figure. While there may have been conceptual differences in defining labor in the censuses, this does not explain such a large difference in the returns of the two censuses taken only one year apart. If temporary labor is also defined as wage labor, the ratio of wage labor to total agricultural labor force would come to around 37 percent*—a result I find hard to accept. However, the differentiation between permanent and temporary wage labor is not clear in the Agricultural Census. According to that census, permanent wage labor is composed of those who are involved in farm operations throughout the year, while temporary labor consists of those who work only part of the year in farm operations. What makes the situation more perplexing regarding this group is their distribution by size of the farm as it appears in table 8.3. Are they wage labor from outside the family farms who participate in some farm operations or are they members of the households who participate intermittently in some farm operations? The first possibility is excluded on two grounds: first, around 43 percent of temporary labor is on farms below 5 feddans, which already absorb 75 percent of the permanent agriculture labor force; and, second, contrary to permanent wage labor, the size of temporary labor declines as the farm size increases, while the reverse should be the case. Moreover, the unit of measurement in the Agricultural Census is the farm, which makes it difficult to account for the size of casual labor at this point of time. I believe, therefore, that this element of the labor force represents double counting, which is why I exclude it.

To arrive at an estimate of the labor force in agriculture in 1976, one could base an estimate on two alternative assumptions: (1) the constancy of the size of the labor force between 1961 and 1976; or (2) the decline in the labor force by 10 percent,[38] which would make the agricultural labor force in 1976 equal to 4,281,000 and agricultural wage labor equal to 538,200.

The third method of estimating agricultural wage labor is shown in table 8.4 and starts by estimating landless agricultural families and, hence, the landless agricultural population, and then deduces the landless labor force in 1976. We start with the rural population, and assume that the ratio of the nonagricultural labor force to total rural labor force is equal to the ratio of nonagricultural population to the rural population.[39] Taking the average size of the family in the 1976 census, we arrive at the number of agricultural rural families. By subtracting the number of agricultural landed families, we arrive at the agricultural landless families. By assuming a participation rate of 30 percent, we arrive at the landless labor force.

Since, among landless families, one would expect the female ratio to be

*In table 8.3, the sharp drop in wage labor was due to the fact that only permanent wage labor was included to make the 1961 census comparable with the previous two censuses, and only those of age six and over are included. In table 8.2, temporary labor was added to all groups age twelve and over.

TABLE 8.4.
*Estimation of Landless Labor Force in 1976*
*(In thousands)*

| | |
|---|---|
| Rural population | 21,446 |
| Agricultural population | 16,513 |
| Agricultural families | 3,303 |
| Agricultural landed families | 1,857 |
| Agricultural landless population | 7,230 |
| Agricultural landless labor | 2,160 |

TABLE 8.5.
*Distribution of the Cropped Area in 1976*
*(Thousand Feddans)*

| *Crop* | *Area* |
|---|---|
| Wheat | 1,396 |
| Barley | 104 |
| Beans | 298 |
| Lentils | 64 |
| Fenugreek | 34 |
| Chick peas | 9 |
| Lupine | 10 |
| Winter onions | 28 |
| Garlic | 12 |
| Flax | 48 |
| Birsīm (perennial) | 1,711 |
| Winter vegetables | 215 |
| Other winter crops | 70 |
| Orchards | 313 |
| Cotton | 1,248 |
| Sugarcane | 242 |
| Sīfī summer maize | 1,490 |
| Autumn maize | 401 |
| Sīfī summer millet | 45 |
| Autumn millet | 28 |
| Rice | 1,078 |
| Ground nuts | 32 |
| Sesame | 31 |
| Sīfī summer vegetables | 443 |
| Autumn vegetables | 529 |
| Summer onions | 31 |
| Other summer crops | 114 |
| Birsīm (Tahrīsh) | 105 |
| Total | 11,199 |

SOURCE: Ministry of Agriculture, Department of Economics and Statistics

*TABLE 8.6.*
*Male and Nonmale Labor Input per Crop*

| *Crop* | *Man Days* | *Nonman Days* |
|---|---|---|
| Cotton | 42.0 | 87.0 |
| Sugarcane | 98.0 | 31.0 |
| Rice | 35.0 | 40.0 |
| Maize | 25.0 | 10.0 |
| Beans | 19.0 | 5.0 |
| Fenugreek | 20.0 | 2.5 |
| Chick peas | 22.0 | 2.0 |
| Flax | 34.0 | 17.0 |
| Birsīm (perennial) | 19.5 | 1.0 |
| Birsīm (Tahrīsh) | 11.75 | ... |
| Millet | 42.0 | 9.0 |
| Sesame | 28.0 | 4.0 |
| Ground nut | 41.0 | 35.0 |
| Wheat | 27.0 | 4.0 |
| Barley | 18.25 | 3.0 |
| Lupine | 20.0 | 2.0 |
| Lentils | 21.0 | 2.0 |
| Garlic | 39.0 | 43.0 |
| Onions | 33.5 | 70.0 |
| Winter vegetables | 45.0 | 60.0 |
| Summer vegetables | 45.0 | 60.0 |

SOURCE: Ministry of Agriculture, Department of Economics and Statistics

above the average, I thus assume 15 percent as a female ratio to agricultural wage labor. The ratio of those between the ages of six and twelve is also assumed to be 10 percent, as in all censuses. The agricultural wage labor will be divided as follows:

| Men | Women and Children |
|---|---|
| 1,626,000 | 542,000 |

However, in the rest of the chapter, the estimate of agricultural wage labor that will be used is the first estimate, which relies on the 1976 Population Census, while using the ratios of the 1960 census. (We shall refer to the other two estimates when necessary.)

## III. Levels of Employment of Wage Labor

Having estimated the wage labor force, we now turn to estimating the number of working days per wage laborer. This is an important step before estimating labor's share in agricultural income.

The only source of income for landless wage laborers is selling their labor power in the labor market. Thus the ultimate determinant of their annual income is their level of employment throughout the year.

The demand for labor is determined by the level of technology employed, the size of the farm, and the type of the crop. The last factor is very important since labor intensity varies a great deal among different crops. Moreover, the demand for labor for each crop varies with the farm operations. Some farm operations like cotton-worm picking, cotton harvesting, and harvesting of winter crops require a large amount of labor, while others like sowing (except rice) and irrigation or hoeing require smaller amounts of labor. Since there are time lags between different farm operations, the demand for labor fluctuates and reflects labor's seasonal nature.

To estimate the seasonal demand for labor, I started with the area cultivated by each crop for 1976 (see table 8.5). I obtained information on labor input per crop per farm operation for men, women, and children (table 8.6). This division of labor input between men, women, and children is so important because they perform different farm operations and at different times of the year. That is why, as we observe in tables 8.7 and 8.8, the peaks of the demand for each category are different, May in the case of men and September in the case of women and children. This also reflects the sex division of farming labor in Egypt, where substitution is infrequent.

The Ministry of Agriculture publishes the *Farm Diary,* in which it specifies the timing of the farm operation for each crop. On the basis of the above information, area cultivated under each crop, labor input per farm operation, and the timing of every farm operation, we have been able to calculate the total labor input for each crop distributed over the year. Thus, if five days of labor input are spent in preparing the land for cultivation for wheat and this was carried out in October, then the area under wheat is multiplied by the labor input (5 men days) and the result was put under the month of October. Accordingly, the seasonal profile of labor input for each crop was carried out in this way: By adding the labor input for each crop under each month, we get the seasonal profile for labor input for men, women, and children for each month of the year. This is indicated in tables 8.7 and 8.8. However, it should be noted that the timing for each farm operation that was used is a theoretical, not an actual, one. That is to say, we used the timing specified in the *Farm Diary* of the Ministry of Agriculture, and this might, to a certain extent, differ from what happens in reality.[40] For example, the time specified for preparation of land for cotton cultivation is December. The farmers might delay the operation until January or even February to take advantage of several harvestings of bersim. For this reason our peaks might be flatter than the actual peaks.

To arrive at the number of days employed each month for men, women, and children, we divided the number of days worked by the size of the labor force.

We have three estimates of the agricultural labor force. The first

TABLE 8.7.

*Labor Input Requirement of Men on Monthly Basis*
*(Thousand Man Days)*

| *January* | *February* | *March* | *April* | *May* | *June* | *July* | *August* | *September* | *October* | *November* | *December* | *Total* |
|---|---|---|---|---|---|---|---|---|---|---|---|---|
| 25,760 | 11,270 | 26,084 | 39,084 | 54,745 | 28,600 | 10,304 | 25,118 | 33,118 | 29,947 | 21,200 | 15,100 | 322,030 |

TABLE 8.8.

*Labor Input Requirement of Women and Children on Monthly Basis*
*(Thousand Nonman Days)*

| *January* | *February* | *March* | *April* | *May* | *June* | *July* | *August* | *September* | *October* | *November* | *December* | *Total* |
|---|---|---|---|---|---|---|---|---|---|---|---|---|
| 2,576 | 8,243 | 4,885 | 9,791 | 49,490 | 44,515 | 25,509 | 34,528 | 65,191 | 5,926 | 8,245 | 773 | 257,672 |

TABLE 8.9.

*Seasonal Employment Profile for Men, Women and Children in Agriculture in 1976*
*(In Work Days)*

| | *January* | *February* | *March* | *April* | *May* | *June* | *July* | *August* | *September* | *October* | *November* | *December* | *Total* |
|---|---|---|---|---|---|---|---|---|---|---|---|---|---|
| Men | 7 | 3 | 7 | 11 | 15 | 8 | 3 | 7 | 9 | 8 | 5 | 4 | 87 |
| Women and Children | 4 | 14 | 8 | 16 | 83 | 71 | 43 | 58 | 109 | 10 | 14 | 1 | 431 |

source, the 1976 Population Census, shows the male labor force to be 3,629,000, while women and children represent 595,000. The latter estimate is based on 6.2 percent female ratio and 7.9 percent male children in the age group six to twelve. The number of days of employment for men, women, and children is indicated in table 8.9. It is clear from that table that there is huge underemployment throughout the year in the case of men and an acute shortage in the case of women and children from May until the end of September. The surplus labor in the case of men amounts to 44 percent[41] of the male agricultural labor force. However, this degree of underemployment represents a great deal of overestimation. This is due to the fact that the area cultivated for fruits and other crops is excluded. Besides, labor employed in animal production, which in 1976 represented 25 percent of agricultural production, was also excluded. Moreover, time spent in preparing animal manure and cleaning canals and drains is also excluded. For this reason, the figure for male employment should be adjusted by 25 percent to be 109 days per year.

I carried out two studies on surplus labor, one in 1966[42] and the other in 1975.[43] They show that a surplus exists among men, and a shortage prevails among women and children. Moreover, surplus labor dominates in small family farms (below 5 feddans), while acute shortage prevails in medium and large farms. Shortages and surpluses coexist so long as no substitution takes place between the labor of men and that of women and children. Moreover, surplus labor in small farms was assumed to be trapped within family farms (due to institutional factors) and is not available for work outside their farms.

It should be noted in this context that the above seasonal profile of men, women, and children seems inconsistent, as we shall see later, with the development of money wage rate for both categories of labor. The data show that the rate of increase of money wage rate for both categories of labor is the same. If this is the actual situation, then one would not expect such a pattern of seasonal profiles of employment where there is surplus of men and acute shortage of women and children. If there is surplus among men of the magnitude mentioned, the rate of increase of the money wage rate should be far slower than the case with women and children, where there is acute shortage.

Table 8.10 compares the seasonal profile estimate for 1976 with some earlier estimates. While these estimates are carried out for different years, they are still comparable. The difference in the total number of working days for men among the three estimates is due to the method of calculation used for 1961. As a result of the large cultivated areas under large and medium farms, the total labor input when divided by a small size of the labor force will result in a large number of working days per laborer.[44] As shown in Table 8.11, the case for women and children is different. We have now a larger number of working days per year (1976). Moreover, the

TABLE 8.10.

*Some Estimates of Seasonal Employment Profile in Egyptian Agriculture for Men*
*(In Work Days)*

| | *January* | *February* | *March* | *April* | *May* | *June* | *July* | *August* | *September* | *October* | *November* | *December* | *Total* |
|---|---|---|---|---|---|---|---|---|---|---|---|---|---|
| Mohie-Eldin (1976) | 7 | 3 | 7 | 11 | 15 | 8 | 3 | 7 | 9 | 8 | 5 | 4 | 87 |
| Mohie-Eldin (1970) | 7 | 3 | 7 | 10 | 14 | 7 | 3 | 7 | 9 | 8 | 6 | 4 | 85 |
| Mohie-Eldin (1961) | 5 | 8 | 9 | 16 | 16 | 7 | 7 | 10 | 10 | 10 | 8 | 4 | 110 |

SOURCE: Estimate for 1970 in "Underemployment in Egyptian Agriculture," in *Manpower and Employment in Arab Countries; Some Critical Issues* (ILO: Geneva, 1976). Estimate for 1961 in "Agricultural Investment and Employment Problems in Egypt since 1935" (London, 1966), typescript.

NOTE: The number of working days per month and over the year is weighted average of the number of days of work in small farms below 5 feddans, medium farms (5–20) feddans, and large farms over 20 feddans. The weights used are the ratios of labor force in every category of the farm size.

TABLE 8.11.

*Some Estimates of Seasonal Employment Profile in Egyptian Agriculture for Women and Children (In Work Days)*

| | *January* | *February* | *March* | *April* | *May* | *June* | *July* | *August* | *September* | *October* | *November* | *December* | *Total* |
|---|---|---|---|---|---|---|---|---|---|---|---|---|---|
| Mohie-Eldin (1976) | 4 | 14 | 8 | 16 | 83 | 71 | 43 | 58 | 109 | 10 | 14 | 1 | 431 |
| Mohie-Eldin (1970) | 2 | 5 | 3 | 6 | 31 | 27 | 16 | 21 | 41 | 4 | 5 | 0.5 | 161 |
| Mohie-Eldin (1961) | 2 | 7 | 4 | 7 | 12 | 39 | 33 | 11 | 44 | 5 | 9 | 2 | 175 |

SOURCE: Estimate for 1970 in "Underemployment in Egyptian Agriculture," *Manpower and Employment in Arab Countries; Some Critical Issues* (ILO: Geneva, 1976). Estimate for 1961 in "Agricultural Investment & Employment Problems in Egypt since 1935" (London, 1966), typscript.

NOTE: The number of working days per month and over the year is weighted average of the number of days of work in small farms below 5 feddans, medium farms (5–20) feddans, and large farms over 20 feddans. The weights used are the ratios of labor force in every category of the farm size.

peak period is more intense and of longer duration (from May until September). This is one of the consequences of the High Dam, that is, the increase in the area cultivated under rice. As a result of the increase in the supply of water made possible by the High Dam, the area cultivated under rice increased approximately three times between 1961 and 1976 (from 300,000 feddans in 1960 to 1,078,000 feddans in 1976). Moreover, since rice is one of the most labor-intensive crops, the number of days of work required from women and children is quite large.[45] The intensity of the peak is due to the fact that the demands for labor of different farm operations for different crops (particularly rice and cotton) conflict. In the case of men, one observes a slight labor reduction in the relative position of April and a slight increase in May. This is due to the transfer of large areas in Upper Egypt from basin irrigation (where harvesting of winter crops usually takes place between the end of March and April) to perennial irrigation (where harvesting takes place in May and sometimes even in part of June).

Two important points should be mentioned regarding the above calculations: First, the time distribution of farm operations is carried out on the basis of the theoretical time distribution as specified by the Ministry of Agriculture in its *Farm Diary*. In practice, the situation might differ a great deal. Late cultivation is a known practice in Egypt, in particular with regard to winter crops, which are preceded by *bīrsīm* (fodder). This is carried out because small farmers like to have several cutting of birsīm before starting other winter crops. Late cultivation of winter crops sometimes results in the harvesting of several crops together. Thus the harvesting of winter crops might occur in May instead of being distributed between April and May. This will lead to a sharper labor peak than the one that appears in the calculations and hence to a lower volume of surplus labor in the technical sense.

The second point is that the above calculation of the seasonal profile of employment in agriculture was carried out on the assumption that we do have two distinct categories of labor, male and nonmale (women and children). Moreover, I assumed that social institutions are so rigid that the possibilities of substitution are nearly absent. That is why we have acute surplus in one type of labor and acute shortage in another. If we relax this assumption and assume that the labor force in agriculture is homogeneous and that its entities are substitutable for one another, there will be no shortage or surplus, and the labor force will be fully employed at the peak season. Each category will be working around twenty-five days per month in the peak season. If we allow for allied activities, there might appear a slight shortage at the peak. The coexistence of shortages and surpluses (either among different farms or among different categories of labor), as our previous calculation shows, cannot continue. The organizational framework in agriculture has to create a device somehow to take care of that disequilibrium.[46]

However, what we really need is the calculation of the actual number of working days for the agricultural wage laborer in order to be able to calculate his income and hence his share in agricultural income. To do this, we follow three methods:

The first method is to assume that wage laborers will work the same number of days as other members of the agricultural labor force. Moreover, we will assume complete mobility and homogeneity of the agricultural labor force, as well as equal productivity of labor by men, women, and children. Thus the assumption of a rigid sex division of labor and nonsubstitutability between men, women, and children will be removed. In this case, we add up all labor inputs and divide them by the total labor force. This will mean that each member of the labor force will be employed 137 days per year. In such a case there will be no surplus labor; the labor force will be nearly fully employed at the peak season. (Each one will be working twenty-five days in May and September.)

The second method is to calculate the number of shortages[47] of women and children's days during the peak months (from May until September) and then distribute them among the male labor force—first, on the assumption of equal productivity by men, women, and children and, second, on the basis that male productivity is double that of women and children. The second assumption was based on the ratio of the average wage rate of men to women and children, as will appear in the next section. Of course, we are assuming here that the women's and children's labor forces are fully employed during the peak months (thus each one of them is supplying twenty-seven days of work per month). On the basis of the first assumption, the days of employment for the labor force will be as follows:

| Men | Women and Children |
|---|---|
| 125 [147] | 202 |
| days | days |

The figure within brackets reflects the case where we adjust the original eighty-seven days by 25 percent to take care of the other agricultural activities. On the basis of the second assumption, the total days of employment will be as follows:

| Men | Women and Children |
|---|---|
| 107 [129] | 202 |
| days | days |

It should be noted that the second method of estimation assumes that wage labor will work the same number of days as other categories of labor.

The third method of estimating employment of labor starts, like the second method, by calculating the number of days that represent the shortage of labor of women and children in the peak agricultural season and assumes that these shortages are filled by wage labor only. The logic behind such an assumption is the fact that wage labor, particularly male wage labor, is the most mobile category of labor in agriculture, particularly when compared with family labor. In such a situation, the number of days of employment of wage labor will be as follows:

Employment of Wage Labor (days)

| Men | Women and Children |
|---|---|
| 180 | 202 |

In such a case, the agricultural wage labor force cannot completely fill the gap in both May and September. In such a case, the gap will be filled by family labor on tiny farms below one feddan since they usually offer their labor in the outside market as a way of adding to their low levels of income generated on such small farms. Family labor on small farms below one feddan represented 17 percent of the total permanent agricultural labor force in 1961. I believe that the third method of estimating employment of wage labor is the most reliable. It reflects what actually takes place in Egyptian agriculture.

Using this last estimate of wage labor in agriculture, we turn now to examine the level of employment in the labor force. The number of days of employment on the basis of that agricultural labor force will be as follows:

Employment of Wage Labor (days)

| Men | Women and Children |
|---|---|
| 150 | 202 |

This was also based on the assumption that the shortages of labor of women and children will be met through the employment of landless wage labor. In such a case, with the exception of May, June, and September, wage laborers will be working less than the normal twenty-seven days per month. However, it should be noted here that the above estimation of employment excludes the possibility of employment in the off-season such as cleaning of canals and drains. Thus, adjusting the above two estimations of employment by 10 percent would still be within the normal bounds.

### IV. The Share of Wage Labor in National Income

We now turn to estimating the share of wage labor in agricultural income. Table 8.12 shows the development of average money wage rate for

*TABLE 8.12.*

*Seasonal Wage Rate in Egyptian Agriculture in Selected Years*
*(Piasters)*

| | Year | January | February | March | April | May | June | July | August | September | October | November | December | Average |
|---|---|---|---|---|---|---|---|---|---|---|---|---|---|---|
| Men | 1963 | 14.0 | 14.0 | 14.0 | 15.0 | 15.5 | 15.5 | 16.0 | 16.0 | 16.0 | 16.5 | 16.5 | 16.0 | 16.0 |
| | 1966 | 24.0 | 24.0 | 24.0 | 24.0 | 26.0 | 26.0 | 26.0 | 26.0 | 27.0 | 25.0 | 25.0 | 25.0 | 25.0 |
| | 1968 | 24.0 | 23.0 | 24.0 | 24.0 | 25.0 | 25.0 | 25.0 | 24.0 | 25.0 | 24.0 | 24.0 | 24.0 | 24.0 |
| | 1970 | 25.0 | 25.0 | 25.0 | 25.0 | 26.5 | 27.0 | 26.0 | 26.0 | 26.0 | 25.5 | 26.0 | 25.0 | 26.0 |
| | 1972 | 30.0 | 30.0 | 30.0 | 29.5 | 30.0 | 31.0 | 31.5 | 31.0 | 32.0 | 33.0 | 31.0 | 30.0 | 31.0 |
| | 1973 | 30.0 | 31.0 | 32.0 | 31.0 | 31.0 | 32.0 | 33.0 | 33.0 | 33.0 | 35.0 | 35.5 | 31.0 | 33.0 |
| | 1974 | 35.0 | 35.0 | 35.0 | 39.0 | 39.0 | 41.0 | 44.0 | 45.0 | 45.0 | 45.0 | 43.0 | 40.0 | 40.5 |
| | 1975 | 44.0 | 43.0 | 45.0 | 48.0 | 54.0 | 56.0 | 56.0 | 56.0 | 57.0 | 57.5 | 58.0 | 58.0 | 53.0 |
| | 1976 | 62.0 | 64.0 | 64.0 | 65.0 | 69.0 | 72.0 | 72.0 | 72.0 | 72.0 | 72.0 | 73.0 | 73.0 | 69.0 |
| | 1977 | 76.0 | 77.0 | 80.5 | 83.0 | 84.0 | 88.0 | 92.0 | 92.0 | 92.0 | 92.0 | 93.0 | 93.0 | 88.0 |
| Women & Children | 1963 | 7.0 | 7.0 | 7.0 | 7.0 | 7.0 | 7.5 | 8.0 | 8.0 | 9.0 | 9.0 | 8.5 | 8.0 | 8.0 |
| | 1966 | 12.0 | 12.0 | 12.0 | 12.0 | 12.0 | 12.0 | 12.0 | 13.0 | 13.0 | 13.0 | 12.0 | 12.0 | 12.0 |
| | 1968 | 12.0 | 12.0 | 11.0 | 11.0 | 12.0 | 12.0 | 12.0 | 12.0 | 11.0 | 12.0 | 12.0 | 12.0 | 11.5 |
| | 1970 | 12.0 | 12.0 | 12.5 | 12.5 | 12.0 | 13.0 | 13.0 | 13.0 | 13.0 | 13.0 | 13.0 | 12.5 | 13.0 |
| | 1972 | 15.0 | 15.5 | 16.0 | 15.0 | 16.0 | 15.5 | 15.0 | 16.0 | 16.0 | 16.0 | 16.0 | 16.0 | 16.0 |
| | 1973 | 15.0 | 15.5 | 16.0 | 15.0 | 16.0 | 15.5 | 15.0 | 16.0 | 16.0 | 16.0 | 16.0 | 16.0 | 16.0 |
| | 1974 | 15.5 | 16.5 | 17.0 | 20.0 | 20.0 | 20.0 | 20.0 | 22.0 | 22.0 | 22.0 | 20.0 | 20.0 | 19.5 |
| | 1975 | 21.0 | 21.0 | 22.0 | 22.5 | 23.5 | 24.5 | 24.0 | 24.0 | 25.5 | 28.0 | 29.0 | 29.0 | 24.0 |
| | 1976 | 27.5 | 30.0 | 20.5 | 29.0 | 31.5 | 33.0 | 33.0 | 33.0 | 33.0 | 35.0 | 36.0 | 37.0 | 32.0 |
| | 1977 | 38.0 | 37.0 | 38.5 | 39.5 | 40.0 | 42.0 | 42.0 | 44.0 | 45.0 | 45.0 | 45.0 | 45.0 | 42.0 |

SOURCE: Ministry of Agriculture, Institute of Agricultural Economics and Statistics (Cairo, 1978).

men, women, and children. Thus, between 1966 and 1977, average wage rate for men increased by 252 percent at an annual compound rate of 13.4 percent.

The rate of increase of money wage rate actually shot up after 1972. Thus, between 1962 and 1972, the average money wage rate increased by 63 percent at an annual rate of 6.5 percent, while it remained more or less constant between 1966 and 1972. After 1972, the rate of increase of money wage increased. Between 1972 and 1977, the increase was on the order of 267 percent at an annual rate of 27.5 percent per annum. However, it should be noted that, while between 1966 and 1972 the real wage rate in agriculture declined by 16 percent (this represents money wage rate deflated by index of consumer prices in rural areas: 1966/1967 = 100), the real wage rate after 1973 increased until 1977. The wage series presented in table 8.12 was adjusted upward since 1972 by 15 percent.[48]

One should remember that the deflator that was used for the money wage series represents the official price index. The World Bank estimates the Gross National Product (GNP) implicit deflator as equal to 18 percent, while other estimates put the rate of inflation as equal to 20 percent. In this case, the rate of inflation would explain a great deal of the increase in agricultural wage rate. This is particularly so because there has been no reporting of any incident of crop failure or delay of harvesting due to labor shortage. It is true that the situation of labor abundance no longer exists, nor has it been replaced by a situation of acute labor shortage. (There are other factors besides inflation that will explain the increase in agricultural wage rate; they will be discussed shortly.)

The share of wages in value added in agriculture showed a steady increase from 1959 until 1966, when there began a steady decline until 1974. After 1975, the share rose again. While the share of wages to value added in agriculture fluctuated, the share of wage labor in agricultural income showed a steady increase throughout the period. Its share increased from 8 percent to 10 percent in 1976. Moreover, the share of wage labor in the total agricultural wage bill, while declining from 32.5 percent in 1960 to 25 percent in 1966, jumped back again in 1976, reaching 37 percent of the total agricultural wage bill.

This trend in both money and real wage rate since 1973 reflects a changing situation in Egyptian agriculture. Several factors have led to a new situation when compared with that in the 1960s. The first factor is the growth in the size of the army and its working as a transformation mechanism, moving labor from agriculture to services. Jobs are guaranteed in the service sector for those who end their period of conscription. This represents a continuous drain on agriculture. That part of the labor force most affected is landless wage labor.

The second factor is the external migration of Egyptian labor to neighboring Arab countries. Direct labor emigration from agriculture to the Arab world does not represent an important element of the labor force in agriculture. Labor availability in agriculture was affected through the process of external emigration in an indirect way, that is, through the process of construction labor emigration. The emigration of construction labor reached about 40 percent of the working force in construction in 1976.[49] A process of replacement took place in the construction sector through drawing labor from agriculture,[50] either partially or totally. The labor drawn out of agriculture is wage labor that has a high degree of mobility when compared to other categories of agricultural labor. While these two factors may not affect the size of the agricultural labor force, they are bound to affect the proportion of wage labor to total agricultural labor force.

In the 1960s there was a surplus of labor on small farms and a shortage on large farms. Large farms depended largely on wage labor. When that labor was insufficient, these farms had to rely on the pooling of family labor from small farms. The dependence on family labor was very limited. Wage rates did not increase, and real wage rate even declined. In the 1970s the proportion of wage labor was affected, and the dependence of large farms on the supply of family labor from family farms increased a great deal. As a result of the existence of technical, as well as institutional, factors that constrain the supply of labor from family farms to outside work, the labor market in agriculture became tighter. The wage rate rose. This situation takes place whether or not there is a surplus of labor on family farms. It is the degree of perfection of labor supply from family farms that ultimately determines the degree of tightness in the labor market, and hence governs the movement of wages.

It is clear from the last section that the estimation of seasonal profiles of employment in agriculture in 1976 shows a huge surplus of men and an acute shortage of women and children. This situation seems inconsistent with the development of wages already described. If this situation persisted, the pattern of increased wages would be different. The rate of increase of the money wage for men should have been far lower than that for women and children, yet the pattern is different. The rate of increase of the money wage rate is the same for men, women, and children. Thus something must have happened in Egyptian agriculture to create this pattern of wage increase. In fact, the old institutional divisions of labor and wage determinations according to sex are giving way to a new system of more rational work allocation, where the wage is determined according to farm operation, regardless of the individual worker.

Given the number of days of employment for men, women, and children, the average annual per capita income in 1976 was £E125 for men and £E65 for women and children. However, it should be mentioned here that the Labor Force Sample Survey of 1975 shows that 31 percent of the families in agriculture have an income below £E200 a year. While this fact confirms our results concerning the size of the agricultural wage labor force, it might show, on the other hand, that our estimation of income of

TABLE 8.13.
*Factor Shares and the Share of Wage Labor in Agricultural Income 1959–1976 (£E million)*

| Year | Value Added | Wages | % | Wage Labor | % |
|---|---|---|---|---|---|
| 1959/1960 | 405.0 | 98.0 | 24.2 | 31.9 | 7.9 |
| 1960/1961 | 402.7 | 99.0 | 24.5 | ... | ... |
| 1961/1962 | 373.0 | 117.0 | 31.3 | ... | ... |
| 1962/1963 | 425.2 | 126.3 | 29.7 | ... | ... |
| 1963/1964 | 475.0 | 139.3 | 29.3 | ... | ... |
| 1964/1965 | 528.3 | 167.4 | 31.7 | ... | ... |
| 1965/1966 | 608.5 | 196.1 | 32.9 | ... | ... |
| 1966/1967 | 612.3 | 206.6 | 32.9 | 53.5 | 8.7 |
| 1967/1968 | 644.4 | 201.3 | 31.9 | ... | ... |
| 1968/1969 | 688.3 | 210.7 | 30.6 | ... | ... |
| 1969/1970 | 771.9 | 218.4 | 28.2 | ... | ... |
| 1970/1971 | 774.1 | 223.4 | 28.8 | ... | ... |
| 1971/1972 | 854.6 | 226.8 | 26.5 | ... | ... |
| 1973 | 1,062.4 | 252.1 | 23.1 | ... | ... |
| 1974 | 1,280.0 | 298.1 | 23.2 | ... | ... |
| 1975 | 1,468.0 | 449.2 | 28.3 | ... | ... |
| 1976 | 1,747.0 | 455.0 | 28.3 | 169 | 9.7 |

SOURCE: Value added and wages are from the Ministry of Planning's follow-up reports.

NOTE: The share of wage labor was calculated on the basis of 202 days of work for nonmen and 180 days for men.

this class is biased downward. This, however, might be due to lack of consideration of the employment opportunities in the off-season.

Having estimated the share of wage labor in agricultural income, we now estimate its share in national income (Tables 8.13 and 8.14). It is clear that the share of agricultural wage labor in the total labor force declined between 1960 and 1976 from 19 percent to 15 percent, while its share in national income increased from 2.4 percent to 3 percent. However, this

TABLE 8.14.
*The Share of Agricultural Wage Labor in National Income, 1960–1976 (percent)*

| Year | Share of Agricultural Wage Labor in Total Labor Force | Share in Agricultural Income | Share in National Income |
|---|---|---|---|
| 1960 | 19 | 7.9 | 1.9 |
| 1966 | 17 | 8.7 | 2.4 |
| 1976 | 15 | 9.7 | 3.0 |

SOURCE: Taken from the Censuses of 1960, 1966, and 1976.

represents a very negligible change in the share over a long period of time. Actually, the increase in the share during the period 1960–1966 is noticeable when compared with the next period, 1966–1976.

## V. Socioeconomic Portrait of the Agricultural Wage Labor

In this chapter we have made an attempt to calculate the income from agricultural employment for the agricultural wage labor. We have also calculated the share of this class in the GNP. In this section we try to describe the consequences of that income for this particular class. For instance, what standard of living would this level of income allow for the wage labor class? What level of nutrition could be commanded by that level of income? What are the levels and patterns of nonfood consumption enjoyed by the members of this class? In what degree would the level of income enjoyed by the members of this class allow them access to basic needs like housing, education, health?

Since the household is the basic income sharing unit, it would appear appropriate for the analysis to be carried out in terms of the household. In reality, the £E125 annual income for men and the £E65 annual income for nonmen do not represent the income enjoyed by the members of this class, but represent the earners' income. Two points need to be made prior to analyzing the standard of living enjoyed by the members of this class. The men's annual income, while adjusted upward, does not take into account the income earned from off-season agricultural employment. It might be appropriate to adjust the income again by 20 percent to allow for off-season income from nonagricultural employment.[51] The second point is to determine the size of the family and the earning members and the nonearning members. In a sample survey of 1,000 rural households carried out by the International Labor Office (ILO) in 1977 it was found that 25 percent of the poor and marginal households engaged in agriculture were landless. The age structure of households termed poor and marginal is quite interesting when compared to the nonpoor families. These poor households support a proportionately larger number of the young than do the nonpoor. People less than fifteen years old were 48 percent of poor households as compared to 41% for the nonpoor. The average size of the family for poor and marginal households was 6.4, the average annual household income was £E305, and per capita income was £E48.[52] Since, according to the survey, farm laborers have an average annual household income of £E217, they clearly fall within the group of poor and marginal households. Moreover, the dependency ratio in large laborers' households amounts to 2.9.[53]

If one assumes an income for the head of a household equal to £E150 plus one earning member of the family (the housewife), the total average income of the household for agricultural wage labor would be £E215. This is nearly equal to the finding of the ILO survey concerning farm laborers.

If one assumes an average size of the family of five (which is less than the finding of the survey for poor households) the per capita income of that class would be £E43. Even if we assume two earning members of the household plus the head of the family, the household income would be £E280, which is still within the poor and marginal households as defined by the survey.

One can, therefore, safely assume that the analysis of living standards and consumption levels and patterns of the poor and marginal households (within which the category of farm laborers fall) would apply to an agricultural wage laborer's household. The ILO poverty survey has calculated the caloric gap[54] of this class as the shortfall of caloric intake of a household from the requirements of its members given their age, sex, and the work they perform. According to this criterion, poor households suffer from a caloric shortfall of 20 percent of their caloric intake from cereals and starches, while meat, eggs, and dairy products contribute only 6.3 percent of the total caloric intake. Poor households suffer from serious protein deficiency.[55]

If one examines the consumption pattern of poor households, one finds that 78.5 percent is spent on consumer goods as compared to 69 percent of nonpoor households. Expenditure on food accounts for 68 percent of total expenditure of poor households compared to 53 percent of nonpoor households, while expenditure on cereals and starches accounts for 24 percent as compared to 14 percent of nonpoor families. Clothing accounts for 8 percent of the family budget for poor families, while expenditure on medical care and education accounts for 2 percent and 0.8 percent, respectively.

To complete the picture, we tried to look at the family budget survey data of 1974/1975. According to our previous calculation, the household income of agricultural wage laborers was £E215 based on the assumption[56] where per capita income was £E43. The household income based on the other assumption was £E280, and per capita income amounted to £E55. We looked at the pattern of expenditure of the per capita group of £E50 to £E60 per year as revealed by the Family Budget Survey (FBS). This corresponds to household expenditure group £E250–£E300.

The pattern of per capita consumption of this group shows that the share of food is 65 percent, similar to the finding of the ILO poverty survey. However, 40 percent is devoted to cereals and starches, compared with 24 percent as revealed by the poverty survey. The difference in the cereals and starches ratio will show different results regarding caloric intake.

Among the nonfood items, the share of textiles and clothing is the highest, around eleven percent. According to prices prevailing in that year, this means the consumption per head of six meters of textile and one pair of shoes. The share of housing expenditure seems surprisingly high, 10 percent of total expenditure[57]. This annual expenditure is more than

*TABLE 8.15.*
*Food Consumption per Person (kg/year) for Per Capita Expenditure Group £E50–60*

| *Food Item* | *Annual per Capita Expenditure (£E)* | *Price (Piastre/kg)* | *Daily per Capita Consumption (Grams)* | *Calories* |
|---|---|---|---|---|
| Grain & Starches | 11.5 | 4.0 | 786.0 | 2,813 |
| Dry Beans | 1.4 | 11.5 | 31.5 | 117 |
| Fresh & Preserved Vegetables | 2.5 | 4.9 | 137.0 | 54 |
| Fresh & Preserved Fruit | 1.0 | 13.5 | 20.3 | 9 |
| Meat & Poultry | 6.5 | 98.0 | 19.2 | 34 |
| Eggs | 0.6 | 99.0 | 1.6 | 3 |
| Milk & Products | 2.0 | 16.0 | 27.4 | 24 |
| Oil & Fats | 3.3 | 10.0(R) | 90.4 | 797 |
| Sugar & Sweets | 2.1 | 10.0(R) | 57.5 | 182 |
| Total | ... | ... | ... | 4,033 |

SOURCE: Annual expenditure compiled from CAPMS, FSB, 1974/1975, table 5.

NOTE: R = rationed prices. The prices for grain and starches are weighted averages, the weights being the ratio of expenditure breakdown of table 15 in FBS (1974/1975). The weights are as follows: wheat 31%, maize 26%, millet 7%, flour and bread 21%, and rice (second group) 14%. For meat and poultry, the weights are 0.75% and 0.25%, respectively.

£E32, half going to fuel and light (equal to one-half ton of kerosene), and the other half to rent. This is an exceptionally high rate for rent given the fact that nearly 90 percent of the rural families own their mud houses.

The per capita expenditure on medical care, medicine, and education services looks extremely low, 2 percent of total expenditure which is lower than the results of the poverty survey.

We attempted to transform the expenditure on food by this per capita income group into physical quantities. The latter is again transformed into its caloric equivalent using the Nutritional Institute conversion ratios. The prices used are those consumer prices published by the Ministry of Planning and the Central Price Agency for 1975.

The results, shown in table 8.15, are exceptionally high (in terms of caloric intake). They approximate North American food consumption and completely contradict the results of the poverty survey of the ILO[58] which indicated that the per capita caloric intake of this group was equal to 2,332 calories and was deficient by about 20 percent of the requirements for that group.

This exceptionally high rate of caloric intake in this class can be explained by the fact that the prices used are very low,[59] or there has been an overstatement of the consumption of grains and starches in the FBS.

TABLE 8.16.
*Percentage Distribution of Preschool Children in Egypt, 1978, by Height for Age, Class, and Geographic Area*

| Geographic Area | Percent of Stunting Severe < 85.0 | Moderate 85.0–88.9 | Total < 90.0 |
|---|---|---|---|
| Lower Egypt (rural) | 4.6 | 17.2 | 21.8 |
| Upper Egypt (rural) | 6.7 | 20.8 | 27.5 |
| Large villages | 4.6 | 19.7 | 24.3 |
| Small towns | 2.9 | 11.9 | 14.8 |
| Small cities | 1.7 | 8.9 | 10.6 |
| Total representative sample | 4.5 | 16.7 | 21.2 |
| Cairo-Giza | 3.5 | 15.5 | 19.0 |
| Alexandria | 2.9 | 12.8 | 15.7 |
| Special groups | 0.1 | 1.0 | 1.1 |

SOURCE: Arab Republic of Egypt, *National Nutrition Survey,* carried out by the Office of Nutrition, Development Support Bureau, AID, and the Nutrition Institute, Ministry of Health, Egypt, table 4 and p. 27.

Moreover, we did not have an appropriate extraction factor to transform the amount of wheat and maize into their equivalent in bread. Thus the entire amount of grains consumed was supposed to be transformed into the equivalent amount of calories.

However, if we use the prices for grains applied by the poverty survey, the caloric intake for that item will drop by around 50 percent, and the total caloric intake will be in the vicinity of 2,400. To show that the caloric intake of that group as indicated by the FBS is illogical, we compared this result with the results of other studies of quality of life indicators of the rural poor. A nutrition survey carried out in Egypt in 1977[60] shows that, in rural areas, fully one-fourth of the children are stunted, with the problem being more acute in some governorates in some occupational groups.

Tables 8.16 and 8.17 indicate how widespread is stunting (chronic malnutrition).

Stunting ranges from 10.6 to 27.5 percent among various geographic areas. It affects over one million preschool children. The problem is more serious in rural areas, especially Upper Egypt, than in cities, although it is also serious among the urban poor in Cairo, Giza, and the Alexandria area.

Table 8.17 shows that stunting in Egyptian children starts at infancy (10.2 percent of six- to eleven-month-olds are stunted) reaches its peak in the age group twelve to thirty-five and then starts to decline. What is really more revealing is the correlation between stunting and the occupation of the father, as shown in table 8.18.

It is clear that children of unskilled workers in urban areas and of most

*TABLE 8.17.*
*Percentage Distribution of Preschool Children in Egypt, 1978, by Height*

| | Percent of Stunting | | |
|---|---|---|---|
| *Age in Months* | *Severe (< 85.0)* | *Moderate (85.0–89.9)* | *Total (< 90.0)* |
| 6–11 | 9.2 | 8.0 | 10.2 |
| 12–23 | 5.7 | 20.5 | 26.2 |
| 24–35 | 6.1 | 20.4 | 26.5 |
| 36–47 | 5.6 | 17.0 | 27.6 |
| 48–59 | 3.5 | 12.8 | 16.3 |
| 60–71 | 1.0 | 15.0 | 16.0 |
| Total | 4.5 | 16.7 | 21.2 |

SOURCE: Arab Republic of Egypt, *National Nutrition Survey*, 1978, table 7, p. 34.

rural farmers are at particular risk from chronic malnutrition. It is also clear from the table that the children of agricultural (landless) wage laborers have the highest ratio of chronic malnutrition. Moreover, contrary to what is assumed, children of owners of farms of 0–5 feddans also have a high ratio of malnutrition. Besides malnutrition, the National Nutrition Survey indicates that Egypt's other major forms of malnutrition result in anemia. According to the survey, about 1.4 million or 25 percent of preschool children are anemic.[61] Moreover, among adults there is evidence that malnutrition is predominant among low-income, rural families, especially adult males.[62]

As for accessibility to other basic needs, the situation is no better. The ILO rural poverty survey shows that 87 percent of the poor live in mud brick houses, 3–7 percent live in huts. The unavailability of pure water

*TABLE 8.18.*
*Children Suffering from Chronic Malnutrition (Height for Age in Less than 90th Percentile) by Fathers' Occupational Categories*

| *Category* | *Percentage of Children* |
|---|---|
| Professional/managerial | 4.9 |
| Clerical/skilled | 16.2 |
| Semiskilled/unskilled | 19.8 |
| Farm owner (5+ feddans) | 19.3 |
| Farm owner (0–5 feddans) | 23.0 |
| Landless laborer/share cropper | 25.4 |
| Others | 20.0 |

SOURCE: Arab Republic of Egypt, *National Nutrition Survey*, July 1978, table 18A, p. 60.

*TABLE 8.19.*
*Access to Potable Water by Households*
*(percent)*

| | *Cairo* | *Alexandria* | *Other Urban* | *Rural* |
|---|---|---|---|---|
| Tap in dwelling | 70.1 | 77.8 | 66.6 | 3.7 |
| Tap outside dwelling but in building | 16.6 | 11.5 | 8.6 | 1.8 |
| Source outside building | 17.0 | 9.0 | 19.6 | 58.2 |
| No source | 1.6 | 0.0 | 12.3 | 36.3 |

SOURCE: CAPMS, 1976 Population Census, Preliminary Results.

and the predominance of poor sewage systems result in poor health, prevalence of parasitic diseases, and high infant mortality rates.

As shown in table 8.19, in rural areas, over 36 percent of the households have no access to pure water. Even for those who have access to potable water (58 percent), the source is outside the building. With respect to this important basic need, the rural areas are at a disadvantage when compared to urban areas. According to the Ministry of Planning report, only 23.2 percent of rural households in Lower Egypt and 10 percent of rural households in Upper Egypt are connected to a sewage system. Given the above conditions, it is no surprise that the WHO found about 50 percent of the cases of death in the two age groups 0–1 and 1–5 were due to diseases of the digestive system (including diarrheal diseases not established as infectious).[63]

To examine the extent to which these conditions affect agricultural wage labor, we attempt to relate some of the indicators of basic needs with levels of income and geographical areas (see table 8.20). Rural areas suffer most from the absence of basic needs requirements. Table 8.20 demonstrates how low-income families (below £E250) correlate with the degree of basic needs availability. The higher the ratio of poor families, the lower the level of basic needs satisfaction. Moreover, a high ratio of poor families (below £E250) results in a low index of the physical quality of life, which combines most of the indicators of basic needs such as infant mortality, pure water, availability of electricity, education, and so forth.

TABLE 8.20

*The Relationship between Some Basic Needs Indicators and Level of Income and Region*

| *Governorate* | *% Urban* | *Literacy* | | *% of Households with Electricity* | *% of Households with Pure Water* | *Households with Annual Income Below £E 250* | *PQLI* |
|---|---|---|---|---|---|---|---|
| | | *Total* | *Female* | | | | |
| Urban | 100 | 64 | 53 | 84 | 83 | 30 | 70 |
| Lower Egypt | 27 | 41 | 25 | 38 | 22 | 46 | 36 |
| Upper Egypt | 30 | 33 | 19 | 29 | 18 | 52 | 24 |
| National | 44 | 43 | 29 | 45 | 34 | 45 | 39 |

SOURCE: J. O. Field and G. Rapes, *Infant Mortality: The Birth Rate and Development in Egypt* (MIT, Cairo University Health Care Delivery System project, Governorate data study, 1980). The percentage of families below £E250 is taken from Lance Taylor's estimation of income distribution in Egypt, World Bank report, 1976.

NOTE: The PQLI is the physical quality of life index, which is a weighted index of indices of quality of life such as literacy, infant mortality, availability of electricity, and pure water. See J. O. Field and G. Rapes, "Development in the Egyptian Governorate: A Modified Physical Quality of Life Index," *L'Égypte Contemporaine*, April 1978.

## Notes

1. A. al-Qalqashandī, *Kitāb Subh al- A'shā fī Sinā^c^a al-Inshā*, 1519, vol. 4, p. 50. Also see al-Maqrīzī, *al-Mawā^c^iz wa-l-I^c^tibār bidhikr al-Khitār wa-l-Athār*, al-Nīl Publication, no. 1324 H, vol. 1, pp. 138, 156.

2. I. A. Tarkhān, *Misr Fi 'Asr Dawla al-Mamālīk al-Jarākisa*, ("Egypt in the Age of the Circassian Mamluk State,") (Khartoum, 1959), p. 222.

3. Ibid., p. 223.

4. Ibid., pp. 224–225.

5. Al-Maqrīzī, *Al-Khitat*, vol. 1, pp. 157–165.

6. Al-Qalqashandī, *Subh Al-A'shā*, vol. 3, p. 458.

7. I. A. Tarkhān, *Al-Nuzum Al-Iqtā^c^īya fi Sharq al-Awsat fī al-^c^Usūr al-Wustā, (The Feudal Systems in the Middle East During the Middle Ages)* (Cairo, 1968), pp. 261–294.

8. Al-Maqrīzī, *Al-Khitat*, vol. 2, pp. 153–154.

9. Al-Qalqashandī, *Subh al-A'shā* vol. 3, p. 548.

10. Tarkhān, *Al-Nuzum* (The Feudal Systems . . .), p. 200.

11. Historians differentiate between national public works and regional public works. The participation of the feudal prince is through provision of labor needed for public works, while the government provides the expenditure; the regional public works were the whole responsibility of the feudal prince and the peasants in their estate. See I. A. Tarkhān, *Al-Nuzum* (The Feudal Systems), p. 201.

12. Ibid., pp. 239–241. This is apart from other taxes and fees the peasant was asked to pay.

13. Al-Maqrizī, *Ighāthat al-Umma bi kashf al-Ghumma*, p. 48.

14. Al-Maqrizī, *Al-Khitat*, vol. 1, p. 138; Al-qalqashandī, *Subh al-A^c^shā*, vol. 3, p. 134.

15. Al-Maqrizī, *Al-Khitat*, vol. 1, p. 138.

16. G. Baer. "The Dissolution of the Egyptian Village Community," in *Studies in the Social History of Egypt* (University of Chicago Press, 1969).

17. ^c^Abd al-Fattāh, *Al-Qarīya al-Misrīya* (The Egyptian Village) (Cairo, 1973), vol. 2, p. 30.

18. G. Baer, *A History of Land Ownership in Modern Egypt* (London, 1962), pp. 12–19. See also ^c^Alī Barakāt, *Tatawwur al-Milkīya al-Zirā^c^īya fī Misr 1813–1914, wa athruhu ^c^Alā al-Haraka al-Siyāsīya* (The development of the agricultural ownership in Egypt and its influence on the political movement) (Cairo, 1977), pp. 29–39.

19. ^c^Abd al-Fattāh, *Al Qarīya* (The Egyptian Village) p. 39.

20. ^c^Alī Barakāt, p. 29; Baer, *Land Ownership*, p. 6.

21. ^c^Alī Barakāt, p. 30; ^c^Abd al-Fattāh, p. 6.

22. ^c^Alī Barakāt, p. 35.

23. G. Baer, *Land Ownership*, p. 10.

24. ^c^Ali Barakāt, pp. 286–300. This reference shows in great detail how the formation of large estates in the form of Ibādīya, Jifliks, and ^c^uhda land was carried out at the expense of peasants' land, and hence the process of formation of these large estates led to the expulsion of large numbers of peasants from their land.

25. ^c^Abd al-Fattāh, p. 220.

26. ^c^Ali Barakāt, p. 311.

27. Ibid, p. 309.

28. Ibid.

29. G. Baer, *Land Ownership*, p. 34.

30. For detailed information of dispossession of land of small peasants by moneylenders and Mixed Courts during the period 1858 till 1912, see ᶜAlī Barakāt, p. 313–322.

31. G. Baer, *Land Ownership,* p. 28.

32. The year 1966 may be an exception, but it is not comparable with the rest of the year since it is based on a sample census.

33. The Ministry of Planning and Follow-up Report for 1976 puts the agricultural labor force twelve years of age and over at 4,062,000. The basis of such estimation is not known to me.

34. Table 30 in the 1960 census, and table 7 in the 1966 census.

35. The census definition of wage labor was "those working for wage," while the Labor Force Sample Survey definition was "those who work for wage in kind or money." However, the definition does not make it clear whether or not those who work partly for money wage rates outside their farms are excluded.

36. The ratio in the 1966 census is also similar to 1960 data, that is, 6 percent.

37. The agricultural labor force in the age group 6–12 was excluded from the 1961 census results to make it comparable to the 1939 and 1950 censuses, which only included those above 12 years.

38. This assumption was made so that the result would be consistent with the results of the 1976 census.

39. The ratio was taken from the 1975 Labor Force Sample Survey.

40. This fact has an important implication for the seasonal profile of employment. Thus a delay in the cultivation of winter crops and hence delay in its harvesting, which may be a common practice, might raise the level of employment in May for men from 15 days to 26 days, and they would be fully employed if those crops that were supposed to be harvested in April were harvested in May.

41. This was estimated in the following way: The number of days the labor force is able to supply is assumed to be 27 days. This is multiplied by the labor force (men); so we get the total available supply. From this the amount actually worked in the peak months is subtracted. We then obtain the surplus labor days at the peak, which is again divided by 27 to get surplus laborers.

42. *Employment and Investment Problems in Egyptian Agriculture Since 1935,* (London, 1966).

43. "Underemployment in Egyptian Agriculture," in ILO. *Aspects of Employment Problems in Some Arab Countries* (Geneva, 1976).

44. Thus the number of working days for men in the first, second, and third groups were 64, 169, and 463 working days. However, the weight of the third group is small, and it is bound to affect the average. The 463 working days on large farms (above 20 feddans) does not mean that each laborer worked this number of days, but these are results of the division of total labor input by the size of the labor force. See *Agricultural Investment and Employment in Egypt Since 1935* (London, 1966), p. 138.

45. See table 8.5. Moreover, some of the *nili* (autumn) crops, like maize, were transferred to be *sifi* (summer) crops. Thus, the area cultivated by summer (sifi) maize increased from 128,000 feddans in 1960 to 1,426,000 feddans in 1976, while the area under nili maize declined from 1,433,000 to 404,000 feddans.

46. I shall discuss this point later in examining the development of wages.

47. The shortage is calculated by assuming that each member of nonmale labor force will be able to supply 27 days per month. By multiplying that with the nonmale labor force, we get total supply. By subtracting total supply from total demand at peak months, we get the actual volume of nonmale labor shortage.

48. This procedure was carried out because I found some discrepancy between the

reported figures of the Ministry and some other figures in some parts of rural areas. (The difference was about 10% to 15%.) When I consulted some people at the Department of Economics, they reported that their figures represented a simple average for the economy as a whole. Moreover, there is wide variation around the mean.

49. N. Choucri, R. Eckaus, A. Mohie-Eldin, *Migration and Employment in the Construction Sector: Critical Factors in Egyptian Development* (Cairo: Cairo University/Massachusetts Institute of Technology Program, 1978), p. 81.

50. The construction wage rate, as a result of emigration, increased about fourfold between 1971 and 1977.

51. The poverty survey shows that among low-income families the off-farm income or that from nonfarm activities reaches over 20% in certain cases.

52. Samir Radwan and Eddy Lee, *The Anatomy of Rural Poverty,* (Egypt, 1977), draft chap. 5, and "Nutrition and Basic Needs," (Geneva; ILO, 1977) table 5–17, p. 49.

53. Poor households are those with household incomes of £E327, while marginal households are those with a household income of £E267. See Radwan and Lee, "Nutrition and Basic Needs" p. 9, table 5–2, and p. 48, table 5–16.

54. The expenditure on food by this class was transformed into quantities using consumer prices prevailing for 1977; the latter was converted with calories equivalent using FAO conversion ratio. See Radwan and Lee, *The Anatomy of Rural Poverty,* chap. 5, p. 23.

55. Ibid., table 5–9.

56. The first assumption is that the family has two earning members and three dependents; the other is that the family has three earning members and two dependents.

57. CAPMAS, *Family Budget Survey in Arab Republic of Egypt (ARE). Computer Results for the Four Rounds, 1974/75* (Cairo, September 1978), table 5, p. 23–24. The poverty survey shows the share of rent to be equal to 1.5 percent, while in the FBS it is more than 5 percent.

58. The IBRD study of the Egyptian FBS came to the same conclusion as mine, that the consumption levels treated by the survey are too high. See Arab Republic of Egypt, *Economic Management in a Period of Transition,* World Bank (Report No, 1X15-EGT), 1978, vol. 1, appendix 1.2.

59. The ILO poverty survey used the price for flour, which is double the price of wheat. The latter weights heavily in an estimation.

60. Arab Republic of Egypt, Nutrition Status Survey, Ministry of Health, Nutrition Institute, Cairo (with technical assistance from AID, Cairo and the Center for Disease Control, Atlanta) July 1978.

61. Arab Republic of Egypt, "National Nutrition Survey," with AID, 1978.

62. Y. B. Ghali and L. Taylor, "Basic Needs Strategy for Egypt," a report to the World Bank, 1980, p. 56.

63. World Health Organization, *World Health Statistics,* 1976.

# CHAPTER 9

# *Income Distribution in Egyptian Agriculture and Its Main Determinants*

Mohaya A. Zaytoun

## Introduction

A striking degree of inequality has been a major characteristic of the distribution of income in Egyptian agriculture for a long time.[1] Several studies have been carried out in the past with the object of estimating the pattern of income distribution and the changes that it has exhibited, particularly as a result of the agrarian reforms that Egypt has witnessed since 1952. Owing to the lack of data on income, these studies centered on the distribution of land that emerged from the agricultural censuses and attempted in various indirect ways to arrive at estimates of the distribution of income. Regrettably, no agricultural census has been carried out since 1961, with the result that even this type of indirect information on the distribution of agricultural income became impossible to obtain—or, if attempted, could only yield highly questionable findings. Up-to-date information on the distribution of income in Egyptian agriculture is, therefore, lacking. Fortunately, I have been able to collect some data from different sources that will hopefully enable us to update our knowledge of how income is distributed among landholding groups in Egyptian agriculture, and throw some light on the major factors that affect this distribution.[2]

## I. Agrarian Reform and the Pattern of Land and Income Distribution

### *Land Distribution after the Agrarian Reform*

Three agrarian reform laws were enacted in the years 1952, 1961, and 1969. Several decrees and amendments were also issued to supplement these laws. Unfortunately no census data are available on the distribution of land after 1961. The latest data available on the distribution of landownership relate to the year 1965.[3] Therefore, there is no way to assess the effect of the third reform. However, it is most likely that it had the least effect on the distribution of land since the area redistributed following that reform was very limited.[4]

The developments that took place in the distribution of land ownership from 1952 until 1965 are summarized in table 9.A.1 in the chapter appendix. The figures clearly demonstrate that the first two agrarian reforms have significantly influenced the position of two classes of landowners, namely, the small and big landowners. The position of small peasants (< 5 feddans) taken as one group has certainly improved. Their share in the area cultivated increased from 35.4 percent before the 1952 reform to 57.1 percent in 1965. Also their average ownership increased from 0.8 feddan before the reform to 1.2 feddan in 1965. It is probable, however, that a large part of this improvement was enjoyed by the upper ownership bracket of this class—those owning 2 to less than 5 feddans.[5]

The most radical impact of the first two reforms was obvious in the case of the group of large ownerships (> 50 feddans). The complete elimination of the ownerships over 200 feddans was mainly responsible for the substantial reduction in the share of this class of big landowners from 34.2 percent of the total cultivated area before the 1952 reform to 12.6 percent in 1965. In contrast, the reduction of the share of landowners with 50 to less than 200 feddans was fairly moderate. They owned 12.6 percent of the total cultivated area in 1965 as compared with 14.5 percent in 1952 before the reform.[6] Therefore, I tend to agree with D. Warriner's statement that "the abolition of feudalism—the main theme of all official statements—is a more exact description of the reform than at first sight appears."[7]

With regard to the medium ownership (5–< 50 feddans), the reform measures did not directly (through expropriation) or indirectly (through crash selling to smaller owners) reduce the share of this class in cultivated area. A possible explanation for the lack of indirect effects is that landowners belonging to this class were confident that no future action was likely to affect their ownerships. Actually some categories within this group managed to increase their share in the cultivated area after the reform. In particular, as a result of the reform, those owning 20–< 50 feddans received an indirect gain of land that is estimated at 161,000 feddans. This gain was mostly due to crash selling of land by big landowners who feared further expropriation.[8] The distribution of landholdings after the reform exhibits a pattern quite similar to that of the distribution of ownership, as can be seen from table 9.A.2 in the chapter appendix, which describes the distribution of landholdings before and after the 1952 land reform.

In view of the foregoing it is probably safe to conclude that the agrarian reform was rather moderate in character considering that a larger section of the rural population could have benefitted from the reform had more radical measures been enacted.[9] The need for a further reduction in the ceiling on land ownership is, indeed, worth considering. As one Western writer put it: "Given the quality of Egypt's land, 50 feddan is a substantial holding."[10] The need for a more radical reform would have been more evident if the objective of the reform had been to achieve greater equality not only among landholders but also between landholders and the landless.[11] Nonetheless, the reform remains the most significant measure taken to alleviate inequality of landownership and to improve the economic and social position of small peasants *vis-à-vis* big landowners since the establishment of private ownership in Egypt.

## *Income Distribution after the Agrarian Reform*

One of the early studies of the effect of the land reform on the distribution of agricultural income was made by D. Mead.[12] He examined the changes in the distribution of income between 1950 and 1960. Another attempt was made by R. Mabro to assess distributional changes between 1950 and 1965.[13] The estimates in question are shown in tables 9.A.3 and 9.A.4 in the chapter appendix. The group of peasantry who benefitted most (in terms of income) from the agrarian reform are those in the upper bracket of the class of small landowners. The position of the middle class of peasantry was maintained or moderately improved. A drastic deterioration occurred in the position of big landowners.

A more recent study that made extensive use of the 1961 agricultural census data was undertaken by M. Abdel-Fadil in the mid-1970s.[14] The results of this study indicate a significant improvement in the overall distribution of income in 1961 as compared with 1950 (See table 5 in the chapter appendix). The share of small peasants in total income also greatly improved over the period. The gain per capita was, however, much lower for this group due to the substantial increase in their number.[15] As regards middle peasants, their share in total income shows a significant increase. The result contrasts, however, with the analysis of section I, where the position of this group of peasantry improved only slightly so far as land distribution is concerned. The class of big peasants on the other hand, is the only class that suffered a great deterioration in its relative position.

It should be noted that the findings from the studies reviewed above should be cautiously interpreted because they suffer from a number of shortcomings that arose either from data inadequacy or from methodological defects or both. Identification of those shortcomings was essential for the design of the methodology adopted in this chapter, which attempts to avoid at least the most serious ones. The main shortcomings of previous studies may be briefly stated as follows:

1. The socioeconomic stratification of agrarian classes is not sufficiently detailed. Such limitation is particularly evident in the studies made by Mead and Mabro. This no doubt conceals some of the income differential that might exist within the highly aggregated classes.[16]
2. Most of the studies made on income distribution in the agricultural sector were concerned only with income differential among different groups of

peasantry in terms of the area held by each group. They completely ignore differentiation in terms of the different kind of assets, wage labor, and crop mix characterizing the different groups.

3. No explicit statement was made in any of the studies reviewed as to whether or not the income per feddan used in the calculation of income of the different categories of peasantry included livestock production. If the latter was in fact excluded, the estimates obtained would then represent the distribution of income from crop production only.
4. None of the studies on agricultural income distribution considered additional sources of income, that is, income from off-farm activities. There are some indications, however, that off-farm income represents an important part of the income of the different classes of peasantry (see section III of this chapter).
5. The method of estimating income distribution suffers from some obvious shortcomings. These, for instance, include the use of arbitrary or unrealistic assumptions (for example, the assumption made by Mead that the share of wages in the agricultural value added remained constant between 1950 and 1960). They also include the calculation of the relative area of a large group of peasantry as a residual (for example, the share of landholders with five to less than a hundred feddans was calculated by Mabro as a residual). Third, they include a misspecification of the income share of the different groups of landholders on one hand and absentee landowners on the other hand as a result of double counting the income share of absentee landowners. This share was once included as part of the income of landholders and was considered once more, and in the same distribution, as income of the absentee landowners (as in the study of Abdel-Fadil).
6. Most previous studies tended to focus on the effects of the 1952 reform on the distribution of agricultural income. This applies even to the most recent study by Abdel-Fadil, in which the 1961 distribution of income does not capture the effects of the 1961 reform, being based on the distribution of landholdings in the 1961 agricultural census.[17]

## II. The Methodology of This Study

### *Some Definitions*

It may be appropriate to start by answering the following two questions. First, what is the concept of income used in this study? Second, who are the people whose incomes are the subject of our analysis? With regard to the first question, it is desirable to use a fairly broad concept of income. That is, income should not be confined to that from crop production but should also include income from livestock and dairy production. Furthermore, income should not be restricted to that derived from farming activities but should also cover income from nonagricultural activities. Also, a distinction should be made between gross income and net income.

Data limitations, however, do not allow such a broad definition of income. The analysis will, therefore, be confined to gross income from plant and livestock production, that is, gross agricultural income.

As to the second question, the people whose incomes are to be examined are the landholding population who own or rent land. Landholding and not landownership will, therefore, be the basic unit of analysis in the present study. This is because the up-to-date data available on land distribution relate to the distribution of holdings rather than to ownerships on the one hand, and because tenancy is a widespread practice in Egyptian agriculture on the other hand.

Two remarks should be made here with respect to the use of the landholding statistics. The first remark relates to the difference between the definition of holding and ownership in the agricultural statistics. Thus, one large ownership may be actually cultivated by several small tenants. This land would be included in the small holding bracket in a landholding distribution, whereas it would be included in the large ownership bracket in a land ownership distribution. The opposite may also occur; that is, several small ownerships may actually be cultivated by one large tenant. The degree of inequality of the landholding distribution may, therefore, differ from that of landownership distribution.

The second remark relates to the treatment of rental payments. Thus, so long as the unit of analysis is landholding, an elaborate analysis of rental payments should be made dealing with the following two important questions: (1) Which group of landholders is a net recipient of rental payments and which group is a net payer? (2) What is the amount of rental payments received by landholders and what is the amount received by absentee landowners? The analysis of these two aspects of rental payments requires very detailed information on the conditions of tenancy for the different groups of landholders. Since these data are not readily available, our attention will be confined in this study to the concept of gross income, before the deduction of rental payments and other production costs.

The above definition of the people whose incomes are to be examined in this study means that no attempt will be made in this chapter to estimate the income share of the landless since that is the subject of chapter 8 by A. Mohie-Eldin.

## *The Data Used*

There are two approaches to the estimation of income distribution in the agricultural sector, depending on the kind of data used. The first is the direct approach, where income distribution can be estimated directly from data on the income received by each household in the agricultural community (or in a sample of the agricultural community). Data of this sort were never previously collected for the Egyptian agricultural sector on a large or a small scale, whether officially or otherwise. There might be several reasons behind avoiding this important area in the field of data collection. One reason may be political. Collecting and disseminating information on income may attract attention to sensitive sociopolitical issues about which the political authorities may not desire to generate much public debate. Another reason is the difficulties involved in collecting such data; household members do not usually respond accurately to questions related to the amount of income they earn.

According to the second approach, income distribution is estimated indirectly using more easily collected data on the distribution of land and other farm assets. This approach depends on the close relationship that normally exists between the distribution of land and farm assets on the one hand and income distribution on the other.

Given the above considerations, and given the absence of direct income data, the present study uses the indirect approach to the estimation of income distribution. The data used for this purpose and for the analysis of the main determinants of the income distribution include:

1. Data on the distribution of landholdings in 1974/1975 and 1977/1978. These data are collected by the Ministry of Agriculture from the records on the size of holding kept by the credit and land reform cooperatives. It is worth noting that the 1977/1978 distribution consists only of landholdings registered in the credit cooperatives, which represent about 95 percent of all landholdings in Egypt. In order to arrive at the distribution of total holdings, it was, therefore, necessary to add the 1974/1975 land reform cooperatives' holding distribution to the 1977/1978 credit cooperatives' distribution. This procedure was considered reasonable in view of the very limited amount of land that is likely to have been distributed by the land reform authorities between 1974/1975 and 1977/1978.

   One reservation should however be made in relation to the 1974/1975 and the 1977/1978 landholding distributions. These two distributions probably imply some exaggeration of the relative share of the small landholders with 3 feddans and less. The reason is that there has been a tendency toward nominally subdividing the larger holdings into smaller ones ($\leq$ 3 feddans) in order to secure eligibility to tax exemption granted to ownerships of 3 feddans and less, in effect as of 1973.[18]

2. Preliminary results of a sample survey that was especially designed to provide the present study with up-to-date information on income, land, and other assets of the agricultural population. The survey covers 2,000 households drawn systematically from a number of Egyptian villages in the year 1979. However, only one section of the households surveyed concerns the present study, namely, the landholders who represent 37 percent of the total rural households surveyed.

   The results of the survey are preliminary because further processing and testing are necessary before the validity of some of the results is established. Most of the data that need further testing relate to income and monetary variables, which appear highly contradictory in some cases. For instance, income from crop production is found to be greater than income from all sources for many landholding groups. Also, the income from livestock production turns out to be inconsistent with the number of animals sold for some groups of less landholders. It was not clear at the time of writing whether such irregularities are due to erroneous valuation and accounting or to faulty processing, or both. Given these defects, none of the survey results were used in estimating the distribution of income. Only those results that appeared credible in the light of comparison with other sources and careful examination of trends over time were used as supplementary information in the discussion of the determinants of the distribution of agricultural income. The results used include those relating to nonmonetary variables such as the distribution of landholdings, the average size of holding, the crop mix, the distribution of farm machinery and equipment, the tenancy situation, and the sources of income. (This survey will be referred to hereafter as the 1979 survey.)

3. Some ratios and relationships are derived from the 1961 agricultural census. Admittedly census data gathered twenty years ago may be of little relevance to the present situation. In the absence of more recent data I had no choice but to fall back on this source. These ratios and relationships are related to the crop pattern and the distribution of cattle by holding groups. All relationships derived from the 1961 census were, however, subjected to careful scrutiny and adjusted whenever necessary, as will be seen in section III.
4. Assorted data related to gross agricultural income, income from crop and livestock production, and other data from the Ministry of Agriculture and from the findings of various studies of relevance to our subject.

## *Stratification Scheme*

The criterion for stratifying the landholding population into socioeconomic groups that will be used in this study is the size of holding. This criterion is chosen because, though I recognize that there are several determinants of the socioeconomic status of the peasantry, land nevertheless remains one of the most important. Moreover, it can be argued that the distribution of landholdings is strongly related to the distribution of other assets (both material and nonmaterial) that contribute to socioeconomic differentiation of the landholders. Given this criterion, one difficult problem that must be dealt with is the determination of the dividing lines between various groups of landholders. As already noted, arbitrary determination of the socioeconomic groups may lead to errors of group misspecification and difficulties of interpretation.

In this study five groups of landholders are distinguished as follows:

| *Holding Group* | *Size of Holding* |
|---|---|
| Very small holders | 1 feddan or less |
| Small holders | > 1–3 feddans |
| Lower middle holders | > 3–5 feddans |
| Upper middle holders | > 5–10 feddans |
| Large holders | > 10 feddans |

The first two groups are supposed to include the bulk of poor peasants. It may be argued that holders in those two groups share several characteristics and could be aggregated in a single group. Of the common characteristics, the following three are worth mentioning:

1. The income derived from 3 feddans is estimated at £E150 annually.[19] This is a very low income that does not meet the bare necessities of the holder and his family.
2. The holders of this size of holding depend mainly on their own labor to cultivate their land. A very limited amount of wage labor may be used but only on a temporary basis during the peak seasons.[20]
3. The owners of three feddans and less are exempted from the land tax, which can be considered as an official recognition of the poverty of this group of peasants.

However, my analysis of the determinants of the distribution income and the factors of differentiation among the peasantry has shown that those holding 3 feddans or less cannot be regarded as a homogeneous group. Within-group variation in certain characteristics (in the relative share of land as will be shown in section III) appeared to be substantial, particularly between those holding 1 fedden or less and those holding "> 1–3" feddans. Those holding 3 feddans or less were, therefore, accordingly divided into two groups.

The definition of the group of large holders as those holding more than 10 feddans may involve some overaggregation. Nevertheless, given the conditions of Egyptian agriculture, where holdings are fragmented and the average holding is about 2 feddans, 10 feddans may be considered an appropriate lower limit for large holdings. Furthermore, a size of holding over 10 feddans is considered large enough to permit the use of advanced farm tools and machinery. According to the 1961 census data a large proportion of landholders with more than 10 feddans employ wage labor on a large scale on their farms.

The distinction between lower- and upper- medium landholders groups can be justified on the grounds that, according to the 1961 census data, those holding 3–5 feddans use wage labor on a limited scale, whereas holders of more than 5 to 10 feddans tend to use wage labor more intensively.

## *The Method of Estimation*

The two main objectives of this study are to estimate the distribution of income and to analyze its main determinants. These two objectives are not attainable if we start by focusing on the final picture of the distribution of income. The purpose of the study is better served by building up the final picture step by step through a series of successive approximations, each of which is designed to handle one determinant of the distribution of income. The determinants to be examined are those variables that are believed to have a marked effect on the pattern of income distribution. These include:

1. The degree of land concentration
2. The crop pattern
3. Livestock and dairy production
4. Production technique, mainly type of machinery and equipment
5. Tenancy conditions
6. Sources of income

To quantify the effect of each of these determinants on income distribution, detailed data are required. Since data could not be obtained or even safely estimated except for the first three determinants, the quantification process will be confined to them. The effect of land concentration on income distribution will be estimated assuming that the crop mix is the same for all groups of landholders, that is, assuming that gross income per feddan of land cultivated is the same for all groups. In the next step the variation in the crop pattern will be considered through allowing gross income per feddan to vary among different groups in accordance with the variation in the crop mix for these groups. The distribution obtained from this step is that of income from plant production. But since agricultural income constitutes both plant and animal production, the last process of estimation will be concerned with income distribution from animal production.

It should be noted here that the distribution of total gross agricultural income is obtained through adding together two independently estimated income distributions, namely, the plant production income distribution and the animal production income distribution. This procedure ignores the possibilities of interaction between the two distributions. That is, it ignores the relationships that may exist between a given group's share in income from crop production and its share in income from livestock production. For instance, I do not consider the economies that are likely to arise when both animal and crop production are produced on the same farm. Nor is the tendency for such economies to increase with the increase in the size of the herd and the size of the holding taken into account. Ignoring this aspect may lead to misspecification of the income of the different groups, particularly if some of these groups enjoy greater economies than other groups. Unfortunately, available data are not sufficiently detailed to be of use in the analysis of the interaction between the two income distributions in question.

## III. Determinants of the Distribution of Agricultural Income

### *The Degree of Land Concentration*

*Land Holdings Distribution in 1977/1978 and 1979.* In Egyptian agriculture, land remains the most important productive asset. Table 9.1 contains

*TABLE 9.1.*

*The Distribution of Landholdings by Holdings Group 1961–1977/1978**

| Size of Holding | 1961 (1) | | | | | 1965 (2) | | | | | 1974/75 (3) | | | | | 1977/1978 (3) | | | | |
|---|---|---|---|---|---|---|---|---|---|---|---|---|---|---|---|---|---|---|---|---|
| | No. of Holdings (000) | % | Area (000 feddans) | % | Av. Holdings | No. of Holdings (000) | % | Area (000 feddans) | % | Av. Holdings | No. of Holdings (000) | % | Area (000 feddans) | % | Av. Holdings | No. of Holdings (000) | % | Area (000 feddans) | % | Av. Holdings |
| < 1 feddan | 434.2 | 26.4 | 211.2 | 3.4 | .49 | 597.7 | 28.7 | 322.7 | 5.5 | 0.54 | 1,124.3 | 42.6 | 739.0 | 12.4 | 0.66 | 1,458.8 | 48.8 | 919.9 | 15.0 | 0.63 |
| 1 < 3 feddans | 672.7 | 41.0 | 1,153.2 | 18.5 | 1.7 | 966.9 | 46.4 | 1,694.5 | 28.6 | 1.8 | 949.2† | 35.9 | 2,023.5 | 33.6 | 2.1 | 984.3 | 32.9 | 2,017.4 | 33.0 | 2.0 |
| 3 < 5 feddans | 274.3 | 16.7 | 990.0 | 15.9 | 3.6 | 283.2 | 13.6 | 1,041.6 | 17.6 | 3.7 | 354.8 | 13.4 | 1,185.6 | 19.8 | 3.3 | 348.7 | 11.7 | 1,165.6 | 19.1 | 3.3 |
| 5 < 10 feddans | 170.0 | 10.4 | 1,100.7 | 17.7 | 6.5 | 147.5 | 7.1 | 970.7 | 16.4 | 6.6 | 148.5 | 5.6 | 944.4 | 15.8 | 6.3 | 127.6 | 4.2 | 785.9 | 12.9 | 6.2 |
| ≥ 10 feddans | 90.9 | 5.5 | 2,767.7 | 44.5 | 30.4 | 86.7 | 4.2 | 1,891.7 | 31.9 | 21.8 | 65.2 | 2.5 | 1,091.2 | 18.2 | 16.7 | 69.9 | 2.3 | 1,226.9 | 20.0 | 17.5 |
| Total | 1,642.1 | 100.0 | 6,222.8 | 100.0 | 3.8 | 2,082.0 | 100.0 | 5,921.2 | 100.0 | 2.8 | 2,642.0 | 100.0 | 5,983.7 | 100.0 | 2.1 | 2,989.3 | 100.0 | 6,118.7 | 100.0 | 2.0 |

NOTES:

(1) 1961 agricultural census.

(2) CAPMS, al-Hayāza al-Zirāᶜīya, 1974.

(3) Ministry of Agriculture, unpublished data.

*Group stratification for the 1974/1975 and 1977/1978 data is as follows:
0–3 feddans, 3–5 feddans, 5–10 feddans, and 10 feddans.

†The figure given by the Ministry of Agriculture for the number of holdings for this group is incorrect. Thus, the number of holdings recorded in the agricultural cooperatives and the land reform cooperatives for this group adds up to 949,200 feddans, whereas the holdings under these two cooperatives are incorrectly added, according to the Ministry of Agriculture data, to 1,160,100 feddan. The former figure was, therefore, considered in this table.

recent information obtained from the Ministry of Agriculture on the distribution of landholdings among different groups of holders for the year 1977/1978. The data demonstrate that, even after the execution of three land reform laws, land distribution among different groups in 1977/1978 is still fairly skewed. The group of very small holders that accounts for almost half the landholders (48.8 percent) holds no more than 15 percent of the total area cultivated, whereas the group of large holders, which represents only 2.3 percent of the total number of holders, farms 20 percent of the area cultivated. The share of the small holders (> 1–3 feddans) in the area cultivated equals their proportionate number of total holders (33 percent). The lower medium holders group represents 11.7 percent of the total holders and holds 19.1 percent of the land; and the group of upper medium holders represents 4.2 percent of total holders and holds 12.9 percent of the total area cultivated.

This unequal pattern of land distribution, particularly with respect to the relative land share of the very small and the large holders, is also confirmed by the preliminary results of the 1979 survey, which are given in table 9.A.6 in the chapter appendix. The data of this table show that 27.0 percent of the very small holders hold 5 percent of the land, whereas the group of large holders represents 4.6 percent of the total number of holders and holds 35.2 percent of the total area cultivated.

A comparison between landholding distribution based on the 1977/1978 data of the Ministry of Agriculture (table 9.1) and that based on the 1979 survey results reveals a wide divergence with respect to the relative share of the group of large holders in total cultivated area (20 percent according to the Ministry of Agriculture; 35 percent according to the 1979 survey). Such divergence can be partly explained by the slightly different group stratification followed in the two distributions. The group of large landholders in the survey distribution includes holders of 10 feddans, whereas those holders are excluded from this group in the distribution of the Ministry of Agriculture; they are included in the smaller group (< 5–10 feddans). This difference in the group stratification is reflected in the relative number of holders in the large landholders group, which amounts to 2.4 percent in the distribution of the Ministry of Agriculture and 4.6 percent in the 1979 survey distribution. A similar line of reasoning is also applicable to the divergence between the two distributions with regard to the relative share of the very small holders in the total area cultivated. Note also that part of the observed divergence is of course attributable to sampling errors.

*The Changing Position of Different Groups of Holders between 1961 and 1977/1978.* The availability of data on the distribution of holdings in different periods makes it possible to consider the development that has taken place in this distribution between 1961 and 1977/1978. As can be seen from table 9.1, which includes landholdings distribution from 1961 to 1977/1978, this period witnessed a substantial increase in the total number of holdings (the increase amounts to 1,347,200 feddans). This increase is due mainly to the increase in the number of the small and very small holdings over this period. Thus, the increase in the number of the very small holdings (up to 1 feddan), which equals 1,024,600 holdings, represents 76 percent of the increase in total holdings. The increase in the number of small holdings (> 1–3 feddans) over the period amounts to 311,600 feddans and represents 23 percent of the increase in the total number of holdings.

The consistent tendency toward the increase in the small holdings over the period under study is contrasted by a tendency toward a decrease in the number of large holdings (over 5 feddans). These two changes have resulted in a decrease in the average size of holding for the entire agricultural sector from 3.8 feddans in 1961 to 2 feddans in 1977/1978. Also in 1977/1978 small and very small holdings represented 82 percent of the total number of holdings as compared with 67 percent in 1961. This reflects a transformation in Egyptian agriculture toward smaller holdings and a larger number of poor peasants, with fewer and fewer peasants holding a relatively large area of land over time.

In terms of the area cultivated, the very small holders increased their area by 708,700 feddans between 1961 and 1977/1978. Their relative share in the total cultivated area shows a substantial increase from 3.4 percent in 1961 to 15.0 percent in 1977/1978. The improvement in the position of this group of holders over the period is also reflected by the increase in the average size of holding from 0.49 to 0.63 feddan.

The area held by the group of small holders (the group that includes land-reform beneficiaries) increased by 864,200 feddans from 1961 to 1977/1978, which is the largest absolute amount of land gained by any group of holders. Their relative share in the area cultivated increased from 18.5 percent to 33.0 percent. It should be noted, however, that in spite of the increase in the absolute number of holders in this group their relative number significantly decreased. Actually, it can be observed from table 9.A.1 that the relative number of holdings decreased over the period for all groups of holders except the very small holders. As for the average size of holding for the small holders, it increased from 1.7 to 2 feddans.

Two main factors may have contributed to the improvement in the position of the small and very small holders in the land distributional structure—the several land distribution programs that took place between 1961 and 1977/1978, and the Moslem inheritance system, which resulted in the long run in the subdivision of medium holdings into smaller ones.

It should be noted, however, that the increase in the relative share of the small and very small landholders in the total area cultivated is probably exaggerated by the statistics published by the Ministry of Agriculture. This is, as already mentioned, because of the recent tendency to nominally subdivide larger holdings into smaller ones (> 0–3 feddans) so as to take advantage of the tax exemption of the ownerships ≤ 3 feddans.

The lower medium holding group (> 3–5 feddans), which includes also some of the land-reform beneficiaries, gained more land as a result of the different land reform laws. Their share in the cultivated area increased from 15.9 percent in 1961 to 19.1 percent in 1977/1978, though they accounted for a smaller proportion of total holdings (11.7 percent in 1977/1978 against 16.7 percent in 1961). Nevertheless, the average size of holding in this group declined from 3.6 in 1961 to 3.3 feddans in 1977/1978.

A notable drop in the area cultivated by the upper medium holders (< 5–10 feddans) took place between 1961 and 1977/1978. The decrease amounted to 314,000 feddans. The relative share of this group in the total area also decreased from 17.7 percent to 12.9 percent. One should note, however, that the decline in the area cultivated between 1974/1975 and 1977/1978 amounted to slightly more than half the decline that occurred over the entire period. This large drop in the relative as well as in the absolute share of this group in the cultivated area between 1974/1975 and 1977/1978 is somewhat perplexing. The loss of around 160,000 feddans in three years may, however, be partly explained in terms of nominal land transfer from this group to the ≤ 3 holding group so as to acquire eligibility for the tax exemption referred to earlier. Another part of the observed drop could be attributed to the sale of land to other groups, particularly the holders of more than 10 feddans, whose share in the total area also increased both relatively and absolutely during this period.

With respect to the group of large landholders (over 10 feddans), they lost 1,541,000 feddans between 1961 and 1977/1978. Slightly more than half this loss occurred between 1961 and 1965; that is, over the four years following the 1961 land reform. It is believed, therefore, that most of the decrease in this group's area cultivated accrued to landholders with over 100 feddans. It is interesting to note, however, that the declining tendency of the relative and absolute share of this group in the area cultivated over time changed direction after 1974/1975. Thus, for the first time over the entire period the number of large holders increased between 1974/1975 and 1977/1978 by 5,000 holders. The relative share of this group in the area cultivated also increased. This may be attributed to the fact that no legal actions were taken against this group after the land reform law of 1969. Such increase may reflect also the ability of the large landholders to buy land from other smaller holders, and their ability to overcome inheritance laws through greater consolidation of holdings. This tendency must have its roots in the process of capitalist growth that has been accelerated by the implementation of the open-door policy since 1974.

*A Summary of the Changes in Land Distribution.* Table 9.2 summarizes the changes in the position of the five groups of landholders between 1961 and 1977/1978.

It can be seen from table 2 that although the intervening period between

*TABLE 9.2.*
*A Summary of Land Loss and Land Gain by Holdings Group from 1961 to 1977/1978 (Thousand Feddans)*

| Holding groups (feddans) | *1961–1965* Land gain | Land loss | *1965–1974/1975* Land gain | Land loss | *1974/1975–1977/1978* Land gain | Land loss | *1961–1977/1978* Land gain | Land loss |
|---|---|---|---|---|---|---|---|---|
| ≤ 1 | 111.5 | ... | 416.3 | ... | 180.9 | ... | 708.7 | ... |
| > 1–3 | 541.3 | ... | 329.0 | ... | ... | 6.1 | 870.3 | 6.1 |
| > 3–5 | 51.6 | ... | 144.0 | ... | ... | 17.0 | 195.6 | 17.0 |
| > 5–10 | ... | 130.0 | ... | 26.3 | ... | 158.5 | ... | 314.8 |
| > 10 | ... | 876.0 | ... | 800.5 | 135.2 | ... | 135.2 | 1,676.5 |
| Total | 704.4 | 1,006.0 | 889.3 | 826.8 | 316.1 | 181.6 | 1,909.8 | 2,014.4 |

SOURCE: Calculated from data of table 9.1.

the 1961 and the 1965 land distribution is rather short, the changes in land distribution toward greater equality are clearly significant. Small holders in general (the first three groups) gained 704,400 feddans and large holders (the last two groups) lost 1,006,000 feddans over a period of four years. This is clearly a result of the 1961 land reform law.

From 1965 to 1974/1975 a substantial gain was achieved also by the small holders, and large holders suffered a great loss. It is believed, however, that such gain and loss were not totally attributable to the 1961 and 1969 reform laws. It is most likely that, over a relatively long period of ten years, inheritance may have led to a significant subdivision of medium and large holdings into small ones, and of small holdings into very small ones. This is evident from the fact that during this period the highest gain accrued to the group of very small holders, which did not directly benefit from the reform laws (redistribution was made in plots of 2–3 feddans). Some nominal subdivision of large holdings also may have occurred during this period due to large landholders' fear of further reform action against them. That is, part of the reduction in the share of the large holders in the area cultivated may be more apparent than real.

Furthermore, a comparison between the total land gained by small holders in general (up to 5 feddans) from 1965 to 1974/1975 and the total land distributed by the land reform authorities over the same period reveals that the total gain over the period (889,300 feddans) was much larger than the total land distributed (334,000 feddans).

The period 1974/1975 to 1977/1978 is a short period during which no legal action was taken to alter land distribution. This is consistent with the obvious weakening of egalitarian tendencies over this period. Thus, there was for the first time during the entire period under study a significant land gain obtained by large holders. Small holders, on the other hand, suffered a slight loss of 6,100 feddans for the first time over the entire period. Another loss of 17,000 feddans accrued to the lower medium holders.

The trends in inequality of the distribution of landholdings may be summarized also by tracing the changes that took place in the Gini coefficient for the distribution in question over time. The values of this measure of inequality turned out to be as follows:

| *Year* | *Gini Coefficient* |
|---|---|
| 1961 | 0.641 |
| 1965 | 0.527 |
| 1974/1975 | 0.458 |
| 1977/1978 | 0.482 |
| 1979 (Survey) | 0.547 |

It is evident that there was a marked decline in inequality between 1961 and 1965, which can mainly be attributed to the 1961 land reform act. The change in the Gini coefficent between 1965 and 1974/1975 or 1977/1978 (a fall from 0.527 to 0.482) cannot be totally accepted at face value. This is because, as noted earlier, the share of the small landholders in the area cultivated is probably overstated in the 1977/1978 official statistics. In addition, some nominal subdivision of large holdings may have occurred during this period due to large holders' fear of any future reform action against them. Furthermore, part of the increase in the relative area held by the very small holders and the decrease in the relative area held by large landholders over this period may be attributed to the different definitions of the landholding groups in the 1974/1975 and 1977/1978 statistics as compared to the 1965 statistics. Thus the holders of one feddan are included in the group of very small holders in the 1977/1978 land distribution statistics, whereas they are excluded in the 1965 statistics. On the other hand, holders of 10 feddans are excluded from the group of large landholders in the 1977/1978 statistics, whereas they are included in this group in the 1965 statistics.

It can be argued, therefore, that at least part of the decline in inequality between 1965 and 1977/1978 may not be real. It is probable that the degree of inequality in the distribution of landholdings remained more or less constant during most of this period. This proposition is confirmed by the results of the 1979 survey, which gave a Gini coefficient almost identical to the one calculated for 1965 (0.547). If this is, indeed, what happened, the degree of inequality in 1979 is lower than in 1961 but almost the same as in 1965. This reflects the strong impact of the first two land reforms, the weak effect of the 1969 reform, and the lack of any reform measures afterward despite the continuous operation of the forces that make for greater differentiation and polarization in the Egyptian countryside.

*TABLE 9.3.*

*Crop Pattern in Egyptian Agriculture, 1961 and 1977*
*(Crop area, 000 Feddans)*

| | *1961** | | *1977†* | |
|---|---|---|---|---|
| | *Area* | *%* | *Area* | *%* |
| Field Crops | 10,107.9 | 95.0 | 9,875.0 | 88.9 |
| Vegetables | 386.1 | 3.6 | 915.0 | 8.2 |
| Fruits | 141.1 | 1.3 | 321.0 | 2.9 |
| Totals | 10,635.1 | 100.0 | 11,111.0 | 100.0 |

SOURCE NOTE:
*The fourth agricultural census, 1961
†Ministry of Agriculture

*The Crop Pattern*

Income from land is a product not only of the size of landholding but also of the mix of crops grown on this land. The transformation from traditional crops to the more profitable products like fruits is likely to increase income of the landholders capable of effecting such a transformation. It is believed that such transformation proceeded at a fast pace by large landholders in the 1970s in response to the rapid increase in the relative price of this variety of crops. In addition, the information available for the census year 1961 indicates that a large proportion of the subsistence crops were grown on the small holdings while a large proportion of the cash crops were grown on the larger holdings.

The data of table 9.3 illustrate the change that took place in Egyptian agriculture as a whole with respect to the cultivation of traditional and nontraditional crops during the period 1961 to 1977.

It can be seen from table 3 that a significant transformation in the crop pattern occured between 1961 and 1977. The area of fruit and vegetables combined more than doubled, whereas the area cultivated with field crops decreased in both absolute and relative terms. Nevertheless, field crops still dominated the crop pattern as they accounted in 1977 for about 89 percent of the total cultivated area.[21]

No up-to-date information on a national scale is available on the type of crops grown on different groups of holdings. An attempt is made here to estimate the crop mix (the relative area of field crops, vegetables, and fruits) for each group of landholders on the basis of the information available for the census year 1961, and on the data on the 1977 crop mix for the entire agricultural sector given in table 3.

The method of estimation starts by assuming—temporarily—that the crop mix in 1977/1978 for each group of landholders is the same as the crop mix prevailing for the corresponding group in the 1961 census data.

*TABLE 9.4.*
*Crop Mix according to Size of Holding*
*1961* and 1977/1978 (000 Feddans)*

| *Holding Groups (feddans)* | | *Field Crops* | | *Vegetables* | | *Fruits* | | *Total* | |
|---|---|---|---|---|---|---|---|---|---|
| | | *Area* | *%* | *Area* | *%* | *Area* | *%* | *Area* | *%* |
| ≤ 1 | 1961 | 380.3 | 95.7 | 12.5 | 3.1 | 4.8 | 1.2 | 397.6 | 100 |
| | 1977/1978 | 1,447.0 | 86.8 | 151.1 | 9.1 | 68.5 | 4.1 | 1,666.6 | 100 |
| > 1–3 | 1961 | 2,066.6 | 96.7 | 59.9 | 2.8 | 11.4 | 0.5 | 2,137.9 | 100 |
| | 1977/1978 | 3,432.9 | 93.6 | 195.2 | 5.3 | 38.5 | 1.1 | 3,666.6 | 100 |
| > 3–5 | 1961 | 1,748.7 | 96.4 | 55.5 | 3.1 | 8.8 | 0.5 | 1,813.0 | 100 |
| | 1977/1978 | 1,926.2 | 90.8 | 165.2 | 7.8 | 30.8 | 1.4 | 2,122.2 | 100 |
| > 5–10 | 1961 | 1,897.2 | 95.7 | 71.6 | 3.7 | 12.4 | 0.6 | 1,981.2 | 100 |
| | 1977/1978 | 1,228.4 | 85.7 | 172.1 | 12.0 | 32.8 | 2.3 | 1,433.3 | 100 |
| > 10 | 1961 | 4,015.0 | 93.3 | 186.6 | 4.3 | 103.7 | 2.4 | 4,305.3 | 100 |
| | 1977/1978 | 1,840.5 | 82.8 | 231.4 | 10.4 | 150.4 | 6.8 | 2,222.3 | 100 |

*The fourth agriculture census, 1961.

This distribution of the cropped area is then modified to allow for the variation in the crop mix for the entire agriculture that actually took place between 1961 and 1977/1978. The modification consists in distributing the difference between the actual and estimated area under a given group of crops among the holding groups according to each group's relative share of a given crop in the total area cultivated by this group in 1961.[22] The outcome of this estimation process is given in table 9.4.

It can be seen from table 4 that all groups of holders managed to increase the area cultivated by nonfield crops (vegetables and fruits) over the period 1961–1977/1978. The group of large landholders, however, devoted a larger proportion of their land to the cultivation of nonfield crops as compared with all other groups in 1961 as well as in 1977/1978. It can be noticed also that the group of very small holders devoted a larger proportion of their land to the cultivation of nonfield crops as compared with the group of small holders. They also managed to increase their nonfield crops area between 1961 and 1977/1978 at a faster rate. This may be due to the fact that the very small holdings include the small plots of land that exist around the main cities that are fully devoted to vegetable and fruit cultivation.

It should be noted here that, within the category of field crops, no distinction is made between cash crops and subsistence crops. A more detailed analysis of this category is expected to reveal that the larger holders devoted a large proportion of their land for cash-crops cultivation than small holders. This would further intensify differentiation between large and small holders with respect to the crop mix.

Further evidence on the crop mix prevailing for different holding groups is also available from the preliminary results of the 1979 survey. Crops are divided into cash and noncash crops. The former includes the nontraditional crops like fruits and vegetables in addition to other cash crops. The latter includes subsistence crops.

It is obvious from that table that the group of large holders is the only group that devoted to cash-crop cultivation a proportion of their land (57.8 percent) larger than the proportion devoted to subsistence-crops cultivation (42.2 percent). Lower and upper medium groups divided the land almost equally between cash and subsistence crops. The group of very small holders (≤ 1 feddan) contained the lowest proportion of the area under cash crops. They devoted 21 percent only of the area they cultivated to cash crops whereas the rest of their land was cultivated by subsistence crops. The proportional land cultivated by cash crops increased to about 40 percent of the total area in the case of the small landholders (1–< 3 feddans).

The implications of such variation between different groups of landholders with regard to crop pattern for income distribution are quite important. This is obvious from the fact that, according to the national data obtained from the Ministry of Agriculture, average gross income per feddan amounted to £E140 for field crops and over £E400 for nonfield crops. The reader should note, however, that average gross income per feddan of fruits and vegetables (nonfield crops), as officially estimated, is probably biased downward. This is due to the use of official rather than actual market prices in calculating the value of vegetable and fruit output.

## *The Ownership of Farm Animals*

Next to land, farm animals are the most important asset in Egyptian agriculture. Available evidence indicates that farm animals are widely possessed by all groups of landholders. This is due to the fact that these animals are used particularly by small landholders to perform farm work and to provide the family with some dairy products. Only a very small proportion of households raise cattle for commercial purposes.

The value of animal production in 1977 represents 28 percent of the gross value of agricultural production.[23] Therefore, the distribution of farm animals among different holding groups is likely to be one of the basic determinants of income distribution among these groups. Detailed information about this distribution is available only for the census year 1961. Table 7 in the chapter appendix contains this information. As can be seen, there exists a strong positive correlation between the number of cattle and the size of the holding.

This relationship is confirmed in another recent study wherein it is demonstrated that landholders possessing at least 1 head of cattle accounted for 10 percent of all holders in the group of 1 feddan and less.[24] The proportion increased to 69 percent in the next group (1–< 3 feddans)

*TABLE 9.5.*
*The Estimated Percentage Distribution of Cattle by Size of Holding (1977/1978)*
*Size of Holding (Feddans)*

| | ≤ 1 | > 1–3 | > 3–5 | > 5–10 | > 10 | Total |
|---|---|---|---|---|---|---|
| 1) First assumption* | 28.6 | 34.3 | 17.5 | 8.6 | 11.0 | 100.0 |
| 2) Second assumption (1961 distribution) | 12.8 | 33.6 | 19.9 | 16.3 | 17.4 | 100.0 |
| Average (1) and (2) | 20.7 | 33.9 | 18.7 | 12.5 | 14.2 | 100.0 |

*See table 9.A.8 in the chapter appendix for further details.

and to 75 percent in the group holding 3–< 5 feddans. In contrast, 100 percent of those holding 5 feddans and more had at least 1 head of cattle. Moreover, ownership of more than 1 head of cattle does not materialize except for holders of more than 3 feddans.

Due to the lack of recent information on the percentage distribution of the cattle stock by size of holding, and because such information is necessary for the estimation of the distribution of income from animal production, an attempt is made here to estimate the cattle (cows and buffaloes) distribution in 1977/1978.

In the absence of firm grounds upon which the required estimate may be based, it appeared not unreasonable to experiment with the following two alternative assumptions. The first assumption is that the average number of cattle per holding in each holding group remained constant between 1961 and 1977/1978. The second assumption is that the percentage distribution of cattle by holding groups remained unchanged during the period in question. Both assumptions are obviously unrealistic; they are given simply for the sake of stimulating a discussion on the more likely directions of change in the cattle distribution. The two alternative distributions are shown in table 9.5.

Clearly the first assumption implies a drastic redistribution of the cattle stock in favor of the very small holders, whose relative share rose from 12.8 percent in 1961 to 28.6 percent in the hypothetical 1977/1978 distribution, whereas the share of the other groups went down except for the small holders group (1–3), whose share remained almost unchanged.

*TABLE 9.6*
*The Use of Farm Equipment (1977)*

| | *Hand plough* | *Mechannical plough* | *Thresher (Nūrj)* | *Irrigation machine* | *Water wheel (sāqiya)* | *Hand irrigation machine (shādūf)* | *sprayer* | *Threshing machine (Darrāsa)* |
|---|---|---|---|---|---|---|---|---|
| Percent users | 34.5 | 98 | 1 | 46.8 | 97 | 3 | 92 | 98 |
| Percent nonusers | 65.5 | 2 | 99 | 53.2 | 3 | 97 | 8 | 2 |

SOURCE: Rural Development Project, PFPB, 1977

Those changes are of course strongly influenced by the changes in the distribution of landholdings over the period in question. It is, however, highly doubtful that the distribution of cattle follows so closely the distribution of landholdings. After all, the redistribution of farm animals was not among the direct objectives of the land reform laws. Indeed, the land reform itself may have led many large holders to invest more heavily in livestock production, given the limitations on the scope for expanding crop production. This suggests that the first hypothetical distribution overestimates the share of the very small holders and underestimates that of the large ones. In contrast, the second hypothetical distribution errs in the opposite direction by ignoring the improvement in the cattle share of small holders and the deterioration in the share of the large holders following the redistribution of land from the latter to the former. It thus appears that the truth lies somewhere between those two hypothetical distributions. One way of approximating the real distribution of cattle may, therefore, consist in averaging the two distributions in question. The resulting distribution is given in row 3 of table 5. In comparison with the distribution of holdings, the distribution of cattle appears less unequal.

### *Use and Ownership of Farm Machinery and Equipment*

Some indications regarding the use of farm machinery and equipment in Egyptian agriculture are available from the results of a sample survey that was undertaken by the Population and Family Planning Board (PFPB).[25] The results are summarized in table 9.6.

It can be seen from table 6 that some modern agricultural tools are now in wide use in some regions of Egyptian agriculture (the survey regions). Some sophisticated equipment like irrigation machines is used by almost half the landholders surveyed. According to this survey, the use of traditional equipment is not widespread. For instance, 66 percent of all surveyed landholders do not use the hand plough, which I believe to be used by many Egyptian peasants.

Nevertheless, because the majority of Egyptian peasants are small landholders, very few of them own such equipment. The results of the survey show that less than 3 percent of the landholders own the mechanical tools they use. The rest of the landholders rent these tools. The information on the sources of equipment rentals is interesting. Around 61.5 percent of all landholders rent their equipment from other households, whereas 3.4 percent only rent their equipment from the cooperatives, and 32.3 percent rent them from both other households and the cooperatives.

There are some indications, therefore, that the use and ownership of machinery in Egyptian agriculture is such that very few families, most probably large landowners, own farm equipment that is rented to the majority of small landholders. This service is usually provided at a very

*TABLE 9.7.*
*The Area Rented by Holding Groups (1979)*

| *Holding Groups* | *Area Rented (feddans)* | *Total Area (feddans)* | *Percent of Area Rented* |
|---|---|---|---|
| <1 feddan | 50.8 | 104.6 | 48.6 |
| 1–<3 feddans | 438.8 | 640.2 | 68.5 |
| 3–<5 feddans | 201.4 | 332.1 | 60.6 |
| 5–<10 feddans | 105.0 | 276.2 | 38.0 |
| >10 feddans | 163.8 | 735.9 | 22.2 |

high price as the report of the PFPB survey indicates. It is also clear that the role played by the agricultural cooperatives, with respect to the provision of farm equipment to small landholders, is very limited.

Some insights into the distribution of different kinds of farm machinery according to different categories of landholders are also available from the preliminary results of the 1979 survey. As would be expected, the share of the small and very small landholders in traditional farm equipment is much larger than of the more advanced machinery. For instance, they possess 64 percent of all hand ploughs, but only 12.5 percent of all tractors and 28 percent of irrigation machines. The large landholders (numbering 33) possess 7 tractors, 7 Qassabiyas (leveling implement), and 9 water pumps. In contrast, those holding less than 2 feddans (numbering 400) possess no tractors, 15 Qassabiyas, and 18 water pumps. The upper medium group (numbering 43 holders) possesses 3 tractors, 6 Qassabiyas, and 8 water pumps. It is obvious, therefore, that a strong positive relationship exists between the size of the holding and the ownership and use of modern farm machinery.

## *The Tenancy Situation*

The state of tenancy for different groups of landholders may also be an important determinant of their relative income. Thus to ascertain the impact of tenancy on the distribution of income, it is necessary to determine which groups are net leasers-in and which are net leasers-out and the amount of rent paid and received by each group. It is also important to know the kind of tenancy arrangement practiced by each group—whether rent is paid in cash or in kind, and whether the tenancy is permanent or temporary (by crop or season).

Some useful information on the tenancy situation for the different group of landholders can be obtained from the preliminary results of the 1979 survey. The proportion of the cultivated area rented by holding group is given in table 9.7, which is derived from the survey results.

It can be seen from this table that there are differences among the groups of holders regarding the proportion of their land that is rented. The largest proportion corresponds to the group of small holders (1–< 3 feddans). This is followed by the lower medium holders and then by the very small holders. The lowest proportion, on the other hand, corresponds to the group of large holders (> 10 feddans). This is followed by the upper medium holders.

These differences in the proportion of the area rented are likely to have an important impact on the pattern of income distribution. Thus, if the small holders in general (the first three groups) rent a larger proportion of the area cultivated than large holders in general (the fourth and fifth group), this means that agricultural income distribution after rental payment should be more unequal than agricultural income distribution before rental payment.

The results of the survey on rental payment confirm this argument. They show that the group of small landholders pays the largest share (52 percent) of all rental payments, followed by the lower medium group (21 percent) and the upper medium group (11 percent). The large group of landholders pays a low share (10 percent) in spite of the fact that its share in the area cultivated is relatively large. The lowest share is paid by the very small holders in view of the relatively small amount of land held by this group.

The results of the 1979 survey demonstrate also that the kind of rent dominating Egyptian agriculture is cash rent, which represents 90 percent of all rental cases recorded in the survey. The rest (10 percent) are rental in kind and mixed rental arrangements (partly in kind and partly in cash). As may be expected, the largest number of cases of rent in kind fall within the group of small holders.

Permanent cash rent is the most common arrangement in the case of cash renting. It represents 93 percent of all recorded cash rental cases. Nevertheless, there are some 7 percent cash rentals by crop; the great majority of them fall within the groups of small and very small holders. It should be noted that the rate of rent paid according to the seasonal rental system is much higher than the amount of permanent cash rent. The latter is usually subject to rent control.

It emerges from the 1979 survey that renting according to the rent control regulations is followed in 91 percent of the total area rented. There appears to be no differentiation between the different groups regarding the level of rent. Thus legal rent ranges between a minimum of £E26 and a maximum of £E39 per feddan. The average legal rent is £E30 per feddan, which is higher than the average rent assumed through inaccurate interpretation of the reform law in most of the previous studies on land reform (£E21 per feddan).

It is believed that the area rented according to the black market level of rental is grossly understated in the survey (representing 9 percent only of the total area rented). This is because many landholders may be reluctant to admit illegal rental. The level of black market rent is much higher than the legal one. It ranges from a minimum of £E38 to a maximum of £E100. The average level of illegal rent is £E72. It is worth noting also that no illegal renting occurs in the group of large landholders (> 10 feddan), where all renting is reported in the survey to be carried out on legal terms.

## *Sources of Income*

The distribution of income for the agricultural population depends on the kinds of activities from which income of the different groups is derived. The activities undertaken by the agricultural population can broadly be divided into farm and off-farm activities. The off-farm activities for the landholders comprise all activities other than crop production and livestock raising. They may include agricultural as well as nonagricultural activities. It is believed that off-farm activities have recently become an important source of income for the agricultural population faced with a constant area of agricultural land and limited employment opportunities in the urban sector.

The preliminary results of the 1979 survey provide some information about the sources of income (but not income itself) for the landholding groups. Farming is naturally the dominant activity and the main source of income, accounting for 75 percent of all the work undertaken by landholders (land cultivation 61 percent, and cattle and poultry breeding 14 percent). The remaining 25 percent consists of off-farm activities (23.6 percent) and remittances (1.4 percent). This clearly indicates a significant division of effort of the farming population in Egypt between farm and off-farm activities.

The two most important off-farm activities are working as wage labor in agriculture and having a job in some governmental or semigovernmental organization. Thus, 78 percent of the landholders who practice off-farm activities are engaged in these two types of work. In the case of very small landholders, however, working as wage labor in agriculture is more important (in terms of the number of people working and not the amount of income derived) than having a governmental job. Other off-farm activities in order of their importance are nonagricultural jobs, nonagricultural wage labor, and trade.

Examination of the distribution of different activities among different groups of landholders shows that 61.4 percent of all landholders working as wage labor fall within the group of very small landholders, and 68 percent of the wage labor in nonagricultural activities comes from this group. On the other hand, the proportion of landholders from this group who breed cattle and poultry is only 17.4 percent of all landholders practicing this activity. Working as wage labor in agriculture seems also to be an important activity for the group of small holders, wherein about 33 percent of all holders working as agricultural wage labor are holders of greater than 1 to 3 feddans.

It is of interest to consider the variations in job multiplicity by different groups of landholders. I consider the relationship between the number of landholders in a certain group and the number of income sources recorded for the same group as an indicator of this group's job multiplicity. This is because, in the question related to the source of income in the 1979 survey, the landholder who works in two different activities is considered to have two sources of income. Therefore, if the total number of income sources given by the survey for a certain group is greater than the number of landholders in that group, this means that there are some landholders who practice more than one activity. Using this criterion, I found that the very small holders, more than any other holders, devote much of their effort to off-farm work. The number of income sources for this group of holders is greater than the number of landholders by 57 percent.[26] This is naturally because the income this group of holders derives from their tiny holdings is not sufficient to provide them with the necessities of life; they have, therefore, to sell their labor to gain additional income.

According to the survey results, landholders in the larger holding groups also practice other off-farm activities but to a smaller extent than the small and the very small holders. This does not mean that the proportion of income derived by the larger landholders from off-farm activities is necessarily lower than that derived by the small and the very small landholders. This is because of the different nature of off-farm activities undertaken by the small holders and those undertaken by the larger holders. Further data on the magnitude of the off-farm income earned by the different holding groups are obviously required in order to determine whether off-farm income contributes, on the whole, toward greater or less inequality in the distribution of agricultural income.[27]

## IV. The Estimation of Income Distribution

The effect of the degree of land concentration on income distribution can be separated by assuming that all holdings obtain the same gross income per feddan irrespective of the holding group to which they belong. In other words, it is assumed at this stage that the crop mix is invariable from one group to another, and that the only determinant of income is the area of land held. The uniform average gross income per feddan is calculated from data given by the Ministry of Agriculture.[28] Multiplying the average gross income per feddan by the number of feddans in each holding group, we arrive at each group's hypothetical income and the distribution of income that reflects the inequality of land distribution. The degree of inequality in this distribution is then measured in terms of the Gini coefficient. The results of this first step are given in table 9.8.

The Gini coefficient for this income distribution equals 0.482. It is to be noted that this coefficient is the same as the coefficient that was obtained previously for the 1977/1978 land distribution. This is because income

TABLE 9.8.
*Distribution of Gross Crop Income by Holding Group (The Effect of Land Concentration 1977/1978)*

| *Size of Holding (feddans)* | *Income (£E million)* | *Percent share in income* | *No. of holdings (000)* | *Percent share in holdings* |
|---|---|---|---|---|
| ≤ 1 | 284.2 | 15.0 | 1,458.8 | 48.8 |
| > 1–3 | 625.3 | 33.0 | 984.3 | 32.9 |
| > 3–5 | 362.0 | 19.1 | 348.7 | 11.7 |
| > 5–10 | 244.5 | 12.9 | 127.6 | 4.3 |
| > 10 | 379.0 | 20.0 | 69.9 | 2.3 |
| Total | 1,895.0 | 100.0 | 2,989.3 | 100.0 |

distribution in this step is obtained by multiplying the land distribution by a constant that is the unified gross income per feddan. Note that the distribution of the landholdings used is the national one provided by the Ministry of Agriculture. This distribution was used in preference to the one obtained from the 1979 sample survey because it ensures a more complete coverage of the agricultural sector than the sample, despite the possibility that the degree of inequality may be understated by this distribution in view of the probable overestimation of the share of the small holders, as discussed earlier.

The next step is to quantify the effect on income inequality of the differences among holding groups in the crop mix. A primary distinction to be made is between landholders growing largely traditional crops and those growing largely high-value crops (fruits and vegetables). After having isolated the effect of the area cultivated in the previous step, a comparison between the income distribution calculated in this step and the previous one would thus reveal the separate effect of the crop pattern on income inequality.

The procedure is as follows: The total area cultivated with field crops, vegetables, and fruits is determined for each group as given in table 4. Gross income per feddan for each of these three kinds of crops is then multiplied by the corresponding area for each group. By adding together the group income from the three kinds of crops, the total distribution of income is obtained. The result of this step is given in table 9.9.

It can be seen from the results of table 9 that, taking into consideration differences in crop pattern, the distribution of income is becoming slightly more unequal. The income share of the group of small holders and lower medium holders has decreased, whereas that of the upper medium and large holders has increased. The relative income share of the very small holders shows a slight increase, which means that the effect of the crop mix on this group is not unfavorable. The Gini coefficient calculated for

*TABLE 9.9.*
*Distribution of Gross Crop Income by Holding Groups (The Effect of Crop Pattern) (1977/1978)*

| *Size of holding (feddans)* | *Income field crops** | *Income vegetables** | *Income fruits** | *Total Income** | *% share in income* | *% share in no. of holdings* |
|---|---|---|---|---|---|---|
| ≤ 1 | 202.8 | 62.4 | 28.4 | 293.6 | 15.5 | 48.8 |
| > 1–3 | 481.2 | 80.6 | 15.9 | 577.7 | 30.5 | 32.9 |
| > 3–5 | 270.0 | 68.2 | 12.8 | 351.0 | 18.5 | 11.7 |
| > 5–10 | 172.0 | 71.2 | 13.6 | 256.8 | 13.6 | 4.2 |
| > 10 | 258.0 | 95.6 | 62.3 | 415.9 | 21.9 | 2.3 |
| Total | 1,384.0 | 378.0 | 133.0 | 1,895.0 | 100.0 | 100.0 |

*In million £E

this income distribution reflects the change resulting from the differentiation between different groups of landholders with regard to crop pattern. It increased from 0.482 in the previous step to 0.495 in the present one. Nevertheless, it must be realized that the full effect of the crop pattern is not demonstrated in this step. This is because we have only distinguished among field crops and fruits and vegetables. Within the category of field crops, however, a further distinction should have been made between cash crops and subsistence crops. As is well known, there is a wide price differential between cash crops and subsistence crops, and small landholders tend to allocate a much smaller proportion of the area they cultivate to cash crops as compared to the larger holders. In addition, income per feddan of fruit and vegetables is calculated by the Ministry of Agriculture using the official prices for these two products. The actual market prices, particularly for fruits, are much higher than the official prices. It is believed that a large part of the fruit production is sold according to the higher market prices. Taking this additional differential between income from fruits and vegetables and income from field crops together with the differential between cash and subsistence crops into consideration would certainly increase the value of the Gini coefficient by a greater amount than is found above.

The third and last step is related to income distribution from livestock production. It was my intention to derive this step directly from the survey results, which should give the percentage distribution of income from livestock production. However, due to the unreliability of the data on the monetary variables included in the survey, this direct derivation could not be undertaken. Instead, my estimation of the distribution of income from livestock production is based on the estimated distribution of cattle among the different holding groups that is given in table 5 in the previous section. It is assumed that the distribution of income from livestock production is a function of the distribution of cattle. Distributing gross income from livestock production for the year 1977 in proportion to each holding group's share in the total number of livestock, we arrive at the distribution of income from livestock production. By adding the distribution obtained in this step to the distribution of the previous step, the distribution of gross agricultural income among the different landholder groups, which is the final step in the process of income distribution estimation, is obtained. The result of the final step is given in table 9.10.

*TABLE 9.10.*

*Distribution of Gross Agricultural Income by Holding Group (The effect of livestock production and the final distribution) 1977/1978*

| *Size holding (feddans)* | *Income livestock (million £E)* | *Percent share in livestock income* | *No. of holdings (000)* | *Percent share in no. of holdings* | *Agricultural income (million £E)* | *Percent share in agricultural income* |
|---|---|---|---|---|---|---|
| ≤1 | 151.3 | 20.7 | 1,458.8 | 48.8 | 444.9 | 16.9 |
| >1–3 | 247.8 | 33.9 | 984.3 | 32.9 | 825.5 | 31.4 |
| >3–5 | 136.7 | 18.7 | 348.7 | 11.7 | 487.7 | 18.6 |
| >5–10 | 91.4 | 12.5 | 127.6 | 4.3 | 348.2 | 13.3 |
| >10 | 103.8 | 14.2 | 69.9 | 2.3 | 519.7 | 19.8 |
| Total | 731.0 | 100.0 | 2,989.3 | 100.0 | 2,626.0 | 100.0 |

The Gini coefficient for the distribution of income from livestock activities is calculated and found to be 0.391. This coefficient is significantly lower than the coefficient derived for the distribution of income from crop production, which is 0.495. Taken at face value, this indicates that income from livestock is more equally distributed than income from crop production. Hence adding income from animals to income from crop production gives a distribution of total agricultural income exhibiting greater equality than the distribution of income from crop production only. The Gini coefficient for total agricultural income is 0.465.

However, some reservations should be made concerning the present estimate of the distribution of income from livestock production. It is my belief that the actual distribution is likely to be more unequal than the one estimated here. One of the reasons behind this belief is that a large proportion of the cattle existing on small holdings is shared between small landholders and large landholders and government employees.[29] In addition, the main activity of farm animals on small holdings is the performance of some farm operations. This no doubt reduces the milk and meat productivity of these animals. It is estimated that the loss due to animal work on the farm is about 30–50 percent of its production capacity of milk. This is in addition to the lowering of the quality of meat as a result of farm work.[30] On the other hand, the large landholders are the group that has the facilities and the financial means to breed animals for slaughtering. This kind of animal breeding provides a higher return than breeding animals to keep on the farm for work and milk production, which just meets the basic requirements of the family.[31] The large holders may also enjoy economies of scale on account of the large herds they can maintain—an advantage not available for the small holders. The foregoing suggests that the allocation of livestock income in proportion to each holding group's share in the total number of livestock leads to a distribution of livestock income more equal than is actually the case.

## V. Concluding Remarks

1. My review of the previous studies of the distribution of land and income in Egyptian agriculture has shown that they suffer from several shortcomings that arise either from data limitations or methodological defects or both. In many cases the data used were either out of date or constructed on the basis of questionable assumptions. This is particularly true of data relating to the distribution of landholdings. For example, studies of the distribution of agricultural income in the 1960s or early 1970s on the basis of the distribution of landholdings in the 1961 agricultural census cannot capture the effects of the 1961 and 1969 land reforms. Most of previous studies tended to focus on income from crop production with no consideration given to the impact of livestock production on the distribution of total income. Methodologically, many reservations can be raised concerning the classification of holdings into size groups and the assumptions underlying the estimation process. Though it cannot be claimed that the present study is free of all the defects observed, it attempted to overcome some of the major ones.
2. The landholding distribution in 1977/1978 or in 1979 is fairly skewed. Thus, after a sufficiently long time has elapsed since the execution of the last of the three land reform laws in 1969, a substantial gap still exists between the very small holders and the large holders regarding each group's share in the total area cultivated. In 1977/1978 the very small holders ($\leq$ 1 feddan), though accounting for almost half the landholders in Egypt, held 15 percent only of the land. In contrast the large holders ($>$ 10 feddans) who represented 2.3 percent of the total holders held 20 percent of the land. This clearly demonstrates that the scope for further land redistributive measures has by no means been exhausted by the earlier land reforms.

   My attempt to trace the development in the distribution of landholdings between 1961 and 1979 on the basis of information not previously used has revealed important trends in inequality. It emerged that the distribution of land and income has become more equal in the mid-1970s as compared with 1961. This improvement seems to be well-established between 1961 and 1965, but some uncertainty surrounds the trends between 1965 and 1977/1978. Inequality was either slightly reduced or remained constant during that period. Examination of the trends in recent years suggests that the downward trend in inequality has been reversed in the late 1970s. This suggests that the land reform had a strong equalizing effect on the distribution of income in the 1960s, but that this effect became weaker and weaker over time. This is probably due to the effect of the built-in tendencies toward more land concentration and greater inequality that have been given further impetus by the open-door policy and the lack of offsetting redistributive measures.

The Moslem inheritance system was found to have a significant impact on land redistribution, increasing the number and the area held by the very small holders, and decreasing the number and area held by large holders.

3. It appears that there has been a tendency in Egyptian agriculture toward the cultivation of more profitable crops, particularly in the late 1970s. Large landholders appear to have benefitted from this transformation more than small holders. This development has led to a greater degree of inequality in income distribution. The disequalizing effect of the crop pattern on this distribution is confirmed by the moderate increase in the value of the Gini coefficient relative to its value before considering the variability in the crop mix among the different holding groups. It is believed, however, that a greater degree of inequality of income distribution could have resulted had the crop pattern for each group of landholders been considered in greater detail (by disaggregating the field crops category), and had the return per feddan been calculated according to market rather than to official prices. Existing data did not, however, permit such detailed analysis.
4. Income from livestock production appears to be more equally distributed than income from crop production. The degree of inequality in livestock income distribution is significantly lower than the degree of inequality in crop income distribution. This may be due, in part, to the fact that many Egyptian peasants hold at least one head of cattle. The large number of holders in the small holding groups means, therefore, that these groups hold a good proportion of the total number of cattle. Nevertheless, there are, as already discussed, some indications that the distribution of income from livestock production is likely to be less equal than the distribution of the number of cattle. The assumption used in this study, therefore—that income from livestock production is a direct function of the number of cattle held by each group—may not be quite realistic. It certainly needs to be modified when relevant data on income from livestock production per holding group become available.
5. Some useful insights have been obtained with respect to the characteristics of the groups of small and very small landholders that in the meantime are indicative of the poverty of holders belonging to these groups. These characteristics can be summarized as follows:
   a) An important feature of these two groups of landholders is their dependency on work as wage labor in agriculture and, to a smaller extent, outside agriculture to supplement their meager incomes. It was observed, however, that working as wage labor is particularly common among the very small holders with less than one feddan whose position may be quite similar to that of the landless wage laborers.
   b) Generally speaking, the group of small and very small landholders use

traditional agricultural implements, which they usually own. Nevertheless, those holders use also, though on a limited scale, some advanced agricultural tools that, in the majority of cases, are rented from other (bigger) landholders.

c) Landholders in those two groups rent a fairly high proportion of the land they cultivate. In this respect, the small holders (> 1–3 feddans) are in a relatively inferior position as compared with the very small holders. The area rented by the small holders represents 68 percent of the total area they cultivate. Therefore, they pay the largest amount of rent among all other landholders.

d) Although noncash renting is not widespread in Egyptian agriculture, my study reveals that noncash renting is generally practiced by the group of very small holders. In addition, this group practices cash rent on a temporary basis (cash rent by crop or by season) more than any other group (which implies that they enjoy little security of tenure and pay higher rent).

e) Small and very small holders practice a crop pattern in which the cultivation of traditional crops is given a large weight. This is more evident in the case of small holders, who devote to traditional crop cultivation the highest proportion of their land as compared with all other groups.

f) The distribution of cattle is more favorable from the very small holders' point of view than is the distribution of land. The relative share of this group in the total area cultivated is 15 percent, whereas their relative share in the total cattle stock is 20 percent. In contrast, the relative position of the small holders in land and cattle distribution is almost the same.

g) A substantial degree of inequality exists between the small and very small holders with regard to land distribution. Thus, the very small holders' relative share in the area cultivated is less than half the relative share of the small holders, despite the fact that very small holders represent a much higher proportion of total holders than small holders.

h) It may be concluded from the above that the group of small and very small landholders combined can be considered to represent poor peasants in Egyptian agriculture. For certain purposes, however, it would be more useful to distinguish between the two groups on the basis of the differences just noted in their characteristics.

6. It is of interest to compare the estimate of income distribution arrived at in this study for 1977/1978 with other estimates that have been made for the mid-1970s. The values of the Gini coefficient for two previous estimates are shown below together with my estimate.[32]

| | *Gini Coefficient* |
|---|---|
| Household budget (1974/1975) | 0.35 |
| A. Mohie-Eldin (1976) | 0.24 |
| My estimate (1977/1978) | 0.46 |

It is clear that my estimate provides the highest value in the group. It is closer to the estimate from the household budget survey than to that of A. Mohie-Eldin, which appears to be exceptionally low.

It appears that the surprisingly low value of the Gini coefficient obtained by Mohie-Eldin is the outcome of three factors.[33] First, the share of rent in agricultural value added is probably understated and that of labor overstated. Second, it is implicitly assumed that the value added generated in a given agricultural subsector accrues exclusively to the income groups in that subsector, without allowing for income transfers between the subsectors (agriculture is divided into four subsectors, with three income classes in each). Third, it appears that the three income classes within a given subsector are equated with the corresponding income classes in the agricultural sector as a whole. (The top 10 percent income class in the cotton subsector is not necessarily part of the top 10 percent in agriculture as a whole.)

It should be further noted that the actual difference between the Gini coefficient that should be obtained in Mohie-Eldin's study and the present study is probably larger than indicated by the Gini coefficients given above. This is because my estimate of the income distribution includes the landholding categories only, whereas Mohie-Eldin's estimate covers the landholding as well as the landless population. Including the landless in my estimate would, most likely, increase the value of the Gini coefficient of the distribution.

The degree of inequality of the household budget estimate seems also to be understated. Actually it is believed that the household budget data do not represent the very rich and the very poor, and they mainly reflect the consumption pattern of the middle income classes.[34] Furthermore, the household budget estimate is an estimate of expenditure distribution and not income distribution. Including saving to arrive at income distribution would significantly increase the degree of inequality and hence the value of the Gini coefficient.

7. Finally, it is important to bear in mind the following qualifications with respect to the distribution of agricultural income estimated in this study. It should once more be noted here that income in this study is gross income, that is, it includes the value of agricultural inputs, wages of agricultural workers, and rental payments. To take account of all these factors and to arrive at net agricultural income, stratified data by group of landholders are required for the three components of gross agricultural income. Net agricultural income is certainly a more meaningful indicator for the study of income distribution than is gross income. In particular, wages and rental payments should be separated from the concept of gross income. This is desirable, not only because it is likely to affect the relative position of the different groups in the income distributional structure, but also in order to determine the share of wage labor and of absentee landowners in total agricultural income.

Another aspect that is likely to affect the credibility of the income distributional pattern estimated in this study is the omission of income from off-farm activities. It is shown that off-farm activities represent an important source of income, particularly in the case of the small holdings groups. The main off-farm activity undertaken by these groups is wage labor. That is, a certain part of the total agricultural wage bill is received by these groups. This clearly should have an equalizing distributional effect since a large proportion of the wages received by the group of small and very small landholders is paid by the group of large and upper medium holders who usually employ

> wage labor. However, the final effect of considering off-farm activities on income distribution is not entirely certain. This is because other groups of holders also practice off-farm activities. The income received from the off-farm activities undertaken by larger landholders may be relatively greater than the income received by the small holders. Indeed, further analysis is required of the effect of this source of income on inequality, but this must await the collection of the relevant data. It should be noted, however, that if income from off-farm activities is considered, then the concept of agricultural income will no longer be appropriate. The concept of income will have to be broader, namely, the income of the agricultural population.

Generally speaking, it appears that the actual degree of inequality of agricultural income distribution is likely to be greater than is reflected by the Gini coefficient calculated in this study. The factors that I expect to lead to greater inequality are as follows: (1) more accurate data on landholding distribution (census data), (2) a more detailed analysis of crop mix, (3) a more accurate estimation of the distribution of income from livestock production, (4) using the concept of agricultural income after rent payment, and (5) dropping the assumption of independent crop and livestock distributions and allowing for the probable interactions. On the other hand, I expect a decrease in the degree of inequality if wages are netted from agricultural income. The likely effect of considering income from off-farm activities is not certain yet.

## Appendix

*TABLE 9.A.1*

*Percentage Distribution of Land Ownerships in Egypt, 1952–1965*

| | *1952 (Before Reform)* | | | *1952 (After Reform)* | | | *1961* | | | *1965* | | |
|---|---|---|---|---|---|---|---|---|---|---|---|---|
| *Ownership Groups* | *Owners (%)* | *Area (%)* | *Average ownership (per feddan)* | *Owners (%)* | *Area (%)* | *Average ownership (per feddan)* | *Owners (%)* | *Area (%)* | *Average ownership (per feddan)* | *Owners (%)* | *Area (%)* | *Average ownership (per feddan)* |
| Small ownerships 5 feddans | 94.3 | 35.4 | 0.8 | 94.4 | 46.6 | 1.0 | 94.6 | 52.1 | 1.1 | 95.0 | 57.1 | 1.2 |
| Medium ownerships | 5.3 | 30.4 | . . . | 5.2 | 33.1 | . . . | 5.0 | 32.7 | . . . | 4.7 | 30.3 | . . . |
| 5–<10 feddans | 2.8 | 8.8 | 6.5 | 2.6 | 8.8 | 6.6 | 2.6 | 8.6 | 6.6 | 2.5 | 9.5 | 7.9 |
| 10–<20 feddans | 1.7 | 10.7 | 13.6 | 1.6 | 10.7 | 13.6 | 1.6 | 10.7 | 13.3 | 1.3 | 8.2 | 13.3 |
| 20–<50 feddans | 0.8 | 10.9 | 29.7 | 1.0 | 13.6 | 27.3 | 0.8 | 13.4 | 31.5 | 0.9 | 12.6 | 28.1 |
| Large ownerships | 0.4 | 34.2 | . . . | 0.4 | 20.3 | . . . | 0.4 | 15.2 | . . . | 0.3 | 12.6 | . . . |
| 50–<100 feddans | 0.2 | 7.2 | 71.7 | 0.2 | 7.2 | 71.7 | 0.2 | 7.0 | 71.7 | 0.2 | 6.1 | 65.3 |
| 100–<200 feddans | 0.1 | 7.3 | 145.7 | 0.1 | 7.2 | 145.7 | 0.2 | 8.2 | 100.0 | 0.1 | 6.5 | 105.3 |
| 200 feddans | 0.1 | 19.7 | 588.5 | 0.1 | 5.9 | 177.0 | . . . | . . . | . . . | . . . | . . . | . . . |
| Total | 100.0 | 100.0 | | 100.0 | 100.0 | | 100.0 | 100.0 | | 100.0 | 100.0 | |

SOURCE: CAPMS

NOTE: There is an error in the number of landowners recorded in 1961 and 1965 in the official data for the strata 10–<20. The figures for the landowners in the medium ownership group were thus adjusted, according to S. Radwan, *The Impact of Agrarian Reform on Rural Egypt, 1952–75*, ILO Working Paper (Geneva, January 1977), p. 35.

*TABLE 9.A.2.*
*Distribution of Holdings, 1950 and 1961*

| | *Small Holdings* | | *Medium Holdings* | | *Large Holdings* | |
|---|---|---|---|---|---|---|
| *Census Year* | *Percent holdings* | *Percent area* | *Percent holdings* | *Percent area* | *Percent holdings* | *Percent area* |
| 1950 | 78.5 | 23.2 | 20.0 | 37.7 | 1.5 | 39.1 |
| 1961 | 84.1 | 37.8 | 15.3 | 40.7 | 0.6 | 21.5 |

SOURCE: M. Abdel-Fadil, *Development, Income Distribution and Social Change in Rural Egypt (1952–1976).*

*TABLE 9.A.3.*
*D. Mead's Estimates of Income Distribution, 1950 and 1960*

| | *1950* | | *1960* | |
|---|---|---|---|---|
| | *£E million* | *%* | *£E million* | *%* |
| Wages | 20.0 | 5.4 | 20.0 | 5 |
| Rental payments | 48.3 | 13.1 | 31.7 | 7 |
| Other income, by size of holdings: | | | | |
| below 2 feddans | 24.1 | 6.5 | 28.7 | 7 |
| 2–50 feddans | 160.7 | 43.7 | 218.1 | 52 |
| over 50 feddans | 114.9 | 31.2 | 123.5 | 29 |
| Gross value added | 368.0 | 100.0 | 422.0 | 100 |

SOURCE: D. Mead, *Growth and Structural change in the Egyptian Economy*

*TABLE 9.A.4.*
*R. Mabro's Estimates of Income Distribution, 1950 and 1965*

| *Socioeconomic groups* | *1950* | *1965* |
|---|---|---|
| Landless families | 9.0 | 8.0 |
| Holders of less than 5 feddans | 17.5 | 34.0 |
| Holders of 5–<100 feddans* | 48.5 | 54.0 |
| Holders of 100 and plus feddans | 25.0 | 4.0 |
| Total | 100.0 | 100.0 |

SOURCE: Mabro, *The Egyptian Economy, 1952–1972.*

*The share of this group is calculated as a residual.

TABLE 9.A.5.

*Abdel-Fadil's Estimates of the Distribution of Agricultural Income, 1950 and 1961*

| | 1950 | | | | | 1961 | | | | | |
|---|---|---|---|---|---|---|---|---|---|---|---|
| | | | | | | | | | | Average income per head of family (£E) | |
| Socioeconomic groups | Income (£E million) | Percent income share | No. of families (000's) | Percent of total farm population | Average income per head of family (£E) | Income (£E million) | Percent income share | No. of families (000's) | Percent of total farm population | Money | Real |
| 1. Landless peasants | 20 | 5.3 | 1,217 | 55 | 16.4 | 39 | 9.7 | 970 | 37 | 40 | 30 |
| 2. Holders of less than 5 feddans | 55 | 15.0 | 787 | 35 | 70.0 | 113 | 28.0 | 1,381 | 53 | 82 | 81 |
| 3. Holders of 5 to less than 50 feddans | 92 | 25.0 | 201 | 9 | 458.0 | 130 | 32.3 | 251 | 9 | 518 | 513 |
| 4. Holders of more than 50 feddans | 144 | 39.0 | 15 | 1 | 9,600.0 | 69 | 17.0 | 10 | 1 | 6,900 | 6,832 |
| 5. Rental payments for absentee landowners | 58 | 15.7 | ... | ... | ... | 52 | 13.0 | ... | ... | ... | ... |
| Net Value added in agriculture, at current prices | 369 | 100.0 | 2,220 | 100 | 166 | 403 | 100.0 | 2,612 | 100 | 154 | 152 |

SOURCE: M. Abdel-Fadil, *Development, Income Distribution and Social Change*

*TABLE 9.A.6.*

*The Distribution of Landholdings by Group (1979)*

| *Holding groups* | *No. of holders* | *Percent* | *Area Cultivated (feddans)* | *Percent* | *Average holding* |
|---|---|---|---|---|---|
| <1 feddan | 202.0 | 27.0 | 104.6 | 5.0 | 0.5 |
| 1–<3 feddans | 368.0 | 49.3 | 640.2 | 30.6 | 1.7 |
| 3–<5 feddans | 99.0 | 13.3 | 332.1 | 15.9 | 3.4 |
| 5–<10 feddans | 43.0 | 5.8 | 276.2 | 13.3 | 6.4 |
| ≥10 feddans | 35.0 | 4.6 | 735.9 | 35.2 | 21.0 |
| Total | 747.0 | 100.0 | 2,089.0 | 100.0 | 2.8 |

SOURCE: Preliminary results of the 1979 survey

*TABLE 9.A.7.*

*The Distribution of Cattle (Cows and Buffaloes) by Size of Holding (1961)*

| | *Number of cattle* | *Percent of total* | *Number of holders* | *Percent of total* | *No. of head per holder* |
|---|---|---|---|---|---|
| <3 | 1,482,818 | 46.3 | 1,106,924 | 67.4 | 1.3 |
| 3–<5 | 637,769 | 19.9 | 274,317 | 16.7 | 2.3 |
| 5–<10 | 522,054 | 16.3 | 170,019 | 10.3 | 3.1 |
| 10–<20 | 237,313 | 7.4 | 56,705 | 3.4 | 4.2 |
| Over 20 | 319,741 | 10.0 | 34,195 | 2.1 | 9.3 |
| Total | 3,199,695 | 100.0 | 1,642,160 | 100.0 | 1.9 |

SOURCE: The 1961 agricultural census

*TABLE 9.A.8.*

*Estimated Distribution of Cattle by Holding Groups in 1977/1978 (First Assumption)*

| *Holding groups (feddans)* | *Average number of cattle per holding, 1961* | *No. of holdings, 1977/1978 (000)* | *No. of cattle (000)* | *Percent of no. of cattle* |
|---|---|---|---|---|
| <1 | 0.9 | 1,458.8 | 1312.9 | 28.6 |
| >1–3 | 1.6 | 984.3 | 1574.9 | 34.3 |
| >3–5 | 2.3 | 348.7 | 802.0 | 17.5 |
| >5–10 | 3.1 | 127.6 | 395.6 | 8.6 |
| >10* | 7.2 | 69.9 | 503.3 | 11.0 |

*In calculating the average number of cattle per holding for the group > 10 feddans the average number of cattle per holding for holders with 100 feddans and over in 1961 was excluded.

## Notes

1. See G. Baer, *A History of Land Ownership in Modern Egypt, 1800–1950* (London, 1962), pp. 201–202; Ibrāhīm ᶜAmr, *The Land and the Peasant* (Cairo, 1958) (in Arabic); Charles Issawi, *Egypt in Revolution* (Oxford University Press, 1963); M. Abdel-Fadil, *Development, Income Distribution and Social Change in Rural Egypt (1952–1970); A Study in the Political Economy of Agrarian Transition,* University of Cambridge, Department of Applied Economics, Occasional Paper 45, (Cambridge University Press, 1975). and S. Radwan, "The Impact of Agrarian Reform On Rural Egypt (1952–75)," Working Paper, *World Employment Program Research,* (ILO, Geneva, 1977).

2. See section 3 of this chapter, which discusses the main determinants of the agricultural income distribution.

3. Data on the distribution of land ownership for the year 1965 are given by the Central Agency for Public Mobilization and Statistics (CAPMS).

4. It is estimated that 35,000 feddans were expropriated under this law, which contrasts sharply with 214,132 feddans expropriated under the 1961 reform. On this point, see F. ᶜAbd al-Hamīd, *The Agrarian Question in Developing Countries; The Experience of Agrarian Reform in Egypt* (Cairo, 1973) (in Arabic).

5. Land was distributed in plots of 2 feddans as a minimum size.

6. In spite of the fact that the 1961 law imposed an upper limit on landownership of 100 feddans, ownerships in the category 100–200 feddans still represented 6.5 percent of the total area cultivated in 1965.

7. Doreen Warriner, *Land Reform and Development in the Middle East,* 2nd ed. (London: Oxford University Press, 1962), p. 13.

8. Landowners subject to expropriation were permitted under the 1952 law to sell their land in small holdings to small peasants. About 145,000 feddans were disposed of in this way only after one year of the 1952 law. There are some indications that almost all of this land was purchased by those holding 20–<50 feddans. The decree permitting this sale was terminated in October 1953.

9. The total area of land distributed until 1974 was 831,000 feddans, which represents 13.5 percent of the total cultivated area in 1950. Also, according to Warriner, the proportion of rural families who benefitted from the distribution is estimated at 10 percent of the rural population in 1965. See D. Warriner, "Employment and Income Aspects of Recent Agrarian Reform in the Middle East," *International Labor Review* 101, 1970.

10. J. Waterbury, "The Balance of People, Land and Water in Modern Egypt," *The American Universities Field Staff* 19, no. 1, 1976, p. x.

11. The number of landless families in 1972 and after the execution of the three land reform laws amounted to 1,850,000 families. They represented 50 percent of the total agricultural families. See S. Radwan, "Impact of Agrarian Reform," p. 22.

12. D. Mead, *Growth and Structural Change in the Egyptian Economy* (New Haven: Economic Growth Center, Yale University, 1967).

13. R. Mabro, *The Egyptian Economy 1952–1972* (Oxford: Clarendon Press, 1974), pp. 218–221.

14. M. Abdel-Fadil, *Development, Income Distribution.*

15. It should be remembered that this group contains the new beneficiaries of land distribution whose income has certainly increased much more than the income of other peasants in this group.

16. In T. Byer's view, for instance, small peasants in Abdel-Fadil's definition have the characteristics of middle peasants. Therefore, including them with the class of poor peasants might lead to misspecification of the different classes. See T. J. Byer, "Agrarian Transition

and the Agrarian Question," *Journal of Peasant Studies,* April 1977, vol. 4, no. 3, pp. 258–274.

17. It should be noted that the landholding data of the 1961 agricultural census were collected over the period 15 May to the end of June 1961 (see the introduction to the 1961 agricultural census, Ministry of Agriculture). This means that all the studies that estimated agricultural income distribution from the 1961 landholding statistics excluded completely the effect of the 1961 reform law, which was issued in July 1961.

18. This reservation was strongly stated by the Ministry of Agriculture officials who supervised the collection of the data in question. Note that subdivision of ownerships does not necessarily lead to subdivision of holdings. They may, however, tend to go together in practice.

19. *The 1978–82 Five Year Plan,* vol. 1 (Cairo: Ministry of Planning, 1977).

20. As found in the 1961 agricultural census, Ministry of Agriculture.

21. The share of fruits is certainly higher, if calculated as a proportion of the total cultivated rather than the total cropped area, since the latter is greater than the former and the absolute size of the fruit area is the same in terms of both cultivated and cropped area.

22. The comparison between the 1977 Ministry of Agriculture data (given in table 2) and my preliminary estimation of the crop mix for the entire agriculture revealed that the area cultivated with field crops in my preliminary estimation is greater than the area cultivated with field crops in the data of the Ministry of Agriculture. On the other hand, the area cultivated with vegetables and fruits in my estimation is smaller than the actual area cultivated by each of these two main crops. Such differences are due to my temporary assumption that the crop mix in 1977/1978 is the same as that prevailing in 1961. The modification of my estimation, therefore, aimed at reducing the area cultivated with field crops to the actual area recorded in the Ministry of Agriculture data and increasing the area cultivated with vegetable and fruits to match the actual area cultivated by each of these two crops. For instance, the group of holders who devote a larger percentage of their area to fruit cultivation was allocated a larger percentage increase of the positive difference between actual and estimated fruit area.

23. Information obtained from Ministry of Agriculture.

24. See A. ᶜAbd al-Muᶜatī, *The Distribution of Poverty in the Egyptian Village,* Cairo, 1979 (in Arabic).

25. This survey, which comprises 1,200 rural households, was carried out by the Population and Family Planning Board (PFPB) in 1977 as part of a rural development project in eight villages in the Daqhalīya governorate (Lower Egypt). All eight villages fall within one village council (Burj Nūr al-Hammūs) in this particular governorate. The results of the survey cannot, therefore, be considered as representative of the whole agricultural sector. It should be noted also that the questions of the survey are not related to income of the households, but they concentrate on other aspects of the rural population such as the holding of land and other assets. The results available so far comprise frequency distributions of the different variables included in the survey. Therefore, they are of limited relevance to the purpose of the present study.

26. Note that land cultivation and poultry and cattle breeding together constitute one activity, namely, farming activity.

27. The 1979 survey does not include any information on the magnitude of income from off-farm activities.

28. This average is calculated by dividing the gross crop income by the total area cultivated. It should be noted that area according to which income data are calculated by the Ministry of Agriculture is the crop area. Therefore, by crop income per feddan is meant income per feddan of crop area. In order to estimate the distribution of income from the distribution of landholdings, the latter is calculated in terms of crop area. Multiplying

income per feddan of crop area, which was found to be £E170.55 by the crop area for the different groups of holdings, the first step income distribution is obtained.

29. According to a recent survey of some Egyptian villages, 90 percent of the cattle on small landholdings is jointly owned between small landholders and large holders or government employees. See M. Dewidar, "An Entry Visa to the Egyptian village," *L. Égypte Contemporaine* no. 396 (July 1977), p. 97.

30. PFPB, Rural Development Project, 1977.

31. It should be noted here that small landholders suffer from the problem of high prices of fodder. This is because the fodder sold at official prices is provided mainly for animal breeders who breed at least five head of animals. See PFPB, Rural Development Project, 1977. See also A. Ibrahim "The Impact of Some Agricultural Policies on Income Distribution in Egyptian Agriculture" in chapter 7.

32. The estimate for the household budget survey is given in chapter 4 by I. El-Issawy. It relates to rural areas. Mohie-Eldin's estimate is calculated from his estimate of the agricultural income distribution reported in R. Eckaus et al., *Multi-sector General Equilibrium Policy Models for Egypt* (Cairo University/MIT Technological Planning Program, 1978).

33. See I. El-Issawy's evaluation of Mohie-Eldin's income distribution estimate for the agricultural sector in "Employment Inadequacy in Egypt" (A paper prepared for the ILO Comprehensive Employment Strategy Mission to the Arab Republic of Egypt, 1980).

34. See I. El-Issawy in chapter 4, section II.

# CHAPTER 10

# *Patterns of Urban Growth and Income Distribution in Egypt*

John Waterbury

## I. Introduction

In this chapter we shall pay particular attention to the four factors that shape the relative income shares of the countryside and the cities: the availability of services, the quality of services, levels of public investment in each sector, and the size distribution of income between sectors. After an introductory summary of the process of urbanization in Egypt, these four factors will be assessed. The final section of the chapter consists of an analysis of the distribution of income and services within Greater Cairo.

This sort of exercise will not tell us all that we would like to know about the impact of rapid urbanization in Egypt upon patterns of national income distribution nor about the evolution of income distribution within Egyptian cities. However, it may help us assess the extent to which the material distribution of income, services, and investment reflects or sustains something that can justifiably be called urban bias, that is, an allocation of resources and distribution of wealth that serves neither the goals of equity nor of efficient economic performance. Lipton[1] and others have argued that the relative inattention to the rural areas of Less Developed Countries (LDCs) manifested by urban-based policymaking elites has engendered a severe maldistribution of resources that perpetuates low standards of living among rural populations that comprise the majority of society and, in turn, the inefficiency of infant industries that cannot justify their size in terms of small and stagnant domestic markets. Moreover, the public-policy privileges granted the cities and urban industries may be financed by the rural sector and act as an economically unjustified incentive to further rapid urbanization and industrialization. The key word is *unjustified,* for, even if we are able to identify and measure the sorts of biases that Lipton has in mind, it may be that in both growth and equity terms they are justifiable and probably inevitable. I do not propose to resolve this question with respect to Egypt but rather to provide some of the data that could inform an intelligent assessment.

*TABLE 10.1.1.*
*Population in Urban and Rural Areas in Egypt in Census Years 1907–1976*

| *Years* | *Urban Population* | *%* | *Rural Population* | *%* | *Total* |
|---|---|---|---|---|---|
| 1907 | 2,125,000 | 19 | 9,058,000 | 81 | 11,183,000 |
| 1917 | 2,640,600 | 21 | 10,029,700 | 79 | 12,670,300 |
| 1927 | 3,715,840 | 26 | 10,367,436 | 74 | 14,083,276 |
| 1937 | 4,382,083 | 28 | 11,429,001 | 72 | 15,811,084 |
| 1947 | 6,202,316 | 33 | 12,603,510 | 67 | 18,805,826 |
| 1960 | 9,651,097 | 37 | 16,120,368 | 63 | 25,771,495 |
| 1966 | 12,036,787 | 40 | 17,687,312 | 60 | 29,724,099 |
| 1976 | 16,091,984 | 44 | 20,564,196 | 56 | 36,656,180 |

SOURCE: Calculated from official census data

The exercise is useful as well insofar as it sheds light on the distribution of income within a rapidly growing, rapidly changing Third World megalopolis—Cairo. Here as elsewhere hard data are difficult to come by, and circumstantial evidence and surrogate measures must be marshalled to establish a hold on the question. Two points can be made at the outset: Cairo is better endowed than any other Egyptian city in terms of the availability of public services (let alone their quality), and its pattern of income distribution is probably more highly skewed.

## II. Egypt's Urban Growth

Egypt is rapidly approaching the point where half its population will be officially designated as urban (living in agglomerations of 20,000 or more) and about a third of the population is already living in cities of 100,000 or more (see tables 10.1.1 and 10.1.2). With its 8 million inhabitants, Greater

*TABLE 10.1.2.*
*Comparative Growth Rates: Cairo vs. Egypt*

| *Years* | *Cairo Population* | *Annual Growth Rate (%)* | *Egypt Population* | *Annual Growth Rate (%)* |
|---|---|---|---|---|
| 1897 | 590,000 | . . . | 9,717,000 | . . . |
| 1907 | 678,011 | 1.4 | 11,183,000 | 1.4 |
| 1917 | 791,000 | 1.6 | 12,670,300 | 1.3 |
| 1927 | 1,071,000 | 3.1 | 14,083,276 | 1.1 |
| 1937 | 1,312,000 | 2.1 | 15,811,084 | 1.2 |
| 1947 | 2,091,000 | 4.8 | 18,805,826 | 1.7 |
| 1960 | 3,353,000 | 3.7 | 25,771,495 | 2.5 |
| 1966 | 4,219,853 | 3.9 | 29,724,099 | 2.4 |
| 1976 | 5,084,463 | 1.9 | 36,656,180 | 2.1 |

SOURCE: Calculated from official census data

*TABLE 10.2.*
*Growth of Egypt's Cities of 100,000 and More Inhabitants*

| *City* | *1960 Census (In Thousands)* | *1960–1966 Annual Average Growth Rate (percent)* | *1966 Census (In Thousands)* | *1966–1976 Annual Average Growth Rate (percent)* | *1976 Census (In Thousands)* |
|---|---|---|---|---|---|
| Cairo | 3,353 | 3.9 | 4,220 | 1.9 | 5,084 |
| Alexandria | 1,516 | 2.9 | 1,801 | 2.6 | 2,319 |
| Giza* | 419 | 5.3 | 571 | 8.0 | 1,233 |
| Port Said | 245 | 2.4 | 283 | −0.7 | 263† |
| Suez | 206 | 4.2 | 264 | −3.0 | 194† |
| Tantā | 200 | 2.4 | 230 | 2.2 | 285 |
| Mahalla al-Kubrā | 188 | 3.0 | 225 | 2.7 | 293 |
| al-Mansūra | 167 | 2.3 | 191 | 3.1 | 258 |
| Shubrā al-Khayma* | 101 | 9.4 | 173 | 8.6 | 394 |
| Asyūt | 127 | 3.3 | 154 | 3.3 | 214 |
| al-Zaqāzīq | 125 | 3.2 | 151 | 3.0 | 203 |
| Damanhūr | 127 | 2.3 | 146 | 2.6 | 189 |
| Ismailia | 116 | 3.7 | 144 | 0.1 | 146† |
| al-Fayyūm | 112 | 3.0 | 134 | 2.2 | 167 |
| Aswān | 63 | 12.5 | 128 | 1.2 | 144 |
| al-Minyā | 100 | 2.1 | 113 | 2.6 | 146 |
| Total | 7,165 | 3.7 | 8,928 | 2.6 | 11,532 |

SOURCE:
Calculated from official census results

*Giza and Shubrā al-Khayma are parts of the Greater Cairo area.
†These three cities are situated in the Suez canal zone and were evacuated during 1967/1968 as a result of the June war. The population began to move back in in 1974—hence the decline of population in two of them.

Cairo alone accounted in 1976 for 22 percent of Egypt's population, while Alexandria, with 2.3 million, absorbed another 6 percent. The preliminary results of the 1976 census do not provide a breakdown of the urban population by city. Still, it is known that the populations of Port Said, Ismailia, Suez, al-Zaqāzīq, Damietta, al-Mansūra, Mahalla al-Kubrā, Damanhūr, Tantā, Banhā, al-Minyā, Asyūt, Sūhāj, Aswān, and so forth house close to or well in excess of 100,000 inhabitants each (see table 10.2).

Egypt has a long urban history and has always maintained a large urban population. Not long after its founding over a thousand years ago, Cairo came to rank as one of the largest cities in the world. More recently, at the time of Napoleon's invasion of Egypt in 1798 and after a period of overall population decline during three centuries of Ottoman rule, Cairo's population may have stood at a quarter of a million, a figure that changed little up to 1821, when a first rudimentary census was undertaken. At that level, Cairo may have housed 6 percent of the nation's population.

There is considerable debate regarding Egypt's total population in 1821. The figure most frequently advanced, based on the census of that year, is 2.5 million. Both Justin McCarthy and Gabriel Baer dispute that figure and offer considerably higher estimates of 4.4 and 4.2 millions, respectively. Because of massive military conscription and epidemics, McCarthy believes the population remained unchanged until 1846. Baer, by contrast, argues for a moderate increase to 5.2 million in the same year.[2]

Despite the discrepancy in their estimates for 1846, McCarthy and Baer agree that, in the census years of 1882 and 1897, the total population reached 7.9 and 9.7 million. If the figure of 2.5 million for 1821 is accepted, that would yield an improbable average annual growth rate of 5 percent over the ensuing seventy-six years. The estimates of McCarthy and Baer yield far more plausible rates of 1.6 percent and 1.3 percent per annum for the period 1821–1897. It is important to establish this sort of figure for it shows, depending on one's 1821 estimate, either that Cairo and most other Egyptian cities were growing more slowly than the total population, or somewhat faster. I am inclined to the latter view. Over the entire seventy-six-year period, Cairo's population increased from 225,000 to 590,000, at an annual rate of 1.8 percent. In the period 1821–1882 the city's growth rate (from 250,000 to 398,000, or 0.9% per annum) lagged behind that of the nation as a whole.The lag may be partially explained by the plague of 1835 which killed a third of the city's inhabitants. But over the fifteen years between 1882 and 1897, Cairo's population surged ahead at a rate of 3.2 percent per annum, rising in the latter year to 590,000. This period ushered in a century, at least, of rapid urban growth.

What the nineteenth century witnessed then was primarily steady growth of a rural population that tended to remain rural, either because it was tied to the land through collective debt and other forms of indenturing, or because land resources were rapidly expanded through the extension of the irrigation grid. It was only toward the end of the century, after the British occupation of 1882 and after abolition of collective debt, that rural-urban migration developed in a major and sustained way. And it was not until after the First World War that land scarcity became an important factor in pushing peasants from the land and toward the cities. From 1920 on, Cairo's growth rates clearly reflect this phenonmenon.

As rural-urban migration accelerated, the major targets were Cairo, the three canal zone cities, and Alexandria. All began to experience very high rates of growth in the late 1930s but above all during and after the Second World War, when hundreds of thousands of Egyptians who had been mobilized for the war effort opted not to return to their villages. For instance, between 1937 and 1947, Cairo's population grew by 779,000, of which an estimated 600,000 were migrants. Thus the city's growth over these years was a function of a natural increase rate of 1.3 percent per annum and a net migration rate of 2.8 percent per annum. The canal zone cities underwent a similar experience, one that was sustained until the late 1960s.

There was a long hiatus between the sample census of 1966 and the full census of 1976. This period spanned the 1967 war, the forced evacuation of the canal zone cities (many of whose residents sought refuge in Cairo) and, after 1974, the repopulation of the canal zone. By 1976 Port Said and Ismailia had attained their pre-1967 population levels and showed signs of very rapid growth in the future. Cairo, excluding Giza, Hulwān, and Shubrā al-Khayma, which are jurisdictionally separate from Cairo proper, showed a marked slowing in its growth rate, declining to 1.8 percent per annum. However, the other parts of Greater Cairo continued to grow rapidly so that Greater Cairo's growth rate between 1966 and 1976 was 3.1 percent per annum.

As Abu Lughod and others have shown, the bulk of all migrants to Cairo and other cities has been of rural origin. Since 1917 only 3 percent, on average, of Cairo's population has come from other cities.[3] It is, in general, the Nile Delta governorates that have supplied Cairo most of its migrants, due above all to their proximity to the capital and its industrial suburbs. They have also had more ready access to Alexandria and the canal zone. Migrants from the delta tend to bring their families with them while those from the more distant governorates of Upper Egypt come more frequently as unaccompanied males. Although the delta is numerically the most important source of migrants, it is Sūhāj governorate in Upper Egypt that, as a proportion of its population, has the highest rate of out-migration. It also has the highest rural density level and the lowest literacy rate of any Egyptian governorate.

Cairo has always dominated Egypt's urban scene, with Alexandria running a distant second. There are relatively few other old urban centers in Egypt, and those that do have a lengthy history, such as the Mediterranean port of Damietta, the delta capitals of Tantā and al-Mansūra, or Asyūt, the unofficial capital of Upper Egypt, have always been dwarfed by Cairo.

A common pattern in Egypt has been for the initial growth of cities to come about by decisions from above. Cairo itself was first laid out over a thousand years ago as a warrior's city. For centuries Damietta eclipsed Alexandria as a port until Muhammad ᶜAlī's dynasty decided to resuscitate the latter in the nineteenth century. The decision to excavate the Suez Canal eventually spawned the three canal zone cities as well as the large eastern delta town of al-Zaqāzīq. The decision of Egyptian entrepreneurs in the 1920s to establish a major textile complex at Mahalla al-Kubrā transformed that delta town into the most important textile city of the Middle East. More recently the decision to build the Aswān High Dam stimulated the growth of Aswān City from 63,000 in 1960 to 128,000 in 1966. Similarly, Najᶜ Hammādī in Upper Egypt is undergoing rapid growth as a result of the location of an aluminum smelter there, as is the Red Sea port of Safāja, through which the bauxite is imported. More ambitious plans for urbanization from above have been formulated and may lead to the construction of nine new cities along the fringes of the Nile Delta.

It should be noted, finally, that in Egypt, as elsewhere, classifying agglomerations as rural or urban according to population size may produce some anomalies. The urban threshold commonly employed in Egypt is 20,000 inhabitants. But it is a fact that many villages in Egypt exceed that number. According to Abu Lughod, between 1947 and 1960 twenty-seven agglomerations were reclassified as urban because they crossed the 20,000 threshold. The total urban population in 1947 was officially set at 6.2 million. However, Abu Lughod recalculated this figure—adding the criteria that densities exceed 1,500 people per square kilometer and that no more than one-third of its population be employed in agriculture—and came up with a figure of 5 million urban inhabitants.[4] It is likely that undiscriminating statistical classification has produced similar discrepancies in subsequent censuses.

## III. Shares of Urban and Rural Areas in National Income, Services, and Investment

It has been the intention of planners in several LDCs, of which Egypt is one, to generate a net flow of resources from agriculture to other sectors of the economy above all in order to finance industrial growth. Most observers concur that this has been Egypt's policy for at least two decades. For example, over the period 1960–1971 public investment in agriculture totaled £E893 million (at the then official exchange rate of £E1 = $2.54). This figure includes the water storage component of the Aswān High Dam. Against this the agricultural sector paid £E176 million in taxes, and the state realized net profits of £E736 million on the sale of rice and cotton abroad. Ostensibly then, agriculture was taxed about £E19 million over eleven years.[5] However, agricultural investment exclusive of the High Dam reached £E483 million for horizontal expansion (land reclamation) and only £E193 million for the "vertical" intensification of cropping in areas already cultivated. Yet it is these old lands that generate at least 90 percent of all agricultural income and from which a regular transfer has been extracted. This very summary evidence would suggest that much of the transfer has gone into new, albeit inefficient, agricultural projects. One must not discount the fact that the foreign-exchange earnings from agriculture realized by the state have probably been used to import raw materials and capital goods for industry and basic foods for urban consumption. The International Bank for Reconstruction and Development (IBRD) has undertaken more recent estimates of the implicit tax on the agricultural sector for the period 1973–1976:[6]

*TABLE 10.3.*
*Intersectoral Resource Flow*
*(£E million)*

| | *1973* | *1974* | *1975* | *1976* |
|---|---|---|---|---|
| Transfers to Treasury of Cotton Organization | 64.8 | 136.8 | 54.0 | 92.4 |
| Exchange rate gains | 114.0 | 177.0 | 129.0 | (100) |
| Total transfers out | 178.8 | 313.8 | 183.0 | 192.4 |
| Direct subsidies | 15.8 | 12.7 | 101.5 | 56.8 |
| All public-sector investments in agriculture | 51.0 | 54.0 | 84.0 | 49.0 |
| Current expenditure of Ministry of Agriculture | 16.4 | 19.8 | 21.3 | 26.0 |
| Current expenditure of Ministry of Irrigation | 18.4 | 19.9 | 26.0 | 28.8 |
| Total transfers in | 101.6 | 106.4 | 232.8 | 160.6 |
| Net inflow | − 77.2 | −207.4 | + 49.8 | − 31.8 |

SOURCE: Calculated from official data. Details are set out in World Bank (IBRD) staff paper, "Egypt—Agricultural Prices, Taxes and Subsidies" (Washington, D.C., 1978).

These estimates confirm the general trend of a net transfer out of agriculture, although in 1975 that transfer was positive and in 1976 not very large. However, all the evidence cited so far overlooks one very important input—water, which is delivered to and in many instances drained from the peasants' fields free of charge. This indirect subsidy to agriculture may be equivalent to £E90 million a year.[7] In addition, despite the rising costs of inputs, the state is absorbing considerable losses through subsidization. In 1979 such subsidies amounted to £E62 million for fertilizers and £E31 million for pest control. The state also subsidized interest rates on agricultural credit to the equivalent of £E17 million.[8]

It may be that by the late 1970s there emerged a net transfer of public resources to the agricultural sector. But it may also be that those who have benefitted most from free water and subsidized credit and fertilizer are the middle-class commercial farmers who produce freely marketed crops such as vegetables, fruits, and fodder with far higher net returns than the so-called government crops of cotton, rice, and sugar cane.[9] (See table 7.1 of this book). Cheap credit has allowed these farmers to mechanize to get around rising labor costs, and thus far the state has done little to tax their growing incomes. In sum, one may speculate that the continued emphasis upon low-return investment in land reclamation and the disproportionate benefits drawn by the upper stratum of cultivators from public subsidies explains the continued stagnation of the agricultural sector in terms of its contribution to national income and its levels of production.

Thus far we have looked only at income transfers from the agricultural to the nonagricultural sector. The net transfers out have contributed to a major disparity between urban and rural sectors that overlap but do not duplicate the agricultural and nonagricultural sectors. There is no need to go over here the detailed analysis found in chapter 4 of this book. However, it is important to call attention to some of the ambiguities peculiar to the manner in which intersectoral income data are presented. The problem hinges on the distinction between agricultural/nonagricultural (A/NA) and rural/urban (R/U). Various authors have not always been explicit in their use of this distinction.

One of those who has been explicit is Amr Mohie-Eldin.[10] He is also one of the two analysts to estimate income distribution between A and NA populations as well as within the two groups. (The other analyst is Lance Taylor, to whom we shall return.) Mohie-Eldin does not use the R/U distinction, which pertains mainly to the physical location of individuals and households, but to the occupational distinction between A/NA livelihoods. He assumes that 20 percent of rural households depend on nonagricultural sources of income. On that basis, the proportions of A/NA individuals and households are roughly the inverse of the R/U proportions (see table 10.4.1).

According to which distinction is used, one arrives at substantially different estimates of per capita income between sectors. Although very crude in their derivation, the figures in table 10.4.2 provide a general indication of these differences. I have relied upon the calculations of Mohie-Eldin and Taylor,[11] who both estimate income distribution and use the A/NA distinction. Inasmuch as this analysis is more concerned with the physical location of populations than with their occupational distribution, I have tried to adjust the two sets of figures to measure the R/U cleavage.

Taylor has been criticized for inverting the actual number of rural (2.87 million) and urban (3.84 million) households. His figures (IBRD, *Arab Republic of Egypt,* vol. 1, p. 86) do refer to rural and urban households, but his text mentions "households in agricultural and nonagricultural activities." In that sense his household distribution corresponds fairly closely to the estimates in table 10.4.1. Were his figures to refer to R/U households, then multiplying them through by his own estimates of per household income would produce a U/R income ratio of 3:1, that is, total urban income would be three times the rural. That, in fact, does not appear to conform to reality. The adjusted figures in table 10.4.2 attempt to introduce the needed correction.

What in essence has been done in table 10.4.2 is to return to both Taylor's and Mohie-Eldin's figures the 20 percent of rural population that they added to the nonagricultural population. Then, by using Taylor's

*TABLE 10.4.1.*
*A/NA and R/U Individuals and Households, 1976*
*(In Thousands)*

| | *Agricultural* | *Rural* | *Nonagricultural* | *Urban* |
|---|---|---|---|---|
| Individuals | 16,451 | 20,564 | 20,204 | 16,092 |
| Households | 2,742 | 3,427 | 3,558 | 2,873 |

NOTE: This information utilizes Mohie-Eldin's assumption of 20 percent of rural population in nonagricultural occupations and Lance Taylor's estimates of average rural household size of 6 people and urban of 5.6 people.

income intervals for nonagricultural households (p. 86), the average income of the intervals £E0–1,000 (but no higher) was calculated and multiplied by the number of households returned to the rural sector, to yield £E284 million. This produced the adjusted rural income figure of £E1,391.5 million for 1974/1975. The same £E284 million was inflated by 15 percent and added to Mohie-Eldin's agricultural figure to give an adjusted rural income of £E2,085 million in 1976. The per capita and per household figures for 1974/1975 were derived by adjusting the 1976 population figures downward and dividing them into the income estimates. Note that the emigrant population of Egypt, over one million, is not, unfortunately, included in these calculations because its rural/urban mix is not known to me.

There are obvious discrepancies in the two sets of figures. This is no surprise because Taylor's figures are drawn from the household budget survey of 1974/1975, from which he infers income intervals, and Mohie-

*TABLE 10.4.2.*
*Adjusted Rural/Urban Income Distribution*
*(£E millions)*

| | *Taylor, 1974/1975* | *Mohie-Eldin, 1976* |
|---|---|---|
| 1. Agricultural income | 1,107.5 | 1,759.0 |
| 2. Adjusted rural income | 1,391.5 | 2,085.6 |
| 3. Nonagricultural income | 2,751.1 | 3,473.0 |
| 4. Adjusted urban income | 2,467.0 | 3,146.4 |
| 5. Per capita adjusted rural | 69.5 | 99.0 |
| 6. Per household adjusted rural | 417.7 | 595.6 |
| 7. Per capita adjusted urban | 157.6 | 198.1 |
| 8. Per household adjusted urban | 884.2 | 1,111.1 |
| 9. Urban/rural total income ratio (2/4) | 1.66 | 1.56 |
| 10. Urban/rural per capita ratio (5/7) | 2.26 | 2.0 |
| 11. Urban/rural per household ratio (6/8) | 2.1 | 1.86 |

SOURCE: These calculations are derived from the figures in Amr Mohie-Eldin (note 10) and Lance Taylor (note 11 of this chapter).

Eldin's are derived from estimated sectoral returns to factors in which income is stratified in three broad classes. They do concur on one important dimension: the ratios of total per capita and per household U/R incomes. For the first, the ratio is about 1.6, for the second 2.0–2.2 (agreeing rather well with Issawy's 1.96 in table 4.6 of chapter 4), and per household 1.9–2.1 Thus, the R/U gap is not insignificant, but it is a far cry from 3.0 ratios found in several LDCs.

Estimating the degree of skew within the rural and urban sectors is no less fraught with difficulties. Looking only at household expenditures, we find that there is considerable agreement in calculating the Gini coefficients for expenditure intervals. For example, Taylor and Issawy find that the Gini coefficients for *rural* household expenditures in 1974/1975 are 0.39 and 0.35, respectively, and those for *urban* household expenditures are 0.36 and 0.37. Issawy makes no estimates of income distribution, so we must turn once again to Mohie-Eldin and Taylor. But it must again be noted that in so doing we are moving from the R/U to the A/NA distinction. The two estimates are at variance only with respect to income distribution within the A sector. Mohie-Eldin posits a Gini coefficient of 0.24 while Taylor's is 0.40. For the NA sector they estimate 0.38 and 0.40, respectively.

Both exercises reveal a fairly equitable pattern of income distribution by the standards of most developing countries. But their respective data sources may have failed to capture a deterioration in income distribution that has made itself felt since the mid-1970s. As a result of the economic liberalization measures undertaken since 1973/1974, the share of profits and nonwage revenues in national income has increased significantly. In chapter 4 of this book Issawy has shown that wages as a proportion of Gross Domestic Product (GDP) increased from 45 percent in the late 1950s to 50 percent in the early 1970s but have fallen since 1975 to 44 percent of GDP. Property income has, of course, followed the exact inverse of this trend. On the other hand, Mohie-Eldin has shown that the sharge of wages in agricultural income has been increasing, unevenly, since 1973, although it stood only at 26 percent of agricultural income in 1976, well below its peak of 33 percent in 1966/1967.

One may conclude from this that, to the extent that property income is rising in Egypt more rapidly than wage income, the phenomenon is overwhelmingly urban. Indeed, such a conclusion stands to reason. For at least five years, Egypt has been experiencing inflation rates in excess of 20 percent per annum, which, in combination with the open-door policy, has placed a premium on speculative investment with returns sufficient to outstrip the rate of inflation.[12] Private import-export trade catering to urban markets and urban real estate and housing have been the investment targets of entrepreneurs. In short, it seems probable that urban incomes are now more sharply skewed than the results of the 1974/1975

*Wages and Recurrent Outlays by Governorate, 1977 Budget*

| Governorate | Wages (£E) | Recurrent Outlays (£E) | Total Budget (£E) | % of Total Budget | Provincial Population | % of Total Population |
|---|---|---|---|---|---|---|
| 1. Cairo | 48,278,500 | 10,633,997 | 58,912,497 | 13.7 | 5,084,463 | 13.8 |
| 2. Alexandria | 22,893,800 | 5,889,709 | 28,783,509 | 6.6 | 2,318,655 | 6.3 |
| 3. Port Said | 6,303,100 | 2,718,587 | 9,021,687 | 2.1 | 262,620 | 0.7 |
| 4. Ismailia | 4,811,100 | 1,526,099 | 6,337,199 | 1.4 | 351,889 | 0.95 |
| 5. Suez | 2,993,100 | 1,335,196 | 4,328,296 | 1.0 | 194,001 | 0.5 |
| 6. Qalyūbīya | 14,948,100 | 4,064,927 | 19,013,027 | 4.4 | 1,674,006 | 4.5 |
| 7. Giza | 18,063,100 | 4,977,722 | 23,040,822 | 5.3 | 2,419,247 | 6.5 |
| 8. Aswān | 9,909,100 | 3,456,987 | 13,366,087 | 3.1 | 619,932 | 1.6 |
| 9. al-Sharqīya* | 22,522,000 | 4,699,164 | 27,221,164 | 6.3 | 2,621,208 | 7.1 |
| 10. al-Daqhalīya* | 25,658,000 | 5,727,050 | 31,385,050 | 7.3 | 2,732,756 | 7.4 |
| 11. Damietta | 7,557,400 | 2,035,285 | 9,592,685 | 2.2 | 557,115 | 1.5 |
| 12. al-Minūfīya* | 18,840,000 | 3,571,471 | 22,411,471 | 5.2 | 1,710,982 | 4.6 |
| 13. al-Gharbīya | 23,163,000 | 5,821,460 | 28,984,460 | 6.7 | 2,294,303 | 6.2 |
| 14. Kafr al-Shaykh* | 11,029,100 | 2,689,866 | 13,718,966 | 3.1 | 1,403,468 | 3.8 |
| 15. al-Buhayra* | 16,476,100 | 4,511,739 | 20,987,839 | 4.8 | 2,545,246 | 6.9 |
| 16. al-Fayyūm* | 9,776,100 | 2,287,535 | 12,063,635 | 2.8 | 1,140,245 | 3.1 |
| 17. Banī Suwayf* | 11,602,100 | 2,759,873 | 14,361,973 | 3.3 | 1,108,615 | 3.0 |
| 18. al-Minyā* | 15,883,100 | 3,546,578 | 19,429,678 | 4.5 | 2,055,739 | 5.6 |
| 19. Asyūt* | 14,273,100 | 3,561,679 | 17,834,779 | 4.1 | 1,695,378 | 4.6 |
| 20. Sūhāj* | 16,457,100 | 3,375,427 | 19,832,527 | 4.6 | 1,924,960 | 5.2 |
| 21. Qinā* | 14,630,100 | 3,643,831 | 18,273,931 | 4.2 | 1,705,594 | 4.6 |
| 22. Matrūh | 1,857,900 | 1,354,230 | 3,212,130 | 0.7 | 112,772 | 0.3 |
| 23. Wadī al-Jadīd | 2,763,600 | 994,817 | 3,758,417 | 0.8 | 56,691 | 0.1 |
| 24. Red Sea | 1,532,700 | 1,053,642 | 2,586,342 | 0.6 | 56,191 | 0.1 |
| 25. Sinai | 784,700 | 509,129 | 1,293,829 | 0.3 | 10,104 | 0.02 |
| Total | 343,006,000 | 86,746,000 | 429,752,000 | 99.1 | 36,656,180 | 98.97 |

SOURCE: Ministry of Finance, unpublished data. Population figures are from the 1976 census. A breakdown of this budget by government and service sector is to be found in table 10.A.4.1 appended to this chapter.

*The populations of these governorates range from 85 percent rural in al-Minūfīya to 73 percent rural in Sawhāj.

household budget survey would indicate. This may well be the case for rural incomes also.

Another approach to gauging the extent of official neglect of the rural areas is to look at proportionate sectoral shares in public services and subsidized goods. Again, however, the indicators are ambiguous. Table 10.5 reveals that urban governorates do not absorb a share of recurrent outlays for wages and services significantly greater than their share in total population. The seven heavily urban governorates at the head of governorate column contain 33 percent of the nation's population and receive 35 percent of recurrent budgetary outlays. The eleven provinces marked with asterisks are overwhelmingly rural. They contain 56 percent of the population and receive about 50 percent of such outlays.

There are some privileged governorates, primarily Port Said, Suez, Ismailia, and Aswān. The first three were partially destroyed as a result of war over the period 1967–1969 (the June war and the subsequent "war of attrition"). They were reopened to civilian habitation in 1974, and the large budgetary allocations for 1977 reflect the high priority attached to their rehabilitation. Aswān's favored treatment stems from its designated role as a regional growth pole and from its proximity to the Aswān High Dam.

The figures in table 10.5 include locally generated revenues and centrally budgeted subsidies for services. The latter generally represent for Cairo, by way of example, about two-thirds of all recurrent outlays. While good time-series data have not been available to me, one may note that a decade earlier, in 1965/1966 and 1966/1967, at the height of the socialist experiment and before the succession of economic crises beginning in 1966, Cairo received on average about 21 percent of such subsidies, well in excess of its share in the population. Table 10.5, by contrast, shows that its share had declined in 1977 to about 14 percent of the total budget.[13]

In contrast to the recurrent budget, the investment budget has reflected urban bias. The selected governorates in table 10.6 show the disproportionate investment levels in Cairo, Alexandria, and the canal zone. They represent 22 percent of the nation's population, but they benefitted from 56 percent of all investment. Again the high priority attached to reconstruction of the canal zone cities explains some of the disproportionate share of the urban areas. Indeed, so favored were those cities that they skewed the national per capita share of investment sharply upward to £E39. As a result, the per capita share of Ismailia was £E137 while that of Cairo was £E31, Alexandria £E28, and Asyūt only £E5.

The same bias is manifest in projected outlays for the Five Year Plan, 1978–1982 (see table 10.A.1, chapter appendix). Nearly 40 percent of all proposed public investment will be concentrated in Cairo (not including Giza and Shubrā al-Khayma), Alexandria, and the canal zone cities. Cairo and Alexandria alone are to absorb 57 percent of all investment in housing and 43 percent of all industrial investment. Looked at from a different angle, the projected sectoral investment figures for 1980 confirm the over-

*TABLE 10.6.*
*Public Investment 1975, Selected Governorates*

| *Governorate* | *Percent of Population* | *Investment (£E in Thousands)* | *Percent of all Investment by Governorate* |
|---|---|---|---|
| Cairo | 13.8 | 182,373 | 27.5 |
| Alexandria | 6.3 | 65,038 | 9.8 |
| al-Buhayra | 6.9 | 49,087 | 7.4 |
| Suez | 0.5 | 48,549 | 7.3 |
| Port Said | 0.7 | 38,589 | 5.8 |
| Ismailia | 0.95 | 36,733 | 5.5 |
| Subtotal | 29.15 | 420,369 | 63.3 |
| Remaining governorates | 70.85 | 242,631 | 36.7 |
| Total | 100.0 | 633,000 | 100.00 |
| Total Public Investment | ... | 1,154,000 | ... |

SOURCE: Arab Republic of Egypt, Ministry of Transport, *Egypt National Transport Study, Interim Report: 1977* (Louis Berger International, Inc.), vol. 1, p. 111–127.

all picture. Agriculture and irrigation are earmarked for £E303 million in investment, or 9.6 percent of the total, while industry, petroleum, mining, housing and reconstruction—all predominantly nonagrarian in nature—will receive £E1.055 billion in investment, or 34 percent of the total.

The distribution of public utilities, particularly piped water and electricity, is yet another indicator that highlights rural-urban differences. Seventy-three percent of all dwellings in the four urban governorates listed in table 10.7 have private water taps while only 1.4 percent are without any source of purified drinking water. The proportions are essentially inverted in the rural areas. In the delta, only 5 percent of all rural dwellings have interior taps, and in Upper Egypt that figure drops to 2.3 percent. By contrast, 90 percent of all rural dwellings in the delta and in Upper Egypt have external water sources or none at all.

The same pattern emerges with respect to household electricity. Eighty-five percent of all households in the four urban governorates have electricity while only 23 percent of the rural households of the delta and 13 percent of those in Upper Egypt are so equipped (see table 10.8). Egypt's program of rural electrification may alter this situation within the next ten to fifteen years although provision of electricity is aimed at furnishing power for mechanizing agricultural operations (pumping, threshing, milling, and so forth) rather than for lighting homes.

In absolute numbers, the urban areas in general have less than their population share of schools: 44 percent as opposed to 35 percent. This is particularly striking in the urban governorates with 21.3 percent of the population but only 16.4 percent of the schools. However, as table 10.9

*TABLE 10.7.*

*Percentage Distribution of Households According to the Source of Purified Drinking Water*

| | *Source* | | | | | | | | | | | |
|---|---|---|---|---|---|---|---|---|---|---|---|---|
| | *Tap for Dwelling* | | | *Tap Outside Dwelling but in Building* | | | *Tap Outside Building* | | | *No Source* | | |
| | *Urban* | *Rural* | *Total* | *Urban* | *Rural* | *Total* | *Urban* | *Rural* | *Total* | *Urban* | *Rural* | *Total* |
| *Urban Governorates* | 72.5 | . . . | 72.5 | 10.6 | . . . | 10.6 | 15.5 | . . . | 15.5 | 1.4 | . . . | 1.4 |
| *Lower Egypt Governorates* (al-Qalyūbīya) | 32.2 | 4.1 | 16.2 | 4.6 | 2.8 | 3.6 | 31.5 | 49.5 | 41.7 | 31.7 | 43.6 | 38.5 |
| Total | 54.1 | 5.0 | 19.3 | 6.0 | 1.9 | 3.1 | 20.1 | 63.6 | 50.9 | 19.8 | 29.5 | 26.7 |
| *Upper Egypt Governorates* (Giza) | 51.7 | 6.6 | 33.8 | 6.8 | 4.5 | 5.9 | 15.6 | 23.5 | 18.7 | 25.9 | 65.4 | 41.6 |
| Total | 43.9 | 2.3 | 15.2 | 7.3 | 1.6 | 3.4 | 22.7 | 52.3 | 43.1 | 26.1 | 43.8 | 38.3 |
| *Frontier Governorates* | 26.5 | 0.7 | 14.8 | 2.1 | .3 | 1.3 | 30.3 | 22.0 | 26.6 | 41.1 | 77.0 | 57.3 |
| Grand Total | 60.6 | 3.7 | 30.2 | 8.6 | 1.8 | 4.9 | 18.5 | 58.2 | 39.7 | 12.3 | 36.3 | 25.2 |

SOURCE:
Preliminary Results of the 1976 Population and Housing Census.

NOTE:
Because portions of Giza and al-Qalyūbīya governorates fall in Greater Cairo, they were entered separately.

*TABLE 10.8.*
*Percentage of Households with Electricity*

| | *Urban* | *Rural* | *Total* |
|---|---|---|---|
| *Urban Governorates* | 84.4 | ... | 84.4 |
| *Lower Egypt Governorates* | | | |
| al-Qalyūbīya | 78.6 | 38.0 | 55.5 |
| Total | 74.0 | 23.4 | 38.1 |
| *Upper Egypt Governorates* | | | |
| (Giza) | 79.4 | 38.4 | 63.1 |
| Total | 65.0 | 13.1 | 29.3 |
| *Frontier Governorates* | 62.3 | 7.1 | 37.3 |
| Grand Total | 77.0 | 18.6 | 45.7 |

SOURCE: Preliminary Results of the 1976 Population Census.

reveals, the distribution of classrooms and students is much more nearly in balance with population shares. The explanation is surely that in the countryside we are dealing with one- or two-room schools, whereas in the cities the schools are likely to have several classrooms. It appears that urban areas have more students per classroom than rural areas, but none of these statistics say much about the quality of the education being offered. One may presume that urban areas tend to retain more highly motivated teachers than the rural. Table 10.9 does not cover the distribution of preparatory and secondary schools, but the somewhat dated figures in table 10.10 reveal the urban bias in those categories.

Finally, it is not surprising to find that university education is an entirely urban affair. With 322,000 students in 1977, Cairo and Alexandria account for 71 percent of all university students while the rest are distributed among the major provincial cities.

Egypt is certainly not unusual in that specialized medical services are concentrated in the cities. In 1977 all public general hospitals, specialized hospitals, dental, X-ray, and mental health clinics, all school health units, rabies and outpatient clinics were in urban areas. The rural areas are served by 2,254 multipurpose medical centers. These centers have neither the staff nor the equipment to offer anything more than simple medical services. Complicated cases must be referred to city hospitals or go untreated.

While more recent figures were not readily available, in 1970 the urban governorates enjoyed no greater number of hospital beds per 100,000 inhabitants than the rural. The national average in that year was 56 beds per 100,000 while Cairo offered 53 and Alexandria 38. Al-Minūfīya had 70 and al-Minyā 84 beds per 100,000 inhabitants.[14]

According to the evidence advanced thus far, there is no denying that

*TABLE 10.9.*

*Distribution of Primary Schools, Classes, and Students, 1977*

| | % of Total Population 1976 | No. of Schools | | Urban % of Total Schools | No. of Classes | | Urban % of Total Classes | No. of Students (Thousands) | | % of Total Students |
|---|---|---|---|---|---|---|---|---|---|---|
| | | Urban | Rural | | Urban | Rural | | Urban | Rural | |
| Cairo | 13.8 | 1,038 | ... | 10.3 | 14,249 | ... | 14.4 | 587.7 | ... | 14.7 |
| Alexandria | 6.3 | 505 | 5 | 5.0 | 6,432 | 36 | 6.5 | 282.2 | 1.1 | 6.1 |
| Port Said | 0.7 | 70 | 1 | 0.6 | 837 | 6 | .8 | 30.5 | 0.3 | 0.8 |
| Suez | 0.5 | 57 | 6 | 0.5 | 707 | 58 | .7 | 27.2 | 2.1 | 0.7 |
| **Total Urban Governments** | **21.3** | **1,670** | **12** | **16.4** | **22,225** | **100** | **22.4** | **927.6** | **3.5** | **22.3** |
| Damietta | 1.5 | 56 | 156 | ... | 560 | 1,470 | ... | 22.2 | 59.2 | ... |
| al-Daqhalīya | 7.4 | 167 | 782 | ... | 1,791 | 6,337 | ... | 73.3 | 250.9 | ... |
| al-Sharqīya | 7.1 | 149 | 725 | ... | 1,450 | 5,514 | ... | 62.0 | 222.6 | ... |
| al-Qalyubīya | 4.5 | 153 | 350 | ... | 2,040 | 2,940 | ... | 95.1 | 122.4 | ... |
| Kafr al-Shaykh | 3.8 | 76 | 379 | ... | 731 | 2,717 | ... | 33.2 | 108.7 | ... |
| al-Gharbīya | 6.2 | 144 | 387 | ... | 2,043 | 4,228 | ... | 85.5 | 173.6 | ... |
| al-Minufīya | 4.6 | 91 | 435 | ... | 1,045 | 4,245 | ... | 43.8 | 186.9 | ... |
| al-Buhayra | 6.9 | 123 | 553 | ... | 1,344 | 4,545 | ... | 61.6 | ... | ... |
| Ismailia | 0.9 | 116 | ... | ... | 1,122 | ... | ... | 29.8 | 16.4 | ... |
| **Total Lower Egypt** | **42.9** | **1,075** | **3,767** | **...** | **12,126** | **31,983** | **...** | **506.8** | **1,315.2** | **...** |
| Giza | 6.5 | 143 | 187 | ... | 3,515 | 2,310 | ... | 165.0 | 90.9 | ... |
| Banī Suwayf | 3.0 | 70 | 273 | ... | 791 | 2,273 | ... | 31.3 | 76.8 | ... |
| al-Fayyūm | 3.1 | 55 | 250 | ... | 662 | 1,933 | ... | 28.2 | 70.1 | ... |
| al-Minyā | 5.6 | 114 | 452 | ... | 1,178 | 3,577 | ... | 47.8 | 125.9 | ... |
| Asyūt | 4.6 | 112 | 361 | ... | 1,173 | 2,796 | ... | 49.4 | 108.2 | ... |
| Sūjāj | 5.2 | 114 | 476 | ... | 1,185 | 3,484 | ... | 49.8 | 124.2 | ... |
| Qinā | 4.6 | 89 | 388 | ... | 1,034 | 3,369 | ... | 42.2 | 115.7 | ... |
| Aswān | 1.6 | 73 | 190 | ... | 805 | 1,350 | ... | 34.5 | 49.8 | ... |
| **Total Upper Egypt** | **34.2** | **770** | **2,577** | **...** | **10,343** | **21,092** | **...** | **448.4** | **761.8** | **...** |
| Frontier Governments | 0.5 | 46 | 114 | ... | 479 | 577 | ... | 18.6 | 15.3 | ... |
| GRAND TOTAL | 100.0 | 3,561 | 6,470 | 35.4 | 45,173 | 53,752 | 45.6 | 1,901.6 | 2,095.8 | 47.5 |

SOURCE:

*TABLE 10.10.*
*Proportionate Shares of Various Regions in Three Levels of Education 1966/1967*

| *Region* | *% of Total Population* | *Primary (%)* | *Preparatory (%)* | *Secondary (%)* |
|---|---|---|---|---|
| Cairo | 14.0 | 16 | 22 | 27 |
| Alexandria | 6.0 | 7 | 9 | 9 |
| Canal Zone | 3.0 | 4 | 5 | 5 |
| Lower Egypt | 41.5 | 41 | 39 | 36 |
| Upper Egypt | 34.3 | 31 | 24 | 22 |
| Frontier | 1.2 | 1 | 1 | 1 |

SOURCE:
Muhammad al-ᶜAtrībī and Ibrāhīm Burāᶜī, "Cairo in Figures," *al-Talīᶜa,* vol. 5, (February 1969), pp. 68–75.

NOTE:
For Cairo alone, it was estimated in 1970 that it had 21% of primary, 28% of preparatory, 38% of general secondary level classrooms and 33%, 29%, 39% and 64% of all primary, preparatory, general secondary and university level students. See Central Agency for Public Mobilization and Statistics (CAPMS), *Cairo: 1970,* Report N. 200/01 (January 1971) (in Arabic), p. 105.

Egypt's cities have, to varying degrees, enjoyed greater access to public services and utilities than the countryside. One must add to this the fact that the socioeconomic characteristics of the urban population create demands for goods and services that have a major qualitative impact. The concentration of skilled workers, of the managerial middle class, and of other professional groups in the principal cities is what accounts for the higher urban-income levels and for the cities' corner on the provision of quality services. For instance, table 10.11 shows the dominance of Cairo and Alexandria in manufacturing.

Nearly 6 percent of Cairo's population has had some form of higher education while the average for the delta governorates is 1.3 percent and for Upper Egypt 1.4 percent. Greater Cairo houses 30 percent of all state employees, 52 percent of all doctors, 59 percent of all engineers, and, significantly, 48 percent of all veterinarians and 53 percent of all agricultural engineers.[15] Their presence may have greater implications for the provision of private services than for public services. For instance, they may well shun public medical facilities in favor of fee-based private services. Their housing and transportation will generally be privately owned or built. They may, however, use the public education system, paying out substantial "tutoring" fees to their children's teachers (on tutoring, see Abdel-Fadil in chapter 11 of this volume). This assures a higher success rate in national exams for the offspring of the well-to-do as well as an income incentive for public-school teachers to cling to their urban jobs.

*TABLE 10.11.*
*Percentage Distribution of Manufacturing Establishments by Selected Governorates*

| *Governorate* | *Percentage of Establishments* | *Percentage of Workers* | *Percentage of Production* |
|---|---|---|---|
| Alexandria | 15.4 | 21.8 | 20.7 |
| Greater Cairo | 55.7 | 48.5 | 51.5 |
| Cairo | 34.7 | 24.8 | 21.3 |
| Giza | 11.1 | 11.2 | 19.6 |
| al-Qalyūbīya | 9.9 | 12.5 | 10.6 |
| al-Gharbīya | 6.2 | 8.9 | 6.2 |
| al-Buhayra | 3.8 | 5.7 | 4.7 |
| Subtotal | 81.1 | 84.9 | 83.1 |
| All other governorates | 18.9 | 15.1 | 16.9 |
| Total | 100.00 | 100.00 | 100.00 |

SOURCE: Louis Berger, vol. 1, p. 111–112, as cited in table 10.6.

The same holds true for public-sector physicians, who are allowed a private practice in the cities.

It is probably the case that state subsidies of a broad range of basic consumer goods favor urban populations. Bottled gas for appliances, stoves, and space heaters is heavily subsidized and consumed in cities. Most rural populations use crop residues as fuel. Similarly, gasoline is subsidized predominantly for the benefit of urban automobile owners, taxi drivers, and truckers. One should keep in mind, however, the offsetting subsidies to rural populations in the provision of water and credit and the sales of seed, fertilizer, and pesticides.

The most costly subsidized items in Egypt are wheat and wheat flour. Most of what Egypt consumes is imported. In 1975, of 2.9 million tons of imported wheat, nearly 1.5 million tons were delivered to the mills of Cairo and Alexandria while half of 700,000 tons of imported flour went to the same two cities. The rest is milled or distributed through provincial cities. Virtually all commercial bakeries are urban. It is, therefore, not known how much wheat and flour find their way to rural consumers (although, because subsidized bread was cheaper than market-priced fodder, urban owners of draught animals bought bread in the mid-1970s to feed their animals). Lance Taylor may be stretching the evidence when he asserts that a decline in the incidence of rural pellagra indicates that rural populations are probably enjoying greater access to subsidized wheat and rice at the expense of home-grown maize.[16] Indeed, two Egyptian analysts offer evidence to the contrary. They note that the per capita annual share of imported grains rose from 38 kilograms in 1960/1961 to 92 kilograms in

1975. Most of this impressive increase was absorbed by urban populations. Moreover, Ibrāhīm ᶜĀmr asserts that Ministry of Supply deliveries of imported grain to the nonurban governorates actually declined in the mid-1970s.[17]

To summarize, Egypt's urban areas have been clearly favored by public policy. Whether or not this constitutes urban bias in the sense of a significant misallocation of national resources with deleterious effects on economic performance is not so clear. We have found a major rural-urban gap in average per capita incomes although, as Saad Ibrahim has implied in chapter 12 of this book, the cost of living in urban areas is probably 30 percent higher than in rural areas. There is probably no country in the world where there is not a substantial difference between rural and urban incomes. However, it may be that, as a result of the concentration of speculative investment activity in the cities, much of Egypt's new wealth is urban. To the extent that the countryside has kept pace, the increases in personal income have been confined largely to a middle stratum of commercial farmers who have been able to exploit the rising prices in "free" domestic markets generated by urban middle-class demand.

Throughout the 1960s the agricultural sector was taxed to provide investment for industrialization and other nonagricultural activities. Since the early 1970s, however, this phenmenon may have come to an end because of the state's ever larger outlays for the subsidization of fertilizers, pesticides, seed, fuel, and commercial credit. On the investment side, it is still the case that resources devoted to agriculture tend to be concentrated in land reclamation rather than in the old lands that account for most of Egypt's production. In a way, the old areas are being taxed to pay for the new.

Recurrent budget expenses show no marked bias in any direction, and fairly faithfully reflect the shares of urban and rural governorates in total population. Investment budgets, on the other hand, have revealed a distinct bias toward urban areas in which virtually all housing and reconstruction activities and industrial enterprises are concentrated. The question remains as to whether or not there is anything inefficient or inequitable about this allocation.

The provision of public services and utilities again highlights the privileged position of the cities. Drinking water and electricity are far more available to urban than to rural populations. So too are establishments of secondary and higher education, hospitals, specialized clinics, and doctors. Moreover, the quality of services available in cities is markedly superior to that of rural areas. Public service in the countryside for medical and teaching personnel, and for bureaucrats in general, is seen as a kind of corvée. The best and brightest personnel generally spend most of their rural sojourn planning their escape to the cities. More often than not they succeed.

*TABLE 10.12.*
*Greater Cairo Population, 1947–1976*
*(In Thousands)*

| *Year* | *Total* | *Cairo* | *Giza* | *Qalyūbīya* |
|---|---|---|---|---|
| 1947 | 2,963 | 2,080 | 574 | 309 |
| 1960 | 4,820 | 3,353 | 1,002 | 465 |
| 1966 | 6,113 | 4,220 | 1,293 | 600 |
| 1976 | 8,000 | 5,084 | 1,978 | 938 |

SOURCE: Central Agency for Public Mobilization and Statistics.

## IV. Income Distribution in Greater Cairo

Cairo is, of course, commensurately different from all other Egyptian cities. Greater Cairo has over eight million inhabitants, or 22 percent of the nation's population. It is the country's capital, and it houses all the central ministries. It is as well the economic hub of Egypt, dominating internal trade and transport, conceding only port activity to the likes of Alexandria, Damietta, and Suez. With its northern and southern industrial suburbs of Shubrā al-Khayma (in Qalyūbīya governorate) and Hulwān, Cairo has a relative monopoly of Egypt's industrial production. Greater Cairo contains three major universities: ᶜAin Shams; al-Azhar; and Cairo University, located in Giza (Giza governorate), the city's fast-

*TABLE 10.13.*
*Greater Cairo Population, 1976*
*Administrative Subareas (In Thousands)*

| *Locality* | *Male* | *Female* | *Total* |
|---|---|---|---|
| **Cities** | | | |
| Cairo | 2,607 | 2,477 | 5,084 |
| Giza | 639 | 607 | 1,246 |
| Shubrā al-Khayma | 205 | 189 | 394 |
| **Provinces** | | | |
| Giza | 48 | 46 | 94 |
| Imbāba | 210 | 197 | 407 |
| al-Badrashīn | 103 | 95 | 198 |
| al-Saᶜf | 17 | 16 | 32 |
| al-Qanātir | 74 | 68 | 141 |
| al-Khānka | 81 | 72 | 153 |
| Shibīn-al-Qanātir | 34 | 31 | 65 |
| Qalyūb | 96 | 89 | 185 |
| Total | 4,113 | 3,887 | 8,000 |

SOURCE: Central Agency for Public Mobilization and Statistics. Preliminary Results of the 1976 Census of Population and Housing, Cairo, April 1977, table 14a.

est-growing section on the west bank of the Nile. Cairo is also home for all foreign diplomatic missions in Egypt, United Nations regional agencies, until recently Arab League headquarters, foreign businesmen, and thousands of wealthy Arabs who own urban real estate. In short, it is the kind of people that live in Cairo that determines its real weight in Egypt and the patterns of income distribution among its inhabitants.

One cannot overstate the political menace that Cairo contains, for it is uppermost in the minds of the nation's leaders. Mass violence, even on a reduced level, can bring Cairo and hence the nation to a halt. The monarchical regime fell in 1952 partly as a result of such violence. Gamal Abd al-Nasser consolidated his hold on power in 1954 by manipulating a Cairo transport workers' strike. He faced his most severe civilian challenge during student-worker demonstrations in 1968. Bread and butter issues have come to dominate similar outbursts in the 1970s. In 1975 workers went on a rampage in downtown Cairo because, among other things, the single electrified rail line that carries tens of thousands of workers daily to the factories of Hulwān was closed for repairs. Workers stood to lose a day's pay, a gratuitous penalty that had been inflicted upon them all too often. In January 1977, when the government announced its intention to abolish or lower subsidies on several consumer items, riots took place in all of Egypt's cities. So violent were they that President Sadat was forced to call upon army units to restore order. The fact of hundreds of thousands of university students, industrial workers, and slum dwellers living cheek by jowl in Egypt's capital, easily visible to the international diplomatic corps and press, explains the edginess of the authorities in all matters concerning public welfare and mood. To the outsider, the amount of coddling these urban populations receive may appear modest at best. Inadequate, dilapidated public transport, insalubrious housing, broken water mains, power failures, fair-price shops with long lines and no goods, and crowded hospitals that are the source of M.A.S.H.-like tales of medical abuse hardly add up to public pampering. Yet that is really what is at stake, for, inadequate as these services and goods may be, the rural areas and smaller provincial cities scarcely share in them. Furthermore, it costs the state a great deal to provide these inadequate services. Figures on water delivery costs constitute an eloquent example of Cairo's claims and the relative neglect of rural areas.

In the same vein, the presence of the large foreign business community, coupled with the growing frustration of middle-class telephone users, has led to the diversion of considerable funds to improve Cairo's telephone system. For the period 1978–1982 £E355 million has been designated for improvement of telephone and telex services. That is an amount about equivalent to all proposed investment in agriculture for the same period and reflects the kind of official attention given Cairo's middle-class demand.

Because of the characteristics of its population, we may posit, without much empirical evidence, that the distribution of income in Cairo is more

TABLE 10.14.
*Public Investments in Water Delivery, 1970–1976*
*(In £E Millions)*

| | *1970* | *1971* | *1972* | *1973* | *1974* | *1975* | *1976* |
|---|---|---|---|---|---|---|---|
| Cairo Water Authority | 1.57 | 3.26 | 4.38 | 3.9 | 7.4 | 7.7 | 7.1 |
| Other cities | 1.5 | 1.38 | 2.8 | .7 | 3.1 | 6.5* | 4.9* |
| All rural areas | 2.1 | 1.9 | 4.1 | 2.2 | 1.2 | 3.8 | 3.6 |

SOURCE: unpublished statistics, General Authority for Greater Cairo Water.

*Includes repair and restoration of water delivery systems to canal zone cities. For the period 1978–82, £E95 million has been budgeted for rural water delivery while Cairo alone has been allocated £E134 million.

sharply skewed than in any of the other cities. The upper-income brackets, especially those involved in the private sale of professional services, real estate speculation, commodity trading, and import-export, are not closely monitored. Until the passage of a law in 1976, income from urban rents and sales of buildings was not taxed. Despite an astronomic rise in land values after 1973, Cairo's building tax generated only a couple of million pounds in revenues. An illiterate scrap-metal merchant and speculator in Cairo's Wikālāt al-Balah area is alleged to owe £E1.2 million in delinquent income taxes. Ten others had aggregate arrears of over £E5 million.[18]

These and probably thousands of others are earning relatively large fortunes of which the Ministry of Finance has no direct knowledge or no means to tax and which household budget surveys cannot effectively measure. Nor, as Mona Seragaldin points out, do these surveys cover those who are not "regularly employed," a segment of the urban population that may be as high as 37 percent. Thus the available data overweight the employed, salaried, middle-income groups while underweighting the upper decile and the lower third.[19]

Measurement is rendered still more difficult because of the existence of the large residual labor pools of the informal sector and the unemployed. One can only guess at the former. In the early 1970s there were, by way of example, probably 100,000 horse-drawn carts and flatbed trucks operating in Greater Cairo. About half of these were unlicensed. The number of pushcart vendors must be equally large. I would argue that there must be upward of 200,000 unlicensed "tradesmen" in Cairo whose activities and income are poorly understood. They may sustain a population of about one million. Surveys in the late 1950s produced an estimate of 400,000 household servants in urban Egypt. Cairo would have had the lion's share, and a figure today of 400,000 for Greater Cairo alone would not seem implausible. In addition, there are 560,000 adult males and 1.5 million adult women "outside" the work force who must be considered unemployed. Cairo's active labor force (Cairo governorate) in monitored

*TABLE 10.15.*
*Household Income Distribution, Būlāq Dakrūr, 1972*

| *Annual Income (£E)* | *No. of Households* | *% of Households* |
|---|---|---|
| 0–120 | 1,915 | 14.4 |
| 121–240 | 6,066 | 45.7 |
| 241–420 | 4,283 | 32.3 |
| 421–600 | 807 | 6.1 |
| 601< | 179 | 1.4 |
| | 13,250 | 100.0 |

SOURCE: unpublished UNICEF Survey 1972.

jobs, trades, and professions is 1.3 million.[20] Once again then, one must conclude that, while the mean urban income figures we have at our disposal (Taylor, Seragaldin, and so forth) may be accurate, because the underweighting of the lowest and highest brackets may cancel out each other, the skew is probably more acute than Taylor's Gini coefficients would suggest.

Some insight into the income of populations that are inadequately monitored can be gained from a survey of 13,200 families in Būlāq Dakrūr conducted by UNICEF (United Nations Children's Emergency Fund) and the Egyptian Institute of National Planning in 1972. Būlāq Dakrūr is reasonably representative of the most impoverished sectors of Greater Cairo. It was originally an agricultural village near Giza City and, like a dozen or so villages within ten miles of central Cairo, it has simply been absorbed by the expanding city. Its population has increased at least tenfold in two decades, reaching 322,480 in 1976.* It no longer has any significant agricultural vocation but rather is little more than a dormitory for Cairo's poorest commuters. Like much of Cairo, it has not expanded physically. Its increased population has simply been crammed into existing room space.

Migrants accounted for 86 percent of Būlāq Dakrūr's population, and nearly half had migrated there during the five years preceding the survey. Significantly, 24 percent had migrated from Cairo and Giza. One may speculate that these were salaried urbanites in search of lower rents. The village is also home for thousands of students at nearby Cairo University. The survey showed that there were 1,500 shopkeepers active in the village. Unemployment reached a rate of 11 percent of all household heads and a rate of about 50 percent for all males and females fifteen years old or older. The survey turned up the following figures on income distribution (table 10.15). If we contrast this distribution with that charted in figure

*The figure is for the Būlāq Dakrūr police district, which is probably larger than the original village. The population density is 18,969 per square kilometer.

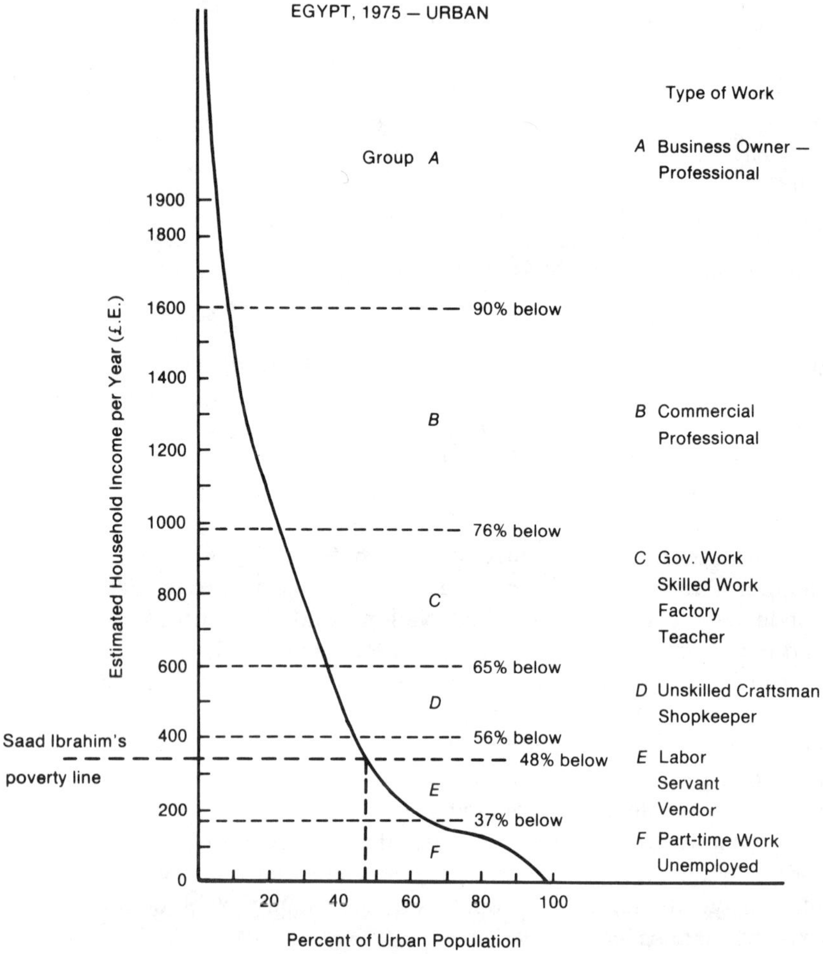


SOURCE: Mona Seragaldin, "Household Income Distribution," Appendix I, *Immediate Action Proposals for Housing in Egypt,* Office of Housing, USAID and Ministry of Housing and Reconstruction and Ministry of Planning, ARE (June 1976) p. 89.

*FIGURE 10.1.*
*Income Distribution*

10.1, we find that about 90 percent of Būlāq Dakrūr's households earn less than £E400 per year while the average for Egypt's cities is 56 percent.

By most standards, that 90 percent must be seen as living in absolute poverty. Saad Ibrahim assumes in chapter 12 of this book that the urban poverty floor in 1975 would be defined by an annual household income of £E350 or less. He estimates that, for all urban areas in 1975, 35 percent of all households fall beneath that floor. Mona Seragaldin's estimates, as represented in figure 10.1, are even more pessimistic, for, according to them, about 48 percent of all urban households fall beneath Ibrahim's poverty line.

By contrast, Ibrahim, through his minisurvey, found that in *Cairo* 11 percent of the population fell well below the line while another 10 percent hovered close to it. So it may be that Cairo's poorest are somewhat less than the poorest of other cities, but much of this is guesswork. My own judgment is that Ibrahim's estimate of 21 percent living at or beneath the poverty line is an absolute minimum. For Greater Cairo it would comprise most of the residents of Būlāq Dakrūr, Imbāba, al-Jamālīya, Darb al-Ahmar, Khalīfa Būlāq, Bāb al-Shaʿrīya. To these we may add segments of the population of Old Cairo, al-Matārīya, Rūd al-Farāj, al-Muskī, Hulwān, and Shubrā, raising the total to two million. While there is no reason to believe that the figure is exact, Cairo's governor in 1973 estimated at one million the population that squatted in the city's elaborate cemeteries.[21] A few hundred thousand more may inhabit illegal rooftop shacks affixed to more substantial housing throughout the city. It would thus appear reasonable to assume that something like 40 percent of Greater Cairo's households can be considered in an income range similar to that of Būlāq Dakrūr and that these four deciles have been significantly underrepresented in household budget surveys. Such a pattern would be in close conformity with Seragaldin's estimates for all cities.

Cairo's intelligentsia are acutely aware of the city's income disparities. Prior to 1952 the issue of rural poverty and exploitation of the peasantry was a predominant theme in all debates about social equity. Since 1952 these equity issues have been increasingly focussed on the city. The sheer visibility of Cairo's problems probably accounts for this shift in concern. There is also the embarrassment, not to say shame, that well-to-do Egyptians feel in exposing urban poverty and blight to resident foreign communities and tourists. Problems that receive constant, occasionally in-depth treatment in the press are transportation, housing, water delivery, and sewage removal. The first two have taken on the proportions of national crises. Both tell us a great deal about how equity issues are reflected in government policy.

Greater Cairo is a big urban agglomeration by any standards, and it is strung out along a north-south axis on both banks of the Nile that is over 30 kilometers long. At least 40 percent of the city's work force must cover substantial distances to reach their place of work. Moreover, about one

*TABLE 10.16.*
*Public Transportation Means Greater Cairo*

| | *1956/1966* | *1968/1969* | *1978* |
|---|---|---|---|
| Buses | 1033 | 1375 | 1363 |
| Trains | 224 | 230 | 157 |
| Trolley buses | 123 | 134 | 74 |
| Nile ferries | ... | ... | 12 |

SOURCE:
*Al-Ahrām al-Iqtisādī,* January 1, 1978.

million people commute in and out of Cairo daily. Cairo's public transportation system is absolutely vital to the city's economic viability.[22] The number of passengers carried by the public system has been growing for over a decade at 10–15 percent each year. The available means of public transport have scarcely grown at all.

These units, administered by the Greater Cairo Transport Authority, in 1978 handled 4 million passenger miles per day or about 1.2 billion passenger miles per year. By 1990 it is anticipated that the system will be called upon to accommodate 13 million passenger miles per day. The Transport Authority in 1979 was operating at a deficit of £E26 million. Interest on its outstanding debt amounted to £E6 million in the same year. The state is thus paying substantial subsidies to operate a service that is grossly inadequate. All buses and trolleys carry passenger loads during peak hours well in excess of theoretical capacity. The city's chaotic traffic and parking patterns reduce the movement of the overcrowded vehicles to a snail's pace. They, in turn, are driven far beyond the life expectancy for which they are designed. At any one time, a third of the bus fleet may be inoperative. Small wonder then that the Transport Authority requested £E168 million for the 1978–1982 Five Year Plan to purchase 1,900 buses, 30 river ferries, and to extend 34 kilometers of tram lines. Despite its decrepit condition, Cairo's public transport receives more public investment annually than the rest of the country combined: in 1978 it was £E19,884 million as against £E9,557 million for the three delta and one Upper Egypt bus lines.

There is a fundamental equity question at stake here that reflects the conflicting interests of the employed urban masses and the better-off professional and administrative strata. The latter are not of one mind on how best to handle Cairo's transportation crisis. Some people advocate placing maximum financial emphasis upon developing public transport at the expense of private convenience. These voices are heard in the Ministry of Transport. The minister in 1979, ᶜAlī-el-Daghistānī, has been a firm supporter of construction of an underground and has urged that the center of the city be closed to private vehicles.

Less vocal, for obvious reasons, but perhaps more powerful have been

*TABLE 10.17.*

*Greater Cairo Motor Vehicle Fleet, 1972–1977*

| *Year* | *Private Autos* | *Private Buses* | *Public Buses* | *Taxis* |
|---|---|---|---|---|
| 1972 | 80,559 | 1,059 | 2,190 | 14,487 |
| 1973 | 83,017 | 1,182 | 1,999 | 15,625 |
| 1974 | 87,388 | 1,397 | 1,599 | 17,714 |
| 1975 | 94,564 | 1,705 | 1,504 | 28,272 |
| 1976 | 109,544 | 2,236 | 1,429 | 30,201 |
| 1977 | 133,599 | 2,849 | 1,363 | 29,359 |

SOURCE: Central Agency for Public Mobilization and Statistics, (unpublished) October 2, 1978.

NOTE: Figures do not include the larger number of private vehicles operating on temporary import, customs plates.

those people who wish to develop the city's transportation infrastructure to the benefit of the private automobile. Some years ago a prominent member of Parliament from Cairo lamented to me that the city, unlike other "modern" cities, devoted only 12 percent of its surface to roads and parking areas. He felt the norm should be more like 30–35 percent. What he failed to note was that Greater Cairo at the time only had about 150,000 private cars circulating in its streets; Rome, by way of contrast, had 1.5 million registered private automobiles. Nonetheless, to some extent Cairo is being ripped apart to cater to its growing private-vehicle fleet, which is expected to grow to 400,000 by 1990. Liberal import and foreign-exchange controls have fostered a massive influx of imported automobiles. During the "socialist" 1960s, these and other luxury imports were strictly curtailed. In 1966/1967 only 1,500 private automobiles were imported; customs records indicate that in 1977 120,000 automobiles entered Egypt.

The general trend in vehicle registration, as table 10.17 shows, is a large steady increase in all private means of transportation and a steady decline in the number of public buses. The addition in 1977/1978 of 200 Ward buses, financed by USAID (U.S. Agency for International Development), does not greatly alter the picture. Thus the number of private automobiles has increased 60 percent in five years, the number of taxis has more than doubled, and private buses now outnumber public buses 2:1. Private buses are not used for general transportation but to service tourists or take public and private sector employees to and from their place of work. They add to the rush-hour traffic jams but stand empty at other times.

Physical planning of Cairo's transportation grid is being substantially determined by 150,000 automobile owners. Financial resources are being diverted from public transport and the millions who use it daily. A major expenditure involves a number of overpasses, elevated roadways, ring roads, and Nile bridges to move, for the most part, private automobiles from middle-class suburbs in Heliopolis, Giza, and al-Maᶜādī to the central business district and to one another. About £E100 million in investment is tied up in such projects. Public buses can, of course, use these roadways, but that is not their primary purpose. Public transport will benefit only insofar as the new roads divert private automobile traffic from the choked arteries connecting Cairo's most densely inhabited districts. On the other hand, the same roadways will reinforce the enclave existence of the well-to-do, joining place of work and residence by the private automobile, and bypassing the decaying "popular" quarters that render the middle classes so uneasy.[23]

One major blow may be struck in favor of Cairo's masses. Ever since the military takeover in 1952, there has been active consideration of building an underground for the city. It offers the major advantage of hauling at least three times as many passengers per hour and over equivalent distances as any other means of transport. Moreover, putting all those commuters below ground would make the remaining surface traffic much less congested. Despite its appeal on these grounds, the project has consistently been assigned low priority.

That situation has reversed itself in the last four or five years. It is now generally, although by no means universally, recognized that the underground is an absolute necessity. If Cairo grows to 14 million by 1990, as the Ministry of Transport anticipates, surface transportation could not conceivably be expanded to meet the projected load of 13 million passenger miles a day. Only the underground could begin to meet the expected demand. The engineering studies have been carried out by French consultants from the Paris Metro, and the current project will utilize French expertise, technology, and equipment. The French government will finance some of the foreign-exchange component involved. In less than a decade, however, estimated construction costs have tripled from £E200 million to £E600 million. The foreign-exchange component is expected to be $545 million. If completed by 1990, the underground would have a north-south axis from Shubrā al-Khayma to Hulwān with a major northeast spur that would serve the area toward which Cairo can expand without encroaching on agricultural land. Lateral spurs would serve both banks of the Nile. No policy on subsidized fares has been fixed as yet, and for the system to function well would require a kind of discipline that Cairo's commuters have never before exhibited. Still, this project represents the only counterweight to the city's growing preoccupation with the private automobile.

On an equal footing with transportation as an equity issue is housing. This is overwhelmingly an urban issue and, from a media point of view, one dominated by Cairo's needs. The government has been involved in rural housing only on a limited scale, such as building new villages for the Nubian refugees flooded out by Lake Nasser or settlements in reclaimed agricultural zones. Village housing is left pretty much to individual families and local private entrepreneurs.

*TABLE 10.18.*
*Housing Production, All Egypt*
*1960/1961–1975*

| | *Public Sector* | | *Private Sector* | | *Total* | |
|---|---|---|---|---|---|---|
| *Year* | *No. Units* | *Cost £E thousands* | *No. Units* | *Cost £E thousands* | *No. Units* | *Cost £E thousands* |
| 1960/1961 | 2,296 | 2,556 | 11,564 | 10,684 | 13,860 | 13,240 |
| 1961/1962 | 16,768 | 12,807 | 25,675 | 14,000 | 42,443 | 26,807 |
| 1962/1963 | 21,288 | 11,498 | 22,590 | 14,770 | 43,878 | 26,268 |
| 1963/1964 | 11,880 | 13,916 | 10,864 | 9,014 | 22,744 | 22,930 |
| 1964/1965 | 9,020 | 10,848 | 8,893 | 8,492 | 17,913 | 19,340 |
| 1965/1966 | 20,509 | 18,380 | 13,000 | 17,400 | 33,509 | 35,780 |
| 1966/1967 | 9,844 | 11,828 | 15,738 | 19,939 | 25,582 | 31,767 |
| 1967/1968 | 10,967 | 5,149 | 29,505 | 40,003 | 40,472 | 45,152 |
| 1968/1969 | 5,299 | 11,077 | 22,710 | 28,570 | 28,009 | 39,647 |
| 1969/1970 | 9,491 | 10,291 | 28,717 | 23,520 | 38,208 | 33,811 |
| 1970/1971 | 5,250 | 5,484 | 22,520 | 19,050 | 27,770 | 29,534 |
| 1971/1972* | 5,789 | 7,489 | 21,540 | 31,300 | 27,329 | 38,789 |
| 1973† | 9,691 | 12,809 | 15,032 | 20,700 | 24,723 | 33,509 |
| 1974† | 6,400 | 10,265 | 8,646 | 15,081 | 15,046 | 25,346 |
| 1975 | 17,700 | 22,400 | 24,000 | 45,600 | 41,700 (est.) | 68,000 (est.) |

SOURCE: Ministry of Housing and Reconstruction and Ministry of Planning, USAID, *Immediate Action Proposals for Housing in Egypt: Statistical Appendix* (June 1976), p. 51.

*18 months
†Exclusive of investments in reconstruction

Urban housing has remained predominantly in the hands of the private sector although the government can influence construction through its own public housing projects, the supply of building materials, and rent controls. In general, the private sector undertakes 60–70 percent of all new construction in Cairo and elsewhere. For reasons that will be more fully explained later, it can make a return on its investment only in middle- and upper-income housing. The public sector undertakes nearly all low-cost housing and has so far failed to meet even a modest portion of demand.

The public sector made its greatest effort during the early 1960s, particularly in the period of the Five Year Plan, 1960–1965. The 21,000 units built nationwide in 1962/1963 have never since been matched. The average for the decade 1960–1970 was 11,000 public-sector units per year. It was, however, when the public sector was most active that private construction began to decline. Public construction reflected the regime's espousal of socialist policies and concern for equity and income distribution while the private-sector slump reflected declining profits and increasingly restrictive legislation. Thus the average number of units built annually, by both the public and private sectors, declined from 52,000 during the period 1952–1960 to 30,000 during 1961–1972.

*TABLE 10.19.*
*Housing Investment*
*1972–1975**

| *Year* | *Housing Investment as % of National Investment* | *Housing Unit Production Rate per Thousand Urban Population* |
|---|---|---|
| 1952–1960 | 28.2 | 7.0 |
| 1960–1972 | 8.5 | 2.5 |
| 1973 | 11.0 | 2.5 |
| 1974 | 8.0 | 0.8* |
| 1975 | 13.8 | 2.5* |

SOURCE: Ministries of Housing and Reconstruction, and Planning; and USAID, *Immediate Action Proposals for Housing in Egypt: Statistical Appendix* (June 1976) p. 89.

*Exclusive of reconstruction investment

Since 1972 there has been some resurgence in public-sector construction (17,700 units nationwide in 1975) and a gradual resurgence of private construction (24,000 units in 1975). The public-sector construction represents growing official concern for Egypt's urban housing crisis while the private construction reflects a combination of private-sector ability to beat the existing legislation and anticipation of more liberal regulation.

There are many varying estimates of urban Egypt's actual and projected housing needs. Given the state of the art, no estimate can be considered authoritative, but that of the Ministry of Housing must, for obvious reasons, be taken seriously. The Ministry believes that Egypt's housing needs between 1981 and 2000 (according to the UN norm of seven units per thousand urbanites) will be as follows:

| | |
|---|---|
| Backlog of demands nat'l. | 831,000 units |
| (estimate of Cairo's share | 400,000) |
| (estimate of Greater Cairo's share | 500,000) |
| Demolition and replacement | 589,000 |
| (estimate of Greater Cairo's share | 400,000) |
| Units needed to meet new demand at current population growth rate | 2,180,000 |
| (estimate of Greater Cairo's share | 1,400,000) |
| Total 1981–2000 | 3,600,000 units |

For the period 1981–1985 alone, it is proposed that both the public and private sectors undertake construction of 675,000 units (25 percent public, 75 percent private) at a total cost of £E3.3 billion or at an average cost per unit of £E4300.[24] These cost estimates, although well above the old norm of £E1000 per unit of public housing, may be conservative. Milad Hanna estimates that a four-room flat of 125 square meters would, in 1977, have cost on average £E7500. Still, if we accept the Housing Ministry's estimate, total costs for housing to the year 2000 would reach £E15.5 billion in 1979 prices. Moreover, construction would have to proceed at a rate of 180,000 units per year. The most that the combined efforts of the public and private sectors have been able to construct in the past were 48,878 units in 1962/1963. It is hard to imagine that Egypt can meet the building and financial challenge that the Ministry of Housing has laid down.

The challenge, however, does not end there. To provide services and utilities to the proposed housing will require outlays of £E1.4 billion for the period 1981–1985 and perhaps £E7 billion until the year 2000. According to the Ministry of Housing, the breakdown for the first five years looks like this:[25]

| | | |
|---|---|---|
| Roads | | £E324 million |
| Water delivery | | £E238 million |
| Sewers and drains | | £E277 million |
| Electricity | | £E151 million |
| Telephones | | £E307 million |
| Transportation | | £E112 million |
| | Total | £E1,409 million |

All of these outlays will have to come from public sources. In sum, the proposals of the Ministry of Housing would entail average annual outlays of £E668 million for construction and £E350 million for services and utilities. For housing construction alone, this would require a level of investment ten times that of 1975 (see table 10.8). Again, there seems little likelihood that funding of such magnitude will become available.

Failing that kind of effort, we may anticipate even greater backlogs of substandard or structurally unsound buildings and even greater crowding as construction rates lag behind urban growth rates. Crowding is already very serious in Cairo. In 1960 the average number of rooms per unit in Cairo, kitchens not included, was 2 and the average number of people per room was 2.3. For 1966 and 1972, I estimated that room densities had increased to 2.7 and 3.1, respectively.[26] On the basis of the 1976 census, the Central Agency for Public Mobilization and Statistics advanced a figure for Cairo of 1.9 people per room without stating their assumption on the average number of rooms per unit.[27] Looking at table 10.20, appended to this chapter, and assuming *(A)* 3 rooms per unit, or *(B)* 2 rooms per unit, we find that for Cairo governorate average room densities would be 2.35 under assumption *A* and 3.32 under *B*. There is frankly little reason to believe that the average number of rooms per unit has increased since 1960, so that I am inclined to accept the figure of 3.32. It should be noted that none of these figures include squatter populations or rooftop dwellers.

Whatever the statistics, there is a general awareness of the combination of deteriorating buildings, overcrowding, and insufficient public invest-

TABLE 10.20.

*Number of Housing Units (Flats and Separate Rooms) According to Usage in Each Kism of Cairo Governorate*[1]

| | | | Number of Flats according to Usage | | | | | Number of Separate Rooms according to Usage | | | | |
|---|---|---|---|---|---|---|---|---|---|---|---|---|
| Kism | Number of Flats | Number of Separate Rooms | Private Habitation | Public Habitation | Work | Habitation and Work | Vacant[2] | Private Habitation | Public Habitation | Work | Habitation and Work | Vacant[2] |
| al-Izbākīya | 12,001 | 4,961 | 9,327 | 312 | 2,049 | 58 | 255 | 3,256 | 262 | 894 | 32 | 517 |
| al-Tabaᶜayn | 7,609 | 1,126 | 6,877 | 56 | 68 | 8 | 600 | 876 | ... | 101 | 12 | 137 |
| Jamalīya | 17,732 | 22,896 | 16,558 | 15 | 684 | 31 | 444 | 19,300 | 3 | 1,134 | 50 | 2,409 |
| Khalīfa | 84,524 | 20,396 | 23,429 | 6 | 104 | 23 | 962 | 17,319 | 6 | 218 | 80 | 2,773 |
| Darb al-Ahmar | 19,384 | 12,670 | 18,343 | ... | 273 | 635 | 133 | 8,954 | 3 | 749 | 1,669 | 1,295 |
| al-Zaytūn | 47,383 | 10,850 | 44,668 | 38 | 207 | 71 | 2,399 | 10,505 | 9 | 33 | 6 | 297 |
| al-Sahl | 69,746 | 19,816 | 66,484 | 10 | 516 | 94 | 2,642 | 18,688 | 1 | 135 | 61 | 931 |
| Sayyida Zaynab | 38,852 | 16,548 | 36,986 | 39 | 648 | 63 | 1,116 | 15,039 | 6 | 395 | 60 | 1,048 |
| Zāhir | 20,417 | 2,815 | 19,554 | 30 | 301 | 30 | 502 | 2,460 | 1 | 58 | 26 | 270 |
| al-Matarīya | 92,004 | 29,773 | 85,753 | 33 | 525 | 182 | 5,511 | 28,081 | 3 | 189 | 93 | 1,405 |
| al-Maᶜādī | 48,613 | 18,428 | 45,295 | 18 | 223 | 54 | 3,023 | 17,330 | ... | 169 | 19 | 910 |
| Muskī | 9,575 | 4,088 | 8,333 | 49 | 959 | 38 | 196 | 2,857 | 55 | 964 | 19 | 193 |
| Nuzha | 28,779 | 1,840 | 26,263 | 12 | 200 | 48 | 2,256 | 1,411 | ... | 41 | 45 | 343 |
| Waylī | 20,026 | 11,134 | 19,026 | 42 | 168 | 30 | 760 | 10,527 | 4 | 75 | 39 | 489 |
| Bāb al-Shaᶜrīya | 16,045 | 6,084 | 15,545 | 5 | 189 | 22 | 284 | 5,539 | ... | 134 | 13 | 398 |
| Būlāq | 19,539 | 21,587 | 18,962 | 1 | 231 | 40 | 305 | 20,466 | 2 | 311 | 21 | 787 |
| Hadīya al-Qubba | 47,625 | 15,207 | 45,296 | 2 | 290 | 431 | 1,606 | 14,645 | ... | 119 | 79 | 364 |
| Hulwān | 41,747 | 28,742 | 39,583 | 28 | 237 | 62 | 1,837 | 27,743 | 1 | 97 | 69 | 832 |
| Rūd al-Farāj | 30,513 | 9,665 | 29,578 | 17 | 359 | 45 | 514 | 9,198 | 10 | 74 | 24 | 359 |
| Shubrā | 18,901 | 8,440 | 18,173 | 20 | 278 | 42 | 388 | 7,834 | 9 | 129 | 43 | 425 |
| ᶜAbdīn | 21,440 | 5,463 | 16,404 | 152 | 4,222 | 103 | 559 | 3,441 | 10 | 1,577 | 23 | 412 |
| Kasr al-Nīl | 14,414 | 1,728 | 11,290 | 246 | 1,580 | 50 | 1,248 | 1,328 | 49 | 248 | ... | 103 |
| Nasr City | 16,818 | 1,010 | 13,947 | 89 | 164 | 46 | 2,572 | 720 | 9 | 27 | 43 | 211 |
| Heliopolis | 32,005 | 4,595 | 29,680 | 44 | 406 | 60 | 1,815 | 3,394 | 20 | 245 | 8 | 928 |
| Old Cairo | 38,835 | 24,527 | 37,587 | 45 | 208 | 81 | 914 | 22,873 | 5 | 252 | 88 | 1,309 |
| al-Sharabīya | 64,607 | 18,477 | 60,728 | 6 | 399 | 122 | 3,352 | 17,825 | 1 | 175 | 86 | 390 |
| Total | 819,134 | 322,866 | 763,669 | 1,315 | 15,488 | 2,469 | 36,193 | 291,609 | 469 | 8,543 | 2,710 | 19,535 |

SOURCE: Preliminary Results of the 1976 Population and Housing Census

ment in housing. In some ways it seems insoluble, so massive are the needs. Milād Hanna has suggested various programs that could have some significance in meeting new demands. USAID and the Ministry of Housing have studied various low-cost credit and financing arrangements. There have, however, been few advocates of radical reform. Gamal Hamdan's suggestion that Cairo's Gezira Sporting Club, refuge for the city's well-to-do, be taken over and used for public low-cost housing was greeted with profound silence.[28] More typical of elite bewilderment is the entire section on housing from the program of the National Democratic party, closely linked to the presidency:

> The housing crisis becomes increasingly difficult year after year and existing laws have been unable to alleviate it. The party will set forth a complete project to deal with this problem to be implemented within a set period of time.[29]

As in other economic domains where state intervention has seemingly been ineffective and where cumulative problems appear insusceptible of public policy solutions, the official attitude on housing is increasingly to let the market place take over. The "socialist" regulation of the housing market that was elaborated in the 1960s has been frequently denounced as benefitting only real estate speculators and black-market operators. The conclusion that is drawn is not that regulations should be improved or applied more rigorously but rather done away with altogether.

Let us look at the regulations controlling the urban housing market so that we can then understand the ways in which they have been violated. The first attempts at rent control came during the Second World War when, under martial law, orders were issued forbidding the expulsion of tenants and fixing rents at the level prevailing on April 1, 1941. Subsequently rents were lowered by 15 percent in 1952 on all apartments built between 1944 and 1952 and then lowered again by 20 percent in 1958 on all apartments built between 1952 and 1958. There was a further sweeping decrease of 20 percent at the time of the Socialist Decrees in July 1961. The most important legislation, however, was issued in Law 46 of 1962. It effectively removed rents from all supply and demand influence and made them a function of administered profits margins. Rents on new buildings could not exceed annually 5 percent of the value of the site and 8 percent of the value of the building. Since the urban real estate market was depressed precisely because of state regulation, and because the state subsidized the cost of building materials, profits remained low in absolute terms as well as steady.

As inflation became a major factor in Egypt's economy toward the end of the 1960–1965 plan, and as private sector entrepreneurs and contractors sought investment outlets, rent controls were increasingly violated. There was (and is) a large pent-up middle-class demand for urban housing. State officials, professionals, private-sector investors—all turned to real estate as the safest investment in a period of rising inflation and growing state control of all sectors of the economy. It was inevitable that this demand would create black-market conditions. For instance, key money became a requisite for access to rent-controlled flats; a second gambit was to require several years' advance rent. By 1974, average (illegal) key money was £E1000 per unit. Commercial leases, such as shoe shops in central Cairo, were worth £E100–£E200,000 in advance rent.[30]

A second phenomenon was the growing resort to the sale of apartments. There was and is nothing illegal about such sales. Their attraction is that they reflect real market value for housing units.

Furnished flats had always been exempted from rent controls. For a limited segment of Egypt's salariat in the 1960s, a sound investment was to pay access to or convert a rent-controlled flat into a furnished apartment that could then be rented to foreigners at whatever the market would bear. In those years it would not have been uncommon for a flat controlled at £E8 per month to rent furnished at £E100. The profit was not taxed. After 1973, with a fairly heavy influx of foreigners and Arabs, the market for luxury housing was strained far beyond its capacity. The flat that rented for £E100 in 1970 would go for anything between £E500 and £E1,000 by 1976. Luxury apartments were frequently sold to wealthy Arabs, and those along the Nile could fetch upward of £E200,000. Urban

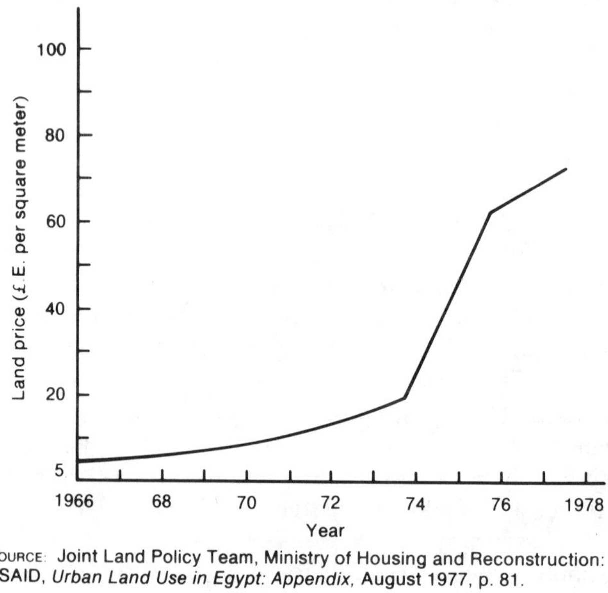


SOURCE: Joint Land Policy Team, Ministry of Housing and Reconstruction: USAID, *Urban Land Use in Egypt: Appendix*, August 1977, p. 81.

*FIGURE 10.2.*

*Land Prices in Newly Developed Residential Areas of Cairo, 1966–1977*

land values began to soar (see figure 10.2). In 1973 land near the Nile in Cairo sold at £E100 per square meter. By 1977 the same square meter of land sold for £E1,000. In poor sections of Cairo, land values rose over the same period from £E2 to £E30 per square meter.[31]

Simultaneously, a booming black market in building materials developed. The supply of cement, construction steel, and glass is controlled by the state. These materials are supplied below real cost to public and private builders. Once they have submitted approved architectural plans, builders receive an allocation of building materials judged sufficient to implement the plan. However, for some materials the waiting time has been months if not years, and frequently the builder has one material on hand but not the others. He will, therefore, buy what he needs on the black market and, when his legal allotment comes through, he will sell it on the black market. His real construction costs, of course, vastly exceed the approved estimates so that he has to violate rent control laws in order to recover his investment. For instance, in 1976 the state sold cement at £E14.5 per ton while importing it at £E35 per ton. The black-market price was £E60 per ton.

Another typical gambit is to bribe city engineers to turn a blind eye to violations of approved architectural plans. A notorious example was that of a building in al-Duqqī, built by Hasan al-Bayyūmī, which collapsed in December 1974. The building exceeded its approved height by four floors, and no steel whatever was used in its construction. The scandal triggered a brief assault upon the "parasites" in the construction sector that manipulated public officials and subsidized goods to reap big, untaxed profits.[32]

The inequities of the prevailing system have been openly recognized, but, as noted, the prevalent official position is to deregulate housing as much as possible. In 1978, the Minister of Housing, Mustafā Hifnāwī, stated that, in order to encourage private investment, housing should be left to supply and demand.[33] The only brake on profits taking was the 1976 tax legislation, which subjects rents and sales of property to income and profits tax. It is not yet clear how thoroughly this law has been applied.

All of this smacks somewhat of a policy of triage where, as with transportation, the poor majority of the city will undergo benign neglect in the hope that unfettered private consumerism will generate a significant "trickle down" effect.

The state for its part will try to mitigate the disparities in the distribution and availability of housing in three ways. The first is to continue to undertake construction of low-income housing at subsidized rents. But, as we have already noted, this effort will probably not even meet new demand let alone address the problems of slum clearance and reconstruction. A second approach is to provide public land and subsidized credit (£E25 million in 1979) to building cooperatives. There are 900 such co-ops nationwide, but there are strong suspicions that many are facades for groups of land speculators and developers who will use public property and cheap credit for private profit.[34]

The third solution being pursued is that of constructing new cities in desert areas proximate to Cairo and Alexandria. The notion is that these would reduce congestion in the major cities, serve as growth poles for development, and reduce urban encroachment upon precious agricultural land. Nine such cities have thus far been proposed and, in at least one instance, engineering studies and even the auctioning off of building sites have been completed. In 1979 about £E170 million was budgeted for the new cities and about 3.2 percent (£E321.6 million) of all investments in the current Five Year Plan is earmarked for them as well. Other than providing utilities and transportation, the state will confine itself to advancing credit, land, and long-term leases so that public and private sector enterprises, with or without foreign participation, can develop these sites.

## V. Conclusion

We have examined two aspects of the impact of urban centers upon income distribution in Egypt: disparities in income and availability of services between urban and rural Egypt; and the distribution of income and services within cities, especially within Cairo. With respect to the first aspect, it was found that, on average, urban incomes were twice those of the rural areas but that services and recurrent public expenditures were not notably biased in favor of cities. There does appear to be such bias with regard to public investment, the quality and nature of the services provided, and in the provision of subsidized goods, especially wheat and flour.

As the proportion of profits and nonwage revenues in national income increases, we expect the disparity between urban and rural incomes to increase as well. We also expect that relatively high-quality medical and educational personnel will remain concentrated in the cities although there may be some spread from Cairo and Alexandria toward secondary centers in the canal zone and the provinces. Public investment may shift marginally from the urban areas, but that shift will probably represent investment in land reclamation, new cities, and the like rather than investment in existing disfavored populations.

Income disparities within Egyptian cities do not appear to be particularly pronounced, but available survey data clearly tend to overweight the salaried middle classes and to underweight the lowest third and the highest tenth of the population. Maldistribution is probably more pronounced than most serious estimates suggest, and, with growing proportions of profits in urban income, is becoming worse. Policy makers and pundits alike are aware of this and fear the peculiarly paralyzing and politically disruptive effects that this inequity has produced or encouraged. The official response so far has been a number of costly holding operations on the service side, pouring money into maintaining the public transport fleet, building more subsidized public housing, and maintaining at ever greater cost the price subsidies of certain consumer essentials. At the same time the middle classes, linked both to the public and private sectors, have been given their head in all forms of consumerism, but nowhere more ostentatiously than in the acquisition of private automobiles. The move away from socialist legislation regulating the housing market has given the middle classes substantial new opportunities for speculative investment and the purchase of rapidly appreciating fixed assets. The official hope is that middle-class earnings, in combination with the resurgence of market forces, will generate new economic activity that will have far-reaching spread effects. The notion of greater rather than less public intervention to effect income redistribution within the cities enjoys little favor among Egypt's policymakers. Peace, private-sector dynamism, foreign investment, and judicious use of public funds to hold the least privileged in check is the package of elements that the regime hopes will be the agent to a more equitable distribution of urban assets.

## Appendix

*TABLE 10.A.1.*

*Recurrent Outlays by Service Sector, 1977*

| *Governorate* | *Gen. Admin. (dīwān al-ᶜām)* | *Education* | *Health* | *Housing* | *Social Affairs* | *Supply* | *Agriculture* | *Labor* | *Total (rounded nos.)* |
|---|---|---|---|---|---|---|---|---|---|
| Cairo | 16,058,726 | 30,720,430 | 8,963,000 | 688,780 | 1,589,901 | 442,290 | . . . | 449,370 | 58,000,000 |
| Alexandria | 6,558,511 | 14,892,650 | 4,900,000 | 534,915 | 728,583 | 253,710 | 345,230 | 269,910 | 23,000,000 |
| Pt. Said | 3,786,462 | 3,342,870 | 1,245,000 | 192,740 | 289,364 | 66,960 | 40,030 | 58,261 | 9,000,000 |
| Ismailia | 2,180,355 | 2,268,090 | 1,089,000 | 185,180 | 134,840 | 51,410 | 377,270 | 51,054 | 6,000,000 |
| Suez | 1,742,361 | 1,290,570 | 870,000 | 150,635 | 127,630 | 39,930 | 64,310 | 42,860 | 4,000,000 |
| al-Qalyūbīya | 4,457,646 | 8,315,080 | 3,899,000 | 348,655 | 390,947 | 99,240 | 1,368,700 | 132,759 | 19,000,000 |
| al-Sharqīya | 6,727,666 | 12,498,120 | 4,691,000 | 532,065 | 703,179 | 225,280 | 1,723,690 | 120,164 | 27,000,000 |
| al-Daqhalīya | 8,131,778 | 14,746,840 | 4,730,000 | 784,260 | 799,712 | 268,730 | 1,778,560 | 145,170 | 31,000,000 |
| Damietta | 2,646,748 | 4,091,500 | 1,429,000 | 104,200 | 244,607 | 43,640 | 388,900 | 44,090 | 9,000,000 |
| al-Minūfīya | 5,206,463 | 11,101,060 | 3,195,000 | 495,810 | 523,757 | 165,280 | 1,636,050 | 88,051 | 22,000,000 |
| al-Gharbīya | 7,904,234 | 13,303,840 | 4,537,000 | 553,100 | 659,007 | 185,660 | 1,667,670 | 173,949 | 28,000,000 |
| Kafr al-Shaykh | 3,474,102 | 5,994,750 | 2,624,000 | 136,890 | 300,394 | 145,550 | 980,290 | 62,990 | 13,000,000 |
| al-Buhayra | 5,412,214 | 8,744,350 | 4,033,000 | 273,395 | 457,256 | 137,380 | 1,801,710 | 128,594 | 20,000,000 |
| Giza | 5,817,791 | 10,750,080 | 4,244,000 | 318,100 | 640,865 | 137,420 | 1,001,790 | 130,775 | 23,000,000 |
| al-Fayyūm | 3,137,408 | 4,666,900 | 2,600,000 | 185,850 | 297,447 | 79,360 | 1,052,490 | 44,180 | 12,000,000 |
| Banī Suwayf | 3,812,066 | 6,292,270 | 2,629,000 | 274,920 | 371,552 | 99,930 | 814,170 | 68,065 | 14,000,000 |
| al-Minyā | 5,199,166 | 8,020,970 | 3,676,000 | 474,540 | 490,304 | 135,170 | 1,328,080 | 105,448 | 19,000,000 |
| Asyūt | 4,134,248 | 8,649,640 | 3,311,000 | 361,580 | 367,792 | 95,850 | 840,460 | 74,209 | 17,000,000 |
| Sūhāj | 4,259,807 | 10,126,420 | 3,297,000 | 442,020 | 407,081 | 116,940 | 1,050,840 | 133,919 | 19,000,000 |
| Qinā | 4,948,837 | 8,469,070 | 3,105,000 | 427,325 | 385,060 | 92,930 | 749,610 | 96,099 | 18,000,000 |
| Aswān | 3,281,996 | 5,826,780 | 2,336,000 | 329,565 | 650,629 | 63,150 | 512,250 | 80,147 | 13,000,000* |
| Matrūh | 1,411,697 | 941,190 | 587,000 | 58,960 | 78,442 | 28,090 | 81,020 | 25,810 | 3,000,000 |
| Wadī al-Jadīd | 1,359,066 | 1,267,510 | 779,000 | 68,370 | 106,985 | 24,940 | 129,950 | 23,596 | 3,000,000 |
| Red Sea | 1,017,251 | 908,090 | 465,000 | 58,825 | 58,446 | 23,940 | 19,930 | 34,860 | 2,000,000 |
| Sinai | 626,830 | 222,830 | 296,000 | 49,320 | 54,519 | 13,800 | . . . | 30,530 | 1,000,000 |

SOURCE: Draft Budget for 1977

*Includes £E285,070 for Aswān regional plan

TABLE 10.A.2.

*Distribution of Public Sector Investment of the Five Year Plan 1978–1982 to Sectors and Governorates*

*(Value in Thousand Pounds)*

| | Agriculture | | Irrigation & Drainage | | Industry | | Petroleum | | Transportation | | Electric Power | |
|---|---|---|---|---|---|---|---|---|---|---|---|---|
| Governorate | Investment | % | Investment | % | Investment | % | Investment | % | Investment | % | Investment | % |
| Cairo | 16,479.0 | 4.6 | 6,500.0 | 1.3 | 611,916.7 | 25.5 | 3,357.0 | 0.6 | ... | ... | 56,103.6 | 6.0 |
| Alexandria | 30,222.4 | 8.4 | 21,100.0 | 4.2 | 407,022.4 | 16.9 | 212,065.0 | 37.7 | ... | ... | 137,849.8 | 14.8 |
| Port Said | 42.0 | ... | ... | ... | 18,053.0 | 0.8 | ... | ... | ... | ... | 2,078.5 | 0.2 |
| Suez | 25.0 | ... | ... | ... | 45,899.0 | 1.9 | 17,876.0 | 3.2 | ... | ... | 178,603.5 | 19.2 |
| Damietta | 461.7 | 0.1 | 6,058.0 | 1.2 | 2,782.0 | 0.1 | ... | ... | ... | ... | 377.1 | 0.1 |
| al-Daqhalīya | 1,531.6 | 1.4 | 17,700.0 | 3.5 | 43,957.3 | 1.8 | ... | ... | ... | ... | 11,957.0 | 1.3 |
| al-Sharqīya | 4,170.4 | 1.2 | 14,544.0 | 2.9 | 6,265.0 | 0.3 | ... | ... | ... | ... | 426.9 | ... |
| al-Qalyūbīya | 5,861.0 | 1.6 | 5,100.0 | 1.0 | 75,582.0 | 3.1 | 8,956.0 | 1.6 | ... | ... | 1,568.6 | 0.2 |
| Kafr al-Shaykh | 7,292.2 | 2.0 | 18,741.0 | 3.7 | 61,171.0 | 2.5 | ... | ... | ... | ... | 570.6 | 0.1 |
| al-Gharbīya | 913.1 | 0.3 | 17,000.0 | 3.4 | 47,831.0 | 2.0 | 850.0 | 0.2 | ... | ... | 300.0 | ... |
| al-Minūfīya | 599.2 | 0.2 | 10,300.0 | 2.0 | 35.0 | ... | ... | ... | ... | ... | 326.1 | ... |
| al-Buhayīa | 41,246.0 | 39.5 | 66,335.0 | 13.2 | 88,259.0 | 3.7 | ... | ... | ... | ... | 3,537.0 | 0.4 |
| Ismailia | 6,141.2 | 1.7 | 725.0 | 0.1 | 14,333.0 | 0.6 | ... | ... | ... | ... | 75,773.5 | 8.2 |
| Giza | 7,634.1 | 2.2 | 7,900.0 | 1.6 | 56,097.0 | 2.3 | 14,986.0 | 2.7 | ... | ... | 17,651.2 | 1.9 |
| Banī Suwayf | 793.4 | 0.2 | 16,250.0 | 3.2 | 19,989.0 | 0.8 | ... | ... | ... | ... | 297.1 | ... |
| al-Fayyūm | 417.1 | 0.1 | 5,500.0 | 1.1 | 9,033.0 | 0.4 | ... | ... | ... | ... | 143.9 | ... |
| al-Minyā | 4,850.8 | 1.4 | 23,042.0 | 4.5 | 436.0 | ... | ... | ... | ... | ... | 642.6 | 0.1 |
| Asyūt | 491.5 | 0.1 | 11,920.0 | 2.3 | −46,034.0 | 1.9 | ... | ... | ... | ... | 384.4 | 0.1 |
| Sūhāj | 781.5 | 0.2 | 11,920.0 | 2.3 | 50,600.0 | 2.1 | ... | ... | ... | ... | 486.6 | ... |
| Qinā | 706.1 | 0.2 | 18,448.0 | 3.6 | 58,414.0 | 2.4 | ... | ... | ... | ... | 364.5 | ... |
| Aswān | 18,439.2 | 5.2 | 5,774.0 | 11.4 | 57,143.0 | 2.4 | ... | ... | ... | ... | 2,578.5 | 0.3 |
| Red Sea | 15.0 | ... | ... | ... | 6,154.0 | 0.3 | 34,005.0 | 6.0 | ... | ... | 71.4 | ... |
| Wadī al-Jadīd | 8,948.3 | 2.5 | 7,945.0 | 1.6 | 101,890.0 | 4.2 | ... | ... | ... | ... | 16,956.3 | 1.8 |

TABLE 10.A.2. (continued)

| Governorate | Agriculture Invest-ment | % | Irrigation & Drainage Invest-ment | % | Industry Invest-ment | % | Petroleum Invest-ment | % | Transportation Invest-ment | % | Electric Power Invest-ment | % |
|---|---|---|---|---|---|---|---|---|---|---|---|---|
| Matrūh | 332.5 | 0.1 | 1,690.0 | 0.3 | 112.6 | ... | 31,594.0 | 5.6 | ... | ... | 175.5 | ... |
| Sinai | 5,305.0 | 1.5 | 3,700.0 | 0.7 | ... | ... | 18,634.0 | 3.3 | ... | ... | 3,132.8 | 0.3 |
| The New Cities | 5,000.0 | 1.4 | ... | ... | 16,000.0 | 0.7 | ... | ... | ... | ... | 25,000.0 | 2.7 |
| Distributed Investments | 268,699.3 | 76.1 | 298,192.0 | 69.1 | 1,845,009.0 | 76.7 | 342,323.0 | 60.9 | ... | ... | 537,106.0 | 57.7 |
| Central Investments | 88,927.0 | 24.9 | 156,772.0 | 30.9 | 170,400.0 | 7.1 | ... | ... | 214,300.0 | 100.0 | 2,708.0 | 0.3 |
| Undistributed Investments | ... | ... | ... | ... | 390,971.0 | 16.2 | 220,077.0 | 39.1 | ... | ... | 390,026.0 | 42.0 |
| Grand Total | 357,626.3 | 101.0 | 454,964.0 | 100.0 | 2,406,380.0 | 100.0 | 562,400.0 | 100.0 | 214,300.0 | 100.0 | 929,840.0 | 100.0 |

| Governorate | Transportation & Communcation Invest-ment | % | Commerce & Finances Invest-ment | % | Housing Invest-ment | % | Utilities Invest-ment | % | Services Invest-ment | % | Relative Total Importance Invest-ment | % |
|---|---|---|---|---|---|---|---|---|---|---|---|---|
| Cairo | 596,142.7 | 21.2 | 94,934.0 | 44.0 | 235,413.0 | 41.5 | 213,207.3 | 34.4 | 236,661.1 | 24.2 | 2,070,714.4 | 10.3 |
| Alexandria | 231,979.9 | 8.2 | 28,132.0 | 13.0 | 65,670.0 | 11.6 | 108,017.2 | 17.4 | 55,683.9 | 5.6 | 1,298,242.6 | 12.7 |
| Port Said | 10,991.3 | 0.4 | 9,538.0 | 4.4 | 3,970.0 | 0.7 | 4,913.3 | 0.8 | 9,091.2 | 0.9 | 58,677.3 | 0.6 |

| | | | | | | | | | | | | |
|---|---|---|---|---|---|---|---|---|---|---|---|---|
| Suez | 56,657.4 | 2.0 | 18,450.0 | 8.6 | 5,140.0 | 0.9 | 5,607.2 | 0.9 | 10,466.5 | 1.1 | 338,724.6 | 3.3 |
| Damietta | 10,187.6 | 0.4 | ... | ... | 4,768.0 | 0.8 | 6,065.9 | 1.0 | 6,585.8 | 0.7 | 37,198.4 | 0.4 |
| al-Daqhalīya | 12,690.1 | 0.5 | ... | ... | 6,625.0 | 1.2 | 8,405.3 | 1.4 | 18,664.9 | 1.9 | 121,531.2 | 1.2 |
| al-Sharqīya | 9,730.7 | 0.4 | ... | ... | 26,014.0 | 6.3 | 26,660.7 | 4.3 | 19,494.7 | 2.0 | 117,305.4 | 1.2 |
| al-Qalyūbīya | 9,762.6 | 0.3 | 2,554.0 | 1.2 | 10,010.0 | 1.8 | 9,452.0 | 1.5 | 13,369.6 | 1.3 | 142,215.8 | 1.4 |
| Kafr al-Shaykh | 10,754.9 | 0.4 | ... | ... | 5,167.0 | 0.9 | 9,373.1 | 1.5 | 8,923.0 | 0.9 | 121,992.8 | 1.2 |
| al-Gharbīya | 12,894.7 | 0.5 | 1,050.0 | 0.5 | 9,601.5 | 1.7 | 11,661.0 | 1.9 | 19,693.5 | 2.0 | 121,374.8 | 1.2 |
| al-Minūfīya | 8,768.7 | 0.3 | ... | ... | 26,978.0 | 4.7 | 21,047.5 | 3.4 | 19,685.5 | 2.0 | 87,740.0 | 0.9 |
| al-Buhayra | 18,458.0 | 0.7 | 1,757.0 | 0.8 | 9,390.5 | 1.7 | 12,034.2 | 1.9 | 13,906.9 | 1.4 | 354,973.6 | 3.5 |
| Ismailia | 19,278.1 | 0.7 | 2,257.0 | 1.0 | 4,368.0 | 0.8 | 5,015.7 | 0.8 | 18,285.1 | 1.8 | 146,176.6 | 1.4 |
| Giza | 53,216.4 | 1.9 | ... | ... | 4,538.0 | 0.8 | 7,746.0 | 1.2 | 35,881.2 | 3.6 | 205,649.9 | 2.0 |
| Banī Suwayf | 6,473.6 | 0.2 | ... | ... | 3,381.0 | 0.6 | 5,807.2 | 0.9 | 7,607.8 | 0.8 | 60,599.1 | 0.6 |
| al-Fayyūm | 3,597.4 | 0.1 | 696.0 | 0.3 | 5,305.0 | 0.9 | 4,630.7 | 0.7 | 7,023.1 | 0.7 | 36,346.2 | 0.3 |
| al-Minyā | 6,830.2 | 0.2 | 15.0 | ... | 4,617.0 | 0.8 | 5,496.6 | 0.9 | 20,227.0 | 2.0 | 66,157.2 | 0.7 |
| Asyūt | 12,418.0 | 0.4 | ... | ... | 7,233.5 | 1.3 | 7,588.3 | 1.2 | 27,820.5 | 2.8 | 113,890.2 | 1.1 |
| Sūhāj | 5,129.5 | 0.2 | ... | ... | 4,095.0 | 0.7 | 6,802.6 | 1.1 | 11,274.1 | 1.1 | 90,789.3 | 0.9 |
| Qinā | 6,824.7 | 0.2 | 315.0 | 0.1 | 4,121.0 | 0.7 | 7,910.1 | 1.3 | 23,718.5 | 2.4 | 120,781.9 | 1.1 |
| Aswān | 21,797.5 | 0.8 | 415.0 | 0.2 | 7,396.5 | 1.3 | 8,296.2 | 1.3 | 14,782.1 | 1.5 | 188,588.0 | 1.9 |
| Red Sea | 26,482.0 | 1.0 | ... | ... | 600.0 | 0.1 | 2,662.4 | 0.4 | 5,310.8 | 0.5 | 75,300.6 | 0.7 |
| Wadī al-Jadīd | 116,669.2 | 4.1 | 25.0 | ... | 12,986.0 | 2.3 | 16,809.3 | 2.7 | 2,882.2 | 0.3 | 285,210.3 | 2.8 |
| Matrūh | 13,766.7 | 0.5 | ... | ... | 162.0 | ... | 3,248.3 | 0.5 | 2,233.4 | 0.2 | 53,315.0 | 0.5 |
| Sinai | 1,728.3 | 0.1 | 25.0 | ... | 1,136.0 | 0.2 | 1,958.9 | 0.3 | 1,831.6 | 0.2 | 37,451.7 | 0.4 |
| The New Cities | 50,000.0 | 1.7 | 9,000.0 | 4.2 | 600.0 | 14.4 | 85,000.0 | 13.7 | 50,000.0 | 5.1 | 321,600.0 | 3.2 |
| Distributed Investment | 1,333,230.2 | 47.4 | 169,163.0 | 78.3 | 469,286.0 | 98.7 | 605,516.0 | 97.4 | 661,004.0 | 67.0 | 66,670,346.9 | 65.5 |
| Central Investments | 1,386,823.1 | 49.4 | 2,273.0 | 1.1 | 7,114.0 | 1.3 | 15,984.0 | 2.6 | 121,054.0 | 12.3 | 2,166,555.1 | 21.3 |
| Undistributed Investments | 86,646.4 | 3.1 | 43,867.0 | 20.3 | ... | ... | ... | ... | 204,937.0 | 20.7 | 1,336,224.4 | 13.1 |
| Grand Total | 2,806,699.7 | 99.9 | 215,303.0 | 99.7 | 476,400.0 | 100.0 | 621,500.0 | 100.0 | 986,995.0 | 100.0 | 10,173,126.4 | 99.9 |

## Notes

1. Michael Lipton, *Why Poor People Stay Poor: A Study of Urban Bias in World Development* (Cambridge: Harvard University Press, 1977).

2. Gabriel Baer, "The Beginnings of Urbanization" in his *Studies in the Social History of Modern Egypt* (Chicago: Chicago University Press, 1969), 133–148, esp. p. 136. Justin A. McCarthy, "Nineteenth Century Egyptian Population," *Middle Eastern Studies* 12, no. 3 (October 1976): 1–40. In general, see Gamal Hamdan, *Studies in Egyptian Urbanism* (Cairo: Anglo-Egyptian Bookshop, 1959); Janet Abu-Lughod, *Cairo: 1001 Years of the City Victorious,* (Princeton: Princeton University Press, 1971), and Alphonse Said, "The Growth and Development of Urbanization in Egypt" (Cairo, American University/Social Research Center, 1960), mimeographed.

3. Abu Lughod, "City Victorious," in *Cairo,* p. 174; ᶜIzzat Hijāzī, *Cairo: A Study of an Urban Phenomenon* (Cairo: National Center for Sociological and Criminological Research, 1971) (in Arabic), pp. 16–30; CAPMAS, "Cairo and its Population Explosion" supplement to *al-Ahram al-Iqtisadi,* Cairo, June 15, 1974, p. 24; and Subhi Abd al-Hakim, "Internal Migration in Egypt" *Population Studies,* Cairo, no. 17, February 1975.

4. In 1960 there were two cities with over one million inhabitants, twelve in the range 100,000–200,000 and seventy-two in the range 20,000–99,000. It is these latter that may in some instances be superficially urban. See Janet Abu-Lughod, "Urbanization in Egypt: Present State and Future Prospects," *Economic Development and Cultural Change* 13 (April 1965): 313–343, esp. 320–322.

5. Essam Muntasser, "Agricultural Growth, Prices, and Sectoral Terms of Trade in Egypt," FAO/SIDA Seminar on Agricultural Sector Analysis in the Near East and North Africa, Cairo, October 20–26, 1975. For the period 1970–1975, see Karima Korayem in chapter 6 of this book.

6. This table was published in IBRD, *Arab Republic of Egypt: Economic Management in a Period of Transition,* vol. 3: Productive Sectors, (Washington, D. C., May 1978), p. 38. For similar assessments of policy toward the agricultural sector, see the contributions of Issawi and Korayem in chapters 4 and 6 of this book.

7. On water costs, see ᶜIzz al-Dīn Kāmil, *Mechanized Agriculture,* (Cairo: Dar al-Thiqāfa al-Jadīda, 1976) (in Arabic), p. 123; see also James B. Fitch, et al., "The Economic Efficiency of Water in Egyptian Agriculture: Opening Round of a Debate," paper presented to the Seventeenth International Conference of Agricultural Economists, September 3–12, 1979, Banff, Canada.

8. Figures on direct subsidies are from Minister of Finance Aly Lutfi, "Financial Presentation of the Draft State Budget for 1980," supplement to *al-Ahrām al-Iqtisādī,* January 1, 1980.

9. See Hassan el-Khedr, "Policy Study on Pricing and Taxation of Major Alternative Agricultural Crops," Ministry of Economy, Foreign Trade and Economic Cooperation, Economic Studies Unit, Cairo, 1978; and John Waterbury, "Egyptian Agriculture Adrift," in B. Huddleston and Jon McLin (eds.), *Political Investments in Food Production* (Bloomington: Indiana University Press, 1979): 61–82.

10. R. Eckaus, F. McCarthy, and A. Mohie-Eldin, *Multisector General Equilibrium Policy Model for Egypt* (Cairo: Cairo University/DRTPC, 1978), p. 94.

11. Lance Taylor, "Annex 1.1" in IBRD, *Arab Republic of Egypt,* vol. 1, *Main Report,* pp. 82–95; Osman al-Kholie also reports on the widening rural-urban income gap in "Disparities of Egyptian Personal Income Distribution as Reflected by Family Budget Data," *L'Egypte Contemporaine* 64, no. 354 (October 1973): 33–55.

12. For a general treatment of this phenomenon, see Jan Tinbergen, *Income Distribution* (New York: American Elsevier, 1975), pp. 144–146.

13. 1965–1967 figures are to be found in Galal Bakeer, "Practical Application of Financial Management Practices," (Ph.D. diss., Faculty of Commerce, Cairo University, 1969) (in Arabic). Although at the time of writing a breakdown by governorate was not available, the total recurrent budget for wages and services had ballooned in 1979 to £E633 million from £E429.7 million in 1977. Of that total, £E123 million was raised locally and £E510 million allocated through the central ministries.

14. IBRD, *The National Family Planning Program of the ARE: A Sector Review* (Washington, D. C., August 14, 1972), Annex 39.

15. Wajdī Riyād, "The End of Cairo's Domination of the Regions," *al-Ahrām al-Iqtisādī* 562 (January 15, 1979): 14–15.

16. L. Taylor in IBRD, *Arab Republic of Egypt,* vol. 1, Annex 1.3.

17. ᶜIssām Rifā ᶜat and Ibrāhīm ᶜAmr, "The Crust of Bread: Crisis in Production or Consumption?" *al-Ahrām al-Iqtisādī* 552 (August 15, 1978). There are 30,530 "fair price" cooperatives or shops in Egypt to service 7.8 million Egyptians with ration cards. Although numbers say nothing about the volume and quality of goods distributed, the shops are more numerous in rural areas. For instance, each shop in Cairo serves, on average, 688 families while in most rural areas the average is less than 250. See Joachim von Braun, "Wirkungen von Nahrungsmittelhilfe in Empfängerländen," Institute für Agrarökonomie der Universität Göttingen, February 1980.

18. *Rūz al-Yūsuf* 2659 (May 28, 1979).

19. Mona Seragaldin, "Household Income Distribution," Appendix I, *Immediate Action Proposals for Housing in Egypt,* Office of Housing, USAID: and Ministries of Housing and Reconstruction, and Planning (June 1976) p. 82. Cf. Lance Taylor, *Arab Republic of Egypt,* vol. 1, Appendix B, showing four different Lorenz curves on urban income distribution according to differing estimates of upper decile incomes.

20. For earlier measurements of urban stratification, see IEDES, "La śociété urbaine Egyptienne," *Tiers Monde* (April–June 1961) vol. 2, no. 6, 183–210; Hassan Riad, *l 'Egypte Nasserienne,* Ed. de Minuit, Paris (1962) 60–64; Ceres Wissa Wassef, "Le prolétariat et le sous-prolétariat industriel et agricole en République Arabe Unie," *Orient,* 3–4e Trim., vol. 13, nos. 51 & 52 (1969): 87–112. For current unemployment, see Mona Seragaldin, "Household Income Distribution," p. 85.

21. Governor Hamdī ᶜAshūr, cited in *al-Ahrām* (March 15, 1973).

22. For background, see my two articles, "Transportation" and "Buses and Subways to the Rescue," in John Waterbury, *Egypt: Burdens of the Past, Options for the Future,* (Bloomington: Indiana University Press, 1978), pp. 145–176; and ARE, Ministry of Transport (with SOFRETU) *Greater Cairo Transportation Economic Study,* vols. A, B, C, Paris (May 1973).

23. One finds the same private vehicle bias at the national level. Proposed investments in highway construction and widening over the period 1976–1980 were £E253 million. The Ministry of Transport/Louis Berger International Inc., *Egypt National Transport Study Interim Report: 1977,* v. 1: p. x, states, "There will be an exceedingly low economic return on these investments. . . . It is presumed that they are being carried out for other than economic development purposes." These investment figures were subsequently revised upward in the draft plan for 1978–1982:

Investments in roads and waterways outside main cities: £E100 million

| | |
|---|---|
| other roads: | 47.0 |
| roads in Cairo: | 125.3 |
| roads in Giza: | 38.1 |
| roads in Shubrā al-Khayma: | 3.5 |
| roads in Alexandria: | 3.0 |

24. These figures are drawn from Ministry of Housing, *Facing Housing's Problems,* published as a supplement to *al-Ahrām al-Iqtisādī,* February 1, 1980. See also *al-Ahrām al-Iqtisādī* 537 (January 1, 1978) and "A Quarter Century of Archives on the Housing Crisis," *al-Ahrām al-Iqtisādī,* 540 (February 15, 1978); Milād Hanna, *I Want a Home: A Problem with a Solution,* (Cairo: Rūz al-Yūsuf Press, 1978): USAID and Ministries of Housing and Reconstruction, and Planning, *Immediate Action Proposals,* Statistical Appendix, p. 54; John Waterbury, "Housing and Shelter" in Waterbury, *Egypt,* pp. 177–198.

25. Ministry of Housing, "Facing Housing's Problems," p. 27.

26. John Waterbury, "Housing and Shelter," *Egypt,* p. 182.

27. CAPMS, *Preliminary Results of the 1976 Population and Housing Census,* mimeographed, (in English), table 22.

28. *Al-Ahrām* (July 14, 1973).

29. *Al-Ahrām al-Iqtisādī* 553 (September 1, 1978).

30. Milād Hanna, *I Want a Home,* pp. 90–100.

31. Ibid, p. 31.

32. For example, see Lutfī al-Khūlī, "These Are the Bayyumis," *al-Talī ʿa* 11, no. 1 (January 1975).

33. *Al-Ahrām* (December 27, 1978).

34. "Housing Coops Convert to Land Speculation," *Rūz al-Yūsuf* 2645 (February 19, 1979).

# CHAPTER 11

# *Educational Expansion and Income Distribution in Egypt, 1952–1977**

Mahmoud Abdel-Fadil

The goal of educational policy in most developing countries is usually twofold[1]: to promote economic growth by wiping out illiteracy and upgrading technical skills, and to promote equality of educational opportunities among people over time.

From the income distribution viewpoint, the importance of educational expansion lies precisely in the fact that it can be one of the most important vehicles for increasing the degree of *intergenerational* economic and social mobility in a society, for education provides individuals with extra earning power and enables them to move up the social ladder.

The main thrust of this chapter is to assess the likely impact of the process of educational expansion on income distribution in Egypt over the period 1952–1977. We shall, however, confine our analysis to the examination of some crucial aspects of the relationship between the expansion of formal education and the changes in income distribution in Egypt during the period under investigation.

## I. Global and Structural Trends in the Expansion of Egypt's Formal Educational System

Formal education in Egypt encompasses a complex of primary, secondary, and vocational schools as well as technical institutes, colleges, and universities. Such a system is geared to certificates, diplomas, and degrees; and success at each educational level is measured by passing tests and gaining access to the next level. In Egypt, as in most developing countries, the orientation of formal education is toward more education,

*I would like to thank Dr. Ibrahim Saad Eddine and Dr. Nader Fergany of the Arab Planning Institute (Kuwait), Dr. Gouda Abdel-Khalek of the Faculty of Economics and Politics (Cairo University), Dr. Saad Eddin Ibrahim (of the American University—Cairo), and Professor Robert Tignor (of Princeton University) for extensive and helpful comments on an earlier draft of this paper. I am also greatly indebted to many colleagues and participants of the Luxor Conference (January 1979) and Lisbon Conference (October–November 1979) for their constructive criticism and advice.

as entry into and completion of higher education are the supreme goals that dominate the entire formal educational system.[2]

The development of Egypt's educational system since 1952 was marked by an extraordinary expansion of educational opportunities at all levels. Throughout the 1950s and the 1960s, education received sizeable resources, and the number of students in all stages grew at an unprecedented pace. The expansionary trends in the educational process reflected the new role assigned to the formal educational system in Nasser's Egypt as a major vehicle to achieve a greater degree of equalization of economic and social opportunities.

Nasser expressed his views on this matter, in one of his major speeches, in the following terms:

> I want a society in which class distinctions are dissolved through the equality of opportunities to all citizens. I want a society in which the free individual can determine his own position by himself, on the basis of his efficiency, capacity and character.[3]

As a result, levels of enrollment in schools, as well as the scale of government spending for education, showed substantial increase. In fact, current government expenditure for education has grown from about £E23 million in 1952–1953 (less than 3 percent of Gross Domestic Product [GDP]) to about £E130 million in 1970–1971 (about 4.1 percent of GDP).[4] Capital expenditure has also shown remarkable growth, from £E2.5 million in the first year of the Revolution to £E9.9 million in 1970–1971.

Strenuous efforts were made under the Nasser regime to provide every child with a *primary education,* and the number of pupils enrolled in the primary stage rose from 1.5 million in the school year 1952/1953 to 2.7 million in 1960/1961 and to 3.7 million in 1970/1971. Nevertheless, while the primary stage was supposed to be free and compulsory for all children between the ages of six and twelve, the universalization of primary education was far from achieved.[5]

The pruning usually begins at the *preparatory stage,* when the numbers of students are reduced to about one-fourth, and the students are groomed for either the general secondary schools—paving the way to the university—or for vocational training schools and teacher training institutes. It was estimated that only 40 percent of the pupils who finish the first six years of primary education are permitted to go on to secondary schools.[6]

Over the period 1951 and 1961, the total number of students enrolled in secondary schools rose by about one third, from 92,062 to 124,607, whereas the numbers of students attending secondary-level industrial, commercial, and agricultural schools almost *quintupled,* from 14,356 to 67,895. By the end of the 1960s the number of students enrolled in secondary schools had more than doubled, rising to 298,000, and the number of students receiving technical training quadrupled to 24,159.[7]

It is estimated that only between 10 and 15 percent of pupils who begin

*TABLE 11.1.*
*The Growth in the Numbers of Pupils and Students per Thousand of Egypt's Population at all Educational Levels (1952–1972)*

| *Educational Level* | *No. of Students per Thousand of Population in 1952* | *No. of Students per Thousand of Population in 1972* | *Percentage Increase* |
|---|---|---|---|
| 1. Primary education | 47.0 | 110.0 | 234 |
| 2. General preparatory education | 16.0 | 31.0 | 194 |
| 3. General secondary education | 4.3 | 9.6 | 223 |
| 4. Vocational secondary education* | 0.8 | 9.0 | 1,125 |
| 5. Higher education | 2.4 | 7.8 | 325 |

SOURCE: Yūsuf Khalīl Yūsuf, *The Main Events in the Educational Sector of Egypt: 1952–1975* (Cairo: National Council for Education, Scientific Research, and Technology, August 1975) (in Arabic).

*Covers all types and branches of vocational secondary education (commercial, industrial, agricultural).

the twelve-year school cycle emerge with a secondary school certificate qualifying them for university education. The four major universities in Egypt (Cairo, Alexandria, ᶜAin-Shams, and Asyūt) enrolled 34,842 students in 1950/1951, 77,087 in 1957/1958, and 152,282 in 1970/1971. In the 1970/1971 academic year, 36,414 additional students were attending higher institutes of various types, and another 23,741 students were studying at Al-Azhar (Islamic University), thus making a grand total of 212,437 students.[8]

The whole process of educational expansion in Egypt over the period 1952–1972 may be summarized with reference to a simple *normalized* indicator, namely, the growth in the numbers of pupils and students per thousand of Egypt's population at each educational level, as shown in table 11.1.

We can still gain a better insight into the dynamic features of the process of educational expansion in Egypt from an income distribution point of view by tracing the evolution of the gross enrollment ratios[9] over the period 1950–1975 as shown in table 11.2.

It is easy to see that the number of enrollments at all levels of education has risen tremendously. Nonetheless, it is equally easy to deduce that the process of educational expansion was highly *skewed* in favor of secondary and higher educational levels. This makes the history of educational expansion during the period under review (1952–1977) a history of *unbalanced growth.*

Moreover, the explosion in enrollments that has taken place since 1952

*TABLE 11.2.*
*Number of Students and Enrollment Patterns at Different Educational Levels (1950–1975)*

| Reference Years | Number of Students Enrolled (thousands) | | | Gross Enrollment Ratios (percent) | | |
|---|---|---|---|---|---|---|
| | First Level* | Second Level† | Third Level‡ | First Level | Second Level | Third Level |
| 1950 | 1,310 | 500 | 34 | 41 | 17 | n.a. |
| 1955 | 1,869 | 554 | 67 | 52 | 16 | n.a. |
| 1960 | 2,663 | 594 | 107 | 66 | 16 | 4.9 |
| 1965 | 3,498 | 1,020 | 175 | 75 | 26 | 6.8 |
| 1970 | 3,795 | 1,507 | 233 | 69 | 32 | 7.9 |
| 1975 | 4,121 | 2,108 | 455 | 72 | 40 | 12.5 |
| Corresponding Enrollment Ratios in Western Europe (1975) | | | | 96 | 80 | 25.5 |

SOURCES: UNESCO, *Statistical Yearbook,* various issues; as quoted in Nādir Farjūmī, "Human Resources in Egypt, 1952–1977," (paper, Cairo, June 1978) (in Arabic).

**First level* covers the primary stage (6–<12 years).
†*Second level* covers both the preparatory and secondary stages (12–<18 years).
‡*Third level* covers the cycle of higher education (18–<22 years).

occurred with little attention to existing manpower and physical facilities, so that serious imbalances between training facilities and needs have been common throughout the period under review. The crisis was particularly acute at the primary level, as about 60 percent of primary schools operate on a multishift basis, with insufficient textbooks and materials.[10]

As a result, *overcrowding* continued to be a serious problem throughout the entire educational system in Egypt as can be seen from an increasing average-students' density for class, as shown in table 11.3. The problem seems to be particularly acute in the primary and preparatory cycles. At the university level, the rapid expansion of university education has frequently been at the expense of academic standards. It is estimated that

*TABLE 11.3.*
*The Evolution of Average Pupil Density per Class at Different Educational Levels (Selected Years)*

| Educational Level | No. of pupils per class 1946/1947 | No. of pupils per class 1953/1954 | No. of pupils per class 1973/1974 |
|---|---|---|---|
| 1. Primary | 33.2 | 39.5 | 41.5 |
| 2. General preparatory | n.a. | 36.2 | 40.4 |
| 3. General secondary | 31.1 | 33.7 | 38.2 |

SOURCE: Ministry of Education, unpublished report.

universities, of which there are now ten, enroll on average about four times their intended student capacity, with the highest ratios in the arts, law, and commerce.[11]

On the whole, and apart from the prevailing distortions in the enrollment patterns, Egypt's educational system continues to retain a strong bias toward an academic education with an overemphasis on formal examinations and paper qualifications.[12] This is further strengthened by the government policies linking secure employment opportunities to paper qualifications and formal examinations. In short, Egypt's formal educational system may be regarded, to use Professor F. H. Harbison's metaphor, as a "giant sorting machine which determines access to position of status, wealth and power."[13]

## II. Educational Expansion and Social Selectivity

Linking educational policy to class structure in a certain society presents an interesting line of investigation.[14] This is particularly important for understanding the influence of economic power and class structure on the pattern of receipt of benefits from the process of educational expansion in Less Developed Countries (LDCs). Hence the most pertinent question to ask in this context is: which classes manage to get their children educated, and up to what level, so that they can get access to better earning opportunities in the future?

The class bias of the educational system in Egypt manifests itself in various respects. One important aspect relates to the high *dropout* rates in primary and preparatory schools. For, in the conditions of poverty and large-size families, one would expect that the pupil would find his parents, not only unable to support him for a much longer period than the initial six years of compulsory education, but also in need of his financial contribution to support the rest of the family. The pupil will, therefore, have to discontinue his education and look for a minor job to earn his living.

The *dropout rates* in the primary cycle of education have ranged between 19.4 percent and 23 percent over the period 1963/1964 and 1969/1970.[15] One further evidence in support of our conjecture is the fact that the dropout rate in primary education has reached a particularly high level in some poor Upper Egypt governorates (41 percent in al-Minyā and Asyūt, 38 percent in Sūhāj).[16]

In the light of the available sociological and economic evidence in many LDCs, Professor Jagdish Bhagwati was able to find support to the notion that the lowest-income groups typically have not been able to have the same effective access to primary education as the higher-income groups because, for them, (1) the opportunity cost (of labor) of primary education is higher; (2) the benefit from primary education is lower; (3) the private rate of return to them from such education is, therefore, lower. These three factors contribute to high dropout rates and low enrollments of such children in primary education.[17]

*TABLE 11.4.*

*The Size of Private Education as Compared with Government Education in Egypt, 1976/1977*

| | *(A) Primary Education* | | | *(B) Preparatory Education* | | | *(C) General Secondary Education* | | |
|---|---|---|---|---|---|---|---|---|---|
| | *Government (numbers)* | *Private (numbers)* | *Private as Percentage of Total* | *Government (numbers)* | *Private (numbers)* | *Private as Percentage of Total* | *Government (numbers)* | *Private (numbers)* | *Private as Percentage of Total* |
| 1. Number of schools | 9,697 | 303 | 3.0 | 1,578 | 242 | 13.8 | 323 | 121 | 27.2 |
| 2. Total class rooms | 96,368 | 5,267 | 5.2 | 28,141 | 7,747 | 21.6 | 7,718 | 2,139 | 21.7 |
| 3. Enrollment (thousands) | 3,940 | 212 | 5.1 | 1,134 | 302 | 21.0 | 302 | 91 | 23.1 |
| 4. Teachers | 120,985 | 5,412 | 4.3 | 33,402 | 11,427 | 34.2 | 15,702 | 1,835 | 10.5 |

SOURCE: Computed from Ministry of Education, Statistical Department, *Statement of Total Number of Schools, Classes, Pupils, Teachers, at the Different Stages and Kinds of Education, 1975/1977.*

The class bias of Egypt's educational system is also reflected in the students' performance in the General Secondary Certificate Examination (GSCE) taken at the end of high school, as one's score largely determines which, if any, university faculty one can enter. Data drawn from a sample survey of secondary schools conducted in 1966 indicated that lower-class students were significantly less likely to get good grades than upper-class students,[18] for most of the GSCE students need extra tutoring at home (which only the well-to-do can afford) to perform reasonably well in the final examinations.

On the other hand, the influence of economic power and class structure on the receipt of benefits from the educational process is most institutionalized in Egypt's *dual* educational system, for in Egypt, as in many developing countries, a fully subsidized *public* education sector coexists with a *private* educational sector. In general, publicly subsidized schools, which charge no or very small fees,[19] tend to recruit a student body whose social composition is biased in favor of low-income groups. Conversely, expensive private *elite* schools tend to cater to the needs of high-income groups.

In this respect, it is significant to note that, far from declining, private education in Egypt (and, in particular, private foreign language schools) has grown over the years. In fact, the number of pupils enrolled in preparatory private schools grew from 277,000 in 1965/1966 to 302,000 in 1976/1977, and the number of pupils enrolled in *secondary* private schools grew from 55,000 in 1965/1966 to 91,000 in 1976/1977. Thus, private schooling becomes more significant as one climbs the educational ladder.

While it may be suggested that the presence of a strong and expanding private education sector may help to achieve equity in the provision of education, as the rich pay their way through educational systems, one is more inclined to think that such pronounced "duality" in Egypt's educational system (see table 11.4) is likely to have very serious adverse effects on long-term (intergenerational) equity. For, as soon as the full cost of educational services is charged to some groups, incentives to acquire the most *common* type of education will disappear altogether.[20] Investors in education will then gather together according to their ability to pay and foster differentiation of the *educational product,* as those with the highest purchasing power will be looking for the best service and those with a lower purchasing power will go for cheaper and inferior educational products.[21]

Thus the high degree of privatization and commercialization of educational services in Egypt tend to foster *long-term* income disparities, especially if the size of returns to different qualities of education is positively associated with the increasing importance of the private finance component in educational cost especially under the new open-door policy.

## III. Income Distribution Effects of Higher Education

Of great relevance to our present investigation is the question of the income-distribution effects of higher education. This applies to the effects of higher-education spending and finance on both the intra- and intergenerational distribution of income.

There are two basic competing hypotheses concerning the effect of government education spending and finance on income distribution. One hypothesis is that public spending on higher education leads to income redistribution in favor of the poor. The alternative hypothesis is that the middle class (or stratum) effectively uses university education as an instrument of upward social and occupational mobility. These two hypotheses apply to the effects of higher-education spending and finance on the size and distribution of income within a generation and to the effects upon movement between (relative) income classes between generations.

The primary purpose of this section is to investigate empirically the income-distribution effects of spending on higher education—post-secondary levels of education in the Egyptian case.[22]

### *Higher Education and Career Prospects*

Admission to the higher education system in Egypt is highly competitive, as the main criterion is performance on written examinations at the end of the secondary cycle. There is a heavy demand for higher education relative to available places because of the high social status usually associated with such a type of education. Middle-class values rather than "pure money income" prospects may explain much about the job expectations of university graduates in Egypt.

This tendency—which reflects the legacy of colonialism—is further reinforced by the fact that, in the 1950s and 1960s, while secondary-school leavers took three to four years to find a permanent job, a university graduate was almost guaranteed a white-collar job within a maximum of two years of his graduation. Moreover, as far as promotional opportunities are concerned, it usually took a secondary school leaver ten to twelve years on average to reach the seventh grade in the civil service, the level a university graduate achieves after four successful years of higher education. It is, therefore, easy to understand the strong urge to acquire more formal education, which ignores the pattern of macroeconomic needs for particular types of occupations or different categories of skill.[23]

The vicious circle that exists between formal education and bureaucratic advancement may be further illustrated by the fact that the prospects of promotion for holders of the secondary-school certificate stops at the fourth grade; only those with university and higher qualifications can go beyond the third grade, which marks the frontier of the top specialized and administrative posts held by the *bureaucratic elites*.[24]

TABLE 11.5.
*Father's Occupation of the Educated in Public Employment, 1962*

| *Father's Occupation* | *People with Higher Education (percent)* | *People with Secondary Education (percent)* |
|---|---|---|
| Business | 30.8 | 33.5 |
| Liberal professions | 26.9 | 17.7 |
| Clerical work | 2.7 | 18.0 |
| Salaried technical work | 4.1 | 12.7 |
| Higher administrative posts | 3.9 | 0.8 |
| Science and engineering | 2.3 | 0.7 |
| Manual work | 1.4 | 2.8 |
| Other occupations | 27.9 | 13.8 |

SOURCE: Institute of National Planning, *Research Project on Employment and Unemployment among the Educated—Final Report* (Cairo, 1963), p. 27.

### *Students' Socioeconomic Background: Interuniversity and Interfaculty*

The large private benefits that accrue to those who receive higher education raise the question of the socioeconomic background of the students who receive the highest rewards.

One of the major lacunae of the Egyptian data on education is the availability of information on the socioeconomic background of the students who receive higher education. However, we can make use of some reliable information on the profession of the father of the educated persons in public employment based on a sample survey conducted by the Cairo Institute of National Planning in 1962. The basic findings of this study are reported in table 11.5, which clearly shows the differential socioeconomic background of the recipients of higher and secondary education in the early 1960s.

Another sample survey conducted on 475 students of Cairo University and 175 students of al-Azhar University, carried out in 1966 by an investigating team from the National Center for Social and Criminological Research in Cairo (NCSCR)[25] pointed to the extent to which university education (with the unique exception of al-Azhar University) was still largely confined to offspring of the privileged socioeconomic elites in the Egyptian society, despite the emphasis of the Nasser regime upon democratization in education.

Furthermore, a higher percentage of the students of the prestigious faculties (medicine, engineering, economics and political science), which require higher grades for admission (and which lead to prestigious professions), tend to come from urban, upper-middle-class families. Data drawn from a sample survey conducted in the spring and summer of 1973,[26] indicated that the urban bourgeoisie and elements of the old landed aristocracy dominate the engineering profession in Egypt.

*TABLE 11.6.*
*Class Origins of Subsamples of Professional Engineers, Engineering & Law Students, 1973*

| *Father's Profession** | *Professional Engineers (percent)* | *Engineering Students (percent)* | *Law Students (percent)* |
|---|---|---|---|
| **Urban** | | | |
| Unemployed, proletariat, and subproletariat | 2.8 | 9.2 | 9.6 |
| Clerks | 10.0 | 5.9 | 10.6 |
| Traditional entrepreneurs | 9.7 | 7.6 | 11.7 |
| Middle-level cadres | 26.8 | 18.5 | 17.0 |
| Bourgeoisie and aristocracy | 40.1 | 49.6 | 33.0 |
| **Rural** | | | |
| Small and landless peasants | 2.6 | 7.6 | 7.5 |
| Rich peasants and rural capitalists | 8.0 | 1.6 | 10.7 |
| | 100 | 100 | 100 |
| (Total Number) | (351) | (119) | (94) |

SOURCE: C. H. Moore, *The Class Origins of Egyptian Engineer-Technocrats*, table 1.

*Where, for instance, should one place the respondent who said his father was a civil servant? If he also indicated his father had held a *high* position and was economically well off or comfortable, he was placed in the urban bourgeoisie. If the father did not hold a high post but was economically well off, he was placed with the middle-level cadres. Otherwise, he was placed with the clerks. Or, again, take the person who says his father was a proprietor. If he was urban and comfortably off, he was placed with the bourgeoisie. If not well off, he was placed with the traditional entrepreneurs. The son of a "peasant" who was urban and rich, on the other hand, was placed with the urban bourgeoisie and landed aristocracy, and so forth.

Comparison between engineering and law students suggests that the upper strata in Egyptian society are also the most capable of taking advantage of the good career opportunities offered by the engineering studies, while the sons of clerks and middle landholders are slightly more likely to go into law studies (see table 11.6).

However small—and suspect—the sample size is in the survey cited, the broad fact remains that the children of the relatively well-to-do tend to get an exclusive hold on the places in prestigious faculties such as engineering and medicine, more than do the children of poorer families,[27] for the graduates of engineering and medicine studies have an increasing chance to achieve higher future monetary income than other recipients of higher education.

### *The Incidence of Public Spending on Higher Education*

Egypt's higher education system is funded almost entirely by the government. Consequently, in order to determine the incidence of public spending on higher education, we must examine the distribution of the tax burden implicit in government subsidy to education. This should allow us to see more clearly how the mechanism of interaction between the class bias in the distribution of benefits from higher education and educational expenditures is affecting income inequality in Egypt.

Professor Bhagwati put forward the following hypothesis:

> For each class of education, the State [in capitalist LDCs] will subsidize the cost of education; the benefits of these subsidies will accrue disproportionately less to the poorer groups at each level of education; the higher the educational level being considered, the higher will be the average income-level of the groups to which the students belong; *and the rate of governmental subsidization to higher education will be greater than that to primary education.*[28]

This hypothesis is based on the view that the pattern of governmental subsidization of education will reflect the class bias in society, since the middle- and higher-income groups are likely to benefit disproportionately more from higher education and the masses disproportionately more from primary education.

The hypothesis of increasing rates of subsidization by level of education fits well the Egyptian case, as the state subsidy via education would be greater for those attending higher education than for primary, preparatory, and secondary education (see tables 11.7, 11.8).

In assessing the equitability of government spending on higher education, at least three criteria need to be distinguished[29]:

1. *The equal-opportunity criterion.* By this criterion, a fiscal program is equitable if different socioeconomic groups in the population have access to the program in proportion to their numbers in the population, irrespective of the costs paid by the different groups in relation to benefits received.
2. *The cost-benefit criterion.* By this criterion, a fiscal program is equitable if the costs paid by different socioeconomic groups in the population are proportional to the benefits they each receive, irrespective of access to the program.
3. *The ability-to-pay criterion.* By this criterion, a program is equitable if the cost-benefit ratio of the program rises as a function of income.

All three criteria apply vertically (for comparisons across income classes). Nonetheless, the equal-opportunity criterion refers primarily to *inter*generational distributional effects, whereas the other two are primarily *intra*generational.[30]

By the first criterion, Egypt's higher education system is inequitable intergenerationally, since those who receive higher education benefits are disproportionately the children of the well-to-do, whether measured by income class or various indices of socioeconomic status.

But in order to use the ability-to-pay criterion to judge the equitability of government spending on higher education, we may adopt the simplify-

TABLE 11.7.
*Development of Unit Costs per Pupil by Level of Education, Selected Years*

| Type of Education | Unit Cost (at Current Prices) per Pupil* (£E) 1961/1962 | 1966/1967 | 1973/1974 |
|---|---|---|---|
| **General Education** | | | |
| Primary | 9.97 | 11.74 | 13.81 |
| General preparatory | 29.25 | 30.29 | 30.06 |
| General secondary | 40.56 | 48.94 | 54.20 |
| **Technical Secondary Education** | | | |
| Industrial | 64.66 | 84.01 | 77.91 |
| Agricultural | 56.64 | 77.77 | 86.90 |
| Commercial | 44.69 | 34.22 | 42.84 |

SOURCE: Ministry of Education Department of Statistics, unpublished report based on the final account of the State Budget (Cairo, June 1975) (in Arabic).
*Refers only to public recurrent education expenditure.

ing assumption that each person's (or household's) contribution to the finance of higher education, within a certain income bracket, is equal to his average tax bill multiplied by the fraction of the government budget that is spent on higher education. It becomes clear then that families whose children receive university education are subsidized by the other families whose children are not educated at this level.

It is a well-known fact that different households pay different proportions of their income in tax, depending on their level of income, household

TABLE 11.8.
*Annual Recurrent Public Expenditure per Student in the Various Faculties of University Education, 1961*

| Faculty | £E | Differential Cost Coefficient |
|---|---|---|
| Faculty of Commerce | 37.4 | 1.0 |
| Faculty of Law | 40.7 | 1.1 |
| Faculty of Arts | 51.5 | 1.4 |
| Faculty of Engineering | 101.0 | 2.7 |
| Faculty of Agriculture | 136.6 | 3.6 |
| Faculty of Medicine | 145.7 | 3.9 |
| Faculty of Pharmacy | 163.2 | 3.4 |
| Faculty of Science | 165.8 | 4.4 |

SOURCE: Amir Boktor, *The Development and Expansion of Education in the U.A.R.* (Cairo: The American University in Cairo Press, 1963), p. 114.

circumstances, and expenditure patterns. Most households pay tax on personal incomes from formal employment and from other sources, and all households pay indirect taxes on many of the goods and services they purchase. The information collected in Family Budget Surveys gives details of expenditure patterns on the basis of which the indirect taxes paid can be estimated.

In order to estimate the distribution of tax burdens by various income groups, Dr. M. R. El-Edel, in his attempt to assess the impact of taxation on income distribution in Egypt,[31] adopted a number of simplifying assumptions, namely:

(i) All *indirect* taxes are shifted forward to final consumer in full;
(ii) *Direct* taxes on different types of entrepreneural income (industrial and commerical profits, income from movable property, and income from liberal professions, as well as the social insurance contributions of private and public business enterprises) are assumed to be fully shifted to the final consumer;
(iii) All *personal* direct taxes such as taxes on wages and salaries, general income tax, employees contributions to social insurance, inheritance taxes, are borne totally by the legal taxpayer (no forward shifting).

The main findings of Dr. El-Edel's paper concerning the overall tax burdens (effective tax rates)[32] by different expenditure brackets are summarized in table 11.9 for the three reference years: 1958/1959, 1964/1965 and 1974/1975.

According to the estimated effective tax rates shown in table 11.9, the overall degree of progressiveness of the whole tax structure in Egypt is found to be rather mild. For while the upper-income groups (over £E600 per annum) seem to be more heavily taxed than the lower-income groups, the effective tax burdens (gross and net) tend to remain almost constant over a wide range of the middle-income classes: (£E150–600) in 1958/1959; (£E150–900) in 1964/1965; and a narrower range (£E200–300) in 1974/1975.

The whole picture of the estimated distribution pattern of tax burden (gross and net) for the three reference years under consideration is depicted in figure 11.1. It comes out quite neatly, from this figure, that *food subsidy* played a larger role in 1974/1975 than it did in 1964/1965, and in 1964/1965 as compared to 1958/1959 to improve the overall degree of progressiveness of the distribution pattern of tax burdens. However, it may be observed that the distribution pattern of tax burdens in Egypt is marked by a rather steep increase in tax burdens at low levels of incomes (up to £E250), but the increase in the tax burdens becomes much milder at medium and high levels of incomes. This introduces certain elements of "regressivity" in the distribution pattern of tax burdens in Egypt.

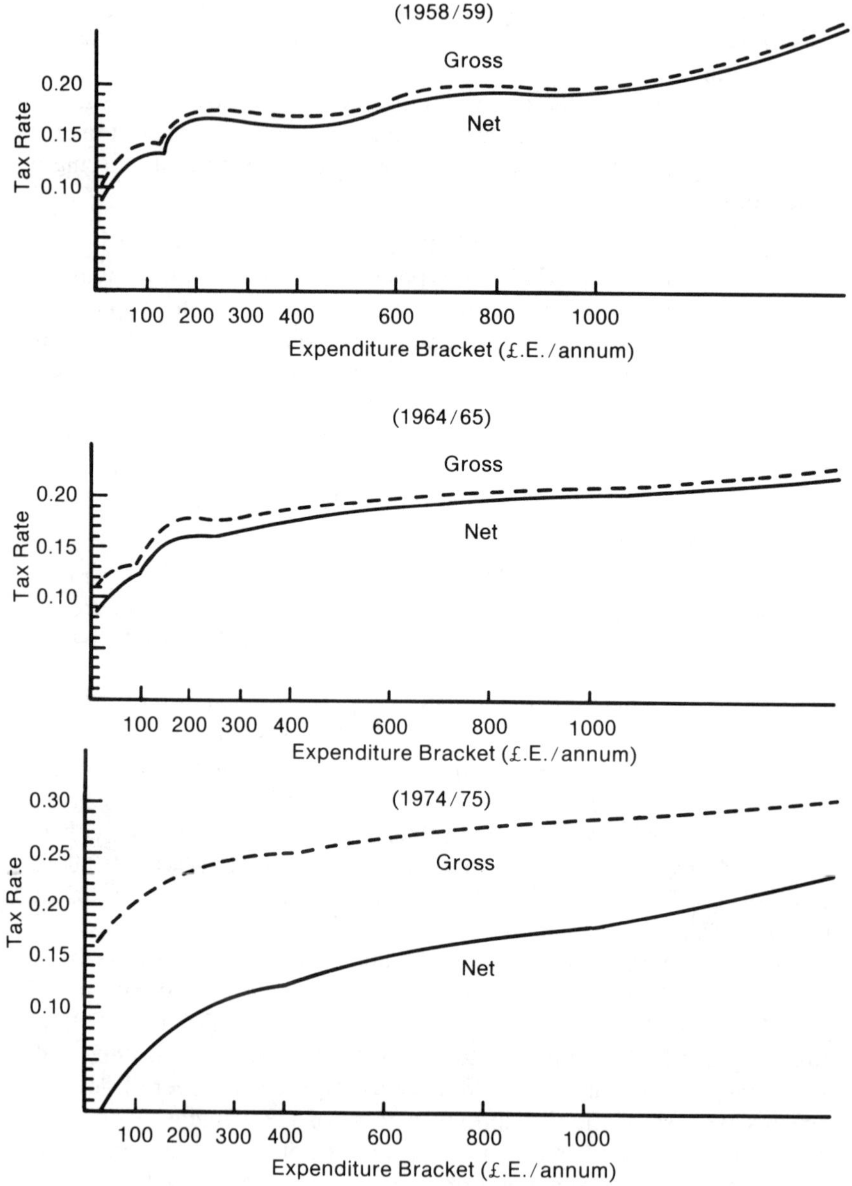


*FIGURE 11.1.*
*Effective Tax Rates by Different Expenditure Groups*

*TABLE 11.9.*
*Effective Tax Rates by Different Expenditure Groups, Selected Years*

| *Expenditure Brackets (£E per annum)* | *1958/1959* | | *1964/1965* | | *1974/1975* | |
|---|---|---|---|---|---|---|
| | *Gross Tax Rates (percent)* | *Net Tax Rates* (percent)* | *Gross Tax Rates (percent)* | *Net Tax Rates (percent)* | *Gross Tax Rates (percent)* | *Net Tax Rates (percent)* |
| 0–< 25 | 0.099 | 0.086 | 0.106 | 0.085 | 0.161 (0–<50) | −0.0002 (0–<50) |
| 25–< 50 | 0.124 | 0.112 | 0.121 | 0.103 | | |
| 50–< 75 | 0.135 | 0.124 | 0.130 | 0.113 | 0.183 | 0.026 |
| 75–< 100 | 0.141 | 0.129 | 0.131 | 0.123 | 0.202 | 0.050 |
| 100–< 150 | 0.143 | 0.132 | 0.163 | 0.147 | 0.222 | 0.077 |
| 150–< 200 | 0.174 | 0.164 | 0.177 | 0.160 | 0.226 | 0.084 |
| 200–< 250 | 0.174 | 0.165 | 0.176 | 0.162 | 0.245 | 0.110 |
| 250–< 300 | 0.175 | 0.166 | 0.178 | 0.165 | 0.249 | 0.119 |
| 300–< 400 | 0.171 | 0.161 | 0.186 | 0.173 | 0.252† | 0.125† |
| 400–< 600 | 0.174 | 0.166 | 0.194 | 0.183 | 0.269† | 0.153† |
| 600–< 800 | 0.197 | 0.191 | 0.205 | 0.196 | 0.279 | 0.172 |
| 800–<1,000 | 0.199 | 0.193 | 0.209 | 0.200 | 0.282 | 0.181 |
| ≥1,000 | 0.259 | 0.254 | 0.231 | 0.224 | 0.310† | 0.231 |

SOURCE: M. R. El-Edel, "Impact of Taxation on Income Distribution," tables.

*By deducting the subsidy benefits received by each expenditure group from the *gross* tax burden of the group, we get the *net* tax burden.

†Refer to the fact that data for tax rates corresponding to expenditure classes 300–<400, 400–<600, and ≥1,000 are simple averages for intervening classes.

According to both the ability-to-pay criterion, and the cost-benefit criterion, it seems clear that middle-class families whose children receive university education are subsidized by both the *low-income families* whose children are not educated at this level, and by the *high-income group* who shoulder a high tax burden relative to income received.[33]

At any rate, it is important to stress the fact that the increasing proportion of government resources that went into expanding the top end of the educational system under Nasser enabled a sizeable fraction of the lower-income groups to educate their children so as to have access to the white-collar jobs reserved for the better educated. In other words, the process of high education subsidization under Nasser helped, despite its class bias, to generate a greater sense of social and economic mobility in the Egyptian society and hence of equity than would otherwise have obtained under the *ancien regime* before the Revolution.

## IV. The Overall Dynamic Relationship between Education and Income Distribution

The period 1956–1970 witnessed a marked process of bureaucratic expansion and a pronounced differentiation in the white-collar occupational categories. For those without access to educational and formal training facilities—that is, the unskilled and the uneducated—the low probability of improving their status and income was in marked contrast with the unusual opportunities open to educated elites and skilled people.

Free public education under Nasser, in a world of unequal incomes, did not mean complete equalization of educational opportunities in the Egyptian society, for students from rich and middle-class backgrounds tended to remain much longer in the educational system than the poor, as the financial and other obstacles to the latter's enrollments were never completely removed.

The generalization of compulsory primary education, together with the diversification of educational opportunities, was designed to spread the educational benefits to the low-income groups. In this regard, it is probably fair to contend that the process of educational expansion under Nasser paved the way for a better distribution of educational opportunities at the bottom of the social ladder.

As a matter of fact, the middle class in Egypt was able effectively to use the higher education system as an instrument of upward social and income mobility. This is witnessed by the importance granted by this social group to university and para-university education (the expanding network of high institutes). In other words, members of the Egyptian middle class were able to maximize their *private returns* through the process of educational expansion while the society as a whole failed to maximize and internalize the *social returns* expected from the process of educational expansion, for instead of providing proper training, which prepares people for more productive high-level work, the expansion of university places sometimes has served as little more than a means of granting the certificates needed to enter the best white-collar jobs.

In the case of Nasser's Egypt, there are good reasons to believe that the expansion of the educational system—and in particular higher education—has been instrumental in enhancing the process of upward social mobility especially in urban areas. This is borne out by indicators on social mobility derived from the Cairo sample survey carried out by Dr. Saad Eddin Ibrahim in 1979. As chapter 12 of this book shows, among three generations—father, respondent, and son—the middle generation enjoyed greater mobility (mostly upward) than did the younger, present generation.

This can be easily gleaned from the following data based on the Cairo Sample Survey:

*TABLE 11.10.*
*Educational Mobility in Cairo*

| | *Generation* | | |
|---|---|---|---|
| *Level of Education* | *I* *Fathers* *(%)* | *II* *Respondents* *(%)* | *III* *Sons* *(%)* |
| Secondary | 4.7 | 16.4 | 34.7 |
| College | 4.4 | 15.1 | 16.3 |
| Postgraduate | 0.6 | 1.6 | 2.1 |
| Total | 9.7 | 33.1 | 53.1 |

SOURCE: Saad Eddin Ibrahim, "Social Mobility and Income Distribution," chapter 12, pp. 410–411 of this book.

It is clear that the middle generation (II) has nearly quadrupled its percentage in secondary and college education *vis-à-vis* generation I (their fathers). On the other hand, generation III (the sons) only doubled its percentage of secondary education and slightly increased its college and postgraduate education *vis-à-vis* generation II. The middle generation (II) was occupationally placed in the 1950s and early 1960s, the younger one (III) in the late 1960s and 1970s.[34]

As Dr. Saad Eddin Ibrahim rightly observed, "Egypt's stratification system reached its maximum fluidity from the mid-1950s to the mid-1960s. Along with ambitious programs in education and industrialization, and with bold socialist policies of equalizing opportunities, the Egyptian society witnessed more social mobility than in any single decade in this century."[35]

On the other hand, the government policies in the 1960s have locked the economy into a vicious circle, in which high expectations of a white-collar job in the civil service and the public sector influenced demand for higher education and thus increased the supply of those who seek a white-collar job in government service.[36] As a result, a new type of structural unemployment has developed, because the expansion of the educational system has outrun the capacity of the economy to provide the sort of jobs that those with secondary-school and university qualifications feel they are entitled to expect—broadly speaking, office jobs.[37]

In other words, there exist important surpluses of certain types of educated manpower that reflect the failure of the educational system to respond fully to the requirements of the economy and its development; for while it is broadly true that *open* unemployment among educated manpower almost disappeared by the mid-1960s, this was achieved at the cost of increasing underemployment and disguised unemployment among the educated in the government sector.[38]

From a developmental viewpoint, one is inclined to think that the gov-

*TABLE 11.11.*
*Pattern of Income Distribution in Egypt according to Educational Status (1974)*

| *Educational Status* / *Annual Income (£E)* | *Illiterate* | *Read and Write* | *Below Intermediate Certificate* | *Intermediate Certificate* | *Above Intermediate Certificate* | *University* | *Postgraduate* |
|---|---|---|---|---|---|---|---|
| <250 | 63.98 | 38.71 | 21.92 | 20.09 | 10.35 | 0.62 | ... |
| 250–< 500 | 29.30 | 43.97 | 48.38 | 43.15 | 45.52 | 18.19 | 8.83 |
| 500–<1,000 | 6.01 | 14.48 | 24.44 | 29.24 | 35.40 | 49.88 | 30.14 |
| 1,000–2,000 | 0.43 | 2.25 | 4.14 | 5.88 | 8.74 | 25.59 | 40.70 |
| ⩾ 2,000 | 0.04 | 0.43 | 0.71 | 1.17 | 0.69 | 5.64 | 21.32 |
| Unclear | 0.23 | 0.14 | 0.40 | 0.48 | ... | 0.06 | ... |

SOURCE: Computed from *The Labor Force Sample Survey,* May Round 1974, (Cairo: CAPMS, 1976).

ernment educational policies during the period under investigation, by putting great emphasis on formal education, encouraged to some extent the diversion of labor from areas where it could have been more productively employed, namely, as technical and skilled workers in industry. For while a substantial number of university graduates (graduates in the humanities and social sciences) found themselves employed in jobs that could have been filled by people with far lower qualifications, it is reported that the annual flow of *technicians* does not exceed 1,800 people while the actual needs of the economy are estimated to be around 8,100 people per annum.[39] Equally, while the annual needs of the industrial sector are estimated to be around 59,300 *skilled workers,* the actual number of graduates of the industrial schools does not exceed 18,700 per annum.[40]

But in order to shed some light on the relationship between the *levels of educational attainment* and the *income earning capacity* in the Egyptian context, we draw upon the only official set of data derived from the 1974 Labor Force Sample Survey relating to the distribution of sample families according to educational status and level of personal income as shown in table 11.11.

In the light of the evidence given in this table, almost two-thirds of the *illiterates* have earnings of less than £E250 per annum, and the absolute majority (93 percent) earn less than £E500 per annum. Incomes of those *who can read and write,* although more concentrated in the £E250–<£E500 income bracket, are also characterized by the presence of a high percentage of those who earn less than £E250 per annum (39 percent).

Nonetheless, the most notable feature of the sample data presented in table 11.11 is that the differentiation by educational status among four

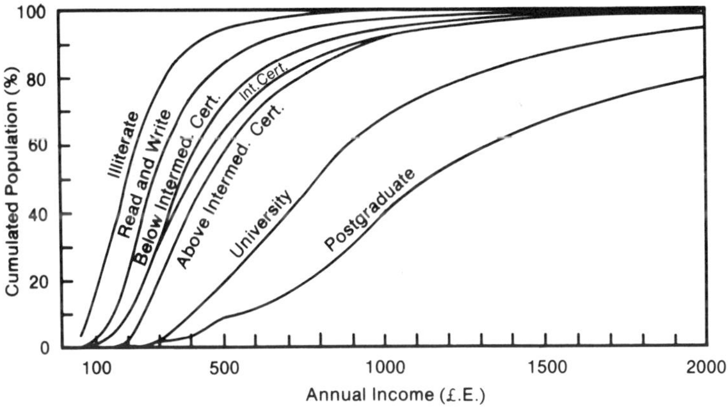


DATA SOURCE: Table 12

*FIGURE 11.2.*
*Egypt: Pattern of Distribution of Personal Income According to Educational Status (1974)*

groups—those who read and write, those with educational qualifications below the intermediate certificate, the holders of intermediate certificate, and those with education above intermediate certificate—*does not seem to be a crucial factor in determining their income-earning possibilities.* For almost 50 percent of the income recipients across the four educational groups fall within the income bracket of £E250–<£E500 per annum.

On the other hand, *university graduates* are more concentrated in the £E500–<£E1,000 income bracket. They are also characterized by a high percentage of income earners in the income class of £E1,000–<£E2,000, if compared with the pattern of income concentrations as observed in the three adjacent lower educational groups. The percentage of holders of university degrees in the top bracket (⩾£E2,000) is also higher than in the case of the three lower educational groups.

As for the holders of postgraduate degrees, it is quite clear that they have a significantly different pattern of income concentration with the highest concentration (41 percent) in the income brackets £E1,000–<£E2,000. Although a 30 percent concentration is observed in the £E500–<£E1,000 income bracket, it is worth noting that the percentage of top income recipients (⩾£E2,000 per year) among this group is significantly higher than the percentages observed in other groups of lower education. In fact, 21 percent of postgraduates earn more than £E2,000 per annum against only 6 percent for ordinary university graduates, and around 1 percent for holders of intermediary certificates.

On the whole, the role of education as a determining factor in shaping the pattern of income distribution comes out quite neatly in figure 11.2, which depicts the cumulative pattern of the distribution of personal income for people with different educational status as reported in May 1974.

It should be noted, however, that some observers contend that this picture might have changed in the second half of the 1970s under the vigorous pursuit of the new open-door policy, as higher education has become less significant in explaining and determining high-income-earning possibilities, especially for certain groups of earners such as artisans, skilled workers, and groups benefitting from different types of "business income."

Distributional data by occupational categories drawn from a national sample survey conducted in 1978,[41] tend to substantiate such impressionistic observations about the rising incomes of craftsmen and self-employed skilled labor (mechanics, carpenters, electricians, plumbers, and so forth), for respondents in these manual occupations reported, on the average, higher annual income than some of the white-collar and college-based occupations.

On the whole, the results of three sample surveys dealing with the relationship between *education* and *income,* and taken successively in 1974, 1978 and 1979 suggest that the association between the two variables is naturally positive, but education, at best, accounts for only 50 percent of the variance in income.[42]

From a longer-term point of view, an increase in the stock of human capital, all other things being equal, may well result in a lower rate of return to education.[43] This rests on the assumption that the ability of education to determine income tends to weaken as education becomes more and more widespread. However, the nature of the technology and the rate of growth of the economy could generate enough demand for educated manpower, which could keep pace with increased supply, thus maintaining the level of relative earnings.

Nonetheless, there is another relevant consideration in the case of Egypt: the extent to which certain sorts of educated manpower provide *tradable services,* for which there is an expanding Pan-Arab market. If that is the case (for doctors, engineers, accountants, and school teachers), even the emergence of excess supplies of educated manpower need not depress per se the earnings of the educated at home.

Finally, it is important to note that the heavy reliance of pupils enrolled in government schools on private tutoring, in response to the crowding of the public education system and the deteriorating quality of classroom teaching, amounts to a gradual but virtual "denationalization" of Egypt's public educational services.[44]

In fact, the issue of private tutoring is becoming an increasingly crucial factor in differentiating accesses to various educational levels. A recent sample survey conducted by the National Center for Sociological and Criminological Research in 1976 points to the crisis dimension assumed by the phenomenon of private tutoring.

*TABLE 11.12.*
*The Relationship between Family Income and the Ability to Pay for Private Tutoring for the Children, 1976*

| *Sampling districts* | | | |
|---|---|---|---|
| *Income (£E per month)* | *Greater Cairo (%)* | *Provinces (%)* | *Total (%)* |
| < 30 | 51 | 72 | 65 |
| 30–<60 | 76 | 62 | 68 |
| ⩾ 60 | 75 | 86 | 80 |

SOURCE: NCSCR, "Sample Survey on Private Tutoring," mineographed (Cairo, July 1978), table 20.

NOTE: The percentages represent the proportion of families *able* to provide private tutoring for their children at each income level.

The sample survey revealed that 63.5 percent of the heads of sampled families in Cairo and 71.7 percent of the sampled families in the provinces resort to private tutoring as a major device to educate their children. The survey also reveals that reliance on private tutoring is most crucial for *secondary education* in Cairo and for *primary education* in provinces, and especially in the final years of each cycle leading to a certificate in order to score the highest marks.

The ability to provide private tutoring for the children at the going rates greatly depends on the family income. This conjecture is strongly supported by the results of the NCSCR sample survey, as can be easily deduced from table 11.12.

This introduces a new dimension to the class bias already existing in Egypt's educational system.

Looking ahead at the future developments, and judging from policy statements made by President Sadat and other top officials, it seems that major changes in the future directions of educational policies in Egypt are likely to occur, the right "to get educated" and the right "to get employed" are going to be fully regulated through the market mechanism. This is likely to stimulate demand for the graduates (products) of private language schools, who are going to have an exclusive hold on certain types of privileged and highly paid jobs in the business sector. In other words, educational services will soon cease de facto to be a *public* good, thus resulting in adverse effects on income distribution in the future.

## Notes

1. Cf. S. Bowles, H. Gintis, and J. Simmons, "The Impact of Education on Poverty: The U.S. Experience," *International Development Review* 18, no. 2, (1976): 6.

2. For a further analysis of formal education systems in developing countries, see Fredrick H. Harbison, *Human Resources as the Wealth of Nations* (New York: Oxford University Press, 1973), chap. 3.

3. Speech delivered on October 16, 1961.

4. CAPMS (Central Agency for Public Mobilization and Statistics), *Statistical Yearbook,* various issues; and World Bank, *Arab Republic of Egypt: Economic Management in a Period of Transition,* Report no. 1815—EGT, vol. 2: *Human Resources* (Washington: May 8, 1978), p. 24.

5. See section 2 of this chapter.

6. Ministry of Education estimates.

7. J. S. Szyliowicz, *Education and Modernization in the Middle East* (Cornell University Press, 1973), pp. 268–269.

8. CAPMS, *Statistical Indicators for U.A.R.: 1952–70* (Cairo, July 1971), pp. 167–169.

9. The gross enrollment ratio may be defined for each educational level (or cycle) as follows:

$$\frac{\text{The number of pupils enrolled in each educational level}}{\text{Size of population in the corresponding age group}} \times 100$$

10. Cf. World Bank, Report no. 1815—EGT, vol. 2, p. 26.

11. Ibid., p. 27.

12. It should be noted, however, that the 1970s witnessed a substantial increase in total number and importance of enrollments in *secondary technical education* as the proportion of students enrolled in secondary technical education to total enrollments in secondary education has increased from about 33 percent in 1966/1967 to 51 percent in 1976/1977. Nonetheless, the majority of these students are enrolled in the *commercial secondary schools,* thus leading to office and clerical jobs.

13. F. H. Harbison, "The Connection between Education and Income Distribution," (paper prepared for the Princeton-Brookings Income Distribution Study, August, 1974).

14. See, in particular, Sam Bowles, "Unequal Education and the Reproduction of the Social Division of Labor," *Review of Radical Political Economics,* (Fall/Winter 1971), and Jagdish Bhagwati, "Education, Class Structure and Income Equality," *World Development,* vol. 1, no. 5, (May 1973).

15. Central Auditing Agency, *The Annual Report for the Financial Year 1969/1970,* part 3, (Cairo, December 1971), p. 639.

16. Ibid., p. 646.

17. Such conjectural analysis rests on the following basic assumption about the lower-income groups: The opportunity cost of education, resulting from the fact that children of primary-school age cannot work during the time that they attend school, is higher because typically these groups can and do use children of this age in gainful work whereas this is not possible (or allowed) with the other, higher-income groups. Cf. J. Bhagwati, "Education, Class Structure and Income Distribution."

18. 80 percent of the lower-class students had poor grade averages, compared to 50 percent of their more upper-class peers. These results were reported by Robert Springborg in "*The Ties That Bind: Political Association and Policy-Making in Egypt,*" (Ph.D. diss., Stanford University, 1974), p. 169, as quoted in C. H. Moore, "The Class Origins of Egyptian Engineer-Technocrats" (unpublished paper, University of Michigan, Center for Near Eastern and North African Studies, August 1974).

19. It should be noted that, while educational fees were abolished in all levels of education since 1962, pupils and students are still required to support themselves. In other words, pupils have to advance their own "means of subsistence."

20. It should be mentioned, however, that there exist in Egypt *a three* (not *two*) tier systems of education: (i) elite *private* schools which embrace private foreign language schools; (ii) *general* publicly subsidized government schools; (iii) low quality *private* schools. The low-quality private schools cater mainly for educational needs of the low-middle income groups who fail to get a place for their children in the general government schools.

21. Cf. J. P. Jallade, "Education, Finance, and Income Distribution," *World Development,* vol. 4, no. 5 (1976), p. 439.

22. The reader should, however, bear in mind the fragmentary nature of the underlying data and interpret what follows with great care.

23. Even those in technical occupations keep, in many cases, trying to obtain academic certificates as "externals," so as to become entitled to a secure desk job.

24. See Ahmad Sādiq Saᶜd, "On Bureaucracy and Socialism" (in Arabic), *al-Kātib* vol. 11 no. 124 (July 1971), p. 106; N. Shaᶜth, *Economic Incentives and Manpower Development in U.A.R.* (Cairo; National Institute for Management Development, May, 1969), pp. 22–24.

25. Cf. M. A. R. Shafshāq, "The Role of the University in forming the Egyptian Elite," (in Arabic), *(National Review of Social Studies),* nos. 2 and 3 (1968), pp. 251–261.

26. The sample consisted of 361 engineering graduates, 128 fourth-year students at the Engineering Faculty, and a control group of 97 fourth-year law students. The students were drawn from arbitrary administrative units so that sample bias was minimized. Each respondent was asked about his father's occupation, the type and level of his job, his wealth, and his principal place of residency. Cf. C. H. Moore, *The Class Origins of Egyptian Engineer-Technocrats.*

27. While the educational fees were abolished since 1962, the students benefitting from higher education need to rely on their own parents (or relatives) both for *maintenance* and for *academic equipment.* Only a very small number of gifted poor students are eligible for small grants. Nevertheless, there exists a *student bank* which lends money for university students, due for repayment after graduation.

28. Bhagwati, "Education, Class Structure, and Income Equality," p. 24.

29. Cf. Gray S. Fields, "Higher Education and Income Distribution in a Less Developed Country," *Oxford Economic Papers,* (n.s.), vol. 27, no. 2 (July 1975), pp. 245–246.

30. Ibid.

31. See: Dr. M. R. El-Edel, "Impact of Taxation on Income Distribution: An Exploratory Attempt to Estimate Tax Incidence in Egypt," in chapter 5 of this book.

32. Expressed, for each expenditure bracket, as a ratio of tax burden to income received. And, in general, the incidence of taxes is usually classified as progressive, neutral, or regressive according to their effect on the post-tax distribution of income. A tax is *progressive* if the amount paid is a higher proportion of income the higher the level of income, *neutral* if the proportion paid in tax is constant over all income levels, and *regressive* if the proportion paid is smaller the higher the level of income.

33. This statement needs to be qualified should we allow for the extensive tax evasion located mainly in high-income levels.

34. Saad Eddin Ibrahim, "Social Mobility and Income Distribution," chapter 12 of this book.

35. Ibid.

36. R. Mabro, "Employment, Choice of Technology and Sectoral Priorities," paper presented to the ILO/ECWA (International Labor Office, Economic Commission for West-

ern Asia), Joint seminar on Manpower and Employment Planning in the Arab Countries (Beirut, May 1975).

37. The ILO Ceylon report provides a thorough analysis of this type of structural unemployment, which was particularly marked among the young educated group. See Dudley Seers: "New Light on Structural Unemployment: Lessons of a Mission to Ceylon," *International Labor Review* (February 1972).

38. See Amr Mohie-Eldin, "Employment Problems and Policies in Egypt," paper presented to the ILO/ECWA Joint Seminar on Manpower and Employment Planning in the Arab Countries (Beirut, May 1975).

39. Figures derived from unpublished report by the Ministry of Labor Forces (Cairo, 1973).

40. Ibid.

41. Cf. S. E. Ibrahim, *Arab Attitudes toward Unification in Ten Arab Countries* (forthcoming) (Beirut: Center for Arab Unity Studies).

42. Cf. S. E. Ibrahim, "Social Mobility and Income Distribution," chapter 12 of this book.

43. The case for falling rates of return to education as the supply of education manpower increases has been indicated by various authors. See, among others, Martin Carnoy, "Class Analysis and Investment in Human Resources: A Dynamic Model," *Review of Radical Political Economics,* vol. 3, no. 4, (Fall, 1971).

44. Dr. Mustafā Kamāl Hilmī (Egypt's minister of education) recently reiterated similar views on the subject. Against the background of the increasing role and scale of private tutoring at all levels, and especially at the secondary level, Dr. Hilmī declared that "The Ministry of Education reached the conclusion that the educational process has become a serious burden for most families, and that 'free education' has become a nominal process." Cf. *al-Ahrām,* March 11, 1979.

# CHAPTER 12

# *Social Mobility and Income Distribution in Egypt, 1952–1977*

Saad Eddin Ibrahim

## I. Introduction

Income distribution is a crucial indicator of class structure in any society. It is both a cause and an effect of class position at any given historical point. One's standing in the dimensions of power and prestige in his society is determined, among other things, by the amount and/or source of his income relative to that of others in the same society. A given income, meanwhile, determines the differential access to goods, services, and other scarce rewards—including power and prestige.

Income rarely operates in isolation from other components of *socioeconomic status* (SES). Together with education, occupation, life-style, and power, it provides a fair measurement of socioeconomic status. Because of this close link, income may be considered as a rough summary index of occupation, education, life-style, and power in most modern societies. By the same token, income may be inferred from these correlates.

When individuals or groups change their SES, it is often because one of the above components has triggered the change. The latter may be an improvement or a deterioration. The change in either direction is what sociologists refer to as "social mobility." Thus change in SES over time, either upward or downward, is effected by a change in income, education, occupation, or power.

During the past quarter-century Egypt witnessed changes in its class structure, income distribution, volume, and direction of its social mobility. The causes and consequences of these changes may be articulated in the following broad questions: How does income correlate with other indices of class—namely, education, occupation, and life-style? What is the overall class configuration in Egypt today? How is it different from what it was before 1952 and the mid-1960s? Who achieved upward mobility, and who was forced downward? And what have the volume and direction of such movement been in the mid-1960s and the mid-1970s?

I hypothesize in this chapter that *rapid social mobility took place in Egypt after 1952*. Consequently, Egypt's class structure was markedly transformed through the mid-1960s as a function of (1) intentional redistributive policies; and (2) rapid expansion of opportunities through planned socioeconomic development. *At the point when these two factors were slowed down or halted in the late 1960s and early 1970s, there was a similar slowdown of collective mobility.*

A new nonrevolutionary system has been taking shape in Egypt since 1970. Since then social mobility has become slower and sporadic rather than rapid and deliberate. The pendulum of change in Egypt had swung from right to its furthermost point left between 1952 and 1965. It slowed down between 1965 and 1970, and has gradually been moving back toward the center since 1970.

Attempting to amplify some of these questions raises various issues, theoretical and methodological. Rigorous treatment of the subject requires more and better data than are presently available in Egypt.

For a multitude of historical and structural reasons, the components of SES (income, education, occupation and power) are differentially distributed in most societies. Social scientists, ideologists, and politicians have vehemently disagreed and debated over such unequal distribution, its underlying reasons, and what to do about it. Without being drawn into polemics, it may suffice to mention that the two most theoretically developed positions are those of functionalism and Marxism. The reader can find numerous treatments of these two and other positions in the social science literature.[1]

The methodological problems of studying stratification and social mobility are the operational side of the theoretical issues raised by functionalism and Marxism. Defining what constitutes a "class" or a "stratum" is theoretically controversial. More difficult, however, is to operationalize the concept and identify its import empirically in the world of everyday experience. Equally difficult is to establish the number of classes in a society like Egypt with multiple modes of production (if we employ Marxism), and with a dual universalistic-particularistic mode of position-reward assignment (if we are functionalist).

Whatever the bases and number of classes or strata we may agree upon, we still have to describe and analyze the inflow and outflow among them—that is, social mobility. The methodological questions here would center on measures of rates, causes, and consequences of social mobility. In the broad sense of the word, *mobility* is akin to the bettering or worsening of one's living conditions. Therefore, it is compelling to consider mobility along several dimensions—income, occupation, education, and life-style.

Previous studies of Egypt's stratification and social mobility have all, in varying degrees, struggled with the above methodological questions. The attempts in this regard fall into three broad categories: macroideological studies,[2] microstructural studies of specific communities,[3] and aggregate socioeconomic studies of Egyptian society.[4]

## *Data Gaps and Limitations*

The above studies, however, reveal serious data gaps. Some theoretical and methodological issues will remain unsettled so long as such gaps persist. Here I am not talking so much of the quality and degree of data refinement. The concern is over basic categories of data. The most obvious gaps in data needed to answer our major research questions are the following:

1. Time-series of income distribution in Egypt;
2. Consistent time-series of occupation distribution (that is, uniform or standard classifications over the past twenty-five years);
3. Intergenerational mobility data (vertical social mobility);
4. Intragenerational mobility data (horizontal social mobility), and
5. Correlational data on income-occupation-education.

One source for some of the data needed may be the Family-Budget Surveys of 1958, 1964, and 1974. But this kind of data would still fall into the category of aggregate studies referred to earlier.

It is obvious that supplementary data especially generated for this study are in order—by means of a national sample survey. The sample survey is to provide data on at least items (3), (4), and (5) above.

As a partial remedy for the data gaps on social mobility in Egypt, two sample surveys have been conducted. The first comprises 4,000 households drawn from several Egyptian governorates. The second is on a much smaller scale and comprises only 634 heads of households, about evenly divided between rural and urban areas. Unfortunately, only the smaller survey was processed in time for this chapter. Since I draw heavily on it, a word about this minisurvey and some methodological precautions are in order.

The urban sample of the survey comprises 322 heads of households drawn systematically from nine wards *(shiyākha)* in Cairo.[5] These wards are considered, by Egypt's Central Agency for Public Mobilization and Statistics (CAPMS), as representative of the population of Cairo proper.[6] Nevertheless, extreme caution must be exercised in generalizing the findings with regard to urban Egypt. For one thing, the sample size is too small for a city of over six million.

Cairo is hardly representative of urban Egypt. Being the country's capital, it does tend to have a greater concentration of power, wealth, goods, services, and high-level manpower. But since our primary concern is with social mobility intergenerationally, such serious limitations remain within reasonable bounds. That is to say, the question is not whether the percentage of the poor is greater or lesser in Cairo than in other cities; the question, from a social mobility perspective, is whether or not the sons of those poor are better off or worse off over time.[7]

The rural sample of the survey consists of 312 heads of households drawn also sytematically[8] from eight Egyptian villages. Two are from Asyūt governorate in Upper Egypt, and six are from al-Daqahlīya governorate in Lower Egypt. Aside from this broad regional representation, we have no grounds to claim that the five villages are typical rural communities. Nor is the sample big enough to warrant hard generalizations. But as was the case with the Cairo sample, such limitations apply mostly to general statements on distribution of income, education, and occupation. However, they do not seriously impede our ability to infer rates and directions of social mobility over time—so long as we are working with percentages and proportions across generational categories of socioeconomic strata.

Along with data findings from this small-scale survey, we shall utilize other aggregate data, notably from the national census series (1947, 1960, 1965, 1976), the Family Budget Survey series (1959, 1965, 1975), Labor Force Sample Surveys (1960, 1966, 1974), and other studies.

## II. An Overview of Egypt's Sociopolitics

To make qualitative sense of the numerous tables and quantitative data in this chapter, a brief overview of Egypt's major sociopolitical change in recent decades is in order.

I propose to begin with the sociopolitical-economic setting on the eve of the 1952 revolution, through Nasser's and Sadat's regimes. Even though it is often said that social history contains no surprises, it is helpful to outline the march and retreat of Egypt's socialist policies. They have had a direct bearing on income distribution and shifting positions of various strata. In other words, these policies are, in a sense, the parameters of Egypt's stratification, income distribution, and social mobility.

The 1952 revolution inherited a society whose socioeconomic transition from "traditionalism" to "modernism" had begun a century and a half earlier. That transition, however, had been frustrated by external and internal factors, resulting in the accumulation of problems and bottlenecks in all aspects of life.[9]

Egypt was characterized by four principal modes of production: capitalist-agricultural; capitalist-industrial; traditional-urban informal sector; and traditional agrarian sector. The size and rate of growth among the four modes was quite unequal, with the capitalist-agricultural dominating in the countryside, and the capitalist-industrial dominating in urban areas. This domination was indicated not as much by the human base involved as by the relative share of each mode in Egypt's national wealth and in the wielding of political power.

The integration of Egypt's economy in the international capitalist system, the slow and imbalanced growth of resources and institutions throughout the first half of the twentieth century, resulted in the accumulation of socioeconomic problems. The failure of the political system to cope with these problems was a principal factor behind the 1952 coup d'etat by the Free Officers.

The revolution of 1952 had to confront many challenges: a land-scarce economy, a surplus population, a lopsided production structure, substantial unemployment, capital shortage, dependence on the outside world, maldistribution of wealth, a half-paralyzed bureaucracy, the British occupation and the task of national liberation, and the Arab-Israeli conflict. Some of these problems had reached crisis proportions on the eve of July 1952, and others were to explode later.

It is beyond the scope of this chapter to deal with how the 1952 revolution attempted, failed, or succeeded in meeting this host of challenges.[10] But the sum of actions, measures, and policies undertaken by the new regime resulted in changing the class structure of Egypt. The intensity and implications of the change varied over the next quarter-century. It is possible to identify distinct phases during this twenty-five year period.

### *A. The Hesitation Phase*

Between 1952 and 1956, the new regime was busy trying to consolidate power, establish legitimacy, and gain full political independence from the British. Socioeconomic policies were, by and large, a continuation of the old regime. A major exception, however, was the issuance and implementation of the Land Reform Law in September 1952, limiting landownership to 300 acres per family. Although its social objective should not be minimized, the Land Reform Law was, to a large extent, aimed at weakening the landed aristocracy of the previous regime.

The changes in the class structure during this phase (1952–1956) occurred primarily at the top and near the bottom. The top ruling elite was completely changed, as a few members of the middle class replaced the old elite of landed aristocracy and big capitalists.[11] The landed aristocracy, but not big capitalists at this point, lost substantial parts of their economic power base. The beneficiaries of this loss were the landless and small peasants near the bottom of Egypt's class structure, as well as the rich peasants, or what Binder calls the "Second Stratum."[12]

### *B. The Consciousness Phase*

Between 1956 and 1960, the leaders of Egypt's revolution became aware of the need to turn their attention to Egypt's economic problems. Such awareness reflected itself in the following measures:

1. The stipulation in the new constitution (1956) that Egypt's economy was to be managed according to a comprehensive national plan. A commission was established in 1957 to prepare the first Five Year Plan (1960–1965).
2. Egyptianization of most foreign interests in Egypt, including the Suez Canal Company, banks, and insurance companies. A public corporation, the Eco-

nomic Organization, was established as a holding company for these interests, and was given mandate to expand its activities alone or in partnership with the private sector. Several new projects were undertaken by the Economic Organization in the fields of cement, fertilizers, and textile industries.

3. The establishment of a new Ministry of Industry, in 1957, to undertake the planning and implementation of an industrial program in the interim period 1957–1960, and subsequently for the first Five Year Plan.
4. Laws issued in 1958 for urban housing rent control, reducing rents by 25 percent and fixing new rentals according to rules favoring tenants.
5. A policy of expansion of agricultural cooperatives and agricultural credit to cover the entire country.

The global impact of these measures in the second phase was the opening up of channels of social mobility. The Egyptianization of foreign interests in 1956–1957 led to the exodus of thousands of foreigners who used to manage these interests. Egyptian professionals, mostly college graduates, came forward to fill the vacuum. The moderate expansion of industrial activities created a greater demand for highly trained managers, engineers, skilled and semiskilled manpower. The latter either existed (but was hitherto underutilized) or had to be drawn and trained from middle- and lower-class pools. The rent control laws had their redistributive effects on both sides of the class divide. Urban landlords lost, and middle- and lower-class tenants gained the equivalent of twenty-five percent of the rentals in annual incomes. Thus, in terms of mobility and sheer improvement in standards of income, the less well-to-do strata gained markedly during the second phase, especially in urban areas—as their counterparts had gained in rural areas in the first phase.

### *C. The Socialist Transformation Phase*

The period between 1960 and 1966 witnessed the height of revolutionary actions in changing Egypt's socioeconomic structure. Among the far-reaching measures effected in this phase were the following:

1. An implementation of the first Five Year Plan for socioeconomic development, aiming at a 40 percent increase of national income (7 percent annual growth); a more equitable distribution of income; and the creation of one million job opportunities.
2. The expansion and consolidation of the public sector to lead the country's economic activities.
3. The nationalization of all big business in industry, banking, insurance, construction, import-export, and tourism—this measure brought over 80 percent of nonagricultural activities under state control.
4. The issuance of a second Land Reform Law limiting land ownership to 100 feddans per family.
5. The issuance of a second rent-control law in urban housing reducing rentals by another 25 percent.

6. The stipulation in the constitution of allocation of 50 percent of the seats in all popular elective bodies to workers and peasants.
7. Decreeing a mandatory election of at least two workers to boards of directors of all companies, and the appropriation of 25 percent of annual profits for workers and employees in these companies.
8. The initiation of a new policy of employing all university and trade-school graduates in state or public-sector jobs.

These measures are known among students of Egyptian society as the *Socialist Laws*. Regardless of their sheer economic meaning, their implications for the shape of Egypt's stratification structure and social mobility were quite significant. They had marked redistributive effects in favor of the middle and lower strata. The vast expansion of the public sector, resulting from both nationalization and the creation of new industries, substantially increased the demand for new talents and skills. The demand was met by a corresponding expansion in public education on all levels. The policy of employing all graduates meant the entry of several hundred thousands into white-collar and civil service jobs. The representation of peasants and workers on elective bodies increased the political power of these two groups as never before. Thus, in terms of income, occupation, education, and power, the third phase resulted probably in the biggest change in Egypt's stratification system in this century.

### *D. The Stagnation Phase*

Between 1965 and 1970, Egypt witnessed serious military-political setbacks. The defeat in the 1967 Arab-Israeli war, the drain of the Yemen war, the termination of American economic aid, among other factors, had a profound effect on slowing down Egypt's socioeconomic march. The envisaged second Five Year Plan never took off, as an increasing percentage of the country's resources were earmarked for military expenditure. The loss of Suez Canal revenues and the Sinai oil fields, the massive destruction of the Suez Canal cities, and the mass displacement of nearly one million people from those cities added to the strain on Egypt's economy. As a result, investments in socioeconomic development declined sharply, and Egypt's rate of growth for the period was no more than 1 percent annually. The public sector stood still during this phase, and under some internal pressures the private sector was allowed some margin for movement.

### *E. The Socialist Retreat Phase*

Between 1970 and 1977, four major events took place: Nasser's death, Sadat's ascendance to power, the October war of 1973, and the institution of the Open-Door policy. That policy, though in the making since 1968, took on explicit official endorsement after the 1973 war. It called for revitalizing the private sector, opening the door for foreign and Arab capital to flow into the country, revoking certain aspects of the Land Reform Law (specifically those regulating land tenure), and indirect measures of Egyptian currency devaluation. The sum of these policies amounted to a reversal of Egypt's socialist transformation. This phase can be characterized as one of mixed economy, progressively tilting toward capitalist "laissez-faire, laissez-passer." The impact on class structure is not definitely clear yet. There are indications, however, that some elements of the prerevolutionary upper and upper-middle class are resurfacing. Upward social mobility is mainly accomplished through (1) private-sector activities or (2) migration to oil-rich Arab countries. Strata with fixed income seem to have suffered the most in this phase.

Against this background, the elaboration of the stratification of income, occupation, and education may be understood.

## III. Stratification of Income

Income is often a summary index of one's earning from wages and salaries, that is, occupation. The latter is determined in turn by one's training or education. Thus both occupation and education are implied by income. Another major source of income is revenue from property (land, real estate, shares, stocks and so forth). Income distribution, therefore, is both a reflection and a cause of stratification in a given society. A separate chapter deals more rigorously with income distribution (Ibrahim H. El-Issawy in chapter 4). My treatment of stratification of income here is only meant to provide the context in which income mobility can be best understood.

### *A. Evolution of Income in Egypt*

As shown in table 12.1, Egypt's national income has risen from £E806 million in 1952 to over £E1.9 billion in 1974 at constant prices. That is more than 137 percent real increase in twenty-two years. Given rapid population growth in Egypt, however, income per capita did not rise as fast. In 1952, the average share of the individual was slightly over £E37. It rose to about £53 in 1974, a percentage increase of 43 during the twenty-two years, that is, at an average growth of slightly less than 2 percent annually for the whole period.

Most of the growth in national and per capita income occurred during the 1955–1965 period, which I referred to in the previous section as the Consciousness and Socialist phases. Between 1955 and 1960, the national income grew from £E881 million to £E1,139 million, that is, over 29 percent, or at an annual average of about 5 percent. Income per capita rose during the same period from £E37.7 million to £E43.3 million, that is, by

*TABLE 12.1.*
*Real National Income and Per Capita Income in Egypt, 1952–1974 (Constant Prices)*

| | *National Income (£E millions)* | *Annual Growth Rate (%)* | *Per Capita Income (£E)* | *Annual Growth Rate (%)* |
|---|---|---|---|---|
| 1952 | 806 | ... | 37.1 | ... |
| 1953 | 871 | 8.1 | 39.1 | 5.4 |
| 1954 | 930 | 6.8 | 40.8 | 4.3 |
| 1955 | 881 | 5.3 | 37.3 | −7.6 |
| 1956 | 897 | 1.8 | 37.5 | −0.5 |
| 1957 | 959 | 6.9 | 39.9 | 6.4 |
| 1958 | 985 | 2.7 | 39.4 | 1.3 |
| 1959 | 1,091 | 10.8 | 42.6 | 8.1 |
| 1960 | 1,139 | 4.4 | 43.3 | 1.6 |
| 1961 | 1,190 | 4.5 | 44.2 | 2.1 |
| 1962 | 1,324 | 11.3 | 48.0 | 8.6 |
| 1963 | 1,416 | 6.9 | 49.9 | 4.0 |
| 1964 | 1,480 | 4.5 | 50.7 | 1.6 |
| 1965 | 1,554 | 5.0 | 52.2 | 3.0 |
| 1966 | 1,559 | 0.3 | 51.8 | −0.8 |
| 1967 | 1,544 | 1.0 | 49.4 | −4.6 |
| 1968 | 1,632 | 5.7 | 51.1 | 3.2 |
| 1969 | 1,746 | 7.0 | 53.2 | 4.3 |
| 1970 | 1,767 | 1.2 | 52.4 | −1.5 |
| 1971 | 1,856 | 5.1 | 53.9 | 2.9 |
| 1972 | 1,789 | 3.6 | 51.4 | −4.6 |
| 1973 | 1,859 | 3.9 | 52.2 | 1.6 |
| 1974 | 1,913 | 2.9 | 52.6 | .8 |

SOURCE: CAPMS, *Bread in Egypt* (in Arabic) (Cairo, November 1977) (Ref. No. 833100/001), p. 61.

15 percent. Between 1960 and 1965, the Socialist Transformation Phase, national income rose from £E1,139 million to £E1,554 million, that is, 36.4 percent real increase averaging over 6 percent average annual growth for the whole period. Despite the continuing population increase, income per capita rose to £E52.2 million, that is, 20.3 percent. Taken together, the 1955–1965 period witnessed the greatest rise in income per capita of Egyptians in this century.[13] In fact, most of the real gains in individual income during the last quarter-century were achieved between 1955 and 1965.

The period 1965–1974, which I referred to as the Stagnation and Socialist Retreat phases, witnessed a zigzagging in per capita income. Thus, per capita income recorded a negative growth in the years 1966, 1967, 1970, and 1972. In the following year, 1972, income per capita recovered to its 1965 level, and in 1974 it showed a slight increase of 1.6 percent (or up to £E52.6 million in constant prices).

*TABLE 12.2.*
*Estimation of Rural and Urban Poverty in Egypt, 1958–1975*

| *Variable* | *Area* | *1958/1959* | *1964/1965* | *1974/1975* |
|---|---|---|---|---|
| Poverty line as measured in £E | Rural* | 93.0 | 125.0 | 270.0 |
| | Urban† | 121.0 | 163.0 | 351.0 |
| Percentage of families below the poverty line | Rural* | 35.0 | 26.8 | 44.0 |
| | Urban† | 30.0 | 27.8 | 34.5 |

SOURCE:
*Samir Radwan, *The Impact of Agrarian Reform on Rural Egypt* (Geneva: ILO, 1977), p. 42.
†My computation on the basis of 30 percent increase in minimum living expenditure in urban areas.

### *B. Poverty and Income Distribution*

In a Third World country such as Egypt, income distribution does not acquire its full social meaning unless it is related to people's needs. The poor are often thought of as those who cannot satisfy their basic needs. But the question of what is basic is quite relative. Nevertheless, it is possible to estimate the monetary value of a least-cost diet, which fulfills the minimum nutritional requirements as set by specialized agencies such as the Food and Agriculture Organization and the World Health Organization.

Egyptian economist Samir Radwan calculated the cost of minimum diet, clothing, and housing for rural Egyptian families.[14] He used that minimum as a benchmark to establish a "poverty line" for the years 1958–1959, 1964–1965, and 1974–1975. His attempt is quite ingenious; I regret that he did not do the same for urban households. To complement his work, I estimated that an urban household requires about 30 percent more than its rural counterpart in order to meet typical urban needs, especially those of housing and transportation in the city.

Table 12.2 shows the two respective poverty lines for rural and urban areas in three successive periods. In 1958–1959, 35 percent of all rural families were below the poverty line. By that date, the first Land Reform Law was implemented, and no doubt several hundred thousands[15] as land recipients and tenants had benefited from it. My estimation is that the percentage of poor families before the 1952 law was well over 40 percent of all rural households. By 1964/1965, the second Land Reform Law was in effect. Along with other policies (credits and cooperatives), there was further reduction of the percentage of poor families to 27 percent of the rural total. During the next ten years, however, economic stagnation and the socialist retreat affected the situation in the countryside. The percent-

TABLE 12.3.
*Income Mobility: Respondents and Fathers, for a Sample of Heads of Household, Cairo, 1979 (N = 255)*

| Income Categories of Respondents | Income Categories of Their Fathers (percent) | | | | | | | | |
|---|---|---|---|---|---|---|---|---|---|
| | 1* | 2 | 3 | 4 | 5 | 6 | 7 | 8* | Total |
| 1 (Lowest) | 34.5 | 34.5 | 20.7 | 6.9 | 3.4 | ... | ... | ... | 11.4 |
| 2 | 29.2 | 26.2 | 24.6 | 1.5 | 15.4 | 1.5 | 1.5 | ... | 25.5 |
| 3 | 18.1 | 20.0 | 28.8 | 8.2 | 16.5 | 7.1 | ... | 1.3 | 33.3 |
| 4 | 6.3 | 16.7 | 22.9 | 12.5 | 25.0 | 10.4 | 6.3 | ... | 18.8 |
| 5 | 13.3 | 20.0 | 33.3 | 13.3 | 13.3 | ... | 6.7 | ... | 5.9 |
| 6 | 22.2 | 11.1 | 11.1 | 11.1 | 11.1 | 11.1 | 22.2 | ... | 3.5 |
| 7 | ... | ... | ... | ... | ... | 50.0 | 50.0 | ... | 0.8 |
| 8 (Highest) | ... | ... | ... | ... | ... | ... | 100.0 | ... | 0.8 |
| Total | 20.4 | 22.0 | 24.7 | 7.5 | 16.5 | 5.5 | 3.1 | 0.4 | 100.0 |

SOURCE: Original survey data

Statistical Measures: $x^2$ = 86.29 P = 0.01 Gamma = 0.35 Contingency coefficient = 0.50
*Different cutting points were used for income categories of the two generations to take inflation into account. See note 17.

age of households below the poverty line jumped to 44 percent, 17 percentage points over the 1964/1965 figure.

In urban areas, poverty was the lot of 30 percent of all households in 1958/1959. There was some improvement in 1964/1965, the figure dropping to 28 percent. But again, during the next two phases (Stagnation and Socialist Retreat), urban poverty climbed to nearly 35 percent of all households. Part of this rise must have been due to the influx of some of the rural poor to urban centers.

### C. Income Mobility

A micropicture of the changing income distribution may be inferred from the findings of the small-scale survey conducted for the purpose of this study in 1979 (see section 1). Respondents were asked to report their annual income, and that of their fathers and their oldest working sons.[16] The three estimates were categorized differently according to the range of income in the three successive generations.[17]

Tables 12.3 and 12.4 show income mobility across three generations. The respondents (heads of household) in the Cairo sample are the points of reference. Table 12.3 compares their distribution by eight income categories cross-tabulated with their fathers' income categories. The two marginal totals reveal the relative improvement attained by respondents *vis-à-vis* their fathers. Thus, while 20.4 percent of the fathers were in the

*TABLE 12.4.*
*Income Mobility: Respondents and Sons, for a Sample of Heads of Household, Cairo, 1979 (N = 75)*

| *Income Categories of Respondents* | *Income Categories of Their Sons (percent)* | | | | | | | |
|---|---|---|---|---|---|---|---|---|
| | *1* | *2* | *3* | *4* | *5* | *6* | *7* | *Total* |
| 1 (Lowest) | 55.6 | 33.3 | ... | ... | ... | ... | 11.1 | 12.0 |
| 2 | 22.2 | 77.8 | ... | ... | ... | ... | ... | 12.0 |
| 3 | 26.1 | 60.9 | 4.3 | ... | ... | 4.3 | 4.3 | 30.7 |
| 4 | 18.8 | 75.0 | ... | ... | ... | ... | 6.3 | 21.3 |
| 5 | ... | 100.0 | ... | ... | ... | ... | ... | 10.7 |
| 6 | ... | 61.4 | 38.6 | ... | ... | ... | ... | 9.3 |
| 7 | ... | ... | ... | 100.0 | ... | ... | ... | 1.3 |
| 8 (Highest) | ... | ... | ... | 100.0 | ... | ... | ... | 2.7 |
| Total | 21.3 | 65.3 | 4.0 | 4.0 | ... | 1.3 | 4.0 | 100.0 |

SOURCE: Original survey data
Statistical measures: $x^2$ = 103.53 P = 0.001 Gamma = 0.49
Contingency coefficient = 0.76

lowest income category, only 11.4 percent of their sons (respondents) fell in the lowest category in 1979, an improvement of 9 percentage points. The combined total of categories 2 and 3 for respondents was nearly 59 percent compared to about 47 percent for their parents. The biggest differences are in categories 3 and 5. Proportionally more of the respondents were in the third income bracket (33.3 versus 24.7 percent of their parents), and proportionally more of the parents were in the fifth income bracket (16.5 versus 5.9 of the respondents).

If we leave the totals and look inside table 12.3 we observe more of the inner dynamics of income mobility. To appreciate the extent and direction of that mobility, the reader may look at the diagonal (underlined) in table 12.3 as the dividing line between upward mobility (below the diagonal) and downward mobility (above the diagonal). The diagonal itself represents income immobility between the two generations. Thus, in income category 1 of the respondents (first row), which is the lowest income bracket, we see that nearly 35 percent are locked in poverty for at least the second generation, as their parents were also in the lowest income category. The other 65 percent of the respondents in this income group have moved downward. In category 2, while 29 percent of the respondents improved by one step over their parents, 26 percent remained the same, and 45 percent moved downward by one to five steps below their parents. In income category 3, nearly 39 percent of the respondents moved upward (one or two steps over their fathers), 29 percent remained the same, and about 32 percent moved downward by one to four steps below their fathers. Thus, in the third income category, more of the newcomers to it (39 percent) are from poorer backgrounds, in contrast with the first and second categories, where more of the respective newcomers had parents who were better off. What we observe in category 3 applies to the next five income categories—more respondents in each category have upward rather than downward mobility. The greatest single difference is in category 5, where nearly 80 percent experienced upward mobility (became better off than their parents), 13 percent remained the same, and 7 percent moved downward. If this category represents the present-day upper middle class, then I suggest that most of its members have ascended to it from various strata immediately below. The same observation applies to category 6.

As for the top two income brackets (categories 7 and 8), the movement, though also substantial, was only one step upward. All of the respondents in category 8 had fathers who were in category 7, and half of the respondents in category 7 had fathers in category 6, the other half remaining immobile.

In summary, what table 12.3 suggests is (1) that income mobility occurred across all income brackets; (2) that this mobility tended to be smaller at the lower income categories and greater at the middle; (3) that in the lowest four income categories the movement tended to be mostly one step in either direction; (4) that none of the respondents whose parents were in the lowest six categories made it to the top income brackets, and (5) that none of the respondents who were in the top bracket slid down to the lowest (1 or 2) categories.

Table 12.4 compares respondents and their oldest working sons. Not all respondents were qualified, not having sons old enough for this comparison. Again, the diagonal represents cases of income immobility. But below it are cases of downwardly mobile sons, and above it are cases of upwardly mobile sons. In the lowest income category, more than half (56 percent) were born to fathers who were also in the lowest income bracket, while the rest (44 percent) have improved their income standing *vis-à-vis* their fathers. In the second income category, nearly 78 percent of the sons have remained immobile; the rest (22 percent) were still below their fathers' income levels. In the third category of respondents, the overwhelming majority of sons (87 percent) are still below the income level of their parents, and only 9 percent have exceeded theirs. The same observation applies to the fourth category of respondents, 94 percent of sons being below and 6 percent above their fathers' income level. None of the respondents' sons in the top four income categories has reached or exceeded his father's income.

In summary, table 12.4 suggests the following: (1) given the fact that most sons have not reached the peak of their earning capacity, the majority are naturally below the income levels of their fathers, and (2) the sons of the more well-to-do are, however, markedly better off than the sons of the less well-to-do.

Looking at the measures of association for the data in tables 12.3 and 12.4, we observe that both Gamma and the contingency coefficient are higher for respondents and sons (0.49 and 0.76, table 12.4), than for respondents and fathers (0.35 and 0.50, table 12.3). The variance in both tables was statistically significant at the 0.001 level. What this implies is that upward income mobility is determined in good part by one's father's income. But this fact was less instrumental twenty years ago than it is at present. In other words, it was relatively easier for more people to improve their income *vis-à-vis* that of their fathers fifteen or twenty years ago than it is today.

In conclusion, it is quite obvious from aggregate data that income distribution in Egypt has been a function of: (1) the overall economic growth, and (2) state policies. Overall growth naturally increases average income per capita, and tends to have a trickling-down effect on the lower strata of the population. This can be seen from table 12.1 for the years 1952–1960, that is, even before the massive socialist measures of 1961. State policies augment or distort income distribution. The Land Reform Laws of 1952 and 1961 had marked distributive effects in favor of the lower strata of Egypt's population up to 1965. The same is true for urban population, which benefited directly or indirectly from both economic expansion and the Socialist Laws of 1961.

Those significant effects, however, were not substantial enough to become self-propelling for further equalization without steady growth or state intervention on behalf of the poor. When both factors ceased to operate between 1965 and 1970, there was a slight increase of inequality. The trend toward inequality picked up after 1970 when the state began to intervene on behalf of the well-to-do.

The microstructural data on Cairo's income mobility support the above conclusion. The respondent's generation, roughly coinciding with the 1950s and 1960s period, had greater opportunities to improve its income standing *vis-à-vis* the previous generation (prerevolution). Their sons, however, remained mostly immobile. The few who attained upward income mobility tend to be the children of the more well-to-do.

## IV. Occupational Mobility

Lipset and Zetterberg assert that "from Plato to the present, occupation has been the most common indicator of stratification. Social scientists have found that occupational categories are one of the major factors which differentiate people's beliefs, values, behavior, and even their emotional expressions."[18] Monitoring change in the occupational structure of a society, therefore, informs us about all these aspects. More important to us, however, is the income implication of occupational mobility.

Occupational mobility may be inferred from differential growth in each type of activity and/or occupational category *vis-à-vis* both overall population growth and growth of the labor force during the period under consideration (1952–1977). The underlying assumption here is that occupational mobility results from (1) the supply of vacant positions generated by expansion of certain socioeconomic activities, and (2) the interchangeability of occupational positions without an overall expansion in socioeconomic activities. Thus any mobility that occurs in society is either a consequence of a change in the absolute supply of job opportunities in certain occupational levels or results from an interchange among levels of the occupational structure. The latter means that, for every move up, there must be a move down. Interchange mobility is determined, to a large extent, by the opportunities that society gives its members of the lower occupational strata to compete with those who enter the structure on a higher level.[19]

### *A. Changing Economic Activities*

Egypt's population grew from 19 to 37 million between 1947 and 1976, an increase of 93 percent in twenty-nine years. Its civilian labor force, however, grew by only 38 percent (from 6.99 to 9.63 million) during the same period. Thus while the population at large grew at an average rate of slightly over 2 percent annually for the entire period, the comparable growth rate of employment was only 1.1 percent. The gap between the two rates may be explained by the rapid expansion of elementary education after 1952, which reduced the entry of children into Egypt's labor force. A similar expansion in the military, especially after 1967, appropriated nearly half a million youngsters who would have otherwise been added to the labor force.

Table 12.5 shows the distribution of Egypt's civilian labor force by broad economic activities between 1947 and 1976. It will be readily observed that those engaged in agriculture have declined steadily over the years. In 1947, agriculture appropriated over 58 percent of the total, and by 1966 it decreased by 5 percentage points. At present the share of agriculture is about 44 percent of Egypt's labor force. This is probably the first time in the country's long recorded history in which the majority are no longer engaged in agriculture.

The share of manufacturing (and related activities) in the civilian labor force has grown steadily from 8 percent in 1947 to 13 percent in 1966. This five-point percentage rise is equal to the percentage drop in the share of agriculture between the same dates. It is fair to assume, therefore, that industry's relatively faster growth in manpower was at the expense of agriculture. The implication of this datum lies in the fact that earnings and

*TABLE 12.5.*

*Employment of Labor Force by Economic Activities*

*(Thousands)*

| | *1947* | | *1960* | | *1966* | | *1971* | | *1976* | |
|---|---|---|---|---|---|---|---|---|---|---|
| *Economic Activities* | *N* | *%* | *N* | *%* | *N* | *%* | *N* | *%* | *N* | *%* |
| Agriculture | 4,086 | 58.4 | 4,406 | 57.0 | 4,447 | 53.4 | 4,471 | 53.2 | 4,224 | 43.9 |
| Manufacturing, mining, and quarrying | 574 | 8.2 | 734 | 9.5 | 1,089 | 13.1 | 1,045 | 12.4 | 1,210 | 12.6 |
| Construction | 113 | 1.6 | 159 | 2.0 | 206 | 2.5 | 195 | 2.3 | 434 | 4.5 |
| Electricity, gas, and water | 23 | 0.3 | 37 | 0.5 | 51 | 0.6 | 26 | 0.3 | 47 | 0.5 |
| Commerce and finance | 590 | 8.4 | 641 | 8.3 | 599 | 7.2 | 803 | 9.6 | 1,016 | 10.6 |
| Transport, communication, and storage | 203 | 2.9 | 260 | 3.4 | 340 | 4.1 | 324 | 3.9 | 422 | 4.4 |
| Other services and unspecified | 1,405 | 20.1 | 1,489 | 19.3 | 1,602 | 19.2 | 1,541 | 18.3 | 2,276 | 23.6 |
| Total | 6,995 | 100.0 | 7,727 | 100.0 | 8,334 | 100.0 | 8,406 | 100.0 | 9,628 | 100.0 |

SOURCES: Population Censuses 1947, 1960, 1966, 1976; Labor Force Sample Survey 1971; CAPMS Ministry of Planning; *1976–1980: Egypt's Five Year Plan*.

TABLE 12.6.

*Percentage Change of Labor Force by Economic Activities, 1947–1976*

| | *1947–1960* | | *1960–1966* | | *1966–1971* | | *1971–1976* | |
|---|---|---|---|---|---|---|---|---|
| *Economic Activity* | *Total Change* | *Annual Average* | *Total Change* | *Annual Average* | *Total Change* | *Annual Average* | *Total Change* | *Annual Average* |
| Agriculture | 7.83 | 0.6 | 0.93 | 0.2 | 0.54 | 0.1 | −5.6 | −1.1 |
| Manufacturing, mining, and quarrying | 27.89 | 2.2 | 48.36 | 8.1 | −4.05 | −0.8 | 15.79 | 3.2 |
| Construction | 40.71 | 3.1 | 29.56 | 4.9 | −5.40 | −1.1 | 122.56 | 24.5 |
| Electricity, gas, and water | 60.87 | 4.7 | 37.83 | 6.3 | −49.02 | −9.8 | 80.77 | 16.2 |
| Commerce and finance | 8.64 | 0.7 | −6.56 | −1.1 | 34.06 | 6.8 | 26.53 | 5.3 |
| Transport, communication, and storage | 28.08 | 2.2 | 30.77 | 5.1 | 30.25 | 6.1 | 30.25 | 6.1 |
| Other services and unclassified | 6.00 | 0.8 | 7.59 | 1.3 | −3.81 | −0.8 | 47.70 | 9.5 |
| Total | 10.46 | 0.8 | 7.86 | 1.3 | 0.86 | 0.2 | 14.54 | 2.9 |

SOURCE: Computed from data in table 12.5.

*TABLE 12.7.*

*Distribution of Labor Force by Occupation 1947–1974*
*(Thousands)*

| Occupation | 1947 | | 1960 | | 1966 | | 1971 | | 1974 | |
|---|---|---|---|---|---|---|---|---|---|---|
| | N | % | N | % | N | % | N | % | N | % |
| I Professional and Technical | 189 | 2.5 | 285 | 3.7 | 400 | 4.8 | 462 | 5.5 | 522 | 5.7 |
| II Administrative and Managerial | 63 | 0.9 | 85 | 1.1 | 150 | 1.8 | 162 | 1.9 | 91 | 1.0 |
| III Clerical Workers | 140 | 1.9 | 285 | 3.7 | 458 | 5.5 | 429 | 5.1 | 507 | 5.5 |
| IV Sales Workers | 476 | 6.4 | 626 | 8.1 | 525 | 6.3 | 480 | 5.7 | 769 | 8.4 |
| Total Non-Manual | 868 | 11.7 | 1,281 | 16.6 | 1,533 | 18.4 | 1,533 | 18.2 | 1,189 | 20.8 |
| V Craftsmen, production, processing* and operators | 1,490 | 20.1 | 1,491 | 19.3 | 1,733 | 20.8 | 1,547 | 18.4 | 1,999 | 22.2 |
| VI Service workers | 630 | 8.5 | 688 | 8.9 | 701 | 8.4 | 765 | 9.1 | 826 | 9.1 |
| Total Nonfarm Manual | 2,120 | 28.7 | 2,179 | 28.2 | 2,434 | 29.1 | 2,312 | 27.6 | 2,825 | 32.3 |
| VII Farmers and related workers | 4,232 | 57.2 | 4,103 | 53.1 | 4,198 | 50.4 | 4,337 | 51.6 | 4,126 | 45.6 |
| Total Manual (V, VI, and VII) | 6,352 | 85.9 | 6,282 | 81.3 | 6,632 | 79.5 | 6,649 | 79.1 | 6,951 | 76.7 |
| VIII Not specified | 175 | 2.4 | 170 | 2.2 | 200 | 2.4 | 227 | 2.7 | 235 | 2.5 |
| Total | 7,395 | 100.0 | 7,733 | 100.0 | 8,365 | 100.0 | 8,409 | 100.0 | 9,075 | 100.0 |

SOURCE: 1947, 1960, 1966 Population Censuses; CAPMS, Labor Force Sample Surveys, 1971 and 1974, Cairo.

*Including transportation workers.

wages in manufacturing are substantially greater than those in agriculture. In the 1960s the average wage in agriculture was £E137 per year, compared to £E208 in manufacturing, that is, a 52 percent difference.[20] In other words, the rise in industrial manpower between 1947 and 1966 meant definite upward mobility for at least 5 percent of Egypt's labor force. The relative share of industry in the mid-1960s has been the biggest ever. It was a clear and direct reflection of the industrialization program during the Consciousness and Socialist Transformation phases (1956–1960, 1960–1965, respectively). During the next two phases (Stagnation and Socialist Retreat) the share of the industrial labor force declined to 12.4 percent in 1971 and 12.6 in 1976.

The other big sectors of the economy are those of services and commerce. The services appropriated slightly over 20 percent of the civilian labor force in 1947. This share declined steadily to reach slightly over 18 percent by 1971. But during the Socialist Retreat phase, which coincided with the capitalist reorientation under the open-door policy, the share of services climbed to an all-time high of nearly 24 percent of Egypt's total labor force. The same thing has happened with employment in commerce and finance. During the Consciousness and Socialist Transformation phases its share in the labor force declined to 8.3 and 7.2 percent in 1960 and 1966, respectively. But by 1976, with the Open-Door policy in full swing, the share of commerce and finance rose to nearly 11 percent of Egypt's total civilian labor force. The share of other sectors in the labor force showed a modest but steady rise, with a tiny halt between 1966 and 1971.

What may be concluded from table 12.5 is that agriculture's share of the labor force has steadily and substantially declined over the period 1947–1976, a net loss of 14.5 percentage points. This decline took place regardless of the prevailing economic orientation, that is, during the Socialist Transformation phase as well as during the Open-Door phase. Most of this net loss, however, seemed to have been primarily a net gain for industry during the Socialist Transformation phase, and a net gain for services, commerce, and finance during the Socialist Retreat (or Open-Door) phase. Table 12.6 provides a clear substantiation for this conclusion.

### *B. Changing Occupational Structure*

Another way of depicting mobility is to examine the changing composition of Egypt's labor force broken down by occupational categories. Official statistics report these categories as shown in table 12.7. Categories I and II include professionals (doctors, lawyers, engineers, scientists, teachers, and the like) and those in commanding government administrative positions as well as executives and managers of both public and private corporations. Together, these two categories represent

TABLE 12.8.

*Percentage Change of Occupational Composition, 1947–1974*

| Occupational Category | 1947–1960 | | 1960–1966 | | 1966–1971 | | 1971–1974 | |
|---|---|---|---|---|---|---|---|---|
| | Entire Period | Average Annual Change | Entire Period | Average Annual Change | Entire Period | Average Annual Change | Entire Period | Average Annual Change |
| I Professional and technical | 50.8 | 3.9 | 40.4 | 6.7 | 15.5 | 3.1 | 29.8 | 9.9 |
| II Administrative and managerial | 34.9 | 2.7 | 76.5 | 12.8 | −16.0 | −3.2 | −17.8 | −5.9 |
| III Clerical | 103.6 | 8.0 | 60.7 | 10.1 | −6.3 | −1.3 | 18.2 | 6.1 |
| IV Sales workers | 31.5 | 2.4 | −16.1 | −2.7 | −8.6 | −1.7 | 60.2 | 20.1 |
| V Craftsmen, production workers, and operators | 36.8 | 2.8 | 59.0 | 9.8 | −10.7 | −2.4 | 29.2 | 9.7 |
| VI Service workers | 9.2 | 0.7 | 1.8 | 0.3 | 9.1 | 1.8 | 7.9 | 2.6 |
| VII Farmers | −3.0 | −0.2 | 2.3 | 0.4 | 3.3 | 0.7 | −5.0 | −1.7 |
| VIII Not specified | −3.0 | −0.2 | 17.6 | 2.9 | 13.5 | 2.7 | 3.5 | 1.2 |
| Total | 10.6 | 0.8 | 8.2 | 1.4 | 0.1 | 0.02 | 8.4 | 2.8 |

SOURCE: Computed from data in table 12.7.

the upper echelons of the occupational structure. In 1947, the date of the last census before the revolution, they totaled 252,000, or 3.6 percent of the civilian labor force. In 1960, eight years after the revolution, their representation rose to 4.8 percent. By 1966, the height of Socialist Transformation in Egypt, these two top categories totaled 588,000, or 6.6 percent of the labor force. After 1966, the professionals continued their absolute and relative growth, to 5.5 percent in 1971 and 5.7 percent in 1974. Administrative executives and managers, however, steadily declined in absolute as well as relative terms, from 150,000 in 1966 to 126,000 in 1971, to 91,000 in 1974, or from 1.8 to 1.5 to 1 percent of Egypt's labor force on the three respective dates.

The third category is that of clerical occupations, which includes white-collar and lower-stratum civil servants with lower than university-level education. In 1947, their number was 140,000, representing 2 percent of the total civilian labor force. By 1966 they more than doubled, to reach 458,000, or 5.5 percent of the labor force. In the following five years, this category declined slightly in both absolute and relative terms, but by 1974 it topped the half-million mark and regained its relative representation of 5.5 percent of the total labor force.

Occupational categories I, II, and III shared basically the same change pattern between 1947 and 1974. They assumed a steady growth in both relative and absolute terms between 1947 and 1966. This substantial change was primarily a function of the expansion of the economy in the first three phases of the 1952 revolution. The rate of change slowed or completely halted between 1966 and 1971 because of the 1967 war and its aftermath. In addition, many of the medium- and highly educated youngsters were drafted into the military between 1967 and 1973. Since my treatment here is confined to the civilian labor force, the data in table 12.8 reflect this deflection in the flow of potential high- and medium-level manpower into the labor force. The data for 1974 (table 12.7) show the early effects of the post-1973 war, as tens of thousands were released from military service. Categories I and III recovered their 1966 position or improved on it. Category II, however, did not. A tentative explanation for the latter may be attributed to (1) the undermining of the public sector under the impact of the new Open-Door policy adopted since 1973, and (2) the out-migration of many elements from this category to neighboring oil-rich Arab countries. Executives and managers, with a high entrepreneurial spirit, would naturally be more prone to migrate for greater fortunes elsewhere once the state ceased to create new opportunities for them. We may expect, however, that many of them will return after accumulating seed capital to start private business, taking advantage of the measures provided by the Open-Door policy.

Category IV in table 12.7 (sales workers), includes those working in commercial, financial, and related activites, whether self-employed or employed by others. In 1947 they numbered 476,000 and made up 6.8

percent of the labor force. They continued to grow in the early years of the revolution since free enterprises remained basically untouched by any contrary government policies. Thus, by 1960 their number topped the 626,000 mark, representing over 8 percent of the total civilian labor force. The 1960s decade, however, was not theirs, as Socialist Transformation began in earnest. The size of this category suffered a serious decline, falling to 525,000, or 6.3 percent of the labor force. But by 1974, the winds of change were in its favor, and sales workers rose to 769,000, or 8.4 percent of Egypt's labor force.

Category V includes skilled and semiskilled workers such as craftsmen, production and processing workers, and machine operators. By 1966, the height of Socialist Transformation, the size of this category was over 1.7 million, or nearly 21 percent of the labor force. There was a slight decline in the 1966–1971 period, as part of this manpower was transferred to the military on the one hand and as expansion in industry was halted on the other. But by 1974, that is, the postwar years, this category more than recovered to reach nearly 2 millions in size and over 22 percent of Egypt's total labor force.

Category VI (service workers) includes all the unskilled outside both industry and farming. Their number has been slightly but steadily increasing, from 630,000 in 1947 to 701,000 in 1966, and to 826,000 in 1974. Their percentage in the labor force, however, slightly dropped in the 1960s decade, from 9 percent in 1947 to 8.4 percent in 1966. But by 1974 their proportion rose again to slightly over 9 percent of the labor force.

Category VII includes farmers, farm workers, fishermen, and forestry workers. The size of this category, though the biggest, seems to have stabilized around 4 million since 1947. But since the total labor force is steadily growing, the proportionate representation of this category has steadily declined. Between 1947 and 1960, it dropped by 7.4 percentage points (from 60.5 to 53.1) of the labor force. With the exception of a slight reversal in the 1966–1971 period, the downward trend continued through 1974 to reach 45.6 percent of Egypt's labor force.

We can look at the data in table 12.7 in terms of manual and nonmanual occupations. Categories I through IV represent the nonmanual occupations, whose combined total rose from 868,000 in 1947 to 1.5 million in 1966 and to 1.9 million in 1974. The relative weight of these four nonmanual occupational categories rose from 12.4 to 18.3 to 20.8 percent in the three periods, respectively. As for manual occupations (categories V, VI, and VII), we observe that the relative weight of their combined total has declined from 85.1 percent in 1947 to 79.5 percent in 1966, to 76.7 percent in 1974, or a drop of 8.4 percentage points in twenty-nine years. All this drop, however, occurred in the farming and related occupations (category VII). The nonfarming manual occupations (categories V and VI) rose from 24.6 percent in 1947 to 29.1 in 1966, to 31.1 percent in 1974, a net gain of 6.5 percentage points. To phrase it differently, Egypt's occupational structure, though still heavily dominated by manual occupations, is changing steadily toward nonmanual occupations. The latter have gained 8.4 percentage points at the expense of the former in the course of the last twenty-seven years. But among manual occupations the net loss was in farming and related occupations, amounting to 15.1 percentage points. Part of this loss went to other manual occupations, namely skilled and semiskilled industrial workers (6.7 percentage points), and to nonmanual occupations (8.4 percentage points).

Table 12.8 shows the percentage change in various occupational categories between 1947 and 1974. I divided this time span into periods that roughly correspond to the successive phases of Egypt's major policy orientations. Thus the 1947–1960 period covers the first eight years after the 1952 revolution. As indicated earlier, the first phase of these years up to 1956 saw the new regime concentrate on political consolidation, improving economic performance without much change in the nature of the economic order. Egypt's labor force as a whole grew at rates higher than the overall average. Highest rates of annual growth were accomplished in clerical (8 percent), professional (3.9 percent), and industrial (2.8 percent) occupations. Lower rates of annual growth were recorded in administrative and managerial occupations (2.7 percent), sales (2.4 percent), and service workers (0.7 percent). Farming occupations registered negative growth of −3 percent for the entire 1947–1960 period, or −0.2 percent annually.

The following period, 1960–1966, is the Socialist Transformation period. The new socialist orientation involved, not only measures of greater equitable distribution of wealth, but also a deliberate policy of planned economic growth, with special emphasis on industry. The labor force averaged an annual growth rate of 1.4 percent. All but sales, farming, and service occupations registered higher rates than this global average. The leading occupations in growth rates during this period were administrative and managerial (12.8 percent), followed by clerical (10.1 percent), industrial (9.8 percent), and professional occupations (6.7 percent). Sales occupations, in contrast, registered negative growth (−2.7 percent annually). Farming and service occupations grew at the very modest rate of 0.3 and 0.4 percent, respectively.

The 1966–1971 period represented stagnation years. The war efforts and the drafting of about half a million people into the military caused not only a halt but also a negative growth in several occupational categories. Training for professional, managerial, and production occupations did continue, but these new trainees, instead of joining the civilian labor force, were inducted into the army. Thus, as soon as the 1973 war was over, a huge backlog of trained manpower was released to join the civilian labor force. We see the impact by 1974, as shown in the last column of table 12.9. The annual growth rate for the entire labor force was the highest (2.8 percent) of all four periods covered in the table. The growth

*TABLE 12.9.*

*Occupational Mobility: Respondents and Fathers for a Sample of Heads of Households, Cairo, 1979 (N=312)*

| | *Occupation of His Father:* | | | | | | | |
|---|---|---|---|---|---|---|---|---|
| *Occupation of Respondent* | *Professionals* | *Executives* | *Clericals* | *Sales* | *Production Workers* | *Service Workers* | *Farming* | *Total* |
| Professional | 10.3 | 17.2 | 10.1 | 13.8 | ... | 13.8 | 34.5 | 9.3 |
| Executive | 4.3 | 25.5 | 17.0 | 19.1 | 6.4 | 10.6 | 17.0 | 15.1 |
| Clerical | 4.2 | 6.3 | 16.7 | 18.8 | 2.1 | 20.8 | 29.2 | 15.4 |
| Sales | ... | 2.3 | 6.8 | 36.4 | 2.3 | 13.6 | 38.6 | 14.1 |
| Production | ... | ... | 13.3 | 20.0 | 20.0 | 40.0 | 6.7 | 4.8 |
| Service | 1.0 | 1.0 | 6.7 | 12.4 | 2.9 | 42.9 | 32.4 | 33.7 |
| Farming | ... | ... | ... | ... | ... | ... | ... | ... |
| Housewives | ... | 8.3 | 12.5 | 25.0 | 12.5 | 16.7 | 25.0 | 7.7 |
| Total | 2.6 | 7.7 | 10.9 | 19.2 | 4.5 | 25.6 | 28.8 | 100.0 |

SOURCE: Original survey data

Statistical measures: $x^2 = 106.41$ P = 0.001 Gamma = 0.22 Contingency coefficient = 0.50

rate for sales occupations was remarkably high (20.1 percent), also reflecting the early thrust of the Open-Door policy of the Sadat regime. But high also were the growth rates in professional (9.9 percent), industrial (9.7 percent), and clerical occupations (6.1 percent). Service occupations grew modestly at 2.6 percent annually; administrative and farming occupations showed negative growth (−5.9 percent and −1.7 percent, respectively).

### *C. Intergenerational Occupation Mobility*

Along with the aggregate data on Egypt's occupational structure, the 1979 survey, conducted for the purpose of this volume, sheds more light on the inner dynamics of occupational mobility.

Table 12.9 compares the occupations of a Cairo sample of heads of households with those of their fathers. The occupational categories are arranged ordinally from "higher" to "lower." The diagonal (underscored values) represent the dividing line between upward (above it) and downward (below it) as well as cases of occupational immobility across two generations.

First, we look at the totals, where the last column refers to respondents' occupations, and the last row to their fathers' occupations. We observe immediately that professionals are nearly four times greater in the respondents' generation (9.3 percent) than in their fathers' generation (2.6 percent). Executives are twice as many in the respondents' generation (15.1 percent) compared to that of their fathers' generation (7.7 percent). There were similar, though less dramatic, increases in the percentages of clerical and sales occupations. In contrast, there were less production and service workers among the respondents than among their fathers. And since table 12.10 contains data on Cairo only, obviously we cannot compare the change across generations with regard to farming occupations. It is interesting to note, however, that as many as 29 percent of our respondents who were engaged in typically urban occupations had fathers who were in farming occupations. This in itself may be construed as a partial measure of rural-urban migration precipitated by and/or resulting in occupational mobility.

If we look at the inner cells of table 12.9, we observe that: (1) As many as 50 percent of the professionals among the respondents (top row) are sons of peasants (34.5 percent) and workers (13.8 percent). Thus the entry into this high occupational category was only partly determined by fathers' occupation. This was also somewhat the case with the next category (executives), in which 34 percent of its ranks had peasant or working class fathers. (2) But since workers and peasants accounted for over 70 percent of Egypt's labor force a generation ago, their sons (my respondents) were still markedly underrepresented in the top occupational categories. (3) Respondents whose fathers were professionals and execu-

TABLE 12.10.

*Occupational Mobility: Respondents and Sons for a Sample of Heads of Households, Cairo, 1979 (N=91)*

| *Occupation of Respondents* | *Occupation of Sons* | | | | | | |
|---|---|---|---|---|---|---|---|
| | *Professionals* | *Executives* | *Clericals* | *Sales* | *Production Workers* | *Service Workers* | *Total* |
| Professional | 87.5 | ... | 12.5 | ... | ... | ... | 8.8 |
| Executive | 28.6 | 57.1 | ... | ... | 14.3 | ... | 7.7 |
| Clerical | 20.0 | ... | 30.0 | ... | 20.0 | 30.0 | 10.9 |
| Sales | 10.5 | 5.3 | 26.3 | 10.5 | 15.8 | 31.6 | 20.9 |
| Production | ... | ... | 33.3 | ... | 33.3 | 33.3 | 3.3 |
| Service | 9.7 | ... | 41.9 | ... | 6.5 | 41.9 | 43.1 |
| Housewives | 23.1 | ... | 46.2 | 7.7 | 7.7 | 15.4 | 14.2 |
| Total | 20.9 | 5.5 | 31.9 | 3.3 | 10.9 | 27.5 | 14.2 |

SOURCE: Original Survey Data

Statistical measures: $x^2 = 91.65$ P = 0.001 Gamma = 0.48 Contingency coefficients = 0.71

tives tended to appear in greater percentages than their proportionate shares in the higher occupations, and in smaller percentages in lower occupations. Thus, only 4 percent of respondents in clerical and 1 percent in working-class occupations were sons of professionals. And only 6 percent of the respondents in clerical, 2 percent in sales, and 1 percent in working-class occupations were sons of executives. This suggests that the entry into higher occupations was relatively greater than exit from them across the two generations under consideration. (4) The middle occupational categories, clerical and sales, tended to be manned primarily by sons of peasants, service workers, and people in the same occupations. (5) Production workers among the respondents heavily tended to have working class fathers (60 percent) or other typically middle urban occupations (33 percent). Very few had peasant fathers (7.7 percent). (6) The primary source of manning the service-workers category was from its own ranks (43 percent of their fathers were also service workers) and from the peasantry (32 percent).

The relationship between respondents' and fathers' occupations is positive in direction, though modest in volume (Gamma 0.22, contingency coefficient 0.50). A weaker relationship implies greater mobility across occupational lines between the two generations. In other words, the data in table 12.9, which are statistically significant at the 0.001 level, suggest a moderate to high degree of mobility. Respondents were generally better off than their fathers for the sample as a whole. Most of the respondents with fathers in higher occupations continued to be in equally high occupational categories. But the opposite was not true. Many respondents with fathers in lower occupations managed to move up in the occupational ladder.

Table 12.10 shows the extent of occupational mobility between respondents and their sons. Here we notice right away that upward mobility has become more difficult for sons of the working class. Only 9.7 percent of the sons of service workers made it to the professional category (compared to 13.8 percent in the previous generation, as shown in table 12.11), and none made it to executive occupations (compared to 10.6 percent in the previous generation). None of the sons of production workers made a change to either one of the two top occupation categories (compared to 6.4 percent, who made it to executive occupations in the previous generation). About the only upward mobility channel that was still open for sons of working-class respondents was clerical occupations (33.3 percent of production workers' sons and 41.9 percent of service workers' sons). Otherwise, they were locked into working-class occupations like their fathers (66.6 percent of production workers' sons and 48.4 percent of service workers' sons).

In contrast, nearly 88 percent of professionals' sons were also professionals, and nearly 86 percent of the executives' sons were either professionals (28.6 percent) or executives like their fathers (57.1 percent). In

TABLE 12.11.

*Distribution of Population (Over Ten Years Old) by Educational Level 1947–1976 (in thousands)*

| | *1947* | | *1960* | | *1966* | | *1976* | |
|---|---|---|---|---|---|---|---|---|
| *Educational Level* | *N* | % | *N* | % | *N* | % | *N* | % |
| Illiterate* | 10,900 | 78.0 | 12,726 | 70.5 | 13,770 | 65.3 | 15,611 | 56.5 |
| Read and write | 2,911 | 20.8 | 4,356 | 24.2 | 5,886 | 27.9 | 6,923 | 25.1 |
| Intermediate certification | 113 | 0.8 | 801 | 4.4 | 1,193 | 5.7 | 4,475 | 16.2 |
| College or higher certificate | 57 | 0.4 | 170 | 0.9 | 235 | 1.1 | 606 | 2.2 |
| Total | 13,981 | 100.0 | 18,053 | 100.0 | 21,084 | 100.0 | 27,615 | 100.0 |

SOURCES: Population Censuses, 1947, 1960, 1966, 1976, CAPMS, Cairo.

*including people not classified

other words, there seems to be a greater consolidation at the top occupational categories, that is, sons inheriting fathers' occupations, and thus restricting entry of newcomers from the ranks of the lower-occupation categories.

Sons of respondents in middle-level occupations (clerical and sales) showed a mixed record, though still on the whole better than those of the working class. Twenty percent of the sons of respondents in clerical jobs managed to join the ranks of professionals, and nearly 16 percent of the sons of respondents in sales occupations managed to rise to the ranks of professionals (10.5 percent) or executives (5.3 percent). But as many as 50 percent of these sons slipped to occupations lower than those of their fathers.

To sum up the picture in table 12.10, we may add up the values below and above the diagonal to show the extent and direction of mobility for the sons of respondents in each occupational category. For sons of professionals, 88 percent continued in top-ranking occupations and only 12 percent experienced downward mobility. For sons of executives, 29 percent moved up, 57 percent remained upwardly mobile, and 14 percent moved downward. For sons of clerics, 20 percent moved up, 30 percent remained in place, and 50 percent stepped downward. For sons of sales-occupation respondents, 42 percent moved up, 11 percent remained in place, and 47 percent moved down. For sons of production workers, one-third moved slightly up, one-third remained in place, and one-third moved down. Finally, for sons of service workers, 10 percent moved higher up, 42 percent moderately up, and 42 percent remained downward mobile.

The relationship between respondents' and sons' occupations is positive in direction, strong in volume (Gamma = 0.48, contingency coefficient 0.71), and highly significant, at the 0.001 level. This suggests that the respondents' occupation made a substantial difference in determining his son's occupational standing, that is, the higher that of the respondent, the higher that of the son, and vice-versa.

Taken together, tables 12.9 and 12.10 show occupational mobility across three generations—father, respondent, and son. While a father's occupation made only some difference in determining a respondent's occupation (Gamma = 0.22), the respondent's occupation made more than twice as much difference in determining a son's occupation (Gamma = 0.48). In other words, the middle generation enjoyed greater mobility (mostly upward) than did the younger, present generation. The middle generation was occupationally placed in the 1950s and early 1960s, the younger one in the late 1960s and 1970s. The respondents' fathers (grandfathers to respondents' sons) were occupationally placed in the pre-1950 decades (1940s and 1930s). Thus, those who started their careers in the 1950s and 1960s had, on the whole, better occupational opportunities than both the preceding and following generations.

The data and analysis presented in this section seem to support my

*TABLE 12.12.*

*Percentage Change in Egyptians' Educational Level, 1947–1976*

| | *1947–1960* | | *1960–1966* | | *1966–1976* | |
|---|---|---|---|---|---|---|
| *Educational Level* | *Change for Entire Period* | *Average Annual Change* | *Change for Entire Period* | *Average Annual Change* | *Change for Entire Period* | *Average Annual Change* |
| Illiterate | 16.8 | 1.3 | 8.2 | 1.4 | 13.4 | 1.3 |
| Read and Write | 49.6 | 3.8 | 35.1 | 5.6 | 17.6 | 1.8 |
| Intermediate certificates | 608.8 | 46.8 | 48.9 | 8.2 | 275.1 | 27.5 |
| College or higher certificates | 198.2 | 15.2 | 38.2 | 6.4 | 157.9 | 15.8 |
| Total | 29.2 | 2.0 | 16.8 | 2.6 | 31.0 | 2.7 |

SOURCE: Computed from data in table 12.11.

hypothesis concerning social mobility in Egypt since 1952. Manual occupations have subsided in favor of nonmanual occupations. Farming activities have steadily declined in favor of nonfarming occupations. In other words, an increasing portion of the labor force has been moving up occupationally, with all the implications entailed with regard to income and prestige. This upward occupational mobility, however, was greatly affected by the prevailing socioeconomic policies in the successive periods of the 1952 revolution. Between 1952 and 1966 most of the upward movement was channeled into professional, managerial, and manufacturing occupations. Then there was a slowdown or complete halt of occupational mobility in the years following the 1967 war, up to the early 1970s. After 1973, upward occupational mobility accelerated again. But with a new socioeconomic orientation under President Sadat, known as the Open-Door policy, most of the upward mobility was channeled into sales occupations. The latter include commercial and finance occupations, which seem to flourish under a free-enterprise system.

This conclusion based on national aggregate data is further sharpened by structural data on intergenerational mobility for a Cairo sample. Strong evidence shows that upward mobility was much greater in the 1950s and 1960s than it was in the pre-1950 decades or in the post-1960s decade. The upward occupational channels were much more open to sons of peasants and workers in the middle period than at any time before or after.

## V. Educational Mobility

Education is one of the principal indicators of socioeconomic status. In modernizing societies, education is the fastest path to social mobility. Modernization implies at least two things: (1) the unfreezing of formerly rigid barriers among various strata, and (2) institution-building and expansion of modern economic activities. Educational achievement becomes a major criterion in manning these institutions and in carrying out those activities. Income, especially in the form of salaries and wages, becomes mainly a function of educational attainment. The channeling mechanism of status, in other words, becomes "achievement" rather than "ascription." The latter implies status determination on the basis of particularistic criteria such as kinship, family, tribal or ethnic background, that is, inherited privileges.

The 1952 revolution was keen from the beginning on undermining such inherited privileges and instituting principles of fairness and equal opportunities (see Dessouki in this volume). One of the earliest acts during the revolution was to abolish aristocratic titles such as *pasha, bey,* and *effendi,* along with titles associated with the monarchy. Another major objective of the revolution was modern institution-building and economic development. Both thrusts meant the primacy of educational achievement as a social-mobility vehicle. The efforts of the revolution to expand education are covered in chapter 11 of this volume by M. A. Fadil. Our concern in this section will be mainly educational mobility, both aggregate and intergenerational.

### *A. Aggregate Educational Mobility*

The expansion of education in Egypt after 1952 allowed new groups in society to send their children to school, enlarged the pool of literate population, and increased the size of those groups in the medium and higher educational levels.

Tables 12.11 and 12.12 show the evolution of and relative changes in population over ten years of age by educational levels from 1947 to 1976. The inference we may draw from these data is that, between 1947 and 1976, greater numbers were being educated at a rate faster than that of annual population increments. Thus, while the population as a whole increased by nearly 98 percent in twenty-nine years, the literate pool increased by 289 percent, nearly three times as much. To assess the aggregate educational mobility, we can assume that zero mobility would obtain if the literate pool grew at a rate similar to that of population in general, that is, 98 percent between 1947 and 1976. That pool in 1947 was 3.1 millions. Had it grown by 98 percent, it would have been 6.1 millions in 1976. Any increase over the latter figure would mean upward educational mobility, and any decrease below the figure would imply the opposite, or downward mobility. Since the actual figure for 1976 was slightly over 12 millions, it means a net increment of 5.9 million, or nearly 97 percent, over the hypothetical figure (6.1 millions) had there been no mobility whatsoever.

The literate pool includes three broad categories: those who read and write (minimally educated), those with intermediate certificates (nine to twelve years of formal schooling), and those with college or higher certificates. We can apply the above method to assess the mobility for each category, that is, rate of entry into it. Thus, had the minimally educated category grown at a rate similar to that of population between 1947 and 1976, its size would have been 5.8 million, meaning no net mobility in or out of this category. But since the actual size in 1976 was 6.9 million, there is a net increment of 1.1 million, about 19 percent higher than the hypothetical no-mobility figure. For the intermediate category, the hypothetical no-mobility figure would have been 224,000 in 1976; the actual figure was 4.2 million higher, about 1,900 percent new entries into that category between 1947 and 1976. For the college-educated category, the new entries in the same period were 463 percent (or 493,000 persons) increment over the expected figure had that category grown at the same rate as the general population.

Another conclusion we can draw from table 12.12 is that the average annual growth rate in the read-and-write category peaked during the

1960–1966 period (5.6 percent). The comparable averages for both intermediate and college categories reached their peak in the 1966–1976 period (at 2.7 and 15.8 percent, respectively). This seems natural, since each educational level represents a pool from which the next higher level will draw in successive years.

### *B. Intergenerational Mobility*

Given the impressive rates of aggregate educational mobility in Egypt in the last quarter-century, the question remains: which of the various strata in the society had greater access to available educational opportunities? This question can ideally be answered by surveying a representative cross-section of all Egyptian families to collect comparative data on the educational level of sons, parents, and grandparents in the same family, along with information on their occupations and incomes (that is, the other two indicators of socioeconomic status). Such data are not available. However, we have a few small-scale studies that shed some light on the question.

The first study was conducted in 1962 on government and public-sector employees.[21] As table 12.13 shows, nearly 43 percent were sons of professionals and managers. The combined total of these two categories in the labor force in 1960 was 4.2 percent. In other words, occupational categories I and II (table 12.13) supplied the government and public sector with university-educated people at a percentage rate ten times bigger than their proportionate representation in the labor force. Category III (businessmen, finance and sales workers, and landowners) represented 10.2 percent of the labor force but supplied government and the public sector with 30.8 percent of the college-educated, three times their proportionate share. The other occupational categories, IV through VII, were all underrepresented in the college-educated employees of the government and public sector. Thus, only 2.7 percent of the latter were sons of parents in clerical occupations, which make up 8.1 percent of the labor force. Slightly over 4 percent of the college-educated were sons of craftsmen and skilled production workers (16.2 percent of the labor force). Service and unskilled workers, with 12.4 percent of the labor force, supplied government with only 1.4 of the college-educated employees. Occupational category VII (all others including small farmers) represented 41 percent of the labor force, but their university-educated children in government represented less than 18 percent of all employees.

The first three categories (I, II, and III) in table 12.13 correspond roughly to the upper and upper middle strata in Egypt. They made up 14 percent of the labor force in the early 1960s. Together, however, they appropriated nearly 74 percent of all the higher-track positions in government and the public sector for their children. Categories IV and V correspond roughly to the lower middle stratum; with a combined total of 24.3

TABLE 12.13.

*Percentage Distribution of Government and Public Sector Employees by Their Educational Level According to Parents' Occupation, 1962*

| Father's Occupation | Percentage of Occupational Category in Labor Force (1960) | Educational Level of Employees: College or Above Percent | Educational Level of Employees: Intermediate Certificate Percent |
|---|---|---|---|
| I Professionals | 3.1 | 39.2 | 18.4 |
| II Administrative and managerial | 1.1 | 3.9 | 0.8 |
| III Business, commerce, and landowners | 10.2 | 30.8 | 33.5 |
| IV Clerical (white collar) | 8.1 | 2.7 | 18.8 |
| V Craftsmen and skilled workers | 16.2 | 4.1 | 12.7 |
| VI Service and unskilled workers | 20.2 | 1.4 | 2.8 |
| VII Other occupations | 41.1 | 17.9 | 13.0 |
| Total | 100.0 | 100.0 | 100.0 |

SOURCES: Institute of National Planning, *Employment and Unemployment among the Educated* (Cairo, 1962; Nazih Auyūbī, *Educational Policy in Egypt* (Arabic), (Cairo: Center for Political and Strategic Studies, 1978), p. 72; 1960 Census.

percent of the labor force, they appropriated less than 7 percent of the high-track positions in the state apparatus. Finally, we may consider categories VI and VII as the lower strata. Their total in the labor force was about 54 percent, but the share of their children in high-track state positions was only 19 percent.

Among state employees with intermediate certificates, there was less lopsidedness. The upper occupational groups (I, II, and III in table 12.13) appropriated for their children 52.7 percent of the medium-track positions in the state apparatus. The middle categories (IV and V) appropriated 31.5 of the medium-track positions; the lower categories appropriated 15.8 percent of such positions. It is clear here that medium and lower occupational categories fared better in medium-track positions than they did with higher-track slots. Their combined share in the former was 26 percent, and in the latter 47 percent.

Another study conducted in 1966 on the students of Cairo University,[22] also offers a partial answer to the question of intergenerational mobility. The data are presented in table 12.14. Being a university student, presum-

*TABLE 12.14.*
*Distribution of Students in Cairo University According to Parents' Occupation, 1966*

| | *Parents' Occupation* | *% of Occupational Category in Labor Force* | *Students at Cairo University (percent)* |
|---|---|---|---|
| I | Professionals, administrators, managers | 6.6 | 33.0 |
| II | Businessmen, landowners | 10.1 | 29.3 |
| III | Clerical (white collar) | 5.5 | 21.0 |
| IV | Craftsmen and skilled workers | 18.4 | 5.6 |
| V | Farmers | 50.4 | 5.8 |
| VI | Others | 9.0 | 5.1 |
| | Total | 100.0 | 100.0 |

SOURCE: M. A. Shafshag, "Role of University in the Formation of the Egyptian Elite," *National Review of Social Research* (Cairo), nos. 2–3, 1968 (Arabic); and 1966 Census.

ably, means that upon graduation the person will occupy a high-track position in the state, public, or private sectors, that is, upper occupational categories. Therefore, we may assume that there is greater upward mobility if the proportion of students whose parents are from middle or lower occupations is rising over time. Categories I and II in table 12.14 may be considered upper-occupational groups since they include professionals, scientists, top administrators, executives, managers, businessmen, and rich farmers. In 1966 they they made up about 17 percent of the labor force, but they appropriated for their children nearly 63 percent of all enrollment slots in Cairo University. Even though still overrepresented, their share in potential high-track positions has dropped (from 74 percent in table 12.13) by about 11 percentage points between the early and middle 1960s.

Students whose parents were in medium occupations (categories II and III in table 12.14) totaled about 50 percent of Cairo University's student body. The farming occupations were still heavily underrepresented. They made up over 50 percent of the labor force, but appropriated only 6 percent of the university slots for their children.

Finally, we have data from the Cairo sample survey conducted in 1979, thirteen years after the previous study. Tables 12.15 and 12.16 show the levels of education for respondents and their fathers, and for respondents and their sons, respectively. Together, they reflect the extent and direction of educational mobility across three generations.

*TABLE 12.15.*

*Educational Mobility: Respondents and Fathers for a Sample of Heads of Households, Cairo, 1979 (N = 318)*

| *Education of Respondents* | *Education of Their Fathers (percent)* | | | | | | | |
|---|---|---|---|---|---|---|---|---|
| | *Illiterate* | *Read and Write* | *Primary* | *Preparatory* | *Secondary* | *College* | *Post grad.* | *Total* |
| Illiterate | 84.7 | 13.9 | ... | 1.4 | ... | ... | ... | 22.6 |
| Read & write | 62.4 | 32.3 | 4.3 | ... | 1.1 | ... | ... | 29.2 |
| Primary | 48.4 | 41.9 | 9.7 | ... | ... | ... | ... | 9.7 |
| Preparatory | 29.4 | 58.8 | 5.9 | ... | 5.9 | ... | ... | 5.3 |
| Secondary | 21.2 | 40.4 | 11.5 | 3.8 | 13.5 | 9.6 | ... | 16.4 |
| College | 4.2 | 39.6 | 20.8 | 2.1 | 10.4 | 18.8 | 4.2 | 15.1 |
| Postgraduate | ... | 20.0 | ... | ... | 40.0 | 40.0 | ... | 1.6 |

SOURCE: Original survey data

Statistical measures: $x^2 = 158.58$   P = 0.001   Gamma = 0.68   Contingency coefficient = 0.58

TABLE 12.16.

*Educational Mobility: Respondents and Sons for a Sample of Heads of Households, Cairo, 1979 (N = 190)*

| | Education of Their Sons | | | | | | | |
|---|---|---|---|---|---|---|---|---|
| *Education of Respondents* | *Illiterate* | *Read and Write* | *Primary* | *Preparatory* | *Secondary* | *College* | *Post grad.* | *Total* |
| Illiterate | 26.6 | 20.0 | 14.5 | 4.3 | 23.6 | 10.9 | ... | 38.9 |
| Read & write | 10.8 | 10.8 | 18.5 | 16.9 | 30.8 | 12.3 | ... | 24.3 |
| Primary | ... | 5.0 | 30.0 | 5.0 | 50.0 | 10.0 | ... | 10.5 |
| Preparatory | ... | ... | 16.7 | 16.7 | 66.7 | ... | ... | 3.2 |
| Secondary | ... | ... | 4.2 | 8.3 | 58.3 | 25.0 | 4.2 | 12.6 |
| College | ... | ... | ... | 15.8 | 21.1 | 47.4 | 15.8 | 10.0 |
| Postgraduate | ... | ... | ... | ... | ... | 100.0 | ... | 0.5 |
| Total | 10.5 | 10.0 | 14.7 | 11.6 | 34.7 | 16.3 | 2.1 | 100.0 |

SOURCE: Original survey data

Statistical measures: $x^2 = 88.95$ P = 0.001 Gamma = 0.50 Contingency coefficient = 0.57

The totals in table 12.15 show the overall improvement in educational attainments of respondents over their fathers. The illiterates among the fathers were proportionately more than twice that among the respondents (48.4 versus 22.6 percent). The college-educated among respondents (15 percent) were nearly four times the number of their fathers (4 percent). The diagonal reveals the dynamics of such improvement. Many of the illiterates among respondents (85 percent) had illiterate fathers (that is, two-generation illiterates). The rest (15 percent) had fathers who were at least literate. Theirs is a case of downward educational mobility. In the next educational level (reading and writing) 62 percent of the respondents had illiterate fathers, that is, one-step improvement; 32 percent were like their fathers, and 4 percent were worse off than their fathers, or one-step downward mobility.

Respondents in the third category (primary education) were mostly better off than their fathers: 48 percent of them had illiterate fathers, 42 percent had fathers who only read and write, and 10 percent had fathers at the same level. In other words, there is no downward mobility in this category.

Respondents with preparatory certificates showed nearly the same overall improvement. Over 29 percent of their fathers were illiterates (that is, three steps up); 59 percent of their fathers read and write (two steps up), and 6 percent of their fathers had primary certificates (one step up). All in all, 94 percent of the respondents in this educational level have experienced upward mobility and only 6 percent moved downward.

Respondents in the category with secondary certificates were mostly sons of illiterates (21 percent) or of barely literate fathers (40 percent). Slightly over 15 percent of the respondents had fathers with primary or preparatory education. All in all, then, about 77 percent in this category have experienced upward mobility (from one to four steps). Nearly 14 percent have remained at the same level as fathers, and about 10 percent have experienced downward mobility.

Among respondents with college education, few (4 percent) of their fathers were illiterates, but the majority of fathers (60 percent) were either barely literate (40 percent) or with only primary-level education (20 percent). For these respondents, the educational mobility was indeed substantial, that is, five and four steps up, respectively. All in all, 77 percent of the respondents with college education were born to fathers who did not exceed the secondary level. The rest (23 percent) were born to fathers with university or postgraduate education.

The relationship shown in table 12.15 is positive in direction, strong in volume (Gamma = 0.68), and highly significant (at the 0.001 level). But it is a complex relationship. Thus, while it is shown that fathers' education is a major determinant of respondents' education, this determinancy varied markedly from one level of fathers' education to another. The channels of upward educational mobility opened up the most to respondents born to fathers not in the very lowest educational level but in the two levels immediately above.

Table 12.16 shows the relationship between respondents' and their sons' education. Again, we notice a continuation of the upward educational mobility for the third generation. Illiteracy among the sons has been reduced to about one-fourth of that of the respondents (10.5 versus 38.9 percent). Sons with secondary certificates were nearly three times more than among their fathers (34.7 versus 12.6 percent). Sons with college education made up over 16 percent compared to 10 percent among their fathers (the respondents).

Of the illiterate respondents, only 24 percent of their sons remained illiterate. The rest (76 percent) of the sons moved up the educational scale: 20 percent by one step, 15 percent by two steps, 7 percent by three, 24 percent by four, and 11 percent by five steps above their fathers.

Of the sons of literate respondents, 78 percent were better off educationally than their fathers, 11 percent remained the same, and 11 percent were worse off. Among those who moved up, 19 percent did so by one step, 17 percent by two, 31 percent by three, and 12 percent by four steps. The middle educational categories of respondents (primary, preparatory, secondary) had no illiterate sons. Most of the latter are concentrated in the middle and upper educational levels. Greater concentration of the sons of college-educated respondents are in the upper-educational end of the scale (college and postgraduate add up to 63 percent). All in all, table 12.16 shows many empty cells below the diagonal, reflecting the general upward mobility for the sons in educational attainment.

The relationship implied by the data in table 12.16 is positive, moderate in volume (Gamma = 0.50), and highly significant at the 0.001 level. But while there is no doubt of the fact that most sons are better off than most fathers (respondents) educationally, we still notice that the degree of betterment varies markedly from one educational level of respondents to another. Thus, while only 11 percent of illiterate respondents' sons and 12 percent of literate respondents' sons made it all the way to college, more than twice as many of the sons of secondary-educated, and four times as many of the sons of college-educated, respondents got to college. This situation is relatively no better than it was a generation earlier (as implied in table 12.16). To clarify this point, we reconstruct the totals of tables 12.15 and 12.16 of the three upper educational levels for the three generations:

| Level of Education | *Generation* I Fathers % | II Respondents % | III Sons % |
|---|---|---|---|
| Secondary | 4.7 | 16.4 | 34.7 |
| College | 4.4 | 15.1 | 16.3 |
| Postgraduate | 0.6 | 1.6 | 2.1 |
| Total: | 9.7 | 33.1 | 53.1 |

We see immediately that the middle generation (II) has nearly quadrupled its percentages in secondary and college education *vis-à-vis* generation I (their fathers). On the other hand, generation III (the sons) only doubled its percentage of secondary education and slightly increased its college and postgraduate education *vis-à-vis* generation II. In other words, the upward educational gains of generation II are substantially greater than those of generation III.

Generation I is mostly made up of persons whose educational opportunities were charted in pre-1952 times (in the 1920s, 1930s, 1940s). Generation II is made up mostly of persons whose opportunities were determined in the 1950s and early 1960s (the height of the 1952 revolution). Generation III is mostly made up of youngsters whose educational opportunities were set in the late 1960s and throughout the 1970s (years of stagnation and socialist retreat).

The national aggregate data as well as the data from the three surveys cited strongly support my hypothesis with regard to Egypt's social mobility in the last three decades. Taking education as an indicator, the volume of upward mobility reached its maximum in the 1950s to the mid-1960s period. Although upward mobility continued through the late 1960s and 1970s, its relative increase has been markedly smaller and more concentrated between the middle and upper educational levels.

## VI. Linkages of Class Components

In this final section an attempt is made to link the various components that determine one's class position—his socioeconomic status (SES). Four components are considered: income, occupation, education, and life-style. The first three were separately elaborated in earlier sections. The fourth, life-style, is operationalized here in terms of acquisition of certain durable goods.[23]

Since income distribution is the focus of this volume, we will first elaborate its linkages with other components of SES separately. Then we shall construct a composite index of all four indicators, including income, and measure it against how people subjectively perceive their own class standing.

TABLE 12.17.

*Distribution of Sample Families according to Activities and Levels of Income (£E per Year), 1974*

| *Levels of Income: Activity* | *<50* | *50–74* | *75–99* | *100–149* | *150–199* | *200–249* | *250–299* | *300–349* | *350–399* | *400–499* | *500–599* | *600–799* | *800–999* | *1000–1399* | *1400–1999* | *2000–* | ** | *Total* |
|---|---|---|---|---|---|---|---|---|---|---|---|---|---|---|---|---|---|---|
| Agriculture | 78 | 184 | 689 | 1,193 | 1,414 | 1,259 | 918 | 658 | 518 | 445 | 300 | 196 | 112 | 51 | 30 | 11 | 11 | 8,067 |
| Mining and quarrying | ... | ... | ... | 5 | 9 | 14 | 13 | 10 | 8 | 6 | 4 | 5 | 2 | ... | 2 | 4 | ... | 82 |
| Manufacturing | 4 | 23 | 95 | 378 | 818 | 905 | 697 | 606 | 497 | 474 | 319 | 297 | 136 | 66 | 52 | 27 | 9 | 5,403 |
| Electricity, Gas, and Water | ... | 1 | ... | 14 | 32 | 27 | 11 | 30 | 13 | 15 | 12 | 16 | 8 | 2 | ... | 1 | ... | 182 |
| Construction | 2 | 6 | 12 | 78 | 157 | 181 | 151 | 118 | 86 | 82 | 65 | 56 | 46 | 19 | 10 | 7 | ... | 1,076 |
| Commerce and hotels | 24 | 54 | 157 | 385 | 669 | 686 | 584 | 507 | 475 | 463 | 311 | 306 | 190 | 100 | 55 | 48 | 6 | 5,020 |
| Transport and communications | ... | 9 | 23 | 95 | 197 | 296 | 237 | 253 | 224 | 224 | 169 | 159 | 79 | 49 | 20 | 9 | 1 | 2,044 |
| Finance and insurance | 1 | ... | 4 | 9 | 40 | 30 | 33 | 37 | 36 | 44 | 49 | 69 | 33 | 29 | 16 | 4 | ... | 434 |
| Services | 22 | 61 | 175 | 430 | 789 | 896 | 643 | 638 | 476 | 560 | 444 | 450 | 299 | 217 | 142 | 69 | 10 | 6,277 |
| Unclassified | 610 | 479 | 796 | 901 | 1,057 | 831 | 566 | 518 | 408 | 435 | 289 | 305 | 188 | 133 | 85 | 48 | 41 | 7,690 |
| Total | 741 | 817 | 1,951 | 3,488 | 5,183 | 5,098 | 3,853 | 3,367 | 2,732 | 2,748 | 1,962 | 1,859 | 1,093 | 670 | 412 | 228 | 78 | 36,280 |
| Percent | 2.0 | 2.3 | 5.4 | 9.6 | 14.3 | 14.1 | 16.1 | 9.3 | 7.5 | 7.6 | 5.4 | 5.1 | 3.0 | 1.9 | 1.1 | .06 | .02 | 100 |

SOURCE: *Labor Force Sample Survey, May 1974* (CAPMS, Cairo, 1976).

**Information unclassified.

TABLE 12.18.

*Relationship between Occupation and Annual Income of a Sample of Heads of Households in Egypt, 1978, in U.S. Dollars (percentages) (N = 1972)*

| | Income | | | | | | | | | |
|---|---|---|---|---|---|---|---|---|---|---|
| *Occupation* | *Less than 1,000* | *1,000–2,000* | *2,000–3,000* | *3,000–4,000* | *4,000–5,000* | *5,000–6,000* | *6,000–7,000* | *7,000–8,000* | *8,000 & above* | *Total* |
| Academic and scientific | 65.1 | 24.3 | 6.9 | 1.6 | ... | 1.6 | ... | ... | 0.5 | 100.0 |
| Medical | 49.7 | 28.2 | 11.9 | 7.3 | 1.1 | 0.6 | ... | 0.6 | 0.6 | 100.0 |
| Engineering | 52.1 | 35.1 | 8.5 | 2.1 | 1.1 | ... | ... | ... | 1.1 | 100.0 |
| Legal professions | 50.5 | 29.0 | 4.3 | 8.6 | 1.1 | 2.2 | 2.2 | 2.2 | ... | 100.0 |
| Mass media | 19.1 | 29.8 | 18.3 | 11.5 | 4.6 | 6.1 | 8.4 | 0.8 | 1.5 | 100.0 |
| Art and culture | 78.0 | 16.0 | 4.0 | 2.0 | ... | ... | ... | ... | ... | 100.0 |
| Education | 80.9 | 16.7 | 2.0 | ... | ... | ... | 0.4 | ... | ... | 100.0 |
| Agronomists | 82.1 | 17.0 | 0.9 | ... | ... | ... | ... | ... | ... | 100.0 |
| Other professional | 43.3 | 10.0 | 3.3 | ... | 3.3 | ... | ... | ... | 40.0 | 100.0 |
| Government administration | 79.4 | 17.6 | 1.5 | ... | ... | ... | ... | 1.5 | ... | 100.0 |
| Commerce | 72.5 | 20.0 | 2.7 | 2.4 | 1.5 | 0.3 | ... | 0.3 | 0.3 | 100.0 |
| Crafts, skilled labor | 68.3 | 24.4 | 2.4 | 2.4 | ... | ... | 2.4 | ... | ... | 100.0 |
| Semi-, unskilled labor | 89.2 | 9.6 | 1.2 | ... | ... | ... | ... | ... | ... | 100.0 |
| Farming | 91.0 | 7.2 | 1.2 | 0.6 | ... | ... | ... | ... | ... | 100.0 |
| Total | 69.0 | 19.0 | 4.9 | 2.7 | 0.8 | 0.8 | 0.8 | 0.3 | 1.7 | 100.0 |

SOURCE: Survey data, S. E. Ibrahim, *Arab Attitudes toward Unification in Ten Arab Countries* (forthcoming) (Beirut: Center for Arab Unity Studies).

Statistical measures: $x^2 = 983.99$ P = 0.01 Gamma = 0.32 Contingency coefficient = 0.58

## A. Social Correlates of Incomes

I made several assertions to the effect that income is determined by and is a determinant of education, occupation, and life-style. Tables 12.17 through 12.25 give data that substantiate these assertions.

1. *Income and occupation:* To suggest that occupation and income are interrelated in a modern or a modernizing society is not new. What would be of greater significance is to reveal the strength of such relationship. Table 12.17 shows the annual income distribution by broad economic activities for a national sample survey of heads of families of Egypt's labor force in 1974. Although economic activities are not occupations per se, it is still obvious that agricultural occupations have their central tendency toward the lower end of the income scale. The "modal category" (circled in table 12.17) is £E150 income per family per annum. Manufacturing, construction, commerce, transportation, and services occupations are included in the same income bracket above. Their modal category is £E200–250 per annum, and they are closer to the middle of the income distribution. Finance and insurance activities have the highest central tendency; their modal category is the £E600–800 per annum.

Table 12.18 shows distributional data by occupational category for another national sample survey conducted in 1978. The income categories here are in U.S. dollars, and the occupational classification is not strictly comparable with similar Egyptian data, since the survey was conducted as part of a comparative attitudinal study in several Arab countries. What matters, however, is the magnitude of the relationship. We observe from table 12.18, for example, that mass media, medical and legal occupations are at the top of Egypt's income scale. They are followed in this respect by engineers, academics, craftsmen, and skilled labor. At the lowest end of the scale (less than $1,000 per year) we find farming, unskilled and semiskilled labor, agronomists, and educational occupations. The lowest income category in this table is at a relatively high cutting point and it, therefore, may contain a greater variance within it than between it and other income categories. This suggests some precautions in drawing any firm conclusions. The findings, nevertheless, substantiate one of the impressionistic observations made in recent years about the rising income of craftsmen and self-employed skilled labor (mechanics, carpenters, electricians, plumbers, and so forth). Respondents in these manual occupations reported, on the average, higher annual incomes than some of the white-collar and college-based occupations. The correlation between occupation and income, as shown in table 12.18, is statistically significant at the 0.01 level, and its magnitude is moderate (Gamma = 0.32, contingency coefficient 0.58). This suggests that income is positively related to occupation, though not always or strictly along manual versus nonmanual lines.

Table 12.19 gives the results of a smaller-scale survey of a Cairo sample

TABLE 12.19.

*Relationship between Family Annual Income and Occupation for a Sample of Heads of Households in Cairo, 1979 (Percentages); N = 320*

| | *Annual Income (£E)* | | | | | | | | |
|---|---|---|---|---|---|---|---|---|---|
| *Occupation* | *(1) Less than 300* | *(2) 300–500* | *(3) 500–1,000* | *(4) 1,000–1,500* | *(5) 1,500–2,000* | *(6) 2,000–3,000* | *(7) 3,000–5,000* | *(8) 5,000 & above* | *Total* |
| Professionals | . . . | 10.0 | 33.3 | 40.0 | 6.7 | . . . | 6.7 | 3.3 | 9.4 |
| Executives | . . . | 10.6 | 27.7 | 38.3 | 10.6 | 10.6 | . . . | 2.1 | 14.7 |
| Clerical | 8.3 | 35.4 | 31.3 | 18.8 | 6.3 | . . . | . . . | . . . | 15.0 |
| Sales | 19.1 | 31.9 | 34.0 | 6.4 | . . . | 8.5 | . . . | . . . | 14.7 |
| Production workers | 17.6 | 47.1 | 23.5 | 5.9 | 5.9 | . . . | . . . | . . . | 5.3 |
| Service workers | 17.0 | 32.1 | 35.9 | 7.5 | 6.6 | 0.9 | . . . | . . . | 33.1 |
| Housewives | 28.0 | 36.0 | 28.0 | 8.0 | . . . | . . . | . . . | . . . | 7.8 |
| Total | 12.8 | 28.4 | 32.2 | 16.6 | 5.6 | 3.1 | 0.6 | 0.6 | 100.0 |

SOURCE: Original survey data

Statistical measures: $x^2 = 117.23$   P = 0.001   Gamma = 0.39   Contingency coefficient = 0.52

TABLE 12.20

*Distribution of Sample Families according to Educational Status and Level of Income (£E/year), 1974*

| *Educational Status* | *1* <br> *<50* | *2* <br> *50–* | *3* <br> *75–* | *4* <br> *100–* | *5* <br> *150–* | *6* <br> *200–* | *7* <br> *250–* | *8* <br> *300–* | *9* <br> *350–* | *10* <br> *400–* | *11* <br> *500–* | *12* <br> *600–* | *13* <br> *800–* | *14* <br> *1000–* | *15* <br> *1400–* | *16* <br> *2000–* | *Un-* <br> *clear* | *Total* | *%* |
|---|---|---|---|---|---|---|---|---|---|---|---|---|---|---|---|---|---|---|---|
| 1. Illiterate | 709 | 743 | 1,697 | 2,697 | 3,392 | 2,863 | 1,993 | 1,501 | 1,127 | 918 | 582 | 385 | 168 | 59 | 22 | 8 | 43 | 18,907 | 52.1 |
| 2. Read and write | 27 | 66 | 224 | 682 | 1,526 | 1,787 | 1,451 | 1,287 | 1,093 | 1,066 | 742 | 577 | 294 | 153 | 98 | 48 | 16 | 11,137 | 30.7 |
| 3. Below intermediate certificate | 1 | 1 | 10 | 23 | 68 | 114 | 88 | 131 | 112 | 148 | 101 | 93 | 48 | 30 | 11 | 7 | 4 | 990 | 2.7 |
| 4. Intermediate certificate | 4 | 7 | 20 | 80 | 188 | 285 | 265 | 322 | 281 | 386 | 293 | 368 | 189 | 109 | 62 | 34 | 14 | 2,907 | 8.0 |
| 5. Above intermediate certificate | ... | ... | ... | 2 | 4 | 39 | 37 | 57 | 40 | 64 | 58 | 56 | 40 | 25 | 10 | 3 | ... | 435 | 1.2 |
| 6. University certificate | ... | ... | ... | 3 | 2 | 6 | 16 | 67 | 78 | 158 | 180 | 364 | 331 | 263 | 186 | 99 | 1 | 1,754 | 4.8 |
| 7. Postgraduate certificate | ... | ... | ... | ... | ... | ... | 2 | 1 | 1 | 8 | 4 | 14 | 23 | 31 | 23 | 29 | ... | 136 | 0.4 |
| Unclear | ... | ... | ... | 1 | 3 | 4 | 1 | 1 | ... | ... | 2 | 2 | ... | ... | ... | ... | ... | 14 | 0.04 |
| Total | 741 | 817 | 1,951 | 3,488 | 5,183 | 5,098 | 5,853 | 3,367 | 2,732 | 2,748 | 1,962 | 1,859 | 1,093 | 670 | 412 | 228 | 78 | 36,280 | 100.0 |
| Percent | 2.0 | 2.3 | 5.4 | 9.6 | 14.3 | 14.1 | 16.1 | 9.3 | 7.5 | 7.6 | 5.4 | 5.1 | 3.0 | 1.9 | 1.1 | 0.6 | 0.2 | | 100.0 |

SOURCE: CAPMS, *Labor Force Sample Survey, May Round 1974*, (Cairo, 1976).

of heads of household conducted in 1979. The occupational classification here is similar to that used in official Egyptian censuses and surveys, and is different from that used in table 12.18. Yet, the magnitude of correlation as measured by both Gamma (0.39) and contingency coefficient (0.52) is very close to that reported in table 12.18. The modal income category for professionals and executives is in the fourth highest income bracket (£E1,000–1,500 per annum), and as many as 16 percent of the professionals and 22 percent of the executives were in higher income brackets. The modal category for clerical occupations and production workers was the second income bracket (£E300–500 per annum) and, except for housewives, they ranked closest to the lower end of the income scale. Between them on the one hand and the professionals and executives on the other hand, we find people in sales and service occupations situated nearly in the middle. The modal income category for sales and services (who tend to be self-employed) is the third income bracket, £E500–1,000 annually.

In summary, the data in the three tables, though not strictly comparable, substantiate the proposition that income and occupation are interrelated. The correlation between the two variables, however, is far from perfect. At best, occupation explains slightly more than 50 percent of the variance in the income of Egyptians surveyed between 1974 and 1979. This suggests that other factors must be introduced to explain the rest of the variance.

*2. Income and education:* Education is thought of as another determinant of income in most societies, that is, the higher the education, the higher the income, and vice versa. Tables 12.20, 12.21, and 12.22 contain data from the same three surveys cited.

The National Labor Survey data (table 12.20) show the modal income category for illiterates to be £E150 annually; the barely literate (second row) are concentrated in the next income category (£E200 per annum). But the next three educational levels jump their modal categories by three steps, that is, £E400–500. The college-educated are concentrated in the upper third of the income scale (modal category £E600–800), with as many as 50 percent in income brackets higher than the mode. The same applies to those with postgraduate education; their modal category is £E1,000–1,400 annually, with as many as 38 percent of them in higher income brackets.

The 1978 Arab Attitudes Survey data for the Egyptian National Sample, shown in table 12.21, give another distribution of income and education. Again, the correlation between the two variables is highly significant (at the 0.001 level), and the measure of association (Gamma) is 0.47. At the lower end of the income scale (below £E1,000), we find 93 percent of the lowest-educated respondents, compared to only 49 percent of the highest-educated. The comparable percentages for respondents with intermediate and college education are 82 and 68, respectively. None in the

*TABLE 12.21.*

*Relationship between Annual Family Income and Education for a Sample of Heads of Households in Egypt, 1978, in U.S. Dollars (Percentages) N = 1972*

| | *Education* | | | | |
|---|---|---|---|---|---|
| *Annual Income* | *Intermediate & below* | *Intermediate* | *College* | *Postgraduate* | *Total* |
| Less than 1,000 | 93.0 | 82.2 | 67.8 | 48.6 | 69.0 |
| 1,000–2,000 | 6.1 | 15.7 | 20.2 | 27.6 | 19.0 |
| 2,000–3,000 | 0.9 | 1.2 | 4.5 | 11.5 | 4.9 |
| 3,000–4,000 | ... | 0.5 | 3.0 | 5.2 | 2.7 |
| 4,000–5,000 | ... | 0.4 | 0.7 | 1.9 | 0.8 |
| 5,000–6,000 | ... | ... | 1.0 | 1.4 | 0.8 |
| 6,000–7,000 | ... | ... | 0.8 | 1.6 | 0.8 |
| 7,000–8,000 | ... | ... | 0.2 | 0.8 | 0.3 |
| 8,000 and above | ... | ... | 1.9 | 1.4 | 1.7 |
| Total | 100.0 | 100.0 | 100.0 | 100.0 | 100.0 |

SOURCE: Survey data from S.E. Ibrahim, *Arab Attitudes toward Unification in Ten Arab Countries* (forthcoming) Beirut: Center for Arab Unity Studies.

Statistical measures: $x^2 = 186.18$ $P = 0.001$ Gamma = 0.47
Contingency coefficient = 0.29

lowest educational level goes beyond the third (of nine) income category, and none in the intermediate level earns beyond the fifth category. In contrast, both the graduates and postgraduates span all income brackets to the top.

Finally, table 12.22 shows the same relationship between education and income for a Cairo sample in 1979. The results are quite consistent with the other two surveys cited. The lowest income category (less than £E300) shows a preponderance of illiterates (57 percent) and the barely literates (31 percent). These lowest two educational levels decline gradually as we go up the income scale until they disappear completely by the fifth and sixth brackets. In contrast, the highest two income brackets are populated entirely by the college-educated and postgraduates. The correlation between education and income is naturally positive in direction and highly significant (at the 0.001 level). But the magnitude of this correlation is moderate (Gamma = 0.51).

The results of the three surveys, taken together, suggest what I expected—a positive relationship between education and income. But as was the case with occupation, this relationship is not perfect. Education, at best, accounts for only 50 percent of the variance in income.

*3. Income and life-style:* In the 1979 Cairo survey, life-style was operationalized by two separate indicators. The first comprised a

TABLE 12.22.

*Relationship of Annual Family Income and Education of a Sample of Heads of Households in Cairo, 1979 (Percentages) N = 322*

| | *Education* | | | | | | | |
|---|---|---|---|---|---|---|---|---|
| | *1* | 2 | 3 | 4 | 5 | 6 | 7 | |
| *Income (£E)* | *Illiterate* | *Read & Write* | *Primary* | *Preparatory* | *Secondary* | *College* | *Postgraduate* | % |
| 1. Less than 300 | 57.1 | 31.0 | 4.8 | 2.4 | 4.8 | ... | ... | 13.1 |
| 2. 300–500 | 29.7 | 34.1 | 13.2 | 7.7 | 11.0 | 1.1 | 3.3 | 28.3 |
| 3. 500–1,000 | 17.5 | 34.0 | 9.7 | 5.8 | 20.4 | 12.6 | ... | 32.1 |
| 4. 1,000–1,500 | 5.7 | 15.1 | 7.5 | 3.8 | 22.6 | 41.5 | 3.8 | 16.5 |
| 5. 1,500–2,000 | 11.1 | 33.3 | 11.1 | ... | 16.7 | 27.8 | ... | 5.6 |
| 6. 2,000–3,000 | ... | 10.0 | 10.0 | 10.0 | 40.0 | 30.0 | ... | 3.1 |
| 7. 3,000–5,000 | ... | ... | ... | ... | ... | 100.0 | ... | 0.6 |
| 8. 5,000 and above | ... | ... | ... | ... | ... | ... | 100.0 | 0.6 |
| Total | 23.1 | 29.3 | 9.7 | 5.3 | 16.2 | 15.0 | 1.6 | 100.0 |

SOURCE: Original survey data

Statistical measures: $x^2 = 133.62$ P = 0.001 Gamma = 0.51 Contingency coefficient = 0.54

*TABLE 12.23.*

*Relationship between Annual Family Income and Acquisition of Durable Goods for a Sample of Heads of Households; Cairo, 1979 (Percentages), N = 298*

| | *Durable Goods* | | | | | | |
|---|---|---|---|---|---|---|---|
| *Income (£E)* | *(Lowest) Category 1* | *Category 2* | *Category 3* | *Category 4* | *Category 5* | *(Highest) Category 6* | *Percent* |
| Less than 300 | 33.3 | 33.3 | 30.0 | 13.3 | ... | ... | 10.1 |
| 300–500 | 17.3 | 18.5 | 44.4 | 18.5 | 1.2 | ... | 27.2 |
| 500–1,000 | 4.9 | 16.7 | 42.2 | 32.4 | 3.9 | ... | 34.2 |
| 1,000–1,500 | 3.8 | 1.9 | 28.3 | 58.5 | 7.5 | ... | 17.8 |
| 1,500–2,000 | 5.6 | ... | 27.8 | 50.0 | 5.6 | 11.1 | 6.0 |
| 2,000–3,000 | ... | ... | 10.0 | 60.0 | 10.0 | 20.0 | 3.4 |
| 3,000–5,000 | ... | ... | ... | ... | 50.0 | 50.0 | 0.7 |
| 5,000 and above | ... | ... | ... | ... | ... | 100.0 | 0.7 |
| Total | 10.7 | 14.4 | 35.6 | 33.9 | 3.7 | 1.7 | 100.0 |

SOURCE: Original survey data

Statistical measures: $x^2$ = 146.54  P = 0.001  Gamma = 0.56  Contingency coefficient = 0.57

TABLE 12.24.
*Relationship between Annual Family Income and Size of Residence for a Sample of Heads of Households, Cairo, 1979 (Percentages), N = 318*

| | Size of Residence | | | | |
|---|---|---|---|---|---|
| Income (£E) | One Room | Two Rooms | 3–4 Rooms | 5 Rooms or more | Percent |
| Less than 300 | 59.5 | 36.2 | 14.3 | ... | 13.2 |
| 300–500 | 16.5 | 50.2 | 27.5 | 5.5 | 28.6 |
| 500–1,000 | 10.8 | 37.3 | 44.1 | 7.8 | 32.1 |
| 1,000–1,500 | 3.8 | 11.5 | 67.3 | 17.3 | 16.4 |
| 1,500–2,000 | ... | 22.2 | 66.7 | 11.1 | 5.7 |
| 2,000–3,000 | ... | 11.1 | 66.7 | 22.2 | 2.8 |
| 3,000–5,000 | ... | ... | 100.0 | ... | 0.6 |
| 5,000 and above | ... | ... | ... | 100.0 | 0.6 |
| Total | 16.7 | 33.3 | 41.2 | 8.8 | 100.0 |

SOURCE: Original survey data
Statistical measures: $x^2 = 135.99$ P = 0.001 Gamma = 0.59
Contingency coefficient = 0.55

weighted scale of certain durable goods (radio, television, refrigerator, private car, and so forth).[23] The second was simply the size of residence as measured by the number of rooms. Tables 12.23 and 12.24 give the relationship between the two indicators and income distribution. Both tables show that the variance on each pair of variables is significant at the 0.001 level. Equally, the magnitude of the two correlations as measured by Gamma are substantial, 0.56 and 0.59. Though they still do not correlate perfectly with income, the two life-style indicators (durable goods and size of residence) show a higher association than did both occupation and education. In other words, the two indicators of life-style are slightly better predictors of income than either education or occupation. This may be of some methodological significance in Third World countries, where income data are either hard to obtain or of suspect reliability.

### B. Stratification Configurations

Of the three surveys cited in the previous section, only the 1979 Cairo study gives data on the four indices I consider important for measuring relative class positions. I have, therefore, constructed a composite index of stratum out of the four indices for each respondent in the sample. I offer the results here, not so much as a generalization about class configuration in Egypt as a whole, but as an attempt to summarize and synthesize the data of the Cairo survey. It is also meant as a methodological contribution that may be useful in future studies on stratification.

TABLE 12.25.

*Relationship between Class Position and Four Indicators of Socioeconomic Status for a Sample of Heads of Households, Cairo, 1979 (Percentages)*

| | *Income (£E), N = 320* | | | | | | | | *Occupation, N = 320* | | | | | | | *Education, N = 321* | | | | | | | *Durable Goods, N = 298 (Life-style)* | | | | | | |
|---|---|---|---|---|---|---|---|---|---|---|---|---|---|---|---|---|---|---|---|---|---|---|---|---|---|---|---|---|---|
| *Class Position (stratum)* | *Less than 300* | *300–500* | *500–1,000* | *1,000 – 1,500* | *1,500 – 2,000* | *2,000 – 3,000* | *3,000 – 5,000* | *5,000 +* | *Professional* | *Executive* | *Clerical* | *Sales* | *Production* | *Service* | *Housewives* | *Illiterate* | *Read & Write* | *Primary* | *Preparatory* | *Secondary* | *College* | *Postgraduate* | *Category 1 (Lowest)* | *Category 2* | *Category 3* | *Category 4* | *Category 5* | *Category 6 (Highest)* | *TOTAL* |
| I Lowest | 12.1 | .. | ... | ... | ... | ... | ... | ... | ... | ... | 2.1 | 6.5 | 17.6 | 8.4 | ... | 4.1 | 1.1 | ... | ... | ... | ... | ... | 3.0 | ... | 10.0 | ... | ... | ... | 11.2 |
| II Low | 31.0 | 18.7 | 2.0 | 1.9 | ... | ... | ... | ... | ... | 8.4 | 16.7 | 21.7 | 41.2 | 29.0 | ... | 24.7 | 10.5 | 12.9 | ... | ... | ... | ... | 39.4 | 14.0 | 1.9 | ... | ... | ... | 10.3 |
| III Low Middle | 47.4 | 34.1 | 23.5 | 11.3 | 11.1 | ... | ... | ... | 6.7 | 8.5 | 33.3 | 41.3 | 41.2 | 47.7 | 20.0 | 42.5 | 35.8 | 32.3 | 5.9 | 19.2 | ... | ... | 33.3 | 46.5 | 34.0 | 11.0 | ... | ... | 26.5 |
| IV Middle | 7.1 | 42.9 | 64.7 | 58.8 | 44.4 | 10.0 | ... | ... | 80.0 | 55.3 | 35.4 | 19.6 | ... | 15.0 | 56.0 | 24.7 | 47.4 | 41.9 | 64.7 | 57.7 | 60.4 | ... | 24.2 | 37.2 | 44.7 | 60.0 | 45.5 | 20.0 | 36.1 |
| V Upper Middle | 2.4 | 4.4 | 9.8 | 26.4 | 44.4 | 90.0 | 100 | 50.0 | 13.3 | 27.7 | 12.5 | 10.9 | ... | ... | 20.0 | 4.1 | 5.3 | 12.9 | 29.4 | 21.2 | 37.5 | 40.0 | ... | 2.3 | 8.5 | 29.0 | 54.5 | 60.0 | 15.3 |
| VI Upper | ... | .. | ... | 1.9 | ... | ... | ... | 50.0 | ... | 2.1 | ... | ... | ... | ... | 4.0 | ... | ... | ... | ... | 1.9 | 2.1 | 60.0 | ... | ... | 0.9 | ... | ... | 20.0 | 0.6 |
| Total | 13.1 | 23.4 | 31.9 | 16.6 | 5.6 | 3.1 | 0.6 | 0.6 | 9.4 | 14.7 | 15.0 | 14.4 | 5.3 | 33.4 | 7.8 | 22.7 | 29.6 | 9.7 | 5.3 | 16.2 | 15.0 | 1.6 | 11.1 | 14.4 | 35.6 | 33.6 | 3.7 | 1.7 | 100 |
| Statistical measures: | $x^2$ = 261.37 Gamma = 0.69 | | | P = 0.001 C.C.* = 0.67 | | | | | $x^2$ = 79.23 Gamma = 0.62 | | | P = 0.001 C.C.* = 0.46 | | | | $x^2$ = 115.94 Gamma = 0.61 | | | P = 0.001 C.C.* = 0.32 | | | | $x^2$ = 174.06 Gamma = 0.70 | | | P = 0.001 C.C.* = 0.61 | | | |

SOURCE: Original survey data.

*Contingency coefficient.

Each of the four indices has a weighted score, and the sum of the four scores represents an Index of SES for each respondent.[24] Respondents were divided into six strata according to their sum of scores on the SES Index. Table 12.25 shows the distribution of the Cairo sample among the six strata as well as how they correlate on each of the four objective indices. It turned out that 21.5 percent of the families fall in the two lowest strata (11.2 percent were destitute, and 10.3 percent were poor), 26.5 percent in the third stratum (low middle), 36.1 percent in the fourth (middle), 15.3 percent in the fifth (upper middle), and less than one percent in the sixth stratum (highest). The SES Index (class position) correlated highest with life-style (Gamma = 0.70), then income (0.69), occupation (0.62), and education (0.61). What follows is a brief description of each of the six strata as it can be inferred from empirical data.

*1. The Lowest Stratum—The Destitute:* This category comprises mostly families whose annual income is less than £E300, who live in one room, own no durable goods or only a radio, and whose breadwinner is unskilled, a production or service worker. He is likely to be an illiterate, born to an illiterate father who was equally poor, a worker or poor peasant. The urban poverty line in 1975 was £E350 (see section II above). Given an inflation rate of at least 10 percent annually in the following four years, the urban poverty line in 1979 would be well over £E500 in 1979. This would suggest that these 11 percent of Cairo's families are rock-bottom poor. If not illiterates like their fathers and grandfathers, the children of these destitute families only read and write, with very few past primary school. All in all, this stratum epitomizes the "culture of poverty,"[25] in which low income is only one manifestation of several in a multitude of vicious circles gripping several successive generations.

*2. The Low Stratum—The Poor:* This category comprises over 10 percent of Cairo's families whose annual income is between £E300 and £E500. The typical family lives in one or two rooms, with a breadwinner who is illiterate or barely literate, and who is a semiskilled worker, vendor, or in a clerical occupation. The breadwinner is generally born to an illiterate worker or a peasant, and has moved up slightly over his father. His children have gained more education and, if working, they are in skilled or clerical occupations, with very few going to college or joining professional and executive ranks. In sheer income alone, these families are immediately below the poverty line. But socially and culturally, they are not as caught up in its vicious cycle. Many of them do not "feel" poor (see table 12.26).

*3. The Low-Middle Stratum—The Border Line:* This category comprises nearly 27 percent of Cairo's families. Their annual income is between £E500 and £E1,000 per family. The typical family lives in two rooms and owns a few durable amenities such as a radio, gas stove, and a black and white television. The breadwinner is likely to be literate or with intermediate education, a skilled worker or in clerical or sales occupations. In most cases, he is better off than his father educationally and occupationally. Nearly half of the heads of household are from rural backgrounds. Their children have attained as much or slightly more educationally. These families "feel" and try to lead a middle-class life-style. Since their income is immediately above the poverty line, they are bound to feel hard-pressed.

4. *The Middle Stratum—The Upwardly Mobile:* This category comprises 36 percent of Cairo's families. The typical family has an annual income of around £E1,000, lives in three or four rooms, and has more than half of the durable items (of the LSS). The heads of households in this stratum are likely to be young professionals, middle executives, or in senior clerical and sales positions. Most of them have had college education. More than half of them are newcomers to the middle class and have ascended to it from lower strata in which the father was a peasant, a worker, a clerk or salesman. Respondents in this stratum have experienced more upward mobility than any other group. Their children seem to have more opportunities than the strata below, but not more than their fathers had a generation ago.

5. *The Upper-Middle Stratum—The Secure:* This group comprises 15 percent of Cairo's families. The typical household has three to five rooms, almost all the durable items, and around £E2,000 to £E3,000 in annual income. The head of the family is likely to be college-educated and an established professional or executive. Most respondents in this stratum are born to fathers who had at least intermediate education, and were themselves in one of the middle strata a generation ago. Their children are continuing on the upward track for the third generation, both educationally and occupationally.

6. *The Highest Stratum—The Rich:* This is the smallest group, consisting of about one percent of Cairo's families. The typical household comprises five rooms or more, enjoys all the urban amenities, possesses all the durable goods (included in the LSS), private car, color television, air conditioners, and so forth. The family income averages more than £E5,000 per annum. The typical head of household is a college-educated, well-established professional, senior executive, or a businessman. Almost all respondents in this stratum were born to college-educated fathers and have college-educated sons. In other words, this group seems to be locked in the highest stratum for the third generation in a row.

This six-strata configuration is based on objective criteria. There may be a degree of arbitrariness in the indices or in the cutting points along the stratification continuum. But this is unavoidable in any such attempt. Nor is this the only approach in depicting class configuration in a community

## TABLE 12.26

*Relationship between Subjective Perception of Own Socioeconmic Status (SES) and Objective Indicators of SES for a Sample of Heads of Households, Cairo, 1979 (Percentages)*

| | Income (£E) N = 321 | | | | | | | | Occupation N = 321 | | | | | | | Education N = 322 | | | | | | | Durable Goods, N = 299 | | | | | | |
|---|---|---|---|---|---|---|---|---|---|---|---|---|---|---|---|---|---|---|---|---|---|---|---|---|---|---|---|---|---|
| Class Position (stratum) | Less than 300 | 300–500 | 500–1,000 | 1,000–1,500 | 1,500–2,000 | 2,000–3,000 | 3,000–5,000 | 5,000 + | Professional | Executive | Clerical | Sales | Production | Service | Housewives | Illiterate | Read & Write | Primary | Preparatory | Secondary | College | Postgraduate | Category 1 (Lowest) | Category 2 | Category 3 | Category 4 | Category 5 | Category 6 (Highest) | TOTAL |
| I Lowest | 7.1 | 2.2 | ... | ... | ... | ... | ... | ... | ... | ... | ... | 2.1 | ... | 3.7 | 4.0 | 2.7 | 2.1 | ... | 5.9 | 1.9 | ... | ... | 12.1 | ... | ... | ... | ... | ... | 1.9 |
| II Low | 28.6 | 16.5 | 9.7 | 1.9 | ... | ... | ... | ... | ... | 6.4 | 8.3 | 14.9 | 17.6 | 12.2 | 28.0 | 20.3 | 16.8 | 6.5 | ... | 3.8 | 2.1 | 20.0 | 21.2 | 18.6 | 11.3 | 1.0 | ... | ... | 11.5 |
| III Middle | 61.9 | 67.0 | 73.8 | 75.5 | 61.1 | 60.0 | ... | 50.0 | 76.7 | 57.4 | 75.0 | 63.8 | 64.7 | 73.8 | 60.0 | 67.6 | 67.4 | 74.2 | 58.8 | 76.9 | 70.8 | 20.0 | 60.6 | 69.8 | 73.6 | 73.3 | 54.5 | 40.0 | 68.9 |
| IV Upper Middle | 2.4 | 12.1 | 12.6 | 15.1 | 27.8 | 30.0 | 100.0 | 50.0 | 20.0 | 25.5 | 8.3 | 14.9 | 17.6 | 10.3 | 4.0 | 8.1 | 11.6 | 16.1 | 29.4 | 13.5 | 16.7 | 40.0 | 3.0 | 7.0 | 13.2 | 19.8 | 36.4 | 40.0 | 13.7 |
| V Upper | ... | 2.2 | 3.9 | 7.5 | 11.1 | 10.0 | ... | ... | 3.3 | 10.6 | 8.3 | 4.3 | ... | ... | 4.0 | 1.4 | 2.1 | 3.2 | 5.9 | 3.8 | 10.4 | 20.0 | 3.0 | 4.7 | 1.9 | 5.9 | 9.1 | 20.0 | 4.0 |
| Total | 13.1 | 28.3 | 32.1 | 16.5 | 5.6 | 3.1 | 0.6 | 0.6 | 9.3 | 14.6 | 15.0 | 14.6 | 5.3 | 33.3 | 7.8 | 23.0 | 29.5 | 9.6 | 5.3 | 16.2 | 14.9 | 1.6 | 11.0 | 14.4 | 35.5 | 33.8 | 3.7 | 1.7 | 100 |
| Statistical measures: | $x^2 = 63.16$ P = 0.001 Gamma = 0.48 C.C.* = 0.41 | | | | | | | | $x^2 = 41.30$ P = 0.02 Gamma = 0.35 C.C.* = 0.34 | | | | | | | $x^2 = 41.10$ P = 0.02 Gamma = 0.35 C.C.* = 0.34 | | | | | | | $x^2 = 70.40$ P = 0.001 Gamma = 0.50 C.C.* = 0.51 | | | | | | |

SOURCE: Original survey data.

*Contingency coefficient.

or in a society at large. One approach is to figure class structure on the basis of relationship to the means of production (ownership of means of production versus hired labor). I opted against this method since most large-scale means of production in Egypt have been state-controlled for nearly twenty years.

Another approach is to construct social stratification on the basis of subjective identification—how people perceive their class standing.[26] The premise here is that, if the concept of "class" is to be a useful analytical tool of general behavior, it matters less where people objectively stand than what whey think of their standing. It is the latter, not the former, that shapes their attitudes and behavior. The objective and subjective may or may not coincide. In the case of my Cairo sample, I did ask the respondents to identify the class they belonged to. Table 12.26 summarizes the answers and correlates them with the objective indices. It is striking that less than 2 percent identified themselves as belonging to the lowest stratum (as compared to 11 percent of the sample who "objectively" belong there). It is equally striking that as many as 69 percent of the respondents perceived their class standing as exactly in the middle. If we add to them those identifying with the upper middle class (14 percent), the total jumps to 83 percent of all respondents identifying with one or another layer of the middle class. In other words, there is a tremendous social-psychological pressure to be members of the "middle class," whether or not people "objectively" qualify as such. This tendency, revealed by the Cairo sample, is not much different from the pattern found in some Western societies.[27] The "middle-classification" tendency has a multitude of sociopolitical implications, not the least of which is the preservation of the status quo. This may be disheartening to those who seek radical change; they would label it as a classical case of "false class-consciousness."

Finally, we take a look at the objective class configuration (based on the SES Index) cross-generationally. Table 12.27 shows the respondents in the Cairo sample broken down by age categories, and compares their class position with that of their fathers and that of their first adult sons.[28] Respondents in the oldest age group (60 or above) had their life-opportunities set in the pre-1952 revolution period (that is, in the 1940s), and respondents in the youngest age group (20–30) had their life-opportunities set in the late 1960s and early 1970s. The middle age categories (30–50) had such opportunities set in the 1950s and 1960s. If we look at their relative representation in the three upper strata (IV to VI), we notice marked differences that are statistically significant (at the 0.05 level or better). Measures of association, such as contingency coefficient, show a higher correlation between age and class position for both fathers (0.37) and sons (0.38) of respondents than for respondents themselves (0.31). This suggests that, on the whole, fathers and sons (generations I and III) were generally worse off than respondents in terms of class

*TABLE 12.27.*

*Relationship between Age of Respondent and His Class Position (SES) and the Class Position of His First Son and of His Father, for a Sample of Heads of Households, Cairo, 1979 (Percentages)*

| | | CLASS CATEGORIES | | | | | | |
|---|---|---|---|---|---|---|---|---|
| *Age of Respondent* | | *(Lowest)* *I* | *II* | *III* | *IV* | *V* | *(Highest)* *VI* | *Total* |
| 20–30 | Son | . . . | . . . | . . . | . . . | . . . | . . . | . . . |
| | Respondent | . . . | 5.3 | 36.8 | 47.4 | 10.5 | . . . | 5.9 |
| | Father | 5.3 | 21.1 | 57.9 | . . . | 15.8 | . . . | 6.0 |
| 30–40 | Son | . . . | 100.0 | . . . | . . . | . . . | . . . | 2.9 |
| | Respondent | . . . | 13.9 | 17.7 | 48.1 | 20.3 | . . . | 24.6 |
| | Father | 6.3 | 21.5 | 40.5 | 29.1 | 2.5 | . . . | 24.8 |
| 40–50 | Son | . . . | 14.3 | 57.1 | 28.6 | . . . | . . . | 20.3 |
| | Respondent | 1.2 | 7.1 | 29.4 | 49.4 | 11.6 | 1.4 | 26.5 |
| | Father | 6.0 | 38.6 | 41.0 | 13.3 | 1.2 | . . . | 26.0 |
| 50–60 | Son | . . . | 16.1 | 71.0 | 12.9 | . . . | . . . | 44.9 |
| | Respondent | 5.0 | 8.3 | 27.1 | 42.9 | 16.7 | . . . | 29.9 |
| | Father | 7.4 | 43.2 | 33.7 | 10.5 | 5.3 | 1.1 | 29.8 |
| 60+ | Son | . . . | 18.2 | 72.7 | 9.1 | . . . | . . . | 31.9 |
| | Respondent | 7.1 | 16.7 | 31.0 | 31.0 | 14.3 | . . . | 13.1 |
| | Father | 4.6 | 41.9 | 46.5 | 4.7 | 2.3 | . . . | 13.5 |
| Total | | | | | | | | |
| | (N = 69) Son | . . . | 18.8 | 66.7 | 14.5 | . . . | . . . | 100.0 |
| | (N = 321) Respondent | 11.2 | 10.3 | 26.5 | 36.1 | 15.3 | 0.6 | 100.0 |
| | (N = 319) Father | 15.3 | 35.1 | 30.4 | 17.4 | 3.4 | 0.3 | 100.0 |

Son: $x^2$ = 11.70 P = 0.05 Gamma = −0.06 Cont. Coeff. = 0.38
Respondent: $x^2$ = 33.09 P = 0.05 Gamma = −0.09 Cont. Coeff. = 0.31
Father: $x^2$ = 46.45 P = 0.01 Gamma = −0.21 Cont. Coeff. = 0.37

SOURCE: *Original survey data*

standing. To put it differently, the middle generation fared better than either of the older or the younger generations. This conclusion was confirmed by other data earlier. But to sharpen the picture further, let us compare the percentages of respondents in strata V and VI in each age group. For respondents in the 20–30 age group there were 58 percent, compared to 16 percent of their fathers, a difference of 42 percentage points. For the next age group (30–40), there were 68 percent of the respondents in the three top strata compared to 32 percent of their fathers, a difference of 36 points. But this age group is 10 points better than the 20–30 age group. As for the 40–50 cohorts, we find 62 percent in the top strata, compared to only 15 percent of their fathers (respondents 47 points better), and 29 percent of their sons (respondents 31 points better). The 50–60 age group of respondents were represented in the upper half of the stratification scale by nearly 60 percent, compared to 17 percent of their fathers (respondents better by 42 points), and to 13 percent of their sons (respondents better by 47 points). Finally, 45 percent of the oldest respondents were in the three top strata, compared to 7 percent of their fathers and to 9 percent of their sons (respondents better 38 and 36 points, respectively).

Respondents who were 30–40 years old in 1979 were 3–10 years old at the time of the 1952 revolution. They benefited the most from the expanded educational and occupational opportunities made available during the 1956–1965 period (the upswing phase of the revolution). The age groups immediately younger and immediately older also benefited greatly but not as much. Older age groups also benefited from these years, but their sons have not benefited as much.

Thus, manipulating the data by age cohorts adds more substantiation of the hypothesis stated in the introductory section of this chapter. Specifically, Egypt's stratification system reached its maximum fluidity from the mid-1950s to the mid-1960s. Along with ambitious programs in education and industrialization, and with bold socialist policies of equalizing opportunities, the Egyptian society witnessed more social mobility than in any single decade in this century. But from the late 1960s on, the class structure appears to have been hardening again. During the last fifteen years, upward mobility has increasingly become "confined" to children of the middle and upper strata. For younger members of the lower rungs, the system does not offer as many opportunities to move up. For them, such opportunities are to be found outside the Egyptian system. It may be a sheer accident of social history that, as Egypt no longer held as bright promise for its dispossessed children, other parts of the Arab world were opening doors of opportunity to them.

## Notes

1. An excellent account of major theories and debates of class structure and inequality can be found in Reinhard Bendix and Seymour Lipset, eds., *Class, Status and Power: Social Stratification in Comparative Perspective* (New York: Free Press, 1966), 2nd ed. For an original statement on functionalism, see Kingsley Davis and Wilbert Moore, "Some Principles of Stratification," *American Sociological Review* 10, no. 2: 242–249. For a classical critique of the functionalist theory of stratification, see Melvin Tumin, "Some Principles of Stratification: A Critical Analysis," *American Sociological Review* 18 (1953): 387–393. For a statement on the Marxist conception of class, see Karl Marx, *Capital: A Critique of Political*

*Economy,* vol. 3 (unfinished chapter), (Moscow: Foreign Language Publishing House, 1962), p. 862. Other Marxists, especially Lenin, have elaborated the concept of class. See V. I. Lenin, *The Complete Works* (Moscow: Foreign Language Publishing House), vol. 29, p. 410. Most recent Marxist accounts of Egypt's class structure would couch it in terms of the "Asiatic mode of production." See Nazih N. M. al-Ayubi, *"Bureaucratic Evolution and Political Development: Egypt, 1952–1970"* (Ph.D. diss., Oxford University, 1975); and E. J. Hobsbawm, *Karl Marx: Pre-Capitalist Formations,* trans. Jack Cohen (London: Lawrence and Wishart, 1964).

2. For typical examples of macroideological studies on Egypt, see Anouar Abdel Malek, *Egypt: Military Society* (New York: Random House, 1968); Mahmoud Hussein, *Class Conflict in Egypt, 1945–1970* (New York: Monthly Review Press, 1973); Samir Amin (under pseudonym Hassan Riad), *L'Egypte Nasserienne* (Paris: 1964); Muhammd al-Jawharī, *ᶜIlm al-Ijtimāᶜ wa Qadīya al-tammīya fi al-ᶜĀlam al-Thālith* (Sociology and Development Issues in the Third World) (Cairo: Dar al-Maᶜrif, 1978), pp. 314–315; Jamāl Majdi Hasanayn, "al-Binā al-Ijtimāᶜī w-al-Tanmīya al-Ijtimāᶜīya fi Mīsr", *Abhāth al-Mu'tamar al-Dawlī al-Thālith Liat-Ihsa' wa al-Alāt al-Hāsiba wa al-Buhūth al-Ijtimāᶜīya* ("Social Structure and Social Development in Egypt" in *Proceedings of the Third International Congress of Statistics, Computers and Social Research*), Cairo, 1978, vol. 1, pp. 95. 108.

3. For examples of microstructural studies, see A. I. ᶜAbd al-Wahab, *Ta'thīr Iᶜadat Tawzīya al-Ard ᶜAlā al-Bina' al-Ijtimāᶜiya Li-Qarīya Misrīya* (The Impact of Land Redistribution on the Social Structure of an Egyptian Village) (M.A. thesis [Sociology], ᶜAin Shams University, Cairo, 1975); ᶜAbd al-Bāsit ᶜAbd al-Muᶜtī, *al-Sirāᶜ al-Tabaqī fi al-Qarīya al-Misrīya* (Class Conflict in the Egyptian Village) (Cairo: Dar al-Thaqafa al-Jadida, 1977).

4. For examples of aggregate socioeconomic studies, see Robert Mabro, *The Egyptian Economy; 1952–1972* (Oxford: Clarendon Press, 1974); Donald C. Mead, *Growth and Structural Change in the Egyptian Economy* (Urbana, Illinois University Press, 1967); Samir Radwan, *The Impact of Agrarian Reform on Rural Egypt, 1952–1975* (Geneva: International Labor Office Working Papers, 1977); ᶜAlī al-Jirītlī, *Khamsa wa ᶜAshrūn ᶜĀman, Dirāsa Tahlīlīya Li-al-Siyāsa al-Iqtisādīya fi Misr* (Twenty-five Years: An Analytical Study of Egypt's Economic Policies, 1952–1977) (Cairo: al-Hī'a al- Misrīya alᶜĀma līl-kitāb, 1977); M. A. Fadil, *Development, Income Distribution and Social Change in Rural Egypt, 1952–1970* (Cambridge: Cambridge University Press, 1975).

5. The ward *(shiyākha)* is the smallest administrative unit in urban areas, and corresponds to a census tract.

6. The nine *shiyākha*'s samples were: Rūd al-Faraj (51 cases); al-Sharqīya (86 cases); Hadayik al-Qubba (60 cases); al-Zaytūn al-Gharbīya (30 cases); Ibn al-Rashīd (18 cases); ᶜAbdīn (10 cases); al-Jamālīya (13 cases); Misr al-Jadīda (27 cases); and Asād al-Sahil (24 cases). A total of 319 cases were drawn using a multiple-stage-probability sampling method. The sample size was set by the project coordinator (300 cases), and it was fractioned among the nine wards according to their relative population (by the 1976 Egypt census). A door-to-door counting of households in each ward was conducted to determine the nth fraction of the systematic samplings. For example, if the ᶜAbdīn shiyākha turned out to have a total of 500 households, then every 50th household was selected for inclusion in the sample, as the relative share of that shiyākha was set at 10 cases (its population being 3.4 percent of the population total of the nine shiakha's combined).

7. For a relevant discussion of this issue, see Thomas Fox and S. M. Miller, "Occupational Stratification and Mobility: Intra-Country Variations," in *Studies in Comparative International Development,* I:1:3.10 (1965).

8. The Asyūt villages are: Maᶜsara; Nazla Mustafa ᶜAbd al Halīm; Nazla Sarājna. The Daqahlīya villages are: al-Sinjā; Kafr ᶜAllām; al-Shibūl; Mit Suwīd; Sallānt, and Kafr Qansūh. The sampling method was the same as that described in note 6.

9. For an analysis of these mounting problems, see Charles Issawi, *Egypt in Revolu-*

*tion: An Economic Analysis* (London: Oxford University Press, 1963) and Robert Mabro, *The Egyptian Economy.*

10. There are tens of scholarly accounts. See, for example: R. Hrair Dekmejian, *Egypt Under Nasser: A Study in Political Dynamics* (Albany: State University of New York Press); Raymond Baker, *Egypt's Uncertain Revolution under Nasser and Sadat* (Cambridge: Harvard University Press, 1978).

11. For an account of the changing elite structure, see R. H. Dekmejian, *Egypt under Nasser,* pp. 167–224, and Robert Springborg, "Patterns of Association in the Egyptian Political Elite," in George Lenczowski, ed., *Political Elites in the Middle East* (Washington: American Enterprise Institute for Public Policy Research, 1975), pp. 83–108.

12. Leonard Binder, *In a Moment of Enthusiasm: Political Power and the Second Stratum in Egypt* (Chicago: University of Chicago Press, 1978).

13. ᶜAlī al-Jirītlī, *Khamsa waᶜAshrūn ᶜAman, Dirāsa Tahlīlīya Lil-Siyāsa al-Iqtisādīya fī Misr* (Twenty-five Years, An Analytical Study of Egypt's Economic Policies, 1952–1977), pp. 118–121.

14. Samir Radwan, *The Impact of Agrarian Reform,* pp. 37–41.

15. Up to 1958, beneficaries of land distribution alone were over 113,000 families. By 1962, this figure was 167,000 families. Tenants benefiting from rent control were 1.1 million. See M. A. Fadil, *Development, Income Distribution and Social Change,* p. 9 (table 1.4) and p. 56 (table 3.8).

16. Reporting one's income accurately is one of the most difficult and, therefore, least reliable items in field surveys in all societies (developed as well as developing). To ask retrospectively, as I did, about fathers' income must compound the unreliability. Nevertheless, I went ahead on the assumption that such inaccuracy cuts across various income brackets randomly—overestimation and underreporting of income canceling each other.

17. The range for fathers' annual income in Cairo was from £E75 to £E6500. It was classified in eight categories, as follows: 0–100, 100–200, 200–400, 400–500, 500–1,000, 1,000–12000, 2,000–5,000, 5000+. The range for respondents' annual income was from £E180 to £E8,400, categorized as follows: 0–300, 300–500, 500–1,000, 1,000–1,500, 1,500–2,000, 2,000–3,000, 3,000–5,000, 5,000+. The range of annual income for the oldest working sons was from £E120 to £E12,000 (a case of a son working in Saudi Arabia), categorized as follows: 0–200, 200–400, 400–600, 600–800, 800–1,000, 1,000–3,000, 3,000+. Even with these classification, there were several empty cells in the respective tables. What matters here is the ordinal ranking of each generational income and not its absolute monetary value.

18. Seymour Lipset and Hanz L. Zetterberg, "A Theory of Social Mobility," in Bendix and Lipset, eds., *Class, Status and Power,* p. 562.

19. Ibid., p. 565.

20. These figures are computed from table I in CAPMS, *Bulletin of Employment, Wages and Working Hours, October 1968,* Cairo, 1973, pp. 3–14.

21. Cited in Nazih N. al-Ayyūbī, *Siyāsa al-Tᶜalīm fī Misr* (Educational Policy in Egypt) (Cairo: Center for Political and Strategic Studies, 1978), pp. 70–72.

22. Ibid., pp. 72–74.

23. The durable goods included in the Life-Style Scale (LSS) are the ten items following, with their respective weighted values: radio (1); gas stove (2); tape recorder (3); black and white television set (4); washing machine (5); refrigerator (6); color television (7); telephone (8); air conditioner (9); private car (10). The range of scores of LSS is 1 to 57. Respondents were classified according to their LSS scores into six categories: I, less than a total score of 5; II, 5 to 10; III, 10 to 20; IV, 20 to 30; V, 30 to 40; VI, 40 and above.

24. The Composite Index of SES was constructed as follows: (a) a weighted score for the respondent's annual income ranging from 1 to 8 according to his income bracket; a weighted score for the respondent's occupation ranging from 1 to 7, with housewives at the lowest end

and professionals at the highest end; a weighted score of education ranging from 1 to 7, with illiterates at the bottom and postgraduates at the top; and finally a weighted score for life-style ranging from 1 to 6 according to the LSS categories described in note 26. (b) The four weighted scores were summed up to make the SES Index with a range of 4 to 28. (c) Respondents were categorized into six strata on the basis of their SES Index as follows: Stratum I (the lowest) comprised respondents who had an SES score of less than 5; Stratum II (low) comprised respondents with scores of 5–10; Stratum III (lower middle), respondents with scores of 10–15; Stratum IV (middle), respondents with scores of 15–20; Stratum V (upper middle), respondents with scores of 20–25; and Stratum VI (highest), respondents with SES scores of 25 and above.

25. The term "culture of poverty" or "poverty subculture" was coined by Oscar Lewis and elaborated by other Western social scientists to describe the pervasive social-psychological facts of poverty along with its economic and physical dimensions. The core element of the concept, however, is its multigenerationality, in which despair of breaking out of its vicious cycle gives in to fatalism. See Oscar Lewis, "The Culture of Poverty", in L. Ferman, Joyce Kornbluh, and Alan Haber, eds., *Poverty in America* (Ann Arbor: University of Michigan Press, 1968), pp. 405–415. For an anthropological account of some of Cairo's poor, see Andrea B. Rugh, *Coping with Poverty in a Cairo Community* (Cairo Papers in Social Science), vol. 2, Monograph 1, 1979.

26. For an elaboration of this approach, see Richard Centers, *The Psychology of Social Classes* (Princeton: Princeton University Press, 1949; A. F. Davies, *Images of Class: An Australian Study* (Sydney: Sydney University Press, 1967).

27. Davies, *Images of Class*.

28. The SES Index for fathers and sons was constructed according to the same technique described in note 27, but on the basis of three indices—education, occupation, and income. I felt that the fourth indicator (durable goods) would not be valid in the case of fathers, since some of the items have only recently been introduced (television), and in the case of the sons because, as quite a few of them are still unmarried, they would be unlikely to have an independent household.

# CHAPTER 13

# *Foreign Economic Aid and Income Distribution in Egypt, 1952–1977**

Gouda Abdel-Khalek

## I. Introduction

This chapter deals with a question that has been neglected by students of the Egyptian economy—what have been the income distribution effects of the heavy reliance by Egypt on foreign aid to finance its economic and social development over the period 1952–1977? This question is important in and of itself; one would like to know whether heavy reliance by Egypt on foreign aid for most of the period was conducive to a more equitable distribution of income.

There are many reasons but three in particular that may lead one to expect heavy reliance on foreign aid to affect income distribution:

1. It is to be expected that aid-financed projects would be quite different from projects financed from other sources—especially domestic savings. Indeed, certain projects may not be undertaken at all without foreign aid. The High Dam is a good case in point.
2. The mechanisms regulating aid usually force the receiving country to adopt priorities more in line with the interest of the donor. Such priorities reflect themselves in many areas, one of which is income distribution.[1]
3. Foreign aid may render it much easier to effect a change in income distribution without risking social tension and political instability. (Outright corruption can also be expected to change income distribution, but this is beyond the scope of this study.) Thus although foreign aid may not be intended to change income distribution, it may yet be redistributive. Through its effect on the rate and pattern of overall growth and the choice of techniques, it is bound to affect the pattern of resource allocation and factor mix, and hence factor rewards.

Since there is no unanimity about the definition of foreign aid,[2] it is important to state what we mean by the term in this study. *Foreign aid* is

*The author is indebted to a large number of individuals for constructive criticism and suggestions. In addition to his colleagues in this project, he owes a special debt to Prof. John P. Lewis, chairman, Development Assistance Committee, OECD, Naim A. Sherbiny of the World Bank, and John Page of Princeton University.

here defined to include grants and medium- and long-term loans contracted on concessionary terms.[3] It is important, however, to recognize that this definition ignores the problems of tying practices.[4] If a loan is tied as to either source or end-use, can it still be considered as aid? The answer to this question is fairly intuitive: unless the recipient was getting more through aid than would be the case through a pure market transfer, there is no reason for accepting the aid transfer. What the tying necessarily implies, therefore, is that the "effective" or *real* aid element in tied resource transfers is usually less than the nominal resource transfer. So, it is implicitly assumed that, even in the case of tied transfer of resources, there is an element of aid.

In the light of Egypt's aid experience, I thus define foreign aid to include grants and medium- and long-term official loans from different countries, as well as grants and concessional medium- and long-term loans from national, regional, and international organizations.

A very important aspect in the study of income redistribution in the course of development is the distribution of the *benefits* of growth.[5] The question then becomes: who has benefitted more? This subsumes the narrower, though more popular, question: who has gained and who has lost? This is a more appropriate question for studying the impact of the financing of development through foreign aid, since foreign aid financing may put the burden of repayment on the socioeconomic groups not benefitting from the aid. Moreover, foreign-aid-financed projects may benefit some socioeconomic groups more than others. This is the rationale for the recent emphasis by the World Bank and other aid donors on the so-called target groups in financing projects through aid.

It is my contention that the foreign aid received by Egypt over the period of the study did affect *income distribution* through both avenues. On the one hand, some socioeconomic groups (particularly small farmers) were made to bear the burden of repaying foreign aid that went to projects that did not benefit them. That means, by implication, that some other socioeconomic group must have gained at the expense of the small farmers. On the other hand, some aid-financed projects benefitted certain socioeconomic groups more than, but not necessarily at the expense of, others.

In this chapter our purpose is to study the effect of aid received by Egypt on income distribution. The problem stems mainly from the fact that there are numerous intervening factors that render it methodologically very difficult to attribute income distribution changes to heavy reliance on foreign aid alone. But before we attempt to do that, a number of questions have to be answered: How much aid did Egypt receive over the period? From what sources? For what purposes? Under what conditions? The answer to these questions paves the way to answering the ultimate one.

*TABLE 13.1.*
*Magnitude and Significance of Foreign Assistance to Egypt 1952–1975*

| *Period* | *Average Annual Inflow (£E million)* | *Average Annual Investment (£E million)* | *Annual Average Imports (£E million)* | *Aid as percentage of* | |
|---|---|---|---|---|---|
| | | | | *Investment* | *Imports* |
| 1952–1959 | 2.1 | 154.8 | 195.1 | 1.4 | 1.1 |
| 1960–1964 | 96.9 | 302.6 | 370.8 | 32.0 | 26.1 |
| 1965–1969 | 89.3 | 349.3 | 405.0 | 25.6 | 22.1 |
| 1970–1975 | 211.1 | 618.2 | 864.0 | 34.2 | 24.4 |

SOURCES: Investment data from Central Bank of Egypt, *Economic Review* 18, nos. 3–4 (1978): 249. Aid and imports data from IBRD, *Arab Republic of Egypt, Economic Management in a Period of Transition,* vol. 6, *Statistical Appendix,* table 3.1.

## II. Magnitude and Significance of Economic Aid to Egypt over the Period 1952–1977

In this section we examine the magnitude of foreign aid received by Egypt over the period 1952–1977.[6] Despite the significance of economic aid to Egypt, only one detailed study of such aid was undertaken previously, dating back to the early 1960s.[7] Moreover, detailed and systematic data are not available in published form. The researcher is forced to comb and sift through much material and to collect and piece together fragmentary data in order to estimate the magnitude of such aid.

Table 13.1 indicates the development of the magnitude and significance of foreign aid over the period 1952–1975.

It must be pointed out that these estimates should be considered with great caution; in fact, they may only indicate orders of magnitude. Having made this explicit caveat, we may note that examination of table 13.1 reveals an interesting feature of the development of aid inflow: a rising trend with a cyclical pattern. Aid inflow starts at a fairly low level, then it rises significantly, then it falls and, finally, it rises again—thus making four phases of a full cycle.[8] Although one cannot be very sure about the turning points, it is safe to say that the first phase started prior to the begining of the period of our study in 1952 and lasted until 1958. During this period, Egypt was riding comfortably on the cushion of the sterling balances, which were accumulated during World War II.[9]

The first Soviet loan for industrialization in 1958 ushered in the second phase, during which Egypt received substantial amounts of aid from all sources, East and West. But the deterioration of relations with the United States in the mid-1960s, coupled with the June 1967 war, marked the beginning of the third phase, which was to last until the October 1973 war.

The fourth phase started perhaps in 1974 and continues through the present.[10]

It is interesting to note that, corresponding to this cyclical pattern of aid inflow, there is a cyclical pattern of growth of the Egyptian economy. After stagnation of The Gross Domestic Product (GDP) until 1957, growth picked up starting in 1958 and continued through 1965, after which it decelerated. It was not until 1974 that growth picked up again.[11] Is this correspondence between growth of GDP and foreign aid inflow apparent or real? To answer this question, note that the growth of GDP was mainly concentrated in manufacturing, electricity, and construction.[12] This growth was made possible directly by Soviet aid to Egypt for industrialization and for the construction of the High Dam, and indirectly by American food aid, which enabled the economy to match investment expenditure with the basic wage goods. These two factors are all the more important in view of two salient features of the development of the Egyptian economy over the period: stagnant exports and a falling savings rate.[13] With this stagnant exports and falling savings propensity, investment and hence growth depended on foreign capital inflow—basically aid transfers—during the period.

Table 13.1 also indicates that foreign aid has financed a larger part of investment, especially with the beginning of the 1960s. To the extent that investment was instrumental for growth, foreign aid must have contributed significantly to growth. It would still be rather difficult, however, to ascertain its exact contribution.

Actually, the positive role of foreign aid in fostering the economic growth of Egypt is borne out by empirical evidence. Thus, projections of the resource gap for the Egyptian economy based on the two-gap model have shown that, for growth rates of GDP above 6 percent, the savings gap becomes dominant.[14] Since GDP growth rate actually achieved during the early 1960s was about 6.5 percent, it may be concluded that foreign borrowing was undertaken to finance a level of consumption much beyond what could be achieved otherwise.

This empirical finding that aid closed the savings gap is significant for the study of the effect of aid on income distribution. For, if foreign aid were not forthcoming, it would have been necessary either to reduce investment or to raise domestic savings. In the first case, growth could have suffered, with the attendant changes in income distribution. In the second case, there would have been concomitant changes in the structure of government revenue and expenditure, and hence in income distribution.

Table 13.2 lists economic assistance to Egypt from all sources from 1952 until mid-1977. Total aid *commitments* over the period amounted to £E4,885.0 million. Of this amount, total *disbursements* represented some 62 percent, or £E3,088.0 million. This amounts to some £E77 per capita, or more than half of per capita GDP. Thus, the first salient feature to the

*TABLE 13.2.*

*Economic Assistance to Egypt from all Sources until June 30, 1977*

| | *Disbursement* | |
|---|---|---|
| *Source* | *£E million* | *Percentage* |
| **Total Bilateral** | **2,686.2** | **87.0** |
| Arab States[a] | 1,066.4 | 34.5 |
| Arab National Development Funds[b] | 85.5 | 2.8 |
| USA | 661.4 | 21.4 |
| Other Capitalist Countries | 324.9 | 10.5 |
| USSR | 391.1 | 12.7 |
| Other Socialist Countries | 156.9 | 5.1 |
| **Total Multilateral** | **401.8** | **13.0** |
| Arab Multilateral[c] | 285.5 | 9.8 |
| Other Multilateral[d] | 116.3 | 3.2 |
| **Total Disbursements[e]** | **3,088.0** | **100.0** |
| Total Commitments | 4,885.0 | |

SOURCES: Ministry of Economy and Economic Cooperation and the Central Bank of Egypt.

NOTES:

[a]Includes assistance from Iran, but excludes Arab support for Egyptian defense effort, which amounted to £E1928.9 million of grants.

[b]These funds are the Kuwait Fund for Arab Economic Development, the Abu Dhabi Fund for Economic Development, the Saudi Fund for Development and the Arab Libyan Bank.

[c]Includes aid from the Arab Fund for Economic and Social Development, the Gulf Organization for Development in Egypt (GODE), the Arab Organization for Industrialization, the Arab International Bank, and the Arab African Bank.

[d]Includes the IBRD (World Bank), IDA (International Development Agency), the African Development Bank, and the OPEC Special Fund.

[e]Official exchange rates were used in calculating £E equivalents.

inflow of aid to Egypt is that it is relatively fairly large. In fact the United States is currently undertaking the largest aid program in the world in Egypt, committing US$1.1 billion of aid to Egypt for 1980.[15]

Another salient feature of foreign aid to Egypt is that it is *concentrated rather than diffused.* Such concentration manifests itself in three respects: type, source, and area of use.[16] Specifically, the bulk of aid received by Egypt is bilateral, coming mainly from the Arab countries, the United States, and the Soviet Union. This may be easily seen from table 13.2. According to the data in this table, 87 percent of total aid disbursements is bilateral, leaving only 13 percent as multilateral. But again, bilateral aid is heavily concentrated, with the Arab countries and Iran contributing 34.5 percent of total aid disbursements, and a still higher 39.4 percent of bilateral disbursement.

The Arab countries are the main donors, with the United States and the Soviet Union following their lead. The fact that aid received by Egypt

*TABLE 13.3.*

*Aid Disbursements to Egypt by Source until June 30, 1977*

| *Source* | *Disbursements (£E million)* | *Percentage* |
|---|---|---|
| *Arab Aid* | *1,436.9* | *46.5* |
| Kuwait | 425.5 | 13.8 |
| Saudi Arabia | 327.8 | 10.6 |
| Iran | 125.0 | 4.1 |
| Abu Dhabi | 92.0 | |
| Libya | 50.0 | 6.1 |
| Qatar | 34.6 | |
| Iraq | 11.5 | |
| Kuwait Fund for Arab Economic Development | 47.5 | |
| Abu Dhabi Fund for Economic Development | 17.6 | 2.8 |
| Saudi Fund for Development | 16.4 | |
| Arab Libyan Bank | 4.0 | |
| Gulf Organization for Development in Egypt | 259.1 | 8.4 |
| Arab Organization for Industrialization | 8.3 | |
| Arab Fund for Economic and Social Development | 5.8 | 0.8 |
| Arab International Bank | 3.9 | |
| Arab African Bank | 7.9 | |
| *Capitalist Countries* | *986.3* | *31.9* |
| USA | 661.4 | 21.4 |
| West Germany | 148.4 | 4.8 |
| Italy | 67.6 | 2.2 |
| Japan | 57.9 | 1.9 |
| France | 21.7 | |
| Spain | 13.7 | |
| Denmark | 7.7 | 1.7 |
| UK | 6.9 | |
| Holland | 1.0 | |
| *Socialist Countries* | *548.0* | *17.8* |
| USSR | 391.1 | 12.7 |
| Czechoslovakia | 44.4 | 1.4 |
| East Germany | 35.8 | 1.2 |
| Yugoslavia | 18.1 | |
| Hungary | 16.8 | |
| China | 14.4 | |
| Poland | 12.5 | 2.5 |
| Romania | 8.8 | |
| Bulgaria | 6.1 | |
| *International & Regional Organizations* | *116.8* | *3.8* |
| IBRD/IDA | 106.4 | 3.5 |
| OPEC Special Fund | 5.7 | 0.18 |
| African Development Bank | 4.7 | 0.15 |
| Grand Total | 3,088.0 | 100.0 |

SOURCES: Ministry of Economy and Economic Cooperation and the Central Bank of Egypt.

over the period 1952–1977 is overwhelmingly bilateral should be very significant for investigating the income distribution effects of financing development heavily through foreign aid. For it is not unreasonable to think that, with bilateral aid, the receiving country will have less freedom to decide, *inter alia,* on the distribution issue than with multilateral aid. There will be concrete evidence on this point in the specific case of Egypt later.

Finally, it is perhaps revealing to note that the bulk of aid to Egypt went into a rather limited number of areas. Thus, Arab aid provided mainly cash transfers for balance of payments support; American aid went mainly to finance consumption, particularly food consumption. Food aid under Public Law (PL) 480 amounted to £E554.1 million, or 84 percent of total aid disbursements by the US.[17] Aside from land reclamation, Soviet aid was used basically to finance the High Dam and industrial development projects.[18] An important question is whether this heavy concentration of aid by type of use was harmful or benefical to income distribution. This is the subject matter of the following sections of the chapter.

## III. The Analysis of Foreign Aid Received by Egypt

### A. *Sources of Foreign Aid to Egypt*

Over the period of the study, Egypt managed to attract foreign aid from many sources. Along with the traditional capitalist and socialist countries that exchanged positions as major aid donors, there emerged recently (after 1973) the Arab oil producing countries and Iran, which swiftly moved to first position among donors.[19] The World bank (IBRD) and its affiliate, International Development Agency (IDA), have also made a small, albeit important, contribution.

It is clear from table 13.3 that aid from Arab sources (governments, national and regional organizations) tops the list, accounting for 46.5 percent of total aid disbursement to Egypt over the period 1952–1977. The United States is the most important single donor, followed by Kuwait, providing 21.4 percent and 13.8 percent, respectively.[20] The Soviet Union is the third largest single donor.

It must be emphasized that the picture provided by table 13.3 is time-aggregated and conceals the development of the relative weight of each donor over time. Until the mid-1960s, the United States occupied a prominent place in Egypt's aid operation, a role that was rivaled only by the Soviet Union. The latter continued to be Egypt's main donor until the early 1970s. But the most significant rise to prominence was in the case of the Arab countries, which quickly established themselves, thanks to the oil boom, as Egypt's main donors. Considering that figures refer to current-price data, there may be an overestimate of the contribution of latecomers.[21] The data in table 13.3 reveal a strong polarity in the overall aid picture, since the Soviet Union accounts for 71 percent of aid disbursed

TABLE 13.4.

*Profile of Foreign Aid Commitments to Egypt by Source and Area of Use until June 30, 1977*

| | Source (percentage) | | | | | | | | | | |
|---|---|---|---|---|---|---|---|---|---|---|---|
| *Area of Use* | *CC* *1* | *SC* *2* | *ALB* *3* | *KF* *4* | *AF* *5* | *SF* *6* | *ADF* *7* | *IBRD/ IDA* *8* | *GODE* *9* | *ADB/ OSF* *10* | *OC* *11* |
| 1. Commerce & Supply | 37.2 | 1.3 | | | | 12.0 | | 2.5 | | | |
| 2. Industry & Petroleum | 12.8 | 35.0 | 100 | 43.2 | 34.2 | | 16.7 | 15.2 | | | 3.1 |
| 3. Housing & Reconstruction | 5.8 | 4.3 | | | 33.5 | | | 13.0 | | | 3.4 |
| 4. Suez Canal | 3.5 | | | 33.8 | | 46.8 | 39.2 | 14.5 | | | 10.1 |
| 5. Agriculture (including High Dam & Land Reclamation) | 2.9 | 19.8 | | | | | | 22.0 | | | |
| 6. Monetary loans | 8.8 | | | | | | | | 100 | 54.8 | 80.0 |
| 7. Electricity | 11.1 | 5.8 | | 17.1 | 21.3 | | 38.6 | | | 45.2 | 0.5 |
| 8. Transportation | 8.4 | 2.6 | | 5.9 | | 41.2 | | 19.3 | | | 2.9 |
| 9. Health | 0.3 | 1.0 | | | | | 5.5 | | | | |
| 10. Aviation & Tourism | 1.1 | | | | | | | | | | |
| 11. Other (including unallocated balances) | 8.1 | 29.5 | | | | | | 13.5 | | | |
| Total | 100 | 99.3 | 100 | 100 | 89 | 100 | 100 | 100 | 100 | 100 | 100 |

SOURCE: Ministry of Economy and Economic Cooperation and the Central Bank of Egypt, unpublished data.

NOTE:

CC: Capitalist countries SC: Socialist countries ALB: Arab Libyan Bank
KF: Kuwait Fund AF: Arab Fund SF: Saudi Fund
ADF: Abu Dhabi Fund IBRD/IDA: World Bank/International Development Agency
GODE/Gulf Organization for Development in Egypt
ADB/OSF: African Dev. Bank and OPEC Special Fund
OC: Oil exporting countries (Abu Dhabi, Kuwait, Qatar, Saudi-Arabia, & Iran)

by the socialist countries while the United States accounts for 67 percent of aid provided by capitalist countries. That leads us to anticipate two important questions. The first is: what are the differences in the terms and areas of use of aid from different sources? The second is: how do such differences reflect themselves on income distribution in the Egyptian economy?

### *B. Areas of Use of Foreign Aid*

The area of use of foreign aid is relevant for investigating its income distribution implication, because alternative uses affect different groups of the population differently. Table 13.4 distinguishes eleven areas for the use of foreign aid resources: agriculture (including High Dam and land reclamation), commerce and supply, industry and petroleum, electricity, transport and communication, housing and reconstruction, Suez Canal, health, aviation, tourism, monetary loans, and other uses. The table also distinguishes eleven sources of foreign aid to Egypt: the group of capitalist countries, the group of socialist countries, the group of Arab oil producing countries and Iran, the Gulf Organization for Development in Egypt, the World Bank and the International Development Association, the Kuwait Fund, the Abu Dhabi Fund, the Saudi Fund, the Arab Fund, the Arab Libyan Bank, and the African Development Bank and the OPEC (Oil Producing and Exporting Countries) Special Fund.

On the basis of the data in table 13.4, some general source-use associations may be noted.

1. The largest single tranche of capitalist countries' aid (37.2 percent) was channeled to commerce and supply. This may be explained by the fact that food aid and commodity loans weighed heavily in this group's contributions. Next was the use of aid resources for industry and petroleum. Aid going to these two areas makes up 50 percent of total aid committed by the capitalist countries.
2. Industry and petroleum absorbed the largest single chunk of aid contributed by the socialist countries. Agriculture (including High Dam and land reclamation) was next in line, with both uses making up more than half the aid commitment by this group of countries. Socialist countries' aid is basically for industrial and infrastructure projects.
3. The whole contribution by the Gulf Organization for the Development of Egypt (GODE) went for balance-of-payments support and for the restructuring of Egypt's debt. This holds true, though to a smaller degree, for contributions made by the Arab oil producing countries and Iran, and the African Development Bank and the OPEC Special Fund.
4. The development funds, both national and regional, focused their assistance, with varying degrees, on industry and petroleum, electricity, transport and communications, and the Suez Canal.

Thus, food and commodity aid weighed rather heavily in the contribu-

*TABLE 13.5.*
*Financial Terms of Aid Received by Egypt from Main Sources*

| *Source* | *Grace (years)* | *Maturity (years)* | *Interest (%)* | *Remarks* |
|---|---|---|---|---|
| | | *TERMS* | | |
| *United States:* | | | | |
| Food aid (PL 480, Title I) | 2.0 | 19.0 | 2.0–3.0 | Until January 3, 1966, was made in pounds |
| AID investment loans | 3.5 | 9.5 | 5.0–5.75 | Loans contracted in 1960 |
| | 9.5 | 30.5 | 0.75 | Loans contracted in 1962–1963 |
| | 10.0 | 40.0 | 2.0–3.0 | Starting 1975 |
| AID commodity loans | 2.5 | 7.5 | 2.5 | Until June 1, 1966 |
| | 10.0 | 40.0 | 2.0–3.0 | Starting 1975 |
| *West Germany* | | | | |
| Reconstruction loans | | 8.0–12.0 | 2.5–4.0 | Loans contracted in 1962 |
| Investment loans | 10.0 | 30.0 | 2.5 | Loans contracted 1973–1975 |
| | 10.0 | 50.0 | 0.75 | Loans contracted 1976–1977 |
| *Soviet Union:* | | | | |
| Project loans | 1.0 | 5.0–12.0 | 2.5 | |
| *China:* | 10.0 | 20.0 | 0.0 | |
| *Czechoslovakia:* | 1.0 | 4.0–12.0 | 2.5–3.0 | Payment in convertible currencies starting January 1, 1977 |
| *Oil Producing Countries* | 1.0–10.0 | 10.0–30.0 | 2.0–6.75 | |
| *IBRD/IDA:* | | | | |
| IBRD | 4.5 | 20.0–25.0 | 6.0–8.85 | Third window loans carry interest of 4% |
| IDA | 10.0 | 20.0–40.0 | 0.75 | IDA gives interest-free loans |
| *Development Agencies:* | | | | |
| GODE | 3.0–5.0 | 4.5–8.0 | 5.0 | |
| National funds | 3.0–5.0 | 10.0–15.0 | 3.0–4.5 | |
| Regional funds | 3.0–6.0 | 14.0–20.0 | 4.0–6.0 | OPEC Special Fund gives interest-free loans |

SOURCES: Compiled and extracted from information obtained from Ministry of Economy, the Central Bank, and the Economic Bulletin of the National Bank of Egypt.

tion of capitalist countries, while industrial and infrastructure projects constituted the bulk of socialist countries' aid. The Arab countries' (and Iran's) aid consisted largely of cash transfers. This is not to imply, however, that one type of aid is superior to another; in the final analysis, aid represents resource flows into the economy. Thanks to the *fungibility* concept, additional resources are made available to the entire economy, regardless of the particular area of use of aid flows. That should not mean, however, that the area of use is inconsequential for income distribution. We shall examine this issue, and others, in section IV of this study.

## *C. The Terms of Aid*

*Terms of aid* refers in the ordinary usage to the financial conditions of the relevant resource transfer. These comprise the grace period, interest rate, and maturity. However, in the confines of this study, we adopt a broader definition that includes the "strings attached" to aid, or simply the nonfinancial conditions (except tying).

### *(1) The Financial Terms of Aid*

The terms of aid are also relevant for determining its income-redistributive implications. Because they do not entail repayment, grants should have no redistributive effects in a zero-sum sense.[22] But they may have differential-distributive effects in the sense that some socioeconomic groups gain more than others. Such differential effects depend largely on the uses made of the additional resources provided by the grants and on the nonfinancial strings attached.

Loans, on the other hand, may have distributive effects of both types—the zero-sum and the differential. Such effects would depend, *ceteris paribus,* on the terms of the loans, both financial (interest, maturity, and grace) and nonfinancial. Although tying practices are also relevant, we shall ignore them for lack of data, except for saying that source-tying may lead to redistribution against factors of production engaged in producing goods competing with those financed by aid.

Table 13.5 summarizes the financial terms of aid received from the main sources. Examination of the data in this table reveals a number of interesting facts. First, there has been an improvement in the terms of aid provided by the United States both in the form of investment loans and commodity loans. However, the terms of food aid under Title I of PL 480 were made harder; starting March 1, 1966, payment was required in dollars. Second, judged by the financial terms alone (grace, maturity, and interest), the Federal Republic of Germany (FRG), and China provide the softest loans. This may be readily ascertained when we express the terms of aid provided by different donors using the grant element concept.[23] The results are reported in table 13.6. Third, on the basis of the financial terms, the hardest loans received by Egypt over the period are those

*TABLE 13.6.*
*Grant Element of Different Aid Sources*

| Donor | Grant Element At 10% Discount | Grant Element At 15% Discount |
|---|---|---|
| United States | | |
| PL 480, Title I aid | 47–42 | 61–57 |
| AID investment loans (1960) | 20–18 | 35–33 |
| AID investment loans (1975) | 65–58 | 76–71 |
| AID commodity loans (1975) | 65–58 | 76–71 |
| West Germany | | |
| Reconstruction (1962) | 30–24 | 43–38 |
| Investment loans (1973–75) | 55 | 68 |
| Investment loans (1976–77) | 76 | 84 |
| Soviet Union and Socialist Countries | 52–15 | 58–32 |
| China | 58 | 69 |
| Arab Countries | 32–28 | 71–49 |
| GODE | 12–18 | 23–30 |
| IBRD | 12 | 30 |
| IDA | 36–65 | 48–75 |
| National Development Funds | 24–32 | 38–47 |
| Regional Development Funds | 26–32 | 42–50 |

SOURCE: Computed by applying grant element formula of note 23 to data of table 13.5, using rates of discount equal to 10% and 15%.

provided by the Agency for International Development (AID) in 1960, those provided by some of the oil producing countries and some of the regional development agencies, and those provided by the World Bank. Other things being equal, we should expect aid offered by those donors to have more influence on the state of income distribution since their financial cost is higher. And with higher financial cost, servicing and repayment require stronger fiscal measures. As a result, we should expect more influence on income distribution than otherwise.

### *(2) The Nonfinancial Conditions of Aid*

The nonfinancial conditions of aid are extremely relevant for the study of the effect of aid on income distribution. This is because such conditions affect the determinants of distribution, that is, resource allocation, pricing, concentration of control over productive assets, technology, and the role of the government.[24] Through their effect on the major determinants of income distribution, they eventually favor some socioeconomic groups of the population *vis-à-vis* the rest.

In the particular case of Egypt, one may distinguish between the (nonfinancial) conditions set by individual donor countries, those set by the lenders' syndicate called the Egypt Consultative Group, and those set by the International Monetary Fund (IMF).

IMF Conditions

The IMF does not give development aid in the sense defined here, but rather as short or medium balance-of-payments support of different types. However, the endorsement of the country's policy by the IMF acts as a green light for aid donors to be forthcoming. So the IMF wields power not so much because of its direct financing but because it speaks for the aid donors.[25]

The IMF conditions are usually stipulated in the Stabilization Program, which is outlined in a letter of intent submitted by the country in question to the executive director of the fund. The elements of the Stabilization Program are carefully negotiated by the fund's representatives with representatives of the country's government.

Egypt has issued a series of letters of intent to the IMF. We only analyze the latest such letter, dated June 10, 1978, which was the basis for the 1978 Stabilization Agreement. According to this agreement, Egypt is to receive IMF assistance of SDR (Special Drawing Rights) 600 million (about $720 million). In return, the government of Egypt undertakes to implement a stabilization program composed of structural reform of the economy plus specific policy measures in different areas.

Succinctly, the elements of the structural reform are: *(a)* "To initiate a process of price rationalization . . . with the aim of placing the operations of the public sector companies on a sound *commercial* basis, *(b)* To encourage the allocation of resources towards agriculture, by giving priority to infrastructure investment, upgrading extension services and reviewing pricing policies for agricultural inputs and outputs, *(c)* To reduce the rate of growth of subsidy expenditure compared with the rate of growth of government expenditure in general, *(d)* To give public sector enterprises and government agencies greater autonomy with regard to hiring. . . ."[26]

This structural reform is supposedly inspired by the quest for efficiency, a reasonably legitimate concern. The social organization of production in Egypt leaves much to be desired. On this basis alone, one may make a strong case for reform. But the IMF-instigated reform goes far beyond the requirements of efficiency. The stress on agriculture is indicative of the prospects envisaged for Egypt in the international division of labor: It is reminiscent of Egypt's nineteenth-century post-Muhammed ᶜAli experience. Also, reducing subsidies without any corrective measures can only accentuate inequality.

What these reform measures really amount to is the reinstitution of market forces as the determinant of resource allocation and the distribution of the social product. Such an orientation is not necessarily a better alternative to the present state of affairs—it may even worsen the distribution of income. This is the more likely since the fiscal system in Egypt (being very weak) cannot be relied upon to correct the negative equity effects of market forces. In fact, if the fiscal system were more effective, it would have been better, from an equity point of view, to balance the budget by raising taxes instead of reducing subsidies.

In addition to these reform measures, certain policies are to be adopted during the program period in the financial, monetary, and exchange-rate areas.[27] The budget deficit is to be curtailed through reducing subsidies. Monetary policy is to be tightened by raising interest rates. The Egyptian pound is to be devalued de facto by shifting the bulk of foreign transactions to the parallel market. Such policies amount to increasing inflationary pressures and raising the prices of basic commodities. Thus, shifting payment for wheat, flour, sugar, tea, edible oil, fertilizers, pesticides, and petroleum products to the parallel exchange rate starting in January 1979 has resulted in an increase in budget deficit of £E2,074.1 million.[28] This deficit is to be financed either by indirect taxes or by banking credit.[29] The former is regressive, and the latter means inflation, which is the worst tax in terms of regressivity.[30]

## Consultative Group Conditions

The Egypt Consultative Group is composed of the countries and international and regional organizations concerned with financing the development of, and providing assistance to, Egypt. It held two meetings, the first in May 1977 and the second in June 1978.[31]

In its first meeting, members of the Consultative Group raised many thorny questions about Egypt's economic and social plans and its priorities in agriculture and manufacturing, the delay in implementing projects with foreign financing, education policy, and foreign exchange policy. They also stressed the importance of government support for the private sector.[32] Consultative Group members went even further and requested "full clarification of the role of the private sector, and recommending that the public sector refrain from large intervention in determining this role."[33] In response to these requests the Egyptian delegation pledged:

- Amending Law 43 for 1974 to provide more incentives for the private sector,
- Approval of a large number of private-sector enterprises in free zones,
- Ending public-sector monopoly of foreign trade,
- Reducing obstacles confronting foreign investors,
- Activating the stock exchange,
- Continuing the new trend of reducing intervention in pricing different commodities so as to increase profit opportunities of the private sector,

- Raising interest rate on savings and exemption of interest income from taxes.[34]

In addition to these measures to encourage the private sector, the Egyptian delegation to the Consultative Group meeting stressed that steps are being taken to design a policy for wages and prices but they are being taken cautiously to arrive at a stable economy without any unfavorable social effects, and *"that there is a full commitment to implementing the agreement signed with the Fund. . . ."*[35]

The same themes as those underlying the IMF program pertain here too: reducing the role of the government and the public sector, increasing the role played by the private sector, and reducing intervention in prices and wages. In other words, more reliance on market forces. As Bela Balassa has aptly put it: "This would entail reorienting government activities from the regulation of prices, production and foreign exchange allocation towards determining the main directions of the economy and the 'rules of the game' applicable to public, private and foreign firms."[36]

*Donor Country Conditions*

Project loan agreements entail conditions that have bearing on income distribution. I shall cite some examples of project loan agreements with the United States, which is the largest donor at present and, perhaps, for some years to come. There is no intention of being exhaustive: I shall only pick some illustrative cases. A very famous example is the *Qattāmīya Cement Project*. According to the text of the loan agreement (signed September 28, 1978), the U. S. Agency for International Development (USAID) is to provide the Egyptian government with a $95 million loan to help finance a project for cement production by the Suez Cement Company in Qattāmīya. Following are the main conditions of this loan that are relevant for income distribution:

- The government of Egypt, in its capacity as borrower, should relend to the Suez Cement Company $58.5 million, and give the balance, $36.5 million, to the company as a grant.
- At least 20 percent of the company's share capital should be sold to the private sector.
- Raising the price of locally produced cement *vis-à vis* imported cement.[37]
- Selling $4.6 million worth of the stock of the public sector to investors.[38]

The above conditions can only be expected to worsen the distribution of income. There are at least three reasons for such expectation: First, the sale of part of the public-sector share capital to the private sector will lead to more concentration of assets and, hence, of income. Second, there is a public-to-private transfer of resources embodied in the government grant to the Suez Cement Company, which will be partly privately owned. This amounts to making a $7.3 million grant to the private sector (20 percent of $36.5 million). Third, raising the price of locally produced cement can only make the housing situation worse, with much of the squeeze put on low- and fixed-income groups.

Another example of project loan agreements is that with USAID for the rationalization of the public sector and reduction of environmental effects. According to the agreement, USAID is to give the Ministry of Industry a loan of $46.445 million, to be supplemented by a $7.5 million grant.[39] The purpose of the loan and the grant is to improve the institutional capacity of the Ministry of Industry for managing resource allocation in industry. The most important conditions related to income distribution questions in this case are:

1. Borrower furnishes the project with at least £E21 million to match the loan, and £E21.5 million to match the grant.
2. Borrower agrees to *adopt a long-term policy to abolish the subsidies which hinder the development of the industrial sector.*

The most important of these conditions is that of abolishing the subsidies. Such measures, if not complemented by other appropriate measures, would lead to some serious negative consequences.

They would lead to higher prices for industrial products. As a result, national enterprises would suffer in competition with imports. This would endanger employment. Thus there would be a double squeeze—inflation coupled with unemployment. This is reminiscent of stagflation, but of a different kind.

One may deduce from the preceding discussion and analysis that aid advanced to Egypt by the nonsocialist donors (those countries and organizations that formed the Consultative Group) leads to negative changes in the state of income distribution. It is interesting to note that such effect of foreign aid comes about through a variety of subtle mechanisms. One such mechanism amounts to what we may term *denationalization*—selling part of the share capital of public enterprises to private investors. Another mechanism is subsidization of the private sector through the government budget: the government *borrows* foreign resources and *grants* some of them to partly privately owned enterprises. A third mechanism is the greater role assigned to market forces—under the euphemisms of liberalization and rationalization. The other side of this mechanism is the smaller role assigned to the government. All of this *may* have something to recommend it but certainly not a more egalitarian income distribution. The undisputable outcome will be the integration of the Egyptian economy into the world capitalist system. Independent national development will be all the more impossible, and social equity will more likely suffer.[40]

## IV. Income Distribution Effects of Major Aid Flows

In this part of the chapter we focus on the analysis of the income distribution effects of the major aid flows only. In particular, we shall restrict the analysis to the aid provided by the Soviet Union and the United States. This choice is justified by two considerations: First, data are not sufficiently available for detailed analysis of the aid provided by other donors. Second, the Soviet Union and the United States are the major donors; they account for about half the total aid disbursements to Egypt.

### *A. Aid from the Soviet Union*

Egypt signed six aid agreements with the Soviet Union over the period 1958–1971.[41] Total commitments under these agreements amounted to £E449.2 million, and actual disbursements until mid-1977 totaled £E391.1 million. Soviet aid to Egypt was concentrated on the High Dam, land reclamation, and industrial projects. We shall examine here only the distributive effects of the High Dam and industrial projects.

1. *The High Dam:* The Soviet Union provided two loans to help finance the High Dam in the amount of £E141 million, of which actual disbursements amounted to £E135 million. This makes up 43 percent of the actual final cost of the project.[42]

It is very interesting to note that the High Dam has become the subject of wide debate in the last few years. Some of this debate is based on technical considerations, but a good deal of it carries political overtones.[43] But, surprisingly enough, the question of the distributive effects of the project was never raised. We take it up here, keeping in mind that only few of the dam's effects have unfolded but many are yet to unfold.

The most important distributive aspects of the High Dam are the following:

- Land reclamation. It is estimated that 650,000–750,000 *feddans,* or some 80 percent of the land reclaimed over the decade 1960–1970, can be attributed to the water made available by the dam.[44] Only 548,900 feddans were cultivated, of which 150,000 were distributed to new owners, 160,000 rented out to tenants, and 240,000 turned into state farms. Some 200,000 workers were employed in the new land sector by 1975, earning £E21.4 million.[45] This is a decided gain to the poor in rural areas.
- Converting 850,000 feddans in Upper Egypt from basin to perennial irrigation. This enabled replacing sugarcane for cotton, thus raising cane acreage by 89 percent and lowering cotton acreage by 18 percent.[46] This is a benefit to the rural population of Upper Egypt: net income per feddan of sugarcane was £E31.5 and £E68.7 in 1971 and

*TABLE 13.7.*
*Structure of Soviet Aid to Industry 1958–1971*

| | | | | Total | |
|---|---|---|---|---|---|
| *Industries* | *1958 (Million Roubles)* | *1964 (Million Roubles)* | *1971 (Million Roubles)* | *Value (Million Roubles)* | *%* |
| *Extractive industries* | *16.5* | *51.8* | . . . | *68.3* | *13.2* |
| *Manufacturing* | *111.3* | *211.3* | *100.1* | *422.7* | *81.7* |
| Food products | 1.8 | . . . | . . . | 1.8 | 0.9 |
| Spinning & weaving | 2.6 | . . . | . . . | 2.6 | |
| Chemicals | 1.3 | 9.4 | . . . | 10.7 | 2.0 |
| Metallurgy | 10.9 | 3.0 | . . . | 13.9 | 2.7 |
| Iron & Steel | 53.1 | 145.7 | . . . | 198.8 | 38.4 |
| Engineering | 24.5 | 5.7 | 6.5 | 36.7 | 7.1 |
| Petroleum | 17.1 | . . . | . . . | 17.1 | 3.3 |
| Aluminum | . . . | 47.5 | 42.6 | 90.1 | 17.4 |
| Cement | . . . | . . . | 51.0 | 51.0 | 9.9 |
| *Electrification* | . . . | *21.3* | . . . | *21.3* | *4.1* |
| *Training* | *1.5* | *3.6* | . . . | *5.1* | *1.0* |
| Total for industry | 129.3 | 288.0 | 100.1 | 517.4 | 100.0 |
| Total Aid | 149.5 | 300.0 | 376.0 | . . . | . . . |

SOURCES: Ministry of Industry, Petroleum, and Mining, the General Organization for Industrialization, *Follow-up Report on Foreign Loans for Industry until June 30, 1978* (Cairo, June 1978), pp. 4–6.

1973, compared with £E28.1 and £E29.3, respectively, for cotton.[47] Thus we estimate that the annual net income from growing sugarcane rose from £E3.5 million in 1971 to £E15.1 million in 1973, and net income from growing cotton fell from £E44 million in 1971 to £E38 million in 1973. The outcome is a net increase from £E47.5 million to £E53.1 million. Thus, the net gain may be estimated at £E5.6 million. The increase in land value due to reclamation and perennial irrigation is estimated at £E350 million.[48]

- Making possible a 65 percent increase in rice acreage, from an average of 654,000 feddans in 1955–1959 to an average of 1,077,000 feddans in 1971–1976. In addition, there has been a net improvement in yield because of the regularity of water supply.[49]
- Electrification of the countryside. In fact, this is one of the most important distributional effects of the High Dam, although it is extremely difficult to assign a money value to it.
- Implementation of the project entailed massive training to provide skilled workers.[50] The skills bestowed on the workers, both through formal and on-the-job training, represent net benefit to them. In addition, there is the wage income, which amounted to 30 percent of the total cost of the project.[51]

- The project had a very positive regional distribution effect, with the Aswan region reaping the benefits. This includes all the utilities and amenities that were established especially for the project and were handed out to the province, such as housing, roads, transportation and communications, hospitals, schools, recreation facilities, bakeries, stores, and so forth. It is estimated that by the end of 1962/1963, only £E7 million were spent for this purpose.[52]
- The unprecedented construction works for the dam brought large gains to firms in the construction sector. It is here, as well as in the first Five Year Plan, that the seeds of the now sprouting Egyptian capitalism may have been sown.
- Electricity generated by the project gave a big boost to industrialization efforts that provided work opportunities for rural migrants, and at the same time involved projects that cater to the needs of the urban population, as we shall see.
- The fish catch in Lake Nasser. This goes primarily to the urban areas, where per capita fish consumption is double that of rural areas.[53]
- Improved navigation benefitted the urban sector more.[54] Thus it may be argued that the High Dam is a good example of a project with diffuse distribution effects. It has benefitted the poor as well as the rich in both rural and urban areas. But perhaps it may be exhibiting some urban bias if we consider such negative externalities as *bilharzia* spreading and interruption of silt.

2. *Industrial Projects:* Aside from the High Dam, the bulk of Soviet aid to Egypt went to complete directly productive projects in industry, particularly manufacturing industry. Table 13.7 indicates the pattern of use of Soviet aid to industry. It shows that loans directed to investment projects for manufacturing industry made up more than 80 percent of loans earmarked for industry.[55] It is interesting to note the industries where these aid resources were used. The follow-up report of the General Organization for Industrialization (GOFI) singles out the iron and steel industry, which attracted 41 percent and 51 percent of aid to industry under the agreements of 1958 and 1964, respectively, and 38.4 percent of total aid to industry. Aluminum projects absorbed 15.8 percent and 42.5 percent of aid resources stipulated under the agreements of 1964 and 1971, respectively, with an overall share of 17.4 percent of total aid. The other industries financed by Soviet aid are mainly either capital-goods or intermediate-goods industries.

Thus the basic distributive effects of these industries[56] are through employment, through the differential benefit of the final products of the industries they help establish, and through the burden of repayment of the funds borrowed. It is important to recognize that payment of Soviet loans takes place in kind—through the exportation of goods to the Soviet Union.

As to employment, I suspect that although Soviet loans opened up precious job opportunities, they did not help much to solve the employment problem in Egypt. For over the period 1960–1971 investment in mining, quarrying, and manufacturing increased by 85.4 percent. Over the same period, employment rose by 42.4 percent only.[57] In fact, this rate of increase in employment is rather misleading; it is an overestimate, being partly a reflection of the employment drive that took place after the nationalization measures of the early 1960s. The true increase in employment warranted by the increase in investment would have been somewhat less. This judgment is based on two grounds: First, the most attractive projects in terms of employment generation (such as handicraft and rural industries) are the least attractive for foreign aid financing.[58] Second, technology used in aid-financed projects is usually capital-intensive. Thus, investment per worker in manufacturing projects averaged £E1,000, shooting up to slightly over £E3,000 for engineering and metal industries.[59]

One may conclude, therefore, that Egypt, perhaps because of reliance on foreign aid financing, was forced to combine two contradictory features in its industrial development: capital-intensive technology and employment promotion. This was an unfortunate mix-up of efficiency and equity considerations, which ultimately resulted, *inter alia,* in a deterioration of labor productivity and, hence, national savings.

Next we examine the differential benefit of the final products of the projects financed by Soviet aid. Let us take a second look at table 13.7. Four industries stand out as major areas where Soviet aid for development in Egypt was used (aside from High Dam and land reclamation)—iron and steel, aluminum, cement, and engineering industries (in order of importance). However, if we recognize that iron, steel, and aluminum are the main feeding industries for engineering industries,[60] it becomes clear that the latter is, indeed, the most important industry financed by Soviet foreign aid to Egypt. We are interested in the final products of these industries.

The main products of the engineering industries in the first Industrialization Project (1957–1960) and those of the first Five Year Plan (1960–1965) include:[61]

| *Industrialization Program* | *First Five Year Plan* |
|---|---|
| Railway wagons | Automobiles |
| Ships | Buses and lorries |
| Buses and lorries | Bicycles |
| Refrigerators | Water heaters |
| Diesel engines | Stoves |
| Household utensils | Sewing machines |
| Bicycles | Springs |
| Pumps | Water meters |
| Water meters | Washing machines |
| Bolts and nuts | |

During the period 1965–1970, investment in the engineering industry included projects that produced machinery and equipment, motorcycles, machine tools, and special tools in addition to expanding production of boilers, bolt and nuts, springs, refrigerators, bicycles, and radiators.

It is significant to note that the bulk of the products mentioned above are either capital goods, intermediate goods, or consumer durables. This determines immediately the socioeconomic groups that stand to benefit most from such products. They are those socioeconomic groups whose per capita incomes enable them to buy consumer durables.[62] We could easily identify them if we had income distribution data. But since reliable income distribution data are not available, we make use of the expenditure data.

Thus, using the household expenditure survey data of 1974/1975, we apply the formula of the benefit index,[63] which indicates the relative benefit to expenditure groups I (top 20 percent), II (middle 30 percent), and III (low 50 percent).

$$d_i = \sum_i \sum_k e_{ik} p_{kj} w_j / \sum_i \sum_j \sum_k e_{ik} p_{kj} w_j$$

$$(i = \text{I, II, III})$$

The logic behind the benefit index is the consumer surplus. This is based on the assumption that, as these products came to be produced by aid-financed projects, their relative prices were reduced, and hence the real incomes of those who consume them are increased. There is some evidence that such an assumption is not unrealistic in the case of Egypt. Industrialization through Soviet aid for industrial projects took place behind high protective walls (composed of tariffs, import licenses, exchange controls, import quotas, and so forth). This rendered the locally produced products relatively less expensive. Moreover, some of the locally produced manufactures were sold at subsidized prices.[64]

The application of the benefit index was made using expenditure data for the urban population only. It is felt that, perhaps for the larger majority rural population, the products produced by the said aid projects are very far from the people's incomes and style of life. The result of the application was as follows:

| *Group* | top 20 percent | middle 30 percent | low 50 percent |
|---|---|---|---|
| *Benefit* | .531 | .223 | .246 |

This means that the richest 20 percent of the population stand to benefit most from the Soviet aid to industrial projects, followed, but rather at a distance, by the poorest 50 percent. This conclusion may not be too shocking if one recognizes the true nature of the economic system that prevailed in Egypt since the early 1960s—basically a system of state

*TABLE 13.8.*
*Share of Exports to the Soviet Union in Main Egyptian Exports, 1967/1968–1971/1972*
*(£E million)*

| *Exports* | *1967/1968* | *1968/1969* | *1969/1970* | *1970/1971* | *1971/1972* |
|---|---|---|---|---|---|
| Raw Cotton | 17.8 | 26.3 | 40.3 | 37.3 | 34.1 |
| Cotton Fabric | 24.6 | 25.5 | 17.4 | 17.2 | 19.3 |
| Cotton Yarn | 47.9 | 45.9 | 48.6 | 53.7 | 52.5 |
| Bleached Rice | 31.9 | 33.2 | 34.2 | 40.2 | 39.2 |
| Fresh Onions | 16.8 | 35.5 | 25.3 | 43.2 | 48.6 |

SOURCE: CAPMS, *Arab Republic of Egypt, Economic Indicators, 1952–1972* (July 1973), pp. 61–67.

capitalism. This provides support to the contention that the effect of aid depends more on the nature of the regime it supports than on its source.[65]

Finally, we consider the effect of Soviet aid on income distribution via the burden of repayment. The economic and technical cooperation agreements between Egypt and the Soviet Union, and the protocols signed thereunder, stipulate repayment in Egyptian goods. Table 13.8 indicates the main Egyptian exports to the Soviet Union over the period 1967–1972, the zenith of Egypto-Soviet economic cooperation. The most important items on the export list are agricultural products such as raw cotton, rice, onions, and agrobased manufactured products—basically cotton yarn and fabrics. Exporting such products for repayment put the burden of repayment on the rural sector, particularly growers of crops subject to compulsory delivery. Cotton, rice, and onions are notable examples.[66]

Miscellaneous export items to the Soviet Union include furniture, leather products, and knitwear. Available evidence suggests that exportation in repayment for aid has boosted these industries and has created employment opportunities. For example, knitwear factories numbered one thousand in the late 1960s, providing job opportunities for some fifty thousand workers. Ninety percent of exports of this industry's output was marketed in the socialist bloc countries.[67] It would appear, therefore, that through its effects on income distribution *via* debt repayment, Soviet aid to Egypt was a mixed blessing.

But since agricultural exports dominate,[68] the negative effect on income distribution may well outweight the positive effect. For, according to the system of marketing agricultural crops, cotton and rice are procured by the Egyptian government at prices often below their world prices.[69] Since the urban population benefits most from Soviet aid to industry, aid therefore helps change the state of income distribution in the wrong direction: taking from the poor (rural population) and giving to the rich (urban population).[70] An interesting question to raise is the place of foreign aid as a link in the political chain of effecting such a change in income distribu-

*TABLE 13.9.*
*American Aid to Egypt until June 30, 1977*

| | *Loans & Grants (£E million)* | *Disbursement (£E million)* | *Disbursement Ratio (%)* |
|---|---|---|---|
| *PL 480 Aid* | *554.1* | *554.1* | *100.0* |
| *USAID Assistance* | *620.1* | *102.9* | *16.6* |
| 1. Investment loans | 147.9 | 20.7 | 14.0 |
| 2. Commodity loans | 365.9 | 58.9 | 16.1 |
| 3. Project grants | 98.9 | 20.3 | 20.5 |
| 4. Technical grants | 7.4 | 3.0 | 40.5 |
| Total[a] | 1,174.2 | 657.0[b] | 56.0 |

SOURCES:
Ministry of Economy and Economic Cooperation and the Central Bank of Egypt unpublished data.

NOTES:
[a]Excludes Export-Import Bank loans.
[b]There is a difference of about £E4 million between this table and table 13.2.

tion. It would seem politically more difficult to change income distribution this way more directly—through fiscal measures. Foreign aid thus masks the *social nature* of the redistribution process under a veil of *national interest*. Soviet aid may have acted as a safety valve by sparing the Egyptian society the social tension that would have arisen for sure otherwise.

### *B. Aid from the United States*

It was mentioned earlier that the United States is the largest aid donor to Egypt. American assistance covered a wide spectrum, from financing final consumption (aid under PL 480) to financing both infrastructure and directly productive activities. Table 13.9 gives the details of American aid to Egypt over the period 1954–1977.[71] It indicates that total aid disbursements amounted to £E657 million, 84 percent of which is in the form of food aid, mainly wheat and wheat flour under PL 480. The rest represents funds provided by the U. S. Agency for International Development. Fifty-seven percent of the funds provided by AID represents commodity loans, and the remainder is allocated to project loans, grants, and technical grants.

*1. Food Aid:* American wheat and flour deliveries to Egypt have assumed significant levels, making up more than 25 percent of total consumption since 1976, as shown by table 13.10. This is about the same level of importance as in the first half of the 1960s, and before the cut-off of American aid to Egypt. There is no doubt that this aid has helped Egypt both to maintain low wheat prices and to implement a decent food subsidy

TABLE 13.10.
American Wheat Aid and Wheat Consumption
1975–1977

| Year | American Wheat/ Flour Aid (million M/T) | Total Wheat Consumption (million M/T) | Wheat Aid to Consumption (%) |
|---|---|---|---|
| | (1) | (2) | (3 = [(1) ÷ (2)]) |
| 1975 | 0.618 | 4.493 | 13.8 |
| 1976 | 1.252 | 4.673[a] | 26.8 |
| 1977 | 1.407 | 4.860[a] | 29.0 |

SOURCES:
Amercan wheat/flour aid: USAID/Controller, *Summary of Economic Assistance to Egypt FY 75 to June 6, 1979* (mimeographed) (July 1979).
Total wheat consumption: Ministry of Agriculture, Department of Agricultural Economics and Statistics, *Food Balances for 1950–1974 Period,* quoted in USAID/Egypt, *A Report on Wheat Consumption in Egypt*, prepared by Farouk Shalaby (December 1978).

NOTE:
[a]Assumes a growth rate of 4% over previous year.

program. In relative terms, the poor stand to benefit more by such aid, since staple food weighs more heavily in their expenditure budget.[72] Whether they have benefitted more, indeed, depends on the extent of their access to subsidized bread through the regular distribution channels. In view of this consideration, one may say with confidence that the urban population has benefitted from this food aid.

But against the benefit to the poor as consumers of food from food aid, one must weigh the likely inflationary effect of the disbursement of counterpart funds,[73] which amounted to £E216.24 million in 1965.[74]

*2. Loans and Grants for Investment Projects:*

Egypt obtained loans and grants given by the USAID for development projects in the amount of $69.6 million until the end of 1963. These included the financing of nine projects covering infrastructure and light-industry projects—a grain-handling facility, the Cairo West power station, expansion of the ᶜIdfīna plant, a *bagasse* plant, a loan for the Industrial Bank, a loan for Misrayon, and a loan to finance a project at Rakta for producing cardboard.[75]

Since the resumption of aid in 1975 and until 1977, total assistance in the form of project loans and grants amounted to $756.3 million.[76] Projects covered mainly infrastructure (power, transport, communication and storage, and tile drainage), with only three industrial projects (cement, textiles, and salines). It may be said that the benefits from infrastructure projects are not widespread; they tend to be concentrated in urban areas. Industrial projects established by American aid, again similar to Soviet aid, mainly produce goods beyond the scope of consumption by the poor, especially the rural poor.

In addition to this, Egypt obtained £E216.2 million worth of aid from American-owned counterpart funds, 84 percent of which went for unified budget support. Of course, the effect of such aid on the distribution of income is to a large extent a function of the fiscal system. There is some evidence that the Egyptian tax system is regressive.[77] Initially, the use of counterpart funds will be beneficial to income distribution, since it will forestall the use of regressive taxes. But repayment may obscure this effect if made through the use of such taxes, or through inflation.

*3. Commodity Import Loans:*

Another important category of American assistance to Egypt takes the form of commodity deliveries. Over the period 1962–1977, commodity import loans amounted to $935 million.[78] These loans are designed to provide machinery, spare parts, and raw materials for industry, and buses, trucks, tractors, and wagons. They represent outright balance-of-payments support. There are no official data on the details of the commodity loans, but buses and trucks, for example, are very visible in both urban and rural areas.

Finally, we should not forget the effect of grants obtained by Egypt on the state of income distribution. Such effects will not be of the zero-sum or compensating type, since there is no repayment required. The grants given by the United States to Egypt are of two types: project grants and technical grants. Until June 30, 1977, disbursement from project grants totalled £E20.3 million. It all went exclusively for Suez Canal and area projects. Such grants must have helped to intensify reconstruction expenditure in the canal area, thereby creating incomes and at the same time inflationary pressure. These pressures manifested themselves in rising wages in the construction industry.

Until June 30, 1977, technical grants disbursements amounted to £E3 million. Such a figure may be too trivial to matter directly for income distribution. However, its indirect effects may not be insignificant. This significance derives from their nature. The grants received cover technology transfer and feasibility studies. Technology transfer grants finance long- and short-term missions to the United States for Egyptian technical experts and administrators, and technical assistance from American sources. These grants "will assist Egypt's efforts to make public sector officials more responsive to free market economic forces."[79] If the said training program proves successful, the effects on the state of income distribution are unlikely to be benign: the unleashing of market economic forces in Egypt in the past has tended toward greater concentration of income and wealth. It was only through interfering with the play of free-market economic forces in the early 1960s that income disparities were narrowed. There are many reasons why free market forces would lead, in Egypt's case, to more concentration of income and wealth. One is the weakness of the fiscal system (especially income taxes) as a stabilizer and regulator. Another is that market forces will be freed in some sectors (manufacturing) and controlled in others (agriculture). A third reason is that external linkages will be stronger for some sectors and weaker for others.

## V. Conclusions

Foreign aid has contributed significantly to the growth of the Egyptian economy over the period. About one-fifth to one-third of the growth achieved over the period of the study may be attributed to foreign aid.

Foreign aid received was heavily concentrated both with regard to source and with respect to area of use. The *source concentration,* through the concomitant dependence, limited the choices that Egypt could have made regarding equity questions. The *use concentration* invoked an urban bias.

The High Dam, the biggest single project financed by the Soviet Union, did have a number of effects in favor of the rural and the urban populations. However, it seems that, on balance, the rural population, and especially small farmers, paid more than others. We could not put a value on such environmental effects as the spread of *bilharzia* in Upper Egypt.

As to industrial projects financed by Soviet aid, they produced capital and intermediate goods that eventually fed consumer goods industries, especially durables. Here it is clear that the farmers, especially cotton growers, subsidized high- and middle-income groups through debt repayment for these industries.

It proved difficult to secure data on the use of American food aid. We can only *speculate* that it was used in the interest of the low-income groups in urban areas.

American aid for industrial projects went mainly to finance infrastructure projects and consumer goods industries. As such, it ties in rather nicely, though indirectly, with Soviet aid. Together, they provided a political safety valve against the risks of social tension that would arise from overt appropriation of the economic surplus by the high-income groups.

Much of the effect of aid on income distribution is rather discrete. This was clear in the case of grants from the United States. Technology transfer grants and feasibility studies are expected to adversely affect the social priorities and, hence, have significant implications for income distribution. Much the same goes for nonfinancial terms of aid.

Finally, one may deduce that foreign-aid finance was for Egypt, perhaps, a blind alley. It did not seem to have favorably affected income distribution. At the same time, it has increased the country's reliance on foreign financing even further. One wonders if foreign aid has necessarily led to craving for encouraging the inflow of foreign direct investment. One also wonders if a self-reliant development effort would at least be more equitable. Perhaps the Egyptian experience is relevant in this regard.

## Appendix
## On the Meaning and Derivation of the Benefit Index

In this appendix I outline a method of relating the benefit from production projects (financed by foreign aid) to different socioeconomic groups. The basic idea is fairly simple. Foreign aid finances production projects. These projects produce output, which may fall into some expenditure pattern. That pattern may be identified with some socioeconomic group. This is shown in the following schematic illustration:

Foreign Aid

Production Projects

Product Mix

Expenditure Pattern

Socioeconomic Groups

Although ideally one would want to base this study on socioeconomic groups, or income groups, data limitation forces the use of expenditure groups. Using household expenditure survey data, we distinguish three expenditure groups:

I The top 20%
II The middle 30%
III The bottom 50%

Four main expenditure items are used to depict the expenditure pattern:*

*F* Food and drink
*H* Housing and amenities, furniture and fixtures
*C* Clothing
*T* Transportation

*The items do not exhaust total expenditure by each group. Thus, the total sum of expenditure proportions for these items is less than one.

In the specific case of Soviet aid for industry, the following product groups were distinguished:

*FP* Food products
*TC* Textiles and clothing
*MP* Metal products
*NE* Nonelectrical machinery
*EM* Electrical machinery
*MT* Means of transport
*CP* Chemical products

We may now proceed to construct the following matrices:

$$\begin{aligned} E &= e_{ik};\ i = I, II, III,\ k = F, H, C, T \\ P &= p_{kj};\ k = F, H, C, T \\ &\qquad j = FP, TC, MP, NE, EL, MT, CP \\ W &= w_j;\ j = FP, TC, MP, NE, EM, MT, CP \end{aligned}$$

*E* is the expenditure matrix, giving proportional expenditure on basic items by expenditure groups. It is easily constructed from household expenditure survey data. *P* is a matrix giving the share of each product group in the different basic expenditure items. *W* is a vector of weight of different product groups in the project's output (product mix).

The formula that I propose for linking the benefit of aid-financed projects to different expenditure groups is the following:

$$d_i = \sum_j \sum_k e_{ik} p_{kj} w_j / \sum_i \sum_j \sum_k e_{ik} p_{kj} w_j$$

$$(i = \text{I, II, III})$$

The numerator is simply the proportion of the *i*th expenditure group's income (= expenditure) spent on the product mix of the aid-financed projects. The denominator is the sum over all expenditure groups; it enables us to obtain a normalized indicator (ranging from zero to unity). We call $d_i$ the *benefit index*.

The *benefit index* indicates the benefit that accrues to the *i*th group from the aid-financed projects. This is a qualitative indicator: the highest $d_i$ implies that the *i*th group stands to *benefit most* from the given project *compared to the other two*.

It is relevant to note the difference between the *benefit index*, $d_i$ described above, and the *summary distribution measure, D,* suggested in a recent World Bank study.** The latter is defined as:

> The increase in total welfare generated when an increment in consumption is distributed among the population in the same way as is current aggregate consumption.

**Lyn Squire and Herman G. von der Tak, *Economic Analysis of Projects,* published for the World Bank (Baltimore: Johns Hopkins University Press, 1975).

Thus $D$ is set at a higher (lower) value *if it is believed* that the increment in consumption arising from the project is improving (worsening) the situation. The $D$ measure is *so subjective* that only the planning authority can decide on its value.

The following data were used to estimate $d_i$:

| $E =$ | $F$ | $H$ | $C$ | $T$ |
|---|---|---|---|---|
| I | 0.462 | 0.158 | 0.134 | 0.061 |
| II | 0.548 | 0.171 | 0.112 | 0.022 |
| III | 0.585 | 0.194 | 0.084 | 0.018 |

It is calculated from the 1974/1975 household expenditure survey data for the urban sector. The implicit assumption is that the rural population's benefit from Soviet aid to industry was negligible.

| $P =$ | $FP$ | $TC$ | $MP$ | $NE$ | $EM$ | $MT$ | $CP$ |
|---|---|---|---|---|---|---|---|
| $F$ | 0.8 | 0 | 0 | 0 | 0 | 0 | 0 |
| $H$ | 0 | 0 | 0.3 | 0.2 | 0.2 | 0 | 0 |
| $C$ | 0 | 0.6 | 0 | 0 | 0 | 0 | 0.1 |
| $T$ | 0 | 0 | 0.1 | 0.2 | 0 | 0.6 | 0 |

The $P$ is based on knowledge of the contribution of each industry's product to basic expenditure items.

$$W = (0 \quad 0 \quad 0.3 \quad 0.3 \quad 0.2 \quad 0.1 \quad 0.1)$$

The $W$ is based on examination of the nature of the industries established with the help of Soviet aid to Egypt.***

***The weight on food processing *(FP)* and textiles and clothing *(TC)* is zero because too small a portion of Soviet aid was allocated to projects in these industries—less than 1% of total Soviet aid to industry over the period 1958–1971. See table 13.7.

## Notes

1. Cf. Cheryl Payer, *The Debt Trap: The International Monetary Fund and the Third World* (New York: Monthly Review Press, 1974); Teresa Hayter, *Aid as Imperalism* (London: Penguin Books, 1971).

2. For a detailed discussion of the different meanings of aid, see: I. M. D. Little and J. M. Clifford, *International Aid* (Chicago: Aldinc, 1965); E. K. Hawkins, *The Principles of Development Aid* (Penguin Books, 1970); R. F. Mikesell, *The Economics of Foreign Aid* (Chicago: Aldine, 1968); J. Bhagwati and Richard Eckaus, *Foreign Aid; Selected Readings* (Penguin Books, 1970).

3. The distinction between short- and medium-term loans is not always clear-cut. However, usually loans of less than three years are considered short-term. Loans of up to five to seven years are usually considered medium-term. The distinction between different loan maturities as a basis for the definition of aid loses importance once we start thinking in terms of the "grant element" of different loans. The grant element, which is a measure of the concessionality of a loan, depends on both the maturity and the interest rate, given the grace period. For a definition of the grant element, see OECD, *Development Cooperation, 1977 Review* (November 1977), p. 240; and for an analysis of the effect of the different loan parameters (maturity, interest rate, and grace period) on the grant element of the loans, see Hawkins, pp. 30–34.

4. For a thorough discussion of tying practices, see J. Bhagwati, "The Tying of Aid," in J. Bhagwati and Richard S. Eckaus, *Foreign Aid: Selected Readings* (Penguin Books, 1970).

5. I use the terms *development* and *growth* interchangeably. In the Egyptian experience, there was no clear-cut distinction between the two.

6. Attention in this study centers around foreign aid for economic purposes only, i.e., foreign economic aid. That includes technical assistance, but excludes military assistance.

7. Said El-Naggar, *Foreign Aid to the UAR* (Cairo: Institute of National Planning, 1963)

8. The data in table 13.1 on average annual inflow of aid may not exhibit this cyclical behavior very clearly. The reason has to do with the division of the period into subperiods rather than years. This aggregation of time smoothes out the cyclical movement. A stronger cyclical pattern would arise if we considered the subperiods: 1952–1957, 1958–1964, 1965–1973, 1974–1977. But data prepared by the Ministry of Planning correspond to plan periods as in the table. Yet, one may still get a stronger feeling of the cyclical behavior of aid if its ratio to investment or imports is examined.

9. See Donald C. Mead, *Growth and Structural Change in the Egyptain Economy* (Homewood, Ill.: Richard D. Irwin, 1967), pp. 184–185. By the end of the war, sterling balance accredited to Egypt amounted to £E430 million; see M. Z. Shafāᶜī, *An Introduction to Money and Banking* (Cairo: Nahda ᶜArabīya, 1964) (Arabic), p. 151.

10. I have tried to estimate the annual flow of aid by consulting various sources such as the Economic Bulletin of the National Bank of Egypt, the *Official Gazette,* the Ministry of Foreign Affairs' *Collection of Treaties,* and various press releases. I arrived at a total of $5,129.2 million over the entire period 1952–1976. Although this may be misleading for the magnitude, it is still very useful for illustrating the cyclical pattern, as the following index number shows:

| Period | 1952–1957 | 1958–1966 | 1967–1973 | 1974–1976 |
|---|---|---|---|---|
| Index | 100 | 3,718 | 1,421 | 10,851 |

11. Actually, growth was negative in 1967. See IBRD, *Arab Republic of Egypt, Economic Management in a Period of Transition, vol. I* (1978): p. 23.

12. Ibid, p. 24.

13. Ibid, pp. 33–34.

14. Gouda Abdel-Khalek, "The Pattern of Development and Growing Dependence on the Outside World," in Société Égyptienne d'Économie Politique, de Statistique et de Législation, *Development and International Economic Relations: Proceedings of the First Conference for Egyptain Economists* (Cairo: General Egyptain Book Organization, 1977, pp. 598–627.

15. Interview with Donald Brown, director of AID-Egypt, *al-Ahrām,* September 3, 1980.

16. We shall examine concentration by area of use in more detail in section III.

17. Data obtained from Ministry of Economy and Economic Cooperation.

18. That should not, and indeed does not, imply that one aid (the American) is inferior to the other (the Russian); consumption is not, *per se* inferior to production. In fact, by virtue of the principle of "fungibility" or "switching," it may be impossible to distinguish aid for consumption from aid to production; see Hans Singer and Javed Ansari, *Rich and Poor Countries* (London: Allen & Unwin, 1977), p. 168. I only wanted to characterize the immediate or direct use of aid resources. More on this point later.

19. The Arab countries suspended their aid to Egypt after its peace treaty with Israel.

20. Kuwait contribution will be 15% if we include the Kuwait Fund for Arab Development (KFAED) loans.

21. I am indebted to Ibrahim El-Issawy for pointing this out to me.

22. There should be no redistributive effects since there is no financial *quid pro quo.* However, if commodity grants depress the price of domestic import substitutes (such as may be the case with food aid), they are bound to have distributive effects of the zero-sum type (i.e, they may benefit urban dwellers at the expense of food producers).

23. The concept of grant element was developed by the Development Assistance Committee (DAC) of the OECD. It is a measure of the concessionality of a loan. See OECD, *Development Cooperation 1977* (Paris: OECD, 1977); and E. K. Hawkins, *The Principles of Development Aid* (1970). The formula for the grant element may be written as:

$$g = \frac{L - \sum_{t}^{T} \frac{C_t + I_t}{1(1+i)^t}}{L} \div 1 - \frac{\sum_{t=1}^{T} \frac{(C_t + I_t)}{(1+i)^t}}{L},$$

where

$g =$ grant element;
$L =$ nominal value of the loan;
$T =$ maturity in years;
$C + I =$ debt service payments (principal and interest);
$i =$ rate of discount;
$t =$ time.

*The calculations reported in the text were based on two alternative values for i* (10% and 15%). The lower value corresponds to the practice of DAC. However, 15% may be more in line with currently observed interest rates.

The calculations reported in the text were based on two alternative values for $i$ (10% and 15%). The lower value corresponds to the practice of DAC. However, 15% may be more in line with currently observed interest rates.

24. Cf. Hollis B. Chenery et al., *Redistribution with Growth* (London: Oxford University Press, 1974), p. 168. Chenery et al. talk about the effect of foreign exchange earnings from exports, but the same goes for "earnings" from aid.

25. For more detail on this point, see Cheryl Payer, *The Debt Trap,* passim; and Teresa Hayter, *Aid as Imperialism,* passim.

26. Gouda Abdel-Khalek, "Development, Self-Reliance and Equity: Queries Inspired by the Egyptian Experience of Over-dependence on Foreign Assistance," paper read to the Fourth Congress of Egyptian Economists, Cairo, 3–5 May 1979.

27. Ibid., pp. 13–17.

28. Statement of the minister of Finance on the Draft Budget for 1979, *Minutes of the 17th Session of the People's Assembly,* dated January 1, 1979, p. 33.

29. Banking Credit was to reach £E.1,197 million, or 45% of the budget deficit for 1979; ibid., p. 23.

30. In fact, IMF conditions in Egypt's case are not unique. There are very similar ones in the cases of countries like India, Brazil, and the Phillipines. See Cheryl Payer, *The Debt Trap*.

31. The first meeting was attended by Canada, France, West Germany, Iran, Italy, Japan, Holland, Britain, the United States, Kuwait, Saudi Arabia, the United Arab Emirates, Qatar, the African Development Bank, the Arab Fund for Economic and Social Development, the Commission of the EEC, the European Investment Bank, the Special OPEC Fund, the OECD, the UNDP, the Gulf Organization for Development in Egypt, the IMF, the IFC, the Islamic Development Fund, and headed by the World Bank.

32. Statement by the deputy premier for economic and financial affairs on the agreement with the IMF and the loan advanced by the Gulf Organization for Development in Egypt, *Minutes of the 51st Session of the People's Assembly,* dated May 28, 1977, p. 12.

33. Ibid., p. 17.

34. Ibid., pp. 16–17.

35. Ibid., p. 16, emphasis added.

36. Bela Balassa, "Towards a Development Strategy for Egypt," in his *Policy Reform in Developing Countries* (Oxford: Pergamon Press, 1977), p. 88.

37. There was some opposition to interference by USAID in determining the price of cement, expressed by some members of the assembly. See *Sabāh al-Khayr,* no. 1229, July 26, 1978.

38. For the text see the *Minutes of the 20th Session of the People's Assembly,* dated 9/1/1979, Appendix 2.

39. *Minutes of the 27th Session of the People's Assembly,* dated January 30, 1979.

40. This is borne out by Egypt's own experience in the nineteenth century. See "Egypt and Europe: From French Expedition to British Occupation" in Roger Owen and Bob Sutcliffe (eds.), *Studies in the Theory of Imperialism* (London: Longmans, 1972), pp. 195–209.

41. These represent the industrialization loan of 1958, the first High Dam loan of 1958, the second High Dam loan of 1960, the land reclamation loan of 1964, the industrialization loan of 1964, and the cooperation agreement of 1971.

42. That was put at £E312 million. See Eng. Tāhir Muhammad Abū Wafā', *The High Dam Project* (Cairo, 1967). This is only slightly different from the figure for total investment allocations for the project over its construction period 1960/1961–1969/1970. See Ministry of Planning, Irrigation and Drainage Branch, "Branch, Basic Data for Preparing the Tentative Frame of the Five-Year Plan 1976–80," memo 103–A (February 1976).

43. The People's Assembly deemed the subject important enough to devote a whole session to discuss the more important aspects. See *Minutes of the 59th Session,* dated December 6, 1976. The secretariat of the Specialized National Councils published a report titled *The High Dam and Its Effects* (Cairo, 1975).

44. Robert Mabro, *The Egyptian Economy 1952–1972* (Oxford: Clarendon Press, 1974), p. 100; Specialized National Councils, *The High Dam and Its Effects,* p. 28.

45. See Ibrahim H. El-Issawy, chapter 4 in this book, pp. 88.

46. Cotton acreage fell from an average of 1,791 thousand feddans for 1955–1959 to an average of 1,454 thousand feddans for 1971–1976, and cane acreage rose from an average of 111,000 feddans for 1955–1959 to 210,000 feddans for 1971–1976. Figures taken from Central Bank of Egypt, *Economic Review* 10 (nos. 3 & 4): 170–171; and CAPMS, *Statistical Yearbook of ARE 1952–1976* (October 1977), p. 29.

47. Rent was included in cost; data from Ministry of Agriculture, Agricultural Research Center.

48. Abū Wafā', *the High Dam Project.*

49. Specialized National Councils, *The High Dam and Its Effects,* p. 30. The High Dam project may have also resulted in lower rice yield on account of rising water table. But there is definitely a net increase in rice yield.

50. For example, the number of welders needed for the project was ten times the total number of welders in the country. Related in a personal interview with Eng. Sidqī Sulayman, former premier and at one time the top High Dam executive.

51. Wages amounted to 30% of the overall cost of the project. See Abū Wafā', *The High Dam Project.*

52. Ibid.

53. Per capita consumption in 1970 was 4.7 kilograms in urban areas and only 2.3 kilograms in rural areas. See Institute of National Planning, *The Economics of Production, Transportation and Marketing of Lake Nasser Fish* (July 1973), table 53.

54. Over the period 1971–1975, the most important cargos shipped through waterways were, in the descending order of weight: petroleum, iron ore, phosphate, cement, coal, fertilizers, clay, molasses, grains and machinery. With the exception of fertilizers and grains, these are either produced or consumed in urban areas. See Arab Republic of Egypt, Ministry of Transportation, Transportation Planning Authority, *Study of National Transportation in Egypt* (1977).

55. I exclude here, of course, loans for High Dam and land reclamation. We have already examined redistributive aspects of the High Dam. It is assumed that land reclaimed through Soviet loan of 1964 was distributed to landless agricultural workers. No data were available to check this.

56. Aside from the burden of repayment of the loans, which will be discussed later.

57. IBRD, *Arab Republic of Egypt, Economic Management,* p. 11, 25.

58. For example, handicraft and rural industries attracted less than 0.5% of total investment in industry in the Five-Year Plan (£E1.9 million). See *Frame of General Plan,* p. 33 Engineering industries were the most important industries financed by Soviet aid.

59. Calculated from Ministry of Industry, *Industrialization Programs* (1961) (Arabic).

60. Eng. Husnī Shākir, "Engineering Industries projects that were Implemented Since the Revolution to Date," paper presented to INF-GOFI-ECA Symposium for the African Conference on Policies and Strategies of Industrial Development, Cairo, 23–26 September 1978 (Arabic).

61. Ibid.

62. Most of the industries established produced durables.

63. For the meaning and the construction of the *benefit index,* see the appendix of this chapter.

64. For example, automobiles were sold officially at half their black-market price. See B. Hansen and K. Nashashibi, *Foreign Trade Regimes and Economic Development: Egypt* (New York: National Bureau of Economic Research, 1975), p. 302.

65. Those who argue that the family budget survey covers only the middle class in the broadest sense would not be surprised by this result. For them, the *d* index would indicate only the distribution of benefit among different *strata* in this class.

66. See Karima Korayem, chapter 6 in this book.

67. This statement was made to the People's Assembly hearings on *infitāh* by Fu'ād Umrān, chairman of the Spinning and Weaving Chamber of the Egyptain Federation of Industries.

68. Egypt's cotton exports to the USSR ranged between 16.5% and 38.8% of total cotton exports over the period 1973/1974–1976/1977. See Central Bank of Egypt, *Economic Review* 18, no. 1 (1978): 82.

69. See Karima Korayem, chapter 6 in this book.

70. Rural per capita income is about half of urban per capita income.

71. Note that American aid to Egypt was discontinued over the period 1967–1973, and was resumed in the second half of 1974.

72. It may be argued also that food aid has depressed wheat price and, hence, the income of wheat growers. (The relative profitability of wheat has declined, according to Hansen and Nashashibi, by 25% between 1961 and 1964. See Hansen and Nashashibi, *Foreign Trade Regimes*, p. 180). But it may be counterargued that wheat growers may be able, thanks to PL 480 aid, to shift to more profitable crops.

73. Said El-Naggar, *Foreign Aid to the UAR* (Cairo: INP, 1963), p. 60. Starting in 1966, repayment was required in dollars.

74. USAID, *U.S. Economic Assistance to the UAR* (1965).

75. Said El-Naggar, *Foreign Aid to the UAR*.

76. Unpublished data from USAID.

77. See B. Hansen and G. Marzouk, *Development and Economic Policy in the UAR (Egypt)* (Amsterdam: North-Holland Publishing Co., 1965) pp. 264–269; M. Abdel-Fadil, "Development of the Tax Structure in Egypt," in Société Egyptienne D'Economie Politique de Statistique et de Legislation, *The Egyptian Economy in a Quarter Century, 1952–1977* (Cairo, 1979). But for an opposite characterization, see Reda El-Edel, chapter 5 in this book.

78. Data obtained from Ministry of Economy and Economic Cooperation and the Central Bank of Egypt.

79. From USAID presentation to Congress in 1977, where it is also mentioned: "The [Inter-Agency] Task Force recommended that the US move vigorously to assist the Egyptians in implementing the 'Open Door' policy to encourage foreign and domestic private enterprise in Egypt." (p. 6).

# CHAPTER 14

# *The Open-Door Economy: Its Roots and Welfare Consequences**

Fouad Ajami

Qadrī Risq was a respectable and loyal follower of the July revolution [of 1952]. It may be impossible to define him in light of working principles but it is easy to do so in light of the Charter: He believes in social justice as much as he believes in private ownership and incentives, in scientific socialism as much as he does in religion, in homeland as much as he does in Arab unity, in the heritage as much as he does in science, in the popular base as much as he does in absolute authority.[1]

Najīb Mahfūz

And he said: "Socialism is an expression of *ressentiment* toward those who excel; our rulers usurped authority with weaponry rather than knowledge." So I asked him what do you think of the problem of poverty in Egypt? He answered with naivete, "Everyone's status is decided according to their abilities and such is Allah's wisdom, praise be to Him."[2]

Najīb Mahfūz

We discussed our economic problems with our Arab friends and colleagues and we have had discussions with the IMF, the World Bank, the U.S. government, Western Europe governments, the EEC, Tokyo, and Iran. In all these discussions we tried to indicate our seriousness about improving our economic conditions and solving our economic problems.[3]

ᶜAbd- al-Munᶜim al-Qaysūnī

At the secondary school I came to realize for the first time what city dwellers were and what class officers meant . . . My classmates

*My debt to the project and its participants is immense. I wish to note, in particular, the help of Gouda Abdel-Khalek, Ali Dessouki, Michael Danielson, Saad Ibrahim, John P. Lewis, Robert Tignor, and John Waterbury. In this project, as in other pursuits, Henry Bienen's help and encouragement were critical.

> were naturally better dressed than I was but I never suffered because of this. Many of my friends came from wealthy families and lived in luxurious houses, yet I cannot recall ever wishing to possess what they had.[4]
>
> Anwar al-Sadat

Qadrī Risq—a character in the fiction of Egypt's most distinguished novelist, Najīb Mahfūz—embodies the ambiguities and contradictions of the Egyptian order that emerged out of the Free Officers' revolt in July of 1952. The revolution's symbols were all-embracing: there was plenty for those in search of radical orders to bless and sufficient ammunition for those who saw nothing but the rise of a new class and the persistence of old arrangements.

The sensibility of Qadrī Risq—his desire to be all things to all people—lives on. As though to underscore the gift of Najīb Mahfūz as Egypt's most penetrating social historian, the secretary general of President Sadat's new political party announced its establishment in the summer of 1978 by describing it as a "national, democratic, socialist, popular, scientific, faithful, revolutionary, nationalist, [Pan-Arab] and humanist party." Its goals, he said, were "social peace, national unity, and socialist democracy. . . . But our socialism is one of affluence, not poverty; one of prosperity, growth and construction, not of destruction."[5]

The opinions expressed in the second quotation are those of another of Mahfūz's characters—an industrious, respectable physician whose work was "disrupted" by the socialist legislations of the Nasser years. Once impervious to politics and secure in his belief in wealth and ownership, the physician became the victim of agrarian reform, losing five hundred acres of land to the state. He felt hatred for the state apparatus, which also denied him the deanship of the medical college, which he believed he deserved. But he lived to witness the defeat of the apparatus in June 1967. It was a national defeat, to be sure, but there was a consolation of sorts. The uncouth, repressive elements that had played havoc with the order of things were defeated; perhaps the old world could be restored and the pecking order be set right again.

The third quotation is from one of Egypt's most respected economic policymakers, a former deputy prime minister for financial and economic affairs. The Egyptian elite no longer bothers to hide behind the trappings of autonomy. Egypt has come a long way from the nationalist instincts and assertions of Gamal Abd al-Nasser. For all practical purposes, Egypt has become a ward of the international community. At one point the Paris-based Consultative Group on Egypt had twenty-five members—states, development funds, international institutions. The new Egyptian dependency was dramatically illustrated during the 1979 Tokyo economic summit of the major industrial countries: the summiteers received a request from President Sadat for a foreign-aid package of $18 billion.[6] The claim was that the package was essential for "development," but development was no longer the issue: the aid was essential to finance a crippling trade deficit, to pay for costly imports, and to provide a minimum economic floor. Where the major Western countries once worried about the radicalism of Nasser's Egypt and its assault on Western economic interests, they now had to worry about Egypt's weakness.

The final of our four opening quotations is President Sadat's reconstruction of his own childhood: an invitation to others to acquiesce in the natural distribution of things and to do it without rage and envy. In President Sadat's universe, *hiqd* (resentment) is a Nasserite legacy, an imported doctrine, hoisted on Egypt that "razed everything to the ground." The fact that President Sadat has come to speak the language of the respectable physician in Mahfūz's fiction explains the thorough reassessment of the Egyptian revolution—its class character, its commitments, its support base—that Egyptians and non-Egyptians alike have been recently engaged in. For scholars, there are interpretive and analytical questions; for those who lived the experiment, there is both the task of making sense of it all and, perhaps, the more fundamental question of what that experiment has left behind and what is to come. Cumulatively, there has been a thorough deradicalization of the Egyptian experiment, a contradiction of its populist model. This conclusion is all the more difficult to escape because the custodians of the Egyptian order have, of late, openly broken with the symbols of that radical interlude in recent Egyptian history, and they will be steadily forced to do so if they wish to legitimate new policy and to avoid too sharp a schizophrenia between deeds and pronouncements. The memory of how the Free Officers overthrew the monarchy is every now and then brandished in the face of "those who would want to take the country back to the past"—a reference to those on the right who can more easily and more naturally assume the mantle of a parliamentary, multiparty system that President Sadat claims he wishes to restore—but the intervening eighteen years between the Free Officers' revolt and Sadat's presidency are no longer the bright years they once were. This act of historical reconstruction is more than an idle, disinterested rewriting of history: it provides the ideological justification for concrete policy changes at home and abroad. Altogether a different sensibility is now at the helm of the Egyptian polity: the political space for issues of equity and distribution has been drastically altered. In this chapter we consider two interrelated themes suggested in the opening quotations: the deradicalization of the Egyptian state and the regional and international context of its choices; to do so, we examine the domestic roots of the open-door economic policy and the role that regional and transitional factors played in it.

## I. State and Economy in Egypt: Some Interpretive Questions

In his *In a Moment of Enthusiasm,* Leonard Binder gives a helpful summary of the changes that have been recently effected in the Egyptian polity. He sketches three conceivable ideal types for the country and, after wisely ruling out a full bourgeois democratic option, focuses on the two that are in the cards: the first program entails the "de-Nasserization" of Egypt while the second is the old Nasserite formula. The de-Nasserization plan would entail what follows:

> The ASU [Arab Socialist Union] must be dismantled, a multiparty system instituted, freedom of expression must be guaranteed to those who can pay for it—at least, corporationism is to be diminished, the public sector of the economy is to be denationalized and agriculture is to become more highly capitalized and less labor intensive. The class base of such a regime would require a coalition of the urban bourgeoisie and elements of the rural middle class. . . . Internationally such a policy would expect and probably receive support from the United States, from the conservative regions of the Persian Gulf and from some European states.[7]

In contrast, the Nasserite formula is primarily mobilizational:

> Its goals are modernization and development, with particular emphasis placed upon enhancing the state administrative and military organizations. The devices are those of increasing the size of the public sector, integrating economic and bureaucratic sectors, controlling political activity through a national union, maintaining a government monopoly over the media, and organizing the occupations and professions in corporativist structuring. . . . Internationally, this policy would receive support from the Soviet Union, from the more radical of the Third World countries, and in particular from the radical Arab states.[8]

Other evaluations of the Egyptian order also sustain the reading of a drastic shift in policies. In chapter 10 of this volume, John Waterbury describes the urban policy as approximating a "triage" of the urban poor. Saad Ibrahim sees an overall pattern of "retreat" and offers a helpful periodization of the Egyptian experiment. In his view, the regime of the Free Officers went through five distinct phases: (1) a hesitation phase, (2) an economic conciousness phase, (3) socialist transformation, (4) stagnation, (5) socialist retreat.

Two analyses, one by Galal Amin[9] and the other by Gouda Abdel-Khalek,[10] see a foreign economic policy at work radically different from the one that prevailed at the height of the Nasserite experiment. The Egyptian economy is being more fully subordinated to the world market system: the result is a dependent economy where loans do the task once assigned to local savings, foreign imports replace local products, and the results are inflation, maldistribution of income, and dependency upon outsiders. Both Galal Amin's interpretive essay and Abdel-Khalek's more useful empirical study recall an important chapter in Egyptian history—the thwarting by European states and industry of Muhammad ᶜAlī's experiment with modernization in 1841. Both see the new open-door economic policy as a reenactment of that old theme: a society long at the receiving end of the power of others once again abandoning its quest for autonomy.

Of course, there is one possible line of interpretation that the recent changes in Egyptian policies are less drastic than they seem, that the Free Officers' regime never really intended to restructure social and economic relations, that Sadatism, so to speak, grows out of the womb of Nasserism. This, essentially, is the perspective of some Marxists. Thus Samir Amin's discussion of the recent changes in economic policy in Sadat's Egypt traces them back to their Nasserite roots. Of what he sees as the mounting inequalities under Sadat, he observes:

> It was the ambiguous and contradictory choices of Nasserism which had created the pre-conditions for inflation and these inequalities. Its bureaucratic style reinforced a class, a part of which eventually revealed itself as openly reactionary. The liquidation of the popular organizations facilitated the transfer of power. Right from the middle of the sixties it was obvious to the more lucid communists that the modernisation and industrialisation strategy could lead only to bankruptcy, that the failure of the five year plan, the emerging inflation and the fragility of foreign dependence represented not just marginal errors but the objective limits imposed by the regime's class nature.[11]

Much of what has come to pass in Egypt presents no serious problems for Samir Amin's analysis. Right at the height of the Nasserite experiment with state capitalism and nationalism, Samir Amin's *L'Égypte Nasserienne* had depicted the Nasser regime as an instrument of the *haute bourgeoisie* and had noted its reliance on the support of the rich peasantry.[12] There is no surprise then. Such was the "class" character of the regime: "petty bourgeois" as it was, its class character decreed its objective limits.

Samir Amin's perspective is too mechanical and wholesale. My own objection to it stems from a general intellectual aversion to historical inevitabilities, to iron laws of development to which all societies and classes must succumb. There is no telling where a given social experiment will end. To be sure, there are limits—geographic, cultural, philosophical, national—within which all societies operate. There is such a thing as a "national situation"—the location of a national society in the world, the resources at its disposal, and so forth. There are also patterns of culture that vary in their attitudes toward authority, equity, and power. But much happens within those limits: choices are made; traditions are improvised upon and reinterpreted; the power of the state is made and remade. There are also the accidents of leadership, foreign defeats, the schemes and desires of allies, neighbors, and more powerful societies. A path opens up, and, conversely, others are blocked, and leaders go beyond their class origins and their original intentions. Sometimes, critical choices are decreed by others—powerful domestic groups, more powerful states—who refuse to cooperate and push a leader elsewhere for support and ideas. And, of particular relevance to the Egyptian experiment, an awesome leader who once intimidated social classes and juggled alliances suffers a devastating military defeat: the classes he once kept at bay suddenly recover; the ideas with which he once mobilized his constituency and intimidated his rivals lose their lure. Then the radical schemes have to be shelved if the order is to survive, and the politics of survival are hardly conducive to great undertakings. Others follow in the leader's footsteps, and they make their own hard choices: they either intensify the radical components of policies, or they come to terms with now assertive classes and squeeze populist gains and welfare subsidies in the name of economic austerity and efficiency.

In the Egyptian case we glimpse the quintessential dilemma of a "populist" economy as groups hitherto dispossessed are brought into the economy:[13] the newly enfranchised lend support to the regime, but populism eventually generates, as Huntington and Nelson note in a relevant discussion, its own "vicious circle." The gains that expand a regime's support base become a drain on the economy "as more groups become participants and attempt to share in a stagnant, or slowly growing economic pie."[14]

Egypt's populist interlude had extended substantial gains to the lower and middle status in the society: there was a growing state, and that meant openings in the bureaucracy and an expanded educational system: there was surplus land expropriated from large landholders and from the dynasty of Muhammad ᶜAlī; there were the possibilities opened up by the departure of the "local foreigners"—the Greeks, the Italians, the Lebanese, Syrian, and Jewish communities.[15] Finally there were substantial infusions of aid generated by the diplomatic skill of Nasser, playing off one camp against the other, receiving aid from both. One camp gave because it initially assumed that the Egyptian order represented a dike against communism; the communist camp gave because it was a rising system bidding for a place in the sun and because it came to accept Nasser's so-called noncapitalist path to development.

All this sustained an expansionist economy that was bound, sooner or later, to make the difficult choice between economic orthodoxy and contraction or going further down the road of socioeconomic radicalism. To the "normal" difficulties of a populist course must be added convergng pressures from outside: the costs of the Yemen War (into which Egypt stumbled in the early 1960s) and the withdrawal of U.S. aid (in 1965). For the Egyptian economy, 1964/1965 marks a turning point in performance. Dependent as it was on a high import component, the country's import substitution and industrialization faltered with idle capacity reaching a level of 25 percent of productive capacity; gross fixed investment, which had shown an appreciable rise during the first four years of the Five Year Plan plummeted.[16]

Now by strict economic criteria, this was a real turning point, and we leave it to economists to make or sustain that argument. But we focus instead on a more political explanation: the decline of "Bonapartist" power, the concessions to more resourceful classes, the general deradicalization of the Egyptian state. It is clear that there was an economic slump, but it is an altogether different matter to argue that the economic slump would have had to be tackled in the manner which unfolded after 1967 and, particularly, after 1973. Even the economic analysis of Robert Mabro concedes the point:

> In Egypt, the Revolution attempted to raise the investment ratio in order to implement its initial development objectives. High rates of economic growth did obtain as long as the balance-of-payment deficit could be financed. But economic growth ground to a halt because the gestation periods of major projects delayed their expected benefits for too long and because aid, in the form of grants or very cheap long-term loans, ceased to accrue in the required amounts. Stagnation need not be more than a temporary phenomenon. The economy will eventually be able to reap the fruit of its past long-term investments and put to use excess capacity in industry, electricity, and other sectors. The redeeming feature of ambitious investment programmes is that they endow the country with durable assets which may become profitably productive after a time.[17]

It was the June 1967 defeat that broke the back of the Egyptian state and helped alter the terms of state-society relations. Not only were the military to be rearmed (the defense burden rose from 5.5 percent of Gross National Product (GNP) in 1960–1962 to 10 percent after 1967), but there was a substantial change in the regime's maneuverability. The weakness of the regime was underscored by massive student unrest in late 1967 and early 1968, by a more assertive Parliament that had been largely quiescent and irrelevant.

Where the Yemen War had been financed out of personal consumption, the post-1967 situation was to be defused at the expense of investment.

During the Yemen War private consumption declined from 72 percent to 68 percent of GNP; it stayed at a steady 67 percent after the June defeat. Gross investment, which stood at 18 percent of GNP prior to the June war, fell to 13 percent in its aftermath.[18] This was a political decision: the regime was in a bind. If it squeezed too hard, it would trigger outright rebellion; if it did not, it would have to compromise developmental goals. The political process being what it is, the regime opted for the second path. The call for austerity was repeatedly made in the aftermath of the defeat, but it did not materialize. Of the £E286 million of world currency slated for imports in 1967/1968, £E130 million went for consumer goods, £E85 went for intermediate goods, only £E75 million for capital goods.[19] The wisdom of that kind of position was questioned at the time, but the political leadership made a critical decision in favor of maintaining private consumption and, as we shall see, in favor of the middle and upper strata. The private sector was given all kinds of breaks and incentives in 1967 so as to help it with export promotion. This was accompanied by a massive assault against the public sector, hitherto beyond the limits of criticism.[20] There was criticism in the media and in Parliament of the public sector's inefficiency, of its losses, of the "illegitimate gains" of the men who were leading the public sector. This was to be but a dress rehearsal for future changes in economic policy, and for changes in the symbols of the Egyptian order.

In 1968 and 1969, the wind was blowing from all directions. On one extreme was the call for domestic austerity, a war economy, and a "people's war of liberation." On the other extreme were the enemies of the regime—both the skeptics and critics at home and its conservative Arab rivals in the region—who saw in the defeat an opportunity to roll back the changes of recent years. In between there was the politically critical bourgeoisie, whose support the regime had to bid for. In more confident times, when the state apparatus and its leader had greater autonomy, the middle class had to toe the line and go along. The ever-present threat was that the leader could tilt to the left, genuinely mobilize the workers and peasants, and strike at the privileges of the middle class. Such a confrontation is easy enough to rule out were one to take seriously the Samir Amin injunction about the "objective limits" and the "class character" of the regime. But insecurity of social classes *vis-à-vis* the state is the hallmark of a Bonapartist order: the leader has the freedom to choose among allies, and the state can go in a number of directions. What the defeat did was to shackle the power of the state and erode its autonomy. With that, it was easy enough for the more resourceful classes to capture state power and check its ambitions. And it is here the "retreat" of the state spoken of by Saad Ibrahim in chapter 12 of this volume can be located.

There were to be tangible as well as symbolic concessions to the more affluent strata. The state drastically curtailed its role in public housing[21] all the way from 21,300 units in 1962/1963 to 20,500 units in 1965/1966, to a low of 5,300 units in 1968. There was a phenomenal rise in the import of private automobiles.[22] Pulled between those who wanted an "intensification of social transformation"—and there were plenty of those in the ASU, among the students—and those who wanted a more steady conservative course, Nasser (and, later, his successor) went with the latter. Nasser reasoned that the left had no place to go and that it would have to stay with him (for the alternative would be a more conservative option), that the left was weak anyway, and that the stability of the social order now depended upon the support of the middle and upper strata.

Anwar al-Sadat's "revisionism" and hindsight references to the important March 30 Declaration—issued in March 1968 in response to student unrest and parliamentary critics—as a "sponge" is too cynical and simplistic.[23] The March 30 Declaration was part of the new bargain between the state apparatus and the more resourceful strata. Three interrelated features stand out in the provisions of the declaration: a greater commitment to political pluralism, to science and technology, a new emphasis on productivity and efficiency in economic matters. The imbalance between the "red" and the "expert" was being rectified in favor of the latter; private initiative was given new and added legitimacy. In a break with the Nasserite conception of earlier years, the importance of "political liberty" was affirmed in the declaration: an "intimate connection" was seen to exist between "political freedom" on the one hand and "socioeconomic freedom" on the other. Homage was paid to the multiplicity of institutions, to the independent role of the legislature, and so forth.[24]

A unique source that helps illuminate the change in the self-defined role of the Egyptian state in the aftermath of 1967 are the three-volume memoirs of Sayyid Marᶜī,[25] an *ancien regime* parliamentarian who served as minister of agriculture and agrarian reform under Nasser then lost his position on charges of corruption, returned after 1967, and went on to become one of the pillars of Sadat's order. The fortunes of Marᶜī, who was born in 1913 to a rural gentry background, say a great deal about the twists and turns of recent Egyptian politics. Mr. Marᶜī was elected to Parliament in 1944, managed to cooperate with the new order (despite the fact that he struck Nasser as a snob, part of a smug, self-satisfied world) by lending it his skills and education as an agricultural engineer, barely survived the radical moment of enthusiasm (1961–1967) when the apparatus was bent on penetrating two countrysides, then lived on to prosper in Sadat's order, serving as speaker of Parliament and enjoying close links to President Sadat cemented through the marriage of his son to President Sadat's daughter. Because of his crucial domain in agriculture and agrarian reform, Marᶜī was a target of the *apparatchiki,* who saw him as part of the old order prone to side with the landholders, hostile to the restructuring of social and economic relations in the countryside. A mere few months before the June defeat, Marᶜī and his family were being investigated by the Committee for the Liquidation of Feudalism—a body set up by the apparatchiki after the famous Kamshīsh incident, when a rich landholder was charged with the murder of an ASU official. The Kamshīsh incident had served as a pretext, as well as a genuinely felt incentive, for those who wanted a "new revolution" in the countryside. Marᶜī and his class had survived and prospered in Nasser's Egypt, but there were many who took the revolution seriously who were bent on resolving the revolution's ambiguity by attacking the interests of Marᶜī and his kind. For several years in the political wilderness on charges of corruption, unable to gain even an audience with President Nasser for a long time, Marᶜī knew the capricious side of a Bonapartist order. But the June defeat gave Marᶜī a breathing spell: only two weeks after the defeat a new cabinet was formed, and Marᶜī ended up with two ministries. At the swearing in of the new cabinet, President Nasser would say to Marᶜī that "we committed a lot of errors and the committee on Feudalism was one of them."[26]

Some years back Nasser and Marᶜī had clashed on the possibility of a revolution in the countryside: Nasser had maintained that he wanted agrarian cooperatives to serve as the "nucleus of a new society" while Marᶜī had made the typically conservative argument that it is impossible to revolutionalize an old society, that the best you can do is introduce some minor reforms. The times had changed: the populist charismatic leadership was hemmed in; its troubles had borne out Marᶜī's conservative skepticism. Marᶜī and others like him bounced back after 1967: they returned armed with the certitude that their way was the right way, that the radicals who had played havoc with the world had had their day, and that history had proven them wrong. The right man was again in his proper place at agriculture and agrarian reform. Muhsin Abū al-Nūr, an officer, an apparatchiki (who was later purged in President Sadat's "corrective movement" of May 1971), lost that critical portfolio.

Marᶜī's account helps clarify the frustrating and earnest debate about the continuity and discontinuity between Nasser's Egypt and Sadat's. Many of the things that Sadat was to embrace were faced up to by Nasser, but always with great hesitation. Restoration would have been too much for Nasser to contemplate and live with: that awaited his successor. What Nasser did was to rein in the radicals, to accept a subdued coming to terms with the world. Full-scale restoration was Sadat's choice, a choice more in accord with his temperament than with Nasser's. Nasser brought Marᶜī back into the cabinet: Sadat made him a relative and a pillar of his order.

It was Nasser himself, however, who initiated the deradicalization. Much has been made of the desequestration of land under Sadat as an indication of a drastic shift in policies. But it was Abdul Nasser himself who began it only one month after the June defeat when he ordered the desequestration for 88 individuals who were targets of the Committee for the Liquidation of Feudalism. He did it against the advice of many in the party and bureaucracy who felt that it was important not to show weakness at that critical juncture and not to suggest to the critics of the state that the state was no longer willing to "protect the social revolution." The bulk of what the committee had done was undone by Nasser: of the 335 cases that had been singled out by the committee, only 25 cases remained for Sadat. The rest were dealt with in Nasser's last three years as really a separate stage of his political career. It was Nasser who urged the toning down of radical symbols: time and again in the sessions of the ASU and the cabinet recalled by Marᶜī, it was Nasser who intervened to ask members of the apparatus to drop their references to "feudalism" and "revolution," to pay greater attention to efficiency and profits: "We must," he observed in one of these sessions, "think of management, for if management is not sound the people would turn away from socialism."[27]

Two symbols battled one another for ascendancy in the aftermath of 1967—"the revolution" and "eliminating the consequences of aggression"—and Marᶜī would draw comfort from the tilting of the balance in favor of the national question. Time and again in the meetings of the ASU, Nasser's prestige was thrown against those who argued that there was a counterrevolution in the making and that the symbols of national unity were being used to undermine the social achievements of the revolution. Nasser's spokesman in the media, Muhammad Haykal, hammered away at the same themes: the need for "scientific management," the importance of toning down the talk about counterrevolution: "It is not true to say that profit—if it is legitimate—is a crime; that the sovereignty of the law is a limit to revolutionary activity; that the private sector must be absorbed by the public sector."[28]

The Marᶜī memoirs reveal an interesting fight with somewhat predictable symbols: the continuity of the revolution on one side, "scientific management" and "rationalizing the public sector" on the other. The advocates of the first position were engaged in a holding effort: here and there they were able to score some victories, but the battle definitely favored the "liberalizers." In 1968, the left had made it difficult for Zakarīyā Muhī' al-Dīn—one of the most powerful figures in Nasser's Egypt, a man who was said to favor a Western connection for Egypt and orthodox economic policies—and his partner in the cabinet, ᶜAbd al-Munᶜim al-Qaysūnī, to put through conservative monetarist policies. Muhī' al-Dīn and al-Qaysūnī had to go because their programs were blatantly unacceptable: they lost out to the more standard, public sector, expansionist views represented in the cabinet by ᶜAzīz Sidqī and favored by the ASU apparatchiki. But this and other victories were minor in the context of a gradual and steady liberalizing course. In agricultural cooperatives, rich and middle peasantry secured a major victory in their effort to water down radical schemes by stipulating that four-fifths of the membership in the boards of cooperatives had to be drawn from those who owned no less than ten *feddans*, by adding a literacy requirement, by securing a promise from the state not to challenge the rights of ownership.[29] Mr. Marʿī's view that he wanted "complete stability" in the countryside carried the day. The rich and middle peasantry had been the principal beneficiaries of the agricultural policies of the regime: the post-1967 situation only worked to further weaken the state, keep at bay those in the political machine who wanted to penetrate the countryside, challenge the rights of ownership, and push for drastic land reform.

To the general deradicalization at home must be added a policy of regional accommodation with the conservative oil states. It began with a toning down of the Arab cold war in return for modest aid to Egypt. The volume of aid went up under Sadat, but the conditions attached to it were to be more demanding—a change in the country's economic policies. The oil states wanted the ideological battle that raged in the 1950s and 1960s to be brought to its rightful conclusion: In weaning Egypt away from radicalism, there would be proof that the conservative ways of the oil states were the right and proper ones.

## II. The Deradicalization of the Egyptian Polity

The theme of deradicalization can be pulled together with the help of a brilliant work by Franz Schurmann—*The Logic of World Power*. Two long quotations are worth citing because they tell us a great deal about the fate of the Egyptian experiment and the relationship between state and society. The first passage addresses the question of radical ideology that enters a society through the state:

> The key character of ideologies is that they come from below, from some segment of those who are disadvantaged in society. All, even the mildest have some kind of revolutionary character. All reflect a revolutionary process which continues even while it may not produce spectacular outbursts. Operationally, ideology enters the social fabric through the state, and specifically, if funneled through the pinnacle of state power, the chief executive. It becomes institutionalized in its minimal and most mundane form through the creation of new bureaucratic structures, which consume a share of the state budget. In other words, a small-scale redistribution of income takes place which is designed to satisfy the demands of the new ideology. In its maximal form, ideology enters the social fabric by taking over the state entirely, destroying class and bureaucratic interests and creating an entirely new state power. In either case, a remaking of state power has taken place. Since conservatives have

> no desire to remake the state (they own property and interests and merely wish to retain and expand them) and since bureaucracies only tend to expand their own interests rather than create new ones, the only source of bureaucratic change is ideology. And the predominant ideologies of the world are those calling for change, most importantly that the exploited, the oppressed, the poor, those with little or no property, be given a greater share of the scarce property of society.[30]

Equally significant for an understanding of the course of Nasserite radicalism is Schurmann's depiction of the relationship between state power and property relations and what he describes as the "merging" between dominant interests and the state.

> While historically states have often arisen through external conquest, more common in recent times is the rise of new state power through revolutionary pressure from below. At first, the function of the state is the integration of the propertyless people of society into the society as a whole, something it does, because of its nature, along national lines. The state normally arises in opposition to ruling classes and ruling interests. Riding on the strength of popular movements, the new state has an ideological character (nationalist, socialist, fascist, democratic, even religious). However, once in power, it seeks accommodation with the ruling classes and interests, and, conversely, those interests seek to capture the state. The state arises as the realm of ideology but almost immediately is subject to infiltration from the realm of interests, the interests of the classes of property. Thus, the normal course of the formation of state power, a process which occurs very frequently in the life of a nation, is the creation of ideological, political, and military power, which results in a broad class of the dispossessed being integrated into the national entity, followed by a rapid merging with the dominant interests, essentially economic, within the society.[31]

In Schurmann's terms and conception, the Egyptian state that emerged out of the Free Officers' revolt could be classified as a radical state. Radical ideology entered it through the "chief executive"; it fulfilled certain redistributive functions. But then the state sought accommodation under fire as a consequence of both its defeat in 1967 and as a result of its "merging" with the dominant interests.

Much of the discussion of the Egyptian state by Marxists, and some times by others, makes a great deal of the innate conservatism of the Free Officers, and much has been made of their early conservative views and roots. Miles Copeland's *The Game of Nations*[32] gave an insider's account of the close links between the Free Officers and the Central Intelligence

Agency (CIA). It is well known that the first victims of the new regime were two labor activists who were hanged in August 1952; new memoirs establish that the motive behind the execution of the two workers was the strong desire by the Revolutionary Command Council to "reassure" the foreign investors, and to "guarantee stability."

Stripped of the great romance that came to surround it, and of the sound and fury it generated, the thrust of the post-1952 order was to integrate Egypt into the world system on more favorable terms. The state stepped in to arrest economic stagnation, to offer a more favorable investment climate. That required, in today's jargon, a "hard state," one that could provide a dike against chaos and wild-eyed radicals, that could provide the needed discipline to intimidate workers, to force an appropriate rate of savings and investment.

That was what the new Egyptian state proceeded to do. It started out with orthodox economic policies. All its spokesmen repeatedly reiterated their faith in the private sector. They took care to distinguish between their land reform and their overall economic policy. The land reform was presented as the only way of dealing with a major historical predicament; it was not to be part of a broader assault against wealth and property. The private sector was offered the bargain that the "hard state" is best equipped to offer: the state would invest in infrastructure, and it would leave the more profitable activities to the private sector. Thus, from 1952 to 1956, 61 percent of the new required investment went into land reclamation and irrigation and 39 percent into transportation and electricity. There were also incentives for the private sectors in the form of loans to industry, tariff protection and the like, and favorable investment codes for the foreign investor.[33]

With hindsight, it is easy to see that the new order represented an "enlightened capitalist path." Only two thousand landholders were affected by agrarian reform. None of the policies or symbols of the new regime came close to a radical attack against the relationship of production and ownership. Local capital, however, did what it had always done (and what is generally normal) in moments of insecurity: it went into real estate speculations, which showed a phenomenal rise in the years 1954, 1955, and 1956. If the plan was to have the private sector shoulder its responsibility in maintaining an enlightened capitalist path, this had clearly failed by 1956. The "accidental radicalism" of the regime, if you will, was born out of the failure of dominant domestic interests to assume their responsibility. The invitation extended by the new regime to the private sector was turned down: the conservative beginnings of the junta ran into the unwillingness of the privileged strata to play by new rules.

A particularly astute analysis of this impasse is provided by Rifaᶜat al-Saᶜīd (writing under the pseudonym of Muhammad Farīd Shuhdī) in *Ta'ammulāt fi al-Nāsirīya (Thoughts on Nasserism)*. In his view, there was an initial truce between the new regime and the dominant economic interests. Then the truce broke down on the issue of agrarian reform. Hard as the new regime would try to reassure the industrialists that the agrarian reform was not an economic or philosophical assault against private property, it failed to do so. This, as Saᶜīd notes, had to do with the fact that the same individuals straddled both the agrarian and industrial sectors—which precluded playing off the industrial elite against the rural aristocracy: "Thus, the blow that was aimed at the landed aristocracy was also aimed, if unintentionally, at big capitalists who took it in silence and pretended to cooperate in order to gain time."[34] The truce was doomed from the start. Leading Egyptian capitalists had no trust in the officers who had confiscated their agrarian holdings and dissolved the political parties through which the capitalists had worked while calling upon them to undertake the industrialization of Egypt.

This forms an essential background to understanding the accidental radicalism of the Egyptian state: the state had invited the private sector to lead the developmental effort. Turned down by the private sector, the state had to do the leading itself. The "socialism" of the regime emerged out of societal stalemate. A path opened up, and it was pursued. The new course was pushed along by the temperament of the man at the helm. It may be wrong to root ideological changes in psychological theories of "unsettledness" and in the temperament of individuals, but personal accidents do make a great difference. From recent Egyptian memoirs, particularly a detailed set of memoirs by ᶜAbd al-Latīf al-Baghdādī, one of the more powerful of the Free Officers who served in several cabinets and as a vice-president and was forced out of power by 1964, it would appear that Nasser himself was more radical than the mainstream of his colleagues.[35] Even after they had passed the socialist legislation of 1961, there still was no clarity in the ruling group, and no consensus among them. Basic differences surfaced at that stage: Kamāl al-Dīn Husayn and ᶜAbd al-Latīf al-Baghdādī repeatedly expressed their concern over Nasser's gradual "susceptibility" to Marxism and gave the standard indictment of socialism: its incompatibility with Islam, with the "tradition" of the people. Socialism, they both insisted, would not stick on the ground, would offend the sensibilities of Egyptians. But both men were squeezed out, and Nasser prevailed. He went on to organize the ASU, with which he aimed to strengthen the mobilizational system; he admitted the communists into the ruling alliance, and the ASU presumably became his instrument for checking the power of vested interests he worried about.

But the ambiguity that seems to have been the hallmark of Nasser's political career asserted itself. He formed the ASU but constantly interfered to clip its wings and limit its power. Then, too, as Binder tells us in his analysis, the ASU, like so many other radical schemes, was shackled by rural notables—the second stratum—who made their way into it. They made sure that they were amply represented in the ASU and that the power of the central apparatus was checked. The ASU wanted a "political approach" to prevail, but it became a center of power among competing centers of power. Its central apparatus, constantly watched and checked by Nasser, was later emasculated and then finally dismantled by Sadat.[36]

The urge to turn things upside down had exhausted itself after 1967. To the extent that the ASU did provide a vehicle for the more radical elements in the state, its demise is part of the broader phenomenon of deradicalization. There was very little patience and energy left after the defeat to fight over social questions. Student demonstrations and labor unrest raised the specter of pre-1952 disorder. The accent was now on accomodation and social harmony, and that was the world that Nasser's successor opted for. A preview of the much-trumpeted foreign investment laws passed in 1974 was offered in 1971 (with Law 65), and the discussion of *al-infitāh* (the opening) was launched in April 1973. The post-1973 order was not as new as its proponents and critics make it out to be.

Above and beyond the politics of defeat and accomodation, the course of the Egyptian state reveals the dilemmas of state capitalism of the kind that developed in the Third World over the last quarter-century. Briefly the genre we are dealing with emerges out of a particular societal crisis: the upper orders fail to pull off a revolution from above; the bourgeois model is not a possibility because the bourgeoisie is not loyal to its own political pretensions and because the international system often intrudes and overwhelms domestic forces. The state then has to step into the vacuum if it is to arrest economic stagnation.

State capitalism of the Egyptian variety seemed triumphant in the 1960s. It fulfilled tangible economic functions—integration into the world economy, greater autonomy, the expansion of employment, and so forth. There were also noneconomic factors working to its advantage—the lure of nationalism, the desire for a place in the sun. For all the polemics of liberal internationalism against the state, it is the state that serves to create a domestic market and to improve a nation's position in the world economy.

More lately, state capitalism, Third-World style, has run into what seem to be fundamental troubles. Whether in Peru, Algeria, Egypt, or in the older experiment of Mexico, there are few victories to be found. At home the model has come up against the phenomenon of the new class; internationally many of the states that opted for state capitalism seem to have succumbed to deeper and new forms of dependency. This has led to a revisionism of the entire model. Mahbub ul-Haq, director of policy planning at the World Bank, once a firm believer, expresses this kind of revisionism of the mixed economy relied upon by state capitalism:

> In most cases, such a choice has combined the worst, not the best, features of capitalism and socialism. It has often prevented the developing countries from adopting honest-to-goodness economic incentives and using the free functioning of the price system to achieve efficiency in a capitalistic framework, if not equity. In reality, there have been too many inefficient administrative controls and price distortions. At the same time, the choice of the mixed economy has prevented these societies from pursuing their goals in a truly socialistic framework, since mixed economy institutions have often been more capitalistic than not. The end result, therefore, has often been that they have fallen between two stools, combining weak economic incentives with bureaucratic socialism. Neither the ends of growth nor equity are served by such confusion in social and political objectives within the framework of a mixed economy.[37]

The failures of the mixed model will, in ul-Haq's view, force many states to become "either more frankly capitalistic or more genuinely socialist." States, of course, might have to do neither. They may continue to muddle through, combining capitalist practices and socialist incantations, allowing the market to decide the distribution of spoils, but intervening now and then to keep things from falling apart. Each model generates its own troubles. If socialism Egyptian-style ended in bureaucratic feudalism, the advent of a capitalist economy might fall prey to speculations, and to the historic incapacity of the Egyptian elites to develop a genuine and responsible capitalist path. The harvest of the shift might turn out to be greater cultural dualism between the sectors that respond to the new opportunities and those not strategically placed or equipped to do so; a growing and politically dangerous imbalance between the rewards of labor and those of speculation; a weakening of the industrial and economic foundations—however fragile and problematic—developed during Egypt's relatively successful experiment with planning.

The troubles of the Egyptian economy have a built-in intellectual risk of leading observers to conclude that Egypt has for a long time had to live with dependency, that its savings rate has been generally low, that it always has to finance investments from outside sources. But scales do matter; dependency is always a relative condition. Deficit financing, which stood at 3.8 percent of national income in 1953, rose to 17 percent in 1975; foreign financing of new investments, which was a source of weakness in the late 1960s, rose from 35 percent in the late 1960s to nearly 75 percent by 1975.[38] There is a great deal of difference between the low figures and the high ones.

There are also equally troubling "softer" indicators: there is a new legitimation of a culture of dependence on outsiders in Egyptian society today. The new dependency, which has become a pillar of the open-door economy, has deep roots in Egyptian history. To the extent that the post-October 1973 oil revolution revived old propensities toward dependence, this must be taken into account in any serious effort to grapple with political and economic change since October 1973.

## III. The Open-Door Economy and Its Proponents

The open-door economy is a step-child of the 1973 oil revolution and bears its marks: faith in technology, a belief in new possibilities, inflated expectations. Its harvest has been wild rents, land speculations, inflation, and the corruption born out of new possibilities.

A view of the post-1973 culture and its ramifications for questions of equity and welfare is provided by the astute analyst Muhammad Haykal.

> People saw, too, how power in the Arab world was passing to new men. For a generation the men who directed the course of events in the Arab world had been ideologists or officers from the armed forces—or sometimes officers who turned into ideologists or ideologists who tried to behave as if they were officers. Such were Sadat, Assad, Ghadaffi, Boumedienne, Michel Aflaq, Sadam Hussein and many others. Many of these were still there, but they were now being joined by the first installment of a new breed of power brokers, the middlemen, and arms dealers, the wealthy merchants who flitted between East and West, between royal palaces and the offices of oil companies—men like Kamal Adham, Mahdi Tajjir, Adnan Khashoggi and others—and by royalty itself, for who in the Arab world now exercised more power than Prince Fahd or Prince Sultan of Saudi Arabia? Could not individuals such as these, it was argued, achieve more for the Arabs than mass movements and radical revolutions?
>
> It is not surprising if in this changed atmosphere men and women in Egypt and Syria felt that the time had come for them too, to see some improvement in their material circumstances. They had known hardship; now they looked for their reward—for more to eat and for better houses to live in. Of course money would have to be found to pay for this, but who would dare to suggest that the Arabs were short of money? It was being said that the Arabs possessed the power to bring the rest of the world to starvation; surely they must have the power to feed themselves? So eyes turned to the oil-producing countries. Oilfields began to loom far bigger in the public mind than battlefields; *tharwa* (riches), it was said, had begun to take over from *thawra* (revolution).[39]

In the states at the periphery of the oil revolution, it was reasoned that shackled economies could not compete in the new regional order, and these states (true of Egypt as it is of Syria) responded to the new opportunities. Their response was typically bureaucratic: scrap yesterday's laws, ease the hold of the state on the economy, change to symbols of the political order. There were state elites anxious to make the transition to the new climate and to break out of the bureaucratic mold. The doctrinaire distinction between public and private sectors breaks down far easier than the faithful imagine, for as some limited data to be presented at a later stage in this analysis will show, there were many state-based elites in Egypt (and I presume the case to be the same in Syria) who would now use their position in the state bureaucracy to make the leap into the private sector. The classic illustration of this syndrome is the Mexican pattern, where the public sector of one regime is the private sector of the next.

The Egyptian response to the era of petrodollars was a rush to demonstrate a break with the populist interlude. Thus in 1975, the Egyptian bureaucracy reported with great pride that 102 laws had been enacted to create a new economic order.[40] The legislations covered the full range of economic activities: Law 43, the centerpiece of the legislations, paved the way for the foreign investors and gave a generous set of provisions and exceptions: Ministerial Decision number 1058 liberalized import laws, and the import sector was shifted to an open licensing system; banking, which had been nationalized, was thrown open to foreign banks, resulting in twenty-five new banking ventures; foreign exchange transactions were shifted from the official market (£E = US$2.55) to the parallel market (£E = 0.70 = US$1). Most of the crucial legislation was enacted in 1974/1975 at the height of the euphoria with the post-October 1973 order. A little later there had to be an intensification of liberalization. The logic was more of the same. The proponents of *al-infitāh* would repeatedly persist in their view that "capital is cowardly," that there had to be more incentive for the foreign interests and "hidden local capital." Indeed, it was the mandate of one cabinet headed by Prime Minister ᶜAbd al-ᶜAzīz Hijāzī to implement the open-door economic policy; and, when that failed, the task fell to Mamdūh Sālim—a man with a background in the police services, a former governor of Alexandria—to achieve what Hijāzī's government had failed to do. In President Sadat's words, "Mamdūh [Sālim] is today blowing up all the rules and obstacles that impede the freedom of economic affairs."[41] To the proponents of *al-infitāh,* intervention by the state was an obstacle, and all obstacles were to be removed.

The relentless attack against the state in the Egyptian liberalizers' arsenal was in part an unwillingness to pay the public costs of the political order. It was also a bit of political and cultural mimicry—an attempt to be more Western than the West—that reflects an inability to understand the rules of the game in Organization of Economic Cooperation and Development (OECD) countries. The result is a "more royalist than the king" kind of situation. While OECD countries regulate their economies, those who wish to appeal to the West urge dismantling of many of the economic functions and responsibilities of the state. And in the aftermath of the October war, the proponents of the new policy based their arguments not only on a vastly changed regional and international configuration—petrodollar, Egypt's geostrategic importance to the American design—but also on the widely perceived failure of what passed for socialism.

In following the voluminous debate on *al-infitāh* and on the broader questions of basic economic choices, as I did for this study, one is struck by a curious simplification of economic issues: economic conditions seem to be of two kinds, *infitāh* (opening) and *inghilāq* (closure). Egypt tried the latter, and it presumably failed; thus it is time to go for an overhauling of the system. In the proponents' depiction of the issues, to oppose *al-infitāh* is to fall prey to a "fear complex." This fits in with the interesting psychologizing of politics in Sadat's Egypt, where politics reduces itself to the search for identity, where all of Nasser's policies are explained by Nasser's "complexes," which President Sadat always refers to but generously refuses to reveal. The "fear complex" appears in President Sadat's important programmatic statement, the October Paper, (April 1974), in connection with the role of foreign capital. The world after 1973, the Egyptian president observed, is not the way it was before: Egypt is strong to rid itself of the "fear complex" vis-à-vis the outside world.[42] The same psychologizing—serving as an escape from concrete discussions—figures in an all too typical statement by Mahmūd Abū Wafīya, a member of Parliament, a brother-in-law of President Sadat who, until the food riots of January 1977, served as secretary general of the Arab Socialist Union. In a discussion of a joint Egyptian-Saudi-Kuwaiti enterprise, one member of Parliament asked whether the terms of the venture violated the gains of the workers and the previous labor legislations; Abū Wafīya's response was to attack what he called "the foreigner's complex." Egypt, he said, must rid itself of "all the complexes that imperialism implanted in our generation."[43]

The political process that brought about the "102 legislative changes" maintained throughout that it was Egypt's laws that stood between the country and access to foreign capital. Here and there dissident voices were heard, but the bureaucracy and interest that pushed those legislators were locked into that proposition. Behind liberalization stood the prestige of the presidency: the authority of President Sadat's October Paper and his promise of a new era of prosperity. And in an authoritarian political setting, the interests that favored the new policy had their way. If critics of the regulatory agencies in the United States focus on the way the regulators end up being "captured" by the interests and industries they are supposed to regulate, Egypt presents a yet more extreme case. The would-be regulated (multinationals, their domestic representatives) helped to make the basic economic policies; the bureaucrats, who are generally entrusted with regulation, had a different mandate in the Egyptian case—that of "blowing up" the rules and promoting the interests of the regulated.

Thus the Investment and Free Zones Authority (whose domain covers foreign investments and joint ventures) was never seen as a regulatory agency. Its task was to "package" the country to pave the way before the foreign investor. Bureaucracies being what they are, the Investment and Free Zones Authority became a domain from which careers could be advanced by those who placed their bets on the new economic policy. Predictably, the authority's indicators were to show its diligent pursuit of its defined objectives. Consider the following introduction to its glossy brochure (printed in Beirut as if to underscore the impact of the open-door economy on local industry):

> The General Authority for Investment and Free Zones has embarked on its new task on the 14th of October 1972 with convening the first meeting of its Board of Directors. Since that day, and until the end of December 1977, the Board held 45 meetings in which they approved 534 projects to be set up in land and in the private free zones. The project's capital amounts to £E2132 at first estimation. The Board of Public Free Zones approved 206 other projects whose capital amounts to £E208 million. . . .[44]

The word *approve* gives away the tactic of the proponents of *al-infitāh* as they held out the promise of massive foreign investment awaiting a favorable political climate. Thus, in 1974, it was announced that £E500 million were approved while the actual committed capital was only £E383,000—in other words, less than 1 percent of approved projects. It was also in the same vein that Prime Minister Mamdūh Sālim announced that one of the achievements of his government was the approval in 1975 of 349 projects with a capital of £E390 million and that another 150 projects were under study. Some of this was wishful thinking; some was a deliberate effort to suggest that a new and bright future beckons for Egypt.

That the basic policy of *al-infitāh* was made by the regulated and by its direct beneficiaries and that its basic pillar was the dismantling of state regulation is borne out by the proceedings of a number of important workshops of multinational business executives and state officials that took place over the 1975–1977 period and by the parliamentary sessions that ratified the key economic decisions. Both these sources afford us a view of the interests represented in the making of the policy (as well as those left out) and of the philosophical base of the policy.

All the workshops—on Legal and Economic Aspects of Foreign Investment held in October 1975, on Exchange Control and the Open-Door Policy held in April 1976, on Banking Control and the Open-Door Policy held in December 1976, and finally the Workshop on Proposed Changes to Law 43 held in February 1977)—were dominated by an unexamined faith in the efficiency of the market. All ritually recommended that primacy should be assigned to removing state barriers. What is immediately evident in all these meetings is the absence of not only those executives who might favor different economic choices but even of those sectors of the bureaucracy—Ministry of Industry officials—that might be committed to a measure of economic nationalism and might have had a vested interest in protecting local industry. The Egyptian officials present at these meetings were invariably the same individuals: representatives of the Investment Authority as well as those of the Ministry of Economy and Economic Cooperation. The officials of the Ministry of Industry, let alone the representatives of affected labor unions, were shut out of the process. Lopsided and pliant majorities in Parliament then ratified the key decisions. In none of the workshops were distributive and welfare questions seriously raised. The reigning economic philosophy can be discerned from the recommendations made.[45] For example, the Workshop on Legal and Economic Aspects of Foreign Investment recommended that

> The structure of relative prices be thoroughly examined and attention be given to the task of making market prices in Egypt more nearly reflect social costs and benefits. . . . It is recognized that private foreign and private domestic investment respond much more to market prices than to direct decisions by the government. It is also noted that public companies are being given more freedom to respond to market incentives. It is therefore necessary that the same review of the relative price structure in Egypt be undertaken that will lead to proposals that make market prices more nearly reflect social costs and benefits.[46]

Behind the tortured verbiage was the familiar call upon the state to "rationalize" things by terminating subsidies—an added bit of pressure to that applied by the International Monetary Fund (IMF) and the Arab oil states. More of the same emerges from the Workshop on Banking Laws, which was attended by virtually the entire foreign banking sector. This time the issue was the convertibility of the Egyptian pound and the exchange rates. It was "recognized" by the participants that there was a "movement to greater reliance on the private sector and the market mechanism." It was concluded that the "current exchange rate policy was a major obstacle, perhaps the major obstacle to private investment entering Egypt." That too was the position underscored by the Workshop on Exchange Control and the Open-Door Policy that recommended floating the

Egyptian pound and shifting imports from the official to the parallel rates: "It was appreciated that the open door policy represents a marked shift in development strategy from that prevailing over the two decades prior to the early 1970s. This shift from the old to the new imposes a variety of demands on the policy maker to effect this transition. At the same time there is a lack of data and full comprehension of how the economy in its present stage will function as new policies are introduced."[47]

One could go on, but the cumulative message is clear. It adds up to a fairly powerful lobby with no countervailing powers. That this lobby's arguments are neither compelling in terms of logic, nor fully thought out, makes no difference whatsoever. The business interests were (naturally) pushing for the most favorable terms they could get, and they invariably came up with the very laws under which they were supposed to operate. The state bureaucracy went along. A sense of the symbiosis between the regulators and the foreign economic interests is conveyed by the following datum: Muhammad Ibrāhīm Dakrūrī, the member of Parliament who headed the parliamentary committee that pushed through the proposed changes to the foreign investment legislations in May of 1977 (changing Law 43 to Law 32) was to show up a while later as a president of one of the banks authorized under the foreign investment codes—Misr-America Bank, in which the Bank of America holds 40 percent interest, Kuwait 9 percent, and Egyptian investors the remaining 51 percent.[48]

The vital changes in foreign investment laws drawn up by a workshop of foreign executives, investment lawyers, and officials of the Ministry of Economy were known to the business community long before they were submitted to Parliament. *Egypt Report,* a newsletter published by investment lawyer Ahmad Shalkānī, had summarized the changes for its subscribers in February 1977—more tax exemptions, more favorable exchange rates, no limits on the repatriation of profits. Mr. Shalkānī attended the meetings that came up with the new legislation. He and other lawyers in his firm (which represents and advises foreign enterprises) lobbied for the most generous of exemptions, in effect for the total absence of state regulation. Mr. Shalkānī's newsletter asserted that it was "believed" that the "introduction" of these amendments will remove the obstacles that have hindered the flow of investments into Egypt up to the present time and create the appropriate investment atmosphere in the Arab Republic of Egypt."[49]

None of this shows a firm understanding of the nature of international political economy, of the dynamics of foreign investment decisions and how they are made. The real problems are wished away. What is at work is faith, an incapacity to realize that economic nationalism asserts itself in countries of conventional leftist ideology like Algeria and rightist ones like Brazil. Having gambled with great exuberance and certitude on the flood of investment awaiting the dismantling of socialism that supposedly frightened away the foreign investor, the proponents of *al-infitāh* held on to their faith in the face of sobering evidence to the contrary.

The parliamentary debates on these matters further reveal the workings of the system: the more reasoned arguments came from the critics; faith and absolutes were the material of the proponents, and they were in the overwhelming majority of that body. Some independent members had specific things to say: Khālid Muhī' al-Dīn questioned the excessive faith in legislation. He rightly noted that the experience of Third World countries confirms that foreign investment is directly correlated with the level of domestic savings and that for Egypt the critical questions were its savings rate, the reform of its infrastructure, and a serious plan for the economy. Unless these problems are tackled, foreign investors will stay away. The few who will come in will do so in sectors of the economy—banking, consulting firms, fast-food chains—that fail to address the basic needs of the society.[50] The relentlessly independent Muhammad Hilmī Murād focused on the generous tax exemptions. Not only were those exemptions unfair—what is the justice in taxing the worker and the employee while exempting investment firms' commercial representatives?—but they were also the wrong issues. Foreign investors, he observed, do not stay away from a particular country or invest there because of taxes. Taxes are one factor among many; it is the overall health of an economy that sways the foreign investor. How does Egypt, he asked, intend to maintain its economy while it erodes its tax base? How will the economy as a whole function when foreign investors have privileges not extended to the Egyptian investor? If foreign investment laws were passed to bring in international technology and capital, then why allow foreign insurance companies to come in when their previous record indicates that they "accumulate domestic savings to serve foreign economies?"[51]

The official position had, of course, many defenders. The views of two members of Parliament may be selected as an indication of the dominant current: one is the position of Dr. Jamal ᶜUtayfī, a deputy speaker of Parliament and a man who could be said to represent liberal professions; the other is that of Kamāl Mustafā Murād, a former Free Officer who seems to speak for the interests of importers. In defense of the open-door policy, ᶜUtayfī reveals its sources of inspiration. He informed his colleagues that he had just returned from a trip to Singapore, Thailand, Indonesia, and the Philippines—countries that are flooded by foreign investment—in order to understand the secret of their success and that he was now firmly convinced that Egypt is amply qualified to attract foreign investments:

> In reality the problem that faced foreign investment in Egypt is providing the right atmosphere that guarantees security for those

> investments. Now that we have finished our quick comparisons . . . we have concluded that Egypt is totally prepared for foreign investment; more prepared than any other country. Let us remind the foreign investor of the fate of foreign investments in Ethiopia, Portugal, Pakistan and in many Latin American countries which are subject to daily disturbances and military coups.[52]

Egypt's comparative advantage is, then, its stability. That ᶜUtayfī uses the "New Society" of President Marcos and the Indonesian "New Order" and the atypical case of Singapore as examples of what Egypt should pursue may tell us a great deal about the conception of equity and its fate in the post-October 1973 order. The journey that ᶜUtayfī took to these countries left no deep impression on him. The troubles of Indonesia and the Philippines, their scale of corruption and inequity, the political repression it takes to secure and maintain these orders, do not appear in ᶜUtayfī testimony. Nor is there a serious sustained inquiry into the relevance of Singapore to Egypt's needs. There is only the overworked reference to the security of the investor, to his need for the right guarantees.

If ᶜUtayfī, a thoughtful, educated legislator, lets the issue of equity fall by the wayside, Kamāl Mustafā Murād's position is yet more extreme. Here we see a pre-New Deal kind of logic at work, and we confront the purposes to which *al-infitāh* was put. For Murād, and for many others like him, *al-infitāh* served as a way of attacking any limits on the freedom of capital and the rights of property: there should be no limits on profit margins; the state should go for maximum exemptions for, in doing so, it would unleash "hidden local capital." What was applied in the 1960s, said Murād, "cannot be applied now for we are in the second half of the 1970s and we should not speak the language of twenty years ago but the language of the time. . . . Capital is abundant around us and the annual surplus in the oil states is US $50 billion. . . . I ask the members to approve this plan and as soon as possible for the Consultative Group meeting in Paris needs such a law. . . . The press services are awaiting an approval."[53] Between Egypt and prosperity stand some "formalities" (to use Murād's term) and the legislations of the 1960s. Dismantle those and all would be well: both hidden local capital and surplus petrodollars would solve Egypt's problems. The extent of the wisdom about economic affairs was evident in Parliament on another occasion when the import laws were being scrutinized. As a proponent of liberalization put it: "The door should be opened before all to import and export as they wish. . . . We will see that the prices will go down and that there will be no deviations."

To go into the debate at such length and to select such passages may seem a bit unkind, but I have insisted on these passages (without selecting the most extreme ones) to unravel the manner in which the new economic policy was formulated and defended. The new economic policy promised salvation to an impoverished society that had been through some very difficult times. Its proponents depicted an external environment of plenty that was Egypt's for the asking if only the "anachronistic" policies of yesterday were pushed aside. At the juncture, both domestic Egyptian interests and foreign economic interests converged. For the former there were new opportunities. For the latter the stakes in Egypt were more substantial than the Egyptian market itself. At stake was the health of the international monetary system, the stability of the Middle Eastern order, and Egypt's unique place in the Arab system. In the aftermath of the October war, the fight between the Arab oil states and the radical ones had been over for some time, concluded after 1967 in favor of the oil states. The phenomenal wealth at the disposal of the oil states that nationalized after 1973 only served to further deepen the dependency of the oil-less Arab lands on the aid of the oil states. Egypt's repudiation of its previous radicalism and its adoption of a pro-American policy stood as the clearest embodiment of that victory.

The promises extended to Egypt by President Richard Nixon, by his Secretary of Treasury William Simon, by David Rockefeller, by the shah of Iran, and by Saudi Arabia, all of whom had inputs into the new policy, were part of a larger game. The particularities of the Egyptian case were of little interest to them. Nor were welfare and distributive questions high priority items to the shah of Iran or to William Simon or to the decision-makers in Saudi Arabia. The shah's record in Iran speaks for itself; William Simon's sermons on private initiative place him on the far right of the ideological spectrum in the United States itself. As for Saudi Arabia, its economic philosophy reflects the accident of its wealth, its isolation from world currents, and its unsophisticated social structure. In the Saudi worldview, concerns with equity and redistribution (beyond the Islamic codes on *Zakat* [alms]) are synonymous with communism. Saudi Arabia was willing to invest in the new Egyptian policy if Egypt would see its way out of its previous "confusions," abandon its "imported" economic doctrines, and join Saudi Arabia in a "stabilization" scheme for the Arab world as a whole.

## IV. The New Economic Policy and Its Social Base

But the motives of foreign interests were only one side of the equation. To the global and regional pull, there was a powerful domestic push. No society is a helpless pawn of others. This much at least could be said of a postcolonial world. Even poor, vulnerable states make their own choices. Third World nationalism may have failed to deliver all that was pinned on it, but it has placed a great deal of sovereignty within the state, and thus it has undermined the view of Third World states buffeted by winds and pressures beyond their control.

More can be learned about the open-door economic policy (both its social base and welfare consequences) through a different route: the list of investors in the companies authorized by the foreign investment codes. These are exhaustive lists of titles of incorporation published in *al-Waqāᶜī al-Misrīya* and *al-Jarīda Rasmīya (The Official Gazette).*[54] A thorough analysis (more systematic than the one here) of these lists may yield significant data about the insights into elite linkages, private-public sector relations, and the relationship between international commerce and state elites. The lists make for interesting reading: predictably, they cover a small set of elites and, if the charge of one member of Parliament that eight hundred families have become the principal beneficiaries of the July 23 revolution of 1952 is true, it is here where the weight of the affluent families is felt. The lists (I checked the full records of 1975 through 1978) substantiate the "merging" of the pre-1952 interests with the beneficiaries of the post-1952 political order. Some old pre-1975 families re-emerge: new families who worked through the Egyptian state after 1952 rise to the top. The lists thus confirm a restoration of sorts combined with the rise of a new class through access to state power.

A great deal of commentary on the Egyptian order is in agreement that a political and social "restoration" of sorts has taken place in recent years. The old interests were pushed aside during the Nasserite interlude, but they survived. Checked against the names of those who were subjected to the socialist and rationalization measures of 1961/1962, the new lists (the 1975–1978 lists of investors) offer a poignant commentary on the fate of many radical claims. The one major difference between the older lists and the new ones is the absence of the "local foreigners" who were so prominent in the old lists. The Greek, Syrian, Lebanese, and Jewish names, so abundant on the first list, do not appear on the new lists. But many native Egyptian families that had substantial assets in 1961/1962 reappear as beneficiaries of the new investment laws. Some examples are in order: Muhammad Munīr Sharīf Sabrī, Zaynab Sharīf Sabrī, and ᶜAisha Sharīf Sabrī held large stocks in two concerns that were subjected to the 1961/1962 measures. They appear as local partners of a Swiss concern represented by an investment of £E150,000. Dr. Muhammad ᶜUwayīs, Ibrāhīm ᶜUwayīs, and Samīn ᶜUwayīs of the 1961/1962 lists appear as investors (with £E220,000 capital) in a tourist-related enterprise authorized on August 11, 1977. The Shalkānī family, present on the old list, had a total of £E325,000 invested in four new concerns. The same is true of the Hasb Allāh', the Marᶜīs and so forth, who also appear on both lists.

By far the most interesting case is that of ᶜUthmān Ahmad ᶜUthmān, who doubles as the country's leading contractor and a frequent minister of housing (his son is marred to President Sadat's daughter) and who often seems in the *Economist's* words to be "in charge of all Egyptian construction."[55] Mr. ᶜUthmān's firm came under the nationalization laws of 1961/1962. At the time, the stocks in his firm were valued at £E400,000 and were held by himself and members of his family: ᶜUthmān Ahmad ᶜUthmān, £E80,000; Husayn Ahmad ᶜUthmān, £E28,000; the heirs of Muhammad Ahmad ᶜUthmān, £E76,000; Ibrāhīm ᶜUthmān Ahmad ᶜUthmān, £E19,444, and so forth. As characteristic of the half-hearted approach of the Egyptian experiment, Mr. ᶜUthmān was left in charge of his own firm.[56] Thanks to his business operations in the Persian Gulf states and to the peculiarities of the intersection of the private and public sectors in Egypt, ᶜUthmān thrived even during the heyday of radicalism. But it was in post-October 1973 Egypt that ᶜUthmān did exceedingly well. His buoyant belief in private enterprise and his dynamism stood out in marked contrast to the seeming inefficiency and lethargy of the public sector. ᶜUthmān was a man who could get things done in a country where things always seem to stall, break down. With his position in the bureaucracy, his links to President Sadat, his international connections, ᶜUthmān was one of the prime movers and symbols of the post-October 1973 order and, it would appear, one of its principal beneficiaries.

Consider the magnitude of Mr. ᶜUthmān's activities. A joint Iranian-Egyptian firm authorized in November of 1975 had a £E500,000 investment by Mr. ᶜUthmān's firm. Two of its directors are relatives of Mr. ᶜUthmān—Husayn Ahmad ᶜUthmān and Muhammad Salāh al-Dīn Hasb Allah. A concern authorized in 1978 with a capital of £E400,000 was owned by Mr. ᶜUthmān and his family. So was a polyester enterprise with £E250,000 capital. Fifteen percent of the Egyptian company for construction and development (a joint British/Egyptian firm) was owned by one of Mr. ᶜUthmān's companies. Specialized Contracting and Industries, a firm capitalized at £E1 million (50 percent Egyptian, 50 percent registered in Luxemburg) is another of Mr. ᶜUthmān's enterprises: its Egyptian shares were held by Muhammad ᶜUthmān Ahmad, £E85,000; Muhammad Husayn Ahmad, £E40,000; ᶜAmr Husayn Ahmad, £E40,000, Isrāᶜīl Ibrāhīm Ahmad, £E20,000; Hadīya ᶜUthmān Ahmad, £E20,000, and so forth. This time the titles of incorporation were a bit more elaborate than usual: the members of the board of the directors were ᶜAmr Husayn Ahmad, twenty-three years of age, Ibrāhīm ᶜUthmān Ahmad, age twenty-five, while its chairman of the board was the twenty-nine year old Muhammad ᶜUthmān Ahmad. This is the phenomenon that Dr. Mahmūd al-Qādī, an independent member of Parliament, refers to as the "young geniuses," sons and sons-in-law of the leading men in Egypt reaching the upper layers of administration and finance in their early twenties; or what Gouda Abdel-Khalek labels "family capitalism." For all the mumbo-jumbo of ideology, there seem to be very few substitutes to being born to the right family. This is as true of Egypt, as al-Qādī and Abdel-Khalek tell us, as it is true of the United States, as the controversial research of Christopher Jencks and his associates persuasively demonstrates.[57] It is also true of the Soviet Union, where members of the bureaucracy and the party pass on to their children the privileges of the new class.

ᶜUthmān's construction firm was also the stockholder of a large tourist-hotel investment. This was capitalized at £E4 million, and the ᶜUthmān-controlled share was forty percent; the ᶜUthmān share represented 50 percent of an aluminum-related investment project capitalized at £E2,240,000. Two of Mr ᶜUthmān's concerns had an investment of £E525,000 in a joint British-Egyptian project capitalized at £E1,500,000.

Mr. ᶜUthmān straddles the private and public sectors. His clan is amply represented in both; he is linked to the president; an associate, ᶜAlī Anwār Abū Sahlī, a lawyer who was blacklisted under Nasser, was reinstated in recent years and appointed in October 1978 as the country's public prosecutor. We learn of the extent of ᶜUthmān's reach from a detailed statement made by Dr. Mahmūd al-Qādi in parliamentary debates: cousins, nephews, and sons-in-law of Mr. ᶜUthmān sit on the board of several joint ventures with foreign companies; they go in and out of the bureaucracy as deputy ministers, heads of public concerns, and prosecutors, creating a powerful network of interlocking directorates. Mr. ᶜUthmān's defense of his activities against the charges of Dr. al-Qādī was put in the reassuring language and symbolism of "the family." All the 35,000 employees of his firms were his "relatives, sons and loved ones." As for his nephew Ismāᶜīl ᶜUthmān, "the young genius," his success was attributed to being a "bright student." Egypt, said ᶜUthmān, had too much to do to be consumed by *hiqd* (resentment) and to succumb to alien doctrines.[58]

The public sector of one era is the private sector of the next. The classic case of this model is that of Mexico—a country whose revolution and its outcome bear more than a superficial resemblance to the Egyptian case. Access to state power provides an opportunity for capital accumulation and extremely valuable experience in mastering the rules of the game. Then the official classes plunge into the private market: the fervor they once displayed for planning and state intervention is channeled into the private market. Official experience thus becomes the base for a new career in the private sector.

Since October 1973 there has been an elite personnel shift of considerable magnitude from the public sector in Egypt to the private sector. Some of those who have made the shift are among Egypt's most powerful and prominent figures. This is the way an Egyptian businessman describes the new competition in the marketplace: "The market is now full of former prominent officials; two former prime ministers in addition to twenty-two former ministers and tens of former heads of public sector companies, deputy ministers and governors."[59]

The businessman adds that it is this group that concludes the big commercial deals and that has a corner on commercial representations of foreign multinationals. The limited data I have substantiate the businessman's claim. We have already encountered the usual example of Mr. ᶜUthmān, but there are others. The two former prime ministers are ᶜAzīz Sidqi, who is the representative of Fiat Motor Company,[60] and ᶜAbd al-ᶜAziz Hijāzī, principal architect of the open-door economic policy and prime minister from 1973 to 1975, who is the local partner of a Saudi-Egyptian investment concern.[61] Former Deputy Prime Minister Muhammad ᶜAbd Allah Marzubān, under investigation in 1979 in a case involving the sale of Boeing jets to Egypt Air, owns 6.25 percent of the stock of Colgate-Palmolive-Egypt with an investment of £E45,250.[62] An Egyptian-Iranian-Abu Dhabian firm capitalized at $6 million and authorized in July 1977 an Egyptian share of £E1,800,000 held by Raᶜūf Yahyā, and Fuᶜād Kāmil Mursī; the same Fuᶜād Kāmil Mūrsī shows up, in January of 1977, in a presidential appointment as deputy minister of civil aviation.[63]

The investment codes and opportunities may have been new, but this is an old theme. For as Mahmūd Mutawalī tells us in his book on the historical roots of Egyptian capitalism, access to state power has been one of the main sources of capital accumulation in Egyptian society.[64] The aspirations of new classes and individuals are expressed through the state; then there is the merging of old and new interests of the kind depicted by Schurmann.

## V. The Workings of the Open-Door Policy: Some Illustrative Ventures

There is, however, a public price to be paid for the private success stories. The large commissions earned by the higher echelons of the state bureaucracy bring public ruin in their train. They either deliver the society into the shackles of foreign dependence—as elites try to generate new resources by trading in on a country's geostrategic importance—or they end up jeopardizing the productive wages of a national economy by eroding its industrial base with a flood of imports that bring in quick profits and large commissions. Large commissions require grandiose, costly projects, while the development needs of a poor society call upon more modest, basic undertakings. Moreover, there are noneconomic kinds of costs associated with large commissions. Engendering as they do a sense of unfairness about how the economic game is played, about the balance between the toil of the many and the good luck of the few—commissions, commercial representations, and large bribes either invite outright rebellion and ruin of the kind that recently played themselves out in Iran and Lebanon, or simply perpetuate stagnation and decline. What one observer called an "Egyptian Watergate"—the Boeing scandal, the Westinghouse affair involving an alleged payment of more than US$300,000 to Deputy Prime Minister Ahmad Sultān, al-Amīrīya project, a grandiose polyester-textile factory, and the Pyramid Oasis Project, an ambitious tourist-related project—has already taken its political toll.[65] The excuse that the system will come through and will cleanse itself is a lame official explanation. What Egyptians refer to as *Nazahāt al Hukm* (the integrity of the political process) has become one of the main political issues in recent years. The "demonstration effect" supplied by the comings and goings in the oil states was bound to spill into Egypt; it ruptured previous limits and encouraged the men in power to go for big stakes. It has always been difficult to practice austerity in a climate where others can hoard and flaunt what they have. None of the attempts to pin corruption on particular cultures, on things like national character, are particularly persuasive. What matters is the *situation* in which men find themselves. Private enrichment is a wholly understandable response to the demise of the public order. It takes political will to instill discipline (always relative, always vulnerable to some violations) in a political order. It takes some fairly good and austere examples at the top of the political system. These have not been in abundant supply in Arab politics of late; this may be one of the prime political casualties of the era of petrodollars in the Arab world.

In all the grandiose projects listed above, large commissions were made by a few individuals; there was also much pomp and ceremony and talk of a new era of prosperity and "civilization." In all the cases, the public interest seems to have suffered. If the aim of the social and economic thought is to locate a country in the world, to define its existential and political predicament, all these projects foster thin illusions and make it possible for the few to escape from Egypt's troubles into some imaginary land. Under the Khedive Ismāʿīl (who ruled 1863–1879), the dream was to make Egypt part of Europe. Some of the proponents of *al-infitāh* aspire to no less and act out their own version of progress, their own version of what Europe and America are all about—in total defiance of the accumulated wisdom about development, about the options open to poor societies in the world system.

Consider some of the debris: One of the most prestigious grandiose projects is a tunnel under the Suez Canal—to be dug by a British firm, Tarmao, in partnership with Mr. ʿUthmān—leading, as the *Economist* put it, into a "fairy city" in the Sinai desert. Here is the *Economist*'s detailed analysis of a project costing more than $100 million:

> Immensely sophisticated and largely untested, digging equipment was brought from West Germany; simpler and more labor intensive method might have suited the Egyptians better. Egyptian steel from Helwan was not strong enough to line the tunnel. Concrete segments were used instead, but it turned out that these had to be made from imported, not Egyptian cement.
>
> Fatal accidents, including the electrocution of a number of distinguished Egyptian engineers, have dogged the project. Mr. Sadat

> proposes to use the equipment to build two more tunnels under the canal. When engineers wonder at how such space-age stuff can be moved, the President speaks of the pyramids.[66]

The Pyramid Oasis project was another piece of showmanship and, again, of private gains and public costs. This was to be a vast 10,000-acre development near the Giza pyramid set aside for luxury hotels and villas. This, as the grandiose ambitions had it, was to be the "spearhead for foreign investment," a supposedly US$500 million project. It was authorized in 1975 as a partnership between Southern Pacific Properties, a firm incorporated in Hong Kong, and a public Egyptian agency. Southern Pacific Properties was to commit US$2,040,000 of capital; the Egyptian agency was to participate in the venture with its commitment of land. But Southern Pacific was mostly a paper entity set up by two Canadian businessmen, Peter Munk and David Gilmore. Munk and Gilmore proceeded to turn the project around and offer the land for sale to real estate developers. Three interested buyers were located: none other than Saudi tycoon and middleman ᶜAdnān Khashoggi, who put up a $12 million investment to acquire 28 percent of Southern Pacific Properties, and two Saudi princes who acquired 23 percent interest in return for US$15 million. In addition to the financial irregularities, the project was vulnerable on archaeological, and ultimately on strict economic, grounds: it represented a clear threat to the area around the pyramids. By building within the "circle of influence" around the Pyramids, it would have prevented further archaeological discoveries. Nor would turning the area into a vast real-estate-development project have aided the cause of Egyptian tourism. Once again, the would-be regulators in the Egyptian state had personal interests at stake: a one-time deputy minister of tourism, Dr. Salāh ᶜAbd al-Wahāb, was the representative of Southern Pacific Properties and the chairman of the board of the project. The fight over the project became a symbol of the underlying battle between the speculators, the middleman, and the "growth-men" behind *al-infitāh* and those worried about the economic and cultural consequences of what has come to pass for a "liberal" economy. Into the fight entered some broader regional considerations: the weight of the Saudi investors and their influence, the need not to do anything that might frighten them and other investors away. Under fire, President Sadat eventually canceled the project.[67]

Roughly the same themes emerge in al-Amīrīya project—a large textile-polyester combine undertaken as a joint venture between Bank Misr and the American firm Chemtex. This time, however, the stakes were bigger—the project required a capital outlay of £E530 million—the extent of the potential danger considerably greater, and the irregularities a bit more stark. This, in summary form, is what emerges as the record of that project: (1) It took only four days to approve the project. Bank Misr, a public sector bank, applied to the Investment Authority on March 23, 1977. Its application was approved on March 27. Approval was granted without consulting the General Organization for Industrialization, the Ministry of Industry, or the existing textile units in the public sector whose output and visibility would be seriously affected by the project. (2) The project, a quite large public investment, had not been part of the 1978 plan or the Five Year Plan that the government is committed to implementing. (3) The proponents of the project claimed that they had the backing of the General Organization for Industrialization; in reality, that agency had been totally opposed to the project. (4) For a joint venture of this scale, the foreign partner had only committed US$3.2 million; the rights were being assumed by Bank Misr. Chemtex, the foreign partner, had nothing to lose; the project stipulated a sale by Chemtex of US$58 million of machinery to the project. The same machinery had been offered to public sector units in Egypt for US$38 million. (5) There were extremely large commissions made by a number of individuals, involving clear and outright conflict of interest. Engineer Sayyid ᶜUwayīs was Bank Misr consultant and project director for ᶜal-Amīrīya; his son Muhammad Sayyid ᶜUwayīs was a commercial representative of Swiss and German concerns supplying machinery to the project. Mr. ᶜUwayīs's commission was something like US$1.6 million; four other individuals made commissions totaling more than US$4.5 million. (6) There was no serious feasibility study. One American-based consulting firm received US$4.5 million for the study. For an unusually high fee, the product was a superficial analysis that gave the proponents of the project the praise and results they wanted. (7) The project was initiated against the combined advice of the experts at the Ministry of Industry and those of the World Bank, who all agreed that there was no foreign market for the projected output and that Egypt would enter into a tough field and would have to compete against such established exporters as Taiwan and South Korea. (8) At the time of the project's inception, the public sector in Egypt had a surplus of textiles valued at £E140 million. (9) The project called for a skilled labor force of 28,000 technicians while the public sector units were suffering from a shortage of skilled manpower. It was clear that luring technical talent away from the old textile firms would be ruinous to the whole industry, and that is why the labor unions joined the fight against the project.[68]

## VI. The Classic Dilemma: Imports versus Manufactures

Beyond the data (some of it fairly tedious) and the scattered projects lie more fundamental issues: the old questions of domestic industrialization, imports versus manufactures, and a country's position in the world economic system. The real danger of the open-door policy is its impact upon local industry, and upon native welfare and employment. The debate for and against industrial protection and economic nationalism is an old one that can neither be settled nor reviewed here.[69] The case for economic nationalism has been made by men like Friedrich List, Alexander Hamilton, and Charles De Gaulle. In extreme formulations, protection of infant industry and economic nationalism rest not only on economic grounds but also on matters of political autonomy and cultural integrity. For some critics these are absolute matters. The dilution of economic sovereignty leads to political subjugation and cultural dependency. The "ideal-type" liberal interpretation can be equally extreme in its advocacy of an open world economy and its denunciation of things that impeded the mobility of men, capital, and technology. Both sides are capable of marshalling a great deal of evidence. The economic nationalists can point to a tough world where societies should not be at the mercy of others, to factors such as a society's level of skills, a technological base that makes a mockery of the laissez faire game and rigs it to the advantage of the strong. The case of the liberals is a familiar one: the protection of infant industry perpetuates inefficiency. In recent times, the advocates of liberalization can point to the poor record of protectionism and import substitution, to the fact that many cases of import substitution have failed, that far too many cases were inspired by national prestige, and that they amounted to the substitution of imports (finished products) by other products (raw materials and capital goods).

It is by the strictures of a moderate version of economic nationalism, which underpins this analysis, that the open-door economy can be faulted. The case for economic sovereignty should not be an absolute one, and in our world that is an impossible thing to aim for. But one does not have to be an uncompromising Gaullist—national grandeur, the right of the state to do what it wants—to note the negative costs of the scale of dependency that Egypt has ended up with. Two things can be singled out: the impact upon national industry—hence upon employment and mass consumption—and the subordination of an economy of debts and deficits to the dictates of others (in Egypt's case the IMF and the oil states).

With the severe ecological limits on its agriculture, the search for a viable industrial base has been a powerful, almost instinctive, theme in contemporary Egyptian history. This was Muhammad ᶜAlī's quest until it was thwarted by European power in 1841; it was also the dream of Talᶜat Harb and the Bank Misr group under British occupation in the 1920s and the 1930s. The Free Officer regime was heir to the same tradition. The slogan "from the needle to the rocket" expressed the ambition of giving Egypt a viable industrial base. Sadat's October Paper continued in the same vein. "The future of Egypt," observed Mr. Sadat, "is linked with industrialization . . . our primary hope in securing food for the increasing millions is for Egypt to export enough of its industrial production so as to enable it to import what it needs in food supplies."[70] The case for the open-door economic policy rested on Egypt's need for more effective, less cumbersome access to outside capital and technology. The proponents of the new policy looked toward the markets of the Persian gulf states: not only would an industrial boom satisfy Egyptian needs, Egypt would also become an "export platform," combining outside technology with cheap Egyptian labor.

But the reality of the policy has been an altogether different matter. A sophisticated industrial base takes a great deal of time to develop; it calls upon a good deal of social discipline, a willingness to save, a capacity to compete in foreign markets (after securing the domestic market) at a time of intense global competition for markets. The quick-kill mentality that moved the post-October 1973 order ruled out the possibility of such an industrial transformation. Nor were the outside markets so easy to penetrate. The abundance of capital in the Persian Gulf states, the hungry competition for those markets by OECD exporters, the kinds of technologies and gadgets that Saudi Arabia and Kuwait were importing, reduced the Egyptian scheme to another of the aborted dreams and possibilities entertained after 1973 by those (in the Arab states and Iran) who were convinced that a new world was in the making.

Thus the laws that were passed to enable Egypt to capture outside markets reduced themselves to what should have been an easy thing to predict; an "import mania" in the Egyptian market, a steady undermining of much of what had been accomplished in Egyptian industry after two decades of systematic bias in favor of industrialization. The relentless attacks—some justifiable, some motivated by personal interests—against the public sector had done their job: the political consensus essential to protect native industrialization was undermined, and the result amounted to a change in the country's view of its economic possibilities. Egypt would generate hard currency through export of its labor to the Arab oil states, from tourism and the Suez Canal and from politically motivated foreign aid; in return it would rely on imports. Strategically placed elites would conduct the transaction; in the process, they would hide behind a laissez faire ideology that they presume and say to be at work in rich capitalist societies. They would also (rather like the Lebanese elites before them) invite those who can not be absorbed in agriculture to emigrate: make their fortunes elsewhere and return to engage in trade, perhaps open a boutique, a travel agency, and so forth. Yesterday's populist experiment had stacked the bureaucracy and the public sector with university graduates to secure the stability of a critical segment of the population. Armed with what they depicted as the dismal record of the populist experiment, the "liberalizers" came back with no policy at all, only with an attack on yesterday's populism and its inefficiency.

The bias in favor of industry has been replaced with a bias in favor of the importer. This more accurately reflects the superior political resources of the importers and the middlemen and their proximity to political power. As ᶜIssām Rifaᶜat, a seasoned analyst at *al-Ahrām al-Iqtisādī* observes, the tariff structure is "killing" local industry: "it has changed from an instrument of protection for infant industry to an instrument for burying the public sector." In several key industries the tax on raw materials is 10–30 percent of value, while finished products are subject to a tax of 5 percent. The import tax on finished generators is 2 percent but 35 percent on raw materials and spare parts; 12 percent on tractors but 17 percent on spare parts; 20 percent on light bulbs but 30 percent on raw materials.[71]

There are abundant examples of industries (as well as agricultural products) in trouble as a result of the unrestricted import laws passed in the 1974–1976 period; the tire, textile, plastics, and paper industries, to name a few. The strategic banking sector is also in trouble; foreign banks were supposedly brought in to help finance investments, but they ended by engaging in regular banking transactions and diverting Egyptian savings outside the country.

The problems of the local tire industry came to light in an exchange between Minister of State for Economic Cooperation Jamāl Nāsir—whose bureaucratic unit is an active proponent of the new economic policy—and Muhammad Ahmad al-Fāqī, the head of a public sector concern that manufactures tires. The local tires had previously met the requirements of domestic consumption and had a decent volume of exports to Arab and African markets when surpluses materialized. But under the new import laws, the public sector was overstocked with tires it could not dispose of. Bureaucratic fragmentation (even within the public sector itself) appears to have aggravated the problem as different bureaucratic fiefdoms scrambled for their own interests. The whole public sector-Ministry of Transportation units were using foreign loans (in this case, Japanese loans) to buy imported tires. Thus in 1977/1978, only one-half of the local tire production was disposed of. Lax enforcement of the free zones was another contributing factor: tires were finding their way, via smuggling, from the free zones into the domestic market.[72] The troubles of the textile industry in the face of cheaper imports from Taiwan and South Korea were again similar and typical.

A mere two years after the formulation of the new economic policy, the agony of local industry was already rupturing the superficial consensus behind the open-door policy. The lines are increasingly drawn between cheaper imports and local manufactures. The political process favors the former, but that victory can be short-lived. The defection from the new policy has familiar features as local national capitalists (who once hailed the open-door policy) begin to suffer its consequences and as sympathetic intellectuals take note of both the welfare consequences and of the sensitive issue of cultural dependency. We see this defection in the position of the Egyptian Federation of Industries whose president, Hāmid Habīb, came out against the hasty import laws favored by other sectors of the bureaucracy. Local industry, he warned, was being undermined by a number of factors: (1) the import laws; (2) smuggling from the free zones; (3) the "import complex," which drives those with purchasing power to buy foreign goods as a badge of their own cosmopolitanism and sophistication; (4) the loss of East European and Soviet markets.

The concern with cultural integrity, always most intimately felt by the intelligentsia, has caused many to take a second look at the open-door policy. The editors and staff of the influential *al-Ahrām al-Iqtisādī,* who once hailed the new policy, appear to have joined its critics—gently and with great caution, for they are part of the country's official media; but their steady coverage and their editorials leave no doubt as to where they stand. In a bitter and sarcastic commentary written in early 1976, editor-in-chief Lutfī ᶜAbd alᶜAzīm expressed cultural and economic grievances that the new policy will have to address if it is to avert a dismal fate. The opening, he said, has been such a "remarkable success": there is plenty of German, Dutch, and Danish beer on the market and plenty of foreign cigarettes on the sidewalks. The opening should be welcomed for there is an abundance of Kentucky Fried Chicken and foreign fast-food chains changing the eating habits of the average Egyptian from eating *fūl* (fava beans) to hamburger; plenty of elegant foreign-made cars relieving the crisis of transportation.[73]

The most penetrating statement of defection by the same editor was made after the food riots of January 1977. His themes were the "new consumer society," the place of the poor masses in it, the alienation from an order that flaunts such waste and wealth in the midst of suffering. The regime's statement on the riots was President Sadat's description of the upheaval as an "uprising of the thieves" and a communist conspiracy. Editor ᶜAbd al-ᶜAzīm gave a deeper explanation that was no doubt held by the majority of Egypt's intelligentsia. "Egyptian society," he observed, "is full of time-bombs; the majority of the Egyptian people has unfortunately come to feel that it is undesirable in the new consumer society." Few individuals, he said, were actively engaged in looting and burning, but there was a "silent majority" that stood by and did not care. There is an "economic apartheid" beween a new class that hoards all the opportunities and the vast majority of the people. Why should the average person, he asked, care whether the casinos on the road to the Pyramids were burned when he hears that a belly dancer makes in one evening what it takes a wage earner a period of five years to earn?[74] The balance between effort and speculation has always bedevilled economies that live off services and international commerce. How to keep the stability of such an economy in the face of a glaring inequality of opportunity may turn out to be the Egyptian order's most taxing challenge.

## *Dependence and Its Costs*

Eventually, ruinous and hasty economic policies have to be paid for. In Egypt and other Third World societies caught in the debt trap (Peru, Zaire, and Turkey, to name a few), states end up paying with their economic autonomy. The outstanding foreign debts accounted for by less-developed countries rose from US$48.4 billion to $206.8 billion in 1976; the external financing needs rose from $13 billion in 1970 to $56 billion in 1977.[75] In country after country, the "politics of creditworthiness" has more to say about the actual conduct of policy than any ideological exhortations. The crisis of foreign debts brings in its train new forms of intervention and dependence, forms that the nationalist leaders did not foresee a generation ago. Subscribing to a primacy of politics, the first-generation leaders sought the trappings of statehood. Today those trappings are there, but sovereignty turns out to be an empty shell. Foreign advisors are practically in control of Zaire's mismanaged economy. Turkey's governments change, but they all end up succumbing to harsh economic reality as left-of-center governments adopt the policies of their conservative predecessors. Peru's populist experiment is now on a conservative course: exhausted in 1975, it took a turn to the right under Morales Bermudez and had to accept the "reform package" of the IMF to gain access to capital markets. In Egypt, the IMF missions come calling regularly with the usual deflationary package.[76] The IMF has some resources to offer, an important rubber stamp of approval; but it also has intellectual capital as well: the familiar prescriptions of a credit squeeze, reduction in governmental expenditures, a very low opinion of state subsidies of services and consumer goods, and usually a devaluation of currency.

Power being what it is, the IMF guidelines subject weak and deficit countries to more powerful economies. The IMF has very little leverage over surplus countries like Germany and Japan. Germany and Japan it can advise; but it can coerce weak economies. This is the way a British economist puts it: "Access to the higher credit tranches in the IMF is only obtained at the cost of the effective elimination of the economic independence of the borrowing countries. This is as true of an industrialized country like Britain as it is for a peripheral country like Mauritius; in both cases, internally determined economic priorities must give way to those established by the need to bring the balance of payments into equilibrium and to repay international credit when it falls due."[77]

The medicine that the IMF recommends can be tough to take. In Peru, Turkey, and Egypt, IMF guidelines had to be enforced by calling in the army. IMF guidelines (backed by the oil states) were behind the Egyptian government's decision to halve its food subsidies in January of 1977. The decision sparked a popular upheaval that was suppressed in a welter of blood and a loss of seventy-nine lives. An excellent report for the U.S.

Senate Foreign Relations Committee notes the connection between IMF guidelines and the grim game of governance in a situation of scarcity and constraints:

> The difficulty with these [IMF-recommended] policies is that while they may be the most effective way of rapidly bringing a deficit country's external accounts into balance, they may also lead to higher unemployment, cuts in social welfare programs, and a generally lower standard of living for the people, at least over the short term. And in desperately poor countries, where the majority of the population may already be living at a bare subsistence level, a decision by the Government to impose a program of stiff economic austerity can create social and political turmoil. The requirement that government spending be reduced and the private sector expanded may also conflict with the long-term social and economic goals of a government or of certain political factions within a country.
>
> If the IMF and the other creditors are not sufficiently responsive to these internal constraints, they may push a government into a position of having to choose between acceptance of the foreign creditors' terms—and perhaps having to use political repression to carry them through—or repudiation of the IMF, the banks, and possibly its debts.[78]

In defense, the IMF can point to the fact that it "confines its conditions to broad economic aggregates," that it does not "dictate details of taxes and spending," and that "the way individual governments choose to meet its conditions reveals much more about them than it does about the IMF."[79] There is no doubt that there is a great deal of merit to this view, but the distribution of power within Third World societies almost invariably dictates the typical way adjustments are made: at the expense of the poor, through cuts in subsidies rather than through vigilant and honest taxation of affluent classes. The way an Egyptian minister explained Egypt's decision on subsidies sums up how governments tackle adjustment problems: "Last year we had a budget deficit of over $2 billion. When we came into the cabinet, we decided this must be reduced. Of the four key budget items—military, investment, subsidies, and debt service—it was decided that the subsidies were the most expendable item."[80]

The relative political weakness of the poor and the ideology of "market pricing" constitute a vicious circle. Subsidies seem expendable because those who benefit from them are disorganized and those who so constantly criticize them are so sure of the efficacy of the medicine they propose. Cross-pressured between those who wanted to phase out the subsidies and the angry Egyptian masses who finally drew a line for their rulers in the January 1977 riots, the Egyptian government retreated and called on the United States to make "the IMF give way."[81] The Egyptian president's strength lay in his weakness: if pushed too far, his regime might collapse.

It is clear from the above that much of Egypt's economic strategy is reliant upon a highly unpredictable and fluctuating foreign policy and geostrategic game. It has been a dangerous trapeze act that, in the aftermath of the Shah's collapse and a rupture between Egypt and Saudi Arabia, ended up with Egypt relying on an Amercan net to keep the act from turning into disaster. The post-October 1973 Egyptian order exaggerated what others would and could do for Egypt: it underestimated what the donors will ask for in return. The oil states were ready to give some help, and they gave it between 1973 and 1977—something like US$1.2 billion a year—for geopolitical reasons. Likewise, they withdrew most of it when the Egyptian state wanted to go its own way on the Arab-Israeli front. The Baghdad summit held in 1978 should have been the moment of reckoning for a policy that put so much faith in outsiders. Egypt's wager was that Saudi Arabia would go along with Egyptian policy, but the Saudis went their own way and agreed at Baghdad to a fairly harsh set of economic measures against Egypt that included a ban on loans, deposits guaranteed, and contributions to the Egyptian government—and a ban on the purchase of Egyptian government bonds.[82] The uncertainties of diplomacy aside, it was wishful thinking to believe that the Arab oil state would finance Egyptian economic recovery. With its sparse population and a long history of Egyptian invasions into the Arabian peninsula (in the nineteenth century under Muhammad ᶜAlī, in the 1960s under Abdul Nasser), Saudi Arabia had no interest in shoring up Egyptian power beyond keeping Egypt barely afloat. "Whoever is responsible for another's becoming powerful," observed Niccolo Machiavelli in *The Prince,* "ruins himself." The Saudis were not interested in their own ruin and in the rise of viable and autonomous Egyptian power. Nor were the expectations of Saudi investments in Egypt and other Arab states particularly realistic. Saudi and other Arab petrodollars responded in an economically rational and predictable way: they went to the capital markets of the West. Of the investment behavior of the oil states, a U.S. Senate report notes:

> The OPEC countries have behaved like other prudent investors in disposing of their financial surpluses; that is, they have invested almost exclusively in low risk, high yield assets such as government securities in the hard currency countries, in stocks and bonds offered by Western corporations, and in deposits with the 15 or so largest multinational banks. Thus, according to the U.S. Treasury estimates, of a total of approximately $133 billion in financial assets accumulated by OPEC in the period 1974–76, that can be accounted

> for, an estimated \$48 billion was invested in government paper, portfolio and long term direct investments in the industrial countries; another \$9.75 billion was loaned to international organizations; and by far the largest amount, \$49 billion, or 37 percent of the total, was deposited with private commercial banks, mostly in New York and London. Only \$16 billion, or 12 percent of the total OPEC surpluses, went directly to the developing countries, mostly in the form of grants to Moslem countries. OPEC did increase its direct lending to developing countries in 1975 and 1976. But this increase may have been largely offset by a cut in 1976 contributions to official international lending institutions, whose chief beneficiaries are the LDC's. The remainder went to the nonmarket economies.[83]

Ideologically, the open-door policy was wrapped in the garb of "Westernization." But men and societies removed from the West rarely seem to understand what is at work in the world they wish to emulate. There is a massive gap between the free-for-all capitalism defended in Egypt and what obtains in today's international political economy. The "open" trading system created in the post-World War II years, sustained as it was by the U.S. economy, has broken down. The will of the preeminent advocate of the free-trade system to assume the burden of the world system's organizer came to an end in April 1971 when President Nixon announced a new foreign economic policy for the United States and, in effect, a new international economic order.[84] This is fully understood in OECD countries. Compare, for instance, the official Egyptian views surveyed in this chapter with the conclusions of an OECD report (the McCracken report) authored by eight prominent economists drawn from major OECD countries. There is, notes the OECD team, some danger that "the edifice of free trade, so carefully built may begin to disintegrate." Of the circumstances that sustained the post-World War II international political economy, the report observes: "This potential for rapid growth would not have been realized . . . had it not been for the favorable economic climate created by governments—first by their assumption of responsibility for the achievement of high employment, and second through their commitment to economic integration in the framework of an open, multilateral system for international trade and payments."[85] The economic troubles plaguing OECD countries, warned the authors of the McCracken report, call upon more "disciplined" governmental policies if the goals of employment, price stability, and reasonable rates of growth are to be realized.

This, unfortunately, is not the first or last time that incantations in non-Western societies about progress and Westernization sharply differ from realities in the West. The curtailment in the role of the Egyptian state is at odds with the increasing role of the state in international economic affairs, a phenomenon repeatedly and fully elaborated upon in the works of

Robert Gilpin. The things that brought about increasing interstate economic competition are apparently here to stay:

> The reasons for this greater government participation in the private sphere are several: (1) the challenges posed by the energy revolution; (2) the increasing cost of technology, especially so-called "high" technology; (3) the concern over "stagflation" itself; and (4) new sets of social demands in areas of social welfare and environment which necessitate greater government intervention in the economy. This change in the role of the government not only has numerous economic consequences but it tends to "politicize" international economic relations. The tendency is for the free market to give way to inter-state negotiations regarding such matters as "orderly marketing agreements" and market shares for domestic industry.[86]

Great expectations pinned on others often culminate in bitterness and recriminations. The "generous Arab brothers" of 1974 and 1975 became, in the words of a writer for the Egyptian daily *al-Akhbār,* "shoeless goatherds" only two years later.[87] Of the large equation that underpinned the post-October 1973 order, there remained American support and American contributions. Whether the recriminations once visited on the Russians and then on the oil states eventually come to be visited on the United States remains to be seen. It is dangerous to patron and client for the client to expect so much of the patron. In today's international system, nations either pay their own way or they fall behind: they make all kinds of "adjustments" to decline and stagnation. Powerful groups help themselves to public resources; many of the gifted emigrate to other lands as despair sets in, and the dominant order abandons any serious commitment to public welfare.

Albert Hirschman's work on "exit, voice, and loyalty" depicts one ominous Egyptian response to politicoeconomic decline[88]—the emigration of some of Egypt's most gifted youth. Choking off the voice option, the Egyptian order has been encouraging the exit option with negative consequences for the quality of the social order and for mass loyalty to the society at large. In one informal survey of university students, nearly 85 percent expressed a desire to leave Egypt upon graduation.[89] This trend set in after the 1967 war; it turned into mass exodus after 1973. The pull of oil wealth was one factor; but there were domestic factors as well. In Egypt, as elsewhere, emigration buys a measure of stability by removing potential dissidents from the system; but it also removes from the society those who would have been more likely to resort to the voice option and to make some contribution to the public interest.

Traditionally, Egypt was a society whose inhabitants were reluctant to venture to other lands. It possessed the stability of an agrarian order where men stayed, normatively and physically, at home. Writing in 1835, E. W. Lane described in his classic *Manners and Customs of Modern Egyptians* the reluctance of Egyptians to leave their native land:

> Love of their country and more especially of home is [a] characteristic of the modern Egyptians. In general they have a great dread of quitting their native land. I have heard of several determining to visit a foreign country for the sake of considerable advantages in prospect; but when the time of their intended departure drew near, their resolution failed them.[90]

More than a century after Lane had made that observation, Jean and Simone Lacouture confirmed it in their book *Egypt in Transition*.[91] It was only in the past decade or so that mass emigration became a widespread Egyptian phenomenon. The private gains are easy to document: but the public costs to productivity and social stability, though harder to specify, are surely considerable. There is a shortage of skilled manpower felt in critical Egyptian industries; there is the cost in productivity that results from those biding their time, waiting to leave. As the Egyptian economic analyst ᶜAdil Husayn put it in an essay that attempts to come to terms with the impact of emigration upon Egyptian society: "It could be said that he who has not emigrated is preparing to do so; that is, he considers himself in transit and we can imagine the impact of such a phenomenon upon his productivity."[92] States can, as Hirschman argues, make it tempting for their citizens to stay at home. They can provide incentives and public services that encourage the citizen to remain. Of interest to this analysis, a fair income distribution is seen by Hirschman as one such incentive: "Social justice, too, may be a public good; individuals may find it enjoyable to live in a society where income distribution is comparatively egalitarian."[93] It then follows that a high level of inequality is an invitation to the more psychologically sensitive to pick up and go elsewhere.

## VII. Conclusion: The Retreat of Egalitarianism

At the root of any sustained fight against inequality lies a certain aesthetic revulsion toward it. This was a sentiment that Rousseau captured in his great work *Emile* long before Marx and Marxists introduced the whole concern with inequality "laws" and "objective conditions." The struggle against inequality begins when some people break with the prevailing sentiment and go against the standard, time-honored injunction that equality is not of this world. Those who make the effort usually know that great crusades may end in failure, that new forms of inequality will arise when you destroy old forms of inequality, that old classes often hang on under new labels; but they make the effort, nonetheless.

Whatever its ideological shortcomings, the Egyptian order made the effort under Abdul Nasser. The radicalism that moved Egyptian order may have been accidental—reflecting the personality of the ruler, the rise of new classes sensing new possibilities, the intransigence of an old order, the pressure of a global system that pushed the experiment further than the Egyptian custodians may have initially intended. Then things took the turn depicted here, and there was the resurgence of the old conservative sensibility about inequality—the kind that lives in all societies and more so in old civilizations that witness the rise and passing of all sorts of claims, the emergence and fading of movements that set out to change the world and then succumb to it.

In one of the most thoughtful analyses of the Egyptian experiment, the noted Egyptian writer Luwīs ᶜAwad writes that the Egyptian revolution has "aged," that it needs a new social contract, a new sense of what it is dedicated to.[94] The dust that revolutions stir eventually settles down. By then, revolutions would have either succeeded in transforming a social order or gone on to become sheer incantation, a cover for inequality, a way of preempting those who might be really interested in social change. All revolutionary changes produce their elites and "new classes."

History—even when brief and compressed—has a way of being unkind to all sorts of radical claims. It either provides testimony to what men claimed, or it can show that their words outran their deeds, that the underlying social realities defied and eluded them. What the Mexicans call the "institutionalization" of their revolution—where revolutionary symbols go hand in hand with one of the most unequal patterns of distribution of the world—shows the fate of many radical quests that try to undo old orders. The Egyptians too have "institutionalized" their more recent revolution. And, as in Mexico, that kind of order sets bounds (perhaps unbreakable) on social policies.

Essentially, the whole concept of income distribution rested on the hopes of a generally buoyant era—the 1960s. In the 1960s it was believed that we could close the gap both within and among nations. Now it is easier to see that income transfers have not worked and that the only large-scale global transfer (the change in the price of oil) took a political decision by a group of states and was done under favorable global circumstances. Likewise, we know that the 2 percent transfer of GNP within poor nations that the World Bank says is essential to tackle the problem of absolute poverty has not materialized either. Generally the sensibility of the 1960s believed in public politics. Today, we lack that belief, so men help themselves to what they can. The prospects for redistribution—within and among nations—are not particularly bright; the prospects for "stalled societies"[95]—like Mexico or Egypt—are more problematic still. Stalled societies escape the grim horrors of great crusades and—given the record of great crusades in our time—that must be judged a positive thing. What they suffer is what Barrington Moore[96] has aptly called the "appalling costs of stagnation."

## Notes

1. Najib Mahfūz, *al Marāya* (Cairo, 1972), p. 345.

2. Ibid., pp. 157–158.

3. ᶜAbd al- Munᶜim al-Qaysūnī, *Middle East Economic Digest*, 13 May 1977, pp. 4–6.

4. Anwar el Sadat, *In Search of Identity* (New York: Harper & Row, 1978), pp. 8–9.

5. *Middle East Reporter*, Augest 12, 1978, p. 13.

6. *Economist*, July 14, 1979, p. 62.

7. Leonard Binder, *In a Moment of Enthusiasm: Political Power and the Second Stratum in Egypt* (Chicago: University of Chicago Press, 1978), p. 399.

8. Ibid., pp. 400–401.

9. Galal Amin, "Some Problems Related to the Economic Opening in Egypt," (Paper presented to the Third Annual Conference of Egyptian Economists, Cairo, 23–25 March 1978); see also by the same writer a trenchant critique of the Arab world's integration into the world market in *al Mustaqbal al-ᶜArabī* (1979): 4–16.

10. Gouda Abdel-Khalek, "The Important Signposts of the Open Door Policy," (Paper presented to the Third Annual Conference of Egyptian Economists, Cairo, 23–25 March 1978).

11. Samir Amin, *The Arab Nation: Nationalism and Class Struggle*, (London: Zed Press, 1978), p. 75.

12. Hassan Riad, *L'Égypte Nasserienne* (Paris: Les Editions de Minuit, 1964).

13. I use the term *populism* in the sense developed by Samuel Huntington and Joan Nelson, *No Easy Choice: Political Participation in Developing Countries*, (Cambridge, Mass.: Harvard University Press, 1976), p. 23. They write of populism: "High and increasing levels of political participation go with expanding governmental benefits and welfare policies, increasing economic equality, and if necessary, relatively low rates of economic growth."

14. Ibid.

15. See Marius Deeb, "The Socioeconomic Role of the Local Foreign Communities in Modern Egypt," *International Journal of Middle East Studies* 9 (1978): 11–22; see also, for a more general discussion, Charles Issawi's *Egypt in Revolution* (London: Oxford University Press, 1963).

16. See Galal Amin, *The Modernization of Poverty* (Leiden: E. J. Brill, 1974), pp. 57–58.

17. Robert Mabro, The Egyptian Economy (London: Oxford University Press, 1974), p. 231.

18. See the excellent paper by Ibrahim El-Issawy and Muhammad Ali Nasser, "An

Attempt to Estimate the Economic Losses of Arab-Israeli Wars Suffered by Egypt Since 1967" (Third Annual Conference of Egyptian Economists, Cairo, March 23–25, 1978).

19. *al-Ahrām al-Iqtisādī,* 15 July 1967, pp. 8–9.

20. See the interesting parliamentary debates—proceedings of the National Assembly (henceforth *Proceedings of Parliament*)—of February 7, 1968.

21. Mahmūd Marāghī, in *Rūz al-Yussif* 56, December 11, 1978.

22. Heba Handoussa, "Public Sector in Egyptian Industry: 1952–1977" (Paper presented to Third Annual Conference of Egyptian Economists, Cairo, March 23–25, 1978).

23. Anwar el Sadat, *In Search of Identity,* p. 195.

24. For a text of the March 30 Declaration, see *Wathā'iq ᶜAbd al-Nāsir* (Cairo, 1973), pp. 371–380.

25. Sayyid Marᶜī, *Awrāq Siyāsīya,* 3 vols., (Cairo, 1978).

26. Ibid., p. 513.

27. Ibid., p. 587.

28. Muhammad Haykal, as cited in Raymond Baker, *Egypt's Uncertain Revolution Under Nasser and Sadat* (Cambridge, Mass.: Harvard University Press, 1978), p. 114.

29. Fu'ād Mūrsī, *This Economic Opening* (Cairo, 1976), pp. 277–278.

30. Franz Schurmann, *The Logic of World Power* (New York, Pantheon), 1974, p. 138.

31. Ibid., p. 135.

32. Miles Copeland, *The Game of Nations* (London: Weidenfeld & Nicolson, 1969), passim.

33. See the work by Mahmūd Mutawalī, *The Historical Roots and Evolution of Egyptian Capitalism* (Cairo, 1974).

34. Muhammad Farīd Shuhdī, *Ta'ammulāt fi al-Nāsirīya* (Thoughts on Nasserism) (Beirut, 1973).

35. ᶜAbd al-Latīf al- Baghdādī, *Memoirs,* vol. 1 and 2 (Cairo, 1977).

36. Binder, p. 399.

37. Mahbūb Ul-Haq, *The Poverty Curtain* (New York: Columbia University Press, 1976), p. 44.

38. See Ibrahim El-Issawy in chapter 4 of this volume.

39. Mohamed Heikal, *The Sphinx and the Commissar,* (New York: Harper & Row, 1978), pp. 261–262.

40. See Fu'ād Mūrsī, pp. 277–278.

41. Ibid., p. 155.

42. Muhammad Anwār al-Sadāt, *Waraqāt Uktubīr* [The October Paper] (Cairo, 1974), pp. 5–6.

43. *Parliamentary Proceedings,* January 18, 1974, p. 2326.

44. Investment and Free Zones Authority, *Report on the Arab and Foreign Investment Until December 12, 1977,* (1978), p. 3.

45. All the citations are taken from Ford Foundation files on the workshops available in the Cairo office.

46. Ibid.

47. Ibid.

48. *Proceedings of Parliament,* May 10, 1977, and *al-Ahrām,* January 16, 1979.

49. *Egypt Report,* February 1977.

50. Muhī' al-Dīn's statement in *Proceedings of Parliament* (May 10, 1977) pp. 34–36.

51. Murād's statement, ibid., pp. 25–28.

52. Ibid., p. 14.

53. Ibid., p. 24.

54. The sources for the new investors lists are *al-Waqā'ī al-Misrīya* and *al-Jarīda al-Rasmīya* [The Official Gazette]. For the 1961 / 1962 list, I used those reproduced by Mahmūd Murād, *Who Ruled Egypt?* (Cairo, 1975).

55. *Economist,* July 14, 1979.

56. See Murād, ibid., p. 76.

57. Christopher Jencks, Susan Bartlett et al, *Who Gets Ahead?* (New York: Basic Books, 1979).

58. *Proceedings of Parliament,* February 10, 1976, pp. 4356–4357.

59. *al-Ahrām,* August 7, 1976.

60. *Proceedings of Parliament,* May 15, 1977, p. 5601.

61. *al-Ahrām,* December 10, 1978.

62. *al-Akhbār,* December 25, 1978, and *al-Waqasai al-Misryya,* May 16, 1978.

63. *Official Gazette,* January 20, 1977, and July 21, 1977.

64. Mutawalī, *The Historical Roots and Evolution of Egyptian Capitalism,* pp. 340–341.

65. Salāh Hāfiz, "Watergate in Egypt," *Rūz al-Yūssif,* December 4, 1978.

66. *Economist,* July 14, 1979, p. 62.

67. Sources on the Pyramid Oasis Project are the *Economist,* May 20, 1978, and June 3, 1978, and Na[c]mat Ahmad Fu'ād, *The Pyramid Oasis Project* (Cairo, 1978).

68. Sources on al-Amīrīya project are Rūz al-Yūssif, December 8, 1978, *al-Ahrām al-Iqtisādī,* January 15, 1979; *al-[c]Umāl* newspaper on the position of labor unions, January 8, 1979. For a good critique of the project, see the article by member of parliament Muhammad Shamīr Abāza in *al-Ahrām al-Iqtisādī,* December 1, 1978.

69. See Robert Gilpin's excellent discussion in his *U.S. Power and the Multinational Corporation* (New York: Basic Books, 1975), particularly pp. 215–262.

70. *The October Paper,* pp. 40–41. See *al-Ahram al-Iqtisadi,* January 15, 1978; also April 1, 1978.

71. *al-Ahrām al-Iqtisādī,* April 1, 1978.

72. *al-Ahrām,* December 21, 1978.

73. *al-Ahrām al-Iqtisādī,* February 15, 1976.

74. Al-*Ahrām al-Iqtisādī,* February 1, 1977.

75. On debts and the debt crisis of the Third World, see the extremely useful survey, "Must Lend, Will Travel," *Economist,* March 4, 1978, pp. 1–82.

76. The *Economist*'s various reports on Zaire, Turkey, Peru, and Egypt provide the empirical basis for this discussion.

77. E. A. Brett, "The International Monetary Fund, The International Monetary System and the Periphery," *International Foundation for Development Alternatives Dossier* 5, (Nyon, Switzerland, March 1979) pp. 1–15.

78. U.S. Senate Foreign Relations Committee, Subcommittee on Foreign Economic Policy, *International Debts, The Banks, and U.S. Foreign Policy* (U.S. Government Printing Office, Washington, D.C.), 1977, p. 6.

79. "After Wittereen's IMF," *Economist,* June 3, 1978, p. 92.

80. *New York Times,* February 26, 1977.

81. "Egypt: Impassivity Rules," *Economist,* March 3, 1979, pp. 71–72.

82. See the *Economist*'s careful assessment in "Egypt Without the Arabs," *Economist,* July 14, 1979, pp. 62–64.

83. U.S. Senate Foreign Relations Committee, p. 36.

84. Robert Gilpin offers a thoughtful assessment of the changes and their implications in *U.S. Power and the Multinational Corporation.*

85. Paul McCracken et. al., *Towards Full Employment and Price Stability: A Report to the OECD by a Group of Independent Experts,* (Paris: OECD, 1977), p. 11.

86. Robert Gilpin, "The Crisis of the World Political Economy: Contrasting American Perspectives," mimeo. Woodrow Wilson School of Public and International Affairs, Princeton University, 1979, p. 20.

87. Cited in the *Economist,* October 7, 1978, p. 79.

88. Albert Hirschman, *Exit, Voice and Loyalty* (Cambridge, Mass.: Harvard University Press), 1970.

89. Cited in ᶜAdil Husayn "Petrodollars as an Obstacle to Unity and Complementarity; *al-Mustaqbal al-ᶜArabī* 5 (1979) p. 28.

90. E. W. Lane, *Manners and Customs of Modern Egyptians* (London: Ward Lock and Co., 1890), p. 272.

91. Jean and Simone Lacouture, *Egypt in Transition* (London: Methuen, 1958).

92. ᶜAdil Husayn, *Economist,* June 3, 1978, p. 28.

93. Albert Hirschman, "Exit, Voice and the State," *World Politics* 31 (October 1978): 90–107.

94. See Luwīs ᶜAwad's sophisticated and fair-minded assessment of Nasserism, *The Seven Masks of Nasseriem* (Beirut, 1976).

95. The concept of "stalled societies" is developed (with emphasis on France) in Michel Crazier's book *The Stalled Society* (New York: Viking, 1973).

96. Barrington Moore, Jr., *The Social Origins of Dictatorship and Democracy,* (Boston: Beacon, 1966).

# *List of Contributors*


MAHMOUD ABDEL-FADIL, Faculty of Economics and Political Science, Cairo University.

GOUDA ABDEL-KHALEK, Faculty of Economics and Political Science, Cairo University.

FOUAD AJAMI, School of Advanced International Studies, Johns Hopkins University.

ALI E. HILLAL DESSOUKI, Faculty of Economics and Political Science, Cairo University.

AMR MOHIE-ELDIN, Faculty of Economics and Political Science, Cairo University.

M. REDA A. EL-EDEL, Instititue of National Planning, Cairo, Egypt.

IBRAHIM HASSAN EL-ISSAWY, Institute for National Planning, Cairo, Egypt.

AHMED H. IBRAHIM, Institute for National Planning, Cairo, Egypt.

SAAD EDDIN IBRAHIM, Department of Sociology, The American University of Cairo.

KARIMA ALY MOHAMED KORAYEM, El-Azhar University, Cairo, Egypt.

ROBERT TIGNOR, History Department, Princeton University.

JOHN WATERBURY, Woodrow Wilson School/Politics Department, Princeton University.

MOHAYA A. ZAYTOUN, El-Azhar University, Cairo, Egypt.

# Index

Italic page numbers indicate material in tables and figures.


ᶜAbbūd, Ahmad, 23, 45, 46
ᶜAbd al-Wahāb, Salāh, 38–39, 500
ACC (agricultural cooperative credit and supply of agricultural inputs), 198, 211, 212
ACCB (Agricultural and Cooperative Credit Bank), 211–21, *212*
ᶜAfīfī, Hāfiz, 23, 46, 47
Agency for International Development (AID), 446
Agrarian reform. *See* Land reform
Agrarian Reform Act of 1952, 199, 200, 203, 210–11
Agricultural Census of 1939, 241ff.
Agricultural Census of 1950, 211, 241ff.
Agricultural Census of 1961, 199, 205, 209, 241ff.
Agricultural and Cooperative Credit Bank (ACCB), 211–21
Agricultural cooperative credit and supply of agricultural inputs (ACC), 198, 211, 212
Agricultural Cooperative Societies, 210, 211
Agriculture: class and, 91–92, *91;* education and, 11; employment in, 125 (*n*. 4, 5, 6), 239–63, 290–91, 389–93, *390–92,* 396–99, *398;* exports of, 456, *456;* foreign aid and, *442,* 443, 451–60, *456, 458;* in GDP, 90–91, *90, 104,* 105–106, 258–63; growth of, 34; investment in, 116–18, *116, 117;* labor in, 35–36, 239–63, 275, 298–99; machinery use in, 287–88, 296–97; subsidies and, 12–13, 114, 169–70, *170,* 324–25; taxes on, 14, 165–93, 312–13; wages in, 6–7, 10, 24, 90–91, *90,* 239–63, 298–99
*Ahrām, al-*, 71, 74
ᶜAin Shams University, 326, 353
Alexandria, 37, 321; employment in, 36, 120; investment in, *118,* 119–120, 318, *319;* population, 6, 13, 35, 309–11, *309*
ᶜAlī, Muhammad, 76, 237, 238, 311, 474, 502, 508
ᶜAmir, ᶜAbd al-Hakīm, 61, 68, 71
ᶜAmirīya, al-, 77, 500–501
Anglo-Egyptian treaty (1936), 31
Arab and International Cooperation Agency, 76
Arab-Israeli war of (1967), 7, 9, 105, 381
Arab Socialist Union (ASU) (1963–1977), 57, 67–68, 72, 74, 213, 472, 477–479, 483–84, 488
ASU. *See* Arab Socialist Union
Aswān (province), 22, 35, 119
Aswān High Dam, 312, 318, 441, 451–53, 460
Asyūt (province), 48
Automobiles, 333–34, *333*
*Azhar, al-* (magazine), 70, 72
al-Azhar University, 326, 353, 359–60

Badrāwī-ᶜAshūr, Muhammad, 45, 46
Baghdādī, ᶜAbd al-Latīf, 71–72, 483
Bahayna, 119
Bank Misr, 43, 45, 70, 491, 500–501
Bank Misr Group, 108, 502
Banks: Agricultural and Cooperative Credit Bank (ACCB), 211–21; Bank Misr, 43, 45, 70, 500–501; Central Bank of Egypt, 18, 181; foreign, 81, 504; National Bank of Egypt (NBE), 70, 108; nationalization of, 70, 108
Banque Belge, 70
Barker, Henry, A., 23, 51 (*n*. 12)
Brussels Tariff Nomenclature, 137
Buhayra, al-(province), 22, 67

Cairo, 28, 37, 55, 321, 326–42; class and, 424–31, *425, 428, 430;* education in, 11, 323, 370–71, *371;* employment in, 120; housing in, 335–42, *338;* income in, *418;* investment in, *118,* 119–120, 318, *319;* migration to, 14, 35; occupational mobility in 389–405, *398, 400, 402, 404;* popula-

tion, 6, 13, 308–12, *308, 309, 326;* social mobility in, 385–88, *386*
Cairo University, 326, 329, 353, 359–60, 408–409, *409*
Capitalism, 108, 378, 484–85, 496–98. *See also* Open-door policy
Capitulations, 21, 47
Cattle, 285–87, *286,* 290, 293–95, *294,* 296, 297. *See also* Livestock
CD. *See* Compulsory delivery (of crops)
Census: agricultural, 5, 22, 199, 205, 209, 211, 241ff.; population, 4, 6, 143, 240ff., 308–12
Central Bank of Egypt, 18, 81
Central Intelligence Agency (CIA), 481–82
Chemtex, 500–501
CIF import price (cost, insurance, and freight), 137
Cities. *See* Urban sector; *individual cities*
Civil service, 9, 73–74, 106, 395; education and, 11–12, 38–39, 113, 358, 381, 408
Class, 101–102, *101;* agricultural income and, 91–92, *91;* in Cairo, 424–31, *425, 428, 430;* conflict and, 60–61; education and, 355–57, *356,* 359–65, *359, 360,* 366; household expenditure and, 92–93, *93,* 95–96, *95,* 100–101, *100;* land ownership and, 5–6; land reform and, 65; perception of, *428,* 429–31, *430;* social mobility and, 375–431
CLUOCR (consolidation of land use and the organization of the crop rotation), 198, 199–203, *202, 226*
CMCDAC (cooperative marketing and compulsory delivery of agricultural crops), 168, 198, 203–10, 214
Committee for Liquidating Traces of Feudalism, 110, 478–79
Commodities: subsidies of, 12–13, 79–80; taxes on, 14, 137–40, *140–41,* 142, 151, 153
Companies, joint stock, 23, 46, 47, 51 (*n.* 11, 12)
Compulsory delivery (CD), 14–15, 17, 166–69, 171, 173, 175, 177, 179, *182, 189–93,* 203–10, *204, 206, 208. See also* Individual crops
Consolidation of land use and the organization of the crop rotation (CLUOCR), 198, 199–203, *202, 226*
Constitution of 1956, 59–60, 379
Constitution of 1958, 60
Constitution of 1964, 60–61
Construction industry, *104,* 106, 341, 453
Consultative Group on Egypt, 448–50, 470–71
Consumption: household, *97,* 98, 100–101, *100,* 102, 258–63
Cooperative marketing and Compulsory delivery of agricultural crops (CMCDAC), 168, 198, 203–210, 214
Cooperatives: agricultural credit and, 198, 211–21; land, 64, 67, 110; marketing, 168, 203–210, 232 (*n.* 10)
Cost of living, urban v. rural, 6, 126–27 (*n.* 20), 325
Cotton: 40–41, 47, 168, 171, 177, 183, 194 (*n.* 11), 200–201, *222–27,* 246, 451–52, 456; compulsory delivery of, 203, *204,* 205, 209, 210; disguised tax on, *172,* 173–75, 179, 180; loan for, 214; production of, *186–88;* subsidies on, 12–13; tariffs and, 25
Crops: 293; compulsory delivery of, 14–15, 17, 166–69, 171, 173, 175, 177, 179, *182, 189–93,* 203–210, *204, 206–208;* crop mix, 283–85, *283, 284,* 305 (*n.* 22); inputs for, *244–45,* 246–48; loans for planting, 213–14, *227–31;* restrictions on, 14–15; rotation of, 5, 14–15, 64, 67, 110, 169, 170, 199–203, *202,* 226. *See also individual crops*
Customs duties, 18, 137–38, *140–41,* 142, 152

Daqhalīya (province), 239
Defense, 475; tax for, 138
Department of Social Support, 32
Duty-free zones, 63, 489

Education, 7, 11–12, 18, 60, 69, 114–15, 351–71, *402, 404;* in Cairo, 11, 323, 370–71, *371;* civil service and, 11–12, 38–39, 113, 358, 381, 408; class and, 355–57, *356,* 359–65, *359, 360,* 366; GDP and, 11, 352; Great Britain and, 37–38; income and, 368–70, *368, 369, 419,* 420–21, *421, 422;* mobility and, 405–14, *408–11;* Nasser and, 352–65; public v. private, 355–57, 370–71, *371;* social mobility and, 366–67, *367,* 405–14, *408, 409–11;* subsidies of, 360–65; taxes and, 360–65, *362, 365;* unemployment and, 11, 38–39, 367; urban v. rural, 319–21. *See also* Literacy
EEC (European Economic Community), 80
Egypt Consultative Group, 448–50, 470–71
Egyptian Communist Party, 78
Egyptian Copper Company, 36

Egyptian Cotton Commission, 168, 195, (*n*. 24)
Egyptian Federation of Industries, 26, 47, 585
Egyptianization, 7, 379–80; defined, 111; impact of, 112–13
Egyptian Workers Communist Party, 78
Electricity, *104*, 105, *116*, *264*, 319, *321*, 325, *346–47*, 452–53
Employment, 120; agricultural, 125 (*n*. 4, 5, 6), 239–63, 290–91, 389–93, *390–92*, 396–99, *398;* distribution of, *118*, 119; foreign aid and, 452–54; government policy for, 113; growth of, 121, *121*, 389–93, *390–92;* industry and, 389–93, 390–92, 397–99, *398;* in service sector, 255, *390–92*, *393;* unemployment and, 11, 36, 38–39, 367
Equipment, agricultural, 287–88, 296–97
European Economic Community (EEC), 80
Expenditure, household: and class, 92–93, *93*, 95–96, *95*, 100–101, *100;* rural sector, 92–93, *93*, *97*, 98, 143–50, *144*, *146*, *148*, 298, 316; surveys of, 3, 4, 6–7, 455–56; urban sector, 6, 95–96, *95*, *97*, 98, 143–50, *145*, *147*, *149*
Export and Import Price Stabilization Fund, 138
Exports: agricultural, 456, *456;* taxes on, 137–38, *140–41*

Family Budget Survey (FBS), 143, 150–52, 259, 363, 377ff.
*Farm Diary*, 246, 251
Faruq, King, 22, 23, 55
FBS. *See* Family Budget Survey
Fellahin. *See* Peasants
Fellah party (Peasant party), 35, 65
Fertilizer, 169–70, *170*, 195, (*n*. 16, 18)
Fertilizer Company, Egyptian, 45
Fertilizers Stabilization Fund, 170
Five Year Plan (1960–1965), 70, 105, 110, 116, 118–21, 335, 379–80, 381, 454–55, 475
Five Year Plan (1978–1982), 13, 119, 318–19, 332, 342, *345–47*, 501
Food: consumption of, 259–62, *260;* foreign aid for, 441, 445, 457–58, 458; poverty and, 260–62, *261*, *262*, 384; shortages of, 200–201, 505; subsidies for, 7, 10, 12–13, 363
Foreign aid, 16–18, 122, 435–63, 470–71; amount of, 437–41, *437*, *439*, *440;* defined, 435–36; employment and, 452–54; for food, 441, 445, 457–58, *458;* industry and, *442*, 443, 451–59, *452;* loans and, 445, 449–50, 458–60, 464, (*n*. 3), 506; sources of, 441–43, *439*, *440*, *442*, *444;* of Soviet Union, 438–43, *439*, *440*, *444*, *446*, 451–57, *452*, *456;* terms of, 445–50, *444*, *446;* of the United States, 437–43, *439*, *440*, *444*, 445, *446*, 457–60, *457*, *458*, 509; use of, 443–45, *442*
Foreign investment, 8, 16–17, 40–41, 43, 62–63, 76–78, 80–81, 488–89
France, 7, 41, 43, 57, 334
Free Officers, 56, 78, 379, 470–71, 481–82, 483, 502
Free Zones, 63, 489

GDP: agriculture in, 90–91, *90*, *104*, 105–106, 258–63; education and, 11, 352; food subsidies in, 13; growth of, 103–106, *104*, 125 (*n*. 1), 128 (*n*. 29), 438; housing in, *104*, 105–106; industry in, *104*, 105–106; service sector in, *104*, 105–106; subsidies in, 114; taxes and, 10, 132; wages in, 5–6, 18, 99–100, *99*, 316
General Federation of Chambers of Commerce, 79
General Federation of Trade Unions, 73
General Organization for Industrialization, 501
General Union for Textile Workers, 29
Gharbīya (province), 22
Government (Egyptian): growth in bureaucracy, 9, 73–74; services of, 2, 185. *See also* Civil service; Taxes and taxation
Great Britain, 7, 21, 27–31, 37–38, 41, 57, 203
Gross domestic product. *See* GDP
Groundnuts, 168, 171, 183; tax on, 177–80, *178*, *192–93*

Hamada, ᶜAbd al-Rahman, 23, 46
Harb, Talᶜat, 42–43, 45
Haykal, Muhammad H., 71, 74, 479, 486
Health services, 7, 115–16, 185, 321–23
High Dam. *See* Aswān High Dam
Hijāzaī, ᶜAbd al ᶜAzīz, 75, 487, 498
Household expenditure: class and, 92–93, *93*, 95–96, *95*, 100–101, *100;* rural sector, 92–93, *93*, *97*, 98, 143–50, *144*, *146*, *148*, 258–63, 298, 316; surveys of, 3, 4, 6–7, 455–56; urban sector, 6, 95–96, *95*, *97*, 98, 143–50, *145*, *147*, *149*
Household savings, *144–49*, 150
Housing, 115, 380, 476–77; in Cairo, 335–42, *338;* in GDP, *104*, 105–106; income and,

424, *424;* investment in, 116, 118–19, 335–42, *335, 336, 338;* rent control and, 339–40, 380; rural, 262–63
Husayn, Ahmad, 30, 32, 65
Husayn, Kamāl al-Dīn, 71–72

ILO (International Labor Office) 10, 258, 259, 262
IMF (International Monetary Fund), 13, 79, 447–48, 490, 506–508
Imports: importance of, 503–505; taxes on, 137–38, *140–41,* 142, 152
Income: of agricultural labor, 239–63, 275, 298–99; crop mix and, 283–85; crop rotation and, 199–203, *202, 226;* data problems of, 3; education and, 368–70, *368, 369, 419,* 420–21, *421, 422;* housing and, 424, *424;* land holdings and, 24, 91–92, *91,* 271–99; livestock and, 5, 285–87, *286,* 293–95, *294,* 299; national v. per capita, 382–83, *383;* occupation and, 414–20, *415, 416, 418–19;* problems of measuring, 327–31; property, 90–91, *90,* 94–95, *94,* 99–100, *99,* 113–14; taxes on personal, 133–34, *140–41,* 142, 155–56; as term, 2; urban/rural, *97,* 98, 127 (*n.* 22), 180–81, *181*
Industrialization Project (1957–1960), 105, 109, 119, 454
Industrial/technical schools, 12, 114–15
Industry: employment in, 389–93, *390–92,* 397–99, *398;* foreign aid and, *442,* 443, 451–59, *452;* in GDP, *104,* 105–106; imports and, 504–505; investment in, 109–10, 116, *116, 118,* 119–20; production v. consumption, 120–21; regional distribution of, *118;* regulation of, 25–26; tariffs and, 25–26
Infitah. *See* Open-door policy
Inflation, 13, 18, 27, 36, 67, 103, 255, 316, 339–40, 450
International Bank for Reconstruction and Development (World Bank), 3, 143, 255, 312–13, 436, 441, 443, 446, 501, 512
International Development Agency (IDA), 441, 443
International Labor Office (ILO), 10, 258, 259, 262
International Monetary Fund (IMF), 13, 79, 447–48, 490, 506–508
Investment: in agriculture, 116–18, *116, 117;* foreign, 8, 16–17, 40–41, 43, 62–63, 76–78, 80–81, 488–89; in housing, *116,* 118–19, 335–42, *335, 336, 338;* industrial, 109–10, 116, *116, 118,* 119–20; public, 112, 318–25, *319, 345–47. See also* Infitah
Investment and Free Zones Authority, 489
Islam, 30, 72
Ismāᶜīl, Khedive, 40, 238, 499
Israel, 7, 9, 80–81, 105, 381

Kafr al-Dawār (city), 37, 38
Khalīl, Muhammad Mahmūd, 23, 51 (*n.* 12)
Khashoggi, ᶜAdnān, 500

Labor, 26, 35–37; agricultural wage, 35–36, 239–63, 275, 298–99; educational mobility of 405–14, *408–11;* income and, 393–99, *394, 398;* industrial, 36; land holdings and, 242, *242,* 243–45, *244;* migration of, outside Egypt, 15–16, 80, 255–56, 511; occupation and, 393–99, *394, 398;* productivity of, 96–97, *97,* 98, 110–12, 113, 239–53, 454, 511. *See also* Trade unions
Labor Force Sample Surveys, 240ff., 378ff.
Labor Party, 79
Land: consolidation of, 199–203; credit and, 211–21; crop rotation and, 199–203; distribution of, 4–6, 8, 22–24, 34, 51 (*n.* 5, 6), 236–39, 276–83, *277, 281,* 295–96, *300;* foreign ownership of, 23; income and, 24, 91–92, *91,* 271–99; labor force and, 242, *242,* 243–45, *244;* reclamation of, 110–11; redistribution of, 278–82, *281,* 295–96, *300;* rental of, 10, 15, 110, 272, 288–90, *288,* 297; taxes on, 47, 65, 135, *140–41,* 155, 181–84, *182,* 237–39, 275, 279
Land reform, 9–10, 59–61, 63–68, 102, 268ff., 482–83; corruption in, 67–68; income and, 89–94; livestock and, 287
Land Reform Law 178 (1952), 4–6, 8, 14–15, 46, 58, 63–67, 109, 110, 116, 379, 384, 388
Land Reform Law 127 (1961), 7–10, 64, 66, 109–10, 116, 281–82, 305 (*n.* 17), 380, 384, 388
Land Reform Law 50 (1969), 64, 66, 109–10, 129 (*n.* 45), 281–82
Lentils, 204, *204,* 208, 209, 210, *222–27*
Liberal Constitutionalists, 31, 65
Liberal Socialist party, 76, 79
Liberation Rally (1953–1956), 57, 58
Literacy, 38, *264, 402, 404,* 406, 412–13, 426, 480. *See also* Education
Literature, 27, 469–71
Livestock, 200–201; income and, 5, 285–87, *286,* 293–95, *294,* 296; loans for, 214–16, *215, 227–29*

Loans: agricultural, 210–21, *212*, 214, *215*, *219*, *227–31*, 313; foreign aid and, 445, 449–50, 458–60, 464 (*n*. 3), 506

Maize, 25–26
Malnutrition, 260–62, *261*, *262*
Marʿī, Sayyid, 22, 23, 64–65, 66, 77, 477–80
Marketing, cooperative, 168, 203–10, 232 (*n*.10)
Migration: outside Egypt, 15–16, 80, 255–56, 511; rural-urban, 5–6, 13–14, 35–36, 310–12
Military: coup of 1952, 55, 56, 78, 379, 470–71, 481–82, 483, 502; expenses of, 7–8; growth of, 255, 389. *See also* Land Reform Laws
Ministry of Agriculture, 4, 5, 47, 170, 199, 246, 251, 273, 274, 278, 279, 285, 291–93
Ministry of *Awkaf* (religious endowments), 68
Ministry of Economy, 4, 490, 491
Ministry of Finance, 328
Ministry of Housing, 336–39
Ministry of Industry, 4, 380, 450, 490, 501
Ministry of Labor, 73
Ministry of National Economy, 32
Ministry of Planning, 207, 260, 263
Ministry of Social Affairs, 32
Ministry of Supply, 138, 170, 207, 325
Ministry of Transport, 332, 334, 504
Minūfīya (province), 35, 67, 203
Minyā (province), 22–23
Misr Spinning and Weaving Company, 37, 45
Mixed Courts, 21, 239
Mobility: occupational, 388–405, *390–92*, *394*, *398*, *400*, *402*, *404*; social, 11–12, 375–431
Muhī' al-Dīn, Khālid, 64, 78, 492
Muhī' al-Dīn, Zakāriyā, 71, 479
Murād, Mustafa Kāmil, 76
Munād, Kamāl Mustafā, 492–93
Muslim Brotherhood, 30, 39, 50, 55, 65, 78

Naguib, Muhammad, 64, 65, 73
Nasser, Gamal Abd al-, 7–10, 56–61, 327, 381, 470ff.; education and, 352–65; land reform and, 63–68; nationalization policy of, 68–75; open-door policy and, 9, 17–18, 76, 82–83, 484–513; socialism and, 59–61, 62, 74
National Bank of Egypt (NBE), 70, 108
National Center for Social and Criminological research, 3, 4, 359, 370–71
National Charter of 1962, 7, 58, 60, 66, 69, 72, 76
National Democratic party, 339
Nationalism, 20–22, 33, 42–49, 501–502
Nationalization, 7–10, 57, 60–61, 95, 102, 380, 454; of banks, 70, 108; defined, 111; impact of, 111–13; laws for, 68–75
Nationalization Acts of 1961, 168
National Progressive Unionist Organization (NPUO), 78, 80
National Union (1956–1962), 57, 71
Naturalization Acts (1961 & 1962), 142
NBE (National Bank of Egypt), 70, 108
NPUO (National Progressive Unionist Organization), 78, 80

Occupation: income and, 414–20, *415*, *416*, *418–19*; labor and, 393–99, *394*, *398*; mobility of, 388–405, *390–92*, *394*, *398*, *400*, *402*, *404*
October Paper (1974), 62, 75, 488, 502
OECD (Organization of Economic Cooperation and Development), 487–88, 503, 509
Oil industry, 15–16, 486–87, 493–94
Onions, 168, 170, 171, 183, *222–27*, 456; compulsory delivery of, 203, *204*, 205, *206*, *207*, 209, 210; disguised tax on, *176*, 177, 179, 180, *190–91*; loans for, 214
Open-door policy (Infitāh), 8–9, 17–18, 62–63, 75–82, 103, 108, 381–82, 393, 486–513

Peanuts, *204*, 205, 209, 210, *223–27*
Peasant party (fellah party), 35, 65
Peasants: early treatment of, 32–50; as instruments of production, 47–48; land distribution and, 64–68, 236–39, 270ff; revolt of, in 1919, 34–35, 39
PFPB (Population and Family Planning Board), 287–88, 305 (*n*. 25)
Political parties, 29–32, 35, 39; banning of, 58, 72, 74; open-door policy and, 78–79; landowners in, 44–45; land reform and, 65. *See also individual parties*
Population, 4, 143, 240ff; of Alexandria, 6, 13, 35, 309–11, *309*; of Cairo, 6, 13, 308–12, *308*, *309*, *326*; growth of, 33–34, 105, 308–12, *308*, *309*, 389
Population and Family Planning Board (PFPB), 287–88, 305 (*n*. 25)
Populism, 8–9, 17, 41–49, 474
Poverty, 505, 507–508; household expenditure and, 258–59; urban v. rural, 331, 384–85, *384*, 386, 426
Prices, 120, 137; inflation and, 13, 18, 27, 36,

67, 103, 255, 316, 339–40, 450; regulation of agricultural, 14–15, 166–70, 173–80, 203–210; tariffs and, 25–26. *See also* Subsidies
Productivity of labor, 96–97, *97,* 98, 110–12, 113, 239–53, 454, 511
Professionals: Egyptianization and, 380; social mobility of, 390–405, *400, 402, 404,* 407; taxes of, 133–34, *140–41,* 142, 151, 154
Profits: of government, on crops, 173–80; taxes on, 47, 49, 134, *140–41*
Public sector, 476; savings and, 122
Pyramid Oasis project, 500

Qāḍī, Maḥmūd al-, 76, 496, 497
Qalyūbīya (province), 24, 35
Qaysūnī, ᶜAbd al-Munᶜim al-, 71, 469, 470, 479
Qinā (province), 22–23, 48
Quotas on crop deliveries, 14–15, 17, 166–69, 173, 175, 177, 179, *182, 189–93,* 203–210, *204, 206–208*

Rent control on housing, 339–40, 380
Revolutionary Command Council, 56, 64, 482
Rice, 168, 170, 171, 177, 183, *222–27,* 251, 452, 456; compulsory delivery of, 203, *204,* 205–207, *208,* 209, 210; disguised tax on, *174,* 175–77, 179, 180, *189;* loans for, 214
Riḍā Commission, 26
Rural sector, 4–6; household expenditure in, 92–93, *93, 97,* 98, 143–50, *144, 146, 148,* 258–63, 298, 316; income distribution in, 89–99, 106–108, *107,* 312–25, 384–85, *384;* policy bias against, 13–14, 156–61

Sadat, Anwar al-, 58, 71, 82–83, 371, 470ff; open-door policies of, 7–10, 17–18, 61–63, 75–82, 381–82, 484–513
Saᶜdists, 31, 65
Sālim, Jamāl, 64, 66
Sālim, Mamdūḥ, 75, 487, 489
Salvago, Michel, 23, 51 (*n.* 12)
Savings, 112–13, 122, 485; estimates of, 3; household *144–49,* 150
Schools: enrollment in, 38, 114–15, 352–55, *353, 354;* industrial/technical, 12, 114–15; urban v. rural, 319–21, *322, 323*
Service sector, 344; employment in, 255, *390–92,* 393; in GDP, *104,* 105–106; investment in, *116;* occupational mobility and, 401
Services, 7, 13–14, 60; taxes on, 137, 151, 153
Sesame, *204,* 205, *223–27*
Sharqīya (province), 24, 239
Shukrī, Ibrāhīm, 65, 79
Ṣidqī, Ismāᶜīl, 28, 39, 47
Sirāj, al-Dīn Shāhīn, Fuād, 31, 32, 65
Sirrī, Ḥusayn, 23, 51 (*n.* 12)
Socialism, 8, 18, 28–29, 30–32, 57–58, 65, 72–73, 78, 108–109, 318, 380–81, 382, 388. *See also* Arab Socialist Union; Nasser; Nationalization
Socialist Laws, 381, 388
Socialist party, 30, 65
Social mobility, 375–431; defined, 375; education and, 366–67, *367,* 405–14, *408, 409–11*
Socioeconomic status, components of, 376. *See also* Class
Soviet Union, 16–17, 472; foreign aid and, 438–43, *439, 440, 444, 446,* 451–57, *452, 456*
Status, socioeconomic. *See* Class
Students, 30, 37–38, 39, 114–15, 477, 484
Subsidies, 79–80, *157–59,* 160, 455, 507–508; agricultural, 12–13, 114, 169–70, *170,* 324–35; on education, 360–65; of fertilizer, 169–70, *170,* 195, (*n.* 16, 18); food, 7, 10, 12–13, 363; on public transportation, 332; taxes and, 13, 154–55
Suez Canal Company, 57, 379
Suez Cement Company, 459–60
Sugar, 43, 45, 169, *222–27,* 233 (*n.* 11), 451–52; loans for, 214; tariffs and, 25
Sugar Company (Egyptian), 23, 43, 45
Sulṭān, Aḥmad, 77, 498

Tariffs, 47, 78, 504; description, 137–38, *140–41;* regulation of, 25–26
Ṭawīl, ᶜAbd al-Fattāḥ al-, 31, 32
Taxes and taxation, 10, 18, 132, 492; agricultural, 14, 165–93, 312–13; business, 47, 49, 134, 137–40, *140–41,* 142, 153–54; education and, 360–65, *362, 365;* estate and succession, 135–36, 155–56; evasion of, 328; excise, 137, *140–41,* 153; on imports, 137–38, *140–41,* 142, 152; income distribution and, 3, 113–14, 142–63, *157–59;* land, 47, 65, 134–35, *140–41,* 155, 181–84, *182,* 237–39, 275, 279; personal income, 62, 69, 133–34, 140–41, 142, 151,

154, 155–56; rates of, 161–63, *161–63, 167,* 363–65, *364, 365;* revenues from, *133, 139, 140–41,* 142; on services, 137, 151, 153; social justice and, 77–79; subsidies and, 13, 154–55
Technical industrial schools, 12, 114–15
Textiles, 504; ᶜAmirīya project, 77, 500–501
Trade. *See* Exports; Imports; Open-door policy
Trade unions, 70, 73–74; formation of, 29, 36–37, 73. *See also* Labor
Transitional Plan of 1974/75, 119
Transportation, 482; investment in, 116; private, 333–34, *333;* public, 327, 331–32, *332,* 333, 334

ᶜUbayd, Makram, 43–44
Unemployment: education and, 11, 38–39, 367; urban, 36. *See also* Employment
Unions. *See* Trade Unions
United States, 16–17, 80, 494; foreign aid and, 437–43, *439, 440, 444,* 445, 446, 457–60, *457, 458,* 509
Universities, 321, 353, 357, *362;* Cairo University, 326, 329, 353, 359–60, 408–409, *409;* graduates of, 9, 114–15; social mobility and, 11–12
Urban sector: growth of, 308–12, *308, 309;* household expenditure in, 6, 95–96, *95, 97,* 98, 143–50, *145, 147, 149;* income distribution in, 94–99, 106–108, *107,* 312–25; policy bias toward, 13–14, *118,* 119–20, 318–25, 435–63; poverty in, *384,* 385, 386; tax impact on, 156–61; wages in, 94–95, *94,* 96–98, *97*
USAID (U.S. Agency for International Development), 335, 339, 449–50, *457,* 457–59
ᶜUthmān, ᶜUthmān Ahmad, 77, 495–97, 499
ᶜUthmān, Saᶜd, 29

*Wafd al-Misrī al-* (newspaper), 28, 29, 31
Wafd party, 31–32, 37, 41, 43–44, 48, 65
Wages, 96–98, *97,* 102; agricultural, 6–7, 10, 24, 90–91, *90,* 239–63, 298–99; in GDP, 5–6, 18, 99–100, *99,* 316; increase in, 12, 15–16, 100; taxes on, 133, *133, 140–41,* 142, 155–56
Watanī party, 31
Water, 313, 325; access to, 262–63, *263, 264,* 319, *320*
Wheat, 168–69, 196 (*n.* 39), *222–27,* 324–25, 457–58, *458;* compulsory delivery of, 203, *204,* 207–208, 209; tariffs and, 25–26
WHO (World Health Organization), 263
Women, 241, 248, *250,* 251, 256
World Bank, 3, 143, 255, 312–13, 436, 441, 443, 446, 501, 512
World Health Organization (WHO), 263

Yahya, ᶜAlī Amīn, 23, 45, 51 (*n.* 12)
Yemen, 7, 17, 105, 381, 475–76
Young Egypt, 30, 39, 50, 55

Zaghlūl, Saᶜd, 41, 42, 43
*Zakāt* (Islamic tax), 78, 494